The Theological Intentions of Mark's Literary Devices

The Theological Intentions of Mark's Literary Devices

Markan Intercalations, Frames, Allusionary Repetitions, Narrative Surprises, and Three Types of Mirroring

DEAN B. DEPPE

WIPF & STOCK · Eugene, Oregon

THE THEOLOGICAL INTENTIONS OF MARK'S LITERARY DEVICES
Markan Intercalations, Frames, Allusionary Repetitions, Narrative Surprises, and Three Types of Mirroring

Copyright © 2015 Dean B. Deppe. All rights reserved. Except for brief quotations in critical publications or reviews, no part of this book may be reproduced in any manner without prior written permission from the publisher. Write: Permissions, Wipf and Stock Publishers, 199 W. 8th Ave., Suite 3, Eugene, OR 97401.

Wipf & Stock
An Imprint of Wipf and Stock Publishers
199 W. 8th Ave., Suite 3
Eugene, OR 97401

www.wipfandstock.com

ISBN 13: 978-1-4982-0988-5

Manufactured in the U.S.A.   10/20/2015

Contents

Preface | ix
Abbreviations | xiv

1   The Two Levels of Interpretation in Mark's Gospel | 1

1.1 Mark and the Jesus Tradition: Surprises in Reading the Gospel of Mark | 1
1.2 Possible Explanations for Mark's Descriptions of the Disciples | 4
1.3 Explanations for Markan Irregularities | 9
1.4 The Difficulty in Discerning Symbolism | 11
1.5 Evidence for Two Levels of Interpretation in Mark's Gospel | 16
1.6 Literary Devices Employed by Mark to Indicate Symbolism | 23
1.7 The Issues Addressed Through the Literary Devices | 26

2   Intercalations in the Gospel of Mark | 30

2.1 Disagreements Regarding the Purpose of Markan Sandwiches | 31
2.2 Mark 3:20–35: Jesus' Family and the Jerusalem Religious Leaders | 36
2.3 Mark 5:21–43: Two Unclean People Healed: A Bleeding Woman and Dead Girl | 41
2.4 Mark 6:7–30: Mission of the Twelve and John the Baptizer Beheaded | 50
2.5 Mark 11:12–25: The Fig Tree and the Temple Action | 54
2.6 Mark 14:1–11: The Jewish Leaders and Judas Plotting versus the Woman Preparing | 70
2.7 Mark 14:53–72: Peter's Denial and Jesus' Confession at the Jewish Trial | 77
2.8 Mark's Role in the Composition of Intercalations | 84

3   The Literary Device of a Markan Framework | 95

3.1 Structural Techniques in the Gospel of Mark | 95
3.2 The Structure of Mark 1:1–15: "The Beginning of the Gospel" | 98
3.3 The Paradigmatic Ministry of Jesus in Mark 1:16(14)–39 | 102
3.4 The Frame around the Controversy Dialogues in Mark 1:40—3:12 | 106
3.5 The Frame around the Accusations from Family and Religious Leaders in Mark 3:13–34 | 120
    Membership in Jesus' Family | 120
3.6 The Structure of the Parable Discourse in Mark 4:1–34 | 123
3.7 The Frame around the Miracle Catenae of Mark 4:35—8:21 | 137
3.8 The Frame around the Discipleship Catechism of Mark 8:22—10:52 | 159

3.9 The Frame around Jesus' Jerusalem Ministry in Mark 11:1—12:40 | 172
3.10 The Frame around the Eschatological Discourse in Mark 12:41—13:37 | 182
3.11 The Frame around the Passion Narrative of Mark 14:1—15:39 | 191
3.12 The Frame around the Burial and Resurrection Narrative of 15:40—16:8 | 194
3.13 Conclusions | 198

4 Markan Allusionary Repetitions | 203

4.1 The Description and Function of Allusionary Repetitions | 203
4.2 The Occurrence of Matched Episodes | 205
    4.2a Preparation for the Triumphal Entry and the Last Supper (11:1–6; 14:13–16) | 205
    4.2b The Wording of the Miraculous Feedings (6:41; 8:6–7; 14:22–23) | 208
    4.2c Times for the Master's Coming (13:35 Fulfilled Initially in 14:17; 14:32–57; 14:72; 15:1) | 211
    4.2d The Threefold Call to Watch (13:32–37; 14:32–42) | 214
    4.2e Eschatological Splitting / Heavenly Confession / Title of Beloved Son (1:10–11; 9:7; 15:38–39; 12:6) | 217
4.3 The Matching of Loaded Terminology | 226
    4.3a The Right and Left Hand of Jesus (10:40, 37; 15:27) and Cupbearer vs. Cup of Suffering (10:38; 14:23, 36) | 227
    4.3b Drinking the Cup in the Kingdom (14:25; 15:36) | 229
    4.3c Suffering and Exalted Son of Man Sayings | 233
    4.3e Eyes/Ears without Seeing/Hearing (4:12; 8:18) | 235
    4.3f Destroying and Building the Temple (14:58; 15:29) | 236
    4.3g From a Distance (ἀπὸ μακρόθεν) with Jesus' Miracles (5:6; 8:3; 11:13) and Passion (14:54; 15:40) | 237
    4.3h The Accusations of Blasphemy (2:7; 14:64) | 238
4.4 Possible Matching Terminology | 239
4.5 The Matching of Old Testament Texts | 243
    4.5a Zechariah 9:9 in Mark 11:7 and Zechariah 13:7 in Mark 14:27 | 243
    4.5b Psalm 118:25-26 in Mark 11:9–10 and Psalm 118:22–23 in Mark 12:10–11 | 244
4.6 The Matching of Characters | 245
    4.6a The Parallel Descriptions of John the Baptizer and Jesus | 245
    4.6b An Inner Circle (Peter, James, and John) See Jesus' Glory and Passion (5:37; 9:2; 13:3; 14:33) | 247
    4.6c Two Characters with the Name of Simon | 247
    4.6d A Young Man Flees Jesus' Passion (14:51–52) and a Young Man Announces Jesus' Resurrection (16:5–7) | 249

5 Markan Narrative Surprises | 256

5.1 The Definition of a Markan Narrative Surprise | 256
5.2 The Omission of Normal Elements in a Miracle Story | 258

5.2a The Omission of the Positive Response of Amazement in Several Miracle Stories | 260

5.2b Astonishment Comes at the Beginning Rather than the End (9:15) | 261

5.3 Fear Becomes a Negative Concept Instead of Awe (9:6, 32; 10:32; 16:8) | 263

    5.3a Discipleship Fear in Mark 9:6 | 265

    5.3b The Addition of Fear to Passion Passages in Mark 9:32 and 10:32 | 269

    5.3c The Surprising Ending of Mark in 16:8 | 272

5.4 An Additional Theme of Misunderstanding Inserted in the Trips across the Sea (Mark 4:40; 6:52) | 288

5.5 Surprising Twists in the Narrative | 292

5.6 The Synoptic Alterations of Later Gospel Writers | 299

6   Markan Temporal Mirroring | 307

6.1 A Summary of the Abuses of Mirroring | 307

6.2 The Sea-Calming Journey with Jesus' Sleeping (4:35–41) | 310

6.3 The Sea-Walking Journey with Jesus Praying on a Mountain (6:45–52) | 313

6.4 The Sea Conversation Journey Seemingly without Bread (8:13–21) | 319

6.5 The Disciples' Inability to Cast Out Demons without Jesus (9:14–29) | 321

6.6 The Night Absence of the Master of the House (13:34–36) | 327

6.7 A Post-Resurrection Journey Following a Crucified "Abandoned" Jesus (16:7–8) | 329

    6.7a A Polemic Against a Theologia Gloriae | 329

    6.7b An Example of Reverse Psychology | 331

    6.7c An Open Existential Ending which the Reader Must Complete | 331

6.8 A Possible Scenario Depicting Mark's Community | 334

7   Geographical Mirroring: Jewish and Gentile Territory | 342

7.1 Jesus and the Gentile Mission | 343

7.2 The Gentile Mission as Understood by the Gospel Writers | 346

7.3 The Problem of Markan Geography | 353

7.4 Mark's Employment of Typology to Designate the Gentile Mission | 356

7.5 The Typology of the Pre-Markan Miracle Catenae: An Emphasis upon the Exodus and the Retaking of the Land | 365

7.6 Mark's Employment of Geographical Mirroring to Designate the Gentile Mission in the Two Miraculous Feedings (6:35–44; 8:1–9) | 371

8   Jewish Ceremonial Ritual Mirroring | 388

8.1 Two Contrary Views Regarding Mark's Attitude toward OT Purity Laws | 388

8.2 The Ceremonial Purity of All Unclean Food (7:14–23) | 391

8.3 The New Wine Must Be Placed in New Wineskins (2:21–22) | 409

8.4 The Sabbath Is Made for Humans to Do Good (2:23—3:6) | 416

8.5 The New Temple and the New Synagogue / House for the New Israel Along with the Replacement of Sacrifices | 429

8.6 An Unclean Menstruating Woman and an Unclean Dead Girl (5:21–43) | 436
8.7 An Unclean Leper (1:40–45) | 442
8.8 Unclean Fluids (7:31–37) | 453
8.9 Conclusions | 457

9 Mark's Symbolic Use of Miracle Stories | 461

9.1 Literary Devices Employed in the Markan Miracle Stories | 461
9.2 Markan Parables as Allegorical Riddles (Puzzles Needing Interpretation) | 463
9.3 Miracle Stories Become Acted Parables (Allegorical Riddles) | 465
    9.3a. Miracle Stories Illustrating Jesus as a Crucified Messiah with a Corresponding Discipleship of the Cross | 466
        9.3a1 The Second Touch Healing of the Blind Man (8:22–26) | 466
        9.3a2 Bartimaeus Following Jesus on the Way (10:46–52) | 466
        9.3a3 The Sea-Walking Journey (6:45–52) | 467
    9.3b Miracle Stories Illustrating the Inclusion of Gentiles into the Community | 468
        9.3b1 The Syrophoenician Woman (7:24–30) | 468
        9.3b2 Healings of the Five Thousand and Four Thousand (6:35–44; 8:1–10) | 469
    9.3c. Miracle Stories Illustrating the Fulfillment of Jewish Ceremonial Rituals | 469
        9.3c1 The Cursing of the Fig Tree (11:12–14, 21–25) | 469
        9.3c2 The Healings of the Bleeding Woman and Dead Girl (5:21–43) | 470
9.4 Growth in the Symbolic Meaning of Miracles Stories in Mark's Narrative | 471
9.5 Mark Envisions Additional Theological Meaning in Jesus' Actions | 472
9.6 Examples Favoring a Two-Level Approach to Mark | 475

Appendix 1: A Summary of Markan Literary Devices | 479
Appendix 2: Examples of Irony in Mark's Gospel | 484
Appendix 3: A List of Possible Markan Intercalations by Various Authors | 489
Appendix 4: Outlines of the Structure of Mark | 497

Bibliography | 533

Preface

What sets this book apart from others? Or what niche does it fill that makes its publication important?

Biblical studies in the last years have concentrated on literary criticism. Since this book examines the literary devices that Mark employs to write his gospel, this volume will interest all those who value a literary approach. In addition, this book will introduce some new literary devices into the research of the Gospel of Mark, like Markan allusionary repetitions and a couple types of mirroring, and then attempt to demonstrate the theological intentions of Mark when he employs these literary devices.

During the dominance of literary criticism, the scholarly community surmised that Mark's literary devices were primarily employed to build suspense and tension into the narratives. Instead I will argue that Mark employs the literary devices of intercalation, framework, allusionary repetition, narrative surprise, and mirroring to indicate where he wants to speak symbolically and metaphorically at two levels.

In chapter 1 I attempt to demonstrate that Mark employs these literary devices not just for dramatic tension and irony (although these are important) but for theological reasons to apply the Jesus tradition to the problems he wants to address in his own day. Specifically, Mark wants to proclaim Jesus' message to the problems of:

1. A crucified martyred Messiah (a suffering servant Son of God);

2. Discipleship failures and struggles at the time of Mark's writing of the gospel, i.e. a crisis of discipleship;

3. The addition of Gentiles into the community;

4. The practice of Jewish regulations and participation in Jewish ceremonies, which are now fulfilled in the ministry of Jesus and demand a new reading of the Old Testament.

The prominence of intercalations or Markan sandwiches has been researched for a long time, but I will demonstrate in chapter 2 the theological purpose that they serve in Mark. Examples of Markan frames have been mentioned here and there in the research, but I will show in an extensive chapter 3 how Mark employs frames to structure his entire gospel. Thus chapter 3 functions almost like a commentary on the entire gospel.

Then in the next two chapters I will introduce the concepts of Markan allusionary repetition and Markan narrative surprise to illustrate how Mark reveals to the reader when he is speaking at two levels in the text. In chapter 4 I will demonstrate through extensive examples how Mark employs a unique set of words to create matched episodes. Mark is purposely employing these intratextual repetitions to address the important issue of Christology. First-century Judaism expected a Messiah of power and conquest who would reign forever and re-establish Israel as the center of the earth. The difficult task of the church involved transforming a symbol of shame and degradation, i.e., the cross, and proving that it was God's intended way to deliver Israel. Mark attempts to accomplish this feat through allusionary repetitions whereby an experience of the exaltation of Jesus the Messiah with authority and power is closely paralleled with another text about the passion and death of Jesus the Messiah.

In chapter 5 I will argue that Mark purposely intrudes into the narrative unforeseen elements and unanticipated ingredients that clash with traditional expectations in order to offer a theological evaluation for the reader. These Markan narrative surprises consist of examples of redaction whereby Mark excludes a conventional element in the narrative and inserts an unexpected twist into the traditional story. This narrative technique reveals where Mark wants to speak to the four issues mentioned above that confronted early Christianity.

Finally, I will utilize three mirroring techniques to demonstrate how Mark employs Jesus' words and deeds to instruct his community in dealing with their most pressing problems. In chapter 6 I will explore temporal mirroring whereby Mark retells the stories of Jesus to speak existentially to the community's sense of the absence of Jesus. The absence of Jesus has become a central issue through four prominent developments within the Christian church, including the loss of leadership with the deaths of the apostles like Peter and Paul, the sudden and temporary cessation in the frequency of miracles, the struggles with the acceptance of a discipleship of the cross in the midst of Nero's persecution, and the potential loss of Jerusalem as the headquarters for the church. The absence of Jesus in the gospel narratives mirrors the feeling of an absent Jesus in the Christian community. Six stories in particular center on this theme. The three sea trips mirror the journey of the community with Jesus sleeping (4:35–41), praying on a far mountain while the disciples are scared for their lives in the storm (6:45–52), and Jesus' rebuke to the community, who visualize their trip across the sea as a journey without bread (8:13–21). In addition, the inability of the disciples to cast out demons without Jesus' presence (9:17–19), the night journey of the absentee homeowner (13:34–36), and the culminating surprise ending of Mark where Jesus can only be seen in Galilee (16:7–8) speak to the community's struggle with the absence of Jesus.

Preface

Chapter 7, "Geographical Mirroring," investigates how Mark foresees in Jesus' ministry the inclusion of Gentiles into the covenant community. Mark establishes the presence of a new community comprised of both Jews and Gentiles in three ways: 1) through Jesus' kingdom miracles in the Gentile territory around Galilee; 2) through the sequence of the miracle catenae which typologically mirror the conquest of the land of Canaan which now includes Gentiles; and 3) through geographical mirroring by locating the two miraculous feedings on Jewish and Gentile territory.

Since Jewish conceptions of purity kept Jew and Gentile apart, Mark must also address the matter of OT cleanliness rites. Whereas Jesus was prophetically critical of the pharisaical purity traditions and emphasized the priority of ethical concerns, Mark discerns in Jesus' sayings a more radical approach to OT regulations. In order to convey this insight, Mark does not manipulate the words and deeds of Jesus, but instead adds explanations like 7:19b on some occasions, but more frequently molds the material through intercalations, frames, narrative surprises, and allusionary repetitions to speak to this relevant issue the early church was dealing with. Just as Mark employed geographical mirroring to address Jew/Gentile relations, so he employs Jewish ceremonial ritual mirroring to tackle the issue of the normativity of the ceremonial law. I begin this chapter with the clearest example in 7:19b, where Mark comments upon Jesus' "parable" (7:15) about defilement, demonstrating that "In saying this, Jesus declared all foods clean." Here Mark openly reveals his agenda that Jesus has transformed all Jewish purity rites. Following an examination of food laws, I turn to other important issues such as Sabbath observance, the temple and sacrifices, touching unclean fluids and dead bodies, and the treatment of lepers. In each case Mark employs one of his special literary devices to demonstrate how Jesus' kingdom words and deeds fulfill various Jewish OT ceremonies and rites. Thus Mark employs literary devices to facilitate a new reading of the Old Testament. All of this is new material and should interest those who have worked intently on the interpretation of the Gospel of Mark.

I believe that John and Mark can be categorized as the two symbolic gospels, whereas Luke is a true historian and Matthew carries on an apologetic with the synagogue. In the final chapter, after reviewing the list of Markan literary devices, I show how Mark employs the miracle stories symbolically to preach to issues in the experience of the early church. This parabolic use of miracle stories adds evidence to the thesis that Mark is not only rehearsing the words and acts of Jesus, but that he has purposely chosen material that speaks relevantly to the problems of the early church.

In this book I cover the topics that a commentary would dwell on, but in a different order to develop the literary devices of Mark. Therefore, for conclusions on introductory matters regarding Mark's gospel, turn to the end of chapter 6. For conclusions about Mark's approach to the law and Jewish ceremonies, see the conclusion of chapter 8. For conclusions on Markan redaction of intercalations and an outline of the pre-Markan passion narrative, see the conclusion to chapter 2. For a description of possible oral sources Mark employed for the controversy dialogues and miracles section, see the ending of chapter 3. Finally, for an outline of the gospel see Structure 12 as well as the ending of Appendix 4.

The appendices give handy charts that should benefit the reader. Appendix 1 lists the specific texts where each literary device can be found. Appendix 2 deals with a literary device that I have not covered in this book, i.e. irony, and offers a summary of other authors' discoveries. Appendix 3 lists the various examples of intercalations that have been put forth by interpreters and then evaluates which meet the criteria.

Finally, Appendix 4 discusses twelve possible outlines of the Gospel of Mark. Here I offer my solution as to how Mark put his gospel together in three stages. First, Mark collected the material from the oral tradition, which had already combined the material of the Jesus tradition by genre. The sayings of Jesus had been collected into controversy dialogues, miracle stories, parable collections, discipleship sayings, eschatological discourses, and a passion narrative, as evidenced by the chiastic structures that were employed as memory devices. Mark then places a frame around each of these sections organized by genre to offer a theological interpretation of this material. Finally, confronted with the difficulties of Nero's persecution, the Roman attack on Jerusalem, the death of the apostles, and the sudden cessation of mighty miracles, Mark superimposes upon these literary units a discipleship structure that narrates the inability of the disciples to remain faithful to a cause to which they had originally dedicated their entire lives. The unfaithfulness of the disciples, Jesus' family, and the women (who are together the heroes of the early church in Acts 1:12–14) must be seen as a foil to both rebuke and encourage the readers of the gospel in their attempts at completing a discipleship of the cross. Each of the five cycles begins with a positive description of the disciples but concludes with a rejection of the ministry of Jesus, which challenges the faith of the disciples. In this progression toward a deepening discipleship, the followers of Jesus are first called to come after Jesus (1:17, 20, then to be with him (3:14), then to go before him (6:45) as he supervises them, and finally to take up their cross and follow him in his passion (8:34) and not to fall back in their commitment to preach a crucified Messiah with all its implications (16:8). True disciples progress from followers to companions to fully authorized agents of Jesus' mission to participants in Jesus' suffering and resurrection.

This discipleship outline of the gospel contents is shown to be particularly relevant to Mark himself. I defend the thesis that the character who would rather surrender his clothes than lose his life (14:51–52) is Mark himself. Then a second discipleship failure for Mark occurs in Acts 13:13, where he not only abandons the missionary work because of its difficulties but also causes the breakup of the missionary team when Paul and Barnabas endeavor to plan a follow-up journey (15:36–41). Discipleship failure was an issue that Mark personally struggled with and now he can see that the broader Christian community is experiencing the same struggle.

Preface

After this study I can understand as well why Paul wanted John Mark again in his company. Along with the return of his scrolls (1 Tim 4:12), Paul includes instruction about Mark: "Get Mark and bring him with you, because he is helpful to me in my ministry" (4:13). Mark is a gifted writer and he is able to deal in creative ways with issues that confront the community. So today the Gospel of Mark is particularly relevant to cultures that are struggling with various forms of persecution. For North America the Gospel of Mark is a call for a deeper discipleship, an appeal to recognize the implications of a crucified Messiah.

This book feels like my *Mona Lisa*, a work that has taken years to complete whereby a very lifelike figure emerges. The sixteenth-century painter and historian Vasari discerningly commented, "The mouth, with its opening, and with its ends united by the red of the lips to the flesh-tints of the face, seemed, in truth, to be not colours but flesh. In the pit of the throat, if one gazed upon it intently, could be seen the beating of the pulse." Mona Lisa comes alive before our eyes. Hopefully the Gospel of Mark comes alive before your eyes as you read this book.

I have wrestled with this material for many years and finally it is coming together. I especially want to thank Katrina Schaafsma, who as my teaching assistant managed all the technical details that are necessary for publication. Special thanks to my students, who at the conclusion of our course on the Gospel of Mark would regularly comment, "We've not read this stuff anywhere else; you ought to write up this material to create a meaningful conversation among interpreters of Mark's gospel." Finally, I want to bless my wife, Julie, who has stood with me through my chemotherapy and radiation treatments and encouraged me to overcome these health issues which demand so much energy. Even though the *Mona Lisa* is a small painting, it is notoriously famous because the onlooker cannot see the lines of the paintbrush. It appears seamless. Hopefully, the discussion of these various literary devices that Mark employs together create a seamless picture. And hopefully through this work, you, the reader, will grow in your appreciation of the art of Mark's narrative.

Abbreviations

AER	*American Ecclesiastical Review*
ASV	*American Standard Version*
b.	*Babylonian Talmud*
BAGD	*W. Bauer; F. Danker; W. Arndt; F. Gingrich, A Greek-English Lexicon of the NT, 2nd ed.*
BBR	*Bulletin for Biblical Research*
BDAG	*W. Bauer; F. Danker; W. Arndt; F. Gingrich, A Greek-English Lexicon of the NT, 3rd ed.*
BDF	*F. Blass, A. Debrunner, R. Funk, A Greek Grammar of the New Testament, 1961*
Bib	*Biblica*
BibLeb	*Bibel und Leben*
BJRL	*Bulletin of the John Rylands Library*
BR	*Biblical Research*
BSac	*Bibiotheca Sacra*
BTB	*Biblical Theology Bulletin*
BTr	*Bible Translator*
BZ	*Biblische Zeitschrift*
CBQ	*Catholic Biblical Quarterly*
CQR	*Church Quarterly Review*
CTJ	*Calvin Theological Journal*
CTR	*Criswell Theological Review*
ETL	*Ephemerides Theologicae Lovanienses*
ETR	*Etudes Théologiques et Religieuses*
EvQ	*Evangelical Quarterly*
ESV	*English Standard Version*
ExpT	*Expository Times*

Abbreviations

GNT	Good News Translation
HTR	Harvard Theological Review
IBS	Irish Biblical Studies
ICC	International Critical Commentary
IDB	The Interpreter's Dictionary of the Bible
Int	Interpretation
ISBE	International Standard Bible Encyclopedia, ed. Geoffry W. Bromiley, 1979
ISV	International Standard Version
JBL	Journal of Biblical Literature
JBR	Journal of Bible and Religion
JR	Journal of Religion
JETS	Journal of the Evangelical Theological Society
JSNT	Journal for the Study of the New Testament
JSNTSS	Journal for the Study of the New Testament Supplementary Series
JSOT	Journal for the Study of the Old Testament
JThS	Journal of Theological Studies
JThSA	Journal of Theology for Southern Africa
KJV	King James Version
LingBib	Linguistica Biblica
LXX	Septuagint
m.	Mishnah
Neot	Neotestamentica
NASV	New American Standard Version
NCV	New Century Version
NEB	New English Bible
NICNT	New International Commentary of the New Testament
NIV	New International Version
NJB	New Jerusalem Bible
NKJV	New King James Version
NLB	New Living Bible
NovT	Novum Testamentum
NRSV	New Revised Standard Version
NThT	Nederlands Theologisch Tijdschrift
NTS	New Testament Studies
PRS	Perspectives in Religion Studies
ResQ	Restoration Quarterly

Abbreviations

REx	*The Review and Expositor*
RSR	*Recherches de science religieuse*
RSV	*Revised Standard Version*
SBL	*Society of Biblical Literature*
SBLASP	*Society of Biblical Literature Annual Meeting Seminar Papers*
SBLDS	*SBL Dissertation Series*
SJTh	*Scottish Journal of Theology*
StEv	*Studia Evangelica*
StTh	*Studia Theologica*
SThR	*Sewanee Theological Review*
t.	Tosefta
T. Levi	*Testament of Levi*
TDNT	*Theological Dictionary of the New Testament* (Kittel)
ThZ	*Theologische Zeitschrift*
TLZ	*Theologische Literaturzeitung*
TNIV	*Today's New International Version*
TS	*Theological Studies*
TTh	*Tijdschrift voor Theologie*
TynBul	*Tyndale Bulletin*
USQR	*Union Seminary Quarterly Review*
VC	*Vigiliae Christianae*
ZAW	*Zeitschrift für die alttestamentliche Wissenschaft*
ZKG	*Zeitschrift für Kirchengeschichte*
ZNW	*Zeitschrift für die neutestamentliche Wissenschaft*
ZTK	*Zeitschrift für Theologie und Kirche*

1

The Two Levels of Interpretation in Mark's Gospel

1.1 Mark and the Jesus Tradition: Surprises in Reading the Gospel of Mark

Luke Johnson begins his discussion of the Gospel of Mark asserting, "the shortest of the gospels is also the strangest and the most difficult to grasp."[1] Although Johnson does not expound on this statement, he surely implies that readers' expectations are overturned. Surprising twists occur in the narrative. Mark purposely intrudes unforeseen elements which clash with traditional expectations, creating theological innovations which the reader must reflect upon and evaluate. The following unexpected turns illustrate the complexity and depth of Mark's gospel.

Surprises confront the reader at the beginning of Mark's gospel. Mark labels Jesus as the promised Messiah in the very first verse, but no angelic announcements, heavenly dreams and visions, or astonishing prophetic fulfillments proclaim a special birth. Instead a secondary person appears front and center, John the Baptizer. In fact Jesus, the main character, needs to be baptized by John, an action which Matthew later tempers to prevent any misunderstanding of their respective roles (3:14–15) and which the fourth evangelist subtly transforms so that Jesus' water baptism is omitted completely from the narrative (1:29–34). The Jewish nation expected a conquering Christ who would live forever. But by combining a messianic psalm (Ps 2:7) with an allusion to the Suffering Servant (Isa 42:1), the voice from heaven in Mark 1:11 introduces a novel theology of the Messiah. Through repetition of vocabulary ($\sigma\chi\iota\zeta\omega$ in 1:10; 15:38) Mark connects the heavenly call of the Messiah with his Passion and crucifixion instead of emphasizing the political, economic, and miraculous powers of the expected Messiah.

---

1. Johnson, *Writings*, 159.

The Theological Intentions of Mark's Literary Devices

Readers of the gospel certainly expect a story highlighting the growing popularity of Jesus, at least until he enters Jerusalem and encounters direct opposition from the temple establishment. Instead, spiritual opposition and human conflict dominate the narrative from the outset. Immediately following his baptism, the Holy Spirit drives Jesus into the wilderness (1:12–13) to confront the devil, and in Jesus' very first sermon in the synagogue (1:21–28) demons interrupt his preaching. Then Mark places five controversy dialogues to inaugurate Jesus' Galilean ministry (2:1—3:6) so that at the very outset of Jesus' ministry two social opposites, the Pharisees and Herodians, combine forces to plot Jesus' assassination (3:6). Already in 2:20 Jesus predicts that the messianic bridegroom will be taken away. As Martin Kähler famously quipped, Mark's gospel becomes "a passion narrative with an extended introduction."[2]

Not only is the beginning of Mark surprising, but also the ending of the gospel is notoriously enigmatic (16:8). Although a young man dressed as a heavenly figure announces that Jesus is alive, no resurrection appearances follow. The message of Jesus' resurrection is not presented evangelistically toward unbelievers in an effort to evoke belief, nor does a missionary commission send the disciples to successfully convert the nations. Instead the failures of the faithful are orated so that, overcome by fear, the woman flee from the tomb conspicuously silent. Instead of concluding on a high point of triumphant joy, the ending of Mark instills uncertainty and self-reflective pondering in the minds of the readers. The lack of resolution with regard to the themes of the Messianic Secret and the disciples' unbelief and hardness of heart creates a bewilderment that must have generated a crisis in the readership.[3] Would a book entitled a "gospel" ("good news") end with human failure, incomprehension, disobedience, and fear? Mark's ending is a surprise grammatically, literarily, thematically, theologically, and stylistically.

In retelling the story of Jesus, one would expect talk about crucifixion to occur near the end of the narrative and to be solely connected with the person of Jesus. Mark, however, introduces the cross at the middle of his gospel and speaks of a cross that the disciples must encounter. The discipleship catechism at the center of Mark's gospel (8:27—10:45) is structured by the threefold Passion prediction of Jesus' suffering in 8:31; 9:31; and 10:33 but culminates in a threefold teaching on discipleship which centers upon the disciples' experience of carrying the cross (8:34), enduring death as salted sacrifices (9:49), and drinking the cup of suffering (10:39). This prominence of the cross early in the narrative creates a double twisting surprise later when Jesus' closest followers fail to follow Jesus to the cross and play absolutely no role in the crucifixion story. This early introduction of instruction about the cross along with the failure to pay attention to this teaching late in the narrative creates a mysterious

---

2. Kähler, *The So-Called Historical Jesus*, 80, n. 11.

3. Authors who posit a lost ending like France (*Mark*, 676) contend that "For Mark's story to have finished with ten of the Twelve as deserters, one a traitor, and Peter blasphemously dissociating himself from Jesus would have undone all that Mark has tried to do."

The Two Levels of Interpretation in Mark's Gospel

questioning in the minds of readers regarding the implications of this theme for their Christian discipleship.

Traditionally, miracle stories provide superlative proof for the distinctive role and differentiating character of the healer whose fame spreads far and wide through these wondrous works. But the Gospel of Mark famously accentuates the Messianic Secret, where Jesus commands utter silence after his most astounding miracles (1:34, 44; 5:43; 7:36; 8:26), his absolute dominion over demonic powers (1:24–25, 34; 3:11–12), and his instruction to the disciples about his true identity (8:29–30; 9:9). Instead of these wonders producing awe and transformational belief in the closest witnesses, the disciples remain faithless and hard-hearted after Jesus calms the storm-tossed sea (4:40) and walks upon the waves (6:52b) like God himself (Job 9:8). His followers fail to comprehend the miracle of the multiplication of bread (6:52a), even when it occurs a second time (8:4, 16), so that at the conclusion of the miracle catenae the disciples are extensively rebuked for their lack of faith, understanding, and hardness of heart (8:17–21). Instead of the normal elements of wonder and acclaim climaxing a miracle story, on several occasions Mark replaces positive awe with negative fear. Shockingly, in the same contexts where "fear" must be understand positively as wonder (4:41; 6:51; 16:5), as in the tradition,[4] this term also takes on a negative connotation (4:40; 6:52; 16:8). Surprisingly, Mark connects fear with lack of faith (4:40–41), insufficient discipleship (9:6; 16:8), and the inability to discern a true understanding of Jesus' identity (6:50–52; 9:32; 10:32).

The traditional picture and purpose of parables as well as miracles is overturned. Normally parables provide simple pictures to make clear, practical, and understandable the more abstract and ethereal religious teachings of the kingdom of God. But for Mark the parables conceal rather than reveal. The purpose of parables according to 4:12 is that the listeners "may be ever seeing but never perceiving, and ever hearing but never understanding." Parables apparently hide the identity of Jesus from the crowd rather than provide the secret to understanding his distinctiveness. What are we as readers to make of this phenomenon?

Readers would certainly expect a book entitled "good news" (1:1) to applaud Jesus with titles that acclaim his exalted nature. Jesus would be identified as the long-expected royal Messiah, a king more renowned than Caesar, and an exalted Son of Man lifted up to God's throne in heaven as Daniel 7:13-14 describes. Instead, at the turning point in the narrative when Peter identifies his master as the Messiah, Jesus immediately changes the title to suffering Son of Man (8:29–31). Instead of ascribing Jesus as king, as both Matthew (2:2; 21:5) and Luke (19:38) proclaim, Mark identifies Herod as the king (6:14, 22, 25–27) so that Jesus is only designated by the term

---

4. Sometimes Mark follows the tradition by connecting the terms amazement (ἐκπλήσσω 1:22; 6:2; 7:37; 10:26; 11:18), astonishment (ἐξίστημι 2:12; 5:42; 6:51), and wonder (θαμβέω 1:27; 10:24, 32; ἐκθαμβέω 9:15; 16:5–6; θαύμαζω 5:20; 15:5; ἐκθαύμαζω 12:17) with Jesus' miracles and extraordinary teaching.

βασιλεύς in his Passion, where the language is consistently mockery rather than respect ("king of the Jews" in 15:2, 9, 12, 18, 26 and "king of Israel" in 15:32). Speaking about Jesus' royal triumphal entry, Ben Witherington poetically explains,

> Mark's account is laden with irony, for the crowd associated the triumphal entry with the promise of coming salvation, whereas, in Mark's view, Hosanna is what happens when the end of the week comes and there are no cries but Jesus' cry of dereliction. Salvation came in a manner no one expected, not during the ecstasy but during the agony, not when everyone was on Jesus' side but when he had been totally abandoned by humankind.[5]

Finally, the repeated chorus of the suffering Son of Man dominates Mark's score (8:31; 9:12, 31; 10:33–34, 45; 14:21, 41) so that he only plays the note of an exalted Son of Man at the end of his composition (13:26; 14:62).[6] Thus Mark alters the traditional coloring of the expected gospel picture of the Savior through all three titles of Messiah, king, and Son of Man.

1.2 Possible Explanations for Mark's Descriptions of the Disciples

If I were composing a gospel, I would certainly exhibit the initial followers of Jesus as powerful models for the world to behold and emulate. Rather than revealing their continuing weaknesses and bumbling mistakes, I would treat them as gifted people and impeccable examples of growing commitment to Christ. But in Mark's gospel the further the narrative progresses, the more negative the disciples appear. In 4:11 Jesus informs his disciples that "the mystery of the kingdom is given to you," but they prove incapable of understanding this mystery during Jesus' ministry (6:52; 7:18; 8:17; 9:32). Their hollow-headedness with regard to the parables is paralleled by their hard-heartedness with regard to Jesus' miracles (6:52; 8:17). Furthermore, when Jesus predicts his Passion (8:31; 9:31; 10:33) they respond with a triad of misunderstandings (8:32–33; 9:33–34; 10:35–39). Finally, their physical actions replicate their head and heart misunderstandings when they desert Jesus in the garden of Gethsemane and run for their lives (14:50–52) instead of offering Jesus companionship in his time of need. Certainly Peter attempts to retrace his steps toward Jesus, but in the process commits graver errors, denying Jesus on three subsequent occasions (14:66–72) and even calling down curses on his master (14:71). The absence of the Twelve at the cross reveals their abandonment of the faith commitment that Mark is advocating. Not surprisingly, this portrait of the disciples is altered by Matthew and Luke because of its one-sidedness in portraying the followers of Jesus. But Mark pursues his agenda with single-minded consistency.

---

5. Witherington, *Mark*, 351.

6. But see 8:38 and 9:9, which show that the suffering Son of Man will end up exalted.

The Two Levels of Interpretation in Mark's Gospel

The tradition depicted the disciples, Jesus' family, and the women as the constituting community, the 120 people who provide the foundation for the church (Acts 1:14). As tried and true followers of Jesus, they gallantly endure persecution as heroes of the faith (Acts 2–5). But in Mark's gospel these three groups end up as failures even though they are introduced positively (1:16–20; 15:40–41). As we have seen, the disciples are transposed from powerful charismatic leaders to mistake-ridden misunderstanding neophytes. In addition, Jesus' mother and family suppose that Jesus is out of his mind (3:21) so that they stand outside Jesus' circle (3:31) and treat him without honor (6:4). Mark teams Jesus' family together with the archenemy teachers of the law (3:22–30), whose accusation against Jesus that he is possessed by an evil spirit sounds conspicuously similar to the remark by Jesus' family. Finally, the women become the characters in the narrative who provide the final picture of discipleship. Instead of icons of stalwart faithfulness, the women conclude the narrative as exhibits of fear, flight, and a failure to proclaim the gospel (16:8). Discipleship failure appears to triumph among those closest to Jesus.

These transformations of the tradition have been explained by a number of hypotheses. Through a harmonization of the Gospels, some scholars contend that Mark is not negative but employs these techniques to emphasize the supremacy of Jesus. The fear of the disciples is interpreted positively as "awe" throughout the gospel, so that the ending in 16:8 is portrayed triumphantly.[7] Craig Evans explains, "Mark's Gospel ends with a dramatic finish, emphasizing once again the awesome power of Jesus, who not only astounded people during his ministry but also astounded people in his death and in his resurrection."[8] In this scenario, each failure of the disciples magnifies the success of Jesus. Robert Gundry, in particular, promotes this approach. In the introduction to his commentary he offers a series of examples:

1. "[T]he disciples' failure to understand yet another passion prediction makes Jesus' fore-sight stand out all the more."

2. "[T]heir fear to ask him what he means implies the awesomeness of a divine being who knows his own fate (9:30–32)."

3. "Since Jesus stays awake in Gethsemane while his disciples fall asleep, his flesh is strong just as his voice will be strong at the very moment of his death."

4. "That all his disciples forsake him increases the unlikelihood that Jesus' predictions will be unfulfilled and thus magnifying the impressiveness of Jesus predictive foresight."

5. "Jesus is Christ, Son of God—a figure of great dignity; so someone else takes up

---

7. See Dwyer, *Motif of Wonder*; Magness, *Sense and Absence*.

8. Evans, *Mark 8:27—16:20*, 540. Evans also envisions Jesus' death in Mark as evidence of triumphant power so that the release of his spirit is awesome and his death shout is so powerful that it tears the temple veil (508–9).

his cross (15:21)."

6. "The women flee away trembling, astonished, and awestruck beyond words because of the power of Jesus' resurrection (16:7–8)."[9]

Therefore, the disciples' failures to understand and follow Jesus do not illustrate an unexpected alteration of the tradition but call attention to the supremacy of Jesus, who predicted these actions. Most of the authors of this persuasion assume a lost ending to Mark in which all the discipleship failures are resolved.[10]

This view does not naturally arise out of the text. As Juel exclaims, "To hear in Mark's elusive ending the strains of Handel's 'Hallelujah Chorus' would require drowning out the music being performed."[11] Since the women's response immediately follows the young man's command to go and tell, their silence reads more naturally as an act of fearful disobedience than an attempt at hurried obedience.[12] Mark consistently constructs the final picture of Jesus' family, the disciples, and the women in negative terms. The last time we encounter Jesus' mother and brothers they stand outside (3:31–32) the circle of disciples who perform God's will (3:34–35). In the climax of the gospel Jesus' disciples are not present at the cross but instead all desert him and flee (14:50, 52 ἔφυγον; ἔφυγεν), which importantly becomes the identical description of the women at the end of the gospel (16:8 ἔφυγον). In fact, the overarching structure of Mark concludes each section with discipleship failure, as I explain at the end of Appendix 4. Instead of employing discipleship failure as a foil for an exalted Christology, Mark parallels Christology and discipleship so that the Passion of Christ enjoins a similar cross-bearing by the disciples.

Since Mark's final picture of these three important groups in the early church (see Acts 1:13–14) is consistently negative, some scholars posit a negative apologetic purpose to explain these Markan innovations. Telford explains, "Polemical theories have the advantage of offering more convincing explanations for the harsh treatment of Jesus' opponents, family, and disciples as well as for the secrecy motif and its Christological motivation."[13] In particular, Theodore Weeden famously concludes that

> Mark is assiduously involved in a vendetta against the disciples. He is intent on totally discrediting them. He paints them as obtuse, obdurate, recalcitrant men who at first are unperceptive of Jesus' messiahship, then oppose its style

---

9. Gundry, *Mark*, 11–14.

10. The long ending of Mark 16:9–20 was the dominant thesis until Wellhausen's commentary in Germany (1903) and Lightfoot's influence in the English-speaking world (1950). The intended ending at 16:8 reigned throughout the second half of the twentieth century, but the landscape is changing in the twenty-first century with evangelical scholars arguing for a lost ending (Craig Evans, Robert Gundry, Grant Osborne, Bob Stein, Richard Swinburne, Ben Witherington, N.T. Wright). See section 5.3c below.

11. Juel, *Master of Surprise*, 120.

12. Cf. Williams, *Other Followers of Jesus*, 27.

13. Telford, *Theology of Mark*, 159.

and character, and finally totally reject it. As the *coup de grace*, Mark closes his Gospel without rehabilitating the disciples.[14]

How are we to evaluate this proposal?

This apologetic approach embraces various variant interpretations. To explain this "vendetta," Weeden proposes that "Jesus serves as a surrogate for Mark, and the disciples serve as surrogates for Mark's opponents . . . Jesus preaches and acts the Markan suffering-servant theology. The disciples promulgate and act out *theios-aner* theology."[15] According to this view, Mark is promulgating an anti-miracle Messiah. Mark employs the miracle stories to refute exaggerations of wonder-working enthusiasts, false disciples of Jesus who preach Jesus as a *theios aner* ("divine man") and themselves as *theioi andres*, thus misunderstanding the gospel.[16]

Since the writing of Weeden's manuscript, this thesis of a divine man theology in the gospels has been completely debunked.[17] As Broadhead explains, "the θεῖος ἀνήρ concept cannot be taken as a fixed assumption. No one has shown that a fixed θεῖος ἀνήρ existed, or that such a concept was widespread, or even that Mark's opponents held this view."[18] Instead the Gospel of Mark avoids any dichotomy between the Jesus of the miracles and the Jesus of the cross. Broadhead eloquently concludes,

> No sharp division exists between the portrait of Jesus in the first and the last half of the Gospel. The narrative develops the failure of the disciples through both miracle stories and the passion account. The opposition of the religious leaders begins in a miracle story and concludes in the passion story. The focus on Jesus' death originates in a miracle story and is fulfilled in the passion narrative.[19]

To posit that Mark polemicized against a θεῖος ἀνήρ Christology is to think unhistorically. Therefore, this formulation of the apologetic approach only leads to a dead end.

A second apologetic explanation posits that the disciples function as representatives of the Jerusalem church, headed by James. As Crossan explains, "The polemic against the disciples and the polemic against the relatives intersect as a polemic against the doctrinal and jurisdictional hegemony of the Jerusalem mother-church."[20] Supposedly, the Jerusalem leadership promulgated a triumphalistic Jewish-Christian

---

14. Weeden, *Mark*, 50–51.
15. Ibid., 113.
16. See Sunderwirth, *Use of Miracle Stories in Mark's Gospel*.
17. See Kingsbury, "'Divine Man,'" 243–57. Marcus (*Mark*, 77) demonstrates that "Divine man does not seem to have been a fixed term in first-century Hellenism and when the term is used, it does not seem to be particularly connected with miracles or with the title Son of God."
18. Broadhead, *Teaching with Authority*, 211.
19. Ibid., 214. Theissen (*Miracle Stories*, 294) adds, "If Mark wanted to warn against belief in miracles, it is hard to see why he should emphasize Jesus' miraculous activity in redactional summaries."
20. Crossan, "Mark and the Relatives of Jesus," 112. Cf. Kelber, *Mark's Story of Jesus*, 90.

Son of David or apocalyptic Son of Man Christology.[21] They only pictured Jesus as the victorious royal Messiah, while Mark advocated a divine but unrecognized Son of God whose suffering and death on the cross were redemptive.

Against this "intramural polemics,"[22] the deceivers described in 13:6–7, 22–23 do not stand within the community but outside of it. To contend that Mark viewed the Jerusalem church negatively undermines the establishment of the church upon the foundation of the apostles and prophets (Eph 2:20).[23] To argue that Jesus' family committed the unpardonable sin (Mark 3:21–22 interpreted by 3:28–29)[24] as represented in the Jerusalem community denies the foundational place of Jesus' family in the early church as narrated by Acts.

Instead of following an apologetic approach, Ernest Best argues that the negative presentation of the disciples favors a pastorally corrective approach.[25] Through the misunderstandings of the disciples, Mark presents a foil for a cross-oriented Christology coupled with a cross-carrying discipleship. Mark addresses a church suffering persecution by presenting a suffering Messiah and using the disciples' misunderstanding as a pedagogic device to present teaching on the true nature of discipleship under such circumstances. The Markan community finds "a recognizable reflection of themselves mirrored realistically in the fallible disciples."[26] This approach fits the facts of Mark's gospel.

Therefore, Mark could be categorized as a symbolic gospel which presents narratives metaphorically to teach the Christian community. Mark sets the memory of the historical Jesus alongside the experience of his community as a pedagogical tool to offer insights into the church's struggles.[27] Despite the attractiveness of this proposal, this view has strong opponents because of the difficulty of determining exactly when Mark is employing symbolism.

---

21. See the description and evaluation in Telford, *Theology of Mark*, 50–52.

22. Anderson ("Trial of Jesus," 107) employs this title. Barton (*Discipleship and Family Ties*, 85) calls this hypothesis an "allegory of ecclesiastic politics in the post-Easter period."

23 Herron (*Mark's Account of Peter's Denial*, 143) notes that "its survival is nothing short of miraculous if it were anti-apostolic." Likewise, Geddert (*Watchwords*, 159) concludes that it is "farfetched to imagine that Mark or his church could have loved the Messiah and hated the twelve."

24 Tyson, "Blindness of the Disciples," 261–68; Trocmé, *Formation of Mark*, 104–9.

25. Cf. Best, *Disciples and Discipleship*, 128–30; and *Following Jesus*, 241; Barton, *Discipleship and Family Ties*, 107; Telford, *Theology of Mark*, 159.

26. Wegener, *Cruciformed*, 69.

27. The book *The Gospels for All Christians: Rethinking the Gospel Audiences*, edited by Richard Bauckham, attempts to demonstrate that the communities addressed by each gospel writer are only scholarly constructs. Although this volume offers a needed corrective, it is by no means convincing since, as Marcus (*Mark*, 27) demonstrates, several ancient Jewish-Christian works are addressed for local purposes. See also Sim, "Gospels for All Christians?," and Esler, "Community and Gospel."

1.3 Explanations for Markan Irregularities

These so-called Markan irregularities can be interpreted by a number of hypotheses. A simple proposal regards Mark as an inept and inexperienced writer. Perturbed by Mark's style of duplicity and his habit of not revealing to the reader the theological implications of his narrative, some authors in frustration proclaim that "The point is settled: the author of Mark was a clumsy writer unworthy of mention in any history of literature."[28] For instance, Nineham, quoting Turner, labels the gospel a "naive and non-logical composition."[29] Chapman, in his volume entitled *The Orphan Gospel*, categorizes this approach as the "Village Idiot Theory."

Regarding grammar and vocabulary, scholars point to paratactic sentences, unwarranted repetitions, double negatives, delayed *gar* clauses, unusual parentheses, and other unorthodox grammatical constructions. From such information Chapman concludes that "Mark has a small vocabulary, his grammar is poor, his style is rough; his preoccupation with miracles suggests a person of limited intelligence."[30] Concerning style, Fowler laments, "One sentence is juxtaposed to another, often with wrenching shifts of direction in the action or with unannounced changes in the subjects of the sentences."[31] Regarding theology, Bultmann concludes that "Mark is not sufficiently master of his material to be able to venture on a systematic construction himself."[32] Regarding the integration of themes, James Williams bemoans the fact that "the author offers broken pieces that the reader cannot quite fit into the total picture."[33] Concerning specific passages, Meagher concludes that 4:1–34 includes content in diametric opposition and "has managed the contradiction not with a finesse that reveals a lesson but with a benumbing baldness that leaves us either bemused or scrambling to our own resources for an explanatory subtlety that is painfully lacking in the text."[34] Cumulatively, these concerns raise the issue of Mark's competency as a writer.[35]

Robert Fowler raises an alternative solution: that Mark is purposefully ambivalent. He contends that the scholarly fox hunt to explain the subtleties of Mark's gospel has never found the prey. Maybe, Fowler proposes, this is precisely Mark's intention.

Fowler suggests that Mark's ambivalence has caused divergent interpretations throughout each section of the gospel. In 1:1 readers are unable to discern if the title "beginning of the gospel" applies to the whole book or the section about John the Baptizer. In Jesus' baptism, several alternative OT scriptures are proposed as the

---

28. Trocmé, *Formation of Mark*, 72.

29. Nineham, *St. Mark*, 215.

30. Chapman, *Orphan Gospel*, 20. Weeden (*Traditions in Conflict*, 140) observes that "Mark must have either been a very careless, inconsistent writer or a very feeble-minded thinker."

31. Fowler, *Let the Reader Understand*, 135.

32. Bultmann, *History*, 350.

33. Williams, *Gospel Against Parable*, 71.

34. Meagher, *Clumsy Construction*, 105.

35. We raise this question again in the second to last paragraph of this chapter.

background for the voice from heaven. The wild animals in the testing of Jesus (1:13) have been applied to a new creation, the wilderness experience of Israel, and the wild beasts of Nero's persecution. The expression "fishers of men" (1:17) is both viewed as a positive title of a missionary evangelist and as a negative description of a judgmental prophet. Likewise, the nicknames "Rock" and "Sons of Thunder" (3:16–17) seem to contain connotations of strength and fervor as well as clamorous judgment. Finally, Jesus' disgustful dismissal of the leper (1:44) is left ambiguous so that the reader is uncertain whether Jesus respects the authority of the Jewish priests in carrying out the ceremonial law of Moses or if he is witnessing against them and usurping their authority to proclaim the leper clean.

Likewise in Jesus' parables and miracles, Fowler explains that ambivalence reigns. Does Jesus recite parables to reveal the meaning of God's kingdom or to conceal it? Does Mark promote Jesus as a great wonder-worker or polemicize against Jesus as miracle worker? Do the geographical descriptions where Jesus' miracles occur entail a symbolism about Jews and Gentiles or is it historical data alone? Regarding the reason why the disciples do not understand Jesus' miracles, Fowler point out,

> Precisely what the disciples dare to understand is left unspecified; in fact, the evangelist never spells it out explicitly anywhere in this part of the gospel. The interpreter of the gospel must admit that even he does not know for sure what the disciples should understand.[36]

The mystery of the kingdom (4:11), the secret understanding of the miracles, and, for that matter, the Messianic Secret itself are never explained.

Similarly, in Jesus' Jerusalem ministry it is unclear whether references to the temple designate a Jewish institution, Jesus' body, or the church. It is difficult to decide if 12:35–37 represents Jesus as a son of David or if Mark intends to undermine any historical connection between Jesus and David.[37] In the Passion narrative, the young man (14:51; 16:5) can be understood as a positive angel or a negative disciple. In the crucifixion narrative the centurion (15:39) is either construed as the ultimate mocker of Jesus or the sole revealer of Jesus' true identity. Notoriously difficult is the ending of Mark, which is understood as a powerful manifestation of Jesus' glory by some, a further negative description of the disciples by others, and an indication of a lost ending by yet another group of commentators.

Fowler contends that the logical interpretation of this phenomenon is that Mark "pulls (and entices) the reader so vigorously (and seductively) in different directions simultaneously that it is ultimately an ambivalent narrative."[38] But why would an author purposely plan ambivalent narratives? James Williams proposes, "The only conclusion I find convincing is that the author intends the audience to be prevented

---

36. Fowler (*Loaves and Fishes*, 110) is speaking specifically about Mark 8:17–21.
37. Fowler, *Let the Reader Understand*, 199.
38. Ibid., 261.

from overconfidence in its ability to fathom the gospel story."[39] But then the disciples become exemplary rather than a foil for discipleship re-education. Then the gospel of Jesus Christ does not increase faith and promote assurance so much as advance tolerance and encourage open-mindedness. These seem like modern-day virtues placed back upon the text. Fowler suggests that Mark has a "parental concern for offspring nearing maturity" and thus is "championing the freedom of the reader to plot her own course through the reading experience."[40] Somehow this solution seems more an introduction to modern reader-response criticism than the purpose for an ancient gospel, almost a palimpsest covering the original text.

Therefore we must look elsewhere for an interpretation of Mark's surprising changes to the Jesus tradition. Bird clarifies the main question: "Certainly the second gospel is an enigma. But is it the child of confusion, or a signpost to mystery?"[41] This pressingly relevant question raises the possibility that Mark's unexpected twists are purposeful literary devices. We will argue that Mark employs literary devices like intercalations, frames, allusionary repetitions, narrative surprises, and mirroring to offer a theological and symbolic interpretation of the events. But several scholars oppose such a hypothesis. Why have symbolic interpretations been dismissed?

1.4 The Difficulty in Discerning Symbolism[42]

The lack of specificity by Mark is the prominent reason why it is difficult to determine if Mark possesses intended symbolism. Unlike Matthew, who consistently quotes the Old Testament to enlighten the events of Jesus' ministry, Mark only alludes to Scripture.[43] As Boring explains, "Only occasionally does the evangelist make his allusions to Scripture explicit. Here, too, the reader must have 'ears to hear.'"[44] Similarly, Mark does not offer explicit signals to notify the reader of intended irony. As Fowler explains,

---

39. Williams, *Gospel Against Parable*, 71. Referring especially to the Markan ending, Juel (*Master of Surprise*, 121) concurs, "The ending produces a tension between disappointment and promise, blindness and insight, concealment and openness, silence and proclamation so that one can only live by promises and be satisfied with questions of meaning."

40. Fowler, *Let the Reader Understand*, 261–62.

41. Bird, "Some γάρ Clauses," 171.

42. Koester (*Symbolism in the Fourth Gospel*, 4) defines a symbol as "an image, an action, or a person that is understood to have transcendent significance." Culpepper (*Anatomy*, 201) states that symbols are "bridges by which the reader may cross in some elusive sense into the reality and mystery, the life, which they represent." We will employ the term in a variety of contexts and ways to speak about a person, place, or thing that comes to represent a more abstract idea or concept. It is anything that stands for something beyond itself.

43. For instance, Matthew adds a fulfillment of scripture to Mark 1:34 (Matt 4:15–16 from Isa 8:23—9:1), Mark 3:12 (Matt 12:18–21 from Isa 42:1–4), the parables of Mark 4:1–20 (Matt 13:34–35 from Ps 78:2), and Mark 11:2–3 (Matt 21:5 from Zech 9:9). A typical Markan allusion is the references to Ps 2:7 and Isa 42:1 in the voice at Jesus' baptism.

44. Boring, *Mark*, 405.

> Verbal signals from the narrator that alert us to the presence of verbal irony are relatively rare. Almost all statements by the characters in the Passion Narrative are ironic, ambiguous, or otherwise oblique, but few are accompanied by explicit interpretive signals from the narrator.[45]

This indirectness of Mark is reinforced by the recurring theme of secrecy in the gospel. Beside the famous Messianic Secret referring to Christology, Mark employs the mystery of the kingdom, the secret only demons know, the secret about miracles, the clandestine instruction to the disciples, and Jesus' attempts to conceal himself from the crowds.[46] Consistent with this emphasis upon secrecy, Mark's symbolism also remains opaque.

Second, the first interpreters of Mark, namely Matthew and Luke, "obviously missed the alleged symbolic contents."[47] Matthew in particular fails to see the significance of Mark's literary devices. For instance, Matthew omits the prominent symbolic miracle story, the two-stage healing of the blind man (Mark 8:22–26), probably because the lack of immediacy of the miracle was thought to diminish Jesus' supremacy and because the method of healing with spit associates Jesus with uncleanness.[48] Likewise, Matthew misses the significance of Mark's frame around the discipleship catechism by the two healings of the blind men (8:22–26 and 10:46–52). Similarly, Matthew dismantles the Markan intercalation around the cursing of the fig tree and the cleansing of the temple (Matt 21:12–17, 18–22 vs. Mark 11:12–14, 15–19, 20–25) as well as missing the Jewish symbolism of the number twelve in the combined stories of the bleeding woman and dead girl (Matt 9:25 vs. Mark 5:42). Thus Matthew overlooks Markan techniques for detecting symbolism.

Instead of following Markan redaction in the miracle stories to include symbolic elements about discipleship, Matthew returns to the original intent of miracle stories expressing the awe and acclaim of a mighty messianic healer. Matthew excludes the misunderstandings after the trips across the sea (Mark 4:40 missing in Matt 9:26–27; Mark 6:52 vs. Matt 14:33), thus transforming the narratives into pure miracle stories. Matthew omits Mark's Jew/Gentile imagery with the feeding of the five thousand on Jewish territory and the feeding of the four thousand in Gentile lands so that the warning to the disciples (Mark 8:11–16) now clearly applies to the teaching of the Pharisees

---

45. Fowler, *Let the Reader Understand*, 159.

46. Examples include the following: 1) the Messianic Secret after revelations to the disciples (8:29–30; 9:9); 2) the mystery of the kingdom (4:11); 3) the secret only the demons know (1:24–25, 34; 3:11–12); 4) the secret after miraculous healings (1:44; 5:43; 7:36; 8:26); 5) secret instruction given to the disciples (4:11–12, 33–34; 7:17–23; 8:31–33; 9:2–8, 28–29; 9:30–32; 10:10–12, 32–34; 13:3–37); and 6) examples where Jesus conceals himself from the crowds (1:35–37, 45; 3:7; 4:35; 6:31, 45–47; 7:24; 9:30).

47. Räisänen, *Messianic Secret in Mark*, 23.

48. Matthew omits both of the Markan healings that employ spit (7:31–37; 8:22–26) or changes them into more generic healings in Matt 9:27–34 along with elements from Matt 12:22–24 and 20:29–34.

and Sadducees (Matt 16:11–12). In addition, Matthew drops the phrase "some came from a distance" (Gentiles in Mark 8:3 vs. Matt 15:32) since Jesus only comes for the lost sheep of Israel in Matthew (15:24). Finally, in the healing of the demon possessed boy, Matthew emphasizes miracle-working faith (17:20) instead of the discipleship action of prayer in the absence of Jesus as emphasized in Mark 9:28–29. Therefore the argument runs: if the closest interpreters neglect possible Markan symbolism, how can modern commentators expect to diagnose its existence?

Third, Mark begins with literal miracle stories and only later in the gospel adds a significant symbolic element. This inconsistency results in the reader's not expecting symbolism to occur since Mark did not begin in this fashion. For instance, the miracle stories in chapter 1 including the exorcism in the synagogue, the healing of Peter's mother-in-law, and the healings of townsfolk from Capernaum (1:23–34) are interpreted as straightforward miracle stories by the consensus of commentators, whereas the trips across the sea and the healings of the blind men are said to be filled with symbolism.

Fourth, the divergent scholarly evaluations of the material make it unlikely that Mark's symbolism is clear enough for the reader to perceive its presence. For instance, Geddert offers thirty-five different interpretations of the rending of the veil.[49] The imagery is so "maddeningly obscure"[50] that it becomes easy to deny its presence altogether.

Not only the opacity of the metaphors but also the scholarly "overinterpretation" of these metaphors has caused conservative scholars to emphasize a literal reading of Mark and to minimize any symbolism. In addition to parallel mania and chiasm mania, symbolism mania can also raise its head. Some authors, justifiably, demand that those enamored with finding symbolism everywhere must rein in their flights of fancy. An overinterpretation of Markan symbolism has resulted in some overly specific conclusions about the provenance and background of the gospel. For instance, from the miracle catenae Achtemeier concludes that these miracle stories "were formed as part of a liturgy which celebrated an epiphanic Eucharist based on bread broken with the θεῖος ἀνήρ Jesus."[51]

The contrasts between Galilee and Jerusalem are especially notorious for resulting in divergent proposals of symbolism.[52] For some Galilee is understood theologically as the place where the *parousia* will occur (14:28; 16:7).[53] For others Galilee becomes the location where Mark's gospel is written and the point of departure for the Gentile mission (7:24, 28, 37; 14:28).[54] For a third group the geographical differences become a

---

49. Geddert, *Watchwords*, 141–43.
50. Fowler, *Let the Reader Understand*, 261.
51. Achtemeier, "Origin and Function," 198.
52. See Van Iersel, *Mark*, 78.
53. Conzelmann, Grant, Lohmeyer, Lightfoot, Kelber, Marxsen, Perrin, Ramsey, etc.
54. See Donald Senior's writings.

means by which Mark expresses a philosophy of history (3:22; 7:1; 10:33; 11:18; 12:12; 13:2; 14:41; 15:38) so that he is "giving expression to the philosophical-theological doctrine that the promised Messiah had to be rejected by his own nation before God's new offer of salvation through the crucified Christ could be freely proclaimed."[55]

Finally, for a fourth group a negatively perceived Jerusalem represents a challenge to the central authority of the Jerusalem church.[56] Jesus' family represents the Torah-observant Jewish Christian church in Jerusalem, which Mark opposes as an exponent of the Torah-free Gentile Christianity.[57] Mark then becomes a representative of a northern Galilean Christianity in opposition to a Jerusalem-type Christianity, "which traced its origin to the relatives of Jesus, considered itself standing in unbroken tradition with the Twelve under the primacy of Peter, and advocated a faith in so Jewish a fashion as to be—in the eyes of Mark, the opponent."[58] This vendetta against the disciples is seen from a number of different angles, with Tyson identifying them with a royal Davidic Christology, Weeden with a miracle-working Christology, Trocmé calling attention to the hierarchal pretensions of the Jerusalem church, Goulder viewing Mark as a Pauline Christian, and Crossan contending for a polemic against the doctrinal and jurisdictional hegemony of the Jerusalem mother church. The multiplicity of explanations demonstrates the overinterpretation of the data.

For many, this variety of proposals weakens the likelihood of ever determining the certainty of Markan symbolism. Likewise, for conservative scholars the positioning of Mark over against other leaders of the church represents a theory which receives no support from the biblical record, and so all symbolic approaches are dismissed.

Robert Gundry is an advocate *par excellence* for a literal interpretation of Mark. On the very first page of his commentary he produces an assault against possible Markan symbolism:

> The Gospel of Mark contains no ciphers, no hidden meanings, no sleight of hand; . . . No ecclesiastical enemies lurking between the lines or behind the twelve apostles, the inner three, and Jesus' natural family. No mirror-images of theological disputes over the demands and rewards of Christian discipleship. No symbolism of discipular enlightenment in the miracles. No "way"-symbolism for cross-bearing. No bread-symbolism for the Eucharist. No boat-symbolism for salvation or for the Second Coming. No Jerusalem-symbolism for Judaism or Judaistic Christianity. . . . None of these. Mark's meaning lies on the surface.[59]

---

55. Burkill, *New Light on the Earliest Gospel*, 237–38; cf. Lambrecht, "Relatives," 254.
56. For instance, Crossen, Goulder, Kelber, Painter, Tyson, Trocmé, and Sunderwirt.
57. See especially Trocmé, *Formation*, 130–37; and Crossan, "Mark and Relatives," 110–13.
58. Kelber, *Kingdom of God*, 64.
59. Gundry, *Mark*, 1.

Gundry is concerned that symbolic interpretations undermine the event character of the narrative so that the *Sitz im Leben Jesu* is downplayed.[60] Certainly it is true that several modern interpreters have poisoned the pot against accepting a symbolic approach to Mark. When Kelber contends that "Mark has taken a decisive step toward identifying the disciples as Jesus' opponents,"[61] scholars like Gundry migrate back to a completely literal interpretation of Mark. Similarly, James Kallas' book *The Significance of the Synoptic Miracles* is a vigorous protest against Alan Richardson's symbolic treatment of the feedings of the multitude. Characteristic of all literal interpreters, Kallas asks, "Why not take the passages for what they say? Simply that Jesus, with practically nothing at all, fed a group of hungry people."[62] Thus for some authors symbolism becomes a flight of fancy away from the true intention of the narrative.

With regard to miracles, many writers emphasize only the kingdom-sign nature of the narratives rather than any symbolic ramifications.[63] The miracle section of 4:35—8:26 details Jesus' triumph over demons, danger, death, and disease. These interpreters concentrate on the *Sitz im Leben Jesu* rather than attempting to discern how Mark is using these narratives to speak to the church. The elements in a typical miracle story take prominence. For instance, when Jesus touches a twelve-year-old dead girl and a sick woman bleeding for twelve years, these authors fail to emphasize the Jewish nature of the numbers and how Jesus fulfills the OT ceremonial legislation regarding touching a menstruating woman and a dead body. Instead, Jesus' power receives prominence through his secret knowledge of her condition (5:27, 30b), the instantaneousness of the cure (5:29a), the healing power streaming from Jesus' body like an electric current (5:30a), and the extraordinariness of the event so that crowd and disciples alike cannot fathom how it could have happened (5:31). The proof of a mighty healing is authenticated by the feeling of wholeness in one's body (5:29b) and the little girl's partaking of food (5:43b). Therefore, the touching is merely a sympathetic method of healing by a holy man combined with special healing formulas like "*Talitha koum*" (5:41). Thus many interpreters prefer a literal, single-dimensional approach to the Gospel of Mark since the identification of Markan symbolism leads to subjectivity and unverifiability.

---

60. Gundry's rejection of symbolism also seems based on his suspicion that an incorrect view of the relationship between a theology of glory and a theology of suffering will result so that the cross is underscored without a victory motif. Therefore, Jesus' cry from the cross is interpreted positively and the ending of Mark is triumphant.

61. Kelber, *Mark's Story of Jesus*, 37.

62. Kallas, *Significance of Synoptic Miracles*, 93. Fuller (*Interpreting the Miracles*, 125) perceptively concludes that "The basic weakness of Kallas' treatment is his failure to distinguish between the various levels in the synoptic tradition."

63. Authors like Twelftree, Koch, Meier, and Van der Loos place the sole emphasis upon this aspect of the story, with the additional redactional stress of Mark receiving only token attention.

1.5 Evidence for Two Levels of Interpretation in Mark's Gospel

I concede that the supposition of Markan symbolism complicates the interpretation of the gospel, but recognizing Markan redaction is crucial to receiving the full impact of his composition. With Geddert I conclude that "There are many ways to go wrong when one watches for subtleties. In the case of Mark, however, the greater danger is to overlook the deeper points and examine only the surface of the texts."[64] The literal historical layer is basic and takes priority, but Mark employs the Jesus tradition to speak to the needs of his community as well. This two-layer approach to the gospel accounts for the redactional symbolism employed in the book.

This fact has been recognized by a series of exegetes who express this truth in various ways:

1. Augustine Stock (*Call to Discipleship*, 33): "Two time frames are superimposed in the narrative: that of the reader and that of the characters in the plotted narrative.... The super-imposition of the two time frames is so handled that the reader is confronted by the same challenge to faith as were Jesus' contemporaries."

2. Heikki Räisänen (*Messianic Secret in Mark*, 190): "On the one hand, he is telling a story of what happened when Jesus of Nazareth was active in Galilee and Jerusalem; on the other hand, he is projecting the story of his own Christian congregation on to the same screen."

3. William Telford (*Theology of Mark*, 132): "In addressing his disciples in private, the Markan Jesus is in actuality addressing the church for whom the gospel was written, and expanding on the tradition in light of the community's contemporary problems and needs."

4. Timothy Geddert (*Watchwords*): "Both the parables and the miracles of Jesus have meanings deeper than whatever appears at the surface of the empirical data" (74). "Mark intends the whole ministry of Jesus to be a model for discipleship in the post-resurrection age" (181). "Mark has found a way of reproducing textually exactly what he is advocating existentially" (178).

5. Joel Marcus (*The Mystery of the Kingdom of God*, 195): "For Mark, the events of Jesus' lifetime are not just events that occurred once-and-for-all, long ago, as in Luke; they are that, but they are also more."

6. Eugene Boring (*Mark: A Commentary*, 160): "The narrative functions at two levels, and the there-and-then account modulates into the here-and-now experience of the readers."

7. Robert Fowler (*Let the Reader Understand*, 225): "We learn through reading this Gospel that narrative can work on different levels simultaneously; that if we read

---

64. Geddert, *Watchwords*, 139.

on one level only, then we may end up as deaf and blind as certain characters in the story."

How do we account for these two levels? Martin Hengel maintains that "the fatal error in the interpretation of the Gospels in general and of Mark in particular has been that scholars have thought that they had to decide between preaching and historical narrative, that here there could only be an either-or."[65] In order not to fall into this interpretative error, it is important to categorize the Gospel of Mark not simply as history or biography but with a combination of terms such as preached history or kerygmatic biography.[66] Mark recounts the story of Jesus in order to shape the beliefs and actions of the community which takes its identity from the Messiah. As Ernest Best explains, "Unlike biography it is concerned to advance an ideological position and move its readers to practice more zealously the faith to which they are committed. In that respect it is more like a sermon."[67]

But notice that I have not reversed the terms to designate the gospel as historicized preaching or biographical kerygma.[68] Mark is not consciously preaching a contemporary sermon in a historical guise. The historical nature of the narratives is the primary emphasis since the noun takes prominence, but the adjective "kerymatic" indicates that Mark is addressing the narratives at the needs of his community, thus creating a double-leveled story. Two layers of tradition are placed on top of each other: the events of the historical Jesus, and the chosen themes of the evangelist. In addition to the biographical events of Jesus' life, the voice of Mark applying these events to his own community can constantly be heard.[69] To call something Markan redaction is not to label it unhistorical. We should not commit the error of confusing a judgment of style with a judgment of history. But through the preaching of the Jesus tradition Mark wishes to touch directly upon the real-life situation of his readers.

---

65. Hengel, *Studies in the Gospel of Mark*, 41.

66. At the end of the twentieth century the categorization of Mark as biography, especially under the influence of Richard Burridge (*What Are the Gospels?*), has generally replaced the Schmidt-Bultmann hypothesis that gospel is a new genre, *sui generis*. But many scholars have misgivings about assigning a genre to Mark that is only described as biography. See Boring, "Mark 1:1–15," 46, 64; Dihle, "Gospels and Greek Biography," 361–86; Guelich, "Gospel Genre," 181; Vines, *Problem of Markan Genre*, 15; Wilder, *Early Christian Rhetoric*, 28.

67. Best, *Mark*, 141.

68. For instance, Elwell and Yarbrough (*Encountering the New Testament*, 72) entitle Mark "expanded biographical sermons." Dowd (*Prayer, Power*, 24–25) employs the more appropriate description "didactic biography." She explains that "sermons end with direct address in the imperative mood unlike Mark," so that Mark should not be categorized as a biographical sermon with "sermon" as the noun but as kerygmatic biography.

69. Watson ("Toward a Literal Reading," 210) argues that whenever a gospel is interpreted in the light of its hypothetical original communal setting, "an *allegorical* reading strategy is employed that systematically downplays and circumvents the *literal* sense of the text." I hope to disprove Watson's theory.

Each of the gospels can be mapped on a continuum from history to preaching. Luke is basically a historian who respectfully reproduces his sources (Luke 1:1–4).[70] Matthew employs the Jesus tradition as an apologist who defends the christological claims of the Christian synagogue over against the Pharisaic synagogue.[71] Mark and John, on the other hand, stand closer to the preaching pole of the continuum and can be categorized as symbolic gospels.

Alan Culpepper perceptively describes the two layers in the Gospel of John with the following enlightening paragraph:[72]

> What seems clear and simple on the surface is never so simple for the perceptive reader because of the opacity and complexity of the gospel's sub-surface signals. Various textual features, principally the misunderstandings, irony, and symbolism, constantly lead the reader to view the story from a higher vantage point and share the judgments which the "whispering wizard" conveys by means of various nods, winks, and gestures. It is the discovery of subsurface signals which had previously escaped the reader's notice that allows the gospel to be read again and again with pleasure and profit. Traffic on the gospel's subterranean frequencies is so heavy that even the perceptive reader is never sure he or she has received all the signals the text is sending.[73]

The confirmation of Markan symbolism comes when we examine its similarities with the Gospel of John.[74] If John is a "whispering wizard," then Mark is a softly speaking sophisticated sorcerer who repeatedly hints at a deeper level of interpretation through his use of literary devices.

In both John and Mark parables become allegorical riddles. The meaning of the dark saying in John 10:1–6 (the Parable of the Good Shepherd) is hidden from Jesus'

---

70. However, in Acts in particular we do encounter a polemic toward Rome that Christianity should be a *religio licita* which never again should be persecuted as well as an apology to Jewish-Christian readers who view Paul with suspicion instead of as a model of orthodoxy.

71. These include 1) an apologetic in the birth narrative against Jesus born out of wedlock and originating from Nazareth not Bethlehem; 2) a polemic in the John the Baptist material against Jesus being a sinner since he was baptized by John thus making John greater; 3) an apologetic in Jesus' ministry that Jesus is greater than Moses and not an antinomian; 4) an apologetic in chapters 21–23 that God did not reject Israel, but instead the Jewish leadership rejected their Messiah; 5) an apologetic in the passion narrative that Jesus truly died (27:36); and 6) in the resurrection narrative arguing that the rumor the disciples stole Jesus' body was a plot of the Jewish leadership so that Jesus is not a deceiver (27:63–64).

72. The most famous study of the two levels of John is Martyn, *History and Theology in the Fourth Gospel*. For opposition see Hägerland, "John's Gospel." Hägerland is certainly correct that "The Gospel itself does not exhibit any desire to present a history of a 'Johannine community'" (321), but it does not follow that there are not two levels.

73. Culpepper, *Anatomy of the Fourth Gospel*, 151.

74. Of course, there are many differences with John as well. The chief disparity involves the cloaking of the identity of Jesus in Mark, whereas Jesus' identity is openly acknowledged by the characters in John from the very beginning. For a chart of differences see Hedrick, *When History and Faith Collide*, 49–53.

disciples (10:6) since it refers to a time when the church will be required to follow Jesus out of the synagogue in order to worship Jesus as God, similar to the blind man in 9:38. Likewise, the Markan expression "to speak in parables" means to teach allegorical riddles. Matthew repeatedly understands the plural "parables" to mean "more than one" and therefore supplements additional parables in the context of Mark 12:1 (Matt 21:28—22:14), whereas "to speak in parables" for Mark is really a technical term meaning an allegorical riddle.[75] Thus in the Parable of the Tenants the owner of the vineyard (God) sends messengers (the prophets) to receive the fruit from the tenants (the Jewish leaders), but they kill the son (Jesus) so that the vineyard is given to others (the church). Thus the parable mirrors a later time.[76]

Second, several of the miracle stories focus upon Christology rather than kingdom signs. A sign in the Gospel of John entails a miracle that displays the specialness of the person of Jesus, so that in the multiplication of the bread Jesus becomes the bread of life, in the healing of the blind man Jesus becomes the light of the world, and in the raising of Lazarus from the dead Jesus becomes the resurrection and the life. Not as obvious and straightforward, but following his habit of allusion, Mark relates the story of Jesus walking on water as a feat which only God can accomplish since Job 9:8 teaches that "God alone stretches out the heavens and treads on the waves of the sea." In the process of the sea walking, Jesus passes by the boat of disciples (6:48), another OT allusion to an epiphany, as when Moses (Exod 33:22; 34:6) and Elijah (1 Kgs 19:11–13) experience the very presence of God. Then when Jesus enters the boat he secretly proclaims the name of God (6:50 "It is I," ἐγώ εἰμι), similar to several "I am" sayings in the Gospel of John. Thus as Kelber proclaims, "In principle, Mark's handling of the miracle catenae is similar to John's appropriation of his miracle source . . . miracles are transformed into signs."[77]

Third, misunderstandings abound in each gospel. In John the characters interpret a saying of Jesus at a literal level whereas he intends it on a more profound symbolic plane.[78] Fowler discerns a similar literary device in Mark 8:14–16: "What we have here is the same kind of play on words and associated misunderstanding that we find repeatedly in the Gospel of John (e.g. John 4:33, 6:33–35). The disciples misunderstand the bread-talk of v. 15 as a reference to loaves of bread; they are oblivious to the true significance of Jesus' words."[79] In both gospels the misunderstanding technique

---

75. Therefore Matthew omits the phrase "speaking in parables" from Mark 3:22 in Matt 12:25–29 when he combines Mark and Q material since there are not multiple parables.

76. See section 9.2 for a multitude of examples. Likewise, in John 16:25 Jesus is speaking figuratively, but a later time will come when figurative language is unnecessary.

77. Kelber, *Kingdom in Mark*, 63, esp. n. 52. Richardson (*Miracle Stories*, 115) states that each of John's lengthy discussions of the signs "is only an underlining or explication of the interpretation which we have seen to be already implicit in St. Mark."

78. John 2:19–21; 3:3–4, 5–9; 4:10–14, 31–33; 6:33–35; 7:33–36; 8:21–23, 32–34, 56–58; 11:11–13, 23–25; 13:8–10; 14:4–6.

79. Fowler, *Loaves and Fishes*, 110. Cf. also Boucher, *Mysterious Parable*, 78.

directs the conversation to a deeper level, so that in John the reader encounters the theological significance of an event, whereas in Mark the misapprehensions lead to a teaching on discipleship.[80]

Fourth, physical characteristics and entities like blindness, bread, fig trees, and the temple take on metaphorical meanings.[81] Physical blindness becomes a foil for spiritual blindness so that sight becomes perception. In John 9 the blind man gradually deepens his spiritual insight into the identity of Jesus until he finally worships Jesus as God.[82] In Mark blind Bartimaeus perceives Jesus as only the triumphant Son of David (10:47–48) until he is healed and follows Jesus along the way to the cross (10:52), thus recognizing Jesus' true mission and identity. In John 6 bread is portrayed as spiritual manna which symbolizes the person of Jesus (6:33, 35, 51). In Mark bread becomes a keyword stitching together the pericopes that stretch from 6:30 to 8:21, culminating in Jesus as the bread:

6:30–44	Multiplication of bread for the five thousand (ἄρτος 6:37, 38, 41 (2), 44)
6:45–56	Sea walking (ἄρτος 6:52; the disciples do not understand about the loaves)
7:1–13	Eating bread without washed hands (7:2, 5 ἄρτος)
7:14–23	A purity proverb: Jesus declares all foods clean (βρώματα 7:19b).
7:24–30	Table fellowship with a Gentile woman (ἄρτος 7:27)
8:1–10	Feeding of the four thousand (ἄρτος 8:4, 5, 6)
8:11–13	Seeking signs is the yeast (making bread) of the Pharisees and Herod.
8:14–21	The disciples forget to bring bread except one loaf (ἄρτος 8:14 [2], 16, 17, 19).

In Mark 8:14 the disciples have forgotten to buy bread but still have one loaf in the boat, which must be a symbolic metaphor for Jesus since, as Stock explains, "the translation 'no bread' is nonsensical when it has just been stated that they had one loaf with them in the boat."[83] Therefore, symbolic meanings are prominent in both John and Mark.

The fig tree represents Israel and its leaders. In John 1:50 Jesus sees Nathaniel under the paradigmatic fig tree since he represents all true Israelites, who become disciples of Jesus and acknowledge him as the new Israel (king of Israel 1:49) and the true Bethel (1:51) or house of God. Likewise, in Mark various elements in Jesus' cursing of the fig tree point to a deeper level of interpretation. The fact that Jesus is hungry means that he is metaphorically hungry for the righteous fruit produced by Israel. However, the fig tree produces nothing but leaves, indicating that Judaism looks fine from the outside but is fruitless in reality. It is no longer the season for figs since the

---

80. For instance, in Mark 4:14–20; 7:19, 21–23; 8:34–38; 9:35–50; 10:42–45.

81. Symbolic water imagery, however, appears uniquely in John.

82. John 9:11, the man called Jesus; 9:17, a prophet; 9:25, 31, not a sinner; 9:29, does not know where he comes from like the Messiah of 7:27; 9:33, from God; 9:35, exalted Son of Man; 9:38, God himself who solely is worshipped.

83. Stock, *Call to Discipleship*, 127.

time for Israel's fruit production is past. As a result the fig tree surprisingly withers from its roots, meaning that the Jewish leadership in charge of the temple is corrupt.

Finally, the temple becomes Jesus' body. John states this truth clearly in 2:19–21, where he develops a theological and symbolic interpretation of the temple as the body of Jesus. Likewise, Mark employs the word "sanctuary" (ναός 14:58; 15:29, 38), not "temple courts" (ἱερόν 11:15–16; 12:35 and 14:49; 13:1–3) to refer to Jesus' death and resurrection, which will symbolically actualize the destruction of the temple and its rebuilding in three days. Both gospels witness a remarkably similar approach to symbolism.

Fifth, the characters in the narrative signify groups of people present in the evangelists' communities.[84] In John the beloved disciple represents the model believer (13:23–26; 18:15; 19:26–27, 35; 20:4–5, 8; 21:7). In Mark Peter represents the half-sighted incomplete disciple who recognizes Jesus as the royal Messiah but not as the suffering Son of Man (Mark 8:22–33). For John the Samaritan woman at the well who was married to five husbands (John 4:16–18) represents the Samaritan nation with its worship of five other gods (2 Kgs 17:24, 29–30), whom Jesus is wooing as his bride at the traditional well (Gen 24:11–27; 29:2–12; Exod 2:15–21). Likewise, the salvation of the Gentiles is epitomized in John by the royal official (4:43–54) who believes that Jesus is the "Savior of the world" (4:42), along with his entire household (4:43), similar to the Gentile conversions in Acts.[85] In Mark, the Syrophoenician woman embodies the Gentiles so that because of her faith the dogs (Gentiles) now eat crumbs at the table (signifying table fellowship) with the family's children (the Jews).

By paralleling incidents in the early church with gospel episodes, both John and Mark trace back events that occur in Acts into the ministry of Jesus. In John 3–4 the Jewish leaders, the disciples of John the Baptizer, the Samaritans, and the Gentiles come to Jesus just as these groups receive the gospel in Acts.[86] Likewise, Mark previews the Gentile mission through Jesus' ministry in the Decapolis, where the healed demoniac becomes the first Gentile missionary (5:19–20), and in Tyre, where the Syrophoencian woman's faith establishes table fellowship between Jews and Gentiles (7:28–29).[87] In

---

84. The best description of Johannine characters is found in Culpepper, *Anatomy of the Fourth Gospel*, 100–148.

85. Acts 11:14; 16:15, 31, 34; 18:8; 1 Cor 1:16.

86. The section from Cana to Cana enclosed by the mention of the first two signs (2:11; 4:54) rehearses the events that will be fulfilled when the new age arrives as evidenced by the abundance of wine in the wedding at Cana (Amos 9:13b) and the continual harvest of 4:35–38 (Amos 9:13a). Cana seems to symbolize Canaan so that the entire land will be retaken once a new temple is established (2:13–22), as evidenced by the coming of the Jewish leaders (2:23—3:21), the disciples of John the Baptizer (3:22—4:3), the Samaritans (4:4–42), and the Gentiles of Palestine (4:43–54) to Jesus. Acts 1:8 states that the gospel will embark from Jerusalem, to Judea, Samaria, and the ends of the earth. In John 2–4 Jesus' ministry begins in Jerusalem (2:13) to the Jewish leaders and then proceeds to Judea (3:22) with the disciples of John the Baptizer, to Samaria (4:4), and finally to the Gentiles in Galilee (4:45).

87. See section 7.4 below. Similarly, the feeding of the four thousand occurs in the Decapolis,

The Theological Intentions of Mark's Literary Devices

Mark 7:20 Jesus declares all foods clean, which does not happen historically until the conversion of Cornelius in Acts 10. In John 5–10 Jesus fulfills all the OT feasts, like the Sabbath (5), the Passover (6), the water ceremony at the feast of tabernacles (7), the light ceremony at the feast of booths (8–9), and the feast of dedication (10:22–42). In Mark Jesus' kingdom actions such as the cleansing of a leper, the healing of a woman with a flow of blood, and the curing of a dead girl all through physical touch fulfill various OT ceremonial regulations against contact with lepers, menstruating women, and all corpses so that as a result the church reads the Old Testament in a new way. Therefore, the fulfillment of OT ceremonies plays a major role in both gospels.[88]

Sixth, the symbolic nature of both John and Mark is evidenced in the predictions made by Jesus which come true in the evangelists' communities. Here the upper room discourse in John 13–17 compares with the apocalyptic sermon of Mark 13. In the final sermon in John's gospel Jesus prophesizes that his followers will be put "out of the synagogue; in fact, a time is coming when anyone who kills you will think he is offering a service to God" (16:2). This "coming time" points to the time of the writing of the fourth gospel so that the blind man's suspension from the synagogue before he can worship Jesus as God represents John's solution to one of the struggles of his community (10:1–6). A second prediction concerns the coming of the Holy Spirit, who will lead the community into all truth and make Jesus' teaching clear and understandable (16:12–15; 14:26). This prophecy as well is fulfilled through the writing of John's gospel. As Moody Smith asserts, "It is by no means unreasonable to surmise that the specific function of the Spirit-Paraclete as described in the Fourth Gospel is actually represented in the figure and words of the Johannine Jesus."[89] Similarly, Jesus' prophecies in the last sermon in Mark are beginning to be fulfilled and experienced by the church as Mark writes his gospel. Brother is betraying brother to death (13:12) during the persecutions of Nero, Christians are on trial before governors and kings (13:9); the gospel is preached to the whole world (13:10); and the antichrists are appearing among the Jewish Zealots in Jerusalem (13:5–6, 21–22). War with Rome is already a reality (13:7), so that the abomination of desolation is standing where it does not belong (13:14).

Seventh, the absence of Jesus becomes a central metaphorical theme in both John and Mark. In John's upper room discourse Jesus' departure (14:28; 16:5, 28) becomes the central theme, with Jesus instructing the community how to live fruitfully in his absence. Jesus comforts his distraught disciples with the promise that he will be constantly with them through the Holy Spirit (14:16–20; 16:7), through his living words

---

where the seven baskets left over is plenty for the seven Gentile nations of the land (Deut 7:1; Acts 13:19).

88. Mark proclaims that the new wine must be placed in new wineskins (2:22b). Likewise in John, the new best wine (2:10) replaces the six stone jars used for ceremonial cleansing (2:6) and Jesus' body becomes the temple (2:20–21).

89. D. M. Smith, *Interpreting the Gospels*, 88.

(15:7–8), through their common love (15:9–17), and through prayer (15:7, 16; ch. 17). In Mark we encounter four events where the disciples falter without Jesus. In the trips across the sea where Jesus is sleeping in the boat (4:38) or praying on the mountain (6:45–46), the disciples display profound doubt and fear so that they are unable to complete the journey of discipleship. When Jesus is absent in the glory of the mount of transfiguration, the disciples cannot cast out the demon in the valley below (9:17–19). Finally, in the ending of Mark the woman flee in fear and forget to spread the gospel message even though they know that the absent Jesus has risen (16:8). These narratives become teaching paradigms for the early church since they mirror their experiences without the physical presence of Jesus during such events as the Neronic persecution and the destruction of Jerusalem.[90]

Therefore in both of these symbolic gospels we must exercise double vision and stereophonic hearing if we are to catch all the artistic overtones of meaning. The writings of John and Mark are not just examples of archivisitic activity. Both authors place the history of Jesus alongside the situation of the community and thus provide the Jesus tradition with a contemporary kerygmatic relevance.

However, despite a multitude of similarities, one basic difference stands out: in John the theological interpretation occupies far more space than the historical account, whereas Mark does not clearly specify the theological interpretations which we contend are clearly in his mind. As Hooker explains, "Unlike the Fourth Evangelist, Mark rarely spells out the meaning of Jesus' miracles. He prefers to set incidents side by side and to leave it to his readers to make the necessary connections."[91] Mark's lack of specificity becomes an invitation to probe and penetrate the gospel more deeply.

1.6 Literary Devices Employed by Mark to Indicate Symbolism

Only on one occasion throughout the entire gospel does Mark as an editor openly reveal his intention for a particular pericope.[92] In Mark 7:19b, after Jesus' logion about uncleanness contaminating a person through inward character qualities and not outward actions, Mark clearly concludes that "in saying this Jesus declared all foods 'clean.'" This unambiguous signal of Markan redaction[93] indicates his desire to instruct the reader how to read the OT ceremonial instructions from a Christian point of view.

---

90. The two symbolic gospels, John and Mark, also employ the literary device of irony in a similar manner so that the characters unconsciously speak the truth. The paradigm example for John is Caiaphas, who proclaims in Mark 11:50 that "it is better that one man die for the people than that the whole nation perishes." For irony in Mark see Appendix 2.

91. Hooker, "Mark's Parables of the Kingdom," 87.

92. In addition, through the phrases "let the reader understand" (13:14) and "what I say to you, I say to everyone, 'watch'" (13:37), we recognize Mark's desire for the reader to grasp his intentions.

93. Even someone like Gundry (*Mark*, 7), who denies a symbolic side to Mark, recognizes the "intrusiveness and awkwardness of the editorial phrase," which "breaks into the middle of Jesus' words and modifies the 'he' in 'he says' five clauses back."

The Theological Intentions of Mark's Literary Devices

Mark envisions the later church's discovery (Acts 10:9–20, 34–35) that kosher food is not integral to the gospel message already happening proleptically in Jesus' proclamation of the kingdom in his parables.

Why does Mark specify this single example to convey his intended meaning but does not employ similar parenthetical devices at other places in his gospel? Does this entail that only here at 7:19b is Mark commenting about the fulfillment of Jewish ceremonies? I think not! It is our hypothesis that Mark employs literary devices like intercalation, framing, allusionary repetitions, narrative surprises, and mirroring to demonstrate that in Jesus' kingdom words and actions the conclusions of the early church are substantiated. But why is 7:19b unique? Why does he not employ a literary technique here? Although not immediately obvious, the fact that Mark entitles the saying in 7:15 a parable (7:17) entails that he understands Jesus' saying as an allegorical riddle that needs an interpretation. Mark aspires to make the interpretation crystal clear since purity rites are so important to a proper understanding of a Gentile's response to the gospel. Therefore, he attaches an explicit editorial comment. Through this procedure Mark clarifies that this entire section speaks about the fulfillment of Jewish ceremonial laws. By inserting a controversy dialogue (7:1–23) in the midst of a series of miracle stories, Mark has transformed the theme into Jesus' teaching on clean hands (7:1–13), clean food (7:14–23), clean people (7:24–30), and clean spittle or fluids (7:31–37).[94]

Normally Mark offers his own theological commentary through literary devices. Just as Mark only alludes to OT references,[95] so he narrates incidents without an interpretation of their significance. As Geddert comments, "Juxtaposing narrative elements without comment but with deliberate intent to influence the readers' interpretations is a favourite Markan technique."[96] The literary devices are Mark's manner of offering a narrator's implicit commentary. Therefore as Fowler points out, "We are given a puzzle to solve and the key to unlock it, but the unlocking is left up to us. He leaves the work for us to do but provides the necessary tools."[97] What are these necessary tools?

First, the Markan hints occur through the intercalation or sandwich, whereby Mark ties together two narratives to shine theological meaning on each other. As Shepperd notes, "It is as though the author uses intercalation as a tool to address the reader's own situation."[98] Therefore Mark sets up a parabolic, metaphorical relationship between two narratives by embedding one within the other. For instance,

---

94. See section 3.7 below.

95. For example: John the Baptizer's prophetic clothing (1:6) as a reference to Elijah (2 Kgs 1:8); the Spirit descending like a dove (1:10) referring back to the new world experienced by Noah (Gen 8:8–12); the significance of the voice from heaven (1:11) from Ps 2:7 and Isa 42:1 (a Suffering Servant Messiah); and allusions to the Psalms in the passion narrative (15:23 = Ps 69:21; 15:24 = Ps 22:18; 15:29 = Ps 22:7; 15:31 = Ps 22:8; 15:34 = Ps 22:1; 15:36 = Ps 69:21).

96. Geddert, *Watchwords*, 256, 129.

97. Fowler, *Let the Reader Understand*, 95.

98. Shepperd, *Markan Sandwich Stories*, 386.

The Two Levels of Interpretation in Mark's Gospel

Mark sandwiches Jesus' Jewish trial (14:55–65) with Peter's threefold denial of Jesus (14:53–54, 66–72). Through this literary device Mark is warning the church about denying Jesus when they are brought to trial. This historical event in the life of Jesus is repeating itself in Mark's time where the disciples are denying any relationship with Jesus rather than going to trial for professing his name.[99]

Second, hints for discerning two levels of meaning occur through the production of frames around a series of pericopes. For example, Mark surrounds the eschatological discourse with two stories of women who offer all they possess to Jesus (12:44; 14:3–5). This speaks to a situation in Mark's day where the Christian community is prepared for Jesus' arrival in all the splendor, glory, and victory of his *parousia* but they are completely resistant to sacrificing their all for Jesus in the required martyrdom of Nero's persecution. The frame around Mark 13 proclaims a theological message which Mark aims at his community to equip them to deal with this situation.

Third, the hints occur through Markan allusionary repetitions whereby he strategically replicates verbal expressions in order to demonstrate that Jesus is both the triumphant Son of David miracle-working Messiah but also the Suffering Servant Son of Man. As Luke Johnson explains, "Mark not only tells a story, he establishes deliberate and meaningful connections between parts of it, signaling those connections to the careful reader."[100] For instance, Mark employs the eschatologically pregnant term "torn" (Matt 27:51b; *T. Levi* 4:1) to link together the tearing of the dome of heaven in divine splendor at Jesus' baptism (1:10 σχιζομένους) with the tearing of the temple curtain (15:38 ἐσχίσθη) at the exact time of the tearing of Jesus' body in death. Theologically and apologetically, Mark is proclaiming to those who refuse to accept the implications of a crucified Messiah that the same person who is exalted by God as the messianic revelation is also sovereignly led by God through forsaken suffering and a crucified death. In these cases Mark is speaking metaphorically through a symbolic literary device.

Finally, the hints occur through Markan narrative surprises especially in the miracle stories. These narrative surprises function like an ideological subcode that surgically opens a narrative to its deeper potencies. For instance, after the feeding of the five thousand Mark neglects to conclude the miracle story with the typical ending of audience astonishment and thunderous praise to the mighty wonder-worker. Instead, the following narrative concludes, with the surprising finale to an astonishing sea crossing, that the disciples "did not understand about the loaves and their hearts were hardened" (6:52). Here again, Mark is writing at two levels and addressing a situation in the early church through the Jesus tradition. In the midst of intense struggles the community yearns for Jesus to perform another deliverance miracle. Instead they must open their hardened hearts to the truth that the breaking of the bread in the

---

99. See Tacitus' *Annals* 15:44, where Christians denounce their faith during the Neronic struggle. We will examine these Markan intercalations in chapter 2.

100. Johnson, *Writings*, 161.

feeding of the multitudes points forward to the broken body of Jesus in the Last Supper. The multiplication, resulting in baskets of spiritual food left over for all, will occur through Jesus' Passion and death and not through a miracle. Thus through the subtle use of these literary devices like intercalation, frame, allusionary repetition, and narrative surprise we are forced to conclude that "Mark is not the simplest but the most sophisticated of the evangelists."[101]

1.7 The Issues Addressed Through the Literary Devices

What are the preaching themes that Mark wants to emphasize from the Jesus tradition through these literary devices? Barton maintains, "It is clear from the seven occurrences of *euangelion* in Mark, that the gospel is something to be preached (cf. 1:14; 13:10; 14:9), something to be believed in (1:15), and something to give up everything for (cf. 8:35; 10:39)."[102] But Mark's contemporaries faced struggles in accepting this gospel, preaching a crucified Christ, and following a discipleship of the cross. These struggles then became the themes that Mark wants to tackle. Mark finds a way to mirror the struggles of the community through a retelling of the history of Jesus and his disciples. This gospel that Mark preached in a written format addresses four prominent areas of contention in the early church.

First of all, the Jewish community resisted a crucified Messiah. Therefore Mark clearly demonstrates that a suffering Messiah was the sovereign design of God as well as Jesus' intended plan from the beginning of his ministry. This Markan purpose explains why the gospel has been entitled a Passion story with a short introduction and why the suffering Son of Man is given an axial place in the gospel. In particular Mark employs the literary device of allusionary repetition to demonstrate that Jesus is both triumphant Messiah and Suffering Servant.

Second, since the Christian community expected that Christ's miracle-working power and victorious resurrection would triumph over any struggle, they did not give proper due to following a crucified Messiah. In response, Mark presents discipleship of the cross as the method by which the church is multiplied. With extremely frank language Mark accentuates the misunderstanding, dullness, and unfaithfulness of the disciples. Through this theme "Mark draws a parallel between the myopia of Jesus' disciples and the spiritual blindness of his own contemporaries."[103] In the midst of the Roman persecution by Nero and the immanent attack on Jerusalem, the church must follow the same route as their leader. Importantly, the first two of these preaching themes are closely related since the disciples must follow a suffering-servant Messiah with a corresponding discipleship of the cross.[104] Enduring suffering becomes the *sine*

---

101. Ibid., 160.
102. Barton, "Mark as Narrative," 231.
103. Stock, *Call to Discipleship*, 130.
104. See Donahue, *Are You the Christ?*, 62.

qua non for being disciples of Jesus (8:34; 10:39; 13:9). "Messiahship and discipleship are cut from the same cloth."[105] The themes of a suffering Messiah and a corresponding discipleship of the cross are especially highlighted by Mark through his employment of the techniques of intercalation and framework.

Third, both the Jewish community and the primitive Christian church had difficulty accepting that Gentiles should be incorporated into Israel without any of the normal entrance rites. Whereas Paul addressed the inclusion of Gentiles into the community through OT quotations and exegesis, as in Romans 9–11, Mark confronts this problem through the additional use of literary devices. Not only does Mark highlight the inclusion of Gentiles through Jesus' future predictions (13:10) and OT prophecies that refer to Gentiles joining Israel (4:32 with Ezek 17:23; 31:6 and Dan 4:12), but he also employs various literary devices. Mark inserts a narrative surprise when a Syrophoenician woman boldly confronts Jesus to receive table fellowship between Jews and Gentiles. Through a Markan repetition the Gentile centurion becomes a third voice from heaven (like 1:11 and 9:7) to proclaim that a crucified Messiah is the Son of God. Likewise, Mark coordinates the phrases "not the season for figs" and a "temple for all nations" in 11:17 to theologically explain that Judaism's time is over and the time for Gentiles has arrived. In addition, Mark employs geographical mirroring whereby just as Jesus' exorcism of a demon out of the synagogue cleanses Judaism (1:21–28) so the demon cast out of the Decapolis (5:1–20) and Syrian Phoenicia (7:30) cleanses Gentile territory. Using similar geographical mirroring, Mark recounts miraculous feedings on both Jewish and Gentile territory (6:34–44; 8:1–10) with the number of baskets left over representing Jesus' ministry to the twelve Jewish tribes and the seven Gentile nations of Canaan (Acts 13:19). Through literary devices Mark supplies his readers with bifocal vision to understand how Jesus' encounters with Gentiles prelude the Gentile mission of the church.[106]

Fourth, through Markan literary devices the OT ceremonial regulations are now read by the early church differently than the original Jewish community.[107] Mark justifies the Christian interpretation of OT ceremonial legislation by demonstrating how purity rites are fulfilled in Jesus' words and deeds. This includes legislation about food laws, leprosy, menstruation, the touching of dead bodies, temple worship, and sacrifice. Just as the first two issues of a crucified Messiah and a discipleship of the cross are tied inseparably together, so the opening of the community to the Gentiles results from a new reading of the OT ceremonial laws. Blount and Charles point out that

---

105. Marshall, *Faith as a Theme*, 142.

106. In chapter 7 will examine geographical mirroring with an emphasis upon Gentiles.

107. After concluding that these were the four theological issues raised by Markan literary devices, I discovered Shepperd's research on Mark's literary device of intercalation, which outlines implications for Markan theology "in the areas of Christology, discipleship, and the relationship of the Gospel of Mark to the Jewish temple and people" (*Markan Sandwich Stories*, 311–12). These are the exact areas that I believe Mark addresses.

> Mark offers a Jesus who embodies and preaches God's boundary-breaking, transformative message for Israel and all humankind. The message is this: God desires a world in which the boundaries that separate people from each other, whether they be holiness and purity codes that separate Jews from other Jews or laws and traditions that separate Jews from Gentiles, be torn down and broken through.[108]

Through the literary techniques of narrative surprises and mirroring, Mark addresses this issue of Jewish ceremonial regulations and how to read the Old Testament. In addition, two intercalations center upon this issue, including the Markan sandwich of the bleeding woman and the dead girl and the encapsulating of the temple action with narrative of the cursing of the fig tree.[109]

In the following chapters we will demonstrate how Mark addresses these four contemporary issues through literary devices. Interestingly, they seem directly related to what Dunn entitles "the four pillars of Second Temple Judaism."[110]

1. The first pillar of Judaism, promoting monotheism, accounts for the difficulty the Jewish community faced with a Suffering Servant Son of God who was worshipped.

2. The second pillar, the election of a covenant people and the promised land of Canaan, indicates why Mark needs to emphasize the inclusion of Gentiles and the conquest of their territory as an integral part of the Promised Land.

3. The centrality of the Torah in Israel's self-consciousness necessitates that Mark focus on the fulfillment of OT ceremonial rites in the kingdom words and deeds of Jesus.

4. Finally, the role of the temple at the center of Israel's national and religious life reinforces the role of Jewish ceremonies in Mark's gospel.

The only issue not covered is the role of suffering in the life of the community, which was an issue in Christianity's relationship with Rome but is not connected with the pillars of Judaism.

With regard to all of these connections, Geddert asks an appropriate question: "How can we be certain we are not being over-ingenious, straining to find subtle meanings where Mark never gave a minute's thought to anything particularly subtle or allusive?"[111] Or, how can we be sure that Meagher is not correct in his assessment that Mark is just plain clumsy in his allusiveness?[112] Maybe these so-called literary devices are placed upon the text by some creative interpreter, forming what Räisänen

---

108. Blount and Charles, *Preaching Mark in Two Voices*, 11.
109. In chapter 8 we will examine Jewish ceremonial ritual mirroring.
110. See Dunn, *Partings of the Ways*, 21, 23, 31.
111. Geddert, *Watchwords*, 129.
112. Remember the title of John Meagher's book, *Clumsy Construction in Mark's Gospel*.

describes as "correlations between elements that are in fact created by readers of the text rather than by its author."[113] These questions heighten the need for the rest of this book. We will attempt to demonstrate how the Markan literary devices of intercalation or sandwich (ch. 2), framing (ch. 3), allusionary repetitions (ch. 4), narrative surprises (ch. 5), and temporal, geographical, and Jewish ceremonial mirroring (chs. 6–8) are employed to offer a theological commentary on the words and events of Jesus' life, especially exemplified in the miracle stories (ch. 9).

Although irony is another important literary device in Mark that speaks at two levels,[114] I will not discuss it since Camery-Hoggatt has already arrived at similar conclusions to my perspective. He concludes that "A survey of the specific ironies would reveal challenges leveled against the institution of the temple, against an exclusivist posture toward the Gentiles, against any piety which rejects as unworthy the 'people of the land'—including tax-collectors and sinners, and against any brand of messianism which disregards or denies the necessity of suffering."[115] All four of my theological reasons for Mark's literary devices are postulated already in the work of Camery-Hoggatt, but he adds a concern for the marginalized, which I contend is not unique to Mark, as evidenced by its prominence in the Lukan material.

Robert Gundry is convinced that "Mark says not a syllable"[116] to convince the reader that he is employing symbolism to speak at two levels, but I will argue that Mark speaks volumes through the literary devices of intercalation, framework, allusionary repetition, narrative surprises, and mirroring. You the reader must in the end decide which solution is preferred.

---

113. Räisänen, *Messianic Secret in Mark*, 27.

114. Camery-Hoggatt (*Irony in Mark's Gospel*, 13) defines irony as "a function of interfacing and conflicting points of view: the points of view of the story's readers set against those of the story's characters."

115. Camery-Hoggatt, *Irony in Mark's Gospel*, 180. See Appendix 2 for examples of Markan irony.

116. Gundry, *Mark*, 1012.

2

Intercalations in the Gospel of Mark

Although a variety of terminology has been employed to describe this literary device,[1] exegetes are unanimously agreed regarding its presence in the Gospel of Mark.[2] The term "intercalation" has the distinct disadvantage of giving the impression that the inner story was "inserted illegitimately."[3] On the other hand, the word "sandwich" implies that the middle section possesses the meat of the narrative, which proves incorrect on occasions as well. So I will employ both terms interchangeably.

An intercalation can be defined as a literary device whereby one story is bifurcated into two sections and a second story is inserted in between to indicate that the two narratives are somehow similar in nature. As Edwards reports, "the whole follows an A1-B-A2 schema, in which the B episode forms an independent unit of material, whereas the flanking A episodes require one another to complete their narrative."[4] The two interconnected narratives have a variety of similar characteristics including recurring vocabulary,[5] parallel actions,[6] dramatized irony between characters,[7] a lack

---

1. Shepperd (*Sandwich Stories*, 1 n. 2) references authors who also use "interpolation" (Kee), "bracketing" (Stock), "dovetailing" (Seargant), "intruded middles" (Synge), or in German, "Ineinanderschactelungen" (Klostermann), "Verschachelungen" (Kuhn), "Verschmelzungen" (Schniewind), and "Schiebungen" (von Dobschütz). Boring (*Mark*, 157) adds "interweaving," "interlocking," or in the jargon of narratology, "heterodiegetic analepsis."

2. See Appendix 3 for a list of authors and their identification of texts.

3. Shepperd, *Sandwich Stories*, 350.

4. Edwards, "Marcan Sandwiches," 197.

5. Kee (*Community*, 54) discovers that four out of eight recognized examples have a "recurring Leitwort."

6. Shepperd (*Sandwich Stories*, 327) reports that "Parallel actions are done by contrasting groups or contrasting actions are done by parallel groups in the two stories."

7. Ibid., 121–22, 126, 146–49, 180–85, 217–20, 248–54.

of character crossover,[8] and similar content emphasizing the "Evangelist's particular theology."[9]

2.1 Disagreements Regarding the Purpose of Markan Sandwiches

Although a consensus exists on the presence of intercalations, scholars disagree on the purpose and function of the Markan sandwich.[10] What is the relationship between the two narratives and what outcome does Mark hope to achieve through this literary device? With the rise of literary criticism the majority answer highlights the heightened suspense in the narrative.[11] Intercalations produce a chronological gap[12] so that the action is retarded in order to heighten dramatic tension. Rhoads and Michie explain that "such suspense maintains the readers' interest, enticing them to stay alert through the second episode to find out how the first episode will end."[13] For instance, in 3:20–35 Mark inserts the controversy with the Pharisees after the concern of Jesus' family about his mental welfare to raise the question in the mind of the reader, "Will the relatives succeed in their mission to seize Jesus?" Likewise, when Jesus' mission to save a sick girl is interrupted in Mark 5:25–34, the reader wonders tensely, "Will Jesus arrive in time to save the little girl from death?" As Shepperd points out, "During the inner story, this outer episode is held in suspense in the background, awaiting resolution."[14]

Shepperd, however, moves one stop forward by postulating that this literary function of the intercalation not only affects the narration of events but also the characterization. The purpose then is "to produce a dramatized irony between key characters and their actions."[15] The characters are contrasted or compared in such a manner as to create dramatized irony. This narrative irony is evident in 3:20–35, where Jesus' family hopes to save him from the pressing needs of the crowds only to ironically ally themselves with the Pharisees who also accuse Jesus. Against the Pharisees Jesus argues that a divided house cannot stand, yet Jesus' own household becomes divided since they stand outside the circle of Jesus' new family (3:31–32). In Mark 5 a bleeding

---

8. Ibid., 318–19. For a summary of narrative features, see ibid., 327–28; and Van Oyen, "Intercalation and Irony," 965.

9. Stein, "Proper Methodology" 184.

10. See Edwards, "Marcan Sandwiches, 195.

11. Those who see it only as a literary technique to heighten suspense or to create the illusion of passing time usually trace their research back to Dobschütz, "Zur Erzählungskunst des Markus."

12. A few authors propose that the reason for the intercalation is purely chronological. Referring to Mark 5:21–43, Burkill (*Mysterious Revelation*, 121) states that "sometimes the intercalation seems simply to signify a lapse of time." See also Van Oyen, "Intercalation and Irony," 951.

13. Rhoads and Michie, *Mark as Story*, 52.

14. Shepperd, "Narrative Function," 525.

15. Shepperd, *Sandwich Stories*, 328. For a description of the irony in each intercalation, see ibid., 338–39; and idem, "Narrative Function," 539–40.

woman touches Jesus (5:27) while Jesus reaches out his hand to a dead girl (5:41). Both gestures result in uncleanness yet, ironically, instead of Jesus becoming tainted the women become clean. Through the intercalation in Mark 6:7–32 the end of John the Baptizer's ministry is ironically linked to the beginning of the disciples' mission. In Mark 11:12–25 the cleansing of the temple can only occur through a destruction of the temple, as suggested by the withering of the fig tree from its roots. Likewise, in 14:1–11 the actions of the outside religious leaders and the insider Judas Iscariot are contrasted with the missionary confession of a nameless woman so that surprisingly "the nefarious plot becomes Good News."[16] Finally, when Jesus institutes the new covenant (14:22–25), the disciples and especially Peter are dramatically singled out as covenant breakers (14:17–21, 27–31). Then at the exact time Jesus offers the good confession of his own identity in the middle of the sandwich (14:61–62), Peter refuses to confess any knowledge of his master on three occasions (14:53–54, 66–72).

Thus the intercalations reveal a multiplicity of functions. Kee even posits a different function for each sandwich, including to change miracle stories into controversy stories (2:1–12; 3:1–6), to shift the onus for Jesus' rejection from his family to the scribes (3:20–35), to add suspense to a healing (5:21–43), to allow for a vivid digression on John the Baptist's denouement (6:6b–30), and to emphasize the fulfillment of Scripture (Mark 11:12–25 = Isa 56:7 Jer 7:11; Mark 14:53–72 = Ps 110:1 and Dan 7:13; Mark 15:6–32 = 1 Macc 1:9 and 11:13).[17] But as we shall see in the exegesis below, Mark's primary purpose in employing intercalations is threefold: to heighten narrative tension, to employ dramatic irony, and to offer theological comment.[18]

Certainly Markan intercalations add narrative tension, character comparison, and ironic overtones, but I will argue that Mark's motive is primarily theological. Since irony entails that an author is dealing at two levels,[19] Mark employs intercalations to offer the reader a theological perspective on the events historically narrated. As Fowler points out, "The intercalations exhibit a hermeneutical function for duality."[20] The meaning and content of the irony are more important than just the presence of

---

16. Shepperd, "Narrative Function," 539. See Burkill, *Mysterious Revelation*, 121.

17. Kee, *Community*, 55. See also Burkill, *Mysterious Revelation*, 121 n. 10.

18. Another hypothesis by Wendling suggests that Mark employs intercalations to indicate the employment of sources with Urmarkus in the middle and Markan redaction surrounding it. But such precision is doubtful, and Mark never intends the surrounding incidents to dominate the commentary. See Wendling, *Entstehung des Markusevangeliums*, 238. For specifics see Van Oyen, "Intercalation and Irony," 956 n. 34. Others simply contend that the intercalations express historical happenedness and chronological order, but the omissions of several sandwiches in Matthew and Luke argue against this thesis since neither follow Mark 3:20–35 (see Matt 12:22–32, 46–50 and Luke 11:14–23; 12:10; 8:19–21) or Mark 11:12–22 (see Matt 21:12–20 and Luke 19:45–48).

19. Camery-Hoggatt (*Irony*, 61) explains, "Irony requires that there be two or more levels of discourse, one available to the victim of the irony, the other to the observer."

20. Fowler, *Let the Reader Understand*, 143.

irony. Therefore, "Irony is the rhetorical medium through which Mk conveys his message of faith."[21]

Even Shepherd who emphasizes the literary function of the Markan sandwich admits that "when the intercalations are read as depicting dramatized irony, they make statements to the reader about one or more of the major theological themes of the Gospel."[22] Agreed on this, scholars disagree whether the intercalations highlight any particular Markan subject matter. George Wright in his dissertation concludes that Markan intercalations "unfold the identity of Jesus and reveal various responses to him."[23] Although he recognizes more intercalations than most modern scholars, each of the examples testifies to a Markan emphasis upon Christology and discipleship. Here is a chart of Wright's findings:

Intercalations that emphasize the authority and identity of Jesus[A]

1:21–28	An authoritative teacher
2:1–12	Jesus' authority over sickness and sin
3:1–6	An authoritative interpretation with regard to Sabbath regulations
3:20–35	The authority to redefine family
4:1–20	The authority to establish the criterion for insiders and outsiders
5:21–43	The authority to overcome sickness and death
6:6–30	Determining the correct identity of Jesus
11:12–21	The authority of Jesus over the temple
14:1–11	Jesus' true identity shown through the woman's anointing
14:53–72	Jesus reveals his identity while Peter hides it.
15:6–32	The titles of Jesus portrayed ironically in mockery
15:40—16:8	Responses to an authoritative Jesus

A. Ibid., 222–24.

Intercalations that emphasize the response of followers[A]

1:21–28	Amazement
2:1–12	Claims of blasphemy by the religious leaders
3:1–6	Anger and plotting by the religious leaders
3:20–35	The disciples do the will of God
4:1–20	Those who hear and understand the word of Jesus are the insiders.
5:21–43	Those who see Jesus as their only source of hope and help
6:6–30	The absence of the disciples pointing to the close relationship of John and Jesus[B]
11:12–21	The crowds amazed; the Jewish leaders agitated; the disciples hear (11:14)

---

21. Donahue, "Temple, Trial, and Royal Christology," 79.
22. Shepperd, *Sandwich Stories*, 343.
23. Wright, *Markan Intercalations*, 222.

14:1–11	Contrast between the response of a woman and a disciple
14:53–72	Those closest to Jesus fail him.
15:6–32	The way of Jesus represented in the cross
15:40—16:8	The noble deed of requesting and burying the body of Jesus in contrast with the inappropriate response of the women

A. Ibid., 236–43. Edwards ("Markan Sandwiches," 196) gets more specific about the content: "faith, discipleship, bearing witness, and the dangers of apostasy."

B. Here Wright overlooks the fact that Jesus' disciples take the place of John the Baptizer in the mission, which would be a more appropriate summary of the response in the Markan sandwich.

John Donahue progresses a step further than Wright by narrowing the theme of the intercalations to "underscore two major themes of his gospel, the way of suffering of Jesus and the necessity of the disciples to follow Jesus on this way."[24] He argues that Mark employs the intercalated material "to cast over the whole gospel the shadow of the cross, and all intercalations contain some allusion to the suffering and death of Jesus."[25] Donahue is certainly correct that the rejection theme dominates the intercalations. In 3:20–35 Jesus' own family, who seem like insiders, become outsiders along with the Jewish leaders so that both reject Jesus' mission.[26] The rejection and murder of John by Herod in 6:6b–30 previews what will happen with Jesus.[27] The temple action coupled with the cursing of the fig tree (11:12–21) prepares both for Jesus' death, when the veil of the temple is destroyed, and for the resurrection, which rebuilds the temple in three days (14:58). In 14:1–11 the rejection of Jesus by the Jewish leaders and Judas the betrayer is contrasted with a woman who prophetically anoints Jesus' body for burial. Similarly, in 14:17–31 Jesus' offering of his body and blood at the Last Supper is contrasted with the predicted rejection by Judas and the denial by Peter. This is fulfilled in 14:53–72 when Peter rejects Jesus at his trial, while Jesus himself faithfully offers the true confession of his identity in the midst of interrogation. Each of these intercalations centers on the Passion of Jesus and the corresponding discipleship of the cross.

Donahue gets in trouble, however, when he discerns a more specific structural pattern in the intercalations where "sections leading to the suffering and death of Jesus are framed by discipleship material"[28] in the intercalations. He reports that "while the B-element has in one way or another to do with the suffering of Jesus, all framing A-elements are related to discipleship (except for Mark 5:21–43 which does not

---

24. Donahue, *Are You the Christ?*, 62.

25. Ibid., 60.

26. As Shepperd (*Sandwich Stories*, 343) points out, "The opposition which Jesus meets in this intercalation, which is tied to the question of his true 'household,' connects with the Gospel theme of the growing opposition to Jesus which culminates in the crucifixion."

27. Again Shepperd (*Sandwich Stories*, 344) seems to support such an hypothesis when he explains, "In Mark 6 the identification of Jesus with John foreshadows the cross and the resurrection."

28. Donahue (*Are You the Christ?*, 62) claims that the framing material is concerned either with the instruction of the disciples or their reaction of Jesus.

fit very well with Mark's normal use of intercalation)."[29] Here Donahue skews the interpretation of passages in order to force the intercalations to fit his theological pattern. The application to discipleship in 14:1–11 obviously stands on the inside of the intercalation, and the sandwiches in 11:12–21 and 5:21–43 (as Donahue admits) concentrate on Jewish practices and institutions rather than the Passion of the Messiah. We want to use Donahue's insight without narrowing Mark's purpose and straightjacketing his employment of literary techniques.

Literary critics have reacted negatively to Donahue's suggestion. Joanna Dewey champions this position when she concludes that

> Donahue's use of literary techniques as a direct indicator of theology ignores the reality of the gospel as narrative. Intercalation is primarily a literary device and should be studied first in rhetorical terms, to see how the intercalation affects the progression of the narrative. Only when its literary function is understood, can one correctly interpret how an intercalation may add to our understanding of Mark's theology.[30]

Dewey's evaluation is helpful if it is categorized as a methodological comment and not a refusal to see theology in Mark's intercalations. Certainly an intercalation is a literary device, and Shepperd has done a masterful job in demonstrating "the narrative characteristics of intercalation in Mark and to delineate its function in Markan storytelling."[31] However, we hope to demonstrate that Markan literary devices such as intercalation and framework offer a theological perspective to the reader as well.

Positively, Wright's and Donahue's analyses of the significance of Markan intercalations corresponds with the two major themes of Mark's gospel: Christology and discipleship.[32] However, if Mark emphasizes these two themes throughout his material, then the specific reason for including intercalations only on certain occasions is not apparent. Why does Mark employ this literary device only here and there in specific narratives? We will argue that Mark uses these literary devices as a codeword to let the readers know that he is addressing a problem in their situation. Scholars have sensed this phenomenon, but have not admitted its full significance. Shepperd, for instance, states offhandedly, "It is as though the author uses intercalation as a tool to address the reader's own situation."[33] Fowler discerns "a parabolic, metaphorical relationship"[34] so that Mark speaks at two levels. Kee likewise claims that "when the intercalations are real as depicting dramatized irony, they make statements to the reader about one or

---

29. Ibid., 59 n. 3. Therefore, Donahue suggests that Mark found this one intercalation in the tradition.

30. Dewey, *Markan Public Debate*, 22.

31. Shepperd, *Sandwich Stories*, 108.

32. Stein ("Proper Methodology" 184) recognizes as well that intercalations call attention to the "Evangelist's particular theology."

33. Shepperd, *Sandwich Stories*, 386.

34. Fowler, *Let the Reader Understand*, 146.

more of the major theological themes of the Gospel."³⁵ Therefore, although the narrative function of intercalations creates a worthy story, we will show through an exegesis of the intercalations that a theological purpose cannot be ignored. Mark employs intercalations for narrative tension, dramatic irony, and theological insight.

2.2 Mark 3:20–35: Jesus' Family and the Jerusalem Religious Leaders

In this first example of a Markan intercalation the list of similarities between these two stories (3:20–21, 31–35³⁶; 3:22–30) is quite impressive:

1. In each section Mark employs all the normal elements of the genre of controversy dialogue. Jesus' actions in each case initiate a conflict. Jesus' family thinks he is out of his mind because of his hectic lifestyle, and in response to Jesus' exorcisms the teachers of the law come from Jerusalem with the double accusation that "He is possessed by Beelzebul"³⁷ and "by the prince of demons he is driving out demons." In each case Jesus responds with a question. Regarding the presence of his family he inquires (3:33), "Who are my mother and my brothers?" (3:33), and to the scribes he asks (3:23), "How can Satan drive out Satan?" As usual, a memorable pronouncement climaxes each controversy. Regarding his true family Jesus concludes, "Whoever does God's will is my brother and sister and mother" (3:35). Likewise, his parable in 3:27 demonstrates to the teachers of the law that his exorcisms are plundering Satan's house: "No one can enter a strong man's house and carry off his possessions unless he first ties up the strong man. Then he can rob his house."

2. Jesus is the central actor on both ends of the intercalation as well as in the interior of the sandwich, so that Shepperd claims that each story is chiastic with regard to characters.³⁸

---

35. Kee, *Community*, 56.

36. Hartmann, "Mark 3,20f"; Wansbrough, "Mark iii.21; and Schroeder, *Eltern und Kinder in der Verkündigung Jesu* (110ff.) claim that 3:31–35 are separate from 3:20–21 since the earlier verses refer to the disciples (οἱ παρ' αὐτοῦ), and ἐξέστη does not normally refer to madness in Mark but instead wonder or amazement, in this case being the enthusiasm of the crowd which is curbed by the disciples. See Wenham, "Meaning of Mark III.21," 295–96; and Best, "Mark III.20, 21, 31–35," 311–14, for a negative critique of this proposal. The negative characterization of Jesus' family, the disciples, and the women is central to Mark's purpose.

37. Instead of the NIV 1984's Beelzebub, following the KJV and ASV, we will follow the TNIV and NIV 2011 with its change to Beelzebul, like the NASV, RSV, NRSV, ESV, GNT, NET, NAB, NCV, NJB, etc.

38. Shepperd, *Sandwich Stories*, 125, n. 1.

Outer story	Jesus	3:20a
	crowd	3:20b
	relatives	3:21
	relatives	3:31
	crowd	3:32
	Jesus	3:33
Inner story	scribes	3:22
	Jesus	3:23–30a
	scribes	3:30b

The employment of chiastic structures is reinforced by an a-b-b'-a' chiastic structure apparent in the delineation of charges in the middle section. The first accusation, "He is possessed by Beelzebul" (22a), is not dealt with until 3:28–30, while the second accusation, "By the prince of demons he is driving out demons" (22b), is responded to immediately in 3:23–27. The resulting structure forms a chiasm:[39]

a	3:22a	Accusation 1: He is possessed by Beelzebul.
b	3:22b	Accusation 2: By the prince of demons he is driving out demons.
b'	3:23–27	Answer to 2: Satan cannot cast out himself (23–26) but only a stronger one can plunder his house (the parable in 3:27).
a'	3:28–30	Answer to 1: The Jewish leaders are guilty of the unpardonable sin.

3. The setting for both controversies consists of a house with Jesus surrounded by a crowd (3:20, 32). The terms "house" and "household" (οἶκόν, οἰκία) even become a *Leitwort*, with the physical location of a house in the outside pericope (3:20, 31 outside) balanced by sayings about "a house divided against itself" (3:25) and "a strong man's house" (3:27) inside the intercalation.[40]

4. Jesus' mother and brothers constitute his physical family, and the religious leaders would be expected to be Jesus' spiritual family.[41] Contemporary Jews would imagine that both groups would be advocates of an up-and-coming rabbi. Ironically, these presumed insiders become outsiders.

---

39. Cf. Barton, *Discipleship and Family Ties*, 71, for similar conclusions.

40. Another tie to the term "house" is the name Beelzebul, which may mean "lord of the heavenly dwelling." See Guelich, *Mark*, 174–75.

41. Shepperd ("Narrative Function," 529) thinks of the scribes from Jerusalem as Jesus' enemies so the two groups are contrasted, but they should be seen as leaders of his faith community in the early days of Jesus' ministry. At the narrative level, of course, they are hostile since their introduction in 2:6–12, 15–17.

5. Both audiences level a serious charge against Jesus. His family accuses him of fanaticism while the teachers of the law complain of satanic inspiration.[42] Is Jesus crazy? Is Jesus demon possessed? These are serious questions in themselves, but Shepperd heightens the import by contending that "the challenge to Jesus' sanity and the accusation about the source of his power are challenges to the claim of Messiahship."[43] Therefore, Mark demonstrates that neither charge is grounded in reality. Instead, in plundering Satan's house (3:27) and introducing an eschatological family (3:34), Jesus as Messiah is proclaiming the arrival of the age to come.

6. Strategically Jesus overturns their accusations by exposing the fallacy of each of these groups with authoritative statements about the unpardonable sin (3:28–29) and true family membership (3:35).

What is the meaning and purpose of these interconnections? Certainly narrative tension is heightened since the reader wants to know if Jesus will have an answer to his family's murmurings concerning his psychological makeup. Likewise, the reference to his family with the vague description οἱ παρ' αὐτοῦ (3:21) "keeps the reader in suspense with regard to the identity of the 'associates,' which is resolved surprisingly in 3,31."[44] Therefore, one purpose is narrative suspense.

The intercalation creates dramatic irony as well. Shepherd advocates an ironic purpose since "there is also the symbol of the divided house in Jesus' comments in the inner story and the irony of his own division from his blood relatives in the outer story."[45] But the greater irony involves the readership. Only the reader can see the connection of the two stories, not the characters themselves, implying that the message must be aimed at the reader.[46] Mark's portrayal of Jesus' family is exceptionally harsh especially considering the sandwich which ties them closely with the Jewish leaders, who have previously plotted to kill Jesus (3:6) and who will in the end take his life. What is Mark intending to say?

A band of modern interpreters hypothesize a polemic against the church of Jerusalem as exemplified in the leadership of James, the brother of Jesus.[47] Crossan,

---

42. Shepperd (ibid.) points out differences: "The charge of the relatives is more on a psychological level, that of the scribes more on a spiritual level," and the charge of insanity does not even achieve the honor of an explicit rebuttal.

43. Shepperd, *Sandwich Stories*, 129.

44. Van Iersel, "Concentric Structures," 524, n. 10. Barton (*Discipleship and Family Ties*, 71) points out that the "bridge between vv. 20–21 and 31–35 is an editorial means of identifying οἱ παρ' αὐτοῦ with Jesus' mother and brothers."

45. Shepperd, *Sandwich Stories*, 333.

46. This observation does not deny the historicity of the event. Marcus points out, "Mark's portrait of strained relations must be historical; it is probably not the sort of depiction that the church would have created out of thin air" (*Mark 1–8*, 279).

47. See the writings of John Dominic Crossen, Michael Goulder, Werner Kelber, Joseph Tyson, Etienne Trocmé, Alfred Sunderwirth, and Theodore Weeden.

for instance, contends that Mark provides a manifesto "against the jurisdictional and doctrinal hegemony of the Jerusalem church."[48] Since the Jewish scribes are described as "coming down from Jerusalem" (3:22; 7:1), Mark is polemicizing against that place and therefore connecting Jesus' relatives with Jerusalem through the intercalation. Just as the early church defended itself against the accusations of Jewish leaders, so also Mark is "an exponent of Torah-free Gentile Christianity" against the "Torah-observant Jewish Christian church in Jerusalem."[49] Evidence that Mark is equating the relatives of Jesus with the culpable scribes is seen in the symmetrical structure of the accusations which employ a verb of saying with a ὅτι clause (21b ἔλεγον γὰρ ὅτι ἐξέστη; 22b ἔλεγον ὅτι Βεελζεβοὺλ ἔχει). Therefore, "He is possessed by Beelzebul" functions as the equivalent of "He is out of his mind," since all mental disorders were ascribed in those days to possession by an evil spirit. Thus Jesus' relatives are actually accusing him of being possessed by Satan, so that Jesus' warning about the unpardonable sin (3:28–29) applies both to the Jewish leaders and his own family.[50]

Although Mark employs an intercalation to compare Jesus' relatives and the Jewish scribes, he is not equating them. In an intercalation the two scenes by definition contain a different set of characters (except for the figure of Jesus) that do not interact. Therefore the contention that the unforgivable sin applies to both groups is mistaken. Similarly, the accusations must be distinguished. As Lambrecht maintains, the charge in "21b as contrasted with that of v. 22b does not imply an accusation openly expressed; it only gives the motivation of the initiative"[51] as indicated by the unique construction of a γὰρ clause. Finally, the Markan ending of this pericope with a positive exclamation regarding the disciples as Jesus' family (3:35) indicates that Mark's "primary interest does not lie negatively in an attack on a party within the church but positively on the nature of true discipleship."[52]

In confronting the claims of Crossan, Lambrecht offers the alternative thesis that Jesus' family mirrors unbelieving Israel: "The relatives of Jesus, however, do not stand on the side of the disciples; they belong to the unbelieving Israel. . . . They neither understood nor accepted Jesus."[53] Evidence for this thesis could derive from Mark 6:1–6a, where Jesus' family (6:4) is tied closely together with the hometown people of Nazareth who reject him. But Lambrecht wants to separate Mark's picture of Jesus' family from his negative description of the disciples at other places in the gospel. In reality, Mark paints the Twelve, the woman disciples at the end of the gospel, and

---

48. Crossan, "Mark and Relatives of Jesus," 111. It is further claimed (112–13) that Joseph is nowhere mentioned in the Markan gospel because Jesus' brother James is the intended target of attention, nor is Nazareth mentioned in Mark 6:1–6a since the apologetic was indirectly aimed at Jerusalem. For a useful negative critique see Lambrecht, "Relatives," 241–58.

49. See Marcus (*Mark 1–8*, 280) for a description of this view.

50. Cf. Trocmé, *Formation*, 135–36.

51. Lambrecht, "Relatives," 245.

52. Best, "Mark III: 20 21, 31–35," 317.

53. Lambrecht, "Relatives," 256–57.

Jesus' family in matching colors. Although Jesus appoints the Twelve as apostles who will remain with him (3:14) as his family, he concludes this list of disciples with Judas, who will betray him (3:19). In fact, at the end of the story all the disciples desert Jesus (14:50) and even Peter, the rock of the disciples, denies Jesus three times, climaxing in a curse (14:71). Similarly, when Jesus' family appears a second time they are pictured as standing outside of Jesus' company (3:31). This description is then picked up in Mark 4:11–13, where now the disciples because of their lack of understanding are warned about becoming outsiders. The women as well neglect to obey the angel and out of fear refuse to proclaim the kerygma (16:8). Through these descriptions Mark creates a pattern so that regarding Jesus as out of his mind (Jesus' family), deserting Jesus in his time of need (the disciples), and fearfully neglecting to proclaim the gospel (the women) are paralleled as illustrations of discipleship failure. It is no coincidence that these three groups constitute the early church described in Acts 1:13–14. Mark "plays with" the most respected leaders of the church to educate his readership about the pointed possibility that insiders can become outsiders.

Therefore, Mark's purpose in creating this intercalation involves the situation of his readers. The alienation of Jesus from his family replicates the estrangement of some Markan Christians from their own family members in their struggle to live the Christian life in a time of persecution. Jesus' prophecy in Mark 13:12–13, which predicts that his disciples will be betrayed to death by their own relatives and "hated by all on account of my name," is beginning to be fulfilled.[54] As Best explains, "Such an alienation from family must have been the experience of many of Mark's community, as was the experience of vi.1–6; their families will have thought them out of their minds for becoming Christians."[55] Mark employs this incident about Jesus' family to speak homiletically to the church, which is in danger of rejecting the lifestyle of Jesus as fanaticism.[56] Just as Jesus' family became outsiders, so the Christian community of Mark's day can become outsiders. Mark is therefore employing the intercalation as a signal that he is speaking at two levels and mirroring the community's experience in the narrative.

The two central issues of Mark's gospel, a suffering Christ and a discipleship of the cross, become prominent themes in Mark's intercalation. As Shepherd points out, "The opposition which Jesus meets in this intercalation, which is tied to the question of his true 'household,' connects with the Gospel theme of the growing opposition to

---

54. See Marcus, *Mark 1–8*, 280; and *Mystery*, 93–94.

55. Best, "Mark III. 20–21, 31–35," 317. Notice that this theology of Jesus' family is a consistent emphasis of Mark. Likewise in 6:4, the prophets are not honored by their relatives whereas Matt 13:57 and Luke 4:24 eliminate this saying (also omitted in John 4:44 and Thomas 31) indicating that the logion is Markan redaction (cf. Lambrecht, "Relatives," 253).

56. The offensive character of the accusation of Jesus' family members should not be eliminated as is done in the KJV and ASV by speaking of Jesus' friends which is countered by Lambrecht ("Relatives," 244–45, n. 6). The description "out of his mind" should be associated with Jesus' extra-committed lifestyle as evidenced by the abstention from normal activities like eating in 3:20.

Jesus which culminates in the crucifixion."[57] Jesus is misunderstood, criticized, and rejected by the Jewish leaders as well as by his own family in this Markan sandwich. As an alternative, Mark advocates a discipleship which is based upon a family relationship that does God's will (3:35) and is not sidetracked by accepting the accusations leveled against Jesus. Mark is calling his community to a discipleship that accepts a radical break with family and religious tradition. A rejected Messiah and a discipleship of the cross become the highlighted themes of this Markan sandwich.

2.3 Mark 5:21–43: Two Unclean People Healed: A Bleeding Woman and Dead Girl

What is the purpose of this intercalation? Beyond the obvious link of combining two miraculous healings, the characterization stands out. Through a whole series of verbal and thematic connections Mark compares the two central female characters and contrasts the father Jairus with the woman experiencing a flow of blood. Verbal links include the following:

1. Both female characters are called "daughter" (5:34, 35 Θυγάτηρ), although the diminutive Greek term (θυγάτριόν) is employed in the first part of the intercalation (5:23).

2. Significantly, Mark calls attention to the girl's age as twelve years old (5:42) and the length of the woman's illness as twelve years (5:25). This seemingly insignificant data must play a role in Mark's purpose of narrating these incidents.

3. Approaching Jesus, both Jairus and the woman with the vaginal discharge fall at his feet (5:22, 33).[58] Fear is present in each situation (5:33 φοβηθεῖσα; 5:36 φοβοῦ) but faith wins out.

4. The woman's faith plays a significant role in her healing (5:34), and Jesus' advice for the frightened household of the young girl is to merely "believe" (5:36).[59] As a result their hope for salvation (σώζω 5:23, 28) becomes a reality (5:34).

5. In addition, a large crowd (ὄχλος πολὺς) appears in both stories (5:21, 24b), but as Shepherd remarks, "their role is really as a prop and not as a character. They never make a statement or carry out an action which expresses a viewpoint."[60]

6. In each case the healing is immediate (εὐθὺς 5:29, 42). As a result the menstruating

---

57. Shepherd, *Sandwich Stories*, 343.

58. Camery-Hoggatt sees a contrast: "The woman falls at Jesus' feet out of fear of repercussions for her unseemly act of having touched Jesus. Jairus falls at his feet at (sic) a way of expressing deference in a moment of extreme crisis" (*Irony*, 138).

59. Schweizer emphasizes faith contending that "Mark has produced this story within a story in the expectation that faith will be created in the reader" (*Mark*, 120).

60. Shepherd, *Sandwich Stories*, 144.

woman can now bear children, and the twelve-year-old stands on the threshold of puberty, marriage, and family.[61] Both can now participate in their expected social roles.

7. But the concept of touching (ἅπτω 5:27, 28, 30, 31) or laying hands upon someone (5:23 ἐπιθῇς τὰς χεῖρας; 5:41 κρατήσας τῆς χειρός) receives the most emphasis.[62] Not only is this data mentioned in both parts of the outer story, it dominates the conflict in the inner narrative through its four occurrences. The woman sets her mind to touch Jesus' garment (5:27–28). Jesus responds by calling attention to the touching (5:30), and the disciples protest that a touch would be imperceptible with this thronging multitude (5:31). The touching is culturally and religiously significant since the bleeding woman and dead girl would be considered unclean in Jewish society, the one by a menstrual disorder, the other by death. "Yet in both cases this uncleanness is boldly ignored, in the one case by the woman, who touches the garment of Jesus, in the other case by Jesus, who touches the girl's corpse."[63]

Beyond these verbal connections, the plot of each healing narrative contains similar twists, with the greater miracle of resurrection from the dead occurring at the end. As Edwards points out, both characters "are victims of desperate circumstances, and apart from Jesus they have no hope."[64] In their desperate situations Jesus' all-knowing superiority supplies comic relief to each story. In contradistinction from the flabbergasted disciples, Jesus knows precisely about the healing power that secretly works its magic over the bleeding women (5:30–31). Over against the wailing despair of the mourners, Jesus alone realizes that the girl is only sleeping (5:39). In each case the onlookers doubt Jesus' discernment so that in 5:31 Jesus' disciples question his judgment since everyone is touching him, while at 5:40 the mourners laugh at Jesus when he concludes she is only resting. Likewise, in each healing the contrast between public and private actions takes prominence, so that the private touching of Jesus results in a public exposure of the woman cured (5:32–33) and the public mockery of the crowd results in a private raising of the dead girl (5:40–41).

Finally, a healing takes place at various levels in both incidents. At a literal level a medical healing occurs. But the healing is pictured as a transformation from death to life. Haber notes, "In physical terms both the girl and the woman are associated with death, the former because she purportedly dies and the latter because her condition not only threatened her life, it also precluded the possibility that she would bring new life into the world by bearing children."[65] Regarding cultural background, a social

---

61. See Boring, *Mark*, 158.
62. For a complete analysis of these words in Mark, see section 8.5 below.
63. Marcus, *Mark 1–8*, 364.
64. Edwards, "Markan Sandwiches," 204.
65. Haber, *They Shall Purify Themselves*, 139.

border is broken in each story, with the unclean woman's touch resulting in Jesus' ritual impurity in the inner story and Jesus' handling of a dead corpse breaking a social boundary in the outer story. But surprisingly the uncleanness is inverted; instead of Jesus becoming unclean, the kingdom miracles produce purity and wholeness that can only be described as salvation (σώζω 5:23, 28, 34).

Other scholars call attention to the contrasts in the narrative.[66] With regard to literary style, the sentence structure varies dramatically. The Jairus episode employs short, paratactic sentences in the historical present while the woman's story is dominated by long, participle-filled sentences in the aorist tense.[67] The complexity of the sentence structure stands out, with seven participles parading in a row (5:25–27) concluding with the main verb that she touched his garment.

With regard to descriptive details, the appeal of Jairus is narrated through words whereas the woman's request comes only in action. Jesus initiates the healing of Jairus' daughter by taking her hand and commanding her to rise, but the woman initiates her own healing. Jairus asks in public but the healing occurs in secret, whereas the woman asks in private but the healing is exposed in public. The foreknowledge of Jesus in the frame is contrasted with Jesus' ignorance as to who touched him in the inner story.[68] Finally, "the report of the representatives stands in a contrasting relationship to the benediction of Jesus in 5:34."[69] Jesus' exhortation to the woman to "go in peace" certainly calls attention to a different atmosphere from the commotion, loud wailing, and sarcastic mockery in 5:38–40.

With regard to the approach of the narrator, "the outer story is character elevating with its delay in telling us of the girl's death and the mourning which has begun, as well as her age, while the inner story is very reader elevating with the reader knowing about the woman's healing before anyone else."[70]

Finally, with regard to the description of characters, Jairus is personally named and enjoys a prominent position as leader of the synagogue whereas the woman lacks both identification[71] and recognition since she is excluded from the synagogue because of her uncleanness.[72] Whereas Jairus is socially secure and materially rich, as evidenced by the ostentation over the death of his daughter, the unclean unattached woman is socially ostracized. The woman journeys from secrecy to openness while

---

66. Prominent among scholars is Guelich, *Mark 1—8:26*, 291–92.

67. See Marcus, *Mark 1-8*, 364; Marshall, *Faith in Mark's Narrative*, 92.

68. Supported by Taylor (*Mark*, 292) and Mann (*Mark*, 285), but the feminine ἰδεῖν τὴν τοῦτο ποιήσασαν ("to see who had done this") in 5:32 could indicate Jesus' knowledge or the narrator's hand.

69. Shepherd (*Sandwich Stories*, 156, n. 1) is referring to 5:35, the verse immediately following Jesus' exhortation to peace.

70. Ibid., 166.

71. Tradition (Acts of Pilate 2) graciously bestowed names upon the two women characters, Bernice and Veronica respectively.

72. See Edwards, "Markan Sandwiches," 204.

Jairus travels toward ever more secret (that is closed) locales.[73] In this manner a striking contrast is developed between a religiously honored, married, named male and a poor, outcast, unnamed, homeless single female.[74] They live and operate at the opposite end of the social, economic, and religious spectrum.

How do these comparisons and contrasts lead to a recognition of Mark's purpose for including these stories in his gospel? Here we will just outline the various suggestions and argue for a theological purpose, but in chapter 8 we will connect this passage with a series of themes throughout the gospel to demonstrate that according to Mark Jesus is fulfilling the required OT ceremonial laws of uncleanness by contact with blood and corpses through these kingdom healing actions.[75]

The literary purpose of this intercalation emphasizes dramatic tension. As Camery-Hoggatt explains, "The painfully slow march toward Jairus' house, the interruption, the report of the servants that the girl has died in the interval, all combine to make this also one of the most suspenseful episodes in the tradition."[76] The suspense adds dramatic irony to the narrative as well.[77] Ironically the little girl dies exactly while Jesus is healing the woman.[78] A third suggestion for the purpose of the narrative concentrates upon the characterization. Since unclean women dominate the narrative, Jesus is offering a social critique about the marginalized of society. Myers suggests that already in Jesus' healing of Peter's mother-in-law (1:29–31), "Mark is serving notice that patriarchal theology and the devaluation of women will be overturned!"[79] In like manner, the reversal of the social status of women and children would be at stake in the intercalation in 5:21–43. A social political critique is seen in the fact that the woman was "bankrupted by profiteering physicians who exploited her."[80]

Shepherd points to additional theological reasons for the presence of an intercalation, suggesting that Mark addresses three important themes: Christology, the secrecy/revelation motif, and the fear/faith theme.[81] Kelber emphasizes the first of these themes, Christology, in particular the resurrection. He describes in detail the skillful dramatic tension which leads up to the miracle of the resurrection.

---

73. Shepherd, "Intercalation and the Synoptic Problem," 693.

74. Shepherd, *Sandwich Stories*, 333. Shepherd, following Lev 15:25–27, points out that "If she had been married, she was probably divorced since she could not have had sexual intercourse with her husband" ("Narrative Function," 529, n. 21).

75. See section 8.6 below.

76. Camery-Hoggatt, *Irony*, 139. But see Kazen (*Jesus and Purity Halakhah*, 130) who argues that this explanation is not satisfactory as exemplified in Matthew's version.

77. Shepherd, *Sandwich Stories*, 146. See his tables on pp. 147–48.

78. Shepherd says, "One 'daughter' finds health in his presence, the other comes to death in his absence" ("Intercalation and Synoptic Problem," 693).

79. Myers, *Say to this Mountain*, 15.

80. Ibid., 64. However, we will argue in section 3.3 that at the beginning of his gospel Mark is merely developing the pattern of Jesus' ministry which included preaching (1:14–15), discipleship (1:16–20), teaching (1:21–22), deliverance (1:23–28), healing (1:29–34), and prayer (1:35–38).

81. Shepherd, *Sandwich Stories*, 149, 157, 344.

> When Jairus approaches Jesus, his daughter is still alive. She is near death, but there is still hope that she could be healed. Then Jesus allows himself to be distracted by the hemorrhaging woman and passes up the chance to rescue the girl from death. No sooner is the woman with an issue healed than the news arrives of the death of Jairus's daughter. Now it is in the face of death that Jesus performs not merely a healing but his greatest miracle on behalf of a human, the resurrection of a dead person.[82]

In this scenario the connection of the two stories would be their genre, that of miracle story. Thus both stories depict Jesus bringing the women from death to life, one literally, the other symbolically.[83] Mark's intended result then becomes the recognition of Jesus' authority over disease and death.[84] No symbolic significance is recognized. The touching of the fringe of a holy man's garment[85] by an unclean woman and the grasping of the hand of a dead corpse are merely healing techniques.

Others emphasize the faith theme as prominent. The tie to Christology is obvious since faith is the proper human response to the words and deeds of Jesus. Christopher Marshall contends that the Jairus story is structured "in five scenes in which the theme of faith in Jesus' saving power is steadily elaborated."[86] Furthermore, the healing of the bleeding woman records as its climax Jesus' saying on the saving power of faith (5:34), whereas the healing itself takes place halfway through the story (5:29).[87] However, the final word to the woman is not "your faith has healed you" (34a) but "go in peace and be freed from your suffering" (34b), which entails the peace and freedom that comes from the elimination of the social ostracism resulting from obeying the ceremonial legislation regarding continued menstruation. Furthermore, Marshall's exegesis treats each story separately and therefore does not inquire into the purpose of Mark's intercalation. Why does Mark employ this particular literary device to unite these two specific types of healing stories?

We will argue that through this intercalation Mark is addressing the deeper issue of the legitimacy of following Jewish ritual regulations prohibiting contact with

---

82. Kelber, *Mark's Story of Jesus*, 32.

83. Loader, *Jesus' Attitude toward the Law*, 61.

84. Certainly Matthew (9:18–26) treats these two narratives solely as miracle stories since he places ten miracles together into Matt 8–9 (like Num 14:22) so that Jesus' word ministry in Matt 5–7 is followed by his deed ministry here. Matt 8–9 contains three sets of three miracle stories (8:1–17; 8:23—9:8; 9:18–34) followed by three calls to deeper discipleship based upon Jesus' authority (8:18–22; 9:9–17; 9:35–38). But Matthew fails to notice Mark's symbolic treatment of miracle stories as evidenced by his omission of Mark 8:22–26; 6:52; 7:19b; 8:14; and the phrase "along the way" in 9:52 as well as the changing of the order of Mark 4:39–40 (Matt 8:26) and Mark 9:6 (Matt 17:6). See below in section 9.3c.

85. For Jewish background reflecting the popular belief that the fringe of a holy man's coat possessed magical powers see Evans, "Who Touched Me?" 366, n. 33.

86. Marshall, *Faith in Mark's Narrative*, 94.

87. Ibid., 101. However, the mentioning of faith in the other story does not occur as the climax of the story but earlier in 5:36.

a bleeding woman and touching a corpse.[88] This does not deny the importance of Christology, since the flow of Markan material demonstrates that Jesus is lord over nature (4:35–41), lord over the demons (5:1–20), master of illness (5:24–34), and victor over death itself (5:25–43). However, Mark wants to instruct his readers on how to read the Old Testament in the age of the kingdom.[89] Evidence that Mark is alluding to Jewish purity rituals begins with the parallel terminology in Leviticus as demonstrated by the fact that ἡ πηγὴ τοῦ αἵματος (Mark 5:29)[90] is never employed for vaginal bleeding except in Leviticus 12:7 LXX (cf. 20:18).[91] This OT background would leap out of the text to anyone who was familiar with the OT regulations about uncleanness from bleeding and dead bodies.

Second, impurity is transmitted through physical touch, and Jesus' contact with the bleeding woman and dead body is repeated in each of the three parts (A1, B, A2) of the intercalation at 5:23, 27, 28, 30, 31, 41. Especially significant is the fact that "touched" is the first finite verb after a series of seven participles in the middle story (5:25–27). From this Marcus contends that "'touched' thus gains extraordinary intensity as the climax of the string of participles."[92] This concentration of references calls attention to the social irregularity in Jewish culture of touching a woman with a flow of blood or a dead girl. Jesus is crossing the purity border and contaminating himself. However, instead of Jesus becoming unclean, the women become clean. Kingdom miracles for Mark thus have theological implications for reading the Torah. The purpose of the intercalation is to demonstrate how Jesus' kingdom actions fulfill the OT regulations about touching menstruating women and dead bodies. Instead of OT ceremonial regulations providing the verification for someone's ritual purity, Jesus makes people clean. Therefore, the purity laws lose their force since the Messiah is on the scene.

Now it must be admitted that Mark employs different verbal expressions in the two stories, using ἅπτω in the framed narrative (5:27, 28, 30, 31) and laying hands upon someone (5:23 ἐπιθῇς τὰς χεῖρας; 5:41 κρατήσας τῆς χειρὸς) in the outer frame. However, this is a common procedure for Mark, who in the similar healings with

---

88. Stein (*Mark*, 263) contends that "issues of ritual purity and impurity did not play any significant role" since Mark does not specifically raise this issue, but we will demonstrate that the literary device of an intercalation indicates to the reader that Mark is speaking at two levels. The topic of Jewish ceremonial regulations is also raised in the Markan sandwich of the cursing of the fig tree and the temple action.

89. Derrett ("Mark's Technique," 476) also believes that allusions to the OT tie this intercalation together (Ps 62:8–9 LXX and references to Canticles and Ruth), but he suggests that fertility issues construct the passage into a divine sacred marriage (480, 487), a cryptic view which has not attracted much attention.

90. Furthermore, the expression ῥύσις τοῦ αἵματος is employed in Mark 5:25 and Lev 15:25.

91. See Kazen, *Jesus and Purity Halakhah*, 134; Boring, *Mark*, 159; and Kahl, "Jairus und die verlorenen Töchter Israels," 66, n. 20. Fonrobert ("Woman with a Blood-Flow," 130) and Sariola (*Markus und das Gesetz*, 70–71) minimize their importance.

92. Marcus, *Mark 1–8*, 367.

spittle in 7:31–37 and 8:22–26 employs both terms in each narrative.[93] Dissident scholars further point out the peculiarity that Mark never explicitly calls attention to purity issues in the narrative. As Loader exclaims, although this passage bristles with issues of purity, "it is all the more striking that Mark shows so little interest."[94] Yet interpreters are continually overwhelmed with the subtlety of the gospel. Mark expects his readers to know when he is alluding to the Old Testament and depending upon its content to enlighten the narrative.[95] The complete dismissal of ceremonial mores by the woman and Jesus would stand out in striking contrast to contemporary Judaism, which emphasized circumcision, Sabbath keeping, diet regulations, and cleanliness rites. Therefore Davies and Allison observe that "it is possible that the woman comes up 'from behind' precisely because she is unclean and must accordingly try to touch Jesus without anyone observing."[96] Although Mark does not make the connection with purity rites obvious, the allusion to the Old Testament is just below the surface.

Finally, it must be conceded that the mentioning of "touching" by Mark does not inevitably bring with it the subject of the fulfillment of Jewish purity rituals. In fact, in the very next pericope at 6:5 the touching is merely a healing technique, and 6:56 mentions touching the edge of Jesus' garment within a summary of healing incidents. However, since Jewish purity becomes the major theme throughout the whole of chapter 7, this "touching" motif causes Mark to focus his final attention on OT purity issues. In fact, Jesus' touch is connected regularly by Mark with incidents that would result in ritual impurity, like touching a leper (Mark 1:41 and Lev 13–14), a menstruating woman (Mark 5:24–28 and Lev 15:19–33), a corpse (Mark 5:41 and Lev 22:4; Num 5:2; 6:6,11; 9:6–7,10; 19:11–22), and bodily emissions like spittle (Mark 7:33; 8:23 and Lev 15:8; Num 12:14).[97] In chapter 8 we will investigate these examples in an orderly format to demonstrate that Jesus' fulfillment of impurity rites is a major theme in Mark's gospel.

Of primary importance is the prominence of the fulfillment of Jewish regulations and cultic institutions in the other Markan intercalation which involves a miracle. In 11:12–25 Mark ties the "destruction" of the temple with the cursing of the fig tree. Just as the fig tree miraculously withers from its roots, so will temple worship be destroyed. Therefore in both intercalations that center on miracle stories Mark emphasizes the

---

93. 7:32 ἵνα ἐπιθῇ αὐτῷ τὴν χεῖρα; 7:33 ἥψατο; 8:22 ἵνα αὐτοῦ ἅψηται; 8:23 ἐπιθεὶς τὰς χεῖρας αὐτῷ; 8:25 ἐπέθηκεν τὰς χεῖρας.

94. Loader, *Jesus' Attitude*, 61.

95. See Juel, *Master of Surprise*, 38. Here the "flow of blood" (5:25) and the "fountain of blood" (5:29) are allusions to Lev 15:25–27, 33 and Lev 12:7 respectively. (5:25 ἐν ῥύσει αἵματος; Lev 15:25 ῥύσει αἵματος; 15:33 ἐν τῇ ῥύσει αὐτοῦ; 5:29 ἡ πηγὴ τοῦ αἵματος; Lev 12:7 ἀπὸ τῆς πηγῆς τοῦ αἵματος αὐτῆς).

96. Davies and Allison, *Matthew*, 2:128.

97. Selvidge offers feminist support: "Mark 5:25–34 may stand preserved because it remembers an early Christian community's break with the Jewish purity system, which restricted and excluded women from cult and society" ("Mark 5:25–34 and Leviticus 15:19–20," 619) since "Jesus does not reprimand this woman for being in the middle of a crowd or for touching Jesus" (ibid., 622).

fulfillment of Jewish practices. As a result the Christian is no longer made unclean through touch nor cleansed by temple sacrifices but becomes a member of the new fig tree vineyard (Mark 12:9; Matt 21:43) where temple service is replaced by faith, prayer, and forgiveness (Mark 11:22–25).[98]

The fact that Jewish regulations play a major role in this intercalation is supported as well by specific references to Jewish life. The twofold emphasis on the number twelve (5:25, 42) calls attention to the nation of Israel,[99] and the mention of Jairus as the leader of a synagogue (5:22 εἷς τῶν ἀρχισυναγώγων) accentuates the cultic life of Judaism. In addition, Jesus journeys from Gentile territory in 5:1–20 to Israel territory to speak about these specifically Jewish issues.[100] Other suggestions for the use of twelve, such as an explanation for why the girl could walk,[101] the prevention of confusion that "little girl" is simply a term of endearment,[102] or mere historical remembrance[103] "to add to the human interest of the story,"[104] require more exegetical support. Although Vincent Taylor asserts that twelve years is probably only a round number to describe a longstanding affliction,[105] there are enough passages in both the Old and New Testaments to make it apparent that twelve is Israel's number (Matt 19:28; Jas 1:1; Rev 12:1,21).[106] Certainly the appointment of twelve apostles in Mark 3:16 signifies the formation of new leaders for Israel. Likewise twelve contains symbolic meaning in the multiplication of bread for the five thousand where the twelve baskets leftover means "enough for all of Israel." Therefore, the twelve-year-old girl and the woman diseased for twelve years both call attention to all of Israel as the surrounding context also indicates.[107]

---

98. See section 2.5 later in this chapter.

99. Edwards states, "Twelve, moreover, may signify Israel to Mark's readers, indeed, Israel coming to faith in Jesus" ("Markan Sandwiches," 205, n. 32). For a systematic presentation of the evidence see section 8.4.

100. Boring concludes, "That Jesus is now back in Jewish territory is made clear by the virtual repetition of the setting of 4:1, by the assumed concern with purity roles, by the approach of the leader of a synagogue, by the use of Aramaic, and by the repeated 'twelve'" (*Mark*, 158).

101. Taylor, *Mark*, 297. Gundry (*Mark*, 275) calls attention to the diminutives in the context that could be misunderstood.

102. Hendriksen, *Mark*, 214.

103. Cranfield, *Mark*, 191.

104. France labels it a "trivial comment" (*Mark*, 240).

105. Taylor, *Mark*, 290. This is a common interpretation when it is combined with her long and fruitless search for a cure.

106. Bird concludes from the reiteration of twelve and the allusive *gar* clause that "This was New Israel coming to life—don't you see, she was 12 years old" ("γάρ clauses in Mark," 182).

107. Farla (*Jezus' Oordeel over Israel*, 122) believes that these two stories were originally separate with the outer story from a Palestinian environment and the inner narrative from an Hellenistic origin, but the contrast between Jew and Gentile occurs between the bleeding woman and the Syrophoenician woman, not the two characters in this intercalation.

Finally, the context surrounding 5:21–43 supports an emphasis upon Jewish rituals.[108] In the Gerasene demoniac passage, immediately preceding the intercalation, we encounter an unclean man, unclean pigs, and therefore an unclean land. Thus the exorcism cleanses the whole of Gentile Decapolis (5:20) so that this territory now becomes a portion of the Promised Land which becomes clean through Jesus' kingdom action. Furthermore, in the context following the intercalation, after a rejection by Jesus' own people (6:1–6) the Twelve are sent throughout Israel, which is then followed by the feeding of the five thousand, where enough bread is left over for all of remaining Israel (twelve baskets). This leads to discussions in Mark 7 about clean hands (7:13), clean food (7:14–23), clean people (7:24–30), and clean fluids (7:31–37). Mark forthrightly reveals his agenda in 7:19b, where he explains that "in saying this, Jesus declared all foods clean." From the context it becomes obvious that Mark is addressing issues of Jewish ritual cleansing.[109] Thus, by inference, Jewish cleansing rituals must be foremost in Mark's mind in the touching of 5:21–43. The concluding words of this pericope, where the girl is given something to eat (5:43), resemble as well the emphasis upon bread encountered in the new purity regulations of chapter 7.[110] Thus Mark is proclaiming a message that indicates the significance of Jesus' kingdom healing ministry for his readers.[111] Jesus' cleansing replaces the cleansing rites of Judaism so that touching a menstruating woman or a corpse no longer results in ritual uncleanness. This, of course, is Markan theology. Matthew, on the other hand, emphasizes the continuity between Judaism and Christianity and thus omits the attachment of Jairus to the synagogue,[112] the girl's age, and Jesus' final command about food since these details are insignificant to his preaching.

---

108. Marcus suggests that Levitical purity restrictions are "seen in the order of the scenes which follow Num 5:1–4 where God commands Moses to remove from the Israelite camp 1) the person with scale-disease (1:40–45), 2) the *zāb* or "oozer" (5:25–34) and 3) anyone who is unclean by contact with a corpse (5:35–43)" (*Mark 1–8*, 367–68). But the distance between these pericopes and references to other purity issues like food laws (7:1–23) and fluids (7:31–37) argues against this postulation.

109. In section 3.7 we will argue that Mark 4:35—8:10 contains two sets of five miracle stories with a trip across the sea and a miraculous feeding at the beginning and end of the series with three miracles symbolizing the replacement of Jewish purity rites with the message of the kingdom placed in the middle. In the first set neither pigs, Gentile territory, the flow of blood, nor a dead body will make one unclean in the kingdom. In the second set, neither spittle nor table fellowship with Gentiles makes one unclean.

110. Normally the eating is considered proof of the girl's recovery as in a normal miracle story, but her walking proves her recovery. The eating must serve another function. Cf. Achtemeier, "Isolation," 279.

111. By means of attaching a change of location and/or an audience to several kingdom miracles (5:37, 40b; 6:31–32; 7:24, 33; 8:23; 9:2, 28, 30–31) as well as kingdom parables (4:10, 34; 7:17) and other teaching (10:10; 13:3), Mark shapes the purpose of the narrative into a discipleship training session also aimed at the reader. The expulsion of everyone from the house except for the parents and three disciples could be such a device to indicate that this miracle has implications for discipleship, in this case the following of OT purity rituals.

112. See Moiser, "Twelve Years Old," 181. Regrettably the TNIV, NRSV, and NLT of Matt 9:18 read "synagogue leader."

Therefore the emphasis upon touching, the connections with the other miracle intercalation in 11:12–25, the verbal repetition of twelve and its typological connection to Israel, and the context surrounding the intercalation conclusively argue for a symbolic emphasis on the fulfillment of OT Jewish regulations through Jesus' ministry. Jesus' healing ministry parallels his habits of eating and socializing with the ritually impure. As Evans concludes, "all of these activities—healing, eating, fraternization—are set in a context of purity concerns."[113] Therefore, along with a literary reason for the intercalation (dramatic tension and irony) comes not only the thematic issue of Christology and the response of faith, but also discipleship instruction about how to interpret the OT regulations about purity.

2.4 Mark 6:7–30: Mission of the Twelve and John the Baptizer Beheaded

With no verbal connections[114] or analogous details of plot, this Markan sandwich diverges strikingly from the last intercalations. Thus far the genres have been identical; now the outer story functions as a mission narrative, while the inner story reads as a passion account.[115] The outer narrative about the disciples builds upon past narratives where the disciples are called (1:16–20), appointed as the new Israel (3:13–19), and now send out as missionaries (6:7–13). But the inserted drama (6:14–29) introduces a new character, Herod, so that this is the only narrative in the gospel where Jesus is not the central character. Furthermore "the language is somewhat more cultivated than is usual for Mark, and the story is therefore more ponderous."[116] Shepherd observes that "in the outer story, the narrator is reporter-like, giving no internal views. But in the inner story the narrator reports the inner thoughts of both the king and the queen."[117] Similarly, the spatial settings diverge with the disciples visiting villages in the countryside while Herod remains stationary within his palace. The meager rations and simple attire of the disciples (6:8–9) contrasts dramatically with the lavish feast thrown by King Herod.[118] Finally, good wins out in the flanking episodes, where the disciples triumph over demons and disease (6:12).[119] However, evil overcomes good in

---

113. Evans, "Who Touched Me?" 375.

114. Shepherd does note one verbal connection: "Jesus sends (ἀποστέλλειν) the Twelve on a mission of preaching the Gospel of repentance. Herod sends (ἀποστείλας) to seize John the Baptist and then sends (ἀποστείλας) to have him beheaded" ("Narrative Function," 530).

115. Shepherd (*Sandwich Stories*, 192–93) posits a connection in that the rumors heard by King Herod in 6:14 are a result of the mission work of the Twelve which spreads the fame of Jesus.

116. Camery-Hoggatt, *Irony*, 144.

117. Shepherd, *Sandwich Stories*, 203.

118. Fowler contrasts the "blundering butchery of Herod from the innate benevolence of Jesus" and the use of the serving dish for the head of the Baptizer versus the lack of dishes used with the hungry in the wilderness (*Loaves and Fishes*, 86).

119. Therefore Van Oyen is incorrect when he concludes that "the mission of the disciples

the middle section, with John's righteous preaching falling on deaf ears and his tragic imprisonment, beheading, and burial terminating his ministry.

Instead of calling attention to the interconnections between the two halves of the Markan sandwich, the dominant scholarly opinion states that "the most obvious and important motif is the parallel between the death of the Baptist and the death of Jesus."[120] Mark is preparing proleptically for the climax of his gospel by presenting the tragic death and burial of John. Marcus succinctly summarizes the vivid interconnections:

1. Each is "eagerly heard" (6:20; 12:37).
2. John and Jesus become an object of curiosity for the ruler (6:12; 15:9–10, 14–15).
3. The leader tries unsuccessfully to save them (6:20; 15:4, 9–14).
4. They fall victim to the enemy's murderous intention (6:19; 3:6; 14:1).
5. Each is arrested and bound (6:17; 14:46; 15:1).
6. Each is executed and buried (6:27–29; 15:16–47).[121]

In fact, throughout his gospel Mark has paralleled the lives and ministries of John and Jesus.[122] Both participate in charismatic ministries where the entire countryside of Judea and Jerusalem come out to see both John (1:5) and Jesus (3:8).[123] When John is placed in prison Jesus begins his ministry (1:14), and when John is executed the disciples take a leading role. Herod even believes that Jesus is John the Baptizer raised from the dead (6:16). This acknowledgment prepares for the closer bond that is established between John and Jesus in 9:11–13, where John is the promised Elijah who must come first.

But the foremost connection between John and Jesus involves the typological correlation of their passion and death. Of prominent importance, as Boring points out, is the fact that "The key word *paradidōmi* (hand over, betray, deliver up) connects the destiny of John (1:14), Jesus (3:19; 9:31; 10:33; 14:10–11, 18, 21, 41–44; 15:1, 10, 15), and the disciples (13:9, 11–12)."[124] The opportune time to murder John (6:21 ἡμέρας εὐκαίρου) anticipates Judas' search for an opportunity to betray Jesus (14:11 εὐκαίρως). In the intercalation itself, the phrase "in prison," which frames the entire story of the Baptist's demise (6:17, 27), foreshadows Jesus' incarceration. With regard

---

(6:6b–13) does not prohibit them from misunderstanding Jesus (6:34–44, 45–52), so that it becomes clear that their mission did not succeed" ("Intercalation and Irony," 962).

120. Edwards, "Markan Sandwiches," 205. Cf. Fowler, *Loaves and Fishes*, 120–24.

121. Marcus, *Mark 1–8*, 404.

122. Instead of a Markan sandwich this is the literary device of a Markan allusionary repetition which will be discussed in section 4.6a below.

123. Camery-Hoggatt explains, "The deeply seated enthusiasm of the crowd for John's message anticipates the enthusiasm they will later show for Jesus during his early ministry" (*Irony*, 94).

124. Boring, *Mark*, 178.

to their suffering, Edwards points out that "John is righteous and suffers silently, and the same will be true of Jesus." Likewise, the officials, Herod and Pilate, who condemn them to death are both "vacillating and pusillanimous in the face of social pressure."[125] Furthermore, each death is prophesied by Scripture as demonstrated in 9:12–13. Not only is it written that "the Son of Man must suffer much and be rejected" (9:12), but Elijah must come first and "they have done to him everything they wished, just as it is written about him" (9:13). Thus the theme of Israel rejecting its prophets ties the two figures together, "for if a prophet like John is without honor and is put to death, how much more will Jesus, who is the greatest of the prophets and the Son of God, face a similar fate!"[126] To summarize the Christology, Jesus "is not only a Royal Messiah (antithetically parallel to Herod in the inner story) but also a suffering Messiah (parallel to John in the inner story)."[127]

Therefore, a passion Christology links together John and Jesus, but what theme holds together the two stories involved in the intercalation? Some interpreters again center on the character of Jesus, who sends out the apostles. Shepherd proposes that "Jesus is a 'sender' as is Herod, but the missions they each send people on are diametrically opposed."[128] Jesus dispatches his apostles to share the good news while Herod sends emissaries to behead John the Baptist. In both cases Jesus triumphs since he is given authority over the successful mission of the apostles as well as power over the thoughts of Herod, who hauntingly proclaims that John is alive from the dead just as Jesus will be raised some day. On the other hand, Gundry proposes that the miracle-working power of Jesus holds the passages together. Jesus sends out his disciples with authority to continue his miracle performing ministry and Herod is so astounded by the rumor of Jesus' miracles that he becomes convinced of John the Baptizer's resurrection.[129]

However, both of these hypotheses are founded upon the false premise that Jesus is the main character in both of these episodes. The disciples' ministry dominates the outer frame and Herod's execution of John keynotes the framed story. Therefore, Mark's purpose for sandwiching these stories together must center on the relationship between John's death and the disciples more than on the passion of John and Jesus or the kingship of Herod and Jesus.

So what is the purpose of this intercalation? Certainly one narrative objective is to create a subtle chronological pause for reflection upon the part of the reader. Will

---

125. Edwards, "Markan Sandwiches," 206. See also Boring, *Mark*, 179 and Stein, *Mark*, 304.

126. Stein, *Mark*, 288.

127. Shepherd, *Sandwich Stories*, 184. Herod is identified as the king in the narrative of John the Baptist's death, but Jesus will be proclaimed the king through ironic mockery at his death. Interestingly, Herod was deposed by Caligula in 39 CE because of his aspiration to have the title of "king" (Josephus *Ant.* 18,7,2) so that the title is historically incorrect (Herod was entitled "tetrarch") indicating that Mark is developing a literary contrast with Jesus.

128. Shepherd, *Sandwich Stories*, 205.

129. Gundry, *Mark*, 10.

Jesus' ministry through his disciples succeed even though John the Baptist's mission is over? Yet Fowler rightly responds, "To say that the story is used 'to fill the gap' is, however, merely to use a circumlocution for the term intercalation.... The question is why he did this."[130] A prominent answer to this question centers on the presence of irony. Camery-Hoggatt discerns a fourfold irony in the intercalation:

1. The sarcastic irony of the designation of Herod as king (14, 22, 25, 26, 27) whereas Jesus is the real king.[131]

2. The comic irony that Herod is now worried about John being resurrected from the dead so that "the old fox has been outfoxed."

3. The "dissonance between the content of the story—which is horrifying—and the tenor of the story—which is understated and dispassionate."

4. The dramatic irony that Herod "executes John to save face, but in that act exposes his debauchery."[132]

Certainly this verbal, dramatic, and sarcastic irony pervades the pericope as it does the entire gospel, but this explanation does not reveal why Mark combined these two passages. The irony demonstrates Mark's skill in creating narratives but does not account for the intercalation. All of the irony, in fact, permeates only the middle story. The key connection, therefore, cannot be only Christology but must involve the discipleship and mission of Jesus' followers. Edwards demonstrates astute perception when he notes that "the rather awkward appending of the return of the Twelve (in only one verse!) to the story of the Baptist's death must mean that Mark saw a relationship between missionaries and martyrdom, between discipleship and death."[133]

Certainly in the inner story "John is a foil for Jesus."[134] Throughout Mark, the stories about John serve to bring the fate of John and Jesus into close proximity.[135] But the intercalation adds the disciples' passion to the mix. As Wright observes, "Thus, John's martyrdom not only prefigured Jesus' death, it also prefigures the death of anyone who would follow after him!"[136] Mark skillfully employs the verb "delivered" ($\pi\alpha\rho\alpha\delta\iota\delta\omega\mu\iota$) to tie the experience of John, Jesus, and the apostles together. John the Baptist is handed over to death (1:14) to prepare in turn for Jesus' death (9:31; 10:33), which will also be the future experience of the disciples (13:9). Their ministries and fate are strategically aligned by Mark. The imprisonment of John initiates Jesus' min-

---

130. Fowler, *Loaves and Fishes*, 115.

131. Five of the twelve occurrences of "king" in Mark apply to Herod whereas six refer to Jesus in his passion (13:9 to kings in general).

132. Camery-Hoggatt, *Irony*, 145.

133. Edwards, "Markan Sandwiches," 206.

134. Camery-Hoggatt, *Irony*, 144–45.

135. Cf. Marxsen, *Mark the Evangelist*, 42–43 and chapter 4 section 4.6a.

136. Wright, *Markan Intercalations*, 239.

istry (1:14) and his calling of disciples (1:16–20). The death of John launches the ministry of the apostles (6:7–30) and foreshadows Jesus' death. Finally, the crucifixion of Jesus will give birth to the new apostolic community.[137] Thus this pericope serves as an "analepsis pointing back to the beginning of the gospel and a prolepsis pointing ahead to the fate of Jesus"[138] and of the apostles. The mission of the Twelve combined into an intercalation with the death of John points to suffering discipleship,[139] while the inner story of the execution of John foreshadows a suffering Messiah.

Therefore, the narrative allusionary repetitions between John and Jesus proclaim the upcoming passion of Jesus while the intercalation itself calls attention to the discipleship of Jesus' followers who must be prepared to suffer the same fate as John. Since a Jewish audience had difficulty accepting a crucified Messiah and a Christian audience struggled with a discipleship of the cross, these become the two themes that Mark broadcasts to his readership in this pericope.

2.5 Mark 11:12–25: The Fig Tree and the Temple Action

In this lengthy exegesis of a notoriously difficult passage, we will first examine the themes that hold the Markan sandwich together, then the metaphorical significance of the fig tree, followed by the meaning of the temple action (whether it constitutes a cleansing or a prophetic action symbolizing its destruction), and finally discuss the significance of the addition of Mark 11:22–25 with its mentioning of a mountain thrown into the sea and the alternative cultic practices to temple sacrifices. We will conclude that this intercalation is a Markan literary device that proclaims a theological message concerning the fulfillment of OT Jewish institutions with new forms.

The cursing of the fig tree (11:12–14, 20–25) and the temple action (11:13–19) along with the triumphal entry (11:1–11) create a triad of dramatic prophetic actions by Jesus[140] occurring on three separate days (11:12, 20). So the genre ties this intercalation together along with the authoritative nature of Jesus' words and actions. As judge and prophet Jesus takes charge of the primary Jewish redemptive institution, the temple, as well as the creation order by cursing the fig tree. The OT background plays an important role in each of the stories as well with an explicit quote from Psalm

---

137. See Kelber, *Kingdom in Mark*, 54.

138. Wright, *Markan Intercalations*, 239.

139. Shepherd suggests that "the intercalation teaches in an acted out form the words of Jesus in 8:34–38" (*Sandwich Stories*, 193).

140. Shepherd (ibid., 228) entitles the temple action a controversy story probably following Bultmann (*History*, 36) who categorizes it as a biographical apophthegm, but the temple action does not include all the elements of a controversy dialogue as found, for example, in 2:1—3:6. On the other hand, the cursing of the fig tree has been entitled a nature miracle story, an aetiological legend that developed from a well-known withered fig tree, and a legend that derived from the parable in Luke 13:6–9. Mark's use of triplicates as well as the presence of an intercalation argues for a similar genre. For scholarly support see Evans, *Mark 8:27—16:20*, 150, 165.

118:25–26 and an allusion to Zechariah 9:9 in the triumphal entry, a reference to various OT symbolic uses of the fig tree in the miracle story, and a Scriptural quote of Isaiah 56:7 and Jeremiah 7:11 in the temple action. Jesus is the Messiah who possesses authority over the temple and fulfills the OT narratives. Thus Christology is one theme that holds the intercalation together.

In addition, the customary building of suspense occurs through the employment of an intercalation. Jesus commands the fig tree, "May no one ever eat fruit from you again" (11:14), but the disciples and the readers must wait expectantly until the following morning (11:20) to see if Jesus' words come true. This creation of episodic tension generates an effectively crafted narrative. In addition to fashioning suspense, Adela Collins contends that "the Markan technique of intercalating stories is a way of allowing one story to function as an inclusio for the second, thus aiding the listener in determining when both stories have concluded."[141]

However, this purpose of creating narrative suspense is a simplistic explanation which overlooks thematic connections. An emphasis upon the destruction of the temple coheres perfectly with the cursing and withering of the fig tree and serves as a prominent and continuous thematic emphasis throughout Jesus' Jerusalem ministry (12:11, 33; 13:1–2; 14:58; 15:38). We will demonstrate how Mark highlights surprises in the text like the expectation of fruit when it is not the season for figs (11:13) and the withering of the tree from its roots (11:20) rather than the shriveling of its leaves. These important narrative surprises indicate that Mark is supplying a metaphorical meaning rather than just remaining at the literal or literary level.

Gundry offers an alternative purely literal interpretation to the surprises in the temple action by denying a symbolic reading of Mark on almost every page of his commentary. Gundry proposes that the phrase "for it was not the season for figs" is not about the fruitlessness of Israel but merely a horticultural statement expressing Jesus' reason for approaching the tree to find something other than fruit, namely edible buds.[142] However, the delight of figs was the initial reason why the fig tree became a symbol for God's shalom in Israel (Mic 4:4; Zech 3:10). Likewise, the tragedy of rotten figs and the dreadful destruction of treasured fig trees became a standard imagery for the judgment of Israel (Jer 5:17; Hos 2:12; Joel 1:7; Mic 7:1; rotten figs Jer 29:17). With regard to the fig tree withering from its roots, Gundry claims that Mark is writing as an omniscient narrator to accent the power of Jesus' curse: "Even the roots have dried up despite the soil's shielding them from the sun and surrounding them with moisture

---

141. Collins, *Mark*, 524 quoting Achtemeier, *Omne Verbum Sonat*, 21. Collins ties the cursing of the fig tree to the triumphal entry, but the intercalation is with the temple action: "The tension between Jesus' searching for figs and it not being the season for figs is analogous to the tension created by the account of his entry into Jerusalem" (526) where the Jewish leadership does not receive Jesus.

142. Gundry, *Mark*, 673.

from the spring rains of the Passover season."[143] Through literal interpretations Gundry undercuts any symbolic applications to these events.

In particular Gundry denies any application of this intercalation to a transformation of cultic rites in Israel. Gundry claims that Mark does not "indicate that the selling, buying, money-changing, and vessel-carrying had anything to do with the sacrificial cult."[144] He joins Hamilton, who contends that "if Jesus had wished to oppose the sacral function of the temple, he would have passed through the court of the gentiles to make his protest where the sacrifices were actually offered."[145] In a similar manner Gundry refuses to allow the parable of the vineyard in 12:1–11, the prediction of the destruction of the temple in 13:1–2, and the rending of the temple veil in 15:38 to shine any retroactive light upon the temple action.[146] However, precisely these references to the temple hold the Jerusalem ministry and passion narrative together in the Gospel of Mark.[147]

In opposition to Gundry, the mention of doves (11:15) brings to the fore the subject of temple offerings.[148] Likewise, as Evans points out, Jesus' condemnation of the traffickers in goods shows that the "animals were to be bought and sold for purposes of the sacrificial offerings."[149] Furthermore, the ties between the temple action, the elimination of the fig tree (11:20), and the mountain cast into the sea (11:23) demand a symbolic interpretation whereby the temple becomes like the cursed fig tree and departed mountain. Gundry contends that the symbolic approach "puts incredible demands on Mark's audience."[150] Although this might be true for the first reading of the gospel, the Gospel of Mark which is packed with both symbolism and irony was meant to be heard again and again. Bottom line, Gundry is worried that the interpretation of the Markan sandwich will indicate "that Mark has fabricated an unhistorical chronology."[151] However, a proper interpretation of Mark demands that one must separate the symbolic level from the historical without denying the results of either.

Therefore neither a purely literal interpretation, nor a literary view concentrating on suspense, nor a christological perspective fully account for the employment of this Markan sandwich. By placing these two stories into an intercalation, Mark is speaking volumes more.[152] A Markan sandwich calls attention to another level of discourse;

---

143. Ibid., 648.

144. Ibid., 675.

145. Hamilton, "Temple Cleansing," 372.

146. Gundry, *Mark*, 676.

147. The theme of prediction and fulfillment could be added to the theme of the temple as the two integrating concepts in Mark 11–15.

148. Cf. Lev 1:14; 5:7, 11; 12:6–8; 14:22, 30; 15:14, 29.

149. Evans, *Mark 8:27—16:20*, 172.

150. Gundry, *Mark*, 674.

151. Ibid., 681. Gundry even entitles his critique of the intercalation, "Excursus on the Chronology of Mark 11."

152. Collins (*Mark*, 516–17) even thinks that the names of the two villages, Bethany and Bethphage,

Mark is speaking metaphorically and creating a symbolic relationship between the temple and fig tree. To demonstrate this we will illustrate first how the fig tree was employed metaphorically in the Old Testament and then secondly show how Mark turns a temple cleansing into a temple destruction narrative as well as offering alternative practices which replace temple sacrifices.

The perceptive reader grounded in the Old Testament understood that the fig tree referred somehow to Israel.[153] For example, Hosea 9:10 reports, "When I found Israel . . . it was like seeing the early fruit on the fig tree." This promising beginning, however, concludes with the prophecy that "Ephraim is blighted, their root is withered, they yield no fruit" (9:16).[154] Jeremiah picks up this tradition to speak about the southern kingdom so that Judah is pictured as "poor figs that are so bad they cannot be eaten" (29:17) but need to be destroyed. Now in Mark 11 history is repeating itself a third time when Jesus comes looking for early fruit but the fruitless fig tree withers from its roots (11:20). Traditionally the fig tree served as an emblem of peace and prosperity in Israel. To experience shalom meant to sit in security under one's vine and fig tree (1 Kgs 4:25; Mic 4:4; Zech 3:10). But now the fig tree withers, becoming a symbol of judgment. As Stein concludes, "It is so used in judgment statements against Israel (Isa 28:4; Hos 2:12; 9:10; Joel 1:7; Mic 7:1), Judah (Jer 5:17; 8:13; 24:1–10; 29:17; Hab 3:17), Nineveh (Nah 3:12), and the nations in general (Isa 34:4)."[155]

Although the fig tree generally represents Israel as a nation, it is more nuanced in Mark to conclude that the fig tree parallels both the Jewish leadership and the temple establishment.[156] The intercalation is further interpreted by Jesus' sayings in the con-

---

have symbolic meaning with Bethphage alluding to the surprise of leaves and no figs though its meaning, "house of early figs."

153. Robin states: "Only in two contexts in the O.T. do figs directly symbolize the nation of Israel . . . In Hos ix. 10, the nation in the wilderness is likened to the first ripe fruit in the fig tree at her first season, and in Jer xxiv and xxix.17 we have references to the exiles and those left in Jerusalem as the good and bad figs respectively" ("Cursing of the Fig Tree," 279–80). The New Testament reinforces this identification. In John 1:47–50 the true Israelite, Nathanael, is seen under a fig tree, certainly a symbol for Israel, as indicated by his confession of Jesus as King of Israel and the promise to see a new Israel (Jacob) in a reoccurring Bethel experience. Gaston states that "the fig tree represents Israel, as in the parable of Luke 13:6–9" (*No Stone on Another*, 83). The early Christian writing, the Ethiopic Apocalypse of Peter 2, reads "the fig-tree is the house of Israel" and envisions the fig tree as an eschatological symbol whose growth symbolizes the end of the world. See Schneemelcher, *New Testament Apocrypha*, 2:626 and Lapham, *Introduction to the New Testament Apocrypha*, 101. Other secondary support for all Israel and not just the official representatives include Best (*Following*, 223, n. 32) and Giesen ("Der verdotted Feigenbaum," 99, 102–3). However, as we shall see, the fig tree cannot represent Israel in general since at this point in the gospel a large portion of the people ("the whole crowd" 11:18) is still responsive to Jesus. Cf. Marcus, *Mark 8–16*, 790.

154. For a series of interconnections with Mark 11 see Geddert, *Watchwords*, 126.

155. Stein, *Mark*, 513.

156. Geddert (*Watchwords*, 126–27) claims the Jewish leadership is primarily in mind. But Geddert should recognize that just as the twelve can represent both the new nation of Israel and the new leadership, so the metaphor of the fig tree is ambivalent and can refer to both. The fig tree should not be matched only with the tenants in 12:1–12 and not with the vineyard in the parable as Geddert

texts following the temple action. A leafy tree without fruit which ultimately withers from its roots matches the teachers of the law who "walk around in flowing robes" (12:38) but refuse to turn over the fruit of the vineyard to the son (12:1–12) and are thus destined for destruction (12:9, 40).[157] In these contexts Jesus encounters various groups of Jewish leaders (11:27 chief priests, scribes, and elders; 12:13 Pharisees and Herodians; 12:18 Sadducees; 12:28 teachers of the law) and wins every argument so that in the end they are silenced (11:33; 12:17b, 27b, 34b, 37b). Therefore Jesus replaces the leaders of Israel just as the Jewish leaders symbolized as the roots of the fig tree wither away.

Because the Markan sandwich connects temple and fig tree, the withering from its roots must refer to the institution of the temple as well. Then the parabolic imagery would identify the leaves of the fig tree as the magnificent exterior of the temple (13:1), the fruitlessness as the corruption and secularism of the temple establishment (11:15), and the withering from its roots as the destruction of this predominant institution of Judaism (13:2).[158] In addition, the experience of shalom in Israel pictured as a fig tree is closely connected with the vitality of temple worship. Finally, since Mark 11:17 specifically refers to Jeremiah 7:11 in the temple narrative, the context in Jeremiah 7:1–15 must be investigated to observe the connections with the cursing of the fig tree.

Recalling the destruction of the sanctuary at Shiloh, Jeremiah proclaims to Jerusalem, "I will thrust you from my presence, just as I did all your fellow Israelites, the people of Ephraim" (7:15). Jeremiah employs the destruction of the tabernacle at Shiloh to mirror the plight of the Jerusalem temple, and Jesus in turn applies this message to the rebuilt temple in his day. Then 8:13 specifies that "there will be no figs on the tree, and their leaves will wither." Because God's house has become a den of robbers (Jer 7:11), the same disastrous results will occur as the destruction of the temple at Shiloh (Jer 7:12).[159] The robbers are specifically identified in Jeremiah 8:1, 9, 10 as the kings, officials, wise men, prophets, and priests of Israel. Because of their faulty leadership, the land will forfeit its prosperity and shalom through the withering of the

---

proposes on page 289, n. 41. He is overly concerned not to portray Israel in a negative manner. Hamerton-Kelly states that "the tree is a symbol of the sacrificial system whose time is now passed" ("Sacred Violence," 467). The sacrificial system, of course, is managed by the temple establishment and occurs at the temple so they are closely related. But the parallel with the sacrificial system is more vivid in the activities of prayer, faith, and forgiveness mentioned in 11:22–25. These symbolize and replace the sacrificial system for Mark. See section 8.4 below.

157. Geddert, *Watchwords*, 289, n. 39. Brooke ("4Q500 1," 268–94) states that the vineyard is Jerusalem and the tower is the temple as evidenced by 1 En 89:50 and the Targum of Jonathan on Isa 5:2. Then the parable would be an apologetic against the Jewish leaders as well as the cult (284). However, one problem with this evidence is that fragment 1 is only 7 lines long and does not mention Jerusalem or the temple, so other texts must clarify its meaning.

158. As Fowler says, "The fate of the fig tree is a figure for the fate of the temple" (*Reader*, 96).

159. As Edwards explains, "The leafy fig tree, with all its promise of fruit, is as deceptive as the temple, which, with all its bustling activity, is really an outlaw's hideout (v. 17)" ("Markan Sandwiches," 20).

fig trees. Thus both the leaders and the temple establishment cause the downfall of Israel. Since the intercalation of Mark 11 parallels the imagery described in Jeremiah 7–8, the prosperous shalom of the land is tied closely to temple worship and faithful leadership.

Should the temple action in Mark be considered a cleansing of the temple or a prophetic action describing the destruction of the temple? Although the narrative is normally entitled "the cleansing of the temple," we will argue that its tie with the cursing of the fig tree in a Markan sandwich demands that a symbolic destruction of the temple is in our author's mind. First, we will demonstrate that the theme of eschatological judgment pervades both sections of the Markan sandwich.[160] The OT Scriptures describe both the destruction of the temple and the destruction of the fig tree as judgments from God.[161] Micah 7:1–6 stands as the likely background since it begins with a woe saying, contains the specific verbal tie, "there is no first-ripe fig for which I hunger" (7:1), and includes a saying in 7:6 which is alluded to in Mark 13:12 and Matt 10:35–36.[162] Since the theme of Micah is judgment, Mark likewise employs the language of curse (11:14 the imprecative optative φάγοι)[163] and the casting out of demons (11:15 ἐκβάλλειν) to describe Jesus' reaction to a fig tree without leaves and a secular nationalistic temple. In Mark the fig tree has the appearance of life but contains no fruit; likewise the temple is supposed to be a house of prayer but has become a den of robbers. Therefore, Jesus condemns the Jerusalem leadership for both what the temple has become, namely a den of robbers, and for what it has failed to produce, i.e., a house of prayer for all nations.[164]

In other passages in Mark's gospel the fig tree and temple are connected as well with eschatological judgment as prophesied in Scripture. The eschatological parable in Mark 13:28–29 describes the signs of the times before the heavens and earth pass away by examining a fig tree and its leaves. Here the likely OT background is Isaiah 34:4, which reports that "All the stars in the sky will be dissolved and the heavens rolled up like a scroll . . . like shriveled figs from the fig tree."[165] Likewise, the eschatological expectations regarding the temple center upon a destroyed sanctuary, which the Messiah will rebuild (*1 En.* 90:28–29; 11QT 29:8–10; *Lam Rab.* 1:51; *Num Rab.*

---

160. As Evans proclaims, "The fig tree, in full leaf but devoid of fruit, symbolizes the temple, while the temple, busy with religious activities but devoid of spiritual fruit, stands in danger of judgment" (*Mark 8:27—16:20*, 154).

161. Jer 5:17; Hos 2:12; Joel 1:7; Mic 7:1; rotten figs in Jer 29:17.

162. See Birdsal, "Withering of the Fig Tree," 191; Collins, *Mark*, 526; Robin, "Cursing of the Fig Tree," 280.

163. Dowd (*Prayer, Power*, 58) concludes that only Peter in 11:21 entitles Jesus' saying a curse, while Jesus himself interprets this word as a prayer (11:23–24), but Meier (*Marginal Jew*, 2:981, n. 45) offers convincing proof against this interpretation.

164. So Mark alone of the evangelists completes Isaiah's sentence, "My house shall be called a house of prayer *for all the nations*" (Isa 56:7).

165. However, as Collins (*Mark*, 523) explains, the context of the oracle is against the nations, not against Israel. But this does not deny the fig tree's connection with eschatological judgment.

18:21; *Pirqe R. El.* 48; *Tg. Isa.* 53:5; *Tg. Zech.* 6:12).[166] Therefore, Jesus' statement at his Jewish trial about the destruction of the temple results in the question, "Are you the Messiah, the Son of the Blessed One"? (Mark 14:57–61). Based upon this evidence we must conclude that Mark intends καιρὸς (11:13) in an eschatological sense so that Israel's religious caretakers have failed to respond in the set time of God's redemptive plan.[167]

Second, since Mark 11:17b alludes to Jeremiah 7:11, which predicts the destruction of the temple as had happened previously at Shiloh (7:13–14), Mark narrates a prophetic action symbolizing the cessation of the physical temple.[168] Jesus ben Ananias even used Jeremiah 7 to predict the destruction of the temple in 62–69 CE.[169] Literature in the apocalyptic tradition as well had predicted the judgment and destruction of the temple (*1 En.* 89:73–90:29; 4QFlor. 1:1–12). In addition, Juel contends that by employing the term ληστής the phrase "a den of robbers" implies revolutionaries as in Mark 14:48 and 15:27. Therefore it is possible that Mark is alluding to the Zealots who took over the temple premises in the Jewish revolt and caused its destruction.[170]

Third, the unique grammatical details in the Markan account evidence an emphasis upon the destruction of the temple. Through the shutting down of the business and religious functions of the temple (11:16),[171] Jesus dramatically prophesies that the temple will be destroyed (13:2). The event is not a protest against abuses and injustice since Jesus drives out both the buyers and sellers (11:15 ἤρξατο ἐκβάλλειν τοὺς πωλοῦντας καὶ τοὺς ἀγοράζοντας), whereas in the social protest in Luke 19:45b only the sellers are expelled (ἤρξατο ἐκβάλλειν τοὺς πωλοῦντας). Furthermore, Mark is not against the use of Tyrian shekels with the insignia of the god Melkart since Mark does not offer any hints regarding the images of the coins as he does for the Roman coin in 12:16. Finally, the word καταστρέφω (11:15) typically means to destroy

---

166. Gundry (*Mark*, 899) claims that contemporary Judaism did not expect an eschatological prophet to cleanse and restore the temple (it was a divine action), but the linking of destroying the temple and the Messiah in Mark 14:57–61 disprove this contention for Mark. For debate in the literature see Juel, *Messiah and Temple*, 189–209 and Gaston, *No Stone*, 147–54.

167. See Giesen, "Der verdotted Feigenbaum," 105.

168. Watty argues that "the context of the prophecy is as significant for the understanding of the quotation as the quotation itself" ("Jesus and the Temple," 238).

169. See Evans (*Mark 8:27—16:20*, 177) for a thorough and enlightening comparison of Jesus of Nazareth and Jesus ben Ananias.

170. Juel (*Messiah and Temple*, 133) believes that the phrase is not appropriate to dishonest merchants in the *Sitz im Leben Jesu*. Gaston (*No Stone on Another*, 85) translates the phrase a "Zealot stronghold." Hamerton-Kelly supports this view since "λῃσταί is Josephus' word for the military opponents of Rome" ("Sacred Violence," 468). See also Buchanan, "Brigands in the Temple," 169–77.

171. See Kelber, *Kingdom*, 101. Ford ("Money Bags," 249–53) and Matthew (*Temple-Criticism in Mark's Gospel*, 145–47) argue that σκεῦος in 11:16 designates money bags instead of cultic vessels, but the context is cultic and "this interpretation would make more sense if Mark put this prohibition right after the overturning of the moneychangers' tables" (Gray, *Temple in the Gospel*, 28).

a place or building so that Mark describes Jesus' action with the provocative image of destruction.[172]

Fourth, other incidents in Mark's gospel demonstrate that destruction of the temple stands foremost in Mark's mind in 11:13–19. The reference to a millstone thrown into the sea in 9:42 (βέβληται εἰς τὴν θάλασσαν) certainly entails destruction, especially since it is connected with the eschatological "thrown into Hell" in 9:43–48 (βληθῆναι εἰς τὴν γέενναν 9:47).[173] The parable of the tenants concludes with the vineyard given to others (12:9) and "the stone which the builders rejected becoming the head of the corner" (Ps 118:22 in Mark 12:11), which imply both a new temple and a new community. The controversy about the greatest command teaches that following the love command is more important than all whole burnt offerings and sacrifices (12:32–33), thus exposing the unimportance of the physical temple. In addition, Hamerton-Kelly maintains that "the institution of the eucharist is intended as a parallel to and a replacement for the temple sacrifices, just as the room is a counterpart to the temple."[174] Likewise, in the eschatological discourse Jesus predicts forthrightly the destruction of the temple (13:2) so that Mark includes both a prophecy in word and a prophecy in action (11:13–19). Finally, the term "made with hands" (χειροποίητος) is employed fourteen times in the LXX, in each case describing idols. Therefore, Jesus' condemnation of a temple made with hands (14:58) does not entail merely a human temple but instead an idol. When the temple action is interpreted as a symbolic action predicting the destruction of the temple, the fear and concern from the Jewish leadership about Jesus' prediction of a destroyed and rebuilt temple (Mark 14:57–58; 15:38; cf. Acts 6:14) suddenly becomes understandable.

But the encapsulation of the temple narrative within the story of the cursing of the fig tree offers the conclusive piece of evidence. The story of the fig tree is the only miracle of destruction by Jesus and the temple event is his only violent act. Through the intercalation Mark coordinates the phrases "not the season for figs" with a "temple for all nations" to theologically explain that Judaism's time is over and the time for Gentiles has arrived. Thus the title "cleansing of the temple" fails to encapsulate the meaning of this passage for Mark. This prophetic action against the temple, which originally may have referred to a reformation,[175] now through the Markan device of intercalation becomes a proleptic act of judgment.[176] Jesus himself probably understood

---

172. Gray, *Temple in the Gospel*, 37.

173. Gundry claims that "in 9:42 being thrown into the sea would be better than judgment and therefore is not equivalent to it," but he neglects to connect 9:42 with the verses that follow it (*Mark*, 678).

174. Hamerton-Kelly, "Sacred Violence," 484.

175. Evans, for instance, says, "His actions did not signify the imminent destruction and replacement of the temple; they were meant to display disapprobation with respect to certain aspects of the trade" (*Mark 8:27—16:20*, 181–82).

176. Stein, "Proper Methodology," 47.

his action as a protest against both injustice[177] and secularism[178] with messianic overtones.[179] But Mark sees in Jesus' action an additional divine theological agenda. By halting the temple activities, Jesus demonstrates prophetically that God is discontinuing temple service.[180] Just as the fig tree is not pruned in the story to bear fruit, so Jesus is not just purging the temple.[181] Both the fig tree and the temple (the institutional worship and leadership of Judaism) are cursed and no longer usable. Therefore in 13:2 Jesus predicts that not one stone of the temple will remain in place, but every block will be thrown down.

Now that we have established that Mark is speaking about the destruction of the temple, it logically follows that new forms of worship must be established. We will now argue that this becomes Mark's theme in the conclusion of the intercalation in 11:22–26. The temple mount is thrown into the sea (11:23),[182] and as a result true worship in the new sanctuary now takes place through the exercise of faith (11:22), prayer (11:24), and forgiveness (11:25).

This conclusion, however, is not universally accepted since the reference to a mountain cast into the sea in Mark 11:23 could be a reference to the Mount of Olives.[183] France points out that the "geographical situation of the narrative would suggest not the temple mount but the Mount of Olives (with the Dead Sea, visible from its summit, as the sea into which it is thrown)."[184] Dowd argues that the Mount of Olives is thus the closer mountain geographically, and if the temple mount were in view the reference would have to be to that mountain (ἐκείνῳ), not this mountain (τῷ ὄρει

---

177. Jesus overturned the tables of the money changers since they sold at abnormally high prices so that the temple became a den of robbers with its exploitation of the poor. Ker. 1:7 offers an historical example where Simeon ben Gamaliel protested on the temple steps the overcharging for doves resulting in an immediate drop in prices.

178. Similar to the temple renewals during the times of Hezekiah and Josiah as well as the Maccabean reversal of the abomination of desolation, Jesus is fighting secularism and idolatry. The temple was no longer mainly a house of prayer for all nations (Isa 56:7) since the Gentile court was taken over with the business aspects of the Passover feast. A polemic against secularism is evident if Jesus is protesting the use of the Tyrian half-Shekel with the god Melkert (Herakles) on one side and the Tyrian (Ptolemic) eagle on the other.

179. See Shepherd, *Sandwich Stories*, 212.

180. See Wright (*Markan Intercalations*, 150) and the writers mentioned by Marshall (*Faith*, 161, n. 4). Kelber (*Story*, 59) suggests that the designation "temple disqualification" is more accurate than temple destruction since the physical Jewish temple does continue its service until 70 CE, but we will employ both terms to describe Mark's intention in this intercalation.

181. Achtemeier, *Mark*, 32–33.

182. The parallel phrase in Rev 18:21 indicates that the temple will be thrown down never to be found again.

183. For a list of scholars who envision a reference to the Mount of Olives see Evans, *Mark 8:27—16:20*, 188 and page 189 for those supporting a temple mount allusion. For additional names see Marshall, *Faith*, 168, notes 3 and 4.

184. France, *Mark*, 449.

τούτῳ 11:23).[185] In this scenario the Mount of Olives constructs an inclusio around the three prophetic actions (11:1, 23). More to the point, the expected eschatological climax would occur at the Mount of Olives, where it would "split in two from east to west, forming a great valley, with half of the mountain moving north and half moving south" (Zech 14:4). Thus this moving of the mountain is reminiscent of Mark 11:23. Furthermore, Jesus' temple action against the merchants and his forbidding anyone to carry merchandise through the temple (11:16) is frequently viewed as an allusion to the pots in Zechariah 14:20–21.[186] Finally, both Zechariah 14 and Mark 11 are connected with feast days,[187] have eschatological overtones,[188] and mention the relationship of Israel to the Gentiles (Mark 11:17; Zech 14:16–19).

A second alternative interpretation contends that moving mountains refers to "feats of an exceptional, extraordinary or impossible nature" connected with the power of faith.[189] The uprooting of a mulberry tree (Luke 17:6) or a fig tree (Matt 21:21) or a mountain (Matt 17:21; 1 Cor 13:2) were thus originally all proverbial statements of performing the impossible. With this in mind the statements in Mark would originally have been used as a call to faith in miracles (11:22–23), the power of prayer (11:24), and the abundance of forgiveness (11:25). Dowd believes that this ἀδύνατα interpretation about the power of faith (unconnected from any eschatological overtones) is precisely Mark's meaning.[190] Although she is certainly correct that Mark is offering an example of a "feat of exceptional, extraordinary or impossible nature," a literal reading fails to incorporate all of Mark's meaning.[191] As Marshall explains, "the saying's figurative language should not be 'flattened out' in this one-dimensional way."[192] Dowd's

---

185. Dowd, *Prayer, Power*, 73.

186. For supporters see Evans, "Jesus' Action in the Temple," 252, n. 52. The "Canaanite" of Zech 14:21 can be understood as a merchant. For translators and commentators who render it as trader and their reasons for doing so, see Meyers and Meyers (*Zechariah 9–14*, 489–90). "Trader" is the reading in the targum as well and b. Pesah 50a combines Zech 14 with Hos 12:7 (using false balances to oppress) which could offer support for a temple cleansing of injustice in the *Sitz im Leben Jesu*.

187. Zech 14:16, 18, 19 speak about the Feast of Tabernacles whereas Jesus comes to Jerusalem for the Passover feast, but several scholars tie the historical pilgrim processional of Mark 11 to the Feast of Tabernacles. See Charles Smith, "No Times for Figs," 315–27.

188. At least seven "on that day" sayings occur in Zech 14.

189. Telford (*Barren Temple*, 109–19) offers legal, thaumaturgical, legendary, and eschatological examples from rabbinic writings supporting this view. This quote from page 115 is his title for these feats.

190. But then one would expect a reference to great obstacles like mountains in general, whereas the demonstrative "this" (11:23 τῷ ὄρει τούτῳ) destroys attempts to force "mountain" to apply to difficulties in general.

191. For instance, in her interpretation of the Talmud reference B. Bat. 3b, Dowd (*Prayer, Power, and the Probelm of Suffering*, 72–73) shows that uprooting a mountain is treated as an impossible feat, but she neglects to make the additional application that the reference is to a specific mountain, that is the temple Herod was destroying and rebuilding.

192. Marshall, *Faith*, 166.

distaste for allegory controls her interpretation.[193] Certainly there must be definite markings that demonstrate an authorial intention for allegory, but a Markan intercalation is just such a literary indication for symbolism.

Dowd overlooks the differences between Mark's intention and the traditional understanding of these sayings offered by Matthew. Matthew's omission of the intercalation (21:12–17, 18–22) indicates that he does not envision a theological connection between the stories and thus narrates a temple cleansing rather than temple destruction.[194] By destroying the sandwich Matthew also interprets Mark 11:21–25 as a demonstration of the power of faith rather than a list of alternative worship rites in a new temple. Likewise, in Matthew 21:20 the immediacy of the withering is emphasized whereas Mark 11:20 omits this element from the story. Through this alteration Matthew highlights the miracle nature of the event rather than its symbolic character in order to parallel the earlier saying from Q in Matthew 17:20.[195] There in the conclusion to the exorcism of the epileptic boy, Matthew also changes Jesus' answer to the disciples' question as to why they were unable to cast out the demon. Instead of the Markan application, "This kind can come out only by prayer" (9:29), Matthew 17:20 reports, "because you have so little faith," followed by the mountain-moving logion.

---

193. See Dowd, *Prayer, Power, and Problem of Suffering*, 74, n. 26.

194. Matthew also places the temple cleansing on the same day as the triumphal entry which again is likely a tradition that Mark changes to construct an intercalation and to have Jesus reconnoiter the temple before the prophetic action. See the convincing arguments of Jeremias (*Eucharistic Words*, 90–91) as well as the reasons enumerated by Gundry (*Mark*, 671–72) which he later dismisses (679) versus Evans (*Mark 8:27—16:20*, 150) who thinks that the smoother versions of Matthew and Luke evidence their secondary quality. Further support from scholars for both positions is given by Blomberg ("Miracles as Parables," notes 30 and 31). Matthew regularly chooses the standard oral tradition over Mark as in the following examples: 1) Herod the tetrarch (Matt 14:1) rather than Herod the king (Mark 6:14); 2) Jesus, the son of the carpenter (Matt 13:55), not Jesus the carpenter (Mark 6:3); 3) From Levi son of Alphaeus (Mark 2:14) to Matthew (Matt 9:9); 4) Matt 4:25 eliminates Tyre and Sidon since it is historically dubious that the Jesus movement was so popular so early (Marcus, *Mark 1–8*, 260); 5) Matthew restores the traditional acclaim after the sea walking miracle at 14:33 (vs. Mark 6:52) as Luke does with the healing of the epileptic boy at 9:43 (vs. Mark 9:15); 6) Matt 15:1–20 changes Mark 7:1–23 so that it is more like the controversy dialogue found in the original oral tradition according to Dunn ("Jesus and Ritual Purity," 37–60); 7) Matt 26:28 understands Mark 9:1 to apply to the *parousia* whereas Mark places it right before the transfiguration; 8) Matt 26:60–61 does not record the charge of Jesus to destroy and rebuild the temple as false but separates it from the appearance of the false witnesses unlike Mark 14:57; 9) At the Jewish trial when the priest asks if Jesus is the Messiah, Mark 14:62 has Jesus reply "Yes, I am," but Matt 26:64 has the more historically correct "You have said so" as in Mark 15:2; Matt 27:11; Luke 23:3; cf. Matt 26:25; 10) The changes made to Mark 16:8 in Matt 28:8 show that the women did originally communicate Jesus' resurrection to the apostles. See Davies and Allison (*Matthew*, 1:112) and Dunn (*Jesus Remembered*, 250, 254) for the importance of the oral tradition instead of Hawkins' suggestion of the use of an *Urmarkus* (Hawkins, *Horae Synopoticae*, 212).

195. Luke 17:6 contains the original Q reference to a mulberry tree, but Matthew changes to the more difficult feat of moving a mountain to consistently emphasize this theme at the end of two miracle stories, i.e., the violent exorcism of the epileptic boy and the cursing of the fig tree. The following story in Matt 17:21–24 interestingly is also about the temple (paying the temple tax), but again the Matthean emphasis is upon the miracle of discovering the coin in the mouth of a fish.

Therefore, Matthew defines prayer as the verbal manifestation of powerful faith, but Mark contains a different emphasis. In the previous context Jesus is glorified on the Mount of Transfiguration while the disciples are alone in the demon-ridden valley below and cannot repeat Jesus' mighty miracles. Thus Mark's story of the epileptic boy begins with the absence of Jesus, whereas at the end of the incident Jesus responds that the answer to their dilemma of divine absence is prayer, not greater faith. Prayer for Mark is calling down the manifest presence of Jesus into difficult trying circumstances, not the medium for performing miracles.[196]

Once we have seen that Mark interprets prayer as the presence of Jesus,[197] the connection between the temple action and 11:22–25 becomes clear. The temple is thrown into the sea (11:23) and replaced by the presence of God in Jesus through prayer (11:24). Through the intercalation Mark applies the imagery of casting a mountain into the sea to a specific "feat of exceptional, extraordinary and impossible nature," namely the difficulty of changing religious institutions and practices. Mark sees in Jesus' kingdom action the turning of the ages so that the physical temple and sacrificial system is now disqualified and replaced by new institutions. Whereas Matthew emphasizes the continuity between Jewish and Christian practices, Mark highlights the discontinuity.[198]

Therefore, it is not the Mount of Olives but instead the temple mount that is in Mark's mind. Since the Mount of Olives is consistently viewed with positive connotations, it cannot be a referent to a mountain that is cast into the sea.[199] Each of Dowd's arguments against the temple mount can be countered. Although the Mount of Olives stood in closer proximity, the temple mount was clearly visible across the valley as Jesus spoke.[200] Even though Dowd is correct that Mark never describes the temple as a mountain, unlike this reference the Mount of Olives is always identified by name (11:1; 13:3; 14:26).[201] Dowd argues that Telford's parallel Talmud references (Pesah 87a; Git. 56b) do not demonstrate "that 'this mountain' would have been understood

---

196. See section 6.5 below.

197. Other Markan references identify prayer with the presence of God as well. Prayer is connected with watching (13:35–37; 14:32, 34, 38) where the opposite is sleeping, i.e., the absence of someone's presence. Jesus' prayer in Gethsemane calls on the presence of Abba Father (14:36) since Jesus will feel the absence of God on the cross (15:34). Therefore Dowd (*Prayer, Power*, 1) is incorrect in identifying Mark 11:22–25 as belonging with the miracle ministry of Jesus found in the first half of Mark and contrasting it with his modeling of prayer in the Garden of Gethsemane.

198. For instance, Matthew omits Mark 7:19b, the replacement of kosher food laws in the Kingdom of God. See chapter 8 below for a systematic approach to this issue.

199. Gray concludes that "The Mount of Olives represents the positive pole over against the negative pole of the temple mount. This polarization between the Mount of Olives and the temple mount represents the conflict between Jesus and the temple" (*Temple in the Gospel*, 51). See also Broadhead, "Which Mountain?" 35.

200. Telford, *Barren Temple*, 115.

201. Cf. Marshall, *Faith*, 168. On all other occasions Mark does not name a mountain (3:13; 5:5, 11; 6:46; 9:2, 9; 11:23; 13:11).

as a reference to the temple as early as the time of Mark."²⁰² However, the OT identification of the mountain of the Lord with the temple (Isa 2:2; Mic 4:1) removes the sting from Dowd's criticism. In response, she points out that in Isaiah 2:2 and Micah 4:1 the mountain of the house of the Lord is established in the messianic age, not removed as in Mark 11:23. However, she forgets about the remaining sections of Mark's gospel where Jesus announces a new temple not made with hands. Placing 11:12–25; 13:2; 14:58; 15:29, 38 together, Mark proclaims both the removal of an old temple and the establishment of a new presence of God.

Furthermore, it seems unlikely that an allusion to Zechariah 14:21 is intended by Mark since the other OT references in this pericope are always introduced as Scripture (Mark 11:17; John 2:17).²⁰³ Gundry points out that Jesus' prohibition of carrying vessels through the temple does not line up with the prophecy of Zechariah 14:21 that every pot will be sacred in that day.²⁰⁴ Nor can the elimination of traders or Canaanites from the house of the Lord easily apply to Jesus' action. If Zechariah 14:21 entails that traders are no longer needed because every cooking vessel is holy, then why would Jesus prohibit the transport of vessels through the temple? Or if Canaanites are eliminated from the house of the Lord, then Jesus' reference to a house of prayer "for all nations" is directly opposed to Zechariah 14:20.²⁰⁵ With regard to verbal identity, Zechariah 14:4 does not specifically envisage a mountain thrown into the sea.²⁰⁶ Therefore a connection with the language and context of Zechariah 14 in Mark's gospel is doubtful.

Finally, Dowd contends that in order to arrive at a reference to the temple mount a scholar like Telford "first has to excise verses 24 and 25 from the Markan text."²⁰⁷ Although Dowd correctly criticizes Telford for this unnecessary elimination,²⁰⁸ a care-

---

202. Dowd, *Prayer, Power*, 72 referring to Telford, *Barren Temple*, 170, n. 65.

203. Barrett, "House of Prayer," 20.

204. Gundry, *Mark*, 643. Roth ("Cleansing of Temple and Zechariah xiv 21," 177–78) interprets the reason for the prohibition about carrying vessels through the temple (Mark 11:16) as a proscription against removing the now sacred vessels (Zech 14:21) from the temple, but the expansion of the sacredness to include all vessels would not be coupled with a restriction that they must remain within temple borders.

205 Roth ("Cleansing of Temple," 180–81) believes that Jesus' reference to the temple as a house of prayer for the Gentiles indicates that he was countering a scribal interpretation of Zech 14:21 that read, "no Canaanite in the house of the Lord" and favoring "no trader" since he cast out the merchants, but if Jesus was exegeting this text, the passage would certainly be mentioned with more verbal transparency.

206. Grant ("Coming of the Kingdom," 300) argues that Jesus misinterpreted המי ("west") as "sea" in Zech 14:4. But Dowd (*Prayer, Power* 74) is correct that the additional moving of the mountain from north to south would make a mistranslation irrelevant.

207. See Dowd, *Prayer, Power*, 74 and 40–45 for her analysis of Telford.

208. Employing Mark 11:26 as a model for inserting material from Matthew into the Markan text, Telford (*Barren Temple*, 49–59) hypothesizes that 24–25 are also interpolations. But the lack of manuscript evidence for this conclusion as well as his curious proposal that the redactor of Mark is responsible for the fig-tree story's position hurts Telford's arguments for a reference to the temple mount

ful examination of the context demonstrates the clear Markan interconnections. At first glance a reference to forgiveness in Mark 11:25 seems awkward,[209] but if faith, prayer, and forgiveness are viewed together as worship acts of piety that replace temple sacrifices then these verses communicate a consistent message. The accompanying statement about the mountain cast into the sea (11:23) only makes sense in this context if the temple mount is in mind.[210] The identical metaphor of a stone thrown into the sea in Revelation 19:21 communicates the destruction of Rome.[211] Therefore, as Wright maintains, the addition of Mark 11:21–25 "present the reader with the alternative to the withered tree and the fruitless temple,"[212] namely a spiritual house of prayer. Only Mark narrates Jesus halting the cultic procession in the temple (11:16) since the appropriate sacrifice is now faith, prayer, and the offering of forgiveness (11:22–25). Mark's conclusion to this narrative argues strongly for a symbolic reference to the destruction of the temple and its replacement with new worship practices.

The switch in vocabulary with reference to the temple confirms that Mark's purpose centers on the fulfillment of Jewish institutions. In Mark 11–13, where Jewish institutions and ceremonies are the subject matter,[213] Mark employs the term ἱερόν to refer to the entire temple complex (11:15–16; 12:35 and 14:49; 13:1–3). However, in the passion narrative when Jesus wants to refer to his death and resurrection as the destruction and rebuilding of the temple, Mark switches the vocabulary to ναός, meaning sanctuary, in 14:58; 15:29, 38.[214] With this alteration of vocabulary comes likewise the change from a prophetic word against Jewish institutions to an eschatological statement pointing toward a new era which requires a new temple.[215] When a temple

---

here. See Marshall (*Faith*, 173–74) for a thorough investigation, also coming to a similar conclusion.

209. See Meier, *Marginal Jew*, 2:888. Juel (*Messiah and Temple*, 135) labels the verses an intrusion. But tied to the destruction of the temple, the forgiveness received through temple sacrifices is now replaced by the forgiveness experienced when Jesus is the temple. Incigneri (*Gospel to the Romans*, 346) offers the plausible hypothesis that forgiveness is included because Mark is extending forgiveness to those who have apotheosized during Nero's persecution.

210. Even Evans (*Mark 8:27—26:20*, 188–89) who concentrates upon the historical situation of Jesus finally admits that the context confirms that the Markan evangelist was thinking of the temple mount.

211. In Ps 46:2 other mountains may be cast into the sea, but "the city of God, the holy place where the Most High dwells . . . will not fall" (46:4–5).

212. Wright, *Markan Intercalations*, 157.

213. In the triumphal entry Jesus becomes the Messianic king; in the temple action and cursing of the fig tree the Jewish leaders and temple will be replaced; in the Parable of the Tenants Jesus becomes the cornerstone; in the controversy dialogues Jesus replaces the leaders of Israel; and in the apocalyptic discourse Jesus predicts the destruction of the temple.

214. See Juel (*Messiah and Temple*, 127–29) versus Michel, who sees "no real distinction between the terms in either meaning or range" (ναός, *TDNT* 4:882), although in note 8 he confesses that Dalman disagrees with him. Trench (*Synonyms of the New Testament*, 10–11) states that this distinction is followed by Josephus, Philo, the Septuagint, and the New Testament. To maintain the distinction in English, the TNIV employs temple courts for ἱερόν and temple for ναός. This same distinction can be seen in the vocabulary change from John 2:14 to 2:19–21.

215. See Wright, *Markan Intercalations*, 151.

(ναός) not built with hands (14:58) is erected in a time frame of three days, Jesus death and resurrection are front and center instead of the physical temple. Whereas the employment of ναός indicates a reference to Jesus' redemptive work, the use of ἱερόν in the Markan intercalation of chapter 11 calls attention to the Jewish institution of the temple.

Having settled the exegetical issues in this passage, we turn finally to the purpose of Mark's intercalation in 11:12–25. At the literary level, it certainly supplies dramatic tension into the narrative. What will happen to the fig tree that Jesus has surprisingly cursed? We have to wait pensively as the temple action is recounted.

Second, the intercalation produces irony. The Jewish religious rulers seek to destroy Jesus but ironically end up destroying their own temple. Jesus condemns the temple because Israel refuses to provide a house of prayer for all nations (11:17), but ironically "the certain demise of the temple will not be the end of prayer. There will be a new praying community"[216] as 11:24 demonstrates.

Third, the cursing of the fig tree is a miracle story or kingdom sign which portrays Jesus as lord of nature.[217] Gundry contends that the glorification of Christ is central to Mark's purpose throughout and that these stories are sandwiched to demonstrate Jesus' authority, "the awe-inspiring power of Jesus' teaching, backed up as it is by his strong actions."[218] Mark, however, transforms a miracle narrative into a prophetic action of eschatological destruction through the intercalation of the withering of the fig tree with the temple action. If this text were only meant as a miracle story, "the capricious nature of Jesus action here seems out of character with his ministry as found in the Jesus tradition."[219] Mark sees in the action of Jesus something more.

The presence of the intercalation indicates that Mark is speaking symbolically. Therefore Jesus' hunger as the narrative begins must be more than just a lack of physical nourishment.[220] Metaphorically Jesus hungers for the righteous fruit produced by Israel,[221] but the tree is barren. Jesus longs for the inclusion of all nations in the prayers of the temple (11:17), but now the temple will not play a further role in the worship of God's people. Mark's γάρ clause in 11:13, "because it was not the season for figs,"

---

216. Shepherd, "Narrative Function," 536.

217. Lohmeyer, *Markus*, 234.

218. Gundry, *Mark*, 641.

219. Evans, *Mark 8:27—16:20*, 151. Funk, for instance, comments "Causing an unproductive fig tree to wither seems uncharacteristic of the historical Jesus. A senseless miracle of retribution, triggered by a petty, even petulant, response is scarcely a mode of behavior that comports with the Jesus who restored a withered limb" (*Acts of Jesus*, 122–23). But a tradition of destructive miracles did exist: Exod 7:14—12:30; 1 Kgs 13:1–5; 2 Kgs 1:4, 10, 12; 2:23–24; 5:27; cf. Acts 5:1–11; 13:6–12 and the destruction of the pigs associated with the story of the healing of the Gerasene demonic can be recalled.

220. Therefore, physical questions like "Would they have exited Bethany without breakfast? Why would Jesus be hungry and not his disciples?" do not seem to be important to the narrative. This applies as well to the comment of Bishop (*Jesus of Palestine*, 217) that eating early in the morning was not a Jewish custom.

221. Goppelt, πεινάω, *TDNT* 6:20; Giesen, "Der verdotted Feigenbaum," 103; Ernst, *Markus*, 325.

entails that the time for Israel's fruit is past;[222] instead, it is time for the Christian community to present its produce of faith, prayer, and forgiveness in a temple not made with hands. The addition of 11:22–25, as Achtemeier maintains, indicates that "The locus of salvation, of God's plan, has shifted from temple to Jesus, and therefore faith and prayer, not temple cults, are the way to God."[223] In addition, since the expression "from the roots" is used in Job 18:16 and Ezekiel 17:9 in metaphorical and symbolic ways to refer to evil people, one would certainly expect a similar meaning in Mark 11:20.[224] Finally, Geddert calls attention to the use of the terms "heard" (11:14), "saw" (11:20), and "remembered" (11:21), which Mark already employed in 8:14–21 "to call the disciples and the readers to discern more in the miracles of Jesus than meets the eye."[225] Therefore, we would expect a symbolic understanding of the mountain thrown into the sea in 11:23 as well. The temple mount is thrown into the sea just as the fig tree representing the temple establishment is cursed.

Therefore the cleansing of the temple when it is intercalated within the cursing of the fig tree demonstrates that the cursing is an eschatological judgment against Israel symbolizing the end of its cult and institutions.[226] But a new beginning is also anticipated. As Charles Smith explains, "Mark's message to them is to abandon the old Jewish institutionalism on which decisive and irrevocable judgment is about to be passed, and to fully embrace the community of the New Age which symbolizes a new, sanctified Temple characterized by the obedience of that community to God."[227] The temple and its sacrificial system are replaced by faith in and prayer to Jesus.[228] Therefore, a replacement motif is introduced to balance the rejection motif.[229] This Markan intercalation symbolically calls attention to the fulfillment of Jewish institutions and cultic regulations as we discovered earlier about the Markan sandwich in 5:21–43.

---

222. Several authors maintain that the mention of fruit instead of figs in verse 14 provides further evidence for the symbolic character of this pericope. See Giesen, "Der verdotted Feigenbaum,"105; Münderlein, "Verfluckung des Feigenbaumes," 95–96.

223. Achtemeier, *Mark*, 26.

224. See Collins, *Mark*, 533. Bildad the Shuhite's second speech in Job 18:16 describes the fate of wicked people and Ezek 17:9 prophecies the destruction of King Zedekiah.

225. Geddert, *Watchwords*, 129.

226. See Donahue, *Are You the Christ?* 42. There is a pressing concern in the literature that this narrative "should not be interpreted as an indictment of Judaism, ancient or modern" (Evans, *Mark 8:27—16:20*, 182). Therefore, it is important to offer a nuanced statement of what we mean by Israel here. Specifically it refers to the Jewish leadership and the temple institution, not at all to Israel as a nation, race, or religion (see Dowd, *Prayer, Power, and Problem of Suffering*, 39). Certainly Mark is not anti-Semitic, although he has been accused of this (see Marshall, *Faith*, 180, n. 3 for a list of scholars).

227. Smith, "No Time for Figs," 190.

228. See Hamerton-Kelly, "Sacred Violence," 468. Hamerton-Kelly attempts to include the renunciation of vengeance with faith, prayer, and forgiveness, but the sayings about piety here do not include that concept as in the Sermon on the Mount.

229. Marshall, *Faith*, 163.

2.6 Mark 14:1–11: The Jewish Leaders and Judas Plotting versus the Woman Preparing

Mark's passion narrative begins with the Jewish religious leaders plotting to eliminate Jesus secretly (14:1–2). Their plan crystallizes with the recruitment of Judas, one of Jesus' own disciples, as the spy to betray his master (14:10–11). This outside bracket of the Markan sandwich sharpens the picture of discipleship in 14:3–9, where an unknown woman divinely sees through the evil plot and exposes God's sovereignty in these events by anointing Jesus for his burial. In summary, as Boring explains, "Both framework (human plotting) and central core (Jesus' sovereignty) are focused on Jesus' death. In 14:1–2, 10–11, Jesus' enemies plot his death; in 14:3–9 Jesus predicts it himself, and interprets the woman's act as anointing his body for burial."[230] We will demonstrate, therefore, that the theological intent of the intercalation centers on the themes of a suffering messiah and a discipleship of the cross. The evidence necessitates a study of the character connections in this Markan sandwich as well as a specification of the type of anointing that Mark intends.

Significantly, at the very outset of the passion narrative Mark sets up a comparison between Judas and a woman who anoints Jesus. An insider disciple, Judas, is contrasted to a woman (a social inferior) at the house of Simon a leper (a social outcast). Both represent discipleship: Judas clearly demonstrates failed discipleship, while the woman illustrates faithful following, which Jesus relates to his passion. In each case unexpected actions dominate the plot. As Shepherd exclaims, "The woman surprises by her lavish gift, the betrayer surprises by his perfidy."[231] A woman newly introduced to Jesus demonstrates extreme affection and loyalty, while a disciple who has walked, ate, and slept with Jesus for three years manifests no connection of intimacy with his master. Their discipleship extends to their attitude toward money. Judas selfishly clings to the promise of an unspecified sum to betray Jesus, while the woman cheerfully pours out almost a year's wages of perfume over Jesus' head. The issue is valuation. As Shepherd points out, "Jesus is highly valued in the inner story, but not even worthy of the specification of a betrayal price in the outer story."[232] Finally, both of their actions anticipate Jesus' passion. The woman's act of love prepares for Jesus' burial while Judas' act of betrayal triggers Jesus' passion.[233]

These commonalities sharpen the contrast between the two and expose the real outsiders to God's plan. Within the expected mores of the culture the named male would take precedence over the undesignated female, but surprisingly the woman

---

230. Boring, *Mark*, 379.

231. Shepherd, *Sandwich Stories*, 246.

232. Ibid., 263.

233. A few verbal connections can be discerned as Shepherd maintains, "Judas takes part in a terrible secret death plot and seeks how he can betray Jesus conveniently (εὐκαίρως 14:11). The anonymous woman's good action (εὖ, καλὸν 14:6, 7) becomes an open memorial in the proclaimed Good News (εὐαγγέλιον 14:9)" (ibid., 334–35).

shines forth as the uncontested hero over the insider Judas. While the woman demonstrates care and concern, Judas models scheming betrayal. An "act of deep devotion" is sharply contrasted with a "heinous malicious act of betrayal."[234] Likewise, "her openness and willingness to risk conflict for Jesus' sake contrasts with the priests' and scribes' secrecy and fear of conflict."[235] It proves deeply ironic that the chief priests are preparing for the sacred feast of Passover and at the same time plotting a murder in stealth. This outward behavior reveals a striking difference of moral character. As Shepherd points out, "In the outer story, the moral background centers on the issue of deceit, killing, betrayal. In the inner story, the moral background has to do with stewardship, the proper handling of resources."[236] In its comparison of characters the literary device of a Markan intercalation again proclaims effectively a message not easily forgotten.

So far we have described the contrast between the murderous Jewish leaders (3:6; 11:18; 12:12; 14:1) joined by the betrayer Judas (3:19) over against the prophetic woman in the inner frame of the intercalation. But an additional contrast within the middle section itself strikes a surprising note. The insiders in the narrative called disciples in Matthew 26:8 evaluate this incident of anointing differently. The disciples' description of the woman's deed as "a wasteful act" (Mark 14:4) stands in sharp contrast with Jesus' estimation of "the beautiful thing she has done for me" (14:6). The disciples downgrade the woman's gift in favor of an offering that should have been given to the poor, while Jesus predicts that her sacrificial offering will be proclaimed around the world. Jesus' closest comrades only recognize the general poverty of the world experienced by every generation, whereas an unsolicited woman demonstrates perceptive insights into the personal poverty of Jesus as he faces the ultimate crisis.[237] The warning that insiders can become outsiders in times of distress is again placed before the reader.

This contrast in the inner story highlights an additional significance to the woman's action. Not only is the woman a model disciple, but she becomes a Christ figure as well. It is precisely through her namelessness that she can represent Christ in the story. The story of the woman parallels the pattern of Jesus' passion including "acts of self-denying service, experiences of conflict which lead to his rejection and humiliation, and glorious vindication signified by the empty tomb."[238] Just like Jesus, the woman freely offers an expensive gift (14:3) but in return is harshly criticized by indignant people (14:4–5). Just like Jesus, she is wonderfully vindicated with the result that her fame will spread throughout the world and her memory live on infinitum (14:6–9). In the breaking of the alabaster box Mark seems to anticipate the smiting of

---

234. Edwards, *Marcan Sandwiches*, 209.
235. Barton, "Mark as Narrative," 232.
236. Shepherd, *Sandwich Stories*, 243.
237. Wright, *Markan Intercalations*, 170.
238. Barton, "Mark as Narrative," 233.

The Theological Intentions of Mark's Literary Devices

Jesus' body. In the pouring out of the expensive ointment Mark possibly envisions a symbolic representation of Christ's blood. Her story is an intricate part of the preaching of the gospel around the world[239] because her breaking of the jar and extravagant pouring out of the precious ointment proclaims in picture form the sacrificial death of Jesus. This occurs amidst verbal abuse and accusation (14:4–5) just as Jesus is mocked and ridiculed on the cross (15:29–32). But the woman is wonderfully exonerated and in a striking change of destiny she becomes famous throughout the world (14:9), as of course is the case with Jesus through his resurrection. Therefore, the Markan sandwich calls attention to the action of the woman and portrays it in a symbolic manner.

The incident that catapults the narrative into a controversy dialogue is the woman's pouring of expensive ointment upon Jesus' head. What is the significance of this episode which we traditionally entitle, "the anointing at Bethany"? Anointing was popular on a number of occasions in Near East culture, including holiday anointing,[240] the consecration to an office or task,[241] and anointing for burial.[242] Since this encounter occurs close to Passover, it may refer to the "familiar mark of festivity and of fellowship"[243] which was customary during feasts. Since the time just before Passover was the traditional occasion for acts of charity to the poor (Pes. 9:11; 10:1), the pouring out of this expensive cosmetic lotion evidenced a disturbing waste of resources. But Jesus silences the disgust of the audience with a ringing acclamation of applause for the woman's loving action.

Historically, this interpretation makes good sense. Since offerings to the poor are mentioned in the context, Lane argues that the woman's act is really an act of charity to the poor man, Jesus.[244] This interpretation fits the literary genre of controversy

---

239. Jeremias ("Mc 14,9," 103–7) argues not for the mission of the church around the world but for a reference to the last judgment where the woman will receive the acclaim of God, but A. L. Moore (*The Parousia in the New Testament* (Leiden: 1966), 203–6) counters that an angelic proclamation is unlikely as well as a restriction of the audience to only God.

240. Cosmetic lotions were employed as normal acts of hospitality and were especially important during the celebration of feasts. The anointing of the head was common with Gundry (*Mark*, 813) mentioning nine examples from Jewish literature and seven from Greco-Roman works. But the anointing of feet was not unknown with Coakley ("Anointing at Bethany," 247–48) offering six examples from Greco-Roman literature and citing two Jewish works besides Luke 7:38 and John 12:3. These cosmetic lotions became a healing technique as well (Mark 6:13; Jas 5:14).

241. The OT offers examples of the anointing of both kings (1 Sam 10:1; 16:3, 12, 13; 1 Kgs 1:39; 2 Kgs 9:3, 6) and priests (Ps 133:2; Exod 40:15; Lev 10:7; Num 3:3) as well as various objects for consecration (Gen 28:18; 35:14; Exod 40:9 etc.).

242. Perfumes and ointments were used to prepare corpses for burial. Davies and Allison (*Matthew*, 3:447, n. 39) mention 2 Chr 16:14; John 19:39–40; Josephus Ant. 17:199; T Abr. A 20:11; Apoc. Mos. 40:2; Sanh. 23:5 (sic = Shabbath 23:5).

243. France, *Mark*, 552. See Ps 23:5; 45:7; 141:5; Amos 6:6; Cant 1:12; Luke 7:46; b. Hul. 94a.

244. Lane, *Mark*, 493–94. Gundry objects, "Since v 7 distinguishes Jesus from the poor, he is hardly portrayed as the poor man par excellence" (*Mark*, 814), but this is too demanding of a distinction upon the text.

dialogue, where the pronouncement saying stands as the climax to the narrative,[245] in this case Jesus' response, "The poor you will always have with you, and you can help them any time you want" (14:7). In addition, a holiday anointing parallels the larger context. In Mark 11:27—12:37 Jesus participates in a series of debates with various groups of Jewish leaders over the hotly debated theological issues of the day, including the importance of John's baptism (12:27–33), taxes to Caesar (12:13–17), belief in the resurrection (12:18–27), the greatest commandment (12:28–34), and the Davidic Messiah (12:35–37). The debate in 14:3–9 centers on almsgiving, which as one of the three pillars of Jewish piety (Tob 12:8; Matt 6:1–4, 5–15, 16–18) belongs here with the other controversy dialogues involving the major issues in Judaism. Finally, the employment of the phrase "good work" in 14:6 functioned as a common designation for works of charity.[246]

However, the location of this pericope at the head of the passion narrative as well as the intercalation with the plot on Jesus' life demonstrates that Mark has much more in mind than just a holiday anointing. Elliot argues for a messianic anointing based upon "the obvious clue . . . that the ointment is poured onto Jesus' head."[247] Likewise, the placing of the anointing in John 12 immediately prior to the triumphal entry could signify Jesus' anointing as messianic king. On the other hand, the anointing of the head was a normal procedure and would not necessarily connote the anointing of a king since oil was poured upon priests as well.[248] Furthermore, perfume rather than oil is employed here. Finally, the omission of the verb χρίω, which was employed in the significant anointing of kings in the OT (1 Sam 10:1; 16:3, 12, 13; 1 Kgs 1:39; 2 Kgs 9:3, 6), argues against an obvious and prominent place given to a messianic anointing.[249]

Mark has already emphasized the messianic identity of Jesus with Peter's confession in 8:29 and Jesus' arrival in Jerusalem as Son of David in the triumphal entry (cf. 10:47–48; 11:10). Now as he begins the passion narrative, Mark wants to demonstrate that this same Christ purposely arrived in Jerusalem to suffer and die. Therefore Mark's specific intent centers upon the woman's action as an anointing for burial to call attention to a certain type of messiah. Evidence for this position includes 1) the prominent place given to the anointing in the passion narrative; 2) Mark's framing technique where women preparing for Jesus' burial provide bookends for the passion narrative (14:8; 16:1); 3) the intercalation Mark employs to contrast human plotting with the

---

245. See Taylor, *Mark*, 78; Bultmann, *History*, 61, 36; Dibelius, *From Tradition to Gospel*, 56.

246. Daube, "Anointing at Bethany," 315–16.

247. Elliot, "Anointing of Jesus," 107. In an attempt to argue for an original messianic anointing Elliot contends that John's account removed the detail of a royal anointing after Lazarus' resuscitation, but this is extremely unlikely since it naturally fits the mold of a burial anointing.

248. Gundry, *Mark*, 813.

249. Johnson believes that "this was a secret anointing for kingship" and that "the woman was an enthusiast who hoped that Jesus would rule over the nation" (*Mark*, 224). Certainly secrecy is an important theme of Mark, but any concept of a political Messiah is excluded by Mark's changing of the title Messiah to Son of Man in 8:29–31 and 14:61–62.

divine preparation for Jesus' passion exemplified in the woman's action; and finally 4) the inconsistencies with the normal literary pattern of a controversy dialogue.

How does the genre of this narrative relate to the dual themes of Jesus' passion and a discipleship of the cross? Mark's controversy dialogues normally contain five elements: 1) an action or word by Jesus or his disciples raises a controversy; 2) this action or word is disputed by the Jewish leaders with a question; 3) Jesus retorts with a counter-question sometimes accompanied with a proof from scripture; 4) a memorable saying provides the climax of the controversy; and 5) the response of the opponents or onlookers is recorded.[250] The anointing narrative rehearses each of these elements[251] except for the final constituent part with Jesus' evaluation of the significance of this event (14:8–9) replacing the usual response of the astonished crowd.[252] In the previous controversy dialogues in the Jerusalem ministry the final element of the genre has either highlighted the astonishment and delight of the crowd[253] or drew attention to the supremacy of Jesus' authoritative debating skills over the wisdom of the Jewish religious leaders.[254] Now as Mark begins the passion narrative, he allows Jesus himself to designate the significance of the encounter. Mark's addition to a normal controversy dialogue underlines two implications of the woman's act: 1) the anointing was a prophetic prediction of Jesus' burial (14:8) and 2) her act encapsulates the gospel message (14:9) of a faithful disciple who emphasizes Jesus' passion.

Therefore the anointing for burial imagery takes prominence in the conclusion of the narrative, where it states the significance of the woman's action. Since Amen

---

250. For example, the controversy about paying taxes to Caesar includes these five elements: 1) the Pharisees and Herodians, each from an opposite political perspective, come to trap Jesus over his purported views on taxes (12:13–14a); 2) the opponents confront Jesus with a question, "Is it right to pay the imperial tax to Caesar or not?" (12:14b–15a); 3) Jesus responds with a counter-question: "Whose image is this?" (12:15b–16); 4) the pronouncement saying is central: "Give back to Caesar what is Caesar's and to God what is God's" (12:17); and 5) the audience responds: "And they were amazed at him" (12:17).

251. 1) 14:3 Introduction of the characters and the situation inaugurating the controversy; 2) 14:4 a disputing question from the opposition, "Why this waste of perfume?"; 3) 14:6 Jesus' counter question, "Why are you bothering her? She has done a beautiful thing;" 4) 14:7 the pronouncement saying: "The poor you will always have with you, and you can help them any time you want," which is "a thought-provoking revision of Deut. 15:11" (Davies and Allison, *Matthew*, 443).

252. Most scholars (cf. Bultmann, *History*, 37 following Dibelius) consider 14:8 an elaboration of the pronouncement saying of 14:7. However, Schenke and Dormeyer contend that 14:8 is the pronouncement saying, not 14:7. Schenke (*Passiongeschichte Markus*, 108–9) thinks 14:7 was added to address community concerns about almsgiving, but wealth and poverty is a major theme in Jesus' preaching. Dormeyer (*Passion Jesus als Verhaltensmodel*, 77–81) thinks 14:7 is Markan redaction to align the story with the other controversies of passion week, but this coherence is evidence for its authenticity. Against Schenke and Dormeyer, the saying "she did this to prepare for my burial" is not really a pronouncement saying upon which the controversy is built around. As Taylor states, "Anointing for burial is not the woman's purpose, but the interpretation Jesus puts upon her action" (*Mark*, 533).

253. Mark 12:17b "they were amazed at him;" 12:37 the large crowd listened to him with delight."

254. Mark 11:33–34 those who question Jesus' authority are forced to concede that they cannot (or will not) answer Jesus question; 12:27b those who argue with him "are badly mistaken;" 12:34b "no one dared ask him any more questions."

sayings (14:9) are a mark of Jesus' conversational style[255] and since the Johannine account links it with the death, burial, and resurrection of Lazarus (the Lazarus account in John 11 is finished in 12:9–11 with the anointing in between),[256] the connection with burial appears to have historical roots not only in Jesus' words but also in the contemporary events. As a consequence, the anointing for burial interpretation takes priority in the narrative.[257]

The divergences in the four gospel accounts was probably caused by confusion and overlap between two historical encounters with Jesus, one between Jesus and a prostitute in Galilee at the house of Simon the leper, who anoints Jesus' feet resulting in a controversy about purity issues, and the other in Judea at the home of Lazarus, where Mary takes the ointment intended for Lazarus in his burial and instead pours it upon the head of Jesus as a thanksgiving offering, initiating a controversy about social responsibility to the poor.[258] Historically, the ointment seems intended for a burial (Mark 11:8), but Jesus takes the place of the resurrected corpse of Lazarus.

Whatever the historical connections, Mark employs the narrative theologically to define Jesus' messiahship as one of suffering and death. Certainly the interpretation of the event as a burial anointing stands in the foreground, but a messianic anointing seems in the background as well. As Fiorenza explains, "While Peter had confessed, without truly understanding it, 'you are the anointed one,' the woman anointing Jesus recognizes clearly that Jesus' Messiahship means suffering and death."[259] Therefore, Mark's preference for anointing the head (with Matt 26:7) rather than the feet (Luke 7:38; John 12:3) indicates a symbolic messianic gesture. Just as the baptism narrative alludes to the scriptures of Psalm 2:7 and Isaiah 42:1 in order to introduce a Suffering Servant Son of David Messiah, so here the connection of a kingly figure with burial produces a comparable theology. Mark combines the messianic and burial uses of anointing to assert that Jesus' messiahship is demonstrated in his death.[260]

In tying together the messianic and burial imagery of anointing, Mark reshapes the current expectations of a messiah figure. The Jews expected the messiah to live

---

255. Jeremias, *Theology*, 35–36.

256. See Coakley ("Anointing at Bethany") for arguments contending that the Gospel of John contains the more original account.

257. Jeremias (*Salbungsgeschichte*, 110) has shown that the burial of the dead occurs regularly in lists of good works to be performed in times of specific need, so that the argumentation in the story clinches its point with the designation of the deed as an anointing for burial.

258. For a compact description of the evidence for one or two accounts see Gundry (*Mark*, 809–10). Compare also the article by Holst ("One Anointing of Jesus," 435–46) with the commentary by Fitzmyer (*Luke*, 1:684–86).

259. Fiorenza, *In Memory of Her*, xiv.

260. This theology could be visible in John's gospel as well since the incident is both tied to Jesus' burial in 12:7 and also to Jesus as king in the following context through the triumphal entry (see 12:13). Furthermore, the plot of the Jewish leaders surrounds the anointing in 11:57 and 12:9–11 as with Mark.

forever (John 12:34) and certainly not to die upon a shameful cross (Deut 21:23; Gal 3:13). As Kelber explains,

> Jesus' anointment at Bethany dramatically reverses all aspects of the Davidic appointment ceremony. He is not anointed in the temple but at 'his place,' outside of and opposite to Jerusalem and its temple. His is not a celebration in royal glitter and priestly pomp but a table fellowship in the house of a leper. He is anointed not by the priests or the high priest but by an anonymous woman. His anointment is not applauded but criticized. Above all, he is not anointed to power and life but 'beforehand for the burial' (14:8). His is an anointment unto death.[261]

The anointing of a king which is also portrayed as the embalming of a dead man means that the messianic king's throne is a cross.

The anonymous woman's story becomes the gospel in miniature, which consists for Mark in belief in a suffering messiah with whose cross a true disciple identifies. Evidence for this conclusion derives from the following narrative of the Last Supper (14:12–25), which is also a story of table fellowship with a symbolic ritual that exemplifies the gospel message. In each there is a reference to Jesus' body (14:8, 22). Just as the bread and wine at the Last Supper are a proclamation of a gospel that celebrates a crucified messiah, so the anointing by the woman of Jesus' head vindicates a Suffering Servant king. Finally, both episodes end with a logion of Jesus which begins with the pronouncement formula, 'Truly, I say to you' (14:9, 25).[262] The narrative sequence of the anointing followed by Jesus' preparatory supper with his disciples demonstrates the close connection between a suffering messiah and the disciples' participation in the life of the cross.

Certainly this interpretation of Jesus' life spoke a powerful apology both to Jews who demand signs and Greeks who seek wisdom (1 Cor 1:22). The current connotations attached to a cross are dramatically portrayed in Cicero's statement, "Let even the name of the cross be kept away not only from the bodies of the citizens of Rome, but also from their thought, sight, and hearing" (*Rab. Perd.* 5:16). This horror and distain of the cross profoundly affected the cultural view of Christianity at the time of Mark. Minucius Felix in his dialogue *Octavius* called Christianity a sick delusion (11:9), an old-womanly superstition (9:2), and even the destruction of all true religion (13:5), since "To say that their ceremonies centre on a man put to death for his crime and on the fatal wood of the cross is to assign to these abandoned wretches sanctuaries which are appropriate to them and the kind of worship they deserve" (9:4).[263] Mark places the anointing of the woman at the head of the passion narrative to defend Christianity against such views of the cross.

---

261. Kelber, *Story*, 72.

262. Barton, "Mark as Narrative," 232.

263. Cf. Hengel, *Crucifixion*, 3–4, 42.

So what is the purpose of this sandwich at this point in Mark's gospel? As usual, the intercalation heightens the literary tension in the narrative. The passion story commences with the dominant religious leaders plotting the death of Jesus so that the reader inevitably asks, "Will their sly underhanded schemes prevail?" Ironically a nameless woman performing a debatable act of extravagant giving proves that the foresight of God will triumph over the combined efforts of powerful Jewish leaders and a secretive inner traitor. Certainly dramatic irony as well plays a role in Mark's placement of an intercalation at this point. Ironically an unnamed woman carries the secret knowledge of a suffering messiah within her being and exposes it with her extravagant action.

But Mark's theological perspective links this intercalation to the purposes of the entire gospel, which involve both Christology and discipleship. In the face of outward criticism and opposition to a suffering messiah by the Jewish establishment (13:9–11) and an inward inability to sustain a discipleship of the cross by the discipleship community (13:12–14), Mark repeats the story of an anointing for burial that combines Christology and discipleship into one victorious message of good news. By placing the anointing for burial between the plot to betray Jesus, Mark demonstrates how Jesus is prepared for his death but also how the discipleship action of a broken bottle and poured out perfume becomes the encapsulated gospel. Alongside the positive example of discipleship at the center of the Markan sandwich, Mark places a warning in the outside panel that insiders can become outsiders just as Judas joins the plot of the Jewish leaders.

But Mark positions the more subtle warning in the inside story of the intercalation. One can stand with Jesus as a disciple but still be indignant (14:4) about a discipleship that extravagantly pours every ounce of one's life for Jesus. Thus the Markan sandwich addresses two key issues in the life of the early church: 1) an apology for a suffering messiah and 2) the call to follow the crucified Christ in a lifestyle of discipleship. This passage demonstrates that the genre of gospel is preached history.

2.7 Mark 14:53–72: Peter's Denial and Jesus' Confession at the Jewish Trial[264]

Mark begins and concludes the narrative of the Jewish trial (15:55–65) with Peter's threefold denial (1:53–54, 66–72). If Mark's purpose was only to present Christology, the prominence of the disciple Peter is very strange. Why is this intercalation stitched into the middle of the passion narrative? But before we explore the purpose of the intercalation, we will argue that the two segments occur simultaneously rather than sequentially and that the similar development of plot calls attention to two unusual

---

264. See Borrell (*Good News of Peter's Denial*, 47, n. 7) for a list of authors who favor an intercalation beginning with 14:54 rather than 14:53. But the difference is insignificant for the meaning of the passage.

features that stand out in the Markan sandwich, namely Peter's cursing of Jesus and the interconnection between Jesus' prophesying and Peter's denials.

Our first task is to demonstrate that this is indeed a Markan sandwich. Since there is no reference to the denial story in 14:53–54, this section could be categorized as simply an introduction of the characters rather than the first section of an intercalation.[265] But more than an introduction of characters is occurring. Both Jesus in 14:53 and Peter in 14:54 are connected with the high priest to demonstrate that both Jesus' confession and Peter's denials will occur at the same time. Furthermore, the geographical designation of the courtyard ties together 14:54 with 14:66, where the denials begin. Certainly the reason for placing together Jesus and Peter in 14:53–54 is to dovetail the following narratives.

Normally the narratives in an intercalation are temporally successive so that a gap is created in the storytelling. Therefore a literary critic like Shepherd emphasizes the presence of an ellipsis in the present narrative between the inner and outer stories to create suspense through a gap.[266] Since all of Peter's denials follow the Jewish trial, one could argue that the Jewish trial and Peter's denial do not occur simultaneously. But for an intercalation to create dramatic tension, a chronological gap is not required. Van Oyen convincingly demonstrates that simultaneous rather than successive narratives are in view, with the most cogent argument being that "irony and simultaneity go together."[267] Ironically, Jesus is on trial for his life before the Sanhedrin at the same time that Peter is also on trial for his life in the courtyard below.[268] Mark includes no time indicators specifying that the two events occur successively.[269]

To argue for successive narratives, Shepherd concentrates on the different tenses linking 14:53–65 and 14:66–72.[270] Grammatically, he points out that the genitive absolute and the indicative verb in 14:66 employ the present tense, which normally indicates that the actions that follow are subsequent to the previous ones (5:18; 11:27; 13:1). But Mark is renowned for rotating the historical present and aorist tenses throughout a narrative.[271] In addition, Borrell points out that the parallel arrangement

---

265. Ruhland, *Markuspassion*, 9. Then only John 19:15–18, 19–24, 25–27 would contain an intercalation since Peter's first denial occurs before the hearing with Annas, but none would be evident in Mark's gospel.

266. In the interest of fairness, Shepherd recites some very convincing arguments against an ellipsis on pages 274–75, note 1 admitting that Peter is pictured in the same location carrying on the same activity as he was in 14:54 and that he is sitting with the servants in 14:54 who receive Jesus with blows in 14:65.

267. Van Oyen, "Intercalation and Irony," 966–71 especially note 95.

268. See Fowler, *Reader*, 144.

269. See Borrell, *Good News of Peter's Denial*, 48–49.

270. See the discussion in Shepherd, *Sandwich Stories*, 269–74 and both the similarities and differences in his summary, 307–10.

271. Mark employs the historical present 151 times. The alteration of present, imperfect, and aorist within a single pericope occurs at 2:1–3, 16; 3:1–3; 6:7–13, 30–31; 7:27–37; 8:4–9, 19–21, 27–30; 10:13–16, 46–52; 11:1–21; 12:15–19, 41–44; 14:10–16, 55–72; 15:1–3, 11–14, 22–29; 16:1–8 etc. But

of both introductions and the events themselves is "the device adopted by the author to present as simultaneous the double episodes of the trial and the denial."[272] In this case Mark introduces both Jesus and Peter in the short first scene of the intercalation (14:53–54) to raise the question in the mind of the reader how each will respond to the upcoming drama. Resumptive repetition indicates simultaneity as well since 14:55 repeats the characters introduced in 14:53 and 14:66 retells where Peter has seated himself.[273]

Van Oyen also notes that the usual crossover of the character of Jesus in Markan intercalations does not occur here.[274] Luke, on the other hand, introduces Jesus directly into the denials with his convicting glance (22:61) jogging Peter's memory so he remembers the prophecy about the cock crowing. But Luke omits Mark's intercalation. Therefore dramatic tension in the narrative does not require a gap in the chronology or the crossover of Jesus to be effective. Instead the juxtaposition of a similar flow of events with contrasting responses in the characters creates the suspense and irony in this particular Markan intercalation.

The similar sequence in both narratives demonstrates that Mark is both comparing and contrasting the characters of Jesus and Peter.[275] Initially Jesus is led right into the presence of the high priest (14:53) while Peter stands outside in the courtyard (14:54, 66). In stark contrast to Jesus, who is inside confessing his faith before the most powerful male Jew in Israel, Peter stands outside denying his faith before a female servant, a person of no power. Both narratives contain interrogations, with the false witnesses in Jesus' trial previewing the false testimony of Peter. Jesus is accused once by the false witnesses (14:56–57) and twice by the high priest (14:60, 61b) just as Peter is confronted twice by a slave girl (14:66, 69) and once by bystanders (14:70).

Three accusations are followed by three responses in each case. Jesus' antagonists inquire into his claim to destroy and restore the temple in three days (14:58), his silence before serious charges (14:60), and his messianic identity (14:61b). Surprisingly Jesus' response to the false witnesses is not recorded, and when the high priest attempts to further investigate Jesus' reaction, Jesus continues in serene silence (14:61a). In contrast, his lengthier than expected final response is full of clarity, content, and

---

France is correct that "when the climax is reached, the narrative goes consistently into the aorist to indicate Jesus' decisive action" (*Mark*, 222).

272. Borrell, *Good News of Peter's Denial*, 48.

273. Ibid., 51–52. Because of the unusual introduction Borrell, 47–48 labels this an A1-B1-A2-B2 structure instead of an A1-B-A2 intercalation.

274. Van Oyen, "Intercalation and Irony," 967–68 and note 81. Therefore, Wegener (*Cruciformed*, 187) contends this is not an intercalation but a comparison between the priests and Peter, not between Jesus and Peter. But Jesus is the central figure everywhere in the gospel except where John the Baptizer takes precedence (1:1–8; 6:14–29). However, Wegener is correct that Peter's responses are similar to that of the priests so that Peter acts like an outsider.

275. For a chart of similarities see Table II in Shepherd, *Sandwich Stories*, 285.

conviction. Jesus openly claims to be not only the Messiah but also the Son of God and the eschatological Son of Man (14:62).

Similarly, Peter's accusers claim he was with the Nazarene (14:67), that he is one of Jesus' band (14:69), and that he speaks like a Galilean (14:70b). Peter's first two retorts comprise simple denials: "I do not know or understand what you are talking about" (14:68), and the narrator's summary, "he denied it" (14:70a). But like Jesus his final reply is full of intensity and emotion so that he calls down curses and employs an oath (14:71).[276] Peter's first denial is private and evasive; the second is still evasive but public; but the third is direct, public, and the most reprehensible type of renunciation.[277] As a result Peter saves himself from suffering while Jesus is condemned to die. In each case a symbolic gesture demonstrates guilt: the tearing of the high priest's clothes (14: 63) in Jesus' trial parallels the crowing of the rooster (14:72a) in Peter's interrogation.

Finally, the last scene in each half centers on prophecy. The Jewish trial finishes (v. 65) with a description of the temple guards mocking, spitting, and striking Jesus as they blindfold him and demand that he prophesy. Whereas in Matthew and Luke the guards ask Jesus to prophesy who struck him (Matt 26:68; Luke 22:64), Mark fails to specify the content of Jesus' prophecy by not including a direct object. Likewise after Peter's third denial, he remembers Jesus' prophecy and breaks down with weeping contrition (v. 72b). But in the heat of the interrogation Peter curses (14:71). Here again the direct object and content of the curse are left a mystery. In each section of the intercalation one of Jesus' prophecies is fulfilled. The fulfillment of Jesus' passion prediction (10:34) in the Jewish trial parallels the completion of Jesus' foretelling of Peter's triadic denial (14:30) in the outside frame.

What do the parallel endings centering on prophecy and the final climatic response of each main character contribute to the meaning of the Markan intercalation? Two unusual features stand out which reveal Peter's appalling lack of faithfulness. In Peter's oath (14:71) the NIV 1984 translates ἤρξατο ἀναθεματίζειν as "he began to call down curses on himself."[278] Since the direct object is normally stated in a cursing formula,[279] the standard interpretation contends that Peter called down a curse upon himself.[280] However, self-cursing is not found in the LXX, Aquila, Symmachus,

---

276. Matt 26:70, 72, 74 constructs a gradual growth in intensity with an initial denial (ἠρνήσατο) strengthened by an oath (πάλιν ἠρνήσατο μετὰ ὅρκου), and finally climaxing in an oath with a curse (καταθεματίζειν καὶ ὀμνύειν).

277. Gerhardsson ("Confession and Denial," 52) makes the point that the gradation to a plural audience in Mark's third denial makes it more public and thus more grave legally. If we contrast the gradual increase of denial in Matthew, the last denial in Mark stands out like a redwood hovering over a sapling.

278. Likewise the RSV and ESV. However, the NIV 2011 has altered it to "he began to call down curses."

279. In Acts 23:12, 14, 21 the Jews opposing Paul bring a curse upon themselves (ἀνεθεμάτισαν ἑαυτοὺς).

280. Cf. Taylor, *Mark*, 575 and Merkel, "Peter's Curse," 67, n. 6 for a list of scholars from Grotius.

Theodotian, or the extra-biblical literature when the verb is employed intransitively. In a very convincing article Merkel contends that "Mark 14.71 is the one and only support for the absolute use of this verb."[281] The alternative, then, is that Peter is cursing Jesus.

What is the evidence that Peter is cursing Jesus? Certainly there must be a special reason why ἀναθεματίζω (to curse) is mentioned in addition to ὄμνυμι (to swear). The presence of a hendiadys is unlikely since the content of the oath is found in the statement, "I don't know this man you're talking about" (14:71b).[282] Therefore, the direct object of the oath, "this man, Jesus," must be the object of the curse as well. As Allison admits, "the best guess is that Jesus is the object of the curse, just as persecuted Christians were later on asked to curse Jesus."[283] The early Christian document the *Didache* seems to speak of Jesus as the one cursed (16:5).[284] But the clinching evidence is the drama that this creates in the Markan sandwich. Peter curses Jesus at the same time and in the same place that Jesus confesses his messianic identity and is condemned to death.[285] Although Mark leaves the curse intentionally unspecified, the intercalation demonstrates that Mark is setting Jesus and Peter alongside of each other as contrasting figures. Peter employs the strongest means possible to dissociate himself from Jesus. Earlier Peter had proclaimed Jesus as Messiah (8:29), but now while Jesus is suffering and arrested Peter is reneging on his confession. Ironically, this occurs exactly when Jesus is confessing his messiahship.

A second stunning contrast between Peter and Jesus centers on the fulfillment of prophecy concluding each section of the intercalation. Again here Mark is purposefully ambiguous and neglects to indicate the content of the prophecy. In Matthew 26:68 and Luke 22:64 the guards test Jesus' divine insight while blindfolded to declare "who struck him." However, Mark omits this apparently early tradition and states the guards' demand generally, "Prophesy to us, Messiah." What is the content of Jesus' prophecy? Because of the Markan intercalation we must infer that Jesus is prophesying Peter's denials. Therefore, the major theme of this pericope becomes discipleship. The conclusion of each part of the intercalation calls attention to Peter's scathing lack of faithfulness expressed in his cursing and denials of Jesus.

---

281. Merkel, "Peter's Curse," 68. See notes 9–14 for evidence from ancient literature.

282. Cf. Taylor, *Mark*, 575 and Merkel, "Peter's Curse," 68, n. 20. Brown (*Death*, 1:604) points out that Matt 26:72 already had an oath in the second denial, so the addition of a curse in Matt 26:74 also adds another action.

283. Davis and Allison, *Matthew*, 3:548. Cf. also Brown, *Death*, 604–5; Derrett, "Cursing Jesus," 551, n. 9; France, *Mark*, 622; Gundry, *Mark*, 890; Lampe, "St. Peter's Denial," 354; and Stein, *Mark*, 692.

284. "Those who endure in their faith will be saved by the accursed one himself" (τοῦ καταθέματος). Cf. Brown, *Death*, 605, n. 30, although Audet reads "from the curse" to mean the grave (Holmes, *Apostolic Fathers*, 269, n. 45).

285. However, Dewey ("Peter's Curse," 111f) goes a step further and proposes that Peter thus becomes an opponent of Mark, but see Brown (*Death*, 617) for counter arguments.

That the tradition transmits such a negative story about the premier apostle Peter is remarkable.[286] Its applicability to the reader must be a major concern. Markan subtlety in expressing these two exegetical details supports such a viewpoint. Furthermore, we know from the younger Pliny's letter to the emperor Trajan (*Ep.* 10.96.5–7) that cursing Jesus served as proof of innocence before a Roman tribunal when a person was accused of unlawfully being a Christian. In 111/112 CE Pliny, as legate of Caesar for Bithynia and Pontus, took legal action against the church and demanded that those charged with being Christians curse Christ, their God (*Christo maledicere*).[287] Pliny even supplies a rough parallel to the three denials of Peter: "I asked them whether they were Christians, and, if they confessed, I asked them a second and third time with threats of punishment."[288] Similarly, in the Jewish opposition of Bar Kochba in the Second Jewish Revolt, Justin Martyr reports that Christians were executed if they did not deny and curse Jesus.[289] Finally, in the *Martyrdom of Polycarp* 9:2–3 the proconsul attempted to persuade Polycarp to deny (ἀρνεῖσθαι), to swear (ὄμοσον), and to revile (λοιδόρησον) Christ. From similarities like these Allison concludes that "already the synoptic tradition assimilates our story to the persecution of Christians."[290] It seems likely that the expression "to deny" was "already a *terminus technicus* for a description of persecution and apostasy (Matt 10:33; Luke 12:9; Acts 13:13–14; 7:35)."[291] Certainly if Mark intends the above stated ambiguities and plays upon them, he could be mirroring the early experience of Christians in Mark's community. They like Peter have cursed Jesus to save themselves from persecution.

Would there be hope for such deserters of the faith? Again Peter would become a paradigm for the reader. After Peter died a martyr's death in the mid-60s, the story of his denials would be useful for Christian exhortation. As Brown explains, "Mark shows that even the disciple who was the first to be named in the Gospel (1:16) and would be the last named (16:7), and who had been the most forward in confessing Jesus, could not remain faithful until after Jesus had died on the cross."[292] Therefore, forgiveness would be extended to any weaker brother who could not sustain the persecution.[293]

---

286. Dewey, "Peter's Curse," 96.

287. Hengel, "Christological Titles," 359–60. See Sherwin-White, *Letters of Pliny*, 702–10.

288. Therefore, Boring muses that "The threefold form itself may reflect courtroom procedure in which the accused are given three opportunities to deny their membership in the suspect group (cf. Pliny, *Letters* 10.96.3; *Mart Pol* 9–10)" (*Mark*, 415).

289. Justin, *Apol.* 1,31,6 ἀρνοῖντο Ἰησοῦν τὸν Χριστὸν καὶ βλασφημοῖεν ("unless they would deny Jesus Christ and utter blasphemies").

290. Davies and Allison, *Matthew*, 3:548, n. 44.

291. Herron, *Mark's Account of Peter's Denial*, 141. Added exegetical evidence is found in Mark's paradigm parable which compares the rocky ground to persecution (4:17) which Herron (142) relabels as "Peterish-soil."

292. Brown, *Death*, 624.

293. Lampe explains, "Mark intends his readers, who may possibly have experienced for themselves the choice between confession and apostasy in Nero's persecution, to draw the conclusion that, if Peter could fall so far and yet be raised again to the leadership of the Church, then reconciliation

The purpose of this Markan intercalation has been variously interpreted. Certainly the mentioning of both Peter and Jesus in the opening scene of 14:53–54 creates pensive questions in the mind of the reader. How will each respond in the upcoming situation? Irony as well as narrative tension saturates the story. In fact, Shepherd labels this narrative the "sharpest irony of any of the intercalations."[294] By denying his Lord, Peter actually proves that Jesus is the Messiah since this very act was prophesized (14:30). In fact, the shout at Jesus to prophesy becomes ironically the exact point at which the narrator returns to Peter in the courtyard below and relates the three denials just as Jesus predicted them.[295] Likewise, when Jesus' mockers demand a prophecy, ironically Jesus' prediction that he will suffer in these exact circumstances (10:34) is fulfilled as well. By the interweaving of Jesus' trial and Peter's denials, Mark unveils the double fulfillment of Jesus' predictions concerning both his own condemnation to death by the Sanhedrin and Peter's denials.

The theological content of this irony, however, takes precedent since it reveals Mark's purpose in writing the gospel. The two central themes of the gospel, Christology and discipleship, are addressed.[296] The identity of Jesus is central to the investigation of the high priest (14:61). In fact, Jesus' confession before the chief priest is the first time in Mark that Jesus drops the veil of silence and openly confesses his identity.[297] The timing of this event is of utmost importance; the secret can only be broken during Jesus' passion, as is also witnessed in the centurion's confession in 15:39. Through the Jewish trial and Peter's denial Jesus is forsaken by his nation and his disciples.

Just as the intercalation proves that the church serves a Suffering Servant Messiah, so it calls forth a discipleship of the cross. The themes of passion Christology and a discipleship of the cross crisscross each other in the intercalation. A story about failed discipleship encircles a narrative about christological faithfulness. Through his inability to speak the truth under pressure, Peter becomes a false witness like the accusers in the Jewish trial (14:57–60). Peter's blasphemous curses of denial (14:71) likewise parallel the rejection of Jesus' claims as blasphemous by the Jewish leaders (14:63–64). Similar to the intercalation in Mark 3 where the family of Jesus team up with the Jewish leaders to oppose Jesus' mission, here Peter becomes an outsider. Jesus' warning in 8:38 about "being ashamed of me and my words in this adulterous and sinful generation" is realized in Peter's open denials. He must return to 8:34 and fulfill Jesus' command to "deny himself, take up his cross, and follow Jesus."

Now the only question is, "Will Peter remain an outsider?" Since this question is not answered in the gospel, apparently Mark wants that issue front and center for

---

cannot be absolutely refused to weaker brethren" ("St. Peter's Denial," 358).

294. Shepherd, "Intercalation and the Synoptic Problem," 695. See note 28 for a list of authors who recognize the ironic sense of the intercalation.

295. Tolbert, *Sowing the Gospel*, 278. Cf. 217–18 for a discussion about simultaneity.

296. Cf. Shepherd, *Sandwich Stories*, 292.

297. Edwards, "Markan Sandwiches," 212.

his community. Jesus is accused of blasphemy and Peter offers blasphemous words. Interestingly, blasphemy becomes a charge which the Christian community will later face as well (1 Cor 4:13; Rev 2:9; 1 Pet 4:4).[298] In addition, "the juxtaposition of bold confession and cowardly denial forces upon the reader the terrible gap between Jesus and Peter."[299] The community must decide to boldly confess their belief in Jesus in courtroom-type situations or follow the example of Peter. Mark 13:9 predicts, "On account of me you will stand before governors and kings as witnesses to them." Mark, then, employs this intercalation to address crucial issues in his day. Will Peter's blasphemous curse reoccur in the pressurized struggles of the Markan community? Will Jesus' prophecy of Peter's denial replay itself in a community that "will betray brother to death" (13:12)?

The intercalation is a sign that Mark is speaking at two levels. Peter's struggles to confess Jesus while confronted by accusations become the struggles of the readers. In doing so Mark addresses what now should be familiar topics for the reader: a discipleship of the cross that is ready to follow a Suffering Servant Messiah.

2.8 Mark's Role in the Composition of Intercalations

We have investigated the six intercalations that are universally recognized.[300] In order to support the theological conclusions above, we must demonstrate that Mark is the originator of this technique. Therefore, we will discuss how the other gospel writers respond to these Markan sandwiches and produce arguments for a Markan composition of each of these intercalations.

The other Synoptic writers dismantle most of Mark's intercalations. Both Matthew and Luke follow Mark's lead only in the healing of the unclean woman and dead girl (Mark 5:21–43 / Matt 9:18–26 / Luke 8:40–56). Within this pericope Luke follows his Markan source closely and only removes the details of the story that could be interpreted as magic: the power protruding from Jesus (Mark 5:30) and the Aramaic healing formula (Mark 5:41).[301] But Matthew treats the story purely as a healing narrative by strategically placing ten miracles together as Jesus' deeds of the kingdom (Matt 8–9) following his words of the kingdom in the Sermon on the Mount (Matt 5–7). In narrowing the narrative to a single focus, Matthew abandons the dramatic irony so memorable in Mark. As Shepherd explains, "The anxiety and suspense over whether Jesus will reach the child in time is absent."[302] Instead of the little girl dying because Jesus spends so much time with the menstruating woman, the girl is already

---

298. Cf. Donahue, *Are You the Christ*, 97, note 1.

299. Edwards, "Markan Sandwiches," 212.

300. See the end of Appendix 3 for a summary of questionable Markan sandwiches.

301. Shepherd ("Intercalation and Synoptic Problem," 694, n. 25) calls attention to the child's multiple names which are removed as well.

302. Ibid., 693.

dead when the narrative begins in Matthew (9:18). More importantly, Matthew omits any connection of the story with Jewish purity rites by omitting 1) the reference to Jairus as head of the synagogue (ἄρχων instead of ἀρχισυναγώγων in Matt 9:18, 23); 2) the elaboration of the fourfold motif of touching in Mark 5:27–31; and 3) the clever repetition of twelve, since the girl's age is missing in Matthew 9:23–26. Thus Matthew completely ignores any reference to the uncleanness of both of the recipients. The traditional genre of healing story is evident in the Matthean ending as well. In Matthew the news of the child's resurrection spreads throughout the region (9:26), whereas Mark emphasizes the secrecy of miracles (5:43) since he wants to hide Jesus' identity until his passion. Therefore, the change of context, loss of dramatic irony, ignorance of the issues of Jewish purity, and further genre specification as a healing story argue that Mark's purpose is not transferred to Matthew. Even in the one intercalation common to all the Synoptic Gospels, Mark's theme is unique.

In two instances neither Matthew nor Luke replicate the Markan intercalation. In order not to discolor the reputation of Jesus' family, both omit Mark 3:21 with the postulation that Jesus is out of his mind. In the process they overlook Mark's point that insiders can become outsiders and that discipleship failure can infect those who are closest to Jesus. Thus Matthew and Luke separate Jesus' family from the accusations of the Jewish leaders (Matt 12:22–32, 46–50 and Luke 11:14–23; 12:10; 8:19–21). In fact, Luke produces an exemplary role for Jesus' family by placing their search for Jesus after the parable of the sower, so that the good soil (8:15) is represented by his mothers and brothers who hear God's word and put it into practice (8:21). Again the motif of discipleship misunderstanding is only integral to Mark's gospel purposes.

The other intercalation dropped by both Synoptic writers becomes the second instance where Mark mirrors Jewish institutions and their fulfillment in the kingdom age. Whereas Mark sandwiched the temple action between the cursing of the fig tree incident, Matthew (21:12–20) and Luke (19:45–48) alter this procedure since they interpret the temple positively. The events occur for Mark on separate days so that Jesus can reconnoiter the temple before he acts out its destruction.[303] In addition, Matthew transforms the cursing of the fig tree into a pure miracle story as evidenced by the immediacy of the wonder (21:19), the amazement of the onlookers (21:20), and the exhortation to miracle faith (21:21–22). Since Matthew places the reference to moving a mountain before any mention of the temple (21:21), Mark's emphasis upon the destruction of the temple is lost. Finally, Matthew omits Mark's strange notification that "it was not the season for figs" (11:13) and the impossible to verify datum that the tree withered from its roots (11:20). By excluding these two surprising statements, Matthew also ignores the symbolic overtones which Mark cleverly employs through the literary device of an intercalation.

---

303. See Marcus, *Mark 8–16*, 788.

More radically, Luke omits this negative miracle completely, choosing to include the parable of the fig tree (13:6-9) instead.[304] Through this procedure the temple action becomes a temple cleansing rather than a temple destruction, which is certainly closer to the *Sitz im Leben Jesu*. Thus the temple maintains a positive connotation so that it becomes the sanctuary of the early church in Acts 2:46; 3:1; 5:21, 25, etc.[305] From this survey it should be evident that the Mark 11 intercalation serves a role that is important only to Mark's theme of the fulfillment of Jewish institutions and ceremonies.[306]

Matthew stands alone by employing two additional Markan Passion story intercalations, i.e., the narratives of the anointing of Jesus by the woman (Mark 14:1-11; Matt 26:1-16) and Peter's denial sandwiched with the Jewish trial (Mark 14:53-72; Matt 26:57-75).[307] However, Matthew overlooks Mark's prominent emphasis on discipleship. Instead an apologetic against the Jews for killing Jesus the Messiah becomes central in Matthew's passion narrative. The three prominent additions of Matthew to Mark's passion narrative comprising Judas' attempt at repentance (27:1-10), Pilate's washing of his hands (27:24), and the crowd's exclamation, "His blood be on us and on our children" (27:25) all involve the responsibility of the Jewish leaders for Jesus' death. Similar to Mark, Matthew's passion story begins with the initiation of a plot against Jesus by the chief priests and elders (26:3), and the charges brought by the Sanhedrin against Jesus (26:65-66) immediately precede Peter's denials. However, a subtle shift of emphasis away from discipleship occurs when Matthew does not follow Mark in applying the soldiers' demand for a prophecy to Peter's denials but instead adds the direct object, "prophesy who hit you" (Matt 26:68). Thus the Markan emphasis on discipleship stands out from the rest of the Synoptic Gospels. Matthew merely repeats the Markan sandwiches of his source, and not because he desires to tie together the themes of the passion of Jesus and the discipleship of the cross in order to preach to the church community.

Finally, Luke alone repeats the intercalation of the disciples' mission with a description of Herod's questions about John the Baptist and Jesus (Mark 6:7-30; Luke 9:1-10). On the other hand, Matthew places the sending out of the twelve disciples into his second discourse on mission strategy (Matt 10:1-14) while leaving a description of

---

304. Luke regularly eliminates any possible duplicates to make room for other material on the scroll. See Cadbury, *Style and Literary Method*, 83-89.

305. The temple as the location of God's revelations even becomes a structural organizing principle for Luke. Cf. Hultgren, "Interpreting the Gospel of Luke," 185.

306. This is evident from Mark 7:19b as well ("In saying thus, Jesus declared all foods clean"), another detail that both Matthew and Luke purposely omit.

307. This is consistent with the fact that Matthew repeats more of the Markan material than Luke and that Luke rewrites the Markan passion narrative. Cf. Stein, *Synoptic Problem*, 48, 115. Over 97% of Mark's material has a parallel in Matthew, yet the number of words that are identical in Matthew is 4,432 (out of a possible 10,901 or 40%). Over 88% of Mark's material is paralleled in Luke, yet only 2,873 words are identical (26%) according to B. de Solages (*Synopsis*, 1052). Luke's rewriting of the passion narrative is discussed in Fitzmyer (*Luke*, 2:1365-69).

the Baptizer's death in the normal Markan sequence (Matt 14:1–12). Although Luke preserves the intercalation, he completely omits the Baptist's death, which for Mark is a precursor of Jesus' death as well as the starting point of the disciples' mission to follow Jesus. Therefore only in Mark are the passion and discipleship consistently tied together through the literary device of an intercalation.

So far we have witnessed how the other Synoptic writers disassemble or fail to recognize the significance of the Markan sandwiches.[308] This phenomenon implies that only Mark understands the uniqueness and purpose of this literary device. As Meier suggests, the "presence of a set style of storytelling in Mark" speaks in favor of Markan origin.[309] The presence of antecedents in other literature could argue against a Markan origin, but few examples related to Markan themes have been identified. Edwards refers to Homer's *Odyssey* (book XIX) and *Iliad* (book XVI), but the B part in each case is a flashback, not an interpreting story. Similarly, such passages as 2 Maccabees 6:1–11, 12–17, 18; 14:31–36, 37–46, 15:1–11 must be labeled consecutive events, not intercalations. Likewise, mutual interpretation is difficult to discern at 2 Maccabees 8:23–29, 30–33, 34–36.[310] Edwards accepts Hosea 1–3; 2 Samuel 11:1—12:25; and with less certainty 2 Samuel 18:9–15[311] from the Hebrew Bible as intercalations, but he denies any influence upon Mark.[312] Although Hosea does interrupt the narrative of Gomer and her three children with prophetic speech in chapter 2, there is no second set of characters with which Gomer is compared with as in normal intercalation. Instead, Hosea 1–3 functions merely as a prose–poetry–prose alteration which binds together the seer's word-and-deed prophecy. In Edwards' second example, the splicing of the David-Bathsheba story with the Nathan prophecy adds suspenseful intrigue and provides the interpretative key. So at the very least we can concede that the suspension of a narrative through the insertion of similar material was not without precedent in ancient literature. However, the Markan themes are unique as well as the application both to the time of Jesus and the church's experience.

In the next few paragraphs we will proceed through each intercalation to argue for a Markan origin of this device.[313] Each of the intercalations reinforces the major

---

308. Shepherd contends that "to leave out intercalations without a traceable reason is tantamount to admitting that they did not have the Markan text before them when writing" ("Intercalation and Synoptic Problem," 692), but we have attempted above to point out the motivations of Matthew and Luke and assume Markan priority throughout this book. Specifically with regard to the minor agreement of Matt 26:68 and Luke 22:64, the omission in Matthew of the blindfold indicates they are unrelated. But for other explanations see Shepherd (696–97, n. 29) and the article by Frans Neirynck mentioned there.

309. Meier, *Marginal Jew*, 708.

310. Edwards, "Markan Sandwiches," 200 critiqued by Van Oyen, "Intercalation and Irony," 961, n. 58.

311. But it is unclear how Joab's killing of Absalom sheds light on the rebellion, and second, it functions as an elaboration rather than as an intercalated story.

312. Edwards, "Markan Sandwiches," 203.

313. For support from scholars see Van Oyen, "Intercalation and Irony," 959, n. 52.

themes of Mark's gospel. The negative shading of Jesus' family and the dovetailing with the Jewish leaders in the first Markan sandwich points out that insiders can become outsiders. The negative edge assigned to Jesus' family stands prominent in Mark 6:4 as well, whereas Matthew 13:57 and Luke 4:24 eliminate the presence of relatives, and its total omission in John 4:44 and Thomas 31 (POxy 1:30–35) argues for Markan redaction. Likewise, the omission and reordering of the material in Matthew and Luke indicate that this intercalation in Mark 3 failed to serve their thematic purposes.[314] The inclusion of Jesus' family as one third of the early community in Acts 1:14 and the mentioning of a resurrection appearance to James by Paul (1 Cor 15:7) demonstrate a different theological agenda in the rest of the New Testament.[315] Only Mark presents Jesus' family in such negative terms, because of his interest in discipleship failure. This recognizable redactional purpose in the theology of Mark argues for a Markan construction.

No intercalation of Mark receives more support from scholars for its pre-Markan traditions than the two miracle stories in Mark 5.[316] Many exegetes deny Markan redaction since "this is how things happened."[317] Gundry points out the obvious observation that "it is the stuff of life that events are often intertwined,"[318] and Twelftree maintains that "in each case the stories read naturally, as if they had always been re-

---

314. Both omit Mark 3:20–21 so that the pericope is no longer an intercalation. Crossan ("Mark and the Relatives," 86–87) thinks that Mark 3:22–27, 31–35 preserves a pre-Markan unity since the ending to the Beelzebul controversy in Luke 11:27–28 includes a woman's call from the crowd, "Blessed is the mother who gave you birth and nursed you" (11:27) which would compare to the subject matter of Mark 3:31–34 as well as Jesus' reply, "Blessed rather are those who hear the word of God and obey it" which is like Mark 3:35. Furthermore, Matt 12:46–50 which repeats Mark 3:31–35 follows the "return of the evil spirit" pericope just as Luke concludes this saying with the blessing upon Jesus' mother and Jesus' response about true discipleship. Yet even this possibility does not account for the Markan intercalation since Mark 3:20–21 is still Markan redaction. A more likely alternative hypothesis argues that Luke is repeating the ending of the Markan controversy since he employs Mark 3:35 already one time in a new context in Luke 8:19–21. In fact, the wording of Luke 8:21 is much closer to Luke 11:28 than Mark 3:35. Also Luke has a tendency to intrude a voice from the crowd into Q material as in 12:13; 14:15; 13:23; 12:41. Therefore, Luke's purpose would be to concoct a traditional concluding acclamation to a mighty deed to make the crowd respond positively to Jesus since the last response by the crowd is mixed (14–15) with the seemingly winning response being the accusation of 11:15 (which Mark assigns to the Jewish leadership). This conclusion is supported by the fact that whereas Matthew normally interweaves both of his sources together (for example, in the Beelzebul controversy), here in Matt 12:46–50 there is no evidence of the content found in Luke 11:27–28. Even Crossan agrees that the juxtaposition of 3:22–27 and 3:31–35 in Mark takes on very different overtones.

315. However, the historicity of Mark's data is substantiated by the unbelief of Jesus' brothers in John 7:3–5.

316. Cf. Bultmann, *Synoptic Tradition*, 228; Cranfield, *Mark*, 182; Gundry, *Mark*, 268; Taylor, *Mark*, 289 and the list of scholars in Achtemeier, "Isolation," 277, n. 46. For a defense of Markan composition see Kazen, *Jesus and Purity Halakhah*, 131. For scholarly support of Markan redaction see Twelftree, *Miracle Worker*, 373, n. 101, although he argues against it.

317. Latourelle, *Miracles and Theology*, 122, 125.

318. Gundry, *Mark*, 268.

membered and told in this way."³¹⁹ Certainly the similar genre of healing story could easily have tied them together before Mark.

But the divergence of the grammar and style point to separate origins for the two sections of the intercalation.³²⁰ Guelich summarizes the findings of most scholars:

> The stylistic differences in the two stories (Jairus' story with short, paratactic sentences in the historical present; the woman's story in long, participle-filled sentences in the aorist tense),³²¹ the integrity of each story as a unit in itself, and the apparent influence of 5:25–34 on the setting of 5:22–24, 35–43 through the introduction of the crowds, which otherwise play no role in the Jairus story, support this conclusion.³²²

Regarding theme, the catchword "twelve" would not serve any purpose in the combination of two miracle stories before Mark, but it furthers Mark's agenda by suggesting the subject of ritual purity rites among the twelve tribes like touching menstruating women and dead bodies. Finally, we shall demonstrate in the next chapter that these two stories were separated in a pre-Markan miracle catenae by illustrating the similarities that occur through the identification of two five-element chiasms in the ten miracle stories of 4:41—8:26. The two healings were originally not intertwined but only successive narratives, with the healing of an unclean bleeding woman paralleling Jesus' encounter with an unclean Gentile woman (7:24–30) in the center of each chiasm, and the healing of Jairus' daughter through the touching of an unclean corpse corresponding to the healing of a deaf/mute through unclean spit (7:31–39). Within the first miracle chiasm itself the demoniac living in the tombs (5:3) parallels the dead girl (5:35).³²³

The intercalation in Mark 6 fits perfectly into the distinctive discipleship outline of Mark, which begins each new section with a call to deeper discipleship, in this case the disciples beginning their own ministry with Jesus supervising them.³²⁴ Furthermore, the interconnections between John, Jesus, and the disciples strengthens a Markan theme. When John is arrested Jesus begins his ministry; when John is killed the disciples begin their Palestinian mission; and when Jesus is crucified the disciples start their world mission. The keyword "delivered" holds all three characters together

---

319. Twelftree, *Miracle Worker*, 73.

320. Cf. Achtemeier ("Isolation," 277) and Meier (*Marginal Jew*, 778–79), who recites a series of redactional touches that were added when the two stories were joined. For Markan vocabulary see Farla, *Jezus' Oordeel*, 122.

321. Stein (*Mark*, 262, n. 1) objects that the story of Jairus' daughter has some long sentences (5:22–23, 38–39a) and the story of the hemorrhaging woman some relatively short sentences (5:29, 32), but the lengthy list of participles in 5:25–27 prove Guelich's conclusion correct.

322. Guelich, *Mark 1—8:26*, 292.

323. Cf. section 3.7 below. In addition, the ending which narrates the girl's eating (5:43) fits well as an introduction to the feeding of the five thousand which would come next in the pre-Markan miracle catenae (Achtemeier, "Isolation," 279).

324. See Appendix 4 below, outline 12.

so that John the Baptist is handed over to death (παραδίδομαι 1:14) to foreshadow Jesus' crucifixion (9:31; 10:33), which becomes paradigmatic for the future experience of the disciples (13:9). Certainly the intercalation of John's death and the disciples' mission is integral to Mark's purpose, but does not serve other needs in the broader Christian tradition which are important to Matthew or Luke.

Mark's originating the device of intercalations is clearly visible in the interconnection between the temple action and the cursing of the fig tree. Stein points out that in Mark "the cleansing of the temple, which originally may have referred to a reformation (see verse 16) is now apparently portrayed as an act of judgment."[325] This is a unique Markan emphasis. In addition, the parable of the tenants (12:1–11), which reinforces this divine act of judgment on the temple leadership, is placed in the midst of a collection of controversy dialogues (11:27–33; 12:13–37), which is surely Markan.[326] Again the intercalation serves the purposes of Mark but not the positive evaluation of the temple in the other gospels.

The last two intercalations are the most complicated because the Gospel of John contains similar material. The sandwich joining the plot to kill Jesus with the woman's anointing of Jesus (Mark 14:1–11) could emanate from the pre-Markan tradition since the Gospel of John witnesses a similar framework, with the plot to arrest Jesus and Lazarus (John 11:57; 12:9–11) surrounding the anointing by Mary (12:1–8). Likewise, Judas (seen in Mark 14:10–11) pokes his head into the narrative (John 12:4–6), but this time in the inner story as the protagonist who petulantly protests the woman's generous action. Finally, the story is connected with the Passover feast, although the time designation diverges (six days before the Passover in John 12:1 versus two days in Mark 14:1).

However, as Shepherd argues, "the social backgrounds of the two stories are different. The outer story deals with religious leadership and discipleship, while the inner story deals with the social relations of mealtime and the social backgrounds of anointing and burial rites"[327] in Mark. Likewise the characterization diverges, with Mark placing Judas in the outer story while John 12:4–6 inserts Judas into the inner narrative as the one who criticizes the woman's action because he is a thief. Moreover, the placement by John in the Book of Signs (John 2–12), whereas Mark employs the narrative to introduce Jesus' passion, indicates a separate use of the material. Finally, the new paragraph in John 12:1 with time and place and character introductions separates the material from the plot to arrest Jesus in 11:57.

Regarding the dovetailing of the Jewish trial and Peter's denials, Gundry offers the reasonable conclusion that "though the story of the trial might easily have circulated without the story of Peter's denials, the story of his denials could hardly have

---

325. Stein, "Proper Methodology," 194.
326. Ibid., n. 1.
327. Shepperd, *Sandwich Stories*, 243.

circulated apart from the story of the trial."[328] Craig Evans proceeds further and concludes that "the intercalation of these two stories reaches back to the very beginnings of the telling of the passion."[329] But the presence of an intercalation is different from the contention that the stories belong together. In Luke they are placed side by side without an intercalation. Certainly it is peculiar that both John and Mark divide up the story of Peter's denials with the seam that "Peter was warming himself" (Mark 14:54, 67; John 18:18, 25).[330] However, the seam is much more apparent in John's gospel, with the participles ἑστὼς καὶ θερμαινόμενος (standing and warming) concluding the first denial and introducing the second. In Mark the theme of "Peter warming himself" does not emerge until a verse later in 14:67 so that the seam is more likely the place where the event occurred, i.e., in the courtyard (14:54 εἰς τὴν αὐλήν; 14:66 ἐν τῇ αὐλῇ). Furthermore, different traditions in the Johannine account, like the inclusion of Peter's first denial before the Jewish trial (18:15–18), a hearing before Annas (18:19–24), and the divergent wording of the denials, demonstrate the unique ways in which the two authors portray the material.[331] Since Mark only introduces Peter's entrance into the courtyard of the high priest before the Jewish trial whereas John includes the entire first denial, evidence for a pre-Markan tradition is scanty.

Certainly the two stories are linked together as evidenced by the fourfold tradition. However the Markan interconnections are unique and indicate that the dovetailing in Mark has the special purpose of highlighting the theme of discipleship failure. Furthermore, only Mark ties together Jesus' prophecy to the soldiers with the fulfillment of Jesus' prediction about Peter's denial. Uniquely, the challenge to prophesy concludes each section of the intercalation. In distinction from Matthew 26:68 and Luke 22:64 ("prophesy who is it that struck you"), Mark 14:65 does not include an object for the imperative "prophesy" since the prediction Mark has in mind is Jesus' foretelling of Peter's denial. Mark places the emphasis on the disciple Peter by revealing neither the purpose for which the soldiers cover Jesus' face nor what they challenge him to prophesy.[332] The Gospel of John's omission of the call to prophesy in the mocking of Jesus as well as Peter's cursing of Jesus in the third denial at the exact time when Jesus confesses his messiahship (which John also eliminates) demonstrates that

---

328. Gundry, *Mark*, 891. Fortna states that "This is seen in the fact that both stories demand a setting at the High Priest's house" ("Jesus and Peter," 373).

329. Evans, *Mark 8:27—16:20*, 463.

330. Cf. Evans, "Peter Warming Himself," 245.

331. Cf. Fortna, "Jesus and Peter," 372–73 for differences in the intercalation, 375–76 for differences in the trial narrative, and 376–79 for differences in Peter's denials with the conclusion that "there is no reason to suppose that John knew a distinctively Markan form of the tradition" (375). Joel Green (*Death of Jesus*, 126–27) produces seven major differences between the narratives. Donahue (*Are You the Christ*, 56–57) produces an impressive list of unique Markan vocabulary for this intercalation as well.

332. The fact that Mark mentions the blindfolding indicates that he knew the oral tradition Matthew and Luke repeat, but he moves the tradition in a different direction to emphasize discipleship.

The Theological Intentions of Mark's Literary Devices

Mark's purpose in intercalating these narratives is totally different. By interweaving Jesus' trial and Peter's denials only Mark brings out the double fulfillment of Jesus' predictions of his own condemnation to death by the Sanhedrin and of Peter's denials. Thus two themes coalesce on top of each other: the passion of Jesus predicted in 10:34 and fulfilled in 14:65, and the discipleship failure of Peter predicted in 14:30 and brought to fruition in 14:72. These two themes, which the other intercalations underline as well, demonstrate Mark's unique use of this literary device.

Further evidence for the original separation of Peter's denials from the Jewish trial focuses on the scholarly doubt that the Jewish trial was included in any pre-Markan passion narrative, oral or written. Instead, the sequence of events in the Jewish trial appear to be based upon the Roman trial, although the order is not exact.

Question of inquiry

14:61	"Are you the Christ, the Son of the Blessed One?"
15:2	"Are you the king of the Jews?"

Jesus' answer

14:62	Although Mark's direct answer ("I am" ἐγω εἰμι) is unique, Matt 26:64 seems more primitive (σὺ εἶπας).
15:2	Evasive answer: "You have said so" (σὺ λέγεις).

Question about silence

14:60	"Are you going to answer? What is this testimony that these men are bringing?"
15:4	"Aren't you going to answer? See how many things they are accusing you of."

False witnesses make accusations.

14:56–59	"Many testified falsely against him, but their statements did not agree."
15:3	"The chief priests accused him of many things."

Jesus, the righteous sufferer, remains silent.

14:61	"But Jesus remained silent and gave no answer."
15:5	"But Jesus still made no reply, and Pilate was amazed."

Jewish consensus to kill Jesus

14:64	"They all condemned him as worthy of death."
15:13–14	"Crucify him! they shouted."

Jesus is flogged.

14:65b	"And the guards took him and beat him" and 15:1 "handed him over to Pilate."
15:15b	"He had Jesus flogged and handed him over to be crucified."

Jesus is mocked.

14:65	"Then some began to spit at him; they blindfolded him, struck him with their fists, and said, 'Prophesy!'"
15:16–20	The soldiers placed a purple robe and crown of thorns upon Jesus to mock him.

The Markan passion narrative probably had its origin in an oral recitation performed at Eucharist celebrations.[333] What narratives were included in the early church's celebration of Jesus' death? The formulary found in Paul's writing at 1 Cor 11:23b–26 requires that the narratives alluded to there were included in a pre-Markan passion narrative. Since the standard recital states "on the night he was betrayed," the narration would certainly include Jesus' betrayal. Because Paul concludes with "you proclaim the Lord's death until he comes," the pre-Markan passion recitation would end with the crucifixion climaxing in an exaltation into heaven so that Jesus as the Son of God will return. Since an oral "performance" would require repetitive structures for memory, the passion presentation was likely organized by triads. Therefore, the Gethsemane prayer vigil, Peter's threefold denial, and the Roman trial before Pilate with their triplicate structures offer evidence for inclusion, but the Jewish trial is excluded.[334] Similarly, a movement from the twelve disciples at the Last Supper, to three in the garden, to Judas at the betrayal and Peter at the denial, while no disciples are present before Pilate and at the cross, would develop an easy memory pattern. Therefore, the following episodes were in all likelihood included in a pre-Markan passion narration:[335]

1. The Lord's Supper formula (Mark 14:22–25), like 1 Corinthians 11:24b–26.

2. Gethsemane prayer vigil (Mark 14:34–42): Jesus moves away to pray three times and returns three times to discover the disciples sleeping.

3. Betrayal, arrest, and flight (Mark 14:43–46, 50): a simple story in three acts.

4. Threefold denial by Peter (Mark 14:66–72) while Jesus is at the house of the chief

---

333. See Goodacre ("Scripturalization," 42–45) who offers both external and internal evidence to suggest that early church worship provided the context for the development of Mark's passion narrative.

334. Donahue ("Temple, Trial, and Royal Christology," 63–64) considers the possibility that both the Jewish trial and Peter's denial consist of a threefold accusation (14:56; 57–59; 60–64 and 66–68, 69–70a; 70b–71), but in the end agrees with G. Schneider that the evangelist himself has created a diptych contrasting the confessing Jesus inside and the denying Peter outside.

335. Scroggs ("Was There a Pre-Markan Passion Narrative?" 565–66) eliminates various sections of the present passion narrative: anointing story; Passover preparation; Gethsemane vigil; night trial before the Jewish authorities; Peter's denials and the prediction of the denials; attempts to mitigate the fact that Jesus was executed as a revolutionary by Rome; and references to the temple. We suggest that the memory devices indicate that Gethsemane and Peter's denial should be included and that Paul's formula evidences the inclusion of the rending of the temple veil which originally did not involve the destruction of the temple but the journey of Jesus' spirit into heaven as in the theology of Hebrews and Luke 23:45b where the hole created before Jesus' death allows him to enter the heavenly sanctuary.

priest (14:55).

5. The Roman trial before Pilate (Mark 15:1–15), where on three occasions Pilate attempts to release Jesus ("again" at 15:4 and 15:12–13), with Luke using the oral tradition to make it more specific (Luke 23:22 "for the third time").

6. Crucifixion: a ternary design with three designations of hours (third, sixth, ninth; Mark 15:25–34a), climaxing in Jesus entering the heavenly temple (Mark 15:38, but like Luke 23:45 and Heb 10:20) and the confession of Jesus as the Son of God by the centurion (Mark 14:39).

Therefore, the details of the Jewish trial of Mark 14:56–65 were not likely recited but instead are Markan additions to form an intercalation with Peter's denial. If this is true, then all the sandwiches are the work of Mark himself.

This investigation confirms our hypothesis that Mark employs this sandwich technique to place before the reader a Suffering Servant Messiah which in turn demands a discipleship of the cross. The intercalation is a unique literary device developed by Mark to let the reader know when he is both recounting the story of Jesus and speaking to the issues in his own community. In the six intercalations these issues center on the reinterpretation of Jewish regulations for the Gentile church and the following of a Suffering Servant Messiah through the community's willingness to take up their cross and follow Jesus.

3

The Literary Device of a Markan Framework

3.1 Structural Techniques in the Gospel of Mark

A Markan frame or framework consists of a matched pair of episodes that bookend a series of episodes and offer a theological interpretation of the material placed in between. As a literary device, a frame is really an extension of the already discussed Markan sandwich or intercalation.[1] As Wright explains, "An intercalation constitutes a scene; framing in the Gospel consists of a series of scenes."[2] We will argue in this chapter that on several occasions Mark has framed already collected traditional material that was organized in the oral tradition by genre (controversy dialogue, parable, miracle story, discipleship teaching, and apocalyptic) into fivefold chiastic structures easily remembered. As Dewey argues, "frames around an extended concentric structure . . . become Mark's method of putting his gospel together."[3] We will demonstrate that Mark's purpose in composing these frames is to emphasize that the Christ sent by God is a Suffering Servant Messiah to whom the most appropriate response is a discipleship of the cross. Whenever Fowler describes these frames as "metaphorical illumination,"[4] I prefer to portray the Markan framework as a perspective-giving device whereby Mark interprets the meaning of the narratives enclosed within the frame.

The most universally accepted Markan framework consists of the two stories of the healing of blind men (8:22–26; 10:46–52) which frame the teaching on discipleship

---

1. Dewey, "Literary Structure," 147: "The setting off of material by means of a frame seems a natural extension of Mark's 'sandwiching' technique."

2. Wright, *Markan Intercalations*. 16.

3. Dewey, *Markan Public Debate*, 23.

4. Fowler, *Let the Reader Understand*, 146: "The frame episodes provide metaphorical illumination for the framed episodes."

in the central section of Mark.[5] A second widely recognized frame consists of the narratives around the eschatological discourse of Mark 13 which develop two portraits of women disciples who give their all.[6] We will argue that Mark consistently employs this literary device both to surround pre-existent oral traditions collected by genre into fivefold chiastic structures and to encircle material which he organizes into a triadic format or fivefold structures without a chiastic organization. These structures provide a literary organization to Mark's entire gospel.[7]

The reader of Mark is struck by the discovery that controversy dialogues, parables, miracle stories, discipleship teaching, apocalyptic, and passion stories are collected together. Form criticism has demonstrated that this material contained a certain standard oral form so that samples of particular genres could be collected together and easily remembered. We will argue that Mark introduces a frame around the controversy dialogues of 2:1—3:6 on the theme of the Messianic Secret (1:40-45; 3:7-12) to teach his readers that the Messiah can only be recognized in controversy and struggle. In the frame (4:1-2, 33-34) around the parables of 4:3-32 Mark offers a specific interpretation of what it means to speak in parables (i.e., as allegorical riddles) so that the mystery of the kingdom (4:11-12) is inevitably hid from those who have not accepted the explanation given in private to Jesus' disciples. A fivefold chiastic structure of "hiddenness" is contrasted with a larger fivefold chiastic structure of "revealedness." In addition, Mark's frame around two fivefold chiastic miracle cycles in 4:35—8:21 narrates trips across the sea concluded with the disciples' failure to understand (4:40; 8:17-21) in order to demonstrate that Jesus cannot be interpreted as a miracle-working Messiah alone. Finally, the apocalyptic teaching of Mark 13 is surrounded with a frame of two women who offer everything they have to Jesus (12:41-44; 14:3-9) to indicate that preparation for the glory of Jesus' *parousia* only occurs through a total surrender to a discipleship of the cross.

Mark encircles additional material with frames, but the structure of the pericopes consists of triads and fivefold divisions without a chiasm, probably indicating Markan imitation of the oral material and his own preference for threefold structures. It is difficult to decide whether 1:1-15, the "beginning of the gospel," is organized by two triads coordinating the ministries of John and Jesus or by a fivefold chiastic structure. But in either case the frame of preaching the gospel (1:1, 15) indicates that the ministries of John and Jesus display the content of the gospel so that a summary

---

5. Cf. Achtemeier, "And He Followed Him," 115, 132; Camery-Hoggatt, *Irony*, 10; Dewey, *Markan Public Debate*, 23; Fowler, *Let the Reader Understand*, 144; Kelber, *Story*, 44; Marshall, *Faith as a Theme*, 139; Meier, *Marginal Jew*, 2:691; Myers, *Binding the Strong Man*, 239; Stock, *Call to Discipleship*, 136; van Iersel, *Mark*, 79 and *Reading Mark*, 22-23.

6. Dewey asserts that "the parallelism of the two stories is beyond question" (*Public Markan Debate*, 154). See also Barton, "Mark as Narrative," 231; Geddert, *Watchwords*, 134; Hooker, *St. Mark*, 327.

7. See the first outline in Appendix 4 for a sample of how Mark organizes his gospel by sub-genre. For support, see Hultgren, *Jesus and His Adversaries*, 181; Koch, *Wundererzählungen*, 30.

of their parallel relationship centers upon suffering and passion (6:14–29; 9:11–13). A description of the fivefold ministry of Jesus (disciple making, deliverance, teaching, healing, and prayer) holds together Jesus' first ministry campaign in 1:16–39, which becomes paradigmatic for the ministry of the church. The teaching about family in 3:13–35 consists of an intercalation (3:20–34) framed by calls to discipleship (3:13–19; 3:35) constructed into a fivefold chiastic discourse. Mark employs this structure to explain that established religious leadership (3:22–30) and flesh and blood (3:20–21, 31–34) do not create spiritual family, but only doing God's will, which is later described as discipleship of the cross (3:35 θέλημα; 8:34–35 θέλει; θέλῃ). In the final frame of Jesus' Galilean ministry Mark narrates a discipleship catechism organized by three cycles of passion prediction (8:31; 9:31; 10:33–34), misunderstanding (8:32–33; 9:32–34; 10:35–41), and teaching on discipleship (8:34—9:30; 9:35—10:32; 10:42–45) framed by two narratives of the healing of the blind men (8:22–26; 10:46–52). The discipleship catechism becomes the second touch which the disciples must receive in order that, like Bartimaeus, they can see clearly to end their journey following along the way to the cross (10:52).

Then in the Jerusalem ministry the frame of messianic psalms (Ps 118:22–23 in Mark 11:10–11; Ps 110:1 in Mark 12:36) demonstrates that the expected Messiah will arrive at Jerusalem to suffer and be glorified. A triad of prophetic actions (royal entry into Jerusalem, the temple action, and the cursing of the fig tree) each occurring on a separate day (11:1, 12, 20) introduces this section, followed by five controversy dialogues which are the counterpart to 2:1—3:6. These five conflicts centering upon the big issues of the day begin with Jesus walking in the temple (11:27) and conclude with Jesus leaving the temple (13:1). Finally, the passion narrative is framed by women intending to bury the body of Jesus (14:1–11; 15:40—16:1), proving that Jesus' suffering and death was prearranged by God. Mark employs the fourfold temporal expectation of the glorified Christ in 13:35 (evening in 14:12–31, midnight in 14:32–52, crowing of the rooster in 14:53–72, dawn in 15:1–20) and the threefold description of the hours on Friday (15:25, 33, 34) to construct a five-part passion narrative, which becomes Jesus' final ministry campaign parallel to the first fivefold ministry campaign in 1:16–39. Thus every section of Mark displays a triadic or fivefold structure surrounded by a frame.

Before we describe these Markan frameworks in depth, it is important to lay down some criteria for recognizing chiastic structures.[8]

---

8. This is an important groundwork procedure because as Craig Blomberg reports, "Today, parts of almost every book in Scripture have been outlined chiastically, with many of the proposals straining all bounds of credulity" ("Structure of 2 Corinthians 1–7," 4–5). The eight guidelines for discerning a chiasm are taken from the nine criteria of Blomberg, 5–7; Stanley Porter's evaluation in "Philippians as a Macro-Chiasm," 219–20; the eight criteria for macro-chiasms in Wayne Brouwer, *Literary Development of John 13–17*, chapter 7; the five criteria of D. J. Clark, "Criteria for Identifying Chiasm," 63–72; the seven laws for interpretation by Nils Lund, *Chiasmus in the New Testament*, 40–41; and John Breck's summary into four criteria in *Shape of Biblical Language*, 335–40, as well as

1. There must be a problem with the structure of the text that conventional outlines fail to resolve.[9]

2. Clear examples of multiple sets of parallelism must exist.[10]

3. Verbal and grammatical repetitions must be widespread, central to the passage, and unique to the passage.[11]

4. The chiastic outline should follow the natural breaks of content in the text as evidenced by the majority of commentators.[12]

5. The centre or climax of the chiasmus should be recognizably significant for its theological or ethical import.

6. Balanced elements are normally of similar length.

7. Rather than rearranging the text, interpreters should use the text as it stands so that the symmetrical elements are in precisely inverted order.

8. A chiasm should begin and end at natural textual boundaries.

We will employ these criteria to discern the presence of a chiasm as we examine the literary structure of the Gospel of Mark.[13] In each section below we will then discover Mark's outline of material between the frames and display how the frame offers a theological interpretation of this material.

Ian Thomson's tightening of Lund's criteria and the addition of three requirements in *Chiasmus in the Pauline Letters*, 27–29.

9. This is the number one criteria in Blomberg's analysis ("Structure of 2 Corinthians 1–7," 5) as well as in Brouwer (*Literary Development of John 13–17*, 95).

10. Dewey says, "the more congruent symmetries a passage contains, the surer one is that the pattern is one which exists in the text rather than one imposed by the interpreter" (*Markan Public Debate*, 231).

11. Regarding repetitions, Clark concludes, "Rarer words are more significant than commoner words. Identical forms are more significant than similar forms. The same word class is more significant than different word classes formed from the same root. Identical roots are more significant than suppletive roots" ("Criteria for Identifying Chiasm," 69).

12. In light of the fact that the purpose of chiasms is the remembrance of oral traditions, van Iersel contends that "a relatively simple concentric structure takes priority over an intricate one" ("Concentric Structures," 528).

13. Thomson offers the following definition of a chiasm, "chiasmus may be said to be present in a passage if the text exhibits bilateral symmetry of four or more elements about a central axis, which may itself lie between two elements, or be a unique central element, the symmetry consisting of any combination of verbal, grammatical or syntactical elements, or, indeed, of ideas and concepts in a given pattern" (*Chiasmus in Pauline Letters*, 25–26).

3.2 The Structure of Mark 1:1–15: "The Beginning of the Gospel"

Although some scholars contend that Mark 1:1 is a title for the entire gospel,[14] "the beginning of the gospel" must designate the preparation for the preaching of the good news of the kingdom, which is Jesus' ministry. Since 1:1 is intricately attached to the quote from the Old Testament in 1:2–3 and similar introductions occur in extrabiblical literature, the gospel as a whole is not in the author's mind.[15] John's identity, preaching, and baptism point to the coming of the Christ as the beginning of the good news. By analyzing various outlines of this section we will show how Mark preludes the theme of Jesus' passion by linking John and Jesus closely together from the beginning of his gospel.

Scholars disagree as to the extent of the "beginning of the gospel." Dewey limits the introductory section to 1:1–8. She thinks that 1:9 ("Jesus came from Nazareth in Galilee") and 1:14 ("Jesus went into Galilee") mark off the next section with an inclusio.[16] She proposes a fivefold chiastic structure for 1:1–8:

a		1:1	The beginning of the gospel of Jesus
	b	1:2–3	An OT citation about John the Baptizer (Exod 23:20; Mal 3:1; Isa 40:3)
		c	1:4–5	John's baptism of repentance for forgiveness of sins
	b'	1:6	An OT allusion about John the Baptizer (2 Kgs 1:8)
a'		1:7–8	John's preaching concerning Jesus' coming

But if the "beginning of the gospel" in 1:1 does not pertain to Mark's entire work, the "end of the beginning" would most likely refer to Jesus' proclamation of the good news which is narrated in 1:14–15. Significantly, a frame employing the term "gospel" is clearly distinguishable in 1:1 and 1:14–15. Rather than narrating the ministries of John and Jesus separately, they are intricately tied together in the kerygma. Jesus cannot proclaim the good news until John is placed in prison (1:14). John's message concerns the future, so that "after me comes the one more powerful" (1:7), and must relate to Jesus' declaration that "the time has come" (1:15a). John stays in the wilderness to prepare for the retaking of the land, but Jesus transfers his geographical realm to the Promised Land since "the kingdom of God has come near" (1:15b). John proclaims a message of judgment, which lays a foundation for Jesus' preaching, that centers on "believing the good news" (1:16c). Therefore Dewey's hypothesis of a fivefold chiastic structure for 1:1–8 must be altered since this section is incomplete without the coming of Jesus.[17]

---

14. For scholarly support see Guelich, *Mark 1—8:26*, 7.
15. See Guelich (ibid.) who compares similar openings in extrabiblical literature.
16. Dewey, *Markan Public Debate*, 144–45.
17. See the arguments in Guelich, *Mark 1—8:26*, 4.

The Theological Intentions of Mark's Literary Devices

If a geographical outline were prominent in Mark's mind,[18] then the switch to Galilee in 1:14 would set apart 1:1–13 as the beginning of the gospel.[19] But literary devices such as a frame rather than geography provide the structural markers for Mark. The repetition of the term εὐαγγέλιον indicates an inclusio in 1:1, 15, and the reference to a messenger or angel (ἄγγελος) in 1:2, 13, as well as the use of κηρύσσων and repentance (μετανοίας; μετανοεῖτε) to link the preaching of John and Jesus together in 1:4, 14–15, demonstrate the presence of a Markan frame. Furthermore, the characters in this section make only temporary appearances, like Satan in 1:12–13 and John the Baptizer, who later appears again only in brief reminiscences (9:3; 11:30) and a flashback (6:14–29). On the other hand, the important figures like the disciples, the crowd, and the Jewish leadership only enter the cast of characters in 1:16.[20] Since on several occasions Mark begins a new section with a special task for the disciples (3:13–19; 6:6b–12; 8:27–30; 15:40–41), 1:16–20 marks a new section. Therefore, the presence of a frame in 1:1, 14–15 signals that the first fifteen verses belong together.[21]

After establishing the frame of Mark 1:1, 14–15 we must still determine the structure of the contents within the frame. To coordinate the figures of the forerunner and the "one more powerful," Guelich proposes a triadic step parallelism synchronizing the identity (1:2–3, 11), mission (1:4–6, 12–13), and message (1:7–8, 14–15) of John and Jesus.

1. Call: an identifying word from God for John and Jesus (1:2b–3, 11).

Call	John	1:2b–3	A voice in the wilderness (Exod 23:20; Mal 3:1; Isa 40:3)
	Jesus	1:11	My beloved Son in whom I am well pleased (Ps 2:7; Isa 42:1)

2. Mission: the person and work of John and Jesus (1:4–6, 12–13).

Person	John	1:6	Dressed in camel's hair like Elijah the prophet (2 Kgs 1:8); eating locust and wild honey just as Elijah was fed by the ravens
	Jesus	1:11	Son of God (Ps 2:7) and the Suffering Servant (Isa 42:1)
Work	John	1:4	Preaching a baptism of repentance for the forgiveness of sins
	Jesus	1:12–13	Empowered by the Spirit to endure the wilderness

---

18. For a geographical outline of Mark with critique see Appendix 4, outline 5.

19. Wegener argues for literary reasons that the story of Jesus' activities begins after 1:13 whereas before this verse he does "not act on his own but is a passive subject" (*Cruciformed*, 95). Similarly, the characters in the rest of the story are not aware of the events in the prologue. Taylor (*Mark*, 165) argues for grammatical reasons that Mark's μετὰ δὲ construction suggests a certain discontinuity with what has gone before instead of the paratactic καὶ of verses 9–13 and 15–23. With regard to content, the absence of the motif of the Spirit in 1:14–15 could favor a division at the end of 1:13.

20. Marcus, *Mark 1–8*, 138.

21. However, 1:14–15 is transitional in nature and can be tied to the preceding or following sections since preaching is also one of the important dimensions of Jesus' ministry summarized in 1:16–39 as we will see in the next section.

3. Message: the preaching of John and Jesus (1:7–8, 14–15).

| Message | John | 1:7 | The mightier one is coming with the Holy Spirit; |
| | Jesus | 1:14–15 | The eschatological time; the kingdom of God; the gospel |

Since Mark closely ties the ministries of John and Jesus together and regularly employs triadic structures,[22] Guelich's emphasis is attractive. However, upon closer analysis the accent upon John's person and clothing in 1:6 is not paralleled in Jesus' ministry, and Jesus' time of testing in the wilderness does not coordinate with the work of John the Baptist.[23]

As an alternative outline, Michaels transforms a triadic structure into a chiasm.[24]

a		1:1	The gospel of Jesus Christ
	b	1:2–4	The Baptist in the desert in fulfillment of Scripture
		c	1:5–8	John baptizing in the Jordan
		c'	1:9–11	Jesus baptized in the Jordan.
	b'	1:12–13	Jesus driven into the desert to fulfill Scripture
a'		1:14–15	The gospel of God

Thus John in the desert parallels Jesus in the wilderness (b and b'), and John's baptizing ministry climaxes in Jesus' baptism (c and c'). These parallels of vocabulary, content, and fulfillment support this proposal. However, Dewey demonstrates that with chiasms "there is often a change in the trend of the argument in the center, and an opposite idea is introduced, before the original trend is resumed."[25] This feature is not evident in Michaels' chiasm. Furthermore, we will demonstrate in the rest of this chapter that Mark regularly employs a fivefold chiasm.

Therefore the outline of Stenger is preferable since it captures the multiple ties between the ministries of John and Jesus but also demonstrates the switch toward fulfillment at the middle of the chiasm with John pointing ahead as a prophet (1:6) to the mightier one who will baptize with the Holy Spirit (1:7–8).[26] At the middle of the chiasm the superior identity (1:7) and more important eschatological work of the coming one (1:8) is maintained. John compares himself to a slave lacing his master's sandals whereas Jesus is the more powerful one who will baptize with the promised Holy Spirit and not just water.

---

22. Cf. Neirynck, *Duality in Mark*, 110–12.

23. Furthermore, in the middle section the work of John (1:4) is placed before his identity (1:6) while Jesus' identity (1:11) is narrated before his work (1:12).

24. Michaels, *Servant and Son*, 44.

25. Dewey, *Markan Public Debate*, 36. Lund names this "the law of the shift at the centre" (*Chiasmus in the NT*, 40–41).

26. Stenger, "Struktur der Markusevangeliums," 51. Although we have not found any of Stenger's other chiasms convincing (except where he agrees with Dewey on 2:1—3:6), this example is supported by Markan vocabulary, themes, and literary patterns.

Frame	1:1	The gospel of Jesus Christ
a	1:2-4	John in the wilderness
b	1:5	The baptism of the people by John
c	1:6-8	John refers to the mightier coming one who will baptize with the Spirit.
b'	1:9-11	The baptism of Jesus by John
a'	1:12-3	Jesus in the wilderness
Frame	1:14-15	The gospel of God

Since 1:1-15 is not composed of material from the same genre, it probably was not grouped together in the oral tradition. Instead Mark himself creates a fivefold chiastic structure surrounded by a frame.[27] What is Mark's purpose for this frame around this section entitled "the beginning of the gospel?" The title Ἀρχὴ τοῦ εὐαγγελίου suggests either the starting point of the gospel or else the "elementary principles" or "rudimentary elements" exhibited in the gospel.[28] Either way Mark is proposing that John the Baptizer as a precursor and forerunner of Jesus is intimately connected with the gospel. The chiastic structure bonds together the wilderness experiences of John and Jesus (a and a') as well as the baptism by John and Jesus' baptism (b and b').

This comparison becomes a model for future resemblances between John and Jesus when death (9:12-13) and resurrection (6:14, 16) become the central subject matter of Mark. The link between the beginning of Jesus' ministry and John's confinement in prison (1:14) prepares for the fact that both are delivered (παραδίδωμι 1:14; 9:31; 10:33) to the authorities and die a martyr's death.[29] In his life and death John exemplifies and prepares for the ministry and death of Jesus. Thus the frame of the gospel around John and Jesus entitled "the beginning" creates in the reader an expectation of more connections between these two figures. They not only begin the gospel but also exemplify its conclusion in suffering and death according to God's plan in the Scriptures (1:2; 9:11-13). Therefore already in the very first pericope Mark foreshadows the theme of the passion. The purpose of the frame matches Mark's purpose for the entire gospel.

3.3 The Paradigmatic Ministry of Jesus in Mark 1:16(14)-39

Scholars widely diverge over the extent of this section in Mark, with suggestions of 1:14—3:6 as the initial phase of the Galilean ministry,[30] 1:21—3:35 as Jesus' assault

---

27. Marcus concludes that "it is hard to imagine this section existing by itself as a separate collection" (*Mark 1-8*, 138).

28. Cf. Wikgren, "ΑΡΧΗ ΤΟΥ ΕΥΑΓΓΕΛΙΟΥ," 16-19 and Guelich, *Mark 1—8:26*, 8.

29. For evidence that John is a foil for Jesus see sections 2.4 and 4.6a.

30. Lane, *Mark*, 62 with 1:14-15 and 3:7-12 each beginning with a summary statement of the ministry of Jesus indicating a new section. Hooker (*St. Mark*, 52) and Schweizer (*Mark*, 44ff) call

on the Jewish social order in Capernaum,[31] 1:21—3:6 as a double pyramid chiasm,[32] 1:14–45 as a seven episode chiastic sequence,[33] and 1:21–39 as Jesus' day of powerful work in Capernaum.[34] Immediately any connection with the controversy dialogues of 2:1—3:6 should be eliminated because of the strikingly different tone that occurs when the suspicious opponents enter the scene.[35] Instead Jesus' powerful ministry as witnessed by his disciples as well as friends and admirers becomes front and center in Mark 1. In fact, the various dimensions of Jesus' ministry are placed into the chronological sequence of a ministry campaign. These include five narrative descriptions of Jesus' ministry in Galilee:

1. Jesus' calling of disciples (1:16–20)
2. Jesus' authoritative teaching ministry (1:21–22)
3. Jesus' deliverance ministry of victory over demons (1:23–28)
4. Jesus' extraordinary healing ministry (1:29–34)[36]
5. Jesus' regular withdrawal for prayer (1:35–38)

On each side of this successful ministry campaign, a summary frame describes Jesus preaching in Galilee. We encounter parallel vocabulary around the words "preaching the gospel in Galilee": εἰς τὴν Γαλιλαίαν κηρύσσων τὸ εὐαγγέλιον τοῦ θεοῦ (1:14) and κηρύσσων εἰς τὰς συναγωγὰς αὐτῶν εἰς ὅλην τὴν Γαλιλαίαν (1:39). Each functions as a summary statement, with a description of the newness of Jesus' ministry in 1:15 (the message of the gospel and the coming of the kingdom) paralleling a summation of Jesus' word and deed ministry in 1:39 (preaching and driving out demons). Honestly, the similarities are not overwhelming, but once an alert reader of Mark discovers his technique of framing narratives, this connection of 1:14 and 1:39 surfaces as another example. Above we argued that 1:14–15 is a frame for the gospel proclaimed by John and Jesus in 1:2–13, but Mark sometimes employs a passage in a double capacity. For example, the story of the woman who spent a huge amount of

---

attention to the manifestation of the authority of Jesus throughout this section.

31. Myers, *Binding the Strong Man*, 137.

32. Clark ("Criteria," 66–71) fails to notice the change in genre between Mark 1 and 2, the lack of intensification in Mark 1 compared to Mark 2, and the close connection between 1:45 and 3:7–12. Cf. also Dewey, *Markan Public Debate*, 175–79. For a seven-fold chiasm of 1:21—2:12 found in Dideberg and Mourlon Beernaert see Dewey, 172 and her negative critique on 173–75.

33. Van Iersel, *Mark*, 116. He includes 1:40–45 because the leper proclaims what Jesus has done for him after he is healed which parallels Jesus' proclamation of the gospel in 1:14–15. The continuity between 1:45 and 3:7 argues against van Iersel's thesis. See Dewey, "Literary Structure," 142.

34. Pesch, "Ein Tag in Kapharnaum," 114, 272. Cranfield (*St. Mark*, 61) likewise states that "The first complex is 1.21–38, a closely articulated group of four narratives, probably all Petrine in origin, concerned with the ministry of Jesus in and around Capernaum."

35. Cf. Marcus, *Mark 1–8*, 177.

36. Gundry illustrates how "verses 29–31 and 32–34 go together to form a single pericope" (*Mark*, 86).

money to anoint Jesus for his burial serves as a frame for the eschatological discourse through the description of her exuberant giving (14:3–7 with 12:41–44) but also frames the passion narrative through the parallel anointing attempts (14:8–9; 16:1). Mark 1:14–15 serves an identical double function as recognized by several scholars.[37]

Within this frame Mark organizes a fivefold description of Jesus' ministry. However, no evidence is available, either through vocabulary or content, that Mark constructs a chiastic structure.[38] Mark begins with Jesus' practice of disciple making since he will create cycles of material throughout his gospel where the disciples begin with a fervent commitment to the cause of Jesus only to surrender their vital faith when confronted by opposition and rejection.[39] Next, the authority of Jesus stands prominent both in his teaching (1:22) and deliverance ministry (1:27). First the reader marvels that the new characters introduced into the narrative follow Jesus without question, leaving their occupations (1:16–18) as well as their family (1:19–20). Then the reader is overwhelmed by Jesus' authority over the powerful spiritual forces of evil (1:27b) in comparison to the best Jewish leaders (1:22). After an emphasis upon the supreme authority of Jesus in the first three pericopes, Mark highlights the extent of Jesus' popularity in the last two sections. Because of his healing ministry the entire city "brought all the sick and demon-possessed" (1:32) so that "the whole town gathered at the door" (1:33). In addition, Jesus' prayer ministry ends with the acknowledgement that "everyone is looking for you" (1:37). As a result in the next section (1:45) "Jesus could no longer enter a town openly but stayed outside in the lonely places." Combined with this emphasis upon the depth and breadth of Jesus' influence, Mark underscores the surprising speed of Jesus' popularity. Throughout the entire section the term "immediately" (εὐθύς) dominates. The quick start of Jesus' fivefold ministry is not only recognized in 1:18, 20, 21, 23, 28, 29, 30 but this emphasis extends to the preceding context (1:10, 12) as well as the narrative about the healing of the leper (1:42, 43). Thus Mark describes the success of Jesus' word-and-deed ministry through his varied fivefold activities, his authoritative impact, his quick and rising popularity, and the depth and breadth of the response of the crowds.

---

37. Marcus suggests that "Perhaps the wisest course is not to be overly dogmatic but to recognize that 1:14–15 functions transitionally both as the end of 1:1–15 and as the beginning of 1:14–45. (*Mark 1–8*, 138). Cf. also Dewey, 'Tapestry,' 225–26"

38. Van Iersel (*Mark*, 116–17) claims that seven episodes form a chiastic structure where the outside stories about preaching the word (Jesus 1:14–15 preaching the gospel; the leper 1:40–45 preaching the word) develop a frame around a five-fold chiasm (a = 1:16–20 call and follow; b = 1:21–28 teach and cast out demons; c = 1:29–31 heal and minister to; b' = 1:32–34 heal and cast out demons; a' = 1:35–39 leave and call back. But the supposed center of the chiasm does not stand out since Jesus' healing ministry is presented alongside the other dimensions of his work. Van Iersel himself labels it "the least important incident," but hints that the ministry of a woman, Peter's mother-in-law, who serves Jesus might give it prominence (1:31 with 15:40–41). Furthermore, a and a' do not balance each other since the former is a call narrative while the later concerns prayer. Van Iersel attempts to contrast these two passages and place them in opposition to each other, but his explanation is neither clear nor convincing.

39. See Appendix 4, outline 12.

The purpose of this section has received various interpretations. Pesch believes that the references to the village of Capernaum (1:21–28); 1:29–34) or its outskirts (1:16–20; 1:35–39) as well as the figure of Peter (1:16, 29, 30, 36) in each of the individual passages encapsulates a "community-founding tradition" which describes the growth and mission of the church in Galilee.[40] Certainly the progression from two sets of disciples (1:16–20) to Jesus' positive reception in the synagogue (1:27) to the news spreading quickly over the whole region of Galilee (1:28) to the entire population of Capernaum gathered around Jesus (1:33) to the mission in surrounding towns (1:38) and the whole region of Galilee (1:39) is noteworthy. The success of Jesus' mission is prominent.

Gundry emphasizes Christology throughout his commentary. "Having introduced Jesus, Mark now portrays him as magnetic, authoritative, powerful, insightful, and dignified, just as one would expect of God's Son and appointed agent."[41] The success and popularity of Jesus is so striking in comparison to the conflict in the rest of the gospel that Marcus insists that Mark's purpose is to create a honeymoon period in Jesus' ministry. But rather than concentrating upon Christology Marcus emphasizes the effect upon the readers. This successful picture of Jesus "contains an important message for Mark's community, whose members perceive themselves to be undergoing a tribulation unparalleled since the world began, hated by all for the sake of Jesus' name, and pushed to the very brink of extinction (13:13, 19–20)."[42] Marcus concludes that "the tableau of healing miracles in chapter 1 thus provides Mark's readers with a vision to hold on to throughout all the terror of the present."[43] Therefore, the portrait of Jesus' successful mission and the authority of his person contain important discipleship implications which cannot be forgotten. Mark has gathered narratives that illustrate the various dimensions of Jesus' successful ministry under the frame of his preaching in Galilee (1:14–15, 39) to call the disciples to imitate and model Jesus' disciple making, teaching, deliverance, healing, and prayer ministry. Therefore, the historical narratives have a paradigmatic and kerygmatic purpose for the discipleship community.[44]

Mark portrays Jesus' successful ministry campaign through a continuous time frame, which is rare outside the passion narrative. After calling his disciples (1:16–20) Jesus and his followers enter the Capernaum synagogue on the Sabbath (1:21). Following Jesus' teaching and mighty deeds, they retire to Simon's house (1:29) and spend the rest of the evening (1:32) conducting a healing service. To finish the Jewish

---

40. Pesch, "Ein Tag in Kapharnaum," 272–74.

41. Gundry, *Mark*, 5.

42. Marcus, *Mark 1–8*, 178.

43. Ibid., 179.

44. Boring explains, "Mark seems to have created this model day as an example of Jesus' work" (*Mark*, 61). Bultmann (*Synoptic Tradition*, 209) and Stein (*Mark*, 85) describe the exorcism in the temple as a "paradigmatic illustration."

day (early morning 1:35), Jesus retreats to a solitary place for prayer, refreshment, and redirection.[45] The extremely fast pace of Jesus' rising popularity in this first ministry campaign stands in stark contrast with Mark's passion narrative, where Jesus' last week is described in days (11:12, 20; 14:1, 12; 15:42) and Jesus' last day is portrayed in hours (15:25, 33, 34). Mark retards the narrative pace in Jesus' passion to decelerate the reader in order to concentrate full attention upon the importance of the Messiah's death. On the other hand, Jesus' first ministry campaign is dominated by the word "immediately" to contrast this first day of calling followers, teaching with unsurpassed authority, exorcising demons, healing crowds of invalids, and experiencing intimate prayer in the presence of God with Jesus' last day. Both Jesus' initial ministry campaign and his passion are placed in an uninterrupted time sequence. Both are tied with the two most important geographical areas, namely Galilee and Jerusalem, through a series of comparisons and contrasts.[46] Both are composed of five sections (without a chiasm) surrounded by a frame.

Therefore, the success of Jesus' fivefold ministry in 1:16–39 points to the success of his passion ministry. In Mark's theology Jesus' successful earthly ministry cannot stand alone just as Jesus' victory, vindication, and resurrection is never far away from a description of his suffering and death.[47] Jesus' initial popularity and ultimate rejection fit together so that just as Mark structures the book into discipleship episodes beginning successfully but ending with rejection, he begins with Jesus' successful preaching campaign but later ties it closely with the passion narrative. Therefore, the themes of Jesus' passion and the resulting discipleship of the cross should never be separated from the successfully popular ministry of Jesus in 1:16–39.

3.4 The Frame around the Controversy Dialogues in Mark 1:40—3:12

In this section we will argue for a fivefold chiasm consisting of controversy dialogues (2:1—3:6) surrounded by a frame (1:40–45; 3:7–12) whose theme is the Messianic Secret, so that Mark' purpose is to demonstrate that the identity of Christ and the presence of the kingdom is revealed only in the midst of controversy.

---

45. Sergeant entitles the time a "specimen day" (*Lion Let Loose*, 43).

46. See the diagram by van Iersel, *Mark*, 78.

47. The resurrection follows the cross in the three passion predictions (8:31; 9:31; 10:33–34); the vindication of the stone as head of the corner occurs only after the rejection by the tenants (12:7–12); Jesus appears to the disciples in his transfiguration only after instructions to take up their cross and follow (8:34—9:2); Jesus walks on the water like a ghost in the resurrection appearances only after he breaks the bread in the feeding of the five thousand (6:35–52); the center of the five controversy dialogues in Jerusalem is talk about the resurrection (12:18–27) but this must follow the five controversy dialogues in Galilee whose center is the taking away of Jesus in his death (2:20). Likewise the ties between 1:16–39 and Jesus' death narrative indicate that they need to be read together as an inclusio.

The Literary Device of a Markan Framework

Mark 2:1—3:6 is the first occasion where we confront narratives combined together according to genre. Here five controversy dialogues[48] appear in succession just as later parables, miracle stories, discipleship teaching, and apocalyptic material will be grouped together.

a		2:1–12	Forgiving sins (paralytic healed)—again in Capernaum
	b	2:13–17	Eating with sinners (eating at Levi's house)—again by the sea
		c	2:18–22	Fasting and the new age (the center = Jesus being taken away at 2:20)
	b'	2:23–27	Sabbath eating rituals (picking grain on the Sabbath)
a'		3:1–6	Sabbath healings (withered hand healed)—again in the synagogue

Dewey has supplied the scholarly world with a masterful presentation of the interconnections between these five controversy dialogues, arguing that they "form a single literary unit with a tight and well-worked out concentric or chiastic structure."[49] To sustain Dewey's argumentation of a fivefold chiastic format for these narratives, we will outline her presentation of the symmetrical parallels supported by arguments from the content, form, and language of the text.[50]

A. a (healing of the paralytic 2:1–12) is similar to a' (healing of the withered hand 3:1–6)[51]

1. Both healings focus upon a physical handicap which prevents the use of one or two of the limbs. If the withered hand is a form of paralysis, then both passages deal with the identical disease.

2. A healing story is embedded in a controversy dialogue whose mixed form is relatively uncommon, whereas in the three middle controversies no miracles appear. Each is what Dewey entitles a ring composition with a healing narrative (2:1–5, 10b–12; 3:1, 5b–6) surrounding a controversy dialogue (2:6–10a; 3:2–5a).[52]

---

48. Bultmann prefers the term apophthegms, Dibelius, paradigms, and Taylor, pronouncement sayings. Bultmann's choice of terminology fails to communicate to a contemporary audience although he divides them into controversy dialogues (*Streitgespräche*, 39–53), scholastic dialogues (*Schulgespräche*, 54–55), and biographical apophthegms (55–61). Dibelius's term places too much emphasis upon the preacher's application of the story in a paradigmatic manner. The advantage of the term "pronouncement story" is that it calls attention to the climax in a logion of Jesus rather than the controversy itself. However, we have chosen controversy dialogue because it conveys each element in the genre which normally in the gospel literature includes 1) an introduction of the controversy; 2) a question from an opponent; 3) Jesus' return question creating a dialogue; 4) the memorable proverbial saying of Jesus; and 5) the response or impact upon the audience.

49. Dewey, "Literary Structure," 141.

50. Some prominent supporters of this structure include Albertz, *Streitgespräche*, 5–16; Hultgren, *Jesus and His Adversaries*, 151ff; Rhoads and Michie, *Mark as Story*, 52–53; Stenger, *Struktur der Markusevangeliums*, 43; van Iersel, "Concentric Structures," 529.

51. Taken from Dewey, "Literary Structure," 142–43; *Markan Public Debate*, 111–12. No. 1 emanates from Marcus (*Mark 1–8*, 214) and Van Iersel ("Concentric Structures, 522, n. 5); no. 12 comes from Dewey (*Markan Public Debate*, 126).

52. Dewey, *Markan Public Debate*, 70, 101.

3. Regarding vocabulary, the verb ἐγείρω is employed on three occasions in the healing of the paralytic (2:9, 11, 12) and once in the parallel narrative of the withered hand (3:3).

4. There are identical introductions: καὶ εἰσελθὼν (εἰσῆλθεν) πάλιν εἰς . . .

5. Concerning literary repetitions, in each case Jesus' address to the man being healed is reiterated (2:5, 10; 3:3, 5).

6. Both contain a similar setting indoors (in a home and at the synagogue) while in 2:13 Jesus is outside beside the lake and in 2:23 in the grain fields.

7. The cast of characters includes Jesus, the opponents, and a sick man versus Jesus, the opponents, and the disciples in the other controversy dialogues.

8. Jesus' disciples play a role in the middle three controversies but not in a and a'.

9. Regarding the manner of argumentation, Jesus takes the initiative whereas in the three middle conflicts Jesus or his disciples are questioned about their behavior.

10. Instead of Jesus' opponents openly stating their opposition, Jesus discerns the problem in their heart, which is employed here for the first time in the gospel (2:6, 8; 3:5).

11. In proper rabbinic style, Jesus responds to the unspoken opposition with a counter-question (2:9; 3:4).

12. The reaction of the audience at the beginning and end of the controversy dialogues is purposely antithetical. At 2:12 everyone is amazed and praising God, saying, "We have never seen anything like this," whereas at 3:6 the Pharisees and Herodians plot how to kill Jesus.

B. b (eating with sinners 2:13–17) is similar to b' (plucking grain on the Sabbath 2:23–28)[53]

1. The central sections of each controversy are concerned with eating so that ἐσθίω is employed twice in the present in 2:16 and twice in the aorist in 2:26.

2. In b Jesus and his disciples eat with tax collectors, something unlawful in light of rabbinic ordinances, and in b' David and his followers eat from the temple loaves, which is lawful only for priests.

3. Regarding the setting, both occur out of doors (2:13 lake; 2:23 grain fields).

4. Both conclude with a proverb followed by a christological saying.
    a. 2:17: "It is not the healthy who need a doctor, but the sick," followed by "I have not come to call the righteous, but sinners."

---

53. Taken from Dewey, "Literary Structure," 144–45; and *Markan Public Debate*, 112–14.

b. 2:27–28: "The Sabbath was made for man, not man for the Sabbath" followed by "The Son of Man is lord even of the Sabbath."

C. a (2:1–12) and b (2:13–17) are joined as well as b' (2:23–28) and a' (3:1–6)[54]

1. a and b are joined by the concepts "sin" (2:5, 7, 9, 10) and "sinners" (2:15, 16, 17), employed four times in each pericope.

2. b' and a', which are both concerned with the Sabbath law, are joined with the catchwords "it is lawful" (ἔξεστιν 2:24, 26; 3:4) and "on the Sabbath" (2:23, 24; 3:2, 4).

3. b' states that the Son of Man is lord of the Sabbath (2:28) and a' confirms his lordship by healing on the Sabbath.

4. The adversaries are not mentioned in a', implying that the antecedent of the "they" of παρετήρουν (3:2) refers to the Pharisees of 2:24, indicating a continuity of the narrative.

5. b' refers to David entering the house of God just as a' takes place in a synagogue.

D. c (2:18–22) as the center is the emphasis of the chiasm.[55]

1. Each of the other four stories has an explicit setting, but this is missing in the center section of c to call attention to its general nature.

2. Each of the other four controversies specify the opponents, but here in c they are not named (2:18 "some people") to again call attention to its general nature.

3. In between two sayings concerned about eating, c is concerned with fasting.

4. In the center of this passage the taking away of the bridegroom (2:20) refers to Jesus' crucifixion, which is central to the entire Gospel of Mark.

5. The specific order of this pericope with two double sayings (18–19; 20–21) interspersed with a reference to the removal of the bridegroom (20) places the crucifixion at the center of the chiasm in 2:1—3:6.

6. The additional two sayings (2:21–22) on the incompatibility of the old and the new in the kingdom demonstrate this section's importance by attaching additional logia of Jesus in place of the more normal structural element of response from the audience in a controversy dialogue.

This list of symmetrical parallels more than adequately fulfills the requirements for a fivefold chiasm. Of course, with the wealth of research in biblical studies unanimous agreement no longer occurs. Marcus claims that Dewey goes beyond

---

54. Taken from Dewey, "Literary Structure," 144; and *Markan Public Debate*, 100.
55. Taken from Dewey, "Literary Structure," 145–46; and *Markan Public Debate*, 114–15.

the evidence in contending that the whole section is concentrically arranged, since the narratives "do not correspond to each other either structurally or thematically."[56] For instance, 2:1–12 describes a controversy about sin whereas 3:1–6 concerns the Sabbath. As an alternative Guelich prefers a triadic structure since the three central controversies (2:13–28) all concern the theme of eating, similar to the triad of seed parables in Mark 4. In addition, these three exhibit pure examples of the conflict form as well as a consistent cast of characters (Jesus, opponents, and disciples).[57] Mark 2:1–12, on the other hand, continues the theme of authority in 1:21–28, and 3:1–5 is a healing narrative. We agree that the subject matter of the first and last controversies diverge, but the unique combination of healing narrative with controversy dialogue demonstrates the close structural link between these two passages. In addition, the first two conflicts center on forgiving sin (2:5, 7, 9, 10) and sinners (2:15, 16, 17) whereas the last two involve Sabbath observance.

Dewey herself admits that the two Son of Man sayings (2:10, 28) fail to fit the chiastic pattern since they occur in the first and fourth pericopes. This exegetical detail has caused Kuhn to posit a collection of four controversies in 2:1–28 highlighting Christian practices as opposed to Jewish regulations. Conflicts over Jesus' authority to forgive sins, table fellowship with sinners, the praxis of fasting, and transgressing Sabbath commands are all settled by christological arguments featuring an inclusio Son of Man expression binding together the first and last. Kuhn contends that this collection should not include 3:1–6 since no christological conclusion can be discerned, Jesus' opponents are not identified as in 2:6, 16, 18, 24, and the opponent's challenge is not given in spoken form as in 2:7, 16, 18, 24.[58]

In opposition to Kuhn, the christological argument of 3:1–6 involves not the person of the Messiah but his actions.[59] Embedded within the question of 3:4 are the messianic actions of "to do good" and "to save life," so that each of the five controversy dialogues contains a christological emphasis. With regard to opponents, the reader assumes the opposition of the Pharisees from the previous pericope, culminating in the plot of 3:6 where the Herodians join the Pharisees.[60] Granted, the opposition is not verbal, but the silence of the opponents in 3:2 possesses the significance of a statement, and Jesus' response of heated anger and deep distress at their stubborn hearts stands as the climax to this entire section.[61] Furthermore, the opposition of Christian

---

56. Marcus, *Mark 1–8*, 214.

57. Guelich, *Mark 1—8:26*, 83.

58. Cf. Kuhn, *Ältere Sammlungen*, 18–24, 53–98 with his alternative proposal on pages 74–87, especially 80. Pesch (*Markusevangelium*, 1:149–51), on the other hand, suggests that the four controversies of 2:15—3:6 are tied together, but his weak evidence centers upon the omission of the Pharisees in 2:1–12 and the supposed contradiction between the scribes (2:6) and scribes of the Pharisees (2:16). Kuhn's and Pesch's arguments in effect cancel out each other.

59. Cf. Fuller, *Interpreting the Miracles*, 52–53; Hultgren, *Jesus and His Adversaries*, 152.

60. Hultgren, *Jesus and His Adversaries*, 152. Furthermore, the opponents in 2:18a are unnamed.

61. Bultmann, *Synoptic Tradition*, 390–91.

practices to Jewish regulations, which Kuhn himself identifies as the central theme of this collection, is clearly visible in the concern for healing on the Sabbath day. In fact, in Mark 2:23–28 and 3:1–6 we encounter two consecutive conflicts concerning the Sabbath just as in the L tradition at Luke 13:10–17 and 14:1–6.[62] Finally, the twelve interconnections described above between Mark 2:1–12 and 3:1–6 are overwhelming evidence for their parallel structure within the fivefold chiasm of 2:1—3:6. A book with five sections is a traditional manner of dividing material according to genre, especially in Semitic literature.[63]

In addition to the symmetrical parallelism within the chiastic structure, the similar purpose and overarching theme for all five narratives binds 2:1—3:6 together. We propose to view the purpose for combining these controversy dialogues through three related lens: 1) five signs of the presence of the kingdom of God; 2) five images picturing the king of the kingdom; and 3) five descriptions of the subjects of the kingdom which socially demarcate them from their Jewish heritage.

The kingdom of God stands prominently at the center of Jesus' proclamation in parables, miracles, and eschatology but also here in his controversy dialogues with opponents. Jesus demonstrates that the future becomes present in his ability to forgive sins, welcome the marginalized sinners to the eschatological banquet, image the joy of the future marriage feast, offer eternal rest through his concept of the Sabbath, and restore decrepit bodies to their resurrection likeness. The kingdom function of 2:1—3:6 is evidenced in the pithy mashal-like sayings at the center of the controversy:

1. Forgiveness of sins becomes a present reality (saying in 2:9).

2. The marginalized leftovers are welcomed to table fellowship as a preview of the eschatological feast (saying at 2:17a).

3. The eschatological marriage celebration has begun (saying at 2:19a).

4. The eternal rest of the Sabbath has arrived (saying at 2:27).

5. Bodies are healed as at the resurrection (saying at 3:4a).

---

62. Besides the catchword "Sabbath" (13:10; 14:1), the theme of siding with the needy is identical in each section, and the disease is associated with a ritual action. In Luke 13: 1–17 the woman is untied just as it is permissible to untie an animal on the Sabbath; in 14:1–4 the man is healed of a water disease just as it is permissible to remove an animal from a well on the Sabbath. The two passages were separated by Luke through the stitchword "eighteen" in 13:4 and 13:11.

63. The traditional nature of the five-fold organizational structure is witnessed in the five books of Moses encompassing the law, the five books of Psalms, the five divisions of wisdom literature in Ecclesiastes according to Edersheim (cf. Hawkins, *Horae Synopticae*, 163 ff.), the five volumes of Maccabean history by Jason of Cyrene (2 Mac 2:23), the five sections of apocalyptic witnessed in the Book of Enoch, the five Pereqs of Rabbinic literature which comprises Pirke Aboth (the sixth chapter is not original), the exposition of the sayings of Jesus by Papias divided into five συγγράμματα which Eusebius (*H.E.* 3:39) calls βιβλία, the five books of apologetic by Irenaeus in *Against Heresies*, and the cycle of five miracle stories by Hanina ben Dosa (Ta'anith 24b–25a; cf. Achtemeier, "Origin," 204–5).

Each of these controversies calls attention to the authority of Jesus in the kingdom as well. They appeal to Jesus' authority as Son of Man (2:10, 28), physician (2:17b), the bridegroom (2:20), and then to the actions of the Messiah "to do good" and "to save life" (3:4). Since this christological function climaxes each narrative, Taylor labels these controversies "pronouncement sayings." The episode exists for the saying and not visa versa. This christological logion climaxing each controversy dialogue holds the fivefold chiasm together.

Each controversy in 2:1—3:6 describes as well the subjects of the kingdom by highlighting the practices that socially demarcated Christians from their Jewish forebears.[64] In Mark 2:1–12 the Christian community proclaims that forgiveness is available now through Jesus instead of the Jewish expectation of a future salvation. Through the pronouncement saying of 2:13–17 Jesus' followers welcome the marginalized and leftovers of society rather than viewing them as impure sinners excluded from the covenant community. Mark 2:18–22 calls the Christian church to create new wineskins to express the joy of the new age, which entails transposing various OT customs. Furthermore, Jesus' lordship over the Sabbath and the resulting human benefits (2:27–28) replace a legalistic maintenance of Sabbath regulations. Finally, in 3:1–5 the Christian community becomes the group that "does good and saves life," whereas the Jewish community becomes renowned for its defense of their crucifixion of Jesus (3:6). The fact that these three purposes are noticeable throughout 2:1—3:6 demonstrates that all five of these controversies belong together as a group.

Third, these five controversies stand apart from the surrounding context. Mark 3:7 continues exactly where 1:45 left off so that there is a seamless flow of material without the controversy dialogues.[65] At the end of chapter 1 the news of Jesus' extraordinary ministry has spread so quickly that he is not able to enter into crowded towns, but the people flock to him in deserted places. Therefore in 3:7 Jesus withdraws to the lake and crowds from everywhere stream to experience his presence. The controversies of 2:1—3:6 interrupt this narrative so that Jesus is active again in a town (2:1). Full of wit, Dewey muses, "According to the gospel of Mark, the first thing Jesus does after not being able openly to enter a city is to enter a city."[66] This rough interruption indicates that these five controversy dialogues belong together as a separate source which Mark employs.

A fourth set of evidence draws attention to the intensification of the conflict which gradually builds throughout this section.[67] This "linear development of hostility"[68] increases from silent criticism (2:8) to the questioning of Jesus' disciples

---

64. As Theissen affirms, "in the synoptic apophthegms one group affirms its own convictions and behavior by differentiating itself from other surrounding groups" (*Gospels in Context*, 116).

65. Cf. Boring, *Mark*, 96 and Nineham, *St. Mark*, 89.

66. Dewey, *Markan Public Debate*, 67.

67. For a description of the intensification see Cook, *Mark's Treatment*, 32–33, n. 20.

68. Dewey, "Literary Structure," 146.

(2:16) to the interrogation of Jesus himself (2:18) to the condemnation of his disciples' actions (2:24) to watching closely to accuse Jesus himself of some fault (3:2) culminating in a plot of destruction (3:6). Such heated opposition suggests that Jesus will lose the debates and suffer certain elimination. However, as we shall demonstrate later in this chapter, Mark's gospel contains a second series of five controversy dialogues (11:27—12:40) taken from the oral tradition, which exactly reverses this intensification so that in the end Jesus wins the arguments by silencing his critics and receiving the admiration of the crowd.[69]

This second set of conflicts begins with the chief priests, teachers of the law, and the elders pushing for Jesus' death (11:18) just as the first series of controversies concludes with the Pharisees and Herodians planning Jesus' destruction (3:6). This connection with Jesus' death fastens these two sets of controversies together as well as a reference to the unusual connection between Pharisees and Herodians in each set (3:6; 12:13). The Jewish leaders question Jesus' authority with two direct hostile questions (11:28), "By what authority are you doing these things?" and "who gave you this authority to do these things?"[70] The "these things" are not specified and could refer to Jesus' triumphal entry and temple action in 11:1–19[71] or else originally to Jesus' Sabbath actions in 2:28—3:5, if these two sets of five controversies were contiguous in Mark's source. The gradual decrease in hostility is evident in the list of complements that Jesus' contemporaries bestow on him. In the first controversy with the entire Sanhedrin, Jesus' opponents are forced to admit, "We don't know" (11:33). In the second dialogue the Pharisees and Herodians admit that Jesus is a man of integrity who is not swayed by public opinion but teaches the way of God truthfully (12:14). In the third argument where the antagonists are reduced to one group, the Sadducees (12:18), Jesus verifies their inability to understand both the Scriptures and the power of God (12:24). Then in 12:28–34 where the opposition shrinks to only one person, the teacher of the law complements Jesus and in turn is found to be not far from the kingdom of God (12:28, 32, 34). In the end no one dares pose any additional questions (12:35) so that Jesus himself takes the offensive and raises the issue of the Messiah's relationship to David, which none of his opponents has the courage to answer. In contrast to the first set of controversy dialogues, where the Jewish leaders have the upper hand, here the delighted audience sides with Jesus (12:37b). Instead of a plot for Jesus' destruction (3:6), the passage concludes with a judgment upon the Jewish leaders, who receive a greater condemnation (12:40).

---

69. See section 3.9 below where we show how Mark both uses this oral tradition and supplants it with a three-fold structure.

70. Usually we follow the NIV, but by translating the second question, "And who gave you authority to do this?" the NIV and TNIV imply that a single action of Jesus is in mind whereas in the Greek, "these things" is repeated in each question.

71. See Taylor (*Mark*, 469–70) for a discussion of these possibilities.

This linear development of growing hostility toward Jesus in the first set of controversies followed by the reverse phenomenon in the second set argues for their close connection in the oral tradition. If the fivefold chiastic structure was employed as a mnemonic device for remembering oral tradition,[72] then Mark separated these two series of conflicts, placing one in Galilee at the beginning of Jesus' ministry and one in Jerusalem, where Jesus trumps the Jewish leaders and replaces them as the community authority. But the theological link between the centers of each chiasm demonstrates their close connection. Whereas Jesus' death is placed at the center of the five controversies (2:20) dealing with signs of the kingdom in 2:1—3:6, in 11:27—12:40, when Jesus addresses the most important issues in contemporary Judaism, resurrection rather than death stands at the midpoint.[73] These epicenters of death/resurrection not only facilitate easy memorization but also prepare the controversy dialogues for use in the kerygma. These two chiastic series of controversy dialogues enable the gospel of Jesus' death and resurrection to be proclaimed even apart from a passion and resurrection narrative.[74] Later in this chapter we will see how this theme of death/resurrection or suffering/vindication also structures the parables, miracles, and eschatological discourse. Each of these oral collections of genre proclaims the gospel.

So what has caused some scholars to assign this collection of controversy dialogues to Mark's hand?[75] In arguing for Markan composition, Dewey calls attention to the matching emphases in theology: "Healing and eating play a prominent role in Mark's presentation of Jesus' proclamation" throughout the gospel as well as in 2:13–28.[76] In particular, the shadow of the cross already darkens the narrative at 2:20 and 3:6. This coincides with Kähler's famous description of the Gospel of Mark as a passion narrative with an extended introduction and Perrin's contention that every major Markan section concludes on a note pointing ahead to the passion.[77] However, the enemies in 3:6 (Pharisees and Herodians) are not the same group who put Jesus to death, but instead they are silenced in the parallel controversy at 12:13.[78] Fur-

---

72. Cf. Thomson, *Chiasmus in the Pauline Letters*, 34–35; Lohr, "Oral Techniques," 425; Best, *Mark: Gospel as Story*, 106; Dewey, *Markan Public Debate*, 35 and 208, n. 155 for scholarly support. Regarding the lack of evidence for chiasms in ancient handbooks of rhetoric, van Iersel responds, "I suggest that the very absence of such a discussion might be seen precisely as an indication that chiasm was not regarded primarily as a literary device" (but an oral technique) ("Concentric," 527, n. 15).

73. In the chiastic structure a = John the Baptizer's identity; b = the greatest commitment; c = discussion about resurrection; b' = the greatest commandment; a' = the Son of David's identity. For arguments see 3.9 below.

74. Hultgren, *Jesus and His Adversaries*, 177.

75. For scholarly support for a Markan source or Markan composition see Hultgren, *Jesus and His Adversaries*, 166–67, notes 1–2 respectively.

76. Dewey, *Markan Public Debate*, 188.

77. Kähler, *So-called Historical Jesus*, 80, n. 11. Perrin (*Introduction*, 148) refers to 3:6; 6:6; 8:21; 10:45; and 12:44.

78. Hultgren, *Jesus and His Adversaries*, 153 and 167, n. 11 for Kuhn's arguments for Markan redaction and Hultgren's response.

thermore, the similar statements plotting Jesus' death in 11:18; 12:12; 14:1 all employ the verb ζητέω, whereas 2:20 evidences the sole usage of ἀπαίρω in Mark's gospel.[79] Finally, the reader would expect Mark's emphasis upon the misunderstanding of the disciples to surface if Jesus' death is discussed, but this nowhere occurs in either 2:1—3:6 or 11:27—12:40.[80]

Some authors contend that the consistency of vocabulary and style between 2:1—3:6 and the rest of the gospel point to a Markan composition. Dewey suggests that the Sanhedrin trial recalls the healing of the paralytic in 2:1-12 with its charge of blasphemy (2:7; 14:64), and the repetition of vocabulary between Pilate's trial and 3:1-6 suggests a similar hand.[81] However, Albertz points out that the references to an earthly Son of Man in 2:10, 28 completely diverge from Mark's normal usage of passion or eschatological Son of Man sayings.[82] Dunn contends that the connection of material is pre-Markan by showing that "evidence of Markan editorial work on the connecting-links between the narratives is lacking," but Stein offers evidence that the seams (2:1-2, 13, 15, 18, 23) contain Markan vocabulary.[83] The best solution to this dilemma concludes that although Mark found this series of controversies in the oral tradition, he employed his own terminology to inscribe them into their final form. The tight and well-worked out concentric structure, the intrusion into the context of 1:45 and 3:7, and the linear development continuing into chapters 11-12 argue that Mark employed oral tradition within the constraints of his own vocabulary.[84]

Having established a fivefold chiastic structure extending from 2:1 through 3:6, we now want to ask how and why Mark places a framework around this pre-existent structure. Mark 1:40-45 and 3:7-12 act like a box of puzzle pieces that must be put

---

79. However, Dewey (*Markan Public Debate*, 46-47) does point out that both 3:6 and 11:18 employ the verb ἀπόλλυμι. Albertz (*Streitgespräche*, 5) argues for source material since a reference to Jesus' death at 2:20 results in Jesus' first passion prediction (8:31-32) becoming anti-climactic.

80. The misunderstanding and opposition from Jesus' family and disciples is evident in 3:20-21; 6:4; 4:13, 40; 6:52; 8:17-21; and the misunderstandings in the catechism discipleship of 8:27—10:52 where Mark's hand is clearly visible.

81. Dewey, *Markan Public Debate*, 189 (συμβούλιον, κατηγορέω 3:6, 2; 15:1, 3, 4; do evil 3:4 κακοποιῆσαι and 15:14 ἐποίησεν κακόν).

82. Albertz, *Streitsprache*, 5. But there could be a progression in Mark from earthly Son of Man sayings (Mark 2-3) to suffering Son of Man sayings (8:31ff), to eschatological Son of Man sayings (13:26; 14:62) as Gundry (*Mark*, 106) proposes.

83. Dunn, "Mark 2:1—3:6," 398 and Stein, *Mark*, 67-68, 112.

84. Dewey, 42 admits that "scholars, almost without exception, have believed that Mark drew upon an earlier written collection of conflict stories for this portion of the work." However, limited Markan redaction can be seen in the following: 1) the temporal references to "again" in 2:1,13; 3:1; 2) the call of Levi in 2:14 which is not a controversy dialogue but a call narrative (but see the perceptive comments of Knox, *Sources*, 1:13 and Gundry, *Mark*, 107); 3) 2:21-22 in place of the response of the audience as in 2:12; 3:6; 12:17b, 34b, 37b; and 4) 2:26-27 with the addition of an OT proof text, although this is a normal part of Jesus answering a question with another question (2:8b, 19a; 27; 3:4; 10:3; 11:29-30; 12:16, 24; added in Matt 22:42; Luke 10:26 vs. Mark 12:28-34), and a proof from Scripture can be found in the controversy dialogues in Mark 7:1-8; 10:2-9; 12:18-27; Matt 22:34-40; 22:41-46. Cf. Albertz, *Streitgespräche*, 9-14; Dewey, 45, 187; Hultgren, 161.

into place to view a scenic masterpiece. Over a half dozen of puzzle pieces are evident in these passages:[85]

1. A natural narrative flow extends between these two passages where Jesus' avoidance of towns in 1:45 leads to a withdrawal to the lake in 3:7. Mark 2:1 breaks up the flow of the narrative by placing Jesus in the city of Capernaum.

2. Jesus' healing ministry becomes so popular that people come from everywhere (1:45c). In 3:7b-8 Mark employs a series of six prepositional phrases to specify these geographical locations (Galilee, Judea, Jerusalem, Idumea, beyond the Jordan, Tyre and Sidon).

3. Through plot foreshadowing Mark uses 1:44b, describing the potential meeting of the leper with the priestly establishment, to prepare the reader for the nasty encounters with the Jewish leaders in the five controversy dialogues. Likewise, 3:9 introduces a small boat into the narrative, which Jesus will finally employ in 4:1 and 4:36.

4. Both sides of the frame emphasize healings, including the cleansing of a leper (1:40, 42) as well as the healing of many with diseases (3:10a).

5. The healings result from Jesus' touch (1:41; 3:10b). The touching of lepers raised purity issues in Jewish culture, which Mark employs to prepare for the controversies dealing with forgiving sins, close contact with sinners, eating consecrated bread, and Sabbath observance.

6. The frame parallels the healing of a leper with the silencing of unclean spirits (3:11 τὰ πνεύματα τὰ ἀκάθαρτα), indicating that both passages speak about impurity. As Boring states, "In this scene, Jesus does not cast out the unclean spirits, and there are no pictures of people rejoicing in their deliverance from demons."[86] Therefore, the purpose of 3:11–12 is not to demonstrate Jesus' power over the spiritual hosts but to offer another dimension of the Messianic Secret similar to 1:44a. Therefore, both 1:40–45 and 3:7–12 serve a similar purpose for Mark.

7. The most prominent common piece in the frame is the secrecy motif, so that 1:44a ("See that you don't tell this to anyone") parallels 3:12 ("But he gave them strict orders not to tell who he was"). Silence is demanded by Jesus both after miracles and by the demons, who know of Jesus' divine sovereignty. However, several commentators refuse to connect these two instances of silence. Gundry,

---

85. Cf. Dewey, *Markan Public Debate*, 105 and Marcus, *Mark 1–8*, 259. Stein (*Mark*, 159) offers an extensive list of ties between 3:7–12 and the preceding material but opts for an introduction to the following material like van Iersel (*Mark*, 118–19 and "Concentric Structures," 523–24) because of the lack of any hint of the controversies, but this is because 2:1—3:6 has been placed here whereas 1:45 flows seamlessly into 3:7–12. But the introduction of a boat in 3:9 is a Markan insertion that points forward to 4:1, 36 to hold the storyline together, but its reason for inclusion is explained by no. 3 below.

86. Boring, *Mark*, 98.

for instance, interprets the silence after the miracle positively as a call to urgency so that the authentication stands as close as possible to the miracle.[87] The healed leper must not talk to anyone but proceed straight to the priest for verification of the miracle. Gundry contends that this action is simply a part of the miracle story and does not display the hiddenness of the Messiah as is evident in the silencing of the demons. However, when the ex-leper disobeys the command and spreads the news about Jesus (1:45a), doesn't this entail that he has not hurried to Jerusalem? The theme is not urgency but silencing a Christology that promotes Jesus as a miracle worker without acknowledging that the kingdom of God will only arrive in the midst of conflict as in the controversies that will follow.

In all likelihood the secrecy motif in some form emanates from the *Sitz im Leben Jesu*. As Rawlinson contends, "It is probable that our Lord, as a matter of history, did not desire to attract men's attention primarily in the capacity of a wonder-worker, and that both the attempt on His part to secure secrecy, and also the impossibility of doing so, are alike true to the historical situation."[88] Historically, Jesus wanted to avoid publicity as a wonder-worker in order to carry out a discipleship training strategy. But Mark adds a theological dimension to this data.[89] The secrecy theme in Mark's gospel

---

87. Gundry (*Mark*, 97) quotes 2 Kgs 4:29 where in a healing incident Elisha sends Gehazi and instructs him not to greet anyone or to answer a greeting, but here the story involves hurrying to accomplish a healing which is already finished in Mark. Likewise, the similar expression in Mark 16:8 must be interpreted negatively since Mark employs each leader group in the church (Acts 1:13–14, the disciples, Jesus' family, and the women) as a foil for failed discipleship.

88. Rawlinson, *Mark*, 261.

89. Scholarly opinions on the secrecy motif defy simplification. If Mark 1:40–45 is purely a miracle story, the *form-critical view* is attractive since the magical papyri employed commands to silence in order to prohibit the passing on of effective healing formulas (Theissen, *Miracle Stories*, 68–69, 140–45). Then "the demon silenced is part of the defensive language an exorcist used to protect himself against a counterspell by the demon" (Achtemeier, *Mark*, 80). However, as Guelich recognizes, "the strongest argument for the redactional character of this injunction stems from similar injunctions in 5:43 and 7:36 as well as the similarity between 1:44a and 16:8b" (*Mark 1—8:26*, 75). The *ironic view* states that these injunctions to silence function as foils for Mark to highlight the impossibility of hiding Jesus' identity and miracle ministry (Collins, *Mark*, 374; Meier, *Marginal Jew*, 2:701). Some like Wrede have argued for a *christological purpose* to facilitate the transmission of early traditions that were non-messianic into the proclamation of Jesus as the Messiah. The similar *corrective christological approach* argues that the silence corrects a divine man (*theios aner*) Christology (Weeden) or a triumphalistic Son of David or apocalyptic Son of Man Christology (Telford) in the early church. On the same theme of Christology, more conservative scholars posit a *Messianic fulfillment theory* where Jesus like other Jewish messianic figures (Bar-Cochbar) advocated silence about their identity as Messiah until the mission was complete (Longenecker, Flusser, Osbourne) or the *Messianic Transformation view* where Jesus avoided publicity so that he would not be seen mainly as a wonder-worker (Barclay). Although the Messianic Secret as an *apologetic device* to explain the rejection by unbelieving Jews is appealing (Dibelius, Grant, Lightfoot, Boucher, Richardson), this theory offers no explanation why the elect disciples do not comprehend the secret nor a satisfactory justification for the miracle secret. We contend that the secrecy motif is a *theological device* indicating that the full significance of Jesus cannot be realized until his passion. This *theology of the cross interpretation* promotes the pastoral objective to juxtapose a *theologia gloriae* with a *theologia crucis* to encourage disciples to follow not just a miracle-working Messiah but also a Suffering Servant cross-bearer. See Boring, *Mark*, 258, 268,

involves several interconnected motifs but each can be connected with the inevitability of Jesus' passion:[90] 1) the Messianic Secret (8:29–30; 9:9); 2) the secret held by the demons (1:24–25, 34; 3:11–12); 3) the miracle secret (1:44; 5:43; 7:36; 8:26); 4) the secret of the kingdom (4:11–12); 5) the secret of the parables (4:10, 13, 33–34; 7:17–23), which both conceal and reveal depending upon whether one receives the interpretation by joining the instruction at the house church; 6) the secret instruction given to the disciples (8:31–33; 9:2–8, 28–29; 9:30–32; 10:10–12, 32–34; 13:3–37); and 7) the misunderstandings by Jesus' disciples[91] as well as his own family (3:20–35), hometown friends (6:1–6), and the women disciples (16:8).

These secrets begin to be cleared up at the beginning of the discipleship catechism when the narrator reports that Jesus "spoke plainly" (8:32). Suddenly, Peter, who moments before had confessed the truth of Jesus' messianic identity (8:29), now is labeled as Satan (8:33) because he cannot follow a Suffering Servant Messiah (8:31). Jesus' messianic identity must remain a secret (8:30) until Peter no longer acts like the satanic demons.[92] The unclean spirits reveal Jesus' heavenly identity as the "Holy One of God" (1:24) and "Son of God" (3:11) but fail to mention that he must "give his life as a ransom for many" (10:45). Just as the evil spirits must remain quiet since they only speak half-truths about Jesus' identity, so Peter must keep his messianic confession secret and the disciples must not speak about Jesus' glory at the transfiguration (9:9), until finally the centurion freely identifies Jesus as the Son of God after his death

---

270, n. 53.

90. As usual not everyone agrees. Luz ("Messianic Secret," 86–88) divides the miracle secret from the Messianic Secret with the latter (including the demons' silencing and the disciples' misunderstanding) connected only with the person of Jesus. Räisänen (*Messianic Secret*, 73, 242–43) splits the parable theory from the secrecy motif (cf. n. 141 for scholarly support). Trocmé (*Formation*, 124 and n. 1; 164f and n. 3; 168 and n. 2) retreats to a pre-Wrede position where only 8:30 and 9:9 belong together and all other secrecy motifs should be interpreted separately. However, all the aspects of the secrecy motif are connected with passion discipleship: 1) The Messianic secret can only be comprehended when a suffering Son of Man is followed (8:27–34) and the resurrection happens (9:9); 2) Jesus silencing the demons when they refer to him as "Son of God" (3:11–12) and "Holy one of God" (1:24–25) is similar to Peter being silenced and identified with Satan when he entitles Jesus as "Messiah" (8:29–30) but is unable to recognize him as the suffering Son of Man (8:31–33); 3) the secret of the miracles is important only in the first half of the gospel until a Suffering Servant Christology can be introduced; 4) the secret of the kingdom recognizes the need for a crucified Christ and a discipleship of the cross since the new age has arrived in a mysterious way that does not eradicate every trace of the old age; 5) the parables conceal the teaching of Jesus since an interpretation is needed just as the Messianic secret cannot be understood until accepting a new interpretation of the Messiah as a Suffering Servant Son of Man and the miracle secret cannot be revealed until the blind receive a second touch (8:22–26) and follow to the cross like Bartimaeus (10:52); 6) the secret instruction is given when the disciples are by themselves (usually in a house) since the Messianic secret can only be realized when one joins the house church and learns about the crucified Lord; and 7) the disciples' misunderstanding identifies them as outsiders who fail to follow Jesus in a discipleship of the cross.

91. These misunderstandings occur after trips across the sea (4:41; 6:52; 8:14–21), concerning parables as riddles (4:13; 7:18), and concerning a discipleship of the cross (8:32–33; 9:5–6, 9–13, 32, 34, 38; 10:13–14, 32, 35–45).

92. Luz, "Secrecy Motif," 83: "So 8:30 is a complete parallel to 1:34 and 3:11f."

(15:39). Similarly, the secret of the kingdom involves the already-but-not-yet nature of the Messiah's work so that God's rule is not visible to contemporary Israel (or disciples), who expect a conquering king and not a crucified savior.[93] Finally, the secret of the parables demands an interpretation since parables function as riddles that are only revealed to Christian disciples (4:34b) who understand the secret of Jesus' identity. For the secret to be revealed the readers must not imitate the misunderstanding of Jesus' disciples, his family, and the women, but instead embrace a crucified Messiah and a discipleship of the cross. Thus Geddert perceptively explains, "Any secrecy concerning Jesus' identity *per se* is linked inseparably to passion discipleship as the way of the kingdom."[94] The decisive moment in the revelation of the secret is the cross, where the Messianic Secret, miracle secret, and kingdom secret are no longer veiled in the open confession of the centurion. The disciples must accept the cross as the central symbol of the Christian faith or else Jesus' teachings will remain only riddles and the community will continue to misunderstand.

All of this intricate and complex biblical interpretation has been necessary to demonstrate that the purpose of Mark 1:40–45 and 3:7–12 is to frame the controversy dialogues of 2:1—3:6 by supplying a series of identical motifs.[95] Two aspects of the secrecy motif described above, the miracle secret and the secret held by the demons, play a central role in framing the controversy dialogues. Mark introduces the theme of secrecy before the five controversy dialogues to indicate that Jesus' identity as well as the kingdom of God will remain hidden in conflict and controversy. The contemporary messianic expectation of a restored Son of David reigning in a kingdom that conquers every political foe, with Israel experiencing a permanent era of peace and prosperity, did not manifest itself in the life and ministry of Jesus. But Mark's secrecy motif surrounds the five conflicts of 2:1—3:6, where each develops an aspect of the kingdom, a description of king Jesus, and a depiction of kingdom discipleship that demarcates Christians off from their Jewish forebears. Mark's intended theological conclusion is that the kingdom, Christ's authoritative identity, and the nature of discipleship will remain a secret that can only be discovered in the midst of conflict and struggle. Resurrection, vindication, and eschatological victory only come after an experience of crucifixion, humiliation, and temporal suffering in Mark's gospel.

Scholars are agreed that 3:7–12 is an entirely Markan composition.[96] Normally this section is seen as a preview of what is ahead in Mark's narrative,[97] but its func-

---

93. Cf. Ladd, *Theology of the New Testament*, 91–92.

94. Geddert, *Watchwords*, 200. See his sections on "Kingdom Secrecy and Christological Secrecy" and "Kingdom Secrecy and Passion Discipleship" on pages 200–202.

95. See Collins, *Mark*, 182.

96. Cf. Fowler, *Loaves and Fishes*, 187, notes 23 and 28 for scholarly support and evidence.

97. Keck ("Mark 3:7–12 and Mark's Christology," 343–44) accepts our conclusion that 3:7–12 points backwards, but Fowler explains that "This is an unusual claim for Keck to make, since virtually every exegete points to the prospective function of this unit" (*Loaves and Fishes*, 13). See for instance the standard commentary of Taylor (*Mark*, 225) and the list of scholars in Guelich (*Mark 1—6:26*,

tion as a framework with 1:44–45 must be recognized. Distinctive Markan themes are visible likewise in the healing of the leper, including the secrecy motif (1:44a), purity issues which cause conflict between the Jewish and Christian communities (1:41, 43, 44b; touching a leper and the response of the priesthood), and the inability to hide Jesus' miraculous deeds (1:45). In particular, Mark is creating a frame around the controversy dialogues to offer a theological interpretation. Mark employs the literary technique of a framework to indicate that Jesus' messianic identity and healing power over disease and demons must remain hidden in the midst of discord and dissent, as evidenced in the five controversy dialogues between Jesus and the Jewish leadership. Jesus' secret identity as well as the presence of the kingdom are only manifested in conflict. The Christian community can expect nothing different; for them as well the signs of the kingdom and the authority of Jesus will only be manifested in a discipleship of the cross.

3.5 The Frame around the Accusations from Family and Religious Leaders in Mark 3:13–35

Between the first set of controversy dialogues and the seed parables, Mark inserts a short section on membership in Jesus' family. What purpose does this section play in the movement of Mark's gospel? How does the organizational pattern contribute to Mark's theology and thematic development? We will argue that Mark places a frame around an intercalation to compare adequate and inadequate discipleship.

The majority of material in this section we have already discussed last chapter under the literary device of a Markan sandwich. Mark places the accusations and failures of Jesus' own family around the serious charges of the Jewish leaders who journey all the way from Jerusalem (where Jesus will be crucified) in order to confront Jesus face to face. This intercalation becomes a pointed rebuke for the reader, who must recognize that the most intimate insiders to Jesus can in fact become his enemies and join the camp of outsiders who accuse Jesus falsely.

One possible structure forms a chiastic structure of three accusations by Jesus' biological relatives and religious family followed by a triad of refutations.

a	3:20–21	Accusation by family: "He is out of his mind"
b	3:22a	Accusation by the scribes: "He is possessed by Beelzebul."
c	3:22b	Accusation by the scribes: "He casts out demons by their prince."
c'	3:23–27	Refutation of c: Satan does not cast out Satan.
b'	3:28–30	Refutation of b: Jesus possesses the Holy Spirit.
a'	3:31–34(5)	Refutation of a: Jesus and his true family do the will of God.

---

144). Hopefully from now on the framing purpose of this passage will be emphasized along with its connections with 1:44–45.

However, the calling of the apostles (3:13–19) must fit into a discussion of Jesus' family as well. Since Mark regularly employs an intercalation pattern (a, b, a), it is more likely that Mark intended a sandwich with a frame encircling it to form a five-part chiastic structure.

a	3:13–19	Jesus appoints the twelve as his family.	Markan frame
b	3:20–21	The accusation of Jesus' physical family	Markan sandwich
c	3:22–30	The accusations of Jesus' religious family	Markan sandwich
b'	3:31–34	Jesus' physical family stands outside.	Markan sandwich
a'	3:35	Jesus' true family are those who do God's will.	Markan frame[A]

A. Van Iersel ("Concentric Structures," 529) concocts a five-fold chiastic structure from 3:7-12 through 4:1 (a = 3:7-12 preparing a boat; b = 3:13-19 creating the twelve; c = 3:20-30 discussing with the scribes; b' = 3:31-35 creating a new family; a' = 4:1 getting into the boat). Positively, van Iersel recognizes the close connection between 3:13-19 and 3:35. However, he fails to recognize the Markan intercalation by not paralleling 3:20-21 with 3:31-34. In addition, the boat appears again at 4:36 and is incidental to 3:7-12 so that in the next section we will explain how 4:1 introduces the section on parables.

In addition to the normal intercalation of two narratives, Mark employs his framework technique to encapsulate the controversies with his family and the Jewish leaders. Placing the calling of the apostles immediately preceding the two controversies introduces a group of insiders into the narrative. The Twelve function as Jesus' family who remain with him (3:14b) and fulfill God's word and deed ministry (3:14c–15a), so that in 3:35 they are identified as the mother, brothers, and sisters of Jesus. Through this frame Mark indicates that Jesus chooses a spiritual family devoted to God's will over against those one might expect to be intimate colleagues of Jesus, namely his biological family and other religious rabbis.

It must be conceded that the conclusion of the frame in 3:35 is not as obvious as its beginning in 3:13–19 since evidence that 3:35 stands apart from 3:31–34 is not exceedingly strong. But Jesus does appear to offer two answers to the question posed in 3:33. In contrast with his physical family, which is standing outside, Jesus points to those around him and answers, "Here are my mother and my brothers!" The English text regularly concludes the sentence with an exclamation mark to indicate the importance of this statement. Then in 3:35 Jesus states a generalizing conclusion, "Whoever does God's will is my brother and sister and mother." The explanatory γάρ clause in 3:35[98] indicates that Mark is rounding off this pericope with a positive conclusion to parallel the call of the true disciples in 3:13–19.[99] Therefore 3:35 is likely Markan re-

98. In a frequently quoted article on γάρ clauses, Bird explains that "the nuance would best be expressed in English by such an extended sentence as 'And the significant thing about it is'" ("γάρ clauses in Mark's Gospel," 173). The γάρ clause was omitted in Nestle-Aland 25 and is placed in brackets in the following editions, but the overwhelming external evidence (missing in only B (W) 2427 b e bo) as well as the Markan pattern of concluding with a γάρ clause argue for its inclusion in the text.

99. Cf. Crossan, "Mark and the Relatives," 97. Crossan thinks the purpose is to compare Mark 3:35 with later passages about Jesus' relatives like 6:3 and 10:29–30, but a closer parallel would be the introduction to this section at 3:13–19.

daction, as Barton concludes, "So v. 35 appears as an addition, rendering Jesus' specific identification of his true kin applicable to a wider audience including, of course, the readership of Mark's Gospel."[100] Since the fourfold repetition of "mother and brothers" in 3:31–34 is replaced in 3:35 by a divergent pattern, "brother and sister and mother," Mark is attempting to create an image of family similar to the twelve disciples with Jesus in the beginning frame.[101]

In Appendix 4 we argue that Mark's handprint is visible in the structure of the gospel in two distinctive redactions of the material. First Mark places a frame around the stories that were collected together in the oral tradition according to genre. Second, Mark overlays these collections of genre with a series of five discipleship outlines, which begin in each case with a faithful display of extraordinary followership but conclude with conniving plots, rejection, unbelief, and hard-hearted misunderstanding. Mark's two-stage redaction of the material results in the double function that 3:13–19 plays in the narrative. Not only does it begin a frame around material about membership in Jesus' family (3:20–35), but it also supplies an introduction to the second cycle of discipleship (3:13—6:6), which ends with Jesus' own hometown rejecting his ministry, parallel to the Jewish leaders who have already started down this road in 3:6.

Jesus called his disciples in 1:16–20, but now he forms a more intimate band of those twelve people who will be with him (3:14 ἵνα ὦσιν μετ' αὐτοῦ). Previously, the disciples only followed Jesus, but now they enter into his word (preaching 3:14) and deed (driving out demons 3:15) ministry as associates. Significantly, they are now entitled "the Twelve" and sent out as apostles. Typologically this entails that they are the leaders of a new Israel who will carry out God's apostolic mission in the world. Through this description Mark creates a "subtle distinction made between the true Israel recalled by the naming of the twelve, and official Israel represented by the scribes who are carefully described as having come down from Jerusalem."[102] Therefore, Mark's purpose in framing the controversies lies in transforming a negative intercalation of betrayal and accusation into a positive call to remain faithful disciples of Jesus. The danger of insiders becoming outsiders is real, but those who devote themselves to God's will join Jesus' family and become participants in his mission like the apostles.

In this section Mark maintains his pattern of five-element discourses, but with some variety since the frame becomes a part of the fivefold structure. Mark includes this short section on family and discipleship to introduce the notion of insider and outsider so that he can build upon it in the parables discourse. As the readers already know, Jesus' own religious leaders turned against him calling him "satanic." And surprisingly even Jesus' own flesh-and-blood family, who form the original constituency

---

100. Barton, *Discipleship and Family Ties*, 73. Best believes that discipleship sayings beginning with ὃς ἄν as found in 3:35 (also 3:29) "existed as a collection prior to Mark" ("Sayings Collection," 4).

101. Cf. Lambrecht, "Relatives of Jesus," 251, n. 23 and Barton, *Discipleship and Family Ties*, 73. Luke 8:19–21, for instance, has the same order throughout.

102. Thompson, *Disbelief*, 123.

of the church family (Acts 1:14), prove to be outsiders (Mark 3:31–32).[103] This warning will be extended to the disciples in 4:10–13. Then this exact theme is picked up in 13:12, where Jesus predicts that "Brother will betray brother to death, and a father his child." Insiders can become outsiders. The theme of inadequate discipleship is again brought to the forefront through a Markan frame. Yet in spite of these warnings the frame provides hope since Jesus ends the discourse with a call to true discipleship.

3.6 The Structure of the Parable Discourse in Mark 4:1–34

In order to identify the frame and its purpose in the parable discourse, we will first explain the difficulties in interpreting this passage, then suggest a scenario of how the material was organized into its canonical form, and finally analyze the suggested structures and demonstrate how the outline supported by Joanna Dewey enlightens Mark's purpose by creating two related chiastic structures.

According to Meagher, the structure of the parable discourse in Mark 4 is so clumsily constructed that "whichever was Mark's own view, he has incorporated material quite alien to it, and has managed the contradiction not with a finesse that reveals a lesson but with a benumbing baldness that leaves us either bemused or scrambling to our own resources for an explanatory subtlety that is painfully lacking in the text."[104] What exegetical details does Meager have in mind? The trio of seed parables perform a unison melody, but then Mark interrupts the concert by inserting parables about a lamp and a measure right in the middle (4:21–25). At the outset Jesus is comfortably teaching the vast crowds from a boat offshore (4:1), but then suddenly he is alone with his own friends and disciples (4:10) so that we never discover if he returns to finish his sermon, except that at the end of the day there he is again in the boat (4:36).

From start to finish this pericope is saturated with difficulties. Lambrecht points out that "the spontaneous introductory phrase" in 4:2, "he taught them in parables," stands in tension with 4:11–12, where Mark's parable theory concludes that the purpose of the parable was to conceal Jesus' teaching.[105] In particular, the exhortations to listen surrounding the parable (4:3, 9) seem superfluous since according to 4:12 they can be "ever hearing but never understanding." Second, although the parable of the sower (4:3–8) is followed by an interpretation in 4:14–20, each section evidences a different locale (lake shore vs. house), audience (crowds vs. disciples), structure (binary vs. fourfold), and grammatical data describing the four grounds (singular neuter pronouns vs. plural masculine pronouns). Therefore the story could be entitled

---

103. With a play on words Mark contrasts οἱ παρ' αὐτοῦ (3:21 Jesus' family) with τοὺς περὶ αὐτὸν (3:34 Jesus' spiritual family).

104. Meager, *Clumsy Construction*, 105.

105. Lambrecht, "Redaction and Theology," 276, n. 32. Räisänen states, "A tension between this motif and the parable theory is unmistakable" (*Messianic Secret*, 103).

the "Parable of the Sower," the "Parable of the Seeds," or the "Parable of the Soils."[106] Third, Lambrecht laments that verses 10-13 confess to a "notorious unevenness of thought."[107] The disciples ask a question in 4:10, but interpreters are unsure if the answer is cited in 4:11-12; 4:13, which also begins with καὶ ἔλεγεν αὐτοῖς, or by the interpretation in 4:14-20.[108] The disciples are extended the "mystery of the kingdom" in 4:11, but throughout the remaining sections of Mark's gospel the disciples completely misunderstand Jesus' teaching. Likewise, in the passage itself the disciples' inquiry is commendable in 4:10, but they are rebuked in 4:13.[109]

After the parable of the sower, new metaphors suddenly appear in 4:21-25, "drawn from indoor domestic life, as opposed to the outdoor, agricultural setting of the seed parables."[110] Any relationship between seeds and lamps is difficult to discern. Rough spots have been discerned here as well. Whereas the concealment under a lamp seems senseless in 4:21, it receives the purpose of promoting disclosure in 4:22. In addition, the symmetry of 24b ("With the measure you use, it will be measured to you") is broken in 24c by "and it shall be added to you." Likewise, the promise of receiving according to the way one measures (4:24) is undermined by 4:25, where instead of receiving little everything is taken away.[111] Whereas the parables of the lamp and measure refer to the final judgment in Matthew and Luke, here in Mark they are applied to parable theory.

Then in 4:26-32 the reader is introduced again to seed parables but this time without an interpretation. Finally, some view the ending in 4:33-34 as the climax of verses "in diametric opposition."[112] Scholar after scholar concludes that 4:33-34a assumes that the crowd understands the parables, while 4:34b negates this pedagogical purpose by requiring explanations in order to comprehend what Jesus taught.[113] Raisanen sums up the thoughts of many:

> According to v. 33b, Jesus uses parables in order to fit his teaching to the intellectual capability of the people. They make his message more comprehensible. . . . The situation is different in v. 34. Here the parables provide no help for understanding. On the contrary, like riddles thy need an interpretation.[114]

---

106. Cf. Marcus, *Mystery*, chapter 2, especially pages 21, 29.

107. Lambrecht, "Redaction and Theology," 277.

108. Cf. Räisänen, *Messianic Secret*, 115-16 and note 133 for a large group of scholars who agree.

109. Marcus, *Mystery*, 99.

110. Ibid., 126.

111. Ibid., 128-29.

112. Meagher, *Clumsy Construction*, 105.

113. Lambrecht, "Redaction and Theology," 276. Van Iersel concludes that "The two new elements contained in the final verses—'so that they were able to hear' (33) and 'to his disciples he explained everything' (34)—are clearly at odds with one another" (*Mark*, 177).

114. Räisänen, *Messianic Secret*, 104-5. Evidence includes the occurrence of a second δὲ clause in 34b after an initial one in 34a with two differing meanings (Marcus, *Mystery*, 88).

Certainly this complicated combination of material makes it extremely difficult to discover the viewpoint of Mark.

How does an interpreter explain the inclusion of this diverse material into one section on parables? One conclusion is sure: "That the chapter was not composed all at once seems clear."[115] In fact, Mark himself reveals in 4:33–34 that 4:2–32 is a summary collection of Jesus' parables instead of a precise chronological sequence of events in the life of Jesus.[116] Layers of tradition overlay each other.[117] Therefore we will endeavor to create a sequential reading over time. Following Joanna Dewey, we will demonstrate how Mark has woven this material into two chiastic structures, with the larger one encompassing the entire narrative and solving the problem raised by the smaller chiasm in 4:2b–20.

Jesus' contemporaries experienced him as a powerful teacher who spoke with authority and orated compelling stories that engraved unforgettable pictures into their minds and opened their eyes to the truths of God. Therefore, the primary purpose of parables was to reveal, not conceal. Consequently we should posit an initial collection of three kingdom seed parables (without an interpretation) which contrast a small beginning with an extravagant conclusion to make obvious to all the marvelous results of the kingdom of God.[118] All three parables include the sowing of the seed, an intermediate period of perplexity, and a final harvest or kingdom result. But a progression is evident as well, with the parable of the sower concentrating on sowing, the parable of the seed growing by itself belaboring the "interim stage of growth," and the mustard seed similitude describing "the final stage of the process."[119] Since 4:33–34a empha-

---

115. Räisänen, *Messianic Secret*, 137.

116. Stein, *Mark*, 204.

117. Marcus calls them "literary layers" (*Mystery*, 106), but one should not imagine written documents but oral tradition.

118. In addition, similar problem situations are developed in each case: doubts about growth because of repeated loss of the crop (4:4–7); the farmer's lack of action (4:27a); and the minuteness of the seed (4:31). Likewise, the two additional parables are introduced similarly with καὶ ἔλεγεν (4:26, 30; also 4:9 which might have been the original connection which Mark duplicated in 4:26) instead of καὶ ἔλεγεν αὐτοῖς (4:2b, 11, 21, 24) or καὶ λέγει αὐτοῖς (4:13, 35). Cf. Ambrozic, *Hidden Kingdom*, 50. Marcus (*Mark 1–8*, 57) mentions a similar triad of parables in Matt 21:28—22:14; Luke 15; Matt 13:24–33 and 13:44–48; Mark 2:18–22; Thomas 63–65, 96–98. Collections of parables using a common image like seeds were widespread in antiquity: king parables (Rab. Lam 1:1; 2:2; 3:7); palm-tree parables (Rab. Gen 3:1); and the fox parables of Rabbi Meir (b. Sanh. 38b). For scholars who support a pre-Markan collection of parables see Gundry (*Mark*, 187). Lambrecht ("Redaction and Theology," 303) and Räisänen (*Messianic Secret*, 138) think Mark himself added two additional parables to the Parable of the Sower already connected with the interpretation, but the switch of audiences argues against this suggestion. Luke 8 only repeats one parable since the Seed Growing by Itself parable could easily be misunderstood and Luke includes the Parable of the Mustard Seed at 13:18–19 from Q material. Matthew expands the parable series to seven just as he constructs seven woes and seven eschatological parables (Matt 23–25).

119. Jeremias, *Parables of Jesus*, 147. Stein discovers a progression in the Parable of the Sower as well since "the first seed never germinates; the second seed germinates and dies shortly afterward; the third seed germinates but at harvesttime it does not bear fruit; the fourth seed germinates, grows, and

sizes as well the powerful communication and welcome reception of the parables by the crowds, we should attach these verses to this initial parable tradition.

A second experience of the parables involves the believing community. Certainly Jesus not only addressed parables to the multitudes in order to attract them to the wonders of the kingdom, but also lectured the disciples, instructing them in kingdom values and molding their behavior to the norms of his teaching. I see no reason why Jesus could not have employed the parables on another occasion to instruct his intimate followers about discipleship (the so-called interpretation of 4:14–20).[120] Whatever the case, this instruction to the community became the message that the early preachers proclaimed to their congregations, so that the house that Jesus enters to teach his own disciples became the house church in the post-resurrection setting. The truths found in the interpretation of the parable were the secrets of the kingdom which the discipleship community prized.

In the third stage of development the parable to the crowd and the parable to the community became united. Their separate origin is demonstrated by the different locale (lake shore vs. house), audience (crowds vs. disciples), structure (binary vs. fourfold),[121] grammar (singular neuter pronouns vs. plural masculine pronouns), and imagery (seed vs. soils). Furthermore, the purpose of the parable is to invite the crowds to join the kingdom movement, while the function of the "interpretation" centers on continued growth in discipleship. A careful investigation of the structure reveals that an additional line ("hear the word" in 4:15, 16, 18, 20) is added to each of the four soils in the "interpretation," indicating that this telling is aimed at those who have already joined the conventicle.

I placed quotation marks around the term "interpretation" in the last paragraph because, although this is the standard terminology in the literature, it is more accurate to label it as a "retelling" or "clarification" of the parable to a different audience in order to preach a distinctively different message. In fact, we should assign the parables different monikers, the "parable of the seed" in 4:3–8 and the "parable of the soils" in 4:14 -20 . The parable of the seed illustrates the attractiveness of the kingdom to draw the crowds to join the Jesus movement. On the other hand, the parable of the soils warns the disciples that certain conditions like persecution, worry, and wealth can prohibit fruitfulness and growth in the kingdom. Rather than an "interpretation" of an earlier parable, it serves the purpose of a clarification to the community. For

---

bears much fruit at harvesttime" (*Mark*, 199).

120. In fact, the largest category of parables are discipleship or lack of discipleship parables (when compared with crisis parables, judgment parables, kingdom parables, mercy of God parables, parables about the marginalized, and community parables). Payne ("Authenticity of Sower") addresses the issue whether the explanation to the community could have been spoken by Jesus, but he does not discuss the argument of Jeremias (*Parables*, 33–42) that all of Jesus' parables were addressed to the crowds rather than the disciples.

121. The binary structure is proven by the three neuter singular pronouns in 4:3, 5, 7 balanced by the triple ἓν construction in 4:8.

instance, in Matthew 13 the "interpretation" of the parable of the tares (13:36–41) strings together a series of seven allegorical equivalents but neglects to include anything about the weeds and the good plants inhabiting the field together, which is the surprise and central theme of the parable (13:24–30). To the crowd the parable calls for patience in the midst of a world where good and evil are mixed together. To the discipleship community Jesus offers a clarification that even though in the present age the believing community cannot extinguish evil, a time will come when all evil will be judged and the righteous vindicated.[122] Likewise, the "interpretation" of the parable of the sower informs the community that membership does not guarantee fruitfulness. Their soil can become packed down in hard-heartedness, shallow through a lack of mature depth, or strewn with thorns when earthly pleasures and concerns divert one's attention from God's priorities. This clarification to the community was at some point in the oral tradition combined with the three seed parables and 4:33–34a, which served as its conclusion.[123]

An additional community experience underlying the parable discourse of Mark 4 was the vivid memory of opposition to Jesus' teaching. The overwhelming majority of the Jewish nation was blind to the value of Jesus' jewels of the kingdom; it was hidden from them. The early church envisioned this blindness as the fulfillment of Scripture, especially of Isaiah 6:9–10, which is employed by Paul (Rom 11:8), Luke (Acts 28:26–27), John (12:40), and the gospel writers here (Mark 4:12; Matt 13:14–15; Luke 8:10) to explain the blindness of the Jewish community. The insignificant size of the Jesus movement as well as the rejection and persecution of the Christian faith by the Jewish religious establishment resulted in the theological proposition that God had blinded their eyes to Jesus' kingdom teaching. Especially the central Christian teaching of a crucified Messiah was hidden from their view. Only those who joined the movement could decipher this mystery of the kingdom; for the rest the meaning of Jesus' parables was concealed.

The formation of 4:10–13 by Mark as the fourth stage of development must be understood against this background. Between the question introducing the interpretation of the parable (4:10) and the clarification to the community itself (4:14–20), Mark inserts a saying (4:11–12) from the Jesus tradition[124] which describes this obduracy of the opponents compared with the joy experienced by those who have accepted the

---

122. Similarly in the Parable of the Net (13:47–50) the "interpretation" is a clarification to the community that at the end of the age God will surely separate the good from the rotten fish, although in the present all have found a home in the net.

123. Mark does not employ his normal expression "in parables" (ἐν παραβολαῖς 4:2; 12:1; 3:23) in 4:33 but the dative παραβολαῖς which Räisänen (*Messianic Secret*, 88), following H. Koester, contends is preMarkan.

124. Schweizer shows that 4:11–12 is very primitive and "goes back to an Aramaic basis, perhaps to an Isaiah Targum and occurs in the community's tradition outside Mark (John 12:40; Acts 28:26f), where it explains the unbelief of the world" ("Messianic Secret," 68). Cf. also Jeremias, *Parables of Jesus*, 15; Marcus, *Mystery*, 81, 83 and the long list of supporters compiled by Ambrozic, *Hidden Kingdom*, 47, n. 1.

The Theological Intentions of Mark's Literary Devices

teaching of the kingdom. The contents of the parable of the sower itself picture the difficult nature of the mission of those who sow the word as well as the stubbornness of most hearers. The addition of the clarification to the community following the parable to the crowd, however, creates the idea that parables need further interpretation.[125] Therefore Mark's ingenious explanation for teaching in parables quotes the logion of Jesus that "The knowledge of the secrets of the kingdom of heaven has been given to you, but not to them" (Matt 13:11). This is the Matthean formulation, which, based upon its verbal connections with Luke 8:10, evidences a primitive well-established oral tradition which both Matthew and Luke revert to instead of employing the Markan version. Mark changed "secrets" to "secret" to describe the paradoxical division of God's kingdom depicted in the parable of the sower and its clarification. The mystery of the kingdom for Mark consisted in the fact that its coming in Jesus did not result in a sudden overturning which put an end to the old age. Instead, contrary to what was commonly expected, a strange coexistence of the new and old ages resulted.[126] This mystery explained the inability of many to envision the necessity of the crucifixion, an event which originally baffled the disciples, as evidenced in Peter's rebuke of Jesus in 8:32.[127] As Marcus reasons, "Mark did not wish to ascribe understanding to the disciples in the period before the crucifixion and resurrection, so he removed the verb 'to know.'"[128] Instead Mark places the theme of knowing into a newly constructed 4:13, which is transformed into a reproach to the disciples. This warning that the disciples as kingdom insiders could become unfruitful is then illustrated through the interpretation of the parable of the sower.

Markan redaction is thus clearly visible in 4:11–13 through the combination of five unique emphases:

1. The notion of esoteric teaching given to an inner circle
2. The idea of a dichotomy between insiders and outsiders
3. The perception of parables as allegorical riddles
4. The suggestion of a divine blinding of the outsiders
5. The teaching of the incomprehension of the inner circle[129]

---

125. See Räisänen, *Messianic Secret*, 131 for similar reasoning.

126. See Marcus, *Mystery*, 49 and *Mark 1–8*, 297.

127. Therefore, one could say that the mystery of the kingdom for Mark is the cross. All the aspects of the Messianic Secret are connected with the cross as explained in section 3.4.

128. Marcus, *Mystery*, 86. Mark splits "mystery" off from "the kingdom" for emphasis and to compensate for the missing of "to know" so that the saying is given stylistic balance (τὸ μυστήριον δέδοται τῆς βασιλείας instead of δέδοται γνῶναι τὰ μυστήρια τῆς βασιλείας in Matt 13:11; Luke 8:10).

129. Räisänen, *Messianic Secret*, 131. Schweizer explains "But v. 13b is unlikely to have existed at the stage of the tradition where parable and interpretation were linked, i.e. before the inclusion of v. 11f" ("Messianic Secret," 68).

The purpose for this redaction becomes clear if we posit a more specific setting in Mark's social environment. A final experience of the impact of Jesus' teaching that Mark recollects focuses upon the freshly remembered ordeal of apostasy under Nero's persecution, whereby members of the community became outsiders spurning the mysteries of the kingdom as foretold in the prophecies of Mark 13:9–13.[130] Since this is the specific situation that Mark wishes to address throughout his gospel, he attaches the theme of misunderstanding here to warn his readers that they too can become outsiders to the kingdom. This theme gets intensified in the following section involving miracle stories, where this warning to the disciples (4:13) becomes reality in their hard-hearted responses of faithless fear to the miracle epiphanies (4:40; 6:52; 8:17–21).

But this potential rejection of the mystery of the kingdom by Jesus' own followers does not speak the final word for Mark. Mark's most creative and significant redaction (a fifth stage) is to insert 4:21–25, the parables of the lamp and the measure, to create a positive alternative to the opposition of outsiders and potential apostasy of insiders in 4:11–13. Thus 4:21–25 complements 4:11–13,[131] since "both passages contrast the group that 'has been given' with a group that 'has not been given.'"[132] When the lamp is not concealed, the light is revealed to all (4:22). Whoever treasures Jesus' parables will understand their correct interpretation as well (4:25). Therefore, the secret of a suffering Messiah and a discipleship which follows Jesus to the cross should no longer be a secret in the life of the church. Since disciples know the mystery of the kingdom, persecution should not come as a surprise anymore. The lamp, which possibly symbolizes the crucified Christ for Mark, belongs on the lampstand for all to see. These parables become a promise of the ultimate triumph of the gospel.[133] The final result is a positive message: the unveiling of the mystery of the kingdom through a true understanding of Jesus' parables.

Although the individual sections of 4:1–34 are extrapolated from various traditions so that at several places in the narrative they appear to clumsily overlay each other, Mark has devised a grand literary design that overcomes all the complexities and idiosyncrasies of the individual traditions of 4:1–34. Dewey has masterfully diagnosed Mark's structure of the parable discourse. She has demonstrated that Mark positioned one fivefold chiasm within a larger similar symmetrical structure so that the hiddenness of the mystery (4:11–12) as well as the potential misunderstanding by the disciples (4:13) is overcome by the lamp faithfully placed upon the lampstand (4:21–22). Therefore, the revealing element of Mark's parable theory triumphs over

---

130. Therefore as Raisanen explains, "Mark's narrational problems are due to his interweaving two 'worlds' tacitly together, the world of Jesus and that of his own community" (*Messianic Secret*, 135).

131. Lambrecht, "Redaction and Theology," 287.

132. Marcus, *Mystery*, 129. For vocabulary similarities between 4:10–12 and 4:21–25 see Fay ("Literary Structure," 68) and the authors he quotes there.

133. Lambrecht, "Redaction and Theology," 281; Nineham, *Mark*, 141.

the concealing element. We will now analyze Dewey's structure and compare it with other alternatives.¹³⁴

1   Introduction: teaching parables in a boat (4:1–2a)^A
2   Parable material: parable and interpretation (4:2b–20)
        a   Parable of the sower (4:2b–9)
          b   Question from the disciples about its meaning (4:10)
            c   Mystery of the kingdom (4:11–12)
          b   Reproof to the disciples for not understanding (4:13)
        a'   Interpretation of the parable of the sower (4:14–20)
3   Sayings material: do not let the parable remain a mystery (4:21–24)
        a   Parable of the lamp (4:21) and interpretation (4:22)
          b   Exhortation to the audience: "He who has ears to hear, let him hear" (4:23)
          b   Exhortation to the audience: "Consider carefully what you hear" (4:24a)
        a'   Parable of the measure (4:24b) and interpretation (4:25)
2'   Parable material: two kingdom parables (4:26–32)
        a   Parable of the seed growing silently (4:26–29)
          b   Parable of the mustard seed (4:30–32)
1'   Conclusion: discussion of parables and leaving in a boat (4:33–34)

A. Dewey (*Markan Public Debate*, 148) finds a five-fold chiasm of vocabulary in 1–2 with a = teaching (1a); b = crowd (1b); c = boat (1c); b' = crowd (1d); a' = teach (2a), but this could be an evidence of Markan duality.

A conventional outline fails to resolve the compositional irregularities of 4:1–34, but Dewey's chiastic structure highlights Mark's redaction in this pericope.¹³⁵ The main chiasm displays balance, with a simple introduction and conclusion on the outside and a more complex parallel structure within, where a seed parable and its interpretation are mirrored by two additional seed parables.¹³⁶ Since the second elements (b and b') vary in length (eighteen verses in contrast with seven verses), some have doubted Dewey's structure,¹³⁷ but the hodgepodge of traditions have been cleverly arranged into a chiastic structure. Each individual section that Mark employed to build the pericope (i.e., 4:10, 11–12, 13, besides the sower parable and interpretation) finds its place within the chiasm. Mark's unique rebuke of the disciples (4:13) now answers

---

134. Dewey, *Markan Public Debate*, 149–50 supported by Via, *Ethics*, 183.

135. Boring (*Mark*, 113) objects and believes that Mark's structure "is linear and progressive" (n. 55) with three sections on parable theory (10–12; 21–25; 33–34) following the parable, the interpretation, and the third seed parable (33–34). But then the second seed parable is completely omitted and 33–34 apply to the entire pericope.

136. For a series of important verbal catchwords including kingdom of God, seed, sow, earth, bear fruit, and birds, see Dewey (*Markan Public Debate*, 150–51).

137. Cf. Fay, "Literary Structure," 68. Against Dewey, Fay claims that "it seems inconsistent to posit understanding as the broader theme of vv. 2b–20, interposed by the notion of obscurity in vv. 11–12." But both the themes of comprehension and incomprehension surface in 4:11–12. One must consider the audiences with comprehension applied to the disciples but incomprehension to outsiders.

the question in 4:10 that was originally connected with the parable's interpretation in 4:14–20. The chiasm centers the reader's attention upon 4:11–12, which highlight's Mark's distinctive parable theory comprising both the revelation of the kingdom to the chosen ones and concealment to outsiders. In a chiasm the central theme is spotlighted in both the center and the frame. Mark's ending in 4:33–34 captures these exact elements, with the revelation of the parable summarized in 4:33–34a and Mark's peculiar parable theory in 4:34b. Therefore, this outline meets all the requirements for an effective chiasm.[138]

The central element of a chiasm must effectively communicate the intended message of the author if the structure is to prove convincing. This is where Dewey's outline shines. If one recognizes that the three kingdom seed parables once belonged together, then Dewey's suggestion of a parable doublet (the lamp and the measure 4:21–25) now breaking this series up makes perfect sense with regard to genre. More importantly, the content at the heart of the large chiasm reinforces the conceal/reveal parable theory of Mark already discovered at the center of the small chiasm and at the frame in 4:33–34. The parable of the lamp focuses upon the disclosure of the hidden (4:21–22) whereas the ending of the measure parable accentuates the hardening theme (4:25b). Between the two parables is a double exhortation to listen (4:23; 24a), which matches the inclusio around the seed parable in 4:3, 9. The crowds listen but do not understand; now the insiders are warned to place the light upon the stand or a similar situation could develop with them.[139] This emphasis parallels the warning in 4:13 so that the two centers of the separate chiasms match each other. However, the larger chiasm proves more influential since the lamp upon the stand cancels the concealment of 4:11–12. The ἵνα clauses of 4:21–22 overcome the ἵνα clause of 4:11–12. Therefore the gospel light of the lamp, which the disciples measure out to the whole world in the apostolic proclamation, proves victorious over all opposition. This opposition includes the series of obstacles to fruitfulness which surface in 4:10–20, including 1) God's mysterious tendency to conceal (4:11–12); 2) the power of Satan (4:15); 3) difficult historical and social circumstances (4:17b, 19); and 4) the lack of internal staying power in the faith of individual believers (4:16b, 17a, 19).[140]

---

138. See the beginning of this chapter for a list of the eight most important criteria for discerning a chiasm.

139. This entails that 4:21–25 addresses the insiders like 4:10–13. Arguments in favor of this view include: 1) both sections are the center of a chiasm and should parallel each other; 2) Since the parable of the Sower is addressed to the crowd, one would expect that only the other two seed parables would be addressed to the same audience; and 3) the overwhelming support of commentators like Marcus (*Mystery*, 140) who points out that the themes of hiddenness, revelation, and hearing do not parallel the seed parables given to the crowd but 4:10–20. However, Gundry (*Mark*, 187) thinks Jesus returns to teaching the crowds in 4:21, "for according to vv 10–12, 33–34 he speaks in parables to the huge crowd but adds explanations for the disciples only in private," but the explanation of the Parable of the lamp (4:21) is given in 4:22 and the measure (4:24b) is interpreted in 4:25.

140. Via, *Ethics*, 184.

The stiffest competition to Dewey's structure comes from the chiasm of Greg Fay, who proposes that the interpretation of the parable (4:14–20) should receive the center of attention.[141]

a		4:1–2a	Introduction
	b	4:2b–9	Parable material
		c	4:10–13	Parabolic method
			d	4:14–20	Parabolic (in)comprehension
		c'	4:21–25	Parabolic method
	b'	4:26–32	Parable material
a'		4:33–34	Conclusion

Although divergent in structure from Dewey's in some points, both outlines highlight the important interconnection between 4:10–13 and 4:21–25. In Fay's chiasm they balance each other while Dewey envisions them both as the center of different chiasms. To his credit, Fay accents the parallelness of 4:10 and 13, stating that "v 10 is a question to Jesus by the disciples about his understanding (or use) of parables while v 13 is a question to the disciples by Jesus about their understanding of parables."[142] However, by separating the interpretation of the parable from this section, he misses the connection between the warning about apostasy in 4:13 and the examples in 4:17, 19.[143] Furthermore, if the interpretation of the parable was already connected with the parable before Mark arrived on the scene, he would not have completely annihilated any structural connection.[144] In grouping 4:10–13 together into one section, Fay overlooks the different traditions of the material and the close connection of 4:11–12 with the conclusion of the section at 4:33–34, which Dewey's outline highlights. Finally, although Fay complained about the unevenness of material in Dewey's parallel sections of 4:2b–20 and 4:26–32, his outline attempts to balance one parable in 4:2b–9

---

141. Dupont ("Transmission des Paroles," 264) constructs a similar chiasm but employs some different titles. Lang ("Kompositionsanalyse," 8, n. 18) posits a five-fold chiasm (which Mark seems to favor) that places the emphasis upon the esoteric teaching to the disciples at the middle (4:10–25). Although Lang contends that the formula καὶ ἔλεγεν αὐτοῖς at 4:11, 13, 21, 24 divides this material into four sections, he fails to demonstrate how this clarifies the progression of thought within this central section.

142. Fay, "Literary Structure," 71. Fay envisions a chiasm for this section: a = 4:10 question (comprehension); b = 11a positive results (disciples); c = 11b parabolic method; b' = 12 negative results (outsiders); a' = 13 question (comprehension).

143. Fay contends that "If one were to remove vv 14–20, the subject of Jesus' parabolic method would continue coherently in answer to the disciples' question of v 10" (ibid., 69). However, originally the answer to the question of verse 10 was the interpretation itself. Furthermore, the warning of 4:13 leads directly into the examples of 4:14–20 like lack of rootedness (4:17) or the deceit of riches or devastating consequences of worry (4:19).

144. Fay (ibid., 78, 81) does posit a similar internal structure between 4:3–9 and 4:14–20 but his outline fails to account for the binary structure of the Parable of the Seed and the four-fold structure of the Parable of the Soils which is demanded by the grammar.

with two in 4:26–32, which is certainly a more recognizable inconsistency for the average reader or hearer.

The fiercest battle of interpretation, however, involves the center of the chiasm. Is the pivotal turning point in the pericope the interpretation of the parable of the sower or the double parable of the lamp and measure? This decision will determine whether the dominant theme of this parable section is the incomprehension or comprehension of Jesus' teaching. Fay contends that the pivotal center of the chiasm "opens the door to further negative developments in the story of the disciples and thereby introduces the reader to a narrative shift. In this way it functions as an introduction to incomprehension."[145] Evidence for his thesis comes from the growing intensity of misunderstanding in Mark's gospel, from the description of Jesus' biological family as outsiders in 3:31–32, to the warning about misunderstanding in 4:13 and the parabolic examples in 4:17, 19, to the disciples' unbelief after the sea crossings in 4:40 and 6:52, climaxing in Jesus' ten-question rebuke in 8:17–21. However, if 4:13 is included in the theme of misunderstanding, one would anticipate that Fay would include this verse with the material in 4:14–20.

Is the central feature of Jesus' parable ministry the hardening of the opposition and the misunderstanding of the disciples? Certainly with all the Markan fingerprints on 4:1–34 one would expect at the center explicit material that Mark added to the oral tradition. Mark would not have employed the interpretation as the center of attention when that was already combined with the parable in the tradition, as the vast majority of scholars who employ diachronic methods of interpretation maintain. Instead, the insertion of two new parables into the middle of three seed parables is striking and catches the ear of the audience. Furthermore, these parables are given a new interpretation. Whereas earlier in the tradition they spoke about the final judgment,[146] now they exegete Jesus' parable theory. Literary features also speak to the prominence of 4:21–25. In the middle of the parables of the lamp and measure we encounter a duplicate exhortation to pay attention. Dewey comments that "nowhere else in Mark are two exhortations found adjacent to each other, separated only by an introductory formula, 'and he said to them.'"[147] Finally, the middle of a chiasm regularly moves the flow of the passage in a new direction, and certainly the parables in 4:21–25 accomplish this task. Whereas the "conceal" theme has been prominent, suddenly there is a move in the "reveal" direction. Just as in Mark's passion predictions the resurrection always follows the cross, so here the blazing lamp of the clarity of Christ's teaching and mission will overcome any opposition or misunderstanding from friend or foe.

---

145. Ibid., 79.

146. The application of Mark 4:22 is applied to the final judgment in Matt 10:26–27; Luke 12:2–3. For six differences between the Q form and the Markan parable of the lamp, see Marcus (*Mystery*, 131).

147. Dewey, *Markan Public Debate*, 151.

A second alternative structural chiasm is developed by Van Iersel, who like Dewey posits 4:21–25 as its center, but breaks this section into several component parts.[148]

a						2	Teach in images
	b					3–9	The seed
		c				10–13	Reaction to the question for an explanation
			d			14–20	The image of the seed explained
				e		21	The lamp and the measure
					f	22–23	Conceal/reveal
				e'		24–25	The measure's measure
			d'			26–29	The seed growing by itself
		c'				30	What is an apt image for God's kingdom?
	b'					31–32	The large shrub grown from the small seed
a'						33–34	Speak in images, explain to the disciples

Placing the theme of conceal/reveal at the center certainly appears admirable. But unlike Dewey's outline, 4:22–23 is not contrasted with 4:11–12 so the tension in the narrative is lost. Instead, the important parable theory section of 4:11–12 is paired with 4:30, which should not be separated from the parable of the mustard seed.[149] Certainly a legitimate outline would somehow connect the parable of the sower with its interpretation as well. The advantages of Dewey's chiasm are immediately apparent.

How does the discovery of various stages in the composition of this pericope and an analysis of its structure help us determine the purpose of this narrative? If Mark's main purpose was only to preserve the Jesus tradition, he would not have broken up the triad of seed parables. Instead he constructs the passage to proclaim the gospel to his contemporaries. Mark expresses the struggles and opposition which Jesus' teaching faced and at the same time discovers how to bring the mystery of the kingdom into its Easter light. By placing one five-part chiasm about not comprehending the mystery of the kingdom within a larger five-part chiasm where concealment is replaced by the light of revelation, Mark preaches a positive gospel message. As Marcus points out,

> The structure of the 'parable theory' passages suggests that God's 'last word' is not blindness, but sight; not the hiding of the truth from the outsiders, but its revelation to the insiders. Indeed, Mark 4 taken as a whole implies that light rather than darkness is God's 'last word.'[150]

In his structure Mark appears to mimic the oral tradition found in the double fivefold structure of the controversy dialogues in Galilee (2:1—3:6) and Jerusalem (11:27—12:40). There the centers of the chiasms emphasize the cross and resurrection so that

---

148. Van Iersel, *Mark*, 178.

149. If 4:30 is a separate section, 4:26 should be as well since it begins with a similar question and introduction to a parable.

150. Marcus, *Mystery*, 123.

the gospel is proclaimed powerfully even through Jesus' controversies. Likewise, the structure of the parables discourse proclaims that the hardening of the opposition and the unfruitful ground of the disciples' lives will not extinguish the lamp of Christ's teaching. Structure and meaning are inextricably connected.

In the parables discourse the center of each chiasm is more important than the frame. Because the inner structure is so intricate, Mark composes a simple frame so as not to distract from the more important elements of Jesus' teaching. Mark simply explains that Jesus taught (4:2 ἔλεγεν αὐτοῖς ἐν τῇ διδαχῇ; 4:33 ἐλάλει αὐτοῖς τὸν λόγον) many parables (4:2 ἐν παραβολαῖς πολλά; 4:33 παραβολαῖς πολλαῖς) from the pulpit of a boat (4:1 εἰς πλοῖον; 4:36 ἐν τῷ πλοίῳ).[151]

However, the ending frame does reiterate the important theme at the center of both chiasms. Mark 4:34b recalls that the mystery of the kingdom will be hidden, and therefore Jesus has to explain everything to the disciples when they are alone in the house church. On the other hand, 4:33–34a proclaims that Jesus spoke to them the word so that they could understand. The clarity and power of Jesus' unforgettable teaching stands front and center.

The purpose of the frame is therefore to reiterate the centers of each chiasm and call attention to the double feature of Jesus' teaching, namely that it both reveals and conceals. Parables are riddles that produce both insiders and outsiders.[152] When Mark employs the term "parables" in the plural, the reader would naturally expect several, but this does not happen in 4:1; 12:1; or 3:23 where this phrase is employed.[153] "Speaking in parables" has become a technical term for Mark meaning to employ riddles which function as allegorical puzzles.[154] As a riddle, a parable would have a literal, superficial meaning that was obvious to the crowd, but a deeper meaning only detected

---

151. For evidence of a frame see Räisänen, *Messianic Secret*, 103 and Lambrecht, "Redaction and Theology," 273–74.

152. Marcus (*Mystery*, 157–58) discerns a double chiasm of insiders and outsiders:

4:10–11a	insiders	4:24–25a	insiders
4:11b–12	outsiders	4:25b	outsiders
4:15–19	outsiders	4:33–34a	outsiders
4:20	insiders	4:34b	insiders

153. Gundry proposes that "Mark means his audience to understand the following parable as one chosen from among other unreported parables" (*Mark*, 199). Certainly Matthew thinks that more parables are needed since he composes a series of history of redemption parables at 21:28—22:14 to replace Mark's lone Riddle of the Tenants. Furthermore, Matthew omits the phrase in Matt 12:25 corresponding to Mark 3:23, but includes the phrase at Matt 13:3, 10, 13, 34, 35 since he composes a parable discourse. But Mark's definition of parables as riddles fits his parable theory so that Mark must be distinguished from Matthew in their definition of parables.

154. Scholarly support for riddle includes Beasley-Murray, *Jesus and the Kingdom*, 105; Burkill, "Cryptology," 33–34; France, *Mark*, 188; Jeremias, *Parables of Jesus*, 16; Kelber, *Kingdom*, 32ff; Kermode, *Secrecy*, 23f; Marshall, *Faith*, 60; Patten, "Form and Function," 255ff; Räisänen, *Messianic Secret*, 84, n. 34, 133; Rhoads and Michie, *Mark as Story*, 55f; and Telford, *Theology of Mark*, 67.

through an inspired word of interpretation. The parable of the sower is designated a paradigm parable (4:13) because understanding takes place only through an interpretation which occurs in a gathering of the faithful (Jesus alone with his disciples in 4:10, 34; 6:31–32; 9:2, 28; 13:3) or within the boundaries of a house (7:17, 24; 9:28, 33; 10:10) which becomes the house church in the NT age. Thus the frame reinforces Mark's parable theory.

Unique to Mark is the warning that those who are given the mystery of the kingdom (4:11) can become outsiders (4:13). Already at 3:31–32 Jesus' biological family stands at a distance from Jesus.[155] Now the two insider groups, "those around him" (περὶ αὐτὸν 3:32; οἱ περὶ αὐτὸν 4:10) and the Twelve, are warned of potential apostasy through Jesus' penetrating question in 4:13, the interpretation of the parable of the sower at 4:17, 19, and with the double exhortation to listen placed right in the middle of the parables of the lamp and measure. The inclusio to "listen" around the parable in 4:3, 9 (ἀκούετε; ἔχει ὦτα ἀκούειν ἀκουέτω), which is aimed at the crowds, who are not given the mystery of the kingdom, now ironically becomes the center of attention for those who are given the mystery. Mark's theme of discipleship misunderstanding is intensifying so that at the end of this discipleship cycle in 6:1–6 the people from Jesus' home town will become outsiders. Finally, in the next cycle (6:7—8:21), at the close of each trip across the sea (4:40; 6:52; 8:17–21) the disciples themselves will become the outsiders.

Each of these groups becomes a foil for the Markan community and readership, who through the devil's schemes (4:15), persecution (4:17), and the deceit of wealth and ravage of worry (4:19) could become outsiders as well.[156] Persecution is particularly emphasized by Mark as evidenced by the amount of vocabulary and imagery employed to describe the rocky ground (33 Greek words vs 18 and 17 employed on the other seeds).[157] Just as the imperative to "watch out" (βλέπετε τί ἀκούετε 4:24a) is placed at the center of 4:1–34, likewise it becomes the central warning in chapter 13 (vv. 5, 9, 23, 33), which could be called Jesus' "passion prediction for Mark's

---

155. Barton points out that "The relative postures and distance from Jesus symbolize degrees of faith and unbelief (cf. 2.4–5!)" (*Discipleship and Family Ties*), 72..

156. Juel explains that "Jesus' troubling comments about insiders and outsiders, about seeing and not seeing, make sense only to the reader" (*Master of Surprise*, 57).

157. a = the type of ground; b = what happened; c = the result.

a	Some fell along the path,
b	and the birds came
c	and ate it up.
a	5 Some fell on rocky places, where it did not have much soil.
b	It sprang up quickly, because the soil was shallow.
c	6 But when the sun came up, the plants were scorched, and they withered because they had no root.
a	7 Other seed fell among thorns,
b	which grew up and choked the plants,
c	so that they did not bear grain.

community."[158] The mystery of the kingdom (4:11), like the motif of secrecy found throughout the gospel, becomes finally clarified in the cross. Therefore, the outsiders are those who misunderstand a suffering Son of Man Christology as well as a discipleship of the cross.

What then is the purpose of the boat in 4:1, which again enters the narrative as the next narrative begins (4:26)? Through the Markan frame the boat becomes a literary marker that interlaces together the controversy dialogues, teaching on family, parables, and miracles. Mark introduces the boat in the ending frame of the conflicts (3:9). But when the crowds again become so intense that Jesus and his disciples cannot even eat (3:20), Mark has Jesus withdraw to the lakeside and teach from the boat (4:1) to begin the frame of the parables discourse. At the end of the day Mark again employs the boat to introduce the miracle stories through the sea-calming epiphany (4:36). Through the boat, which becomes Jesus' pulpit, Mark holds these sections together and thus indicates that a common message is being emphasized. Therefore, as we now turn to the miracle section of Mark we should expect a similar theme where insiders can become outsiders and comprehension can turn to misunderstanding. Indeed we will see that Mark ends his miracle catenae with this identical theme in 8:17–21. In each case outsiders are those who refuse a discipleship of the cross.

3.7 The Frame around the Miracle Catenae of Mark 4:35—8:21

In the two central sections of Mark's gospel we encounter a series of miracles (6:35—8:21) and a discipleship catechism (8:22—10:52), memorably organized with three sea journey episodes (4:35–41; 6:45–52; 8:14–21)[159] followed by Jesus' three passion predictions (8:31; 9:31; 10:33–34). In the three sea journeys, which I will entitle the sea calming, the sea walking, and the sea conversation trips, the befuddlement of the disciples concerning Jesus' miracle ministry intensifies so that the slight mention of faithless fear in 4:40 converts into the misunderstanding of an entire miracle in 6:52, and finally climaxes in an avalanche of rebukes from Jesus in 8:17–21. Likewise, the passion predictions escalate in the descriptions of Jesus' suffering and opposition until in 10:33–34 every specific detail of his passion is revealed. Each passion foreshadowing is followed with confusion by the disciples as well (8:32–33; 9:32–34; 10:35–38), so that the apprentices misconstrue Jesus' miracle ministry because they are unprepared for Jesus' passion. Within the discipleship catechism each misunderstanding concludes with a teaching on discipleship to offer wise instruction to the novitiate, but within the miracle catenae Mark waits until the termination of the section to prod toward a per-

---

158. Cf. Marcus, *Mystery*, 152. Helen Graham ("Passion Prediction," 18) gives this title to Mark 13.

159. Mark refers to four boat trips to the other side (4:35; 5:21; 6:45; 8:13) and two other side trips (6:32; 8:10b), but only three episodes are portrayed as extended narratives, and each discloses the ignorance of the disciples. Cf. Petersen, "Composition of 4:1—8:26," 195–96 and Meye, *Jesus and the Twelve*, 63.

spective adjustment with his own composition of the material (8:11–21). Therefore, even though one section is dominated by miracles and the other with teaching on discipleship, in reality Mark employs the three sea journeys for didactic purposes.[160] In the sea calming Jesus is addressed as teacher (4:41); in the sea walking the disciples do not understand the message of the loaves (6:52); and the final trip across the sea turns into a sea conversation about discipleship instead of a miracle story (8:17–21). Jesus the teacher is also portrayed as Jesus the Messiah and Lord. Just as in the Jerusalem ministry Mark desires to establish Jesus as the messianic Son of David (11:1—12:40) before the passion narrative (chs. 14–15), so Mark portrays Jesus' lordship through miracles (4:35—8:21) before he predicts his suffering (8:22—10:52). Jesus' healing ministry authorizes his lordship over nature (4:35–41; 6:45–56), spiritual demonic forces (5:1–20), disease and death (5:21–43), daily sustenance needs (6:35–44; 8:1–9, 14–16), human controversy (7:1–23; 8:11–13), both Jews and Gentiles (7:24–30), and the corporal body (7:31–37). Then the discipleship catechism portrays Jesus as the suffering Son of Man. The two sections together establish Jesus as a suffering Messiah.

Although a triad of similar narratives networks the miracle stories with the discipleship catechism, the inner structure of the miracle catenae is quite distinct and substantially more complex. In this section we will demonstrate how Mark employs an already established miracle catena in two cycles to demonstrate Jesus' greatness but then develops a frame around this section to call attention to the insufficiency in viewing Jesus only as a miracle worker. In the process we will explain how and why Mark subtracts the healing of the blind man (8:22–26) from the miracle sequence but adds material about discipleship following rejection (6:1–30) and teaching on the fulfillment of Jewish ceremonial rites like washing hands and eating kosher food (6:53—7:23).

First, we will examine three alternative suggestions for structuring this miracle section before we arrive at the preferred option advocated by Achtemeier. Peterson opts for a triadic structure of three cycles, each containing three miracle stories, by incorporating the parable sequence in chapter 4 and the healing of the blind man in 8:22–26 into the sequence:

Cycle 1   (4:1–34; 4:35–41; 5:1–20) with a triad interval (5:21–43; 6:1–6a; 6:6b–29)

Cycle 2   (6:30–44; 6:45–52; 6:53–56) with a triad interval (7:1–23; 7:24–30; 7:31–37)

Cycle 3   (8:1–12; 8:13–21; 8:22–26)[A]

    A. Petersen, "Composition of 4:1—8:26," 188. Petersen reports that this section is "comprised of three triadically composed cycles, the central one of which is surrounded by triadically composed intervals, each of which contains one triadically composite minimal unit" (200). Thus Mark 6:6b–29 can be subdivided into 6b–13, 14–16, 17–29 and 7:1–23 into 1–13, 14–15, 17–23.

Mark's preference for triads is the major advantage of Petersen's suggested structure. The first unit in each cycle describes Jesus' actions with the crowds on one side of the

---

160. Meye, *Jesus and the Twelve*, 67.

sea, the middle section depicts Jesus and the twelve inside a boat, and the final passage represents Jesus' miracles on the other side following his debarkation.[161] In the two intervals between the cycles the events no longer occur by the sea.

The chief setback for this outline is the strange combination of parable and miracle material. Whereas the first cycle commences with parables, the last two begin with miraculous feedings. Before this structure proves itself a viable option, more thematic parallels are necessary. In addition, although Peterson employs boat trips to hold this section together, he ignores the first reference in 3:9.[162] Finally, Peterson climaxes his outline with the healing of the blind man in two steps (8:22–26), whereas Mark couples this narrative with the healing of blind Bartimaeus (10:46–52) to form a frame encircling the discipleship catechism.

Because summary sections frequently divulge a transition in the narrative,[163] several authors employ Markan summaries as roadmarks to the author's intended structure. For example, both Pesch and Kuhn envision 3:7–12 and 6:53–56 as important transition passages in their respective outlines of this material.

Outline	Pesch[A]		Kuhn[B]	
a	3:7–12	Summary	3:7–12	Summary
b	4:35–41	Crossing of the sea: stilling	3:13–19	Jesus and his disciples
c	5:1–20	Healing of the demoniac	3:20–35	Jesus and his family
d	5:21–43	Intercalation: disease & death	4:1–34	Jesus as teacher
			4:35—5:43	Jesus as wonder-worker
c'	6:32–44	Feeding of 5,000	6:1–6	Jesus and his compatriots
b'	6:45–51	Crossing of the sea: walking	6:7–31	Jesus and his disciples
a'	6:53–56	Summary	6:53–56	Summary

A. Pesch, *Markusevangelium*, I: 277–81.
B. Kuhn, *Sammlungen*, 208-9. Cf. Fowler, *Loaves and Fishes*, 21–22 for an evaluation.

Although the two summaries contain similar material, including the flocking of crowds to Jesus from the entire region (3:8; 6:55), the reference to a boat (3:9; 6:54), and the sick seeking to touch Jesus (3:10; 6:56), the second summary fails to repeat

---

161. Ibid., 196.

162. Meye, *Jesus and the Twelve*, 65. Petersen points out that "prior to 4:1 Jesus had been beside the sea on three occasions (1:16; 2:13; 3:7) but never on it" ("Composition of 4:1—8:26," 194), but the key to this miracle section as indicated by its conclusion in 8:17–21 is the disciples' reaction to Jesus' miracles, not his teaching the crowds as in 4:1.

163. For instance, the summaries which indicate the evangelism of a new people group in Acts (6:7; 9:31; 12:24; 16:5; 19:20; 28:28,31) proposed by C. H. Turner ("Chronology of the NT," 1:421) and the conclusions of Matthew's five discourses (7:28; 11:1; 13:53; 19:1; 26:1 proposed by B. W. Bacon ("'Five Books' of Moses," 56–66).

the themes of withdrawal (3:7), Jesus' deliverance ministry (3:11), and the silencing of the demons (3:12). In particular, the omission of an important pericope in each of these outlines substantially decreases their credibility. Pesch eliminates the parables discourse (4:1–34) and the Nazareth rejection and mission of the disciples (6:1–31) in order to construct a miracle catena, while Kuhn disregards the feeding of the five thousand and sea walking narratives (6:32–52).[164] More importantly, the centers diverge resulting in a contrasting emphasis.

Although the presence of summary statements is frequently significant, these examples are uneven in length, difficult to discern, and cluster in the first half of Mark's narrative. Furthermore, these so-called summaries do not notify the reader of any organizational change but instead provide narrative progress through a series of loose-knit pericopes.[165] The boat, for example, functions as a familiar object that moves the narrative along following the controversy dialogues (3:9) to the parables (4:1) and miracle stories (4:36). Likewise, such summaries as 6:6b and 6:53–56 link the miracles to additional motifs that Mark inserts into the narrative, including teaching on discipleship (6:7–30) and instruction on purity rituals (7:1–23). Therefore, summary statements do not provide the key for unlocking the structure of Mark's gospel.[166]

The most widely followed organization of the miracle stories, suggested by Taylor,[167] pictures a duplicate series of events beginning with the two feedings of the multitudes. Fowler contends that this structure has achieved the status of "scholarly lore."[168]

6:34–44	Feeding of the 5,000	8:1–10	Feeding of the 4,000
6:45–52	Crossing the lake (sea walking)	8:10a	Crossing the lake
6:53–56	Landing at Gennesaret	8:10b	Landing at Dalmanutha
7:1–23	Controversy with the Pharisees (about cleanliness)	8:11–13	Controversy with the Pharisees (about signs)
7:24–30	Dialogue with the Syrophoenician woman about bread	8:14–21	Dialogue with the disciples about the bread miracles

---

164. Kuhn believes that in a pre-Markan source the two miracles of 6:32–52 were included in the collection of 4:35—5:43, but Mark separated them to prevent repetition, thus spoiling the symmetry.

165. Hedrick explains, "The summary statements create an impression of animation and movement in the narrative over broad geographical areas and general time frames" ("Summary Statements," 310).

166. See ibid., 291–94. See Appendix 4, outline 2 for an evaluation of various attempts to structure Mark's entire gospel through summary statements.

167. Taylor, *Mark*, 368; Malley, "Mark," *Jerome Biblical Commentary*, 38. For a longer list of scholars supporting this view see Fowler, *Loaves and Fishes*, 185, n. 2. Jenkins ("Markan Doublet," 91) proposes a similar chart with divergent terminology such as the title "Avoiding Realm of Antipas" for 7:24–30 and 8:13–21 and "Healing East of Lake" for 7:31–37 and 8:22–26.

168. Fowler, *Loaves and Fishes*, 7.

7:31–35	Unusual healing of the deaf-mute (with spit 7:33; two stages 7:33 & 34)	8:22–25	Unusual healing of the blind man (with spit 8:23; in two stages 8:23–24 & 25)
7:36–37	Messianic secret	8:26	Messianic secret

Several excellent arguments have been adduced in favor of this proposal.

1. The progression follows the exact order of Mark.

2. The sequence ties the crossing of the sea to the feedings, followed by a misunderstanding in 6:52 ("for they had not understood about the loaves") and 8:17–21, where the disciples are rebuked for their inability to comprehend the significance of the two feedings.

3. In John's gospel the sea crossing (6:16–24) likewise follows the feeding of the five thousand (6:1–15) in succession.

4. The healings of the deaf-mute and blind man are linked close together through vocabulary, content, and progression in the narrative.[169]

5. Some detect a thematic progression of symbolic interpretations for the miracles, from an emphasis upon death in the feedings (the distribution of Jesus' body) to resurrection in the sea walking (Jesus appears like a ghost), resulting in controversy with Jewish opponents (the debates with the Pharisees) but also a mission to the Gentiles (the Syrophoenician woman and the Decapolis healing),[170] so that the ears of the deaf and the eyes of the blind are opened (deaf-mute and blind man healings). This progression concludes with statements that the gospel remains a secret for many.

However, a substantial series of objections as well as a more attractive solution require us to reject this outline of miracle catenae.[171]

1. If Mark inaugurates the series of wonder stories in 4:35, one would expect his organizational structure to commence there as well, especially since the first two sea crossings (sea calming and sea walking) display such similarities.

2. Beginning each cycle with a miraculous feeding overlooks the background in OT typology, where crossing the water to retake the Promised Land precedes a celebration of an eschatological feast in the stories of Moses/Joshua (Exod 16; Josh 5:10–12) and Elijah/Elisha (2 Kgs 4:42–44).

---

169. Cf. Jenkins, "Markan Doublet," 95–96.

170. Boring (*Mark*, 180) thinks that 7:1–30 stands in the center of the first column in order to facilitate a transition from a Jewish to Gentile mission, but the reader would expect a corresponding emphasis at the middle of the second column.

171. Quesnell offers an historical development of the thesis and concludes that the "results are less than convincing" (*Mind of Mark*, 28–36). Fowler says the evidence is "scant and unpersuasive" (*Loaves and Fishes*, 9).

3. The second lake crossing (8:10a) is just a short summary rather than a narrative like 6:45–52, so that the sea calming in 4:35–41 more closely matches this sea walking incident.

4. The two cycles are completely unbalanced with regard to length, with the first series of miracles consisting of 1,032 words while the second only contains 369 words.[172]

5. If death and resurrection symbolize the movement from the feedings to the sea crossing miracles, certainly the near-death experience of the disciples while crossing the sea (4:38), followed by the eschatological calm (4:39) as well as the transformation of the Gerasene demoniac (5:15) and the resurrection of the young girl (5:39, 42) would require the inclusion of these narratives as well.

6. The content of 7:1–23 is unique and does not parallel 8:11–13 since, as even Taylor admits, it is only "loosely connected with its present context and was probably compiled independently."[173] The more appropriate doublet to the "no sign will be given" saying (Mark 8:11–13) is the sign of Jonah pericope in Matthew 12:39 and Luke 11:29.

7. The conversation about bread in 7:24–30 occurs within a story about exorcism, whereas in 8:13–21 the occasion is another sea crossing.[174] In addition, a land journey contrasts with a boat journey, and the only common vocabulary consists of the verb "they went away" (7:24; 8:13). Finally, the bread motif appears throughout this section, not just in these two passages.

8. Mark 8:22–26 functions as a frame for the discipleship catechism, along with the healing of blind Bartimaeus in 10:45–52, and is not a part of the series of miracles, as evidenced by the links between the two-stage healing and Peter's need for a two-stage christological confession in 8:27–33.

9. This structure fails to explain why the boat leaves for Bethsaida in 6:45 but arrives in Gennesaret in 6:53.

10. Mark patterns the organization of 8:11–21 upon the parable discourse of 4:1–34 (also 7:14–23) and not upon the miracle narrative of Mark 7 as proposed above. Therefore, Markan redaction is the key to the structure of 8:11–21 rather than a pre-Markan miracle catena.[175] The following pattern of texts demonstrates significant parallels between the arrangement of parables in Mark 4 and 7 and the material placed by Mark into 8:11–21: 1) an enigmatic saying (4:3–9; 7:14b–15;

---

172. See Jenkins, "Markan Doublet," 91 for the statistics.

173. Taylor, *Mark*, 631.

174. See Gundry, *Mark*, 395.

175. See section 4.3e below for dramatic parallels in content, vocabulary, and flow of material. See Kelber, *Kingdom*, 59; Lemcio, "External Evidence," 323–38 and Sellew, "Composition of Didactic Scenes," 613–34.

8:15); 2) a change of locale (4:10a; 7:17a; 8:13); 3) a question to Jesus in private about the saying's meaning (4:10b; 7:17b; 8:16–17a); 4) Jesus' retort that they should already understand (4:13; 7:18a; 8:17b–18); and 5) Jesus' interpretation of the material (4:14–20; 7:18b–23; 8:19–21).[176]

Therefore, since this cycle of Markan miracles fails to observe where Mark begins his miracle sequence as well as the parallels between the sea stilling and sea walking, it fails to unveil Mark's purpose in transmitting the miracle catenae.

In contrast to these three structural outlines explained above, Achtemeier has discovered within 4:35—8:17 two series of pre-Markan miracle catenae that brilliantly reveal the Markan seams in the narrative and unveil specific Markan emphases.[177] We will discuss the pattern of Jew and Gentile territory when we discuss Markan geographical mirroring in chapter 7. Here we intend to summarize his findings and argue for their veracity in order to demonstrate how and why Mark places a frame around these miracle stories.

a	4:35–41	Jesus calms the *water* To Gentile territory	6:45–56	Jesus walks on *water* Leaves for Bethsaida, Gentile land (6:45), but arrives at Gennesaret, Jewish land, (6:53)
b	5:1–20	Decapolis exorcism An unclean land is cleansed Gentile territory: pigs	8:22–26	Healing the blind man A two-stage process; healing with spit Gentile territory: Bethsaida (see John 12:20–21)
c	5:25–34	Sick woman An unclean Jewish woman saved Jewish territory: reference to 12	7:24–30	Syrophoenican woman's daughter An unclean Gentile woman receives salvation Gentile territory: Tyre
b'	5:21–23, 35–43	Jairus' dead daughter (Dead bodies are no longer unclean) Jewish territory: reference to 12	7:31–36	Decapolis healing of the deaf/mute (A two-stage process; healing with spit) Gentile territory: Decapolis
a'	6:34–44	*Feeding* of the 5,000 With twelve baskets surplus Jewish territory: reference to 12	8:1–10	*Feeding* of the 4,000 With seven baskets surplus Gentile territory: reference to 7 (see Acts 13:19)

Just as Mark absorbed from the oral tradition two sets of controversy dialogues, each with a fivefold chiastic structure, so he incorporates two miracle catenae with a similar structure. The parallel content and vocabulary, special emphasis upon the middle of each chiasm, and the typological flow of the material indicate the

---

176. See Sellew, "Composition of Didactic Scenes," 620.

177. Achtemeier, "Isolation," 265–91, especially 284 with support from Collins (*Mark*, 258) and Kelber (*Kingdom*, 58).

significance of this structure.¹⁷⁸ Certainly the material was organized in this manner for easy memorization.

In each section of Mark previously discussed, we have witnessed a fivefold structure. Its presence in the miracle stories then should not be surprising and confirms our previous results. Each miracle catena commences with a trip across the sea and ends with a miraculous feeding. Three healings are placed seriatim in the middle of each miracle sequence, climaxing in a command to silence (5:43; 7:36) and a response of amazement (5:42; 7:37). The beginning and concluding elements in each chiasm parallel each other perfectly.

The two sea crossings at the beginning of the chiasms stress the absence of Jesus in sleep or prayer (4:38a; 6:46) and his sudden epiphany to rescue his disciples from the chaotic sea (4:39; 6:48b) when they are unable to reach their destination (4:38b; 6:47b-48a) in their nightlong labors (4:35; 6:47a). In the sea calming and sea walking narratives Jesus performs deeds that were only God's prerogative in the Old Testament. God alone is privileged to control the forces of nature (Ps 89:10-11; 74:13-14; 107:23-30; Job 9:13; Isa 51:9-10)¹⁷⁹ and to command the sea at his bidding (Job 26:11-13; Ps 104:7; Isa 51:9-10; Ps 18:15; 106:9; Isa 50:2). Likewise, only God can walk on water (Job 9:8b; Hab 3:15; Ps 77:19; Isa 43:16; Wis 14:1-4). In each case Jesus initiates the sea journey through his imperative or compulsion (4:35; 6:45). After dismissing the crowd (4:36; 6:46) as evening arrives (4:35; 6:47) a dangerous wind (4:37; 6:48a) instigates such a tumult that the disciples question Jesus' concern for them (4:38; 6:48c). But Jesus causes the storm to vanish (4:39; 6:51a) and then rebukes the disciples for their fear (4:40; 6:52).¹⁸⁰ Based upon the ending of this miracle section in 8:17-21, Jesus appears to have more trouble with the disciples inside the boat than the storm outside.¹⁸¹ Yet in both cases we have a revelation of the true character of Jesus similar to his resurrection, so that his rising from sleep (4:39a) and his sudden coming like a ghost (6:49a; Luke 24:37b) as well as his employment of the phrase *egō eimi* (6:50b; Luke 24:39) have caused some to interpret these events as displaced resurrection narratives.¹⁸²

The two concluding narratives of the feeding of the five thousand and four thousand mirror each other so dramatically that they are frequently entitled duplicates.¹⁸³

---

178. Just like the exodus and the conquest of the land, the miracle catenae display a flow of material from the crossing of the sea to the feeding of the people with several divine miracles in between. We will discuss the typological flow of the material in section 7.6.

179. Latourelle, *Miracles of Jesus*, 108-9.

180. See the diagram in Marcus (*Mark 1-8*, 424-25) for a comparison of the content of the pericopes.

181. Fowler agrees that "the focus of the action is on the disciples of Jesus" (*Loaves and Fishes*, 101).

182. See Marcus (*Mark 1-8*, 433) for a list of nine similar characteristics.

183. Donfried, "Feeding Narratives," 95-101. Against this view France states, "Since the numbers are emphasized in each account, it is hard to believe that tradition would have treated them with such

The nearly identical progression of material indicates that Mark desires the reader to be so expectant of similarities that the divergences stand out.[184] These include the categorization of people as sheep (6:34), the long distance they have traveled (8:3), the division into groups on the green grass (6:39–40), the vocabulary for giving thanks (6:41; 8:6), and especially the divergent numbers (6:44; 8:9). We will study these divergences and explain their function in chapter 7 when we deal with the Jew and Gentile emphasis in Mark. Finally, in the summary section of the miracle discourses (8:17–21) Mark himself combines the two feedings together (8:19–20), indicating that he is now developing a commentary on these two catenae of miracle stories.

The middle elements of the chiasms[185] correspond as well and reveal the overall emphasis of salvation to the Jew first but also to the Gentile. Both main characters are not only women but also unclean, the one with a flow of blood and the Syrophoencian woman as a dog Gentile (7:27). Both fall at Jesus' feet (5:33 προσέπεσεν αὐτῷ; 7:25 προσέπεσεν πρὸς τοὺς πόδας αὐτοῦ) in humble adoration.[186] The Gentile has a daughter (7:25) while the Jewish woman is addressed as daughter (5:34). Both initiate the healing process, but a growth in boldness is apparent when the Gentile woman masterfully outwits Jesus (7:28), thus emphasizing her faith response (7:29) and the appropriateness of a Gentile mission. Likewise, the faith response of the woman with the hemorrhage provides a climax to the narrative in 5:34, "your faith has healed [saved, σέσωκέν] you."[187] Salvation, therefore, comes to the marginalized in Israel as well as to a Gentile woman in Tyre, who is offered table fellowship along with Israel. Because of her word of faith, the demon leaves her daughter (7:29) and presumably the whole territory of Tyre is now cleansed as Jesus retakes the Promised Land in the narrative.

The sections b and b' in the first miracle catena describe two people brought back to life. This is true literally of the daughter of the Synagogue leader (5:42) and metaphorically of the Geresene demoniac, who resided among the tombs with the dead (5:5) until the legion within him drowned in the sea and he was resurrected to a new life as an apostle to the Gentiles (5:18, 20). Purity issues are also central to each story, with Jesus' healing of a dead corpse through touch signifying the fulfillment of OT impurity rituals and the elimination of the unclean pigs denoting the cleansing of Gentile territory for the kingdom of God. Thus, although the second story is thoroughly Jewish as indicated by the role of girl's father as a synagogue leader (5:22, 35), and the first occurs in the Gentile Decapolis, the Jew/Gentile barrier is broken down through the parallelism of the chiasm.

---

negligence" (*Mark*, 306).

184. For a detailed list of similarities, see section 5.5d below.

185. Because of the Markan intercalation it is difficult to determine which narrative came first in the miracle catenae, but Achtemeier ("Isolation," 278–79) argues for this order from the progression of healing a persistent illness to raising one from the dead and the fact that the eating of the girl (5:43) previews the feeding of the five thousand.

186. Marcus, *Mark 1–8*, 467.

187. See also 5:28 "If I touch the hem of his garment, I will be saved" (σωθήσομαι).

The b and b' elements in the second chiasm are both two-stage healings. With the deaf-mute from the Decapolis, Jesus first employs the healing gestures (7:33) of placing his fingers in the deaf man's ears and spitting on the mute man's tongue, which is then followed by the Aramaic incantation, *Ephphatha*, "be opened" (7:34). The healing of the blind man is similarly elongated, with a partial healing whereby he sees people looking like walking trees (8:23–24), followed by a second touch with the result that he sees everything clearly (8:25). The similar order of material is striking:[188]

1. A man is brought to Jesus for healing (7:32 = 8:22).

2. Jesus removes the man from the public eye (7:33 = 8:23).

3. The use of spittle and touch for healing is recorded (7:33 = 8:24, 26).

4. A command for silence is issued (7:37 = 8:26).

5. However, the healing is really impossible to conceal (7:36; 8:22–26 prepares for Jesus speaking plainly in 8:32).

The vocabulary betrays a tight-knit parallel purpose as well:

7:32a	and they brought him a blind man (καὶ φέρουσιν αὐτῷ)		8:22a	and they brought him a deaf man (καὶ φέρουσιν αὐτῷ).
7:32b	and they begged Jesus (καὶ παρακαλοῦσιν αὐτὸν)		8:22b	and they begged Jesus (καὶ παρακαλοῦσιν αὐτὸν)
	to place his hand on him (ἵνα ἐπιθῇ αὐτῷ τὴν χεῖρα)			to touch him (ἵνα αὐτοῦ ἅψηται)
7:33a	and taking him (καὶ ἀπολαβόμενος αὐτὸν)		8:23a	and taking his hand (καὶ ἐπιλαβόμενος τῆς χειρὸς)
	away from the crowd privately			he led him out of the village
7:33b	he spit and touched the man's tongue (καὶ πτύσας ἥψατο τῆς γλώσσης αὐτοῦ)		8:23b	and spitting on his eyes (πτύσας εἰς τὰ ὄμματα αὐτοῦ)
7:34	he looked up to heaven (καὶ ἀναβλέψας εἰς τὸν οὐρανὸν)		8:24	he looked up (καὶ ἀναβλέψας)
7:35	a description of the healing		8:25	a description of the healing
7:35	spoke plainly (ὀρθῶς) in the end			see plainly (τηλαυγῶς) in the end
7:36	Jesus commanded them not to tell anyone.		8:26	Jesus sent him home saying, "Don't even go into the village."

---

188. The list is taken from Guelich, *Mark 1—8:26*, 429. Boring (*Mark*, 215) offers ten similarities: 1) the location of each is specified, in Gentile territory; 2) an anonymous group brings an afflicted person to Jesus; 3) pleading that 4) Jesus will lay his hands on the person; 5) Jesus takes the afflicted person away from the crowd and 6) heals him 7) by touching him and 8) using saliva, then 9) commands the incident to be kept quiet or sends the afflicted person away from the crowd; 10) Both reflect the eschatological saving work of God as portrayed in Isa 35:5–6.

The Literary Device of a Markan Framework

Even though Fowler decides against Achtemeier's proposed structure,[189] he reports, "The two healing stories in 7:31–37 and 8:22–26 possess as much or more verbal similarity than any two stories in Mark, including the two feeding stories."[190] With both stories alluding to Isaiah 35:5–6, commentators are agreed that "Mark found the two paired in the tradition"[191] or that they were "once a pair of twins."[192] This series of parallel content, vocabulary, and progression of material argues for a fabricated chiastic structure.

A twofold theological purpose accounts for these highly structured miracle catenae in the oral tradition before Mark. First, the flow of the material, beginning with a crossing of the sea as on dry ground and concluding with a miraculous feeding of the people, with healing accounts in between, proclaims that Jesus was a figure like Moses/Joshua and Elisha who delivered his people by an exodus and brought them into the Promised Land. Second, the geographical structure of the miracle catenae, where Jesus demonstrates the signs of the kingdom of God in both Jewish and Gentile territory, calls attention to the fact that the gospel is meant both for Jews and Gentiles. These two themes from the pre-Markan narrative we will discuss in chapter 7. Now we want to explain how and why Mark fractured these well-structured chiasms to proclaim his pet theological themes. Therefore, we will study the reasons for the intercalation in 5:21–43, the movement of the healing of the blind man to 8:22–26, the

---

189. Against Achtemeier's pre-Markan structure Fowler protests that "large sections of non-miracle material (Mark 6:1–33; 7:1–23) are too quickly laid aside as Markan compositions" while not acknowledging Markan redaction in the miracle catenae (*Loaves and Fishes*, 27). Employing literary criticism, Fowler is resistant to any source analysis and complains that "hiding in Achtemeier's work is the implicit principle that the miracle catenae are preeminent over the text of Mark" (29). But we have argued that Mark's purpose is brought front and center when his source material is acknowledged. Fowler effectively details the remarkable similarities between the feedings, sea journeys (100ff), and healing stories of the blind and mute man (105–7), but then he inconsistently claims that the first feeding narrative is based upon the second while maintaining that the other doublets are distinct episodes (101–2, 107). He envisions an overlapping chain-like structure (113) connecting all three doublets, but our proposal following Achtemeier of a double cycle from sea crossing to miraculous feast typologically suggests the retaking of the land, a more meaningful theological purpose for the sequence. Through his chain-like structure Fowler creates a frame (108) of healing narratives between the mute (7:31–37) and the blind man (8:22–26). But this totally misses Mark's intention of creating a frame around the discipleship catechism by the two healings of the blind men (8:22–26; 10:46–52). Finally, Fowler only produces a very general purpose for Mark's inclusion of two feeding narratives: "something to do with the person of Jesus" (111), to create irony (176), and "the crux of both stories is the interaction between Jesus and his disciples" (93). This fails to account for Mark's return to the leftover baskets in 8:19–20.

190. See Fowler, *Loaves and Fishes*, 105 and 105–7 for a complete comparison of the Greek vocabulary. Different maladies are present, but they are introduced at the same point in the story (7:32; 8:22). Different expressions are employed for withdrawal from the crowd, but the secret is present in each. Different cognates of the same verb are used (7:33 and 8:23; 7:36 and 8:26), but the two cures are described similarly with an adverb following a verb (7:25 and 8:25).

191. Guelich, *Mark 1—8:26*, 435, 429.

192. Räisänen, *Messianic Secret*, 151.

inclusion of the rejection at Nazareth and mission of the disciples in 6:1–30, and Jesus' controversy with the Pharisees in 6:53—7:23.

Originally the healings of the bleeding woman and the dead girl were in sequence, but Mark regularly constructs certain narratives into intercalations as we demonstrated in chapter 2.[193] In order to develop literary suspense as well as to theologically speak to the issue of ceremonial uncleanness, Mark places the entrance of Jairus prior to the encounter with the hemorrhaging woman and then resumes the story when the girl has died. Mark interlaces the stories of the unclean woman and the dead girl through the use of the number twelve (5:25, 42) in order to demonstrate that through Jesus' kingdom miracles the Jewish purity regulations against contact with menstruating women and dead bodies are fulfilled.[194] This is the first of Mark's adjustments to the miracle catenae.

The most prominent irregularity in Achtemeier's proposal is the transfer of the two-stage healing of the blind man from 8:22–26 to its original position following 6:52. Why would Mark demolish this well-balanced chiastic structure? The answer centers upon Mark's preference for the literary device of the framework. As we shall observe in the following section, the two-stage healing of the blind man is intricately tied to Peter's incomplete profession of Jesus' messiahship and then completed through the healing of a second blind man, Bartimaus, who perceives Jesus' complete identity and follows the way of the cross. To achieve this frame Mark must create a fracture in the narrative after the sea walking so that Jesus embarks for Bethsaida at 6:45 but fails to arrive at this destination until 8:22 for the healing of the blind man.[195] Mark then fills the gap in the narrative with a healing summary (6:54–56) since the miracles have ended[196] and changes the destination to Gennesaret since he inserts material about Jewish purity regulations into 7:1–23, which demands a Jewish provenance. Mark chooses Gennesaret since it is a familiar district that encompasses a three and a half mile plain on the western shore of Sea of Galilee between Tiberias and Capernaum.[197] This breach in the pre-Markan miracle catena entails that the fivefold structure of the

---

193. See the section at the end of chapter 2, "Mark's Role in the Composition of Intercalations."

194. See section 2.3 above and section 8.5 below.

195. Matthew has removed the incongruity by eliminating Bethsaida (just Gennesaret 14:34) while John simply mentions the city of Capernaum (6:21, 34) rather than the broader region of Gennesaret.

196. Mark regularly places summaries of healings after specific miracles when he is changing the genre of the material: 1:32–34 after Peter's mother-in-law; 3:7–12 after the healing of the shriveled hand; and 6:54–56 after the miraculous feeding and sea walking. Stein (*Mark*, 330) demonstrates Markan redaction through the allusion to previous accounts like arriving by boat (5:1, 21, 32–34, 45), people bringing the sick on mats (2:1–12; cf. 1:32), and the diseased touching Jesus' garment and being healed (5:28). See also Achtemeier ("Isolation," 284–85) and Smith ("Bethsaida via Gennesaret," 355–56) for arguments that this is Markan material.

197. Achtemeier ("Isolation," 284) following Snoy contends that Gennesaret belonged to the original catena as the conclusion to the feeding of the five thousand, but Smith ("Bethsaida via Gennesaret," 357) appropriately argues against this supposition with the question, "But how could they cross over to the western shore if they were already there?"

second chiasm vanishes along with the matched pairing of the healings of the deaf mute and the blind man. However, in Mark's new structure the two-stage healing of the blind man not only frames the discipleship catechism but contrasts the full-blown incomprehension of the disciples in 8:17–21. Therefore as a result we now have the complete-hearing and plain-speaking (7:35) former deaf-mute and the perfectly envisioned ex-blind man (8:25) contrasted with the Pharisees (8:11–15) and disciples (8:17–21), who are deaf, dumb, and blind in the enclosed material.

Achtemeier's ingenious explanation for the alteration of the boat trip from Bethsaida (6:45) to the destination Gennesaret (6:53) has not gone unchallenged. The naturalist explanation posits that the boat was simply blown off course through the stormy winds and blustery weather.[198] The obvious problem with this thesis is that the wind ceased when Jesus joined the disciples leaving them every opportunity to get back on course.[199] Certainly Jesus could have just changed his mind and headed for Gennesaret instead, but without any further details this theory lacks conviction.[200] These explanations suppose that both Bethsaida and Gennesaret ensue from the hand of Mark because of the familiar Markan double-step expression:

6:45   εἰς τὸ πέραν / πρὸς Βηθσαϊδάν (to the other side, to Bethsaida)

6:53   ἐπὶ τὴν γῆν ἦλθον / εἰς Γεννησαρὲτ (they came unto the land, to Gennesaret)

However, if Mark employed oral rather than written sources he would certainly retell the traditional stories with his own vocabulary, which would explain the consistent use of terminology throughout the entire gospel.[201]

Others explain this contradiction through the author's geographical incomprehension, claiming that the evangelist himself had no clear picture of the localities in mind since they were little more than names in the tradition.[202] But in chapter 7 we will demonstrate how Mark strategically distinguishes Jewish and Gentile locations to demonstrate that Jesus' kingdom miracles already proclaim the gospel to Gentiles.

A fourth alternative position concentrates on Christology, although its main proponent, Stephen Smith, labels it a plot suspension technique. He concludes that "The two-stage nature of the healing at Bethsaida and the two-stage attempt of the disciples to arrive there are parallel narrative constructions which are intended to underpin

---

198. Cf. Smith, "Bethsaida via Gennesaret," 351, n. 3 for a list of supporters including Swete (*Mark*, 129–30, 140) and Taylor (*Mark*, 332).

199. Smith points out that the phrase in Mark 6:53a (διαπεράσαντες ἐπὶ τὴν γῆν) "suggests that they were still some way off shore" ("Bethsaida via Gennesaret," 352).

200. The western text has Jesus first arrive at Bethsaida and then Gennesaret but this is an obvious compilation. Cf. Smith, "Bethsaida via Gennesaret," 358–62 for various textual alterations, none of which really solve any of the problems involved.

201. Schenke, *Wundererzählungen*, 386.

202. Rawlinson, *Mark*, 89 and Fowler, *Loaves and Fishes*, 66.

Mark's overriding theological purpose."[203] Jesus' delayed arrival in Bethsaida creates suspense in the narrative which emphasizes Jesus' true identity. Already in 6:14–16 Mark has raised the question of Jesus' identity but never answered it. Jesus' late arrival in Bethsaida at 8:22 maintains the narrative tension so that Jesus' complete identity is not revealed until Peter's confession in 8:27 and the subsequent passion predictions. Smith's position is really a subset of the literary view one could entitle an extended object lesson. The purpose of the plot suspension is pedagogical. The disciples will only finish the journey across the lake when they learn the teaching material contained in the events narrated in between. They must learn like Peter that a miracle-working Christ is insufficient Christology without an emphasis upon the necessity of the cross.

For Smith the reason for the plot suspension and insertion of pedagogical material is christological, but for Malbon the object lesson centers on the mission to the Gentiles.[204] She contends that the inability of the boat to arrive at the Gentile city of Bethsaida demonstrates the disciples' unwillingness to accept a gospel mission to the Gentiles. Their hardness of heart demonstrates a rebellious stance against the universalism of Jesus. Mark intends to teach the importance of a mission to the Gentiles, as evidenced by the material within the plot suspension: 1) the fulfillment of Jewish cleansing rituals and restrictive culinary legislation in 7:1–23; 2) the creation of table fellowship between Jews and Gentiles in 7:24–30; 3) the healing of the deaf-mute in Gentile Decapolis; 4) the miraculous feeding of a multitude in Gentile territory (8:1–9) just as he had earlier done on Jewish ground; and 5) the emphasis placed upon the number of baskets left over in the miraculous feedings (8:19–20), which symbolizes ministry to both Jews and Gentiles. However, as Malbon puts it, "In the detour from the journey commanded by Jesus, the disciples display their blurred vision."[205]

The dislocation theory of Achtemeier, which concentrates on Markan redaction of his oral source (a diachronic method), and the literary approach of plot suspension whereby Mark offers an extended object lesson (a synchronic approach) are not necessarily contradictory. The dislocation theory argues for a pre-Markan source so that redaction criticism can be employed to determine unique Markan emphases. Likewise, the literary technique of plot suspension focuses on the didactic material that must be grasped before the discipleship journey can be completed. These two separate methods result in the unfolding of identical Markan emphases. The placing of the healing of the blind man in Bethsaida calls attention to a Gentile emphasis, but

---

203. Smith, "Bethsaida via Gennesaret," 374. Smith labels it, "A Structuralist Solution" (362–65).

204. Malbon, *Narrative Space*, 27–29. Smith argues against Malbon's view contending that "we would surely be entitled to expect the comment in 6,52 to have been placed after the Feeding of the Four Thousand (8,1–10), since it was Jesus' ministry to the Gentiles which the disciples did not understand" ("Bethsaida via Gennesaret," 365). However, the material in Mark 7 and 8 demonstrates the importance of the Gentile mission as when Jesus offers table fellowship to the Syrophoenician woman so that Mark has emphasized both an appropriate Christology (Smith's emphasis) and the Gentile mission (Malbon's emphasis). Both of these are important Markan themes as Smith concedes on page 373.

205. Malbon, "Jesus of Mark," 363.

the two-step healing and its new placement at 8:22–26 emphasizes the necessity of a Suffering Servant Christology. Smith emphasizes the Christology theme whereas Malbon underlines the Gentile mission motif. Both are present, with the Gentile mission the central subject of the pre-Markan miracle catenae, whereas the emphasis upon a suffering Messiah is Mark's favorite theme. As Smith points out, the Gentile theme becomes "a sub-plot which is subservient to the main thrust of the action which, at that point, is concerned with the question of Jesus' true identity."[206] The prevalence of miracle stories in this section entails that the primary lesson must involve the purpose and function of the miracles themselves. The disciples travel toward Bethsaida but they cannot arrive until they understand the correct theology of miracles, which is finally taught through the second touch given to the blind man. The disciples will not understand Jesus' works (4:40; 6:52; 8:17–21) until they accept a discipleship willing to follow Jesus to the cross.

Since the dislocation theory establishes the presence of pre-Markan material, redaction criticism can be employed to reveal the unique Markan emphases found in 6:1–30, 7:1–23; and 8:11–21. Each of these insertions into the pre-Markan miracle catenae introduces the reader to a crucial theme in Markan theology which stands alongside the themes of a suffering Messiah and a Gentile mission.

Mark has separated the healing of the bleeding woman and dead girl from the feeding of the five thousand by the insertion of the rejection at Nazareth (6:1–6a) and the mission of the disciples (6:6b–13, 30) encircling the death of John the Baptizer (6:7–29).[207] Why has Mark interrupted this miracle catena that originally depicted the retaking of the Promised Land through a miraculous crossing of the sea, mighty wonders, and a miraculous feast? Mark's emphasis upon a discipleship that overcomes rejection has caused him to insert Jesus' negative reception at Nazareth (6:1–6a), which completes his second narrative cycle and prepares for the deeper discipleship his devotees experience when they commence their own mission work (6:6b–13, 30–31).[208] Thus Mark concludes the training of the disciples (3:13—5:43) with the reality of the rejection by their own countryfolk (6:1–6a) and then begins a new cycle with a deeper involvement of the disciples in Jesus' mission. Now they perform the ministry while Jesus supervises from a distance. The increase in responsibility requires that the narrative be placed before the feeding of the five thousand and the sea-walking journey across the lake since these are examples of the increased demands of discipleship. In 6:37 Jesus instructs the disciples to feed the multitude themselves; at 6:41 and 8:6 the disciples distribute the bread to the crowds; in 6:45–52 Jesus sends his disciples away by themselves to face the journey over the sea; and at 8:14 the disciples have forgotten to bring bread along for the sea trip. This discipleship "intrusion" at 6:1–30 shapes

---

206. Smith, "Bethsaida via Gennesaret," 373.

207. See Achtemeier ("Insertion," 266–71) for evidence of a thorough Markan editorial activity in this section.

208. See Appendix 4, pattern 12.

and molds the miracles into didactic material which then concludes with the disciples' inability to understand the meaning of the loaves (6:52; 8:17–21).[209]

After inserting the area of Gennesaret (6:53) and concluding the series of miracles with a summary (6:54–56), Mark attaches a second lengthy didactic section of controversies (7:1–23).[210] Smith contends that such an "insertion of a controversy story (7,1–23) into a passage devoted to Jesus' miracle-working activity would be decidedly odd,"[211] but Mark wants to provide a new context for the following miracle stories, the exorcism of the Syrophoenician's daughter in 7:24–30 and the healing of the deaf mute at 7:31–37. Through this added material Mark alters the emphasis from tales of wonder to the fulfillment of Jewish rituals. Mark introduces purity issues since one of the major struggles facing the church is the place of Gentiles in the plan of God as well as the normativity of OT cleanliness rites for Gentiles (Acts 15:5–11, 19–21). Therefore Mark incorporates a section on clean hands (7:1–13) and kosher food (7:14–23) so that the primary emphasis of the following two incidents become controversies about clean people and clean fluids (spittle). The Syrophoenician woman's faith is now not miracle faith but "faith that the barrier between Jew and gentile is overcome, and the gentiles are admitted to the people of God."[212] Regarding the healing of the deaf mute in the Decapolis, Broadhead demonstrates that "the story now tells of the breaking in of God's ransoming mercy to the Gentile people through the life and ministry of Jesus."[213] Earlier in 5:21–43 Mark transformed the third and fourth elements of the first miracle catena into an intercalation which added a purity emphasis regarding the OT regulations about touching menstruating women and dead bodies. Mark's additional transformation here inserts the identical emphasis so that the theme of the fulfillment of OT Jewish purity rites now saturates the entire section on miracles.

Since the two series of miracle catenae conclude with the feeding of the four thousand (8:1–9), the Markan addition of 8:11–21 must be central to the purpose of this entire section of miracle stories. This returns us to the important discussion of a Markan frame. Mark concludes the miracle section with a sea conversation (8:14–21).[214] Whereas earlier the discipleship cycles concluded with the theme of rejection

---

209. It is interesting to note that Mark shapes 6:6b–31 into a sandwich similar to the pericope before in 5:21–43.

210. See Achtemeier ("Insertion," 271–73) for Markan redactional features in 7:1–23. Since 6:54–56 provides a closing summary there is no need for 7:1–23 to relate to the healings that immediately precede it.

211. Smith, "Bethsaida via Gennesaret," 353. However, Smith agrees that "As it stands, the arrival at Gennesaret in 6.53 makes an appropriate setting for the thoroughly Jewish debate on ritual purity" (354–55).

212. Fuller, *Interpreting the Miracles*, 59. Fuller further hypothesizes that "The healing at a distance is perhaps a way of saying that Jesus did not go to the gentiles directly during his earthly ministry; he is now doing it at a distance, from heaven, through his agents on earth" (48).

213. Broadhead, *Teaching with Authority*, 134.

214. Since this passage is modeled on two earlier didactic scenes (Mark 4:3–20; 7:14–23), it must be a Markan composition and not part of the pre-existent miracle catenae. See Sellew, "Composition

by the Jewish leadership (3:6) or the Jewish people (6:1–6a), now the disciples themselves are hard-hearted (8:17), spiritually blind and deaf (8:18a), surprisingly forgetful (8:18b), and theological ignorant (8:21). Mark piles ten questions of Jesus on top of each other to illustrate the unfathomable befuddlement of the disciples.[215]

1. 8:17a   Why are you talking about having no bread?
2. 8:17b   Do you still not see?
3. 8:17c   Do you still not understand?
4. 8:17d   Are your hearts hardened?
5. 8:18a   Do you have eyes but fail to see?
6. 8:18b   Do you have ears but fail to hear?
7. 8:18c   And don't you remember?
8. 8:19   How many basketfuls of pieces at the feeding of the five thousand?
9. 8:20   How many basketfuls of pieces at the feeding of the four thousand?
10. 8:21   Do you still not understand?

What do the disciples not understand? The content of the disciples' misunderstanding has stumped the scholarly community. Countryman points out that "Most commentators have nothing at all to say about v 21, perhaps because the modern reader is forced to answer its question negatively: 'Do you not yet understand?' No, we do not."[216] One can only dare to exegete this passage by discovering the clues to its meaning in Mark's context.

Mark attaches a third narrative about crossing the sea (8:14–16) to the two cycles of miracles. Therefore, the primary intended message must concern a theology of miracles as evidenced in the following flow of material. Immediately after the feeding of the four thousand, Mark moves the story to Jewish territory to bring the Pharisees on the scene (8:10). They demand a sign (8:11–13), which leads to the sea conversation about bread. This talk over a loaf of bread (8:14) results in a warning about the leaven of the Pharisees and Herod in 8:15, which must be linked with the seeking after signs by the Pharisees in 8:11–12. The negative leaven consists of the seeking of signs.[217] This in turn flows back in 8:19–20 to the two feeding narratives and the fact

---

of Didactic Scenes," 613, 617.

215. Marcus counts seven questions: "Is it just a coincidence, or a part of Markan numerology, that 'seven' is the last word in 8:20, which is the seventh question in the passage?" (*Mark 1–8*, 508). But this comment reads too much into the narrative. Latourelle (*Miracles*, 181) envisions eight questions.

216. Countryman, "How Many Baskets Full?" 644. Marcus quips that "even in a puzzling work such as Mark, our passage is singularly cryptic" (*Mark 1–8*, 512).

217. A sign, then, is not a miracle of a higher order but a wonder that offers such concrete evidence that faith is not required. For scholarly support that a sign from heaven refers to a miracle of a special kind, greater than the other miracles performed by Jesus see Linton ("Demand for a Sign," 113–15) and Gundry (*Mark*, 402, 404). But the expression "from heaven" is not crucial to the interpretation

that the disciples do not understand about the loaves (6:52). This obtuseness of the disciples has intensified, as the three sea crossings proceed from a quick note in 4:40 about hard-heartedness to a Markan comment concluding an entire feeding incident in 6:52 to an extensive series of critical questions in 8:14–21. What do the disciples not understand about the feedings? The answer must involve the leaven of the Pharisees and Herod, which centers on the seeking of signs as indicated in the context.

Problematically, Matthew interprets the leaven as the teaching of the Pharisees (16:12) and Luke as hypocrisy (12:1), neither of which fits Mark's context. In Mark the leaven must involve the theology of miracles, as evidenced by the broader context of miracle stories, the demand for a miraculous sign by the Pharisees in 8:11, and the leaven of Herod indicating his desire for a sign in 6:14.[218] The disciples' incomprehension places them in the camp of the outsiders, namely the Pharisees and Herod. Through this episode Mark is challenging his readers not to misunderstand miracles by demanding God's action to alter historical events so that they can avoid suffering and a discipleship of the cross. They misunderstand the miraculous feedings since they have limited their significance to dramatic rescue events and neglected their foreshadowing of the real miraculous feeding, which occurs at the last eucharistic supper and Jesus' crucifixion. A miracle ministry can never be disassociated from Jesus' passion; it is through the third miraculous feeding, the giving of Jesus own flesh, where the real miracle occurs and where there is plenty left over for all.

To confirm this understanding of the leaven, we must review other proposals that have been put forward. If the leaven is the teaching of the scribes and Pharisees, like Matthew 16:12, then the disciples are unaware of their own legalistic, cultic-ritual piety as in Mark 7:1–23.[219] If the leaven is hypocrisy, like Luke 12:1, then the failure of the disciples is their unawareness of their own negative character qualities. If the leaven is faulty eschatology (misguided expectation of apocalyptic signs or failure to recognize the arrival of the eschatological age), then the meaning of the feedings missed by the disciples is the foretaste of the eschatological banquet.[220] If the leaven is unbelief and a continue demand for more proof, then the disciples' failure is a lack of faith in the abundance of Christ's provision.[221] If the leaven of the Pharisees and Herod is their secret service apparatus consisting of observers, hearing posts, Sabbath-watchers, and liquidation commissars, then the disciples do not understand the danger of persecution.[222] If the leaven is Jewish particularism, then the meaning

---

since it is omitted in Matt 12:38–39 but present in 16:1–4.

218. Herod suggests that Jesus is the Baptizer risen from the dead in 6:14 because of the wonders he accomplished. See Luke 23:8 where Herod wants Jesus to "perform a sign" (σημεῖον ἰδεῖν).

219. See Boucher, *Mysterious Parable*, 77, n. 50 for a list of scholars who support this view.

220. See Robbins, "*Dynamis* and *Sēmeia*," 5–20.

221. See Guelich, *Mark 1—8:27*, 426–27; Gundry, *Mark*, 411.

222. See Stauffer, "Realistische Jesusworte," 2:507–8.

of the feedings is Gentile inclusion.[223] Finally, if the leaven is the failure to recognize and accept Jesus as the bread, then the disciples have failed to see Jesus as the one true Bread into whom they have been incorporated, including a recognition of the Eucharist as the presence of Christ.[224] But since the leaven is outward sign-seeking, then the disciples fail to discern the symbolic meaning of the feedings, which point to the passion of Jesus through the similar expressions employed in the Last Supper (6:41; 8:6–7; 14:22–23).[225] As Donfried explains, "What the disciples should already have perceived and understood in Mark 6 and 8 by way of anticipation is now made clear in 14,22ff. The bread symbolizes Jesus as the body, as the one who becomes a ransom for many by means of his death."[226]

Mark's primary emphasis, therefore, is to demonstrate that the Jesus which the community must follow is not just a miracle-working Messiah but a Suffering Servant Son of Man. This then becomes the emphasis of the following discipleship catechism section (8:22—10:52). However, the theme of a Gentile mission remains in the background as a secondary accent. An emphasis upon the Gentiles is evidenced by the recognition of Jewish and Gentile territory throughout the sea journeys. In addition, Jesus calls attention to the number of basketfuls collected in the overflow of the miracle near the end of his interrogation of the disciples (8:19–20). The twelve and seven respectively reflect the twelve tribes of Israel and the seven nations of Canaan, displaying that Mark has discerned the significance of the duplicate feedings in his oral source. However, since the Gentile mission is not a structural element in Mark's gospel, the motif of the passion of Jesus and the theology of the cross must be given prominence. Misunderstanding concludes the section on miracles. If this obduracy involved primarily a resistance to a Gentile mission, certainly Mark would begin the next section with teaching on Jesus' universalism. Instead, the healing of the blind man in two stages introduces the vital necessity of following not just a victorious messianic Son of David but also a suffering Son of Man. To view Jesus only as a sign-giving wonder-worker means the disciples remain half blind. Instead, true followers must discover Jesus' means of multiplying the bread of life through a discipleship of the cross.

What then is Mark's theology of miracles? Mark is not against miracles per se, but against a demand for miracles. Therefore, this section is not a negative foil for

---

223. See Beck, "Reclaiming a Biblical Text," 56; Boobyer, "Miracles of the Loaves," 86; Ernst, *Markus*, 226; Gibson, "Rebuke of the Disciples," 32; Lohmeyer, *Markus*, 157; Kelber, *Mark's Story*, 40–41; Pesch, *Markusevangelium*, 1:413; Reid, *Preaching Mark*, 86; and Stock, *Call*, 127.

224. See Burkill, *Mysterious Revelation*, 106–7; Donfried, "Feeding Narratives," 101–3; Quesnell, *Mind of Mark*, 260; for ancient documents see Hippolytus, *Antichrist*, 59; *Apostolic Constitutions* 2:547.

225. See Best, "Miracles in Mark," 539–54. See also section 4.2b below.

226. Donfried, "Feeding Narratives," 102. Van Iersel adds evidence, "For those who know the rest of the book, Jesus' saying in v. 15 contains an unmistakable but as yet obscure reference to the passover meal that Jesus will celebrate with his disciples (14:22–25)" (*Mark*, 264). Camery-Hoggatt (*Irony*, 201, n. 87) offers additional support.

an attack upon Mark's opponents within the community[227] but a positive foil for a cross-oriented Christology. The two-stage healing of the blind man holds the miracle section and discipleship catechism together since Jesus is both a wonder-worker and a Suffering Servant. This double identity of Jesus begins the gospel with the voice from heaven (Ps 2:7 combined with Isa 42:1), concludes the gospel in the centurion's confession, and is prominent at the center of the gospel in Jesus' response (8:31–34) to Peter's confession of faith (8:29). Therefore the first half of the gospel, which abounds with miracles stories, prepares for the second half, which concentrates on the passion. Miracles are not polemicized against; they are just insufficient.[228] Broadhead offers the correct perspective:

> No sharp division exists between the portrait of Jesus in the first and the last half of the Gospel. The narrative develops the failure of the disciples through both miracle stories and the passion account. The opposition of the religious leaders begins in a miracle story and concludes in the passion story. The focus on Jesus' death originates in a miracle story and is fulfilled in the passion narrative.... Both miracle stories and the passion (14.61–62; 15.26, 39) confirm the messiahship of Jesus.[229]

Therefore, the sea miracles do not produce faith (4:40; 6:52; 8:17–18) because they instill an incomplete picture of Jesus without his passion.[230]

Mark has turned attention away from an epiphanic emphasis toward a teaching emphasis.[231] Even though Mark includes many miracle stories, he does not concentrate on the miraculous. Miracles can lead to amazement but not to commitment. Indeed, miracles are frequently accompanied by blindness and hardness of heart. Since mighty deeds cannot give a complete picture of Jesus' identity, the disciples cannot understand completely. Therefore, Jesus' identity remains hidden in his miracle working since it can only become clear in his passion (14:62) and crucifixion (15:39).

---

227. A range of triumphalistic views have been assigned to the disciples so that scholars posit a polemic against a *theios aner* Christology (Weeden, *Traditions in Conflict*, 50–51; Perrin, *Redaction Criticism*, 51–57; Achtemeier, "Origin," 218–21; Sunderwirth, *Use of Miracle Stories*, 50), a royal Davidic Christology (Tyson, "Blindness," 261–68), an apocalyptic Son of Man Christology (Telford, *Theology of Mark*, 50), or a Hellenistic Son of God Christology (Kelber). But as Marcus argues, "Divine man does not seem to have been a fixed term in first-century Hellenism and when the term is used, it does not seem to be particularly connected with miracles or with the title Son of God" (*Mark 1–8*, 77).

228. Therefore, the conclusion of Sunderwirth cannot be confirmed, "When miracles abound, wrong confessions are made. When true identity and function are declared, miracles are relatively absent" (*Use of Miracle Stories*, 109).

229. Broadhead, *Teaching with Authority*, 214.

230. As Achtemeier points out, "Nowhere in Mark is there any hint that miracles are adequate grounds for discipleship. The only adequate grounds for Mark is readiness for martyrdom" ("And He Followed Him," 135).

231. Stock concludes that Mark "moves from the miraculous to the kerygmatic" (*Call*, 147).

Mark wants to establish the "insufficiency of miracles to identify the true mission of Jesus."[232]

Presumably, the role and importance of miracles is misunderstood by Mark's intended audience as well. As Latourelle points out, Mark "sets up a comparison between the partial blindness of the disciple of Jesus and that of the community of Mark's contemporaries. The passion and death are required for the opening of the eyes of Jesus' true disciples."[233] Mark places a frame of discipleship misunderstanding around the miracles in order to focus the picture of Jesus. He balances the first sea journey (4:35–41) with a sea conversation (8:14–21) so that a discussion of miracles in the life of the church can occur.[234] If Mark is written as a persecution tract to a community recovering from struggle and tragedy, then Mark employs the sea conversation trip as a frame to perform a narrative metamorphosis. Now the miracles become a call to discipleship since the community will misunderstand Jesus' mission until they see him as the loaf that is offered in death (8:14) and follow to learn the discipleship catechism (8:27—10:52).

We still must deal with one objection to the presence of a pre-Markan chiastic structure of miracle catenae, namely the parallel passage in John 6:1–24, where the feeding of the five thousand leads into the sea crossing.[235] If the two miracle catenae began with the crossing of water and concluded with the eschatological feast of the miracle feedings, why does John reverse the order and position the miraculous feeding first? The answer derives from a realization that just as the two sets of five controversy dialogues (Mark 2:1—3:6 and 11:27—12:40) were fused together in the oral tradition through the parallel centers of death and resurrection, so the two miracle catenae are fastened by death and resurrection.[236] This occurs through the flow from one chiasm to the next. The centers of the chiasms triumph the secondary theme of salvation to the Jew first but also to the Gentile, with the paralleling of the Jewish woman who is saved from her impurity and the Gentile woman who is granted table fellowship with Israel. On the other hand, the connection of the two catenae weds the feeding of the five thousand to the sea-walking narrative (Mark 6:30–52). The feeding presents Jesus as offering broken bread to the multitudes, which foreshadows his death on the cross, while the walking over the sea shortly before dawn where Jesus passes by (Mark 6:48; like Exod 33:22; 1 Kgs 19:11) in epiphanic majesty as the "I am" (Mark 6:50; like Exod 3:14) suggests Jesus' resurrection.[237] In fact, several scholars claim that Jesus'

---

232. Broadhead, *Teaching with Authority*, 144.

233. Latourelle, *Miracles*, 184.

234. Fowler quips, "We might say that a storm does take place in 8:14–21, but it is inside the boat!" (*Reader*, 145).

235. For similarities and differences with John see Marcus, *Mark 1–8*, 412–13, 428.

236. Stock explains, "Significantly, in Mark's account, the breaking of the bread, symbol of Jesus' death, precedes the victory over water, symbol of the resurrection" (*Call*, 121).

237. Cf. Boucher, *Mysterious Parable*, 75.

sea walking was in fact a displaced resurrection narrative because of the following connections:[238]

1. A mountain is mentioned as the geographical background (6:46; Matt 28:16).
2. Jesus appears suddenly after a period of separation (6:48; Luke 24:36).
3. The disciples believe Jesus is a ghost (6:49a; Luke 24:37b).
4. The disciples are terrified (6:49a; Luke 24:37a) and troubled (6:50; Luke 24:38a).
5. The narrator points out that Jesus is not a ghost (Luke 24:39 implied by Mark 6:50a).
6. Jesus' greeting instructs the disciples not to be afraid (6:50b; Luke 24:38).
7. Jesus states, "I am here," employing the formula ἐγώ εἰμι (6:50b; Luke 24:39).
8. The disciples respond with amazement (6:51; Luke 24:41a).
9. The narratives include a reference to food (6:52a; Luke 24:41b).
10. Some disciples have hardened and doubting hearts (6:52b; Luke 24:38b).
11. In the Emmaus appearance (Luke 24:13–35) Jesus is made known in the bread, whereas in Mark 6:52 the disciples do not understand the meaning of the loaves.
12. Jesus intends to pass by the two men going to Emmaus just as he intends to pass by the disciples in the boat (but the Greek vocabulary diverges significantly (Mark 6:48 ἤθελεν παρελθεῖν; Luke 24:28 προσεποιήσατο πορρώτερον πορεύεσθαι).

In all likelihood the early church employed these miracle catenae as well as the controversy dialogues to proclaim the gospel message in the oral preaching tradition. Both emphasize death and resurrection, the breaking and taking of Jesus followed by his vindication and revelation.[239] Apparently the Gospel of John employs the central connecting message of these miracle catenae rather than the fivefold chiasms in two cycles which highlight a Jewish and Gentile mission for the church. In John's time the recognition of the Gentile mission has been replaced by the burning issue of removal from the synagogue (John 9:22; 12:42; 16:2) so that these two sets of miracle catenae are no longer relevant. Issues between the church and synagogue rather than between Jews and Gentiles are prominent in John's gospel, so that he emphasizes Jesus as the fulfillment of the Passover feast (John 6:4).[240]

---

238. See Madden (*Jesus Walking*, 36–40) for support and chapter 4 for his arguments in favor of this thesis. We are of the opinion that Dodd's arguments still triumph against this thesis. Cf. Dodd, "Appearances of the Risen Christ," 23–24. The following list is adapted from Marcus (*Mark 1–8*, 433) and the diagrams in chapter 4 of Madden.

239. The only difference is that the death/resurrection theme in the controversy dialogues is called attention to through the coordination of the centers while in the miracle stories it is the connecting link of the two cycles.

240. Therefore the trip over the sea in John 6:1 cannot be to Gentile territory since the feeding of the five thousand has implications for the Jewish Passover.

We have demonstrated that the two miracle catenae are not Markan creations, as evidenced by the transfer of the healing of the blind man to a later place in the gospel (8:22–26) and the addition of passages emphasizing discipleship (6:1–30), purity issues (7:1–23) and the role of miracles in the church (8:11–21). However, Mark does create a frame around these cycles of miracles by paralleling the sea journey at the beginning with a sea conversation at the end which develops Mark's theology of miracles to address his community. Taken together, the three sea narratives increasingly deepen the misunderstanding of the disciples.[241] Therefore Mark consistently employs the frame technique to prepare for a suffering Christ and a discipleship of the cross with the theme of a Gentile mission in the background.

3.8 The Frame around the Discipleship Catechism of Mark 8:22—10:52

In this section we will investigate the structure of the discipleship catechism as well as the frame around it to demonstrate that Mark highlights the double theme of a suffering Messiah and a discipleship of the cross. In the process we will analyze how the triadic structure of the narrative evidences this double theme and how the frame which seems initially to be miracle stories are really discipleship narratives.

Just as the controversy dialogues of 2:1—3:6, the parables of 4:1–34, and the miracle catenae of 4:35—8:21 each contain material unique to its genre, so in 8:27—10:52 twenty-three didactic statements of universal moral directives occur, whereas up to this point the reader has only encountered two such statements (3:29, 35).[242] Although Mark narrates the transfiguration and the healing of the boy possessed by an evil spirit within this instruction, each episode is transformed from epiphany and healing narrative to discipleship teaching. The transfiguration emphasizes discipleship through the placement of Peter's lack of understanding (9:5) at the center of the pericope. The exorcism narrative is transformed at both the beginning and the end when 1) a controversy is added with the teachers of the law (9:14); 2) a response of astonishment is placed first rather than last (9:15); 3) Jesus rebukes the unbelieving generation (9:19); 4) Jesus engages in a discussion with his disciples in a house (9:28), which is a standard Markan reference for discipleship teaching; and 5) the passage concludes with a call to prayer (9:29).[243] Finally, the reference to Jesus as a teacher throughout

---

241. See 4:40; 6:52; and 8:17–21. Latourella explains about the first sea journey in 4:35–41, "If we leave aside v. 40 with its reproach of the frightened disciples, we find the classic literary structure of a miracle story" (*Miracles*, 103). However, this addition has been "superimposed on a miracle story in order to give it a catechetical direction."

242. Quesnell, *Mind of Mark*, 134–36.

243. See section 6.5 below.

the healings in this section[244] indicates that a discipleship catechism is the appropriate title for 8:22—10:52.

The progression of material reveals a twofold purpose of Christology and discipleship, with both centering upon the cross. Just as three boat trips featuring an increasing misunderstanding by the disciples structure the miracle catenae, so a triad of passion predictions (8:31; 9:31; 10:33–34) followed by misunderstandings (8:32–33; 9:32–34; 10:35–38) and teachings on discipleship (8:34—9:29; 9:35—10:32; 10:39–52) organize the material in this passion instruction catechism. Two inclusios as well reinforce these two connected themes. An envelope technique places christological declarations at the opening and ending of this section. Peter's confession of Jesus as the Messiah (8:29) followed by his inability to confess Jesus as suffering Son of Man (8:33) parallels Bartimaeus' acclamation of Jesus as the Son of David (10:47–48) followed by his positive action of following Jesus on the way to the cross (10:52).[245] Second, the theme of "the way" (ἐν τῇ ὁδῷ 8:27; 10:46, 52) highlights the importance of the way of discipleship at each end of the section.

The content of the material focuses upon a suffering Messiah and a discipleship of the cross as well. The triad of passion predictions, which reflects three different geographical locales (Caesarea Philippi; the roads of Galilee, Judea, and Trans-Jordan; and Jesus' approach to Jerusalem via Jericho), intensify in specificity so that 10:33–34 is literally fulfilled in the passion narrative.[246] The three misunderstandings all involve a choice by the disciples for self-aggrandizement rather than self-sacrifice. The disciples want to follow a victorious Messiah (8:32–33) where they can achieve greatness (9:34) and be enthroned with power (10:35–37), but each teaching on discipleship (8:34–38; 9:35–37; 10:42–45) corrects the disciples' misunderstandings through the employment of a paradox in the form of a "whoever" statement:

8:35 "Whoever wants to save their life will lose it."

9:35 "Anyone who wants to be first must be the very last, and the servant of all."

10:43 "Whoever wants to become great among you must be your servant."

In the three teachings on discipleship, the first section focuses on self-denial and cross-bearing (8:34), the second discusses relationships so that the disciples are prepared to be salted sacrifices (9:49–50), and the third cycle concentrates on servant

---

244. In 9:17 Jesus is addressed as teacher which Matthew changes to "Lord" (17:15) as well as in the healing of Bartimaeus (10:51; *Rabbouni*) which both Matt 20:33 and Luke 18:41 alter to "Lord." Also at 4:38; 5:35; 9:38 "teacher" becomes a title in the Markan miracle stories. Cf. Meye, *Jesus and the Twelve*, 78.

245. Therefore Best is correct when reflecting upon the healing of Baritmaeus, "It is perhaps significant that the man uses the title 'Son of David' while he is blind, just as Peter used 'Christ' at the time when he could not see properly" (*Following Jesus*, 140).

246. Van Iersel, *Mark*, 270–71.

leadership and provides a positive example in Bartimaeus, who follows Jesus along the way (10:52b).

The primary argument against this triadic structure focuses upon Matthew and Luke's demolishment of key features of the Markan edifice. Luke omits the first and last misunderstandings (9:22–23; 18:34 but see 22:24–27) while Matthew eliminates the second episode of incomprehension (18:1). However, these changes are not uncommon, since both gospel writers disassemble several of the Markan intercalations[247] as well as expunging the frame for this section consisting of the healings of the two blind men.

Gundry combats a triadic structure by discovering a fourth passion prediction in 9:9–13 and recognizing the lengthier teaching on discipleship in the first cycle. He also attempts to demonstrate that a discipleship of the cross is neither a unique nor consistent theme in these chapters by pointing out that passion predictions spill over into the rest of Mark (3:6, 21; 6:4, 17–29; 14:8, 17–25, 41–42), while Jesus' supernaturalism is highlighted in this section (9:2–8, 38–41; 10:46–52).[248] But this minute analysis demands too much from a structure. Whereas the theme of Jesus' passion increasingly expands within this section, an emphasis upon the cross at other places before the Jerusalem ministry is sporadic, surprising, and unexpected. Certainly the first triad is lengthier, but at the outset Mark wants to emphasize Peter's misunderstanding both of the earthly Jesus' passion prediction (8:32–33) as well as the heavenly vision (9:5–6). Discipleship failure becomes inexcusable when it occurs on two successive occasions.

As an alternative to a triadic structure, Humphrey discerns a lengthy chiastic structure covering the entire discipleship catechism:[249]

[8:22–26]			A blind man receives his sight
a		8:27–30	The contrast between what people say about Jesus and what the disciples say.
	b	8:31–33	A resurrection prediction, an uncomprehending reaction by the disciples.
		c	8:34—9:1	The necessity of death to self.
			d	9:2–8	The blessedness of Jesus the Son.
				e	9:9–13	Jesus interprets the scriptures, against the scribes, for the disciples, privately.
					f	9:14–15	The crowds acclaim Jesus, the scribes are hostile.
						g	9:16–27	Jesus casts out an unclean spirit in response to faith in a faithless age.
							h	9:28–29	Jesus alone with the disciples, in a house, deals with their failure.
								i	9:30–32	A resurrection prediction and the disciples' misunderstanding.
							h'	9:33–37	Jesus alone with the disciples, in a house, deals with their failure.

---

247. See section 2.8 above.
248. Gundry, *Mark*, 440–42.
249. Humphrey, *He is Risen!* 79; the diagram is found in van Iersel, *Mark*, 274.

g'	9:38–50	Jesus permits others to cast out demons; speaks of faith, and of scandalizing that faith.
f'	10:1–9	The crowds acclaim Jesus, the Pharisees test Jesus.
e'	10:10–12	Jesus interprets the scriptures, against the scribes, for disciples, privately.
d'	10:13–16	The blessedness of all who become like children.
c'	10:17–31	The necessity of giving up what one owns for Jesus and the gospel in order to enter the kingdom of God.
b'	10:32–40	A resurrection prediction, an uncomprehending reaction by the disciples, corrected by Jesus.
a'	10:41–45	The contrast between what people say and do and what disciples must do.
[10:46–52]		A blind man receives his sight

Positively, Humphrey recognizes the frame surrounding the instruction and gives prominence to the passion predictions either at the center of the chiasm or around the edges (b and b'). However, why should the second passion prediction stand prominently at the center when the third prediction is the most developed? And what about the parallel triad of misunderstandings and teachings on discipleship? Therefore we conclude with Van Iersel that "a number of correspondences perceived by Humphrey are based on a selective if not arbitrary way of reading the text."[250] Finally, this leading rival outline completely ignores Mark's use of fivefold chiasms as well as his preference for triadic structures.[251]

Having established a triadic structure for the discipleship catechism and the themes that it develops, we now turn to the frame encircling this section. Of all the candidates nominated for this literary device, the healings of the blind men in 8:22–26 and 10:46–52 are by far the most widely recognized and accepted exemplars of a Markan framework.[252] Support for a frame includes the following:

1. The term "blind" (τυφλὸς) is only employed in 8:22–23; 10:46, 49, 51.

2. The pericopes begin identically: "And they are going into Bethsaida/Jericho" (8:22; 10:46).[253]

---

250. See van Iersel, *Mark*, 272 where he offers examples.

251. Cf. Broadhead, *Teaching with Authority*, 161–64; Dewey, *Markan Public Debate*, 38; Neirynck, *Duality*, 110–12; and Rhoads and Michie, *Mark as Story*, 54–55.

252. Scholarly support ensues from a wide range of theological traditions including Achtemeier, "Followed" 115, 132; Burkill, "Strain on the Secret," 32; Camery-Hoggatt, *Irony*, 10; Collins, *Mark*, 391; Dewey, *Markan Public Debate*, 23; Fowler, *Reader*, 144; Kelber, *Story*, 44; *Oral and Written Gospel*, 110; Marshall, *Faith*, 139; Myers, *Binding*, 239; Perrin, "Towards an Interpretation," 4–5; Swartley, "Structural Function," 74; van Iersel, *Mark*, 79.

253. Dewey, "Oral Methods," 40. The only other instances of ἔρχονται εἰς as a pericope introduction are 3:20 and 11:27 with ἦλθον εἰς employed twice (5:1; 9:33).

3. At the conclusion of the two-stage healing Jesus arrives at Caesarea Philippi (8:27), which becomes the northern point of Jesus' journey to Jerusalem, with Jericho (where Bartimaeus is healed) as the southern point.

4. Seeing and hearing are popular metaphors for spiritual perception and understanding in Mark,[254] and blindness as a figure for ignorance is dominant in the Jewish tradition.[255]

5. Mark is establishing an integral relationship between the blind men and the disciples, so that "In these chapters [8–10] Jesus is trying to bring sight to his disciples, analogous to his effort to bring sight to the blind men in the frame episodes."[256]

6. Mark ties healing and discipleship together in each passage. The need for a second touch speaks to Peter's need to receive additional insight into Jesus' identity (8:29–33) and the healing of Bartimaeus climaxes with his discipleship commitment to follow Jesus on the way to the cross (10:52).

7. The healings reveal a progression and intensification. As van Iersel explains,

> The first blind man is unnamed, does not ask for healing himself, and is brought to Jesus by others (8.22). He is healed in two stages (8.23, 25), and is then sent home and told not to go into Bethsaida again (8.26). The second blind man, whose name is Bartimaeus, takes the initiative himself, calls out to Jesus repeatedly, and has to overcome the obstruction of the crowd (10.46–48). He is healed on account of his trust without a therapeutic treatment (10.50–52a), and then follows Jesus on the way (10.52b).[257]

8. Each of the frames serves as a transition. The two-stage healing of the blind man continues the theme of the blindness of the disciples in 8:17–21 but prepares for the discipleship catechism, which will give sight into the true identity of Jesus. Bartimaeus represents the disciple who understands the teaching of the discipleship catechism and follows the Son of David (10:46) along the way, which prepares for Jesus' triumphal entry as the Son of David (11:10).

Having demonstrated the presence of a frame, now we will explain its purpose. Mark employs this frame to persuade his readers to follow a suffering Son of Man through their acceptance of a discipleship of the cross.

---

254. Marshall (*Faith*, 131, n. 1) mentions 4:3, 9, 12, 15ff, 23ff, 33; 6:11; 7:14; 8:18; 9:7; 12:29, 37; 14:40; 15:39.

255. Cf. Klauck, *Allegorie und Allegorese*, 348. Isaiah in particular uses the cure from blindness as spiritual insight (Isa 29:18; 42:7,16) and lack of understanding as blindness (Isa 42:18–19; 43:8; 44:9; 56:10; 59:10; Matt 23:16, 17, 19, 24, 26).

256. Fowler, *Reader*, 144.

257. Van Iersel, *Mark*, 276–77.

Since the epiphany (9:2–13) and exorcism (9:14–29) within this section are transformed into discipleship narratives, it should come as no surprise that the miracle stories which frame this section likewise bear this emphasis. Regarding the double-stage healing of the blind man, Meier calls attention to the missing elements from a normal healing story. First of all, "There is no mention of faith on the part of the blind man or his helpers either before or after the miracle." Second, no reaction of acclaim is reported. "The healed man neither glorifies God nor thanks Jesus nor spreads the news of his healing nor seeks to follow Jesus." Similarly, "There is no larger audience to be astonished, bewildered, shocked, or moved to praise. A 'choral conclusion' is totally lacking." Third, Jesus' order to go home without entering the town does not quite fit the usual Markan demand of silence.[258] Furthermore, although Jesus performs all the action, the beginning verb is plural (ἔρχονται), another indication that the miracle is meant to speak to disciples. In addition, the withdrawal to a private location (8:23a) regularly connotes a teaching for the disciples.[259] Finally, with regard to context Mark places the healing between two episodes of apostolic misunderstanding so that a commentary upon these events is expected.[260]

If 8:22–26 stands as a teaching narrative, what subject matter is Mark proclaiming? Mark's primary contribution to the story's message consists in the pivotal position to which he assigns this passage within the overarching structure of his gospel.[261] The turning point in the gospel, Peter's confession,[262] follows directly this twofold healing of the blind man. In fact, "the Blind Man of Bethsaida is none other than St. Peter."[263] Therefore the two-stage nature of the healing does not reveal the difficulty involved in healing this man,[264] but functions symbolically as an enacted parable calling for enlightenment concerning Jesus' identity.

However, commentators interpret the symbolism differently depending upon the sufficiency or deficiency of Peter's confession of Jesus as the Messiah. Lightfoot and Matera align the healing narrative with Peter's confession in 8:27–30 to demonstrate the competency of his testimony.[265] Then the following parallels occur:

---

258. Meier, *Marginal Jew*, 2:694.

259. Through withdrawals the disciples receive teaching applied to them alone (κατὰ μόνας 4:10; κατ' ἰδίαν 4:34; 6:31, 32; 9:2, 28; 13:3).

260. Marcus, *Mystery*, 145.

261. Cf. Meier, *Marginal Jew*, 2:691.

262. For scholarly support see Johnson, "Blind Man," 375, n. 31.

263. Richardson, *Miracle Stories*, 86.

264. Supported by Ernst, *Markus*, 230; Gundry, *Mark*, 416. Against this proposal Guelich points out that "healing a blind man hardly qualifies as the most difficult or greatest of Jesus' miracles" (*Mark 1—8:26*, 433).

265. Lightfoot, *History*, 90–91: "Then the opening of the blind man's eyes will symbolize also the enlightenment of the disciples by their understanding of the Messiahship of Jesus."

8:23a	"outside the village"	=	8:27a	"to the villages around Caesarea Philippi"
8:23b	"Do you see anything?"	=	8:27b	"Who do people say that I am?"
8:24	The blind man's partial sight	=	8:28	The disciples' acknowledgement that Jesus is someone great like John the Baptist, Elijah, or one of the prophets
8:25	Jesus once more puts his hands on the man's eyes.	=	8:29a	Jesus once more asks a question about his own identity.
8:25b	The blind man's sight is restored.	=	8:29b	Peter confesses Jesus as the Messiah.
8:26	Jesus forbids the blind man to go into the village.	=	8:30	Jesus warns the disciples not to tell anyone that he is the Messiah.

The advantage of this proposal is the coordination between the partial healing by Jesus and the insufficient answer of the disciples about Jesus' identity contrasted with the complete healing and the answer of Peter. With this interpretation Peter's confession points backward to 6:14–16, where Herod wrestles with Jesus' identity like the apostles do here.[266] Then the theological point becomes that "Previous to Peter's confession, the disciples are like the blind man to whom men appear like trees walking. . . . After Peter's confession, the disciples see clearly what has been the main focus of this section, and the first half of the gospel: Jesus is the Shepherd Messiah."[267] According to this view Peter's confession is the climatic description of Jesus' identity.

However, Matera and others have been blinded by Matthew's redaction of this passage.[268] For Matthew, Peter's confession is a combination of growing insight and divine revelation. But in Mark, as Ourisman points out, there is "No praise, no recognition of divine inspiration, no conferral of a new name, no granting of leadership within the church, not even a hint that Peter answered the question correctly."[269] Since in the following verses (8:33) Peter is forcefully rebuked and identified with Satan himself, his confession demands supplementation just as the blind man required a second touch. In fact, since Peter's response is labeled demonic, his confession must parallel the christological utterances of the demons (1:24–25; 3:11–12), which Jesus also silences (8:30) because they omit any reference to his death. The initial unclear vision of the blind man does not correspond to the incorrect an-

---

266. Matera, "Incomprehension," 165. But in reality Herod is wrestling with John's identity, although John' death becomes a preview of what will happen with Jesus.

267. Ibid. Matera qualifies his conclusion by admitting that "This is not to say that they comprehend the mystery of the suffering Son of Man (the subject matter of the second part of the Gospel), but they do see the significance of the feeding miracles" (169). However, Matera contends that "Mark draws a comparison between Peter's confession and the confession of the centurion" (171), but Peter's confession is insufficient since he is not facing the cross like the centurion.

268. Matera even states that "Matthew's material presents the clearest parallel to Mark" ("Incomprehension," 166).

269. Ourisman, *From Gospel to Sermon*, 4.

swers of Peter's contemporaries (8:28); instead the title Messiah is deficient if not juxtaposed with an acknowledgement of the Suffering Servant character of Jesus' mission. Therefore the proper correspondence is between the two-stage healing of the blind man and 8:27–33 (not 8:27–30 alone).[270]

8:22	The introduction of a blind man	=	8:27–28	The question to the disciples indicating they are blind to the identity of Jesus
8:23–24	The blind man can see but not clearly (people look like walking trees).	=	8:29–30	Peter confesses the identity of Jesus as Messiah.
8:25a	The blind man requires a second touch.	=	8:31–33	Peter needs an additional christological insight to see Jesus as a Suffering Servant Son of Man.
8:25b	The blind man sees everything clearly.	=	8:32a	Jesus now speaks plainly.
8:25	The second touch	=	8:34ff.	The acceptance of the implications of a Suffering Servant Messiah as taught in the discipleship catechism

Through the two-stage healing of the blind man Mark creates the expectation that some in the narrative will come to genuine insight. However, the disciples never receive complete sight within the gospel.[271] Therefore the narrative must be primarily aimed at the reader. As Williams points out about 8:34, "Jesus calls 'anyone' or 'whoever' which would include the reader."[272] The two-stage healing intends to elicit from the reader a full confession of Jesus as both triumphant Messiah and Suffering Servant Son of Man. Therefore, instead of positively identifying with the disciples, who continually misunderstand Jesus' identity, the reader is open to the possibility of identifying with the minor characters in the story. Thus Mark guides the reader through the discipleship catechism and concludes this journey with an encounter with Bartimaeus, who leads the parade of minor characters demonstrating a true discipleship of the cross. Just as the two-stage healing of a blind man introduces the need for additional insight for the myopic half-sighted, so Bartimaeus concludes the discipleship catechism with his heroic action of following along the way.[273]

---

270. See Best, "Discipleship in Mark," 325–26; *Temptation and Passion*, 108; Marcus, *Mystery*, 145; and Robbins, "Healing," 39.

271. The disciples are only given complete sight to behold the true nature of Jesus' identity after the resurrection, even though Jesus speaks clearly in 8:32. Cf. Best, *Following*, 137; *Gospel as Story*, 67–68; Guelich, *Mark 1—8:26*, 430–31, 436; Hooker, *St. Mark*, 198; Johnson, "Blind Man," 383.

272. Williams, *Other Followers*, 137. Cf. also Malbon, "Disciples, Crowds, Whoever," 109–10, 124–26.

273. Therefore, when commentators decide for 8:27 instead of 8:22 as the major division in Mark (Guelich, for instance), they miss the close connection between the two-stage healing of the blind

Similar to the healing at the entry port of the discipleship catechism, the healing of Bartmaeus at the exit port does not satisfy the qualifications for the *Gattung* of miracle story. As Marshall explains,

> There is a conspicuous lack of emphasis on the course of the miracle itself. There is no healing word or gesture, no demonstration of a cure, and no choral acclamation. The localization of the event near Jericho, the naming of the petitioner, and the allusion to his subsequent fate, are all details not usually found in miracle stories.[274]

Only remnants of the structure of a healing narrative are evident as in the problem–solution–proof format. Certainly Jesus' response, "your faith has healed you," is a typical feature of healing miracles (1:44; 2:11; 5:19, 34; 7:29; 10:52).[275] However, the blind man's action of jumping to his feet (10:50) is more appropriate to a healing of lameness than blindness. More significant is the fact that "unlike other miracle stories, Jesus and his 'mighty work' are not in the centre of the narrative."[276] As Achtemeier observes, the healing is present in such an abbreviated form that "it appears to have been subordinated to some other intention."[277]

Therefore many exegetes categorize this passage as a call narrative.[278] The repetition of the term "call" (φωνεῖν) three times in 10:49 by Jesus, the narrator, and the crowd offers substantial evidence in this direction.[279] In addition to an introduction and conclusion, Bailey describes five crucial elements in a standard call narrative: confrontation, reaction, commission, protest, and reassurance,[280] with Habel attaching the frequent presence of a sign to these characteristics.[281] On the other hand, Achtemeier discerns seven different but somewhat comparative elements in the passages of Mark 10:46–52 and Luke 5:1–11. However, the terminology differs widely between these two descriptions of call narratives.[282] In addition, the protest is uttered

---

man, Peter's confession and rebuke, and the healing of blind Bartimaeus.

274. Marshall, *Faith*, 124.

275. Gundry, *Mark*, 596.

276. Steinhauser, "Form," 583.

277. Achtemeier, "And He Followed Him," 121.

278. For supporters see the list in Gundry, *Mark*, 596.

279. Williams, *Other Followers*, 156.

280. Bailey (*Literary Forms*, 144) following Hubbard ("Commissioning Stories in Luke-Acts," 103–26) with an acknowledgement that the elements of reaction or protest are frequently missing.

281. Habel ("Call Narrative," 301, 309) for the calls of Gideon, Moses, and Jeremiah, but not for the calls of Isaiah and second Isaiah (319). For a helpful comparison chart with Gideon's call see Cotter, *Christ of the Miracle Stories*, 54.

282. Achtemeier, "And He Followed Him," 122–25 (summarized by Steinhauser, "Form," 592–93, n. 14): 1) Editorial introduction Luke 5:2–3; Mark 10:26b; 2) Setting of the scene: 5:2–3; 10:26b; 3) Dialogue; verbal conflict 5:4–5a; 10:47–48 = confrontation ?; 4) Resolution of the conflict 5:5b; 10:49 = reaction ?; 5) Chief character acts 5:6a; 10:50; 6) Miracle described 5:6b–7; 10:52a; 7) Second dialogue 5:8–10a; 10:51; 8) Word of comfort 5:8b; 10:49 = reassurance ?; 9) Conclusion; reaction of the central

The Theological Intentions of Mark's Literary Devices

by the crowd instead of Bartimaeus himself, and it precedes rather than follows any commission. More significantly, the request of a sign in a call narrative is replaced by the description of a miracle. Since these alterations are not standard features of a call narrative, the healing of Bartimaeus cannot be categorized as a typical calling. Furthermore, the fact that this narrative is balanced by a healing story at 8:22–26 makes the hypothesis of a call narrative more tentative, as does its omission from standard lists of call narratives in the secondary literature.[283] The most fitting conclusion is the observation by Broadhead that Mark 10:46–52 is a "unique narrative production."[284]

Although 10:46–52 does not fit neatly into any form critical category, Marshall observes that this "is, in fact, an important key to appreciating the literary functioning of the narrative as it stands."[285] The structure of the passage reveals that it moves from a call narrative to a healing story and finally to a discipleship genre.

Contact with Jesus	Physical description	Genre
Calling contact (46–49a)	Sitting by the roadside (46)	Call narrative
Healing contact (49b–52a)	Jumped to his feet, came to Jesus (50)	Healing story
Discipleship contact (52b)	Followed along the road (52b)	Discipleship

Therefore 10:46–52 is a miracle story calling Bartimaeus to faith and intending to teach discipleship. But the conclusion places the emphasis upon the genre of discipleship narrative. Certainly the fact that this is the first and only time that a healed person follows Jesus is significant.[286] Furthermore, the address of Jesus as "Rabbouni" (10:51) suggests a teaching purpose[287] as do the symbolic elements in the narrative. The throwing aside of the beggar's garments represents the relinquishment of his worldly goods and his entire way of life to follow Jesus.[288] Likewise, the terms ἀκολουθεῖν and ἐν τῇ ὁδῷ belong to Mark's discipleship repertoire.[289] Finally, since the beginning frame of the two-stage healing conveys a symbolic meaning with regard to discipleship, this

---

character 5:11; 10:52b. But Steinhauser (584) points out the problematic nature of this comparison since Luke 5:1–11 is really a displaced resurrection narrative when compared with John 21:1–11.

283. Cf. Bailey, *Literary Forms*, 146 and Berger, *Formgeschichte des Neuen Testaments*, 315–16.

284. Broadhead, *Teaching with Authority*, 161.

285. Marshall, *Faith*, 125.

286. Lohmeyer, *Markus*, 226.

287. Neither Matt 20:33 nor Luke 18:41 follow the Markan wording but insert "Lord" instead. This demonstrates a Markan emphasis so that "Bartimaeus responds to Jesus like a disciple addressing his teacher" (Williams, *Other Followers*, 158, n. 3).

288. Steinhauser, "Form," 205; Marshall, *Faith*, 129. This relinquishment is similar to the calls to discipleship of Peter and Andrew who leave their fishing nets (1:18), James and John who leave their father (1:20), and Levi who leaves his tax business (2:14).

289. Regarding the term "to follow," Williams (*Other Followers*, 161) explains that metaphorical overtones appear in the vast majority of instances (1:18; 2:14, 15; 6:1; 8:34; 10:21, 28, 32; 14:54; 15:41), but a strictly literal sense is apparent in 3:7; 5:24; 11:9; 14:13. In addition, Marshall points out that "By this stage of Mark's narrative, 'the way' has become a metaphor for the path of obedient suffering" (*Faith*, 131).

type of interpretation carries over to 10:46–52 as well.²⁹⁰ Therefore the genre of discipleship takes prominence over miracle story or call narrative.

The clinching piece of evidence for identifying the genre is the discovery that 10:46–52 exactly parallels earlier calls to discipleship in Mark's gospel. The invitations to discipleship in 1:16–20 and 2:14 share six mutual elements:

1. The identification of the candidates by name (1:16, 19; 2:14)

2. The specification of their vocation (1:16 casting a net; 1:19 preparing their nets; 2:14 sitting at the tax collector's booth)

3. A discernment process whereby Jesus looks (εἶδεν) them over (1:16, 19; 2:14)

4. Jesus summoning his disciples instead of the normal procedure whereby a pupil chooses a rabbi (1:17 δεῦτε ὀπίσω μου, 20 ἐκάλεσεν; 2:14 λέγει αὐτῷ, ἀκολούθει μοι)

5. The relinquishment (ἀφέντες) of something superfluous to a disciple's mission (1:18, 20; implied in the rising (ἀναστὰς) of Levi in 2:14)

6. A decisive movement to follow (1:18; 2:14) after Jesus (ὀπίσω 1:17, 20)

Mark replicates these elements in the beginning of the discipleship catechism, where Peter is called to a deeper commitment and receives the second touch which healed the blind man in the first frame. Mark 8:34 includes these six elements of naming (τις), Jesus' summons (προσκαλεσάμενος), leaving something behind through denial (ἀπαρνησάσθω ἑαυτόν), a new profession, i.e., the cross (ἀράτω τὸν σταυρὸν), and the following after Jesus (ὀπίσω μου ἀκολουθεῖν), with the discerning look of Jesus occurring the verse before in 8:33 (ἰδὼν). Likewise, with Bartimaeus we discover a unique naming of the blind man (10:46b), his profession as a panhandler (10:46c), Jesus' summons (10:49a), the abandoning of his garments (10:50),²⁹¹ and his following of Jesus (10:52), whereas his search for Jesus (10:47–48) reverses the established procedure of Jesus choosing his followers but coincides more with the rabbinic pattern. Therefore every element of Mark's patterned call to discipleship is perspicuous in 10:46–52.

In addition, three surprising elements in the narrative point to the presence of discipleship symbolism. First, the normal place to encounter a beggar would be at the city gate where Jesus enters Jericho.²⁹² But Mark quickly proceeds to Jesus' exit from Jericho (10:46) since he wants the reader to concentrate on Jesus' destination of Jerusalem and the newly enlightened beggar's following toward the cross.²⁹³ Sec-

---

290. Meye explains that there is a "reciprocal relation for interpretation" (*Jesus and the Twelve*, 77).

291. Marshall points out, "A beggar's mantle would represent all his worldly goods, as well as his only means of livelihood, since Oriental beggars commonly spread their cloaks before them to collect alms" (*Faith*, 141). Gundry (*Mark*, 596) simplistically interprets this procedure as getting rid of something that would impede the blind man's healing process.

292. Van Iersel, *Mark*, 339.

293. Scholars differ regarding the destination to which Bartimaeus is following Jesus. As usual

ond, "The reader would expect a character that makes such a sudden appearance in the book, to address Jesus as 'teacher' (4.35; 9.17, 38; 10.17, 20, 35), or 'lord' (7.28), or 'rabbi' (9.5)."[294] Instead Bartimaeus addresses Jesus on two occasions as "Son of David" (10:47–48), which parallels Peter's address of "Messiah" in the beginning of the discipleship catechism (8:27).[295] Therefore, Bartimaeus replaces Peter as the true disciple who exhibits both a christological confession and the appropriate response of following to the cross. Third, Mark names the blind man, which is rare if the story is purely a miracle narrative.[296] In addition, the naming of someone other than Jesus

---

Gundry (*Mark*, 426) disregards all symbolism and merely views the way as the physical road leading outside the village. Three additional views have theological implications. First, Gray maintains that "For Mark, the theology of 'the way' has its primary locus in Jerusalem's temple" in order "to show the prophetic and eschatological significance of Jesus' coming to the temple" (*Temple in the Gospel*, 19, 44). As evidence Gray contends that 1) the original context of "the way" for the citations from Exod 23:20, Mal 3:1, and Isa 40:3 in Mark 1:2–3 is the festal pilgrimage to Jerusalem's temple (16); 2) "Mark takes much care in preparing the reader for seeing Jesus' coming to the temple as the climax of 'the way'" (22) through the slower narrative pace and the absence of any mention of a previous visit of Jesus to the temple in Mark's story; and 3) "The last narrative use of 'the way' (Mark 11:8) serves to highlight further how Jesus' journey reaches its final destination at the temple" (23), whereas this phrase is not employed in the passion narrative. Against this proposal, the exodus passages mentioned in Mark 1:2–3 have their goal as the promised land, not the temple since the temple has not yet been constructed or has been destroyed. Furthermore, the pace of the narrative slows further yet in the hours (15:25, 33, 34) mentioned in the crucifixion narrative. More importantly, the discipleship catechism (8:22—10:52) contains the majority of symbolic references to the way whereas the temple is not even mentioned in this section. In addition, the temple imagery climaxes in the cross (15:38) whereas the temple incident itself connotes the destruction of the temple through a Markan intercalation so that Mark would unlikely be stating that "the way" leads toward destruction.

The second view supported by Swartley ("Structural Function," 79–82) and Kelber (*Kingdom and Parousia*, 109) states that the destination of "the way" is the promised land or in Jesus' terminology, the kingdom of God as derived from the Septuagint's Deuteronomic phrase of "entering into the land" (Deut 1:8; 4:1; 6:18; 16:20). Evidence includes the fact that the "on the way" section ends at Jericho (11:8) just as Israel's journey climaxes at Jericho. Against this thesis, Jesus already enters the promised land at the beginning of his ministry when he leaves the wilderness as demonstrated in his preaching in Mark 1:15. Furthermore, Jesus' trips into Gentile territory signify reclaiming this land as part of the original promised land (see chapter 7 below). Yet this proposal is partly true since Mark pictures Jesus' death on the cross as the kingdom of God (see 14:25 and 15:23).

The third proposal identifying "the way" with Jesus' death and his followers' discipleship of the cross fits the evidence the best and has overwhelming secondary support. Mark 1:2–3 introduces the theme of the way where the Baptizer prepares the way by becoming a martyr (6:14–29; 9:12–13). In addition, ἐν τῇ ὁδῷ serves as an inclusio around the discipleship catechism (8:27; 10:52) which focuses on Jesus' threefold passion prediction and the disciples' response of carrying their cross (8:34). 'The way' is not mentioned in Jesus' passion narrative since Mark connects this theme not only with Jesus' passion but also with the disciples' need to overcome their misunderstandings of Jesus' passion predictions (8:32-33; 9:32-34; 10:35-38) and follow him to the cross (8:34-38; 9:35-50; 10:42-45) which becomes the message of the central section of Mark's gospel.

294. Van Iersel, *Mark*, 341.

295. Fuller explains that "the twice repeated cry, 'Son of David, have mercy on me!' makes it a Messianic miracle" (*Interpreting the Miracles*, 63).

296. Gundry argues that "miracle-stories include personal names (1:29–31; 5:22–24, 35–43; John 11:1–11; Acts 9:36–43; and perhaps Acts 20:7–12; cf. Luke 8:2) and call-stories do not always include personal names (Mark 10:17–22, esp. 21, parr.; Luke 9:59–60)" (*Mark*, 596), but Simon's mother-in-law

focuses the attention on that character and their exemplary actions, in this case upon faith and discipleship.[297]

Finally, the context argues for a discipleship emphasis. Immediately preceding this healing Jesus' disciples are arguing about status, again proving their continued lack of insight. Mark employs Bartimaeus both to underscore the disciples' shortcomings by means of contrast and to serve as a model and remedy for them. Five contrasts highlight the differences between Bartimaeus and the sons of Zebedee:

1. Jesus asks the same question of both (10:36 Τί θέλετέ [με] ποιήσω ὑμῖν; 10:51 Τί σοι θέλεις ποιήσω) but responds in a totally different fashion to their answer.

2. James and John desire sitting at the right hand and left hand of Jesus in glory (10:37 εἷς σου ἐκ δεξιῶν καὶ εἷς ἐξ ἀριστερῶν καθίσωμεν ἐν τῇ δόξῃ σου) while the blind beggar sits along the way (10:46 ἐκάθητο παρὰ τὴν ὁδόν).

3. The disciples seek places of power and prestige (10:37) while Bartimaeus follows along the way of Jesus' passion to Jerusalem (10:52b).

4. The sons of Zebedee cannot receive their wish (10:38) while Bartimaeus does receive his healing (10:52a).

5. The disciples exhibit a naive self-confidence, contending they can make the required sacrifice (10:39), while the blind man recognizes his need for mercy (10:47).

Further back in Mark 10, the encounter of Jesus with the rich seeker displays a second contrast with the Bartimaeus episode. Both men are positioned along the way (10:17a; 10:46) and both initiate contact with Jesus (10:17b; 10:47–48). However, Jesus responds to the rich man with a rebuke (10:18–19) but to the blind man with a call (10:49). The rich man wants to be judged based upon his obedience to the commandments (10:20), while Bartimaeus comes to Jesus in faith (10:52).[298] The rich man refuses to sell his possessions (10:22), but the blind beggar gladly leaves behind his mantle (10:50). Both receive a command to go (10:21, 52), but only Bartimaeus chooses to follow Jesus along the way. Finally, at the end of the narrative the disciples respond, "Who then can be saved?" (10:26). The answer to this question as the narrative progresses must be the blind beggar who is saved on account of his faith (10:52). Thus Bartimaeus embarks in faith on the path of obedient suffering as a full-sighted disciple of Jesus in contrast with the rich inquirer and the sons of Zebedee.

---

is not a name and Jairus is not the person healed but is mentioned as father and synagogue ruler (notice that this function is placed before his name) to assure the passage's Jewish emphasis. Furthermore, Lazarus is named not because of the story's miracle value but because the narrative results in a death plot both against Jesus (11:45–53) and Lazarus (12:10–11). Finally, Tabitha is famous for her discipleship (Acts 9:36) which is again placed in a priority position in the narrative. For the unusual meaning of Bartimaeus' name see chapter 5 below, in the footnotes of section 5.6.

297. Achtemeier, "And He Followed Him," 115.

298. Williams, *Other Followers*, 165.

These exegetical details establish that Mark 10:46–52 is an appropriate frame to the discipleship catechism and fulfills the expectation in the two-stage healing (8:22–26) that a disciple will receive full sight by acknowledging and following Jesus both as the Son of David Messiah and the suffering Son of Man.[299] Mark then employs this narrative for the education of his church "so that the members have always the cross at the centre of their faith."[300] A suffering Messiah demands a discipleship of the cross.

3.9 The Frame around Jesus' Jerusalem Ministry in Mark 11:1—12:40

Again in this section we will analyze the structure of the material in Mark 11–12 and then attempt to discern the presence and purpose of the frame encircling these chapters. Everyone recognizes that Mark begins Jesus' Jerusalem ministry with a triad of prophetic actions: the royal procession[301] of the Son of David followed by the temple action and the cursing of the fig tree. But already here confusion arises since Mark sandwiches the last two prophetic actions together into one section and appears to fit the prophetic actions into a larger organization of the events over three Greco-Roman days beginning in the morning (11:1–11, 12–19, 20–?). These prophetic actions flow into a series of controversy dialogues in the temple, but it is difficult to determine how many controversies our author has in mind since the flow is interrupted by the parable of the tenants (12:1–12) and the last episode (12:35–37) omits a pronouncement saying and is really not a dialogue. The controversies are prompted by a query from the Jewish leaders concerning Jesus' authoritative questioning of cherished Jewish values. The chief priests, teachers of the law, and elders challenge Jesus' jurisdiction to perform "these things" (11:28), whose referent is difficult to determine.[302] The closest narrative focuses upon the cursing of the fig tree, but there is no evidence that the Jewish leaders ever witnessed this event. Since the two prophetic actions are intercalated, Mark appears to allude to the symbolic temple destruction, after which the Jewish leaders plot Jesus' downfall (11:18). However, if Mark employed an oral source of controversy dialogues consisting of two five-element chiasms,[303] then "these

---

299. See the long list of authors produced by Williams that support this conclusion that "Bartimaeus serves as a model of the insight and sacrifice that is necessary for true discipleship" (*Other Followers*, 15, n. 3 and 16, note 1). Gundry and Meye find themselves in the small minority who oppose an emphasis upon discipleship. Meye (*Jesus and the Twelve*, 165) erases any connection of Bartimaeus with discipleship because of his pre-conceived and misguided view that only the twelve are disciples. Gundry (*Mark*, 595–96) refuses an interpretation that does not emphasize Christology by arguing that nowhere in this pericope does Jesus call Bartimaeus to "follow me," but employs "go" (ὕπαγε) instead. He argues that "go" is tied with the ending of miracles stories in 1:44; 2:11; 5:19, 34; 7:29; 10:52. But the parallels with the narrative of the rich inquirer in 10:17–31 indicate that an opportunity to go (ὕπαγε 10:21) and sell and then come is appropriate for a discipleship narrative.

300. Best, *Following Jesus*, 137.

301. France, *Mark*, 428 suggests this title.

302. Cf. Knox, *Sources*, 1:88.

303. See the section above, 3.4.

things" would have originally referred to Jesus' questionable activities on the Sabbath (2:23—3:6). How do we organize this section to solve these interpretive difficulties?

The major obstacle to conceptual unity in this section, as Stephen Smith recognizes, is that the controversy dialogues in Mark 11–12 are "more disparate than the catena of five controversy stories in Mark 2:1—3:6 which has frequently been observed to be the counterpart of the Jerusalem conflict cycle."[304] We have followed the perceptive chiastic structures of Joanna Dewey in outlining the contents of the Galilean controversy dialogues and Mark's parable discourse. For Jesus' Jerusalem ministry she likewise suggests a symmetrical structure and links it with 2:1—3:6 because of the declining evidence of overt opposition in contrast to the surging intensity in the Galilean conflicts. The flow of material is convincing.

The intensification in the first set of controversies results in a plot to kill Jesus.

1	2:6-8	Silent criticism with the scribes questioning in their hearts.
2	2:16	The scribes of the Pharisees complain verbally about Jesus to his disciples.
3	2:18	Complaints are now addressed to Jesus about his disciples by an unspecified group.
4	2:24	The Pharisees now complain to Jesus directly about the unlawful actions in which Jesus and his disciples are participating.
5	3:2, 5	The Pharisees watching Jesus' every move accuse him because of their hardness of heart.
	3:6	As a result the Pharisees and Herodians plot to murder Jesus.

The gradual winning of the controversies in the second set so that Jesus replaces the Jewish leadership.

5	11:33	The chief priests, teachers of the law, and elders admit "we don't know."
4	12:17	The Pharisees and Herodians are amazed at Jesus' answer.
3	12:24	The Sadducees are rebuked because they know neither the Scriptures nor the power of God.
2	12:34	"From then on no one dared to ask him any more questions."
1	12:37	The large crowd listens with delight in approval of Jesus as their leader.
	12:38	Jesus warns his audience to watch out for the teachers of the law.
	12:40	The Jewish leaders will receive the greater condemnation so that their leadership is overturned.

So far we have followed Dewey's conclusions. However, she removes 11:27–33 from the series, not discerning that the question over Jesus' authority is the link between the two sets of controversy dialogues. But if these two sets originally formed a sequence, then the shocking plot of Jesus' death in 3:6 matches the crest of opposition by the entire Jewish Sanhedrin in 11:27, as verified by Mark's repetition of a conspiracy to eliminate Jesus in 11:18. In its place Dewey advocates a seven-member

---

304. Smith, "Literary Structure," 104.

chiasm which diverges from the regular fivefold structuring encountered previously in Mark.³⁰⁵

a		12:1–9	Public teaching: parable of the wicked tenants; threat of judgment
b		12:10–12	Public teaching: psalm citation; audience reaction
c		12:13–17	Public debate: the things of God given to God; audience reaction
	d	12:18–27	Public debate: resurrection
c'		12:28–34	Public debate: the things of God are the commands to love God and neighbor; audience reaction
b'		12:35–37	Public teaching: psalm citation; audience reaction
a'		12:38–40	Public teaching: warning against the scribes; threat of judgment

Dewey correctly discerns the middle of this section as the resurrection, although she fails to correlate it with the crucifixion center in 2:20, whose combination empowers these two sets of controversies to become presentations of the gospel message. She also recognizes "the ring composition"³⁰⁶ where the greatest commitment offered to God (12:13–17) is matched by the greatest commandment given by God (12:28–34). In fact, both passages have a double interchange of dialogue between the questioner and Jesus, whereas the center only has a single exchange of dialogue but a double question and answer. Furthermore, in both dialogues the questioners praise Jesus' teaching (12:14, 32), with the result that the pericopes are joined by the catchwords "with truth" as an inclusio (ἐπ' ἀληθείας 12:14, 32 used only here in Mark).³⁰⁷ Finally, in the debate over revenue to Caesar Jesus declares, "give to God the things of God" (12:17), and in the great commandment debate Jesus spells out what the things of God are: "to love God and neighbor" (12:29–31).

However, the remaining elements in Dewey's chiasm present insurmountable problems. Because the genre of 12:1–9 consists of a parable, it sits uncomfortably next to a series of controversy dialogues as if all elements are of equal structural importance. Furthermore, Dewey attempts to match the parable with Jesus' warning of judgment to the scribes in 12:38–40,³⁰⁸ but this material forms a conclusion to Jesus' debates which proclaims his victory over the Jewish leaders just as the earlier conclusion at 3:6 portrayed an apparent victory of Jesus' opponents over him. Furthermore, 12:10–12

---

305. Dewey, *Markan Public Debate*, 162.

306. Ibid., 158–59.

307. Ibid., 157–58.

308. In favor of this suggestion Dewey (ibid., 161) lists 1) each is an attack on the behavior of the Jewish leaders; 2) each passage ends with a prophesy of doom upon the Jewish leaders; 3) each contains two parts of a debate followed by a condemnation; 4) in each case Jesus diverges from the teaching of Judaism whereas in the other controversies he basically agrees with the Pharisees. However, the first three arguments are far too general and the last one wrongly assumes that Jesus agrees with the Pharisees about not paying taxes to the Roman empire. Furthermore, Mark 12:1–9 is much longer than 12:38–40.

is not a separate pericope but a conclusion to the parable of the wicked tenants.[309] In addition, 12:35–37 is better categorized as an additional controversy dialogue that coordinates with 11:27–33 to discuss the identity of John the Baptizer and the identity of the Messiah as the Son of David. Finally, Dewey loses the symmetrical pattern with 2:1—3:6 by eliminating the fivefold nature of the chiasm.[310]

The following five-element chiastic structures much more neatly match each other.[311]

		2:1—3:6 Kingdom Teaching in Controversy	11:27—12:40	Major Issues of the Day
a	2:1–12	Forgiving sins	11:27–33	Identity of John the Baptizer
		Healing of a paralytic		The Jewish leaders question Jesus' authority
		(Mixed genre of controversy and healing)		Mention "walking in the temple" 11:27
		Conflict: silent criticism (2:8)		Interlocutors: chief priests, scribes, elders
x		Mark's addition: call of Levi (2:13–14)		Addition: Parable of the Tenants (12:1–12)
b	2:15–17	Eating with sinners	12:13–17	The greatest commitment
		Eating with tax collectors and sinners		Paying taxes to Caesar;

---

309. In favor of this parallel Dewey (ibid., 160) argues that an antithetical reaction exists between beginning (12:12 seek to arrest Jesus) and end (12:37 listen to Jesus gladly) and with regard to the audience only the crowd appears in 12:12 and 12:37. But the crowd is employed in summary statements as in 11:18 and the antithetical reaction in 12:12 parallels 11:18 more closely.

310. Therefore Wegener (*Cruciformed*, 169–70) develops a five-fold chiasm that begins after the parable (see also Smith, "Literary Structure," 186, who in the end rejects this structure):

a	12:13–17	Practical argument about paying taxes.
b	12:18–27	Theoretical argument about the resurrection.
c	12:28–34	Sympathetic discussion of the commandments to love God and neighbor.
b'	12:35–37	Theoretical riddle about the Christ being David's Son.
a'	12:38–40	Practical warning against the scribes' avarice.

However, this structure loses the connection between the great commitment and the great commandment and no longer centers the chiasm on the resurrection.

311. A dispute about a pre-Markan collection of controversies in Jesus' Jerusalem ministry has raged since the beginning of form criticism with Albertz (*Die synoptische Streitgespräche*, 5, 35–36) in support, Dibelius (*From Tradition to Gospel*, 218) against a collection, and Taylor (*St. Mark*, 91–92, 101) contending that they are a composition by Mark from a time earlier than the writing of the gospel. For scholarly support advocating two pre-Markan controversy collections see Dewey, *Markan Public Debate*, 47 and 213, n. 39; Kuhn, *Ältere Sammlungen*, 40; and Cook, *Mark's Treatment*, 35. We conclude that Mark used a previous oral collection of controversy dialogues organized into two sets of five-part chiasms, but that he shattered the second set when he combined them with the three prophetic actions to form one section, 11:1—12:44.

The Theological Intentions of Mark's Literary Devices

		Conflict: question Jesus' disciples (2:16)		Interlocutors: Pharisees and Herodians
c	2:18–22	Feasting or fasting in the new age		12:18–27 The resurrection of the dead
		New age imagery of bridegroom, garments, and new wine		Marriage in the resurrection New age imagery of being like the angels
		Conflict: interrogate Jesus himself (2:18)		Interlocutors: the Sadducees
		The center = the crucifixion at 2:20		The center = the resurrection
b'	2:23–27	Sabbath eating rituals	12:28–34	The greatest commandment
		Picking grain to eat on the Sabbath		The Shema and the double-love command
		Condemnation of disciples' actions (2:24)		Interlocutor: a friendly scribe
a'	3:1–5	Sabbath healing activities	12:35–37	Messiah's identity: Son of David
		Healing of a withered hand		Jesus questions the Jewish leaders' authority
		Mixed genre of controversy and healing		Mention of "teaching in the temple" (12:35)
		Watch closely to plot Jesus' death (3:2, 6)		Absent interlocutors
Result	3:6	The Jewish leaders condemn Jesus	12:38–40	Jesus condemns the Jewish leaders
		They plot how they might kill Jesus		"These men will be punished most severely"

Each series consists of five controversy dialogues organized as chiasms, beginning with a question concerning Jesus authority (2:10; 11:28) and concluding with a condemnation of one opponent against the other, first Jesus and then the scribes in the second chiasm. The first set creates a social demarcation between Christians and the Jewish leaders, whereas the second series contrasts Jesus' authority with the authority of the Jewish leaders. The Pharisees and Herodians who appear to triumph in 3:6 submit to Jesus' wisdom in 12:13. Just as the Galilean controversies display signs of the kingdom of God manifested in the midst of conflict, so 11:27—12:40 comprises five contemporary Jewish debates during which Jesus' wisdom emerges as triumphant. Debates raged between the various sects and schools of first-century Palestine over the ministry of John the Baptizer, paying taxes to the Roman Empire, the reality of the resurrection, the greatest commandment in the law, and the identity of the Messiah.[312]

---

312. Cf. Albertz, *Streitgespräche*, 18, 26–27, 35–36 and Gaston, *No Stone on Another*, 82. For examples that the middle three are contemporary issues see also Dewey, *Markan Public Debate*, 157.

The Literary Device of a Markan Framework

Through these debates Jesus is proclaimed by the church as the final authority and ultimate interpreter to whom all owe their allegiance and submission.

The necessary presence of 11:27–33 within this series is verified by the inclusio that it forms with 12:35–37:[313]

1. In 11:27 Jesus is walking in the temple courts and in 12:35 he is teaching in the temple courts.

2. Whereas the full weight of the Jewish Sanhedrin as opposition appears in 11:27, in contrast at 12:35–37 all the interlocutors are absent so that the large crowd remembers all the interlocutors.

3. Whereas in 11:28 the Jewish leaders question Jesus' authority, in 12:35 Jesus questions the authority of the teachers of the law.

4. The first passage mentions John being "from heaven" (11:30–31) and the second envisions the Son of David "at the right hand" of God (12:36).

5. Most significantly, each contains an issue of spiritual discernment about the identity of a particular person so that the distinctiveness of the Baptizer (11:30–32) parallels the peculiar identity of the Son of David (12:37).

So an evaluation of the significance of John begins the series of five discussions and the debate over the authority of a Davidic Messiah concludes the set. In the church's proclamation of this series of controversy dialogues, a link is established between John and Jesus in their ministry and death since John prepares the way for the Messiah (1:1–11; 6:7–29; 9:9–13). After the Jewish authorities cease taking the offensive, finally Jesus goes on the warpath and demonstrates how the leaders fail to understand the Scriptures, as exemplified in their inability to perceive from Psalm 110 (12:35–37) that the Messiah will be David's lord.[314] The absolute delight of the crowd after this fifth controversy (12:37) indicates that all the people have turned their allegiance from the Jewish leaders to Jesus. Then in a stirring conclusion the roles in the narrative are completely reversed so that those plotting to kill Jesus are destined to be punished more severely. Therefore Jesus triumphs in contradiction from the first set of controversy dialogues, where the plots of the enemies conclude the narrative (3:6). To proclaim the gospel through these controversy dialogues all five are needed.

---

313. Dewey (*Markan Public Debate*, 159) argues against this position by contending that whereas ἀποκρίνομαι never begins a unit of narrative in Mark, 12:35 begins with Jesus' answer. Therefore only the three preceding debates must be included in the series. However, to completely reverse the debates so that Jesus stands alone as the victor, this controversy is needed. Admittedly, the structure is not a full controversy dialogue, but the additions in Matthew indicate that it should be interpreted as a separate pericope. Four changes are apparent: 1) the rhetorical question of Mark 12:37 becomes a real query in Matt 22:42a; 2) Matt 22:42b makes the controversy a real dialogue; 3) the charge from opponents in Matt 22:46 is missing in Mark 12; and 4) Mark 12:34 ("no one dared to ask him questions") following the double love dialogue is placed at the end by Matt 22:46.

314. The climatic nature of this story is evidenced by the fact that only here does Jesus start a controversy.

However, Mark's insertion of the parable of the tenants within these five Jerusalem controversy dialogues shatters their cohesiveness.[315] Why does Mark include this pericope at this point in the narrative? Mark connects the dispute over Jesus' authority (11:27–33) with the temple action[316] so that a new structure of action–objection–vindication results, as evidenced by the triple ending with the authorities fearing the crowd at 11:18, 32 and 12:12.[317] The temple action leads to the objection to Jesus' authority in the interrogation by the Jewish leaders, which Mark culminates with the parable of the tenants, where Jesus is vindicated so that the leaders leave him alone because they are afraid of the crowd. This connection of the parable with the prophetic actions dissolves the fivefold structure of the oral controversy dialogues in favor of a new three-day organization by Mark. But this should be no surprise to us since in identical fashion Mark has transformed the five-element miracle catenae into a triad of narratives about crossing the sea. Therefore as Smith contends, we can no longer "force these chapters into the same structural mould as the Galilean controversies."[318] Mark creates a new three-day structure when he combines the triad of prophetic actions with the five controversy dialogues found in the oral tradition.

The three-day structure places the triumphal entry on the first day, with the healing of Bartimaeus serving a transitional role of introducing the title "Son of David" (10:47–48). Then Mark sandwiches together the temple action and cursing of the fig tree on the second day.[319] Finally, the third day begins with the discovery of the symbolic fig tree action and its theological ramifications (11:20–26), continues with the interrogation of Jesus' authority by the Jewish leaders because of his temple action (11:27–33), and concludes with Jesus' vindication as the chief cornerstone of the temple (12:1–12). This arrangement results in a division into three days with approximately the same amount of material in each section.

Two additional triads complete the structure of the third day.[320] In 12:13–34 Jesus is confronted with a triad of difficult questions by three different groups, with the result that "no one dared ask him any more questions" (12:34). Then in 12:35–44 Jesus becomes the assailant of his opponents, where he now propounds the question

---

315. Knox, *Sources*, 1:85.

316. A connection between the temple action and Jesus' authority is also evident in John 2:13–22 with the employment of the Johannine term "sign" instead of "authority," with both Mark 11:28 and John 2:18 using ταῦτα ποιεῖς in a question. Cf. Burkill, "Strain on the Secret," 40, n. 46.

317. Dewey, *Markan Public Debate*, 155.

318. Smith, "Literary Structure," 172.

319. Matthew abandons Mark's intercalation as well as Jesus' reconnoiter of the temple after the triumphal entry to change the narrative back to the traditional three symbolic actions (21:1–11, 12–17, 18–22). The questioning of Jesus' authority (21:23–27) then becomes an introduction to the Parable of the Two Sons (21:28–32) which concerns the mission of John the Baptizer as well.

320. Burkill has caught the flow of Mark 12:13–44 when he reports that "The section also provides yet another illustration of the evangelist's predilection for series of three in his arrangement of the material, for it falls naturally into two parts, each consisting of three pericopes" ("Strain on the Secret," 42).

(35–37), condemns the scribes for their ostentation, rapacity, and hypocrisy (38–40), and contrasts a poor widow's contribution with the conniving self-centeredness of the Jewish leaders (41–44). The resulting three-day outline is captured successfully by Stephen Smith.[321]

	10:46–52	Healing of Bartimaeus (transitional)
Day 1	11:1–11	Triumphal Entry (Ps. 118:26 inclusio)
Day 2	11:12–19	Fig tree and Temple
Day 3	11:20—12:12	Withered fig tree, prayer, and parable (Ps. 118:22–23 inclusio)
	12:13–17	Question on taxes (poll tax)
	12:18–27	Question on the resurrection
	12:28–34	Question on the first commandment
	12:35–37	*Davidssohnfrage*
	12:38–40	Condemnation of the scribes
	12:41–44	Widow's mite (temple tax)
	13:1–2	Temple prophesy (transitional)

This triadic Markan structure is supported by its further and clearer development in Matthew.[322]

---

321. Smith, "Literary Structure," 187–88.

322. One other structure of these chapters that should be mentioned is the analysis of Daube (*New Testament and Rabbinic Judaism*, 158–69) who suggests a Passover Haggadah pattern outlined in b. Niddah 69b–71a whereby the four pericopes of 12:13–37 are modeled on the questions of four sons at the Passover:
Question about wisdom concerning a point of the law posed by a wise son = Pharisees and Herodians.
Question of mockery which frequently bears on the resurrection posed by a wicked son = Sadducees.
Question of conduct which centers on our relationship to God posed by a son of simple piety (a scribe who is not far from the kingdom 12:34).
Question of biblical exegesis which concerns resolving an apparent contradiction between two passages of scripture posed by the head of the family = Jesus himself.
Dewey (*Markan Public Debate*, 61) offers three decisive arguments against this hypothesis:
It is extremely doubtful that the Passover Haggedah had a fixed pattern at this time.
The questions in Mark do not really fit these types of Haggedah questions.
The issue of the Christ as David's son is not a comparison of two scriptures.

1. Three prophetic actions (Matt 21:1–22).

    a. Jesus triumphantly enters Jerusalem, fulfilling the Scriptures (21:1–11).

    b. The Jewish leaders make the temple a den of robbers (21:12–17).

    c. The Jewish leaders are like the withered fig tree (21:18–22).

2. Three "history of salvation" parables emphasize the rejection of the ministries of John, Jesus, and Jesus' disciples (21:23—22:14).

    a. The Jewish leaders do not receive John so the tax collectors and prostitutes enter the kingdom ahead of them (21:23–32).

    b. The Jewish leaders kill Jesus, the son, so that the kingdom is given to a people who produce fruit (21:33–46).

    c. The Jewish leaders refuse to come to the wedding banquet when invited by Jesus' servants, the church, so Jerusalem is burned (22:1–14).

3. Three groups of Jewish leaders lose theological arguments (22:15–46).

    a. Herodians and disciples of the Pharisees: debate about taxes to Caesar (22:15–22)

    b. Sadducees: debate about marriage at the resurrection (22:23–33)

    c. Pharisees: debates about the greatest commandment (22:34–40) and the Messiah as David's son (22:41–46)

Therefore, when Mark combines the three prophetic actions and the five controversy dialogues into one section, he creates a new three-day structure culminating in Jesus becoming the leader of Israel rather than the Jewish authorities. Mark has suppressed the original triad of prophetic actions and the fivefold chiasm of controversy dialogues in the oral tradition to create a daily itinerary of Jesus. Thus, the closer we get to Jesus' passion, the more deliberate and methodical becomes the pace of the narrative. The fast-paced beginning of Jesus' ministry, where the term "immediately" dominates the chronology, gives way to a more retarded day-by-day rehearsal of Jesus' Jerusalem ministry (11:12, 20; 14:1, 12), until finally at the cross Mark almost stops the action (hours in 15:25, 33, 34) to allow the reader to meditate on the significance of these momentous events.

The theological purpose and literary function of Mark 11–12 is further revealed in the framework by which Mark encapsulates these chapters. The simple geographical frame consists of the temple courts, which Jesus enters upon his arrival in Jerusalem (11:11) and leaves at the end of his confrontations with the Jewish leaders (13:1).[323] Within the temple courts Jesus' authority is manifested. Through the prophetic actions of halting the temple activities and cursing the fig tree, Jesus predicts a renewed Israel and temple. Through the conflicts with the Jewish leaders Jesus replaces them as the authoritative voice of God to his people.

---

323. Cf. Dewey, *Markan Public Debate*, 153.

The second aspect of the Markan frame is the title "Son of David."[324] The healing of the blind man as Jesus approaches Jerusalem introduces the messianic title "Son of David" (10:47–48), which is picked up by Mark in the expression at the triumphal entry, "Blessed is the coming kingdom of our father David!" (11:10). The opposite frame (12:35–35) discusses the significance of this term and exalts the Son of David to Lord. Therefore, this frame establishes Jesus as the victorious Son of David, the expected Messiah promised in the Old Testament.

This theme of fulfillment functions as a third element in the Markan frame. Mark employs two royal psalms (Ps 118:22–23 in Mark 11:10–11; Ps 110:1 in Mark 12:36) to demonstrate that this Son of David will triumph over all his enemies. At the triumphal entry Mark utilizes an a-b-b-a structure to call attention to the cry of "Hosanna" and the exalted nature of the blessed one.

a	11:9a	Hosanna!
b	11:9b	Blessed is he who comes in the name of the Lord!
b	11:10a	Blessed in the coming kingdom of our father David!
a	11:10b	Hosanna in the highest heaven!

A comparable messianic scripture finishes the frame so that through the quotation of Psalm 110:1 the Son of David is proven to be superior to David as his lord (Mark 12:35–37).[325] Therefore Mark frames these conflicts with royal psalms to indicate that God's sovereign plans are manifesting themselves, with God's Son exalted as Savior (Hosanna means "save us") and Lord. A triumphant Christology is central.

This Christology of the Jerusalem ministry parallels the glorious splendor poured upon Jesus through his Galilean miracle ministry in 4:35—8:21. But as we have discovered through the two-stage healing of the blind man in 8:22–26, such a Christology leaves the reader only half-sighted. Therefore, the second half of Jesus' experience in Jerusalem centers upon his passion (Mark 14–15) just as the discipleship catechism followed Jesus' miracle ministry. The Markan frame composed of OT royal scriptures and the title "Son of David" establishes the triumphant messianic nature of Jesus' identity. This is affirmed and culminated in the eschatological discourse which follows and proclaims that Jesus will be exalted as the Son of Man coming on the clouds of heaven (13:26). But this is not the end or even the climax of the story. These sections prepare for the passion narrative, where the frame will demonstrate God's sovereign plan in the midst of Jesus suffering and death.

---

324. Cf. Burkill, "Strain on the Secret," 31.

325. Several interpreters contend that Jesus is calling into question the Davidic origin of the Messiah (see the list in Fitzmyer, *Luke*, 1312). But Taylor (*Mark*, 491), Fitzmyer (*Luke*, 1312), and Burkill ("Strain on the Secret," 33) offer a defense against this proposal. Others claim that the Davidic emphasis is unimportant to Mark's Christology (Achtemeier, "And He Followed Him," 115, 130f; Johnson, "Blind Man," 136, 139), but the title is neither negative nor unimportant but only insufficient (Evans, *Mark 8:27—16:20*, lxxix; Witherington, *Mark*, 333).

3.10 The Frame around the Eschatological Discourse in Mark 12:41—14:11

For this section of Mark we will reverse our normal order and first discuss the frame before we investigate the structure of the eschatological discourse. Two passages whose main characters are women surround Mark 13: the widow who places her offering in the temple treasury and the woman who anoints Jesus. Are these episodes related to each other? In the process we will attempt to determine if 12:41–44 refers more naturally back to Jesus' warning against the scribes who devour widows' houses in the previous context.

As we concluded in the last section, Jesus' Jerusalem ministry comprises a triadic structure, with 12:41–44 as the third pericope in the third triad, which reports Jesus' accusations against the Jewish leadership. It is disputed, however, whether 12:41–44 serves as an example of the scribes' devouring of widows' houses or if the woman's financial worship is contrasted with the scribes conniving selfishness. Is the woman a negative example of the scribe's greed or a positive model of altruistic giving? We will demonstrate that the frame with the woman's generous anointing of Jesus in 14:3–9 is the decisive piece of exegetical evidence to establish an exemplary discipleship interpretation to this passage. Mark 12:41–44 then serves the double function of finishing off Jesus' negative critique of the Jewish leadership as well as serving as a frame around the eschatological discourse and contributing a discipleship emphasis to these cataclysmic events.

The new interpretation formulated by A. G. Wright and supported recently by Fitzmyer, C. A. Evans, and Sugaritharajah[326] argues that the woman's contribution of everything she possessed into the temple treasury is a raping of the needy by greedy manipulators to benefit an obsolete institution which God is preparing for destruction. In 12:40 Jesus condemns the scribes for devouring widows' houses, and then in 41–44 he laments the demands of a corrupt temple system, which requires sacrificial donations from the poor rather than financially providing for their well-being. According to this interpretation Jesus condemns the value system that motivates her action. The pericope functions therefore as a lament rather than exemplary discipleship. Their arguments include evidence from the context (both the previous and forthcoming), the grammar (the repetition of widow), and the historical background of Jesus' concern for the marginalized.

The preceding context consists of a series of controversies with the Jewish establishment concluding with an imprecation against the teachers of the law. Mark 12:41–44 then would provide a case in point for this malediction.[327] In this case, "The

---

326. Wright, "Widow's Mites," 256–65; Fitzmyer, *Luke*, 2:1320–21; Evans, *Mark 8:27—16:20*, 281–82; Sugaritharajah, "Widow's Mites Revalued," 42–43.

327. Supporters argue that Mark employs a pattern of two passages in a row against the Jewish establishment as in Mark 7:1–13, 14–23 with Jesus' condemnation of Corban and the Pharisee's outward show of piety as well as 11:15–19, 20–23 with 12–14 where Jesus critiques the temple and Judaism as

story does not provide a pious contrast to the conduct of the scribes in the preceding section (as is the customary view); rather it provides a further illustration of the ills of official devotion."[328] Then in the following context (13:1–2) Jesus proclaims the destruction of the temple. Since any offering toward the temple would be totally ridiculous with the downfall of the temple immanent, this poor woman's contribution to the temple treasury must be "totally misguided."[329] Therefore Jesus disapproves of the widow's gift.

The repetition of the term "widow" (12:40, 42) offers grammatical evidence for a continuation of the theme of 12:38–40. Jesus lambastes the scribal establishment for devouring the homes of widows (presumably through abusive fraud)[330] and then offers an example of such a procedure in 12:41–44. Since OT regulations supported offerings for the widow including the partaking of tithes (Deut 14:29; 26:12–13) and gleaning privileges (Deut 24:19–21), and not offerings from the widow, this view claims that Jesus' statement about the woman's offering is negative.

Finally, the passage repeats a familiar refrain in Jesus' teaching that human need takes precedence over religiosity (Mark 3:1–5; 7:10–13; 12:28–34). As Evans explains,

> Jesus apparently has taken up the cause of the marginalized, and widows were among the most marginalized in his society. Evidently he has leveled a prophetic complaint against the religious establishment for failing to live up to its Mosaic obligations. He has warned of the scribes whose religion devours the poor and enriches themselves. He has pointed to the poor widow who cast her last tiny coins into the temple's coffers as an example of one such person who has been consumed. We have here an important remnant of Jesus' criticisms against the temple establishment and what motivated them.[331]

This view eliminates any exemplary role afforded to the widow since, as Wright concludes, "There is no praise of the widow in the passage and no invitation to imitate her, precisely because she ought not be imitated."[332]

---

a withered fig tree and a mountain cast into the sea. But in each context, a contrast is drawn as well. In Mark 7 the Pharisees' ritual cleanliness is contrasted with the disciples who must recognize that all foods are clean (7:19b), avoid the vices of inner character qualities (7:21–23), and welcome the believing Gentile into the community (7:24–30). In Mark 11 the old temple piety of Judaism is transformed into the Christian practices of faith, prayer, and forgiveness in 11:22–25. Likewise here in Mark 12 the greed of the scribes is contrasted with the generosity of the widow.

328. Wright, "Widow's Mites," 262.

329. Wright, "Widow's Mites," 263. In addition, Miller remarks that Jesus' seat opposite the temple treasury suggests "a position that conveys an attitude of judgment" (*Women in Mark's Gospel*, 116) just as his position in 13:3 opposite the temple prepares for his prediction of its destruction.

330. The exact action causing the devouring of widows' houses is disputed with possible suggestions including fraud (Taylor, *Mark*, 495), the abuse of Jewish inheritance laws (Derrett, "Eating Up the Houses," 1–9), or a pietistic omission of social responsibilities by the Jewish leadership.

331. Evans, *Mark 8:27—16:20*, 285.

332. Wright, "Widow's Mites," 262.

Although this viewpoint effectively employs grammatical and contextual arguments, more overwhelming evidence of the same quality argues against this position. As Malbon points out, this standpoint "seems more ingenious than convincing," since "Wright's narrow contextual focus results in an unfortunate, if not unusual, case of 'blaming the victim.'"[333] The widow is not a passive player in the scribe's evil scheme but a contrasting example of compassionate generosity. Certainly context reigns supreme, but the more natural connection with the following context of Mark 13 centers in the disciples offering their lives in 13:9–13, which will prove to be the chiastic middle of the discourse. The widow who gives everything she has becomes an example for the disciples as they face hardships. This incident offers another example where Mark is preparing for the passion narrative. Just as the withered fig tree in Mark 11 alludes to the destruction of the temple in Mark 13 and previews the ripping of the temple curtain at Jesus' death (15:38), so the widow's sacrificial gift in Mark 12 points to Jesus' offering of his life as well as the disciples' sacrifice of themselves in 13:9–13. Therefore, the widow provides a counterexample for the scribes since she is a model of the true disciple.

Grammatically, the word order suggests that the story climaxes in the ending, "but she, out of her poverty, put in everything—all she had to live on." She literally gave her whole life (ὅλον τὸν βίον αὐτῆς). The wording therefore supports a connection with discipleship, not a condemnation of the scribes. With regard to the historical situation, Jesus normally distinguishes the marginalized from the establishment, which again supports a contrast to the preceding context. Finally, woman characters in Mark are regularly connected with discipleship, including the service of Peter's mother-in-law (1:31), the faith of the bleeding woman (5:34), the insight of the Syrophoenician woman (7:28–29), the sacrifice of the anointing woman (14:8–9), and the presence of women at the cross (15:40–41). Therefore, equally compelling arguments support an exemplary interpretation of the widow's action.

However, the presence of Markan literary features offers convincing proof for the exemplary interpretation of this passage. We have witnessed how Mark regularly employs frames to provide a theological perspective on the enclosed material. In this case the widow giving her entire life (12:41–44) matches the woman generously anointing Jesus for burial (14:3–9).[334] The two stories about women giving their all surround the eschatological discourse to exhibit how disciples can be ready and watching for the eschatological woes and the signs of the end times. This interpretation is supported by vocabulary connections, an identical theme and emphasis, the progression of material, parallel Jewish literature, and the contrasting portrayal of characters.

---

333. Malbon, "Poor Widow," 596.

334. Dewey remarks that "The parallelism of the two stories is beyond question" (*Markan Public Debate*, 154).

The vocabulary and lexical connections are striking.[335] Both employ the term ὅλος (12:44 the widow gives her all; 14:9 the whole world hears the message), use the stitch word "poor" twice in the story (12:42, 43; 14:5, 7), and begin Jesus' logion with ἀμὴν δὲ λέγω ὑμῖν (12:43; 14:9). Furthermore, the wording supports a connection with discipleship, not condemnation of enemies. For instance, the term προσκαλεσάμενος (call to oneself) regularly involves discipleship if we compare 12:43 with 3:13, 23; 6:7; 7:14; 8:1, 34; 10:42. Although Jesus attaches "amen" to sayings condemning Jewish practices (3:28; 8:12; 11:23; 13:30), it is employed with equal frequency in contexts about discipleship (9:41; 10:15, 29; 14:9, 30). Finally, as Malbon points out, "Sitting was the authoritative position of the rabbis while teaching."[336] Therefore Jesus' sitting (καθίσας 12:41) and reclining (κατακειμένου 14:3) support an emphasis upon the teaching of discipleship, similar to the introduction of Jesus' parable sermon (4:1) and eschatological discourse (13:3).

Second, since Jesus praises women who demonstrate the way of self-giving in each narrative, identical themes and parallel emphases are present. In fact, "These are the only two such incidents in Mark in which an individual's act is praised."[337] Furthermore, if the conclusion of each narrative points out the emphasis, then the sacrificial action of the women becomes prominent.[338] Likewise, the grammatical expression "she has done what she could" in 14:8 reads very oddly in the Greek and is literally interpreted "what she had she has done," indicating a deliberate echo of 12:44, where the widow puts in everything she had.[339]

Third, this Markan frame contains a progression of material similar to the frame surrounding the discipleship catechism. There the two-stage healing of the blind man introduces the need for following a suffering Christ, whereas the healing of Bartimaeus completes Jesus' teaching section by exemplifying this following along the way of the cross. Similarly, here in the frame surrounding the eschatological discourse, "there is progression from the giving up of life to burial after death."[340] Therefore both of these narratives point to Jesus, who becomes the prominent example of sacrificial giving in his death and burial.[341] Best expresses it well, "Jesus praises a woman who gives her all to the temple which is about to be destroyed" just as Jesus is about to be destroyed in death.[342]

Fourth, parallel Jewish literature supports a connection between a woman's temple gift and her sacrificial discipleship. *Midrash Rabbah* 3:5 on Leviticus 1:17 states,

---

335. See the helpful diagram in Grassi, *Hidden Heroes*, 36.
336. Malbon, "Poor Widow," 600.
337. Dewey, *Markan Public Debate*, 154.
338. See Malbon, "Poor Widow," 596.
339. Hooker, *St. Mark*, 330.
340. Dewey, *Markan Public Debate*, 154.
341. Cf. Grassi, *Hidden Heroes*, 36–39.
342. Best, *Following Jesus*, 155.

The Theological Intentions of Mark's Literary Devices

> Once a woman brought a handful of fine flour, and the priest despised her, saying: "See what she offers! What is there in this to eat: what is there in this to offer up?" It was shown to him in a dream: "Do not despise her! It is regarded as if she had sacrificed her own life."[343]

Certainly these similar incidents support a theme of exemplary discipleship.

Finally, the portrayal of characters by Mark argues for a frame emphasizing the modeling actions of the two women. As we have already observed, woman characters in Mark are normally tied to the theme of discipleship. But the contrasts in the context stand out; prominent exemplary women are set over against villainous men.[344] The woman's generous feat of preparing for Jesus' death contrasts dramatically with Judas' dastardly act of betrayal (14:10). Likewise, the scribes' conniving greed exemplified in devouring widows' houses (12:40) must be contrasted with the selfless example of the widow. Therefore, Jesus' condemnation of the scribes' avarice and counterfeit piety is antithetically related to his commendation of the widow's behavior. Since Jesus normally contrasts the marginalized with the establishment, the widow becomes the hero in place of the Jewish leadership.[345]

Having demonstrated the presence of a frame around the eschatological discourse, we will investigate the structure of the discourse itself before we analyze the purpose of the frame. Since Mark organizes the Jerusalem ministry into triadic structures, some exegetes prefer a threefold structure for the eschatological discourse. After an initial introduction (13:1–4) Lohmeyer envisions sections on the beginning of trials (13:5–13), the events of the end (14–27), and final exhortations about the end (28–37).[346] Certainly a concluding section on eschatological ethics fits the NT pattern, but 13:14–27 must be divided into a description of the distress on earth (14–23) and the signs in heaven following the distress (24–27) before the occurrence of eschatological ethics. Therefore, Burkill's alternative triadic structure captures this distinction between signs upon the earth (5–23 birth pangs), signs in heaven (24–27), and the resultant exhortations (28–37).[347] However, as we shall see, the repetition of the term βλέπετε (watch 13:5, 9, 23) as well as the distinction between catastrophes you will

---

343. Freedman and Simon, *Midrash Rabba Leviticus*, 40.

344. Cf. Barton, "Story of the Anointing Woman," 231. Miller (*Women Disciples in Mark*, 124) sees an additional contrast between the seeking of public approval by the scribes (three public places are mentioned in 12:38–39) and the secret giving of the woman. In addition, although the widow's mite is contrasted with the huge amount of money the nard is worth, both gifts are surprisingly better than the other options of enormous offerings placed by the rich in the temple treasure (12:41) and giving the money to the poor (14:5).

345. The genre also supports this interpretation since as pronouncement stories, the sayings are central. Both 12:43–44 and 14:9 emphasize the women's exemplary behavior. In addition, the history of interpretation dramatically favors this view as Malbon ("Poor Widow," 593) observes.

346. See Appendix 4, outline 4.

347. Burkill, "Strain on the Secret," 43–44.

hear about (13:7) and events you will see (13:14) subdivide the signs upon earth into a fivefold chiasm.

Geddert has proposed an interesting alternative structure which attempts to parallel chapter 13 with the overall outline of the Gospel of Mark.[348]

1. The beginning of Jesus' ministry (1:21–39) parallels the beginning of the messianic age (13:8).

2. The developing conflict in the controversies (2:1—3:6) mirrors the developing eschatological conflict (13:9).

3. Jesus' ministry in the context of rejection and misunderstanding by family (3:20f, 31–35) and townspeople (6:1–5) now turns into a rejection of the disciples (13:9–11) by family (13:12).

4. Jesus' missionary efforts beyond the borders of Israel (7:24—8:10) parallel the outreach of the disciples to all nations (13:10).

5. Jesus' attempts to correct wrong concepts of Christology, eschatology, kingdom, discipleship responsibilities etc. (9:9–13, 10:35–45) now become the disciples' responsibility to guard against wrong Christologies and eschatologies (13:5–6, 21–22).

6. Just as Jesus breaks with the temple establishment (11:12—12:40), so Jesus' followers must make a break with the temple and its would-be defenders (13:14).

7. The description of Jesus' passion and beyond it the resurrection (Mark 14–16) are paralleled by predictions of a great tribulation (13:19f) and beyond it the final vindication (13:24ff).

However, if the sequence of verses is examined closely, the order of material does not always exactly parallel each other (see 3–5 above). Furthermore, the signs of the time (15:5–8a) really have no parallel in the rest of the gospel. The only valid conclusion to draw from these findings is that "a strong impression is created that the kinds of experiences that characterized the life of Jesus . . . will also characterize the lives of those who follow him."[349] Therefore, this mirroring of material has theological rather than structural implications for the gospel.

Because the repetition of key words normally reveals an author's thinking pattern, the threefold recitation of the term βλέπετε at 13:5, 9, 23 as well as the paralleling of hearing and seeing apocalyptic signs in 13:7, 14 offers clues to the structure of 13:5–23. First, the imperative "watch out" (βλέπετε) serves as an inclusio delineating the passage in 13:5, 23. Then this term is placed at the head of the central section (13:9) so that the passage forms a fivefold chiasm.[350]

---

348. Geddert, *Watchwords*, 193–94.

349. Ibid., 194.

350. Cf. Marshall, *Faith as a Theme*, 146. Wegener (*Cruciformed*, 171–72) offers another alternative

a	13:5-6	Beware of false messiahs (inclusio with 13:21-23 βλέπετε)
b	13:7-8	General signs (things you will hear): the beginning of birth pains
c	13:9-13	Persecution (βλέπετε placed at beginning, middle, and end of 13:5-23)
b'	13:14-20	Abomination of desolation (things you will see): tribulation (θλῖψις)
a'	13:21-23	Beware of false messiahs (inclusio with 13:5-6 βλέπετε)

As a result the emphasis lies upon the persecution the disciples face as they preach the gospel to the nations (13:9-11) and the unfaithfulness within the community (13:12-13). These themes fit perfectly with the emphases throughout Mark's gospel.

Lambrecht accepts this chiasm for 13:6-23 and then endeavors to construct the entire chapter into a fivefold chiasm with smaller fivefold chiasms in the b sections.[351]

a	Two introductory questions (13:4) and a command to watch out (13:5)
b	Earthly signs: 13:6-23 employs a chiasm:
	1 = 6a / 2 = 7-8 / 3 = 9-13 / 2' = 14-20 / 1' = 21-23
c	Heavenly signs: 13:24-27
b'	Parables concerning the earthly signs: 13:28-36 employs a chiasm:
	1 = 28-29 / 2 = 30 / 3 = 31 / 2' = 32 / 1' = 33-36
a'	Conclusion: the readers must watch: 13:37

However, the divergent Greek words (βλέπετε vs. γρηγορεῖτε) argue against an inclusio between 13:5 and 13:37. Second, the two introductory questions of 13:4 have no complementary section in the chiasm. Third, the second shorter chiasm in 13:28-36 seems doubtful since the mentioning of "this generation" in 13:30 is not paralleled in 13:32. Finally, the heavenly signs of 13:24-27 do not stand out as the center of a chiasm but instead parallel the earthly signs of 13:5-23.

Instead, the double introduction of 13:1-4 corresponds to the double paraenetic conclusion using parables in 13:28-37. In between this introduction and conclusion Mark narrates the signs upon earth (13:5-23) composed of a fivefold chiasm followed by the signs in heaven (13:24-27) constructed into a fivefold poetic parallelism.

A. Double introduction (13:1-4)

1. Jesus' prediction of the destruction of the temple (observation and prediction) (13:1-2)

2. The disciples' question about when this will be fulfilled (double question) (13:3-4)

---

outline but this outline misses the chiastic structure, the parallel expressions "when you hear" (13:7) and "when you see" (13:14), and the inclusio between the reference to false christs in 13:6, 22 as well as the imperatives βλέπετε in 13:6, 23.

351. Lambrecht, *Markus-Apokalypse*, 263-97, esp. 273-74. Cf. also "La structure de Mc. XIII," 141-64.

B. Signs of the end (13:5–27)

    1. Signs upon the earth (a fivefold chiasm beginning and ending with (βλέπετε) (13:5–23)

    2. Signs in the heavens (a fivefold poetic parallelism) (13:24–27)

	(But in those days, following that distress)
a	the sun will be darkened,
a	and the moon will not give its light;
b	the stars will fall from the sky,
b	and the heavenly bodies will be shaken.
c	At that time people will see the Son of Man
c	coming in clouds with great power and glory.
d	And he will send his angels
d	and gather his elect
e	from the four winds,
e	from the ends of the earth to the ends of the heavens.

    3. Double paraenetic conclusion using parables: call to watch (βλέπετε, v. 33) (13:28–37)

        a. Parable of the fig tree (the nearness of Jesus' coming) (13:28–31)

        b. Parable of the doorkeeper (the suddenness of Jesus' coming) (13:32–37)

Therefore, although the signs on the earth and in heaven do not each employ a chiasm, they do use an analogous fivefold structure.

Some exegetes prefer two parallel fivefold chiastic structures and therefore extend the heavenly signs to 13:31. They contend that the whole of 13:5–31 concerns the destruction of Jerusalem, based upon the analogy of Isaiah 13:10; 34:4.[352]

a		13:24–25	Signs in heaven = the destruction of a major city or country
	b	13:26	The Son of Man going up (not down) to be enthroned with the Ancient of Days
		c 13:27	Angels gathering the elect = the apostolic mission to the Gentiles as in 13:10
	b'	13:28–29	"It is near" (not "he is near") = the time has come for the destruction of Jerusalem (like 13:26 "at that time")
a'		13:30–31	Heaven and earth passing away during this generation refers to 13:24–25.

---

352. Cf. France, *Mark*, 504.

However, this outline breaks up the two eschatological parables of 13:28–37.[353] Furthermore, the fourfold use of *parousia* in Matthew 24:3, 27, 37, 39 indicates that Matthew, as the canonical interpreter, understood this section to refer to Christ's second coming and not the destruction of Jerusalem. In addition, Mark's nearest reference to the ἄγγελος of 13:26 is 13:32, which refers to angels in heaven (12:25 too) and not to human messengers. Finally, 13:27 mentions not only the ends of the earth as the place of gathering but also the end of the heavens. Will the apostles preach to angels or demons or the dead? A connection between the apostolic preaching mission of 13:10 and the angels gathering the elect in 13:26 cannot be substantiated.

Having therefore demonstrated the presence of a frame and the structure of Mark 13, now we will investigate how these sections tie together. In other words, what is the purpose of the frame around the eschatological discourse?

Within the future predictions of the eschatological discourse, 13:9–13 stands out as the center of the chiasm. Here the emphasis focuses upon the persecution of the community (13:9–11) and their struggle to stay faithful in these tumultuous times without betraying each other to the authorities (13:12). Consequently, as Barton points out, "The addition of the παραδιδόμαι sayings (vv. 9b, 11a, 12a) sets traditional apocalyptic motifs (at vv. 8, 12b) firmly within the *theologia crucis* framework of the passion narrative."[354] In fact, Mark intends to align the experience of the disciples with the suffering and death first experienced by John the Baptizer and then by Jesus. This emphasis at the center of the eschatological discourse parallels the sacrificial giving of the two women in the frame. They become examples of how to endure the end times and how to wait for Jesus' second coming.[355] The consistent emphasis on watching in the eschatological discourse (13:35–37), contrasted with the lack of watching by the disciples in the garden of Gethsemane in preparation for Jesus' death (14:34, 37, 38), reinforces the call in the frame to sacrifice all that you have for Jesus. With

---

353. Boring points out that the parable in 13:32–37 involves "a dramatic shift of perspective, from signs to no signs, from knowing to not knowing" (13:29 "you know that it is near, right at the door;" 13:32 "No one knows about that day or hour") (*Mark*, 376). One explanation for this assumes that 28–31 refers to the fall of Jerusalem and 32–37 to the coming of the Son of Man. Therefore, Stein argues, "That the order 'these things—all these things' in 13:29 and 30 follows exactly the order of 'these things—all these things' in 13:4a, and b indicates that the lesson of the fig tree involves the fall of Jerusalem, not the *parousia*" (*Mark*, 618). Also "when you see" (13:29 ὅταν ἴδητε) corresponds to 13:14 concerning the abomination of desolation. Then the discourse would have an abab structure with the eschatological teaching describing both the destruction of the temple (5–23) and the coming of the Son of Man (24–27) in the same way the parables do (28–31 destruction of Jerusalem; 32–37 coming of the Son of Man). However, since the parable immediately follows the signs in the heavens, it refers more naturally to the immediate context. "That day" in 13:32 is most naturally understood as the day when "he is at the gates." Furthermore, the return of the owner of the house in 13:35 must parallel "he is near, right at the door." Then the first parable (28–31) argues that the coming of the Son of Man is near, but the second parable (31–37) clarifies that we should not attempt to determine the exact timing.

354. Barton, "Story of the Anointing," 110.

355. Danker, "Double-entendre in Mark XIII 9," 162.

the destruction of the temple predicted in Mark 13, the discipleship commitment of the women will replace temple piety.[356] Therefore, Mark places a frame calling for discipleship around the eschatological discourse just as previous frames surrounded controversy dialogues, parables, and miracle stories.

Certainly this call to discipleship was directed to the situation of Mark's own day.[357] Graham even entitles the eschatological discourse "A Passion Prediction for Mark's Community."[358] Likewise, Geddert argues that this section "makes clear just what sort of road the disciple will travel in the post-resurrection age."[359] Mark's community, in the midst of outward persecution and inward unfaithfulness, must face the eschatological trials of the last times with the resolve of the widow and the munificence of the anointing woman, who give their all as a sacrificial offering of discipleship.

3.11 The Frame around the Passion Narrative of Mark 14:1—15:39

First we will consider the organization of the material in the passion narrative and then investigate how Mark's frame around this section offers a theological perspective upon these events. The dominant motif throughout the passion narrative is the theme of prediction and fulfillment, with Mark rehearsing two different types of fulfillment. The first set constitutes ten predictions of Jesus spoken at the Last Supper that materialize throughout the passion narrative.[360] The second sort consists of ten OT prophecies that are fulfilled in the events narrated in the passion story.[361] Although the theme of promise and fulfillment dominates the passion narrative, it does not specifically structure these events. Instead it demonstrates theologically that God has preordained these events and that Jesus as God's representative is sovereignly in control as the sequence of predictions unfolds.

The climatic nature of the passion account is evident through the retardation of the narrative. The gospel begins with a multiple employment of the word "immediately" (εὐθὺς). Occurring eleven times in the first chapter (1:10, 12, 18, 20, 21, 23, 28, 29, 30, 42, 43), Jesus' ministry establishes a breakneck pace. Immediately Jesus' popularity surges and the entire town gathers at his door (1:33); everyone craves his

---

356. This phenomenon is very similar to the intercalation in Mark 11:12–26 where the piety of faith, prayer, and forgiveness replaces the temple ceremonies.

357. Cf. Barton, "Story of the Anointing," 113 and Burkill, "Strain on the Secret," 45. Weeden maintains, "Nowhere else in the Gospel is there an extensive section addressing itself to the post-Easter life of the church in such pellucid fashion" (*Traditions in Conflict*, 71).

358. Graham, "Passion Prediction," 18.

359. Geddert, *Watchwords*, 192.

360. Mark 14:13–15 fulfilled in 14:16; 14:18, 20 in 14:44; 14:21a in 14:27; 14:21b in Matt 27:5; 14:22–24 in 15:24–37; 14:25 in 15:36; 14:27 in 14:50; 14:28 in 16:7; 14:30 in 14:66–72; 14:41 in 14:43ff.

361. Mark 14:34 alludes to Ps 42:6, 12; 14:62 to Dan 7:14; 14:60–61a and 15:4–5 to Isa 53:7; 14:65 and 15:19 to Isa 50:6; 15:23 to Ps 69:22; 15:24 to Ps 22:19; 15:27 to Isa 53:12 and Ps 22:16; 15:29–32 to Wis 2:17–20; 15:33 to Amos 8:9–10; 15:34 to Ps 22:2.

attention (1:37) so that he cannot enter the more populated towns but must stay in the deserted places (1:45). One hurried event follows abruptly upon another until Jesus reaches Jerusalem, where the narrative slows down and Mark describes events day by day (11:11–12, 19–20; 14:1, 12; 15:42; 16:1). Now beginning with the passion narrative Mark breaks up the narrative further into the four watches of the night which he had used to conclude chapter 13: 1) evening (14:17–31); 2) midnight (14:32–51); 3) the time the rooster crows (14:52–72); and 4) dawn (15:1–20).[362] Finally, on the day of Jesus' crucifixion Mark presses firm on the brakes and records what transpires in hours: the third hour (15:25), sixth hour (15:33), and ninth hour (15:34). Through this change of pace the reader stops and reflects upon the events of Jesus' passion. The thread that holds the events of the passion narrative together, therefore, is the descriptions of the watches of the night previewed in 13:35.

Mark employs these four time delimiters to structure the upcoming passion narrative, where the disciples may be ready to receive a triumphant Christ coming in glory but neglect to watch for Jesus' passion and death. In the evening at the Last Supper (14:17–31) the disciples vehemently deny that any event could separate them from Jesus, but Jesus predicts that one of the disciples will betray him and that Peter will three times deny him. Then at midnight the disciples are sleeping on three successive occasions (14:37–42), and finally all flee when Jesus is arrested (14:50), even though Jesus had warned them three times to watch in the eschatological discourse (13:34, 35, 37).[363] By the time the rooster crows, Peter has denied Jesus three times (14:66–72) instead of being ready through watching. Finally, Jesus is abandoned to face the malevolent authorities alone and then die a forsaken death without the disciples' company. Therefore at dawn Jesus stands alone before Pilate (15:1). The disciples are ready and actively waiting for an eschatological victorious Jesus, but they are totally unprepared for Jesus in his passion.

Since the disciples have not obeyed the call to watch, Mark employs the conclusion of the eschatological discourse as a paraenetic call to the readers to watch for Jesus' passion and follow him in his suffering. Nine common themes between chapters 13 and 14–16 conclusively demonstrate that Mark wants to tie together the future discipleship struggles of the church (seen in 13:9–13) with the readiness of Jesus to face suffering.[364] As Geddert explains, "It is by means of cross-referencing between

---

362. Verbally, the ὀψὲ of 13:35 becomes ὀψίας γενομένης in 14:17; the ἀλεκτοροφωνίας is repeated as ἀλέκτωρ ἐφώνησεν in 14:72 (14:68 in some manuscripts) and the πρωῒ occurs again at 15:1. The specific term μεσονύκτιον does not occur, but the midnight hour is implied in the sleeping of the disciples in the Garden of Gethsemane.

363. On the threefold repetition of the term γρηγορέω in 13:34, 35, 37 and 14:37, 40, 41 see Deppe, "Charting the Future," 95.

364. See section 4.2c below for an exposition of the nine similarities and for scholarly support for the use of a Markan literary device which I entitle a Markan allusionary repetition to tie together Mark 13:35 and the structure of the passion narrative.

Mark 13 and the passion narrative that we see most clearly how the passion of Jesus becomes a model for discipleship in the post-resurrection age."³⁶⁵

The fifth section of the passion narrative then becomes the crucifixion narrative, where the four watches of the night now become the hours of Jesus' agonizing death, where the disciples should be watching but are nowhere to be found. Mark organizes this final scene into the triplicate structure of the third hour (15:25), sixth hour (15:33), and ninth hour (15:34).³⁶⁶ Marcus points out that "the orderly progression of third, sixth, and ninth hours, like the series of sevens in the book of Revelation, implies that this dark epoch is nevertheless under the firm control of an all-powerful God."³⁶⁷ Mark has inserted these time demarcations to show how God was methodically taking care of every step, how Jesus was prepared for it and faithfully endured this time of persecution, and finally to make the reader perceive the slow passage of time in Jesus' passion, thus bringing more significance to Jesus' death.

How does the purpose of the frame coincide with the structure and themes of Mark's passion narrative? The frame around the passion narrative portrays women disciples who are closely tied to Jesus' suffering and attempt to anoint Jesus' body (14:8 μυρίσαι; 16:1 ἀλείψωσιν). As Barton points out, "Just as the Passion begins with a woman who anoints Jesus' body for burying (14:8), so it ends with more women who come to do the same (16:1)."³⁶⁸ The woman who anoints Jesus in the beginning frame prophetically announces that Jesus' death and burial are God's chosen plan for his Messiah. But significantly, the women in the final frame are unable to anoint Jesus' body for burial since this event has already occurred in the symbolic anointing by the woman at the beginning of the passion narrative.³⁶⁹ God has prepared everything ahead of time for the death of the Messiah.

Mark contrasts the male and female disciples in the passion narrative. The women are closely aligned with Jesus in his death and burial, whereas the male disciples betray Jesus (14:43–46), deny him on three occasions (14:66–72), and flee from a Jesus who must suffer (14:50–52). Whereas the women who follow Jesus from Galilee personally witness Jesus' death (15:40), the disciples are conspicuously absent from

---

365. Geddert, *Watchwords*, 189.

366. See my proposal at the conclusion of chapter 2 for a structuring of the pre-Markan passion narrative by triplicates so that it was easily remembered when recited at the Eucharist.

367. Marcus, *Mark*, 1050.

368. Barton, "Story of the Anointing," 232. See also Boring, *Mark*, 379; Kelber, "From Passion Narrative to Gospel," 173; Lincoln, "Promise and Failure," 288; and Miller, *Women in Mark's Gospel*, 177 for specific support for a frame.

369. The inability of the women to anoint Jesus has been variously interpreted. Elliot contends that "The early Christians were obviously embarrassed that Jesus' body was buried without the proper Jewish rites of anointing... Mk tries to remove the stigma that Jesus was not anointed at burial" ("Anointing of Jesus," 106). Cf. Nineham, *St. Mark*, 374–75 vs. Evans, *Mark 8:27—16:20*, 359; Hooker, *St. Mark*, 331; and Taylor, *Mark*, 533 who argue that Mark does not compensate for the lack of burial. This apologetic interpretation would fit a Matthean perspective much better, whereas Mark continuously includes material for discipleship purposes.

the cross. In addition Mark closely associates the women with Joseph of Arimathea (15:47), whose bold willingness to attend to Jesus' burial demonstrates that he is "waiting for the kingdom of God" (15:43).[370] This frame then calls attention to the contrast between readiness to follow to the cross, as evidenced by the women and the disciples' blindness and hardheartedness to accompany him.

In summary, the passion narrative is structured according to the four night watches harbingered in 13:35 and concluded with the hourly structure of the crucifixion narrative (15:21–39). Consequently the passion narrative consists of five sections similar to most other framed sections within Mark's gospel, but no chiasm is apparent.[371] Within the passion narrative the necessity of Jesus' death is demonstrated by the fulfillment of OT prophecies, the enactment of Jesus' predictions, Jesus' planning of the Last Supper at the beginning of the narrative (14:12–16), and the frame around the material illustrating the exemplary actions of the woman who anoint Jesus ahead of time for burial and follow Jesus from Galilee all the way to the cross (15:40–41). Jesus' readiness to die is contrasted with the disciples' complete avoidance of a theology of the cross, as evidenced in their unfaithful responses in each of the sections of the passion narrative.

The readers of the gospel would certainly see themselves existentially within the narrative. Mark proclaims that the community must not just watch for Christ's second glorious coming but should be prepared to suffer with Jesus during this long night of distress and persecution. Instead of committing the identical mistakes of the disciples, the readers should be ready to deny themselves, take up their cross, and follow Jesus. The frame again repeats the familiar Markan themes of a suffering Messiah who faithfully endures a time of extreme agony and calls his disciples to imitate his actions.

3.12 The Frame around the Burial and Resurrection Narrative of 15:40—16:8

Several scholars have postulated a Markan intercalation in Mark 15:40—16:8 because the exact characters are mentioned in 15:40 and 16:1,[372] but the first scene occurs on Good Friday with the women at the cross while the ending transpires on Easter at Jesus' tomb. Therefore, the literary device should be labeled a Markan frame instead, with different but similar events serving as bookends for the narrative. The women begin and conclude the narrative, whereas the actions of Joseph of Arimathea and the

---

370. Wright (*Markan Intercalations*, 204–6) offers four connections: 1) the name and the place from which they came is specified for both; 2) Joseph is awaiting the kingdom of God and the women witnessed the kingdom of God in Jesus' death; 3) both are closely tied to the grave; and 4) both contribute an unexpected source of support.

371. Stenger ("Struktur der Markusevangeliums," 16) proposes a five-fold chiastic structure consisting of seven scenes, but the material in the B sections displays little similarity and the climax is certainly Jesus' crucifixion, not his interview by the Sanhedrin.

372. See the chart in Appendix 3.

young man are framed in the middle. We will examine the relationship between the structure of this passage and the frame around its contents.

The structure of 15:40—16:8 depends upon your view of the conclusion of the gospel and whether the original ending is now lost.[373] If the gospel did continue, then the theme might be the gathering of the followers of Jesus, as hypothesized in the following fivefold chiastic structure and frame.

Frame	15:40–41	Introduction of the woman disciples who follow Jesus from Galilee
a	15:42–47	A male disciple who seeks the kingdom buries Jesus
b	16:1–3	The women journey to the tomb to anoint Jesus' body.
c	16:4–6	The announcement of Jesus' resurrection
b'	16:7–8	The women journey from the tomb to tell the disciples first.
a'	?	The male disciples discover that Jesus is not buried but risen.
Frame	?	The women disciples return to Galilee and see Jesus. The church is established and composed of the renewed disciples, including women.

In this scenario, the emphasis of the passage would center upon the resurrection, and the discipleship of the male Jewish leader, Joseph of Arimathea, would parallel the renewal of the eleven in Jesus' band. However, why propose a hypothetical ending if the present conclusion fits admirably? The parallel unfaithful discipleship endings of the male and female characters, as well as the Markan pattern of faithful discipleship at the beginning followed by discipleship unfaithfulness at the end of each section, argues for the original ending of Mark at 16:8.[374]

On the other hand, van Iersel advocates an alternative chiastic structure with an empty center.[375]

Frame	15:40–41	The women are looking on from a distance.
a	15:42–46	Before the Sabbath Joseph buries Jesus' body.
b	15:47	Two of the three women are looking on.
c	Unfilled time	? Jesus, God, or both observe the Sabbath ? God raises Jesus.
b'	16:1	After the Sabbath the three women buy spices.
a'	16:2–7	At the tomb the women hear that Jesus has risen.
Frame	16:8	The women flee in terror from the tomb.

---

373. The longer ending of 16:9–20 was accepted as original until Wellhausen's convincing arguments in 1903 that Mark intended to conclude the gospel at 16:8. This became the dominant sentiment in the English speaking world in the second half of the twentieth century after the 1950 commentary by R. H. Lightfoot (*Gospel Message of St. Mark*, 80–97). Recently, the theory of a lost ending is competing for prominence through the evangelical commentaries of Gundry, Evans, France, Stein, Witherington, and N. T. Wright.

374. See section 5.3c below for the surprises in this narrative and 6.7 for various interpretations on the ending of Mark as well as the discipleship outline 12 in Appendix 4.

375. Van Iersel, *Mark*, 483.

The Theological Intentions of Mark's Literary Devices

However, the theory of an empty center, similar to the proposal of a lost ending, rings hollow and lacks conviction. At no other point in the gospel does Mark attempt the technique of an empty center. Certainly the middle of a chiasm should call attention to an important event or saying, not to a gap in the narrative which the reader as a detective must discern.

Instead, Mark emphasizes the movement of the women disciples from their faithful following from Galilee and presence at the cross during Jesus' suffering, to their lack of recognition of Jesus' passion predictions as they attempt an impossible anointing of Jesus, to their outright response of fright, flight, and fight against proclaiming the gospel. This process, interspersed with the positive response of a forgiven male disciple, structures the narrative into a concentric pattern.[376]

a		15:40–41	The faithful beginning of the women disciples is described.
	b	15:42–46	A forgiven Jewish leader seeking the kingdom of God buries Jesus.
		c 15:47—16:3	The women, not remembering Jesus' prediction of the resurrection, attempt to anoint Jesus' body with spices.
	b'	16:4–6	An angel described like the young man of 14:51–52 makes it appear that a forgiven disciple announces Jesus' resurrection.
a'		16:7–8	As with the apostles, the women forsake their discipleship commitment. Because of fear the women flee without proclaiming the message of the gospel.

It might surprise the casual reader of Mark that the resurrection does not stand at the center of this chiasm. However, the cross climaxes Mark's gospel so that the reader's response to a discipleship of the cross is Mark's culminating message.[377] Through the behavior of the women Mark convicts his readership regarding their anti-passion stance with regard to the gospel as well as offering hope for the future when they meet Jesus in Galilee. The need for a change of behavior as well as the promise of forgiveness is demonstrated by Joseph of Arimathea, who, although a prominent member of the opposition party, boldly chooses the kingdom of God and identifies with Jesus in his death. Parallel to Joseph, Mark cleverly depicts the young male angel at the tomb to recall the young man in 14:51–52, who deserted Jesus in his passion but now in an act of renewal proclaims the gospel of the crucified one (16:6). These forgiven disciples offer hope to the readers that their unfaithfulness (13:12) can be replaced by a new start. They must travel to where the gospel began, meet the risen transformed Jesus, and now read the gospel again without repeating the mistakes of the disciples, Jesus' family, and the women.

---

376. For evidence that Mark describes the young man in 16:4–6 similarly to the young man in 14:51–52 see 4.6d below.

377. Cf. Lincoln who argues that "Mark's resurrection narrative is anticlimatic" and "the structure of the plot deemphasizes the resurrection" ("Promise and the Failure," 298).

The presence of the women in 15:40 surprises the reader since suddenly at the conclusion of the gospel Mark introduces new characters into the narrative.[378] Since the women are one of the three formative groups composing the church (Acts 1:14), Mark desires to relate their story of failed discipleship. As with the male disciples (1:16–20; 2:14; 3:13–19; 6:7–13), the women begin heroically but finish faithlessly when confronted with the demands of a discipleship of the cross.[379] Thus the outer edge or frame around the burial and resurrection events contrasts the discipleship of the women from beginning to end.

The purpose of the frame is therefore to portray the struggle of the women to accept a discipleship of the cross similar to that of the other founders of Christ's church, the apostles and Jesus' family. Mark's renowned negative portrayal of the disciples must be placed alongside his surprising negative description of Jesus' family in Mark 3 and the women encountered in Mark 15–16. Neither Jesus' mother nor father is given any role in salvation history, contrary to the birth narratives of Matthew and Luke. No genealogies trace their lineage back to scriptural heroes. Instead they are characterized as outsiders (3:31–32) who accuse Jesus of being out of his mind (3:21) and finally fail to honor him even as a prophet (6:4). Although these negative depictions have been categorized as a polemic against the Jerusalem church,[380] an apologetic against anti-passion disciples in the community is much more likely because this appraisal fits all three groups. The original readers symbolized by Peter refuse to accept Jesus' passion (8:32–33). The traitorous actions of the community in a time of persecution where "brother betrays brother to death" (13:12) is mirrored in the opposition of Jesus' family. The community is called to preach the gospel in the midst of persecution (13:10) since like the women they have remained silent out of fear that they could experience the same fate as the crucified Jesus.

But the church knows that the apostles, Jesus' family, and the women became the unquestioned heroes of the faith.[381] Even though Mark concludes his description of each group negatively, hope for renewal is hinted at through a series of unmistakable

---

378. Cf. van Iersel, *Mark*, 486. On page 482 he demonstrates that a new section begins at 15:40 as evidenced by a change in place and time as well as thematics, the number of characters arriving on the scene who have so far played no part in the story, and the elaborate introduction of these minor characters compared to Bartimaeus and Simon of Cyrene.

379. As Danova explains, "This analysis reveals that the story of the women re-presents significant elements of the characterization of the (male) disciples of Jesus and establishes narrative grounds for aligning the women with the disciples, from their earlier positive presentation to their final negative valuation" ("Characterization and Narrative Function," 375).

380. Crossan contends, "The polemic against the disciples and the polemic against the relatives intersect as a polemic against the doctrinal and jurisdictional hegemony of the Jerusalem mother-church" ("Mark and the Relatives," 112). See section 1.2 above.

381. Johnson notes, "Although the disciples only have half-sight throughout Jesus' earthly life, the church knows that they did see clearly after the resurrection when they received the Holy Spirit (xiii. 11) and were reunited with the risen Lord" ("Mark viii. 22–26," 383). Jesus' command to keep silent until Easter (9:9) states clearly the timing for the disciples' renewal.

clues. The prediction of a future meeting with the risen Jesus in Galilee (16:7), where Jesus' ministry started, indicates a new beginning for everyone. The separate mention of Peter prefigures his re-establishment as the prominent disciple and communicates hope to the readers who are concerned about their traitorous conduct during the Roman persecution under Nero.[382] Since Peter was forgiven, even his denials offer grace to those who are ashamed of Jesus in this generation (8:35–38) or speak on Satan's behalf (8:33) or even curse Jesus (14:71). The two-stage healing of the blind man (8:22–26) and its connection with Peter's confession (8:27–29) implies that the incomplete perception of the disciples will change.[383] Similarly James and John will in the end be baptized with Jesus' baptism and drink his cup of suffering (10:39). Likewise, the angel described as a young man dressed in a white robe (16:5) offers hope to the naked young man who deserted Jesus in his trials (14:51–52). Finally, I would contend as well that the renewal of Jesus' biological family is evidenced in the fact that Jesus' mother (15:40, 47; 16:1) is one of the three women to whom the angel reveals Jesus' resurrection.[384] She is identified by different titles in 15:40 and 16:1 to continue the foil whereby Jesus' family, the disciples, and the women represent those in Mark's readership who have failed to take sufficient account of the cross of Jesus. However, the reader catches the hint that renewal is promised through the resurrection when Jesus' mother takes part.[385]

Thus the experience of the women in 15:40—16:8 parallels the depiction of the disciples and Jesus' family throughout the gospel. Mark's purpose is to proclaim the necessity of recognizing a suffering Son of Man Christology and responding with a discipleship centered in the cross. Certainly Mark's readership would see themselves mirrored in the story of the gospel and respond appropriately without repeating the discipleship mistakes of these three groups. Mark's audience would realize that there is no resurrection without suffering, no miracle without a prior struggle, no vindication without a discipleship of the cross, and no recognition of the true Messiah without an acceptance of a Suffering Servant Son of David.

3.13 Conclusions

Throughout this chapter we have argued for the presence of Markan frames as an organizational technique within Mark's gospel. Just as a picture frame guides the human eye to focus upon the details of a painting, so these literary frames encapsulate

---

382. See section 6.8 below.

383. Cf. Marcus, *Mystery of the Kingdom*, 145. Reploh (*Markus—Lehrer der Gemeind*, 80) points out that the phrasing of 8:21, "Do you not yet understand?" implies that the disciples' misunderstanding is only temporary.

384. See chapter 5 below, the note in section 5.3c for a discussion of this issue.

385. Mark probably paints a negative picture of Jesus' family in 3:31–34 to prepare as well for 10:29–30 where the disciple is exhorted to leave brother, sister, and mother, terms placed in the exact same order.

the narrative and accentuate the details that the author desires to highlight. Mark employs a variety of framework structures, with most passages encircled by a single frame while several pericopes serve double duty by supplying the frame for two sets of passages. These double-use overlapping frames provide a retrospective view of what has preceded and a prospective view of the events to follow.[386] Mark seems to employ double frames at the end of his gospel especially through the use of woman characters in the narrative.

Single-use frames		Double-use frames	
1:1–15	The beginning of the gospel	11:1—12:44	Jesus' Jerusalem ministry
1:16(14)–39	The dimensions of Jesus' ministry	12:41—14:9	The eschatological discourse
1:40—3:12	First set of controversy dialogues	14:1—16:1	The passion narrative
3:13–35	Jesus and his true family	15:40—16:8	The burial and resurrection narrative
4:1–34	Jesus' parables		
4:35—8:21	Jesus' miracles		
8:22—10:52	The nature of discipleship		

The content within a frame is normally organized into a fivefold chiastic structure, while on other occasions Mark prefers a triadic structure. Ordinarily the frame lies outside the fivefold structure, but sometimes it functions as the outer element in the chiasm.

Fivefold structure encircled by a frame	Fivefold structure including the frame	Triadic structure encircled by a frame
1:1–15	3:13–35	8:22—10:52
1:16 (14) –39	4:1–34	Triad including the frame
1:40—3:12	12:41—14:9	11:1—12:44
14:1—16:1	15:40—16:8	4:35—8:21

Because of Mark's frequent employment of fivefold chiastic structures, one might expect the entire book to be organized in this manner. Van Iersel supports such a suggestion.[387]

    a   Prologue (1:2–13) with its prospective hinge (1:14–15)
       b   Galilee (1:16—8:21)
          c   The way (8:27—10:45) with its frame of the blind seeing (8:22–26; 10:46–52)
       b'   Jerusalem (11:1—15:39)

---

386. The frames function both as entry ports and exit ports in the double use examples.
387. Van Iersel, *Mark*, 84. For other chiastic structures of the entire gospel see Appendix 4, outline 3.

a'   Epilogue (15:42—16:8) with its retrospective hinge (15:40-41)

To substantiate this outline, Van Iersel proposes a series of supposed inclusios that tie together the beginning and end of the gospel.[388] He claims that John's baptism of repentance offered a new beginning from death to life just as Jesus' resurrection, but no exegetical evidence supports this supposition. The depiction of John the Baptizer as the messenger (1:4–9) and the attention given to his dress could possibly correspond to the young man proclaiming the resurrection in 16:5-7. However, the omission of the term ἄγγελος at the end of the gospel and the contrast between prophetic dress and angelic garments argue against any intentional inclusion. Likewise, Mark speaks of "the way" in 1:2-3 and going ahead to Galilee in 16:7, but the term ὁδός is employed by Mark at more significant locations in the middle discipleship catechism. Van Iersel identifies 1:14-15 and 15:40-41 as two hinge passages, but Mark employs other passages to create double-use frames, as we have shown above. Finally, van Iersel wants the wilderness in the John the Baptizer narrative to mirror the tomb at the end of the gospel, but any imagery connection between wilderness and tomb is lacking in the literature of that time.

Similarly, Kim Dewey supports an inclusio of the entire gospel through vocabulary similarities. He points out that Mark includes references to Jesus as the Nazarene at 1:9, 24 and 16:6, names Peter as the first and last disciple (1:16; 16:7), and describes the reaction of the crowd in 1:27 employing θαμβέω in a similar manner to the reaction of the women in 16:5-6 using ἐκθαμβέω.[389] However, Dewey's first two items of evidence are insignificant with regard to the content of these chapters, and the terms θαμβέω (9:15; 14:33) and ἐκθαμβέω (10:24, 32) are employed in more significant locations in Mark's gospel. Therefore, evidence for a supposed inclusio with regard to the vocabulary of Mark's gospel is totally missing. This as well destroys any idea of a chiastic structure for the entire gospel. Van Iersel's fivefold chiastic structure crunches unlike material into huge sections and misses Mark's organization by genre as well as the development of the five cycles of discipleship.[390]

Although we cannot support a macro chiastic structure for the entire Gospel of Mark, fivefold chiasms provide important organizational schemes for sectionalizing the material. Some of these fivefold chiasms emanate from the pre-Markan oral tradition. Evidence for this conclusion derives from the times that Mark breaks up these structures, as in the miracle section and the Jerusalem set of controversy dialogues. In their place Mark creates a triad of crossings of the sea with increased discipleship failure (4:35—8:21) and a three-day structure with Jesus in the temple which combines the prophetic actions of 11:1-26 and the controversy dialogues of 11:27—12:37. What purpose did these memorable chiasms play in the oral tradition? Since the Galilee

---

388. Ibid., 82, 485.

389. Dewey, "Peter's Curse," 99-100.

390. See Appendix 4, structural patterns 1 and 12.

controversy dialogues center in a prediction of Christ's passion (2:20) and the middle of the Jerusalem controversies speak about the resurrection, this oral structure was used to preach the gospel before Mark was written. Likewise, the first set of miracle stories concludes with the feeding of the five thousand, where Jesus breaks the bread and offers it to the people, while the first miracle story in the second set envisions Jesus' resurrection in the sea-walking epiphany and Jesus' sudden miraculous appearance in a form perceived as a ghost (notice the interconnections with the resurrection story of Luke 24). Both of these double sets of five-part chiasms appear to be connected through the theme of death and vindication. Thus the early church proclaimed the gospel through a collection of controversies and miracles in the oral tradition.

The Markan fingerprint on the parable and eschatological sections makes it unlikely that these structural devices derive from Markan oral sources. Therefore Mark is likely imitating his sources when he combines the parabolic material into two interspersed fivefold chiasms, with the center of the smaller chiasm proclaiming the hiddenness of the kingdom (4:11–12) while the larger chiasm emphasizes the disclosure of that which is hidden (4:21–25). Likewise, the eschatological discourse contains a fivefold chiasm describing the apocalyptic signs of disaster upon earth and centering upon the persecution and suffering of the church, followed by a five-part poetic parallelism of signs in heaven that will initiate the glorious appearing of the Son of Man upon the clouds of heaven. These two chiasms also proclaim the gospel in different ways. Therefore, the genres of controversy dialogue, miracle story, parable, and eschatological teaching were employed by the early church to rehearse the death and resurrection, suffering and vindication, defeat and victory of Jesus.

Surrounding these fivefold or triadic structures, Mark employs frames as a repeated literary device to display a consistent theological emphasis. The two recurrent themes are a suffering Messiah and a corresponding discipleship of the cross.[391]

The gospel of the suffering son	1:1, 14–15	Suffering Messiah
Successful preaching ministry	1:14–15, 39	Contrast with passion
Secrecy frame around controversies	1:40–45; 3:7–12	Suffering Messiah
Insider/outsider frame	3:13–19, 33–34	Discipleship
Seed parables frame	4:1–2, 33–36	Discipleship
Sea trips frame	4:35–41; 8:13–21	Discipleship
Blind men healed frame	8:22–26; 10:46–52	Suffering Messiah and discipleship
Royal psalms frame	11:9–11; 12:36 + 13:1	Suffering Messiah
Women's sacrificial action frame	12:41–44; 14:3–9	Discipleship
Burial actions frame	14:3–9; 16:1–8	Suffering Messiah
Success and failure of woman disciples	15:40–41; 16:7–8	Discipleship

---

391. Broadhead remarks that "The intense focus on the identity and mission of Jesus in terms of his death on the cross creates a consequent focus on the radical demands upon those who would follow Jesus" (*Teaching with Authority*, 165).

The Theological Intentions of Mark's Literary Devices

Therefore, the literary device of a frame reinforces the Markan double emphasis upon Christology and discipleship. But Mark also employs another literary device to promote this theme. In the next chapter we will illustrate how Mark employs allusionary repetitions to proclaim this identical message.

4

Markan Allusionary Repetitions

4.1 The Description and Function of Allusionary Repetitions

What is a Markan allusionary repetition and what distinguishes it from normal repetitions throughout the gospel? Scholars have frequently called attention to Markan duality and duplications of style such as double negatives.[1] Stylistic repetition is the "small-scale use of repetition to keep the story tied together for the narratee."[2] Three types are sometimes distinguished.[3] Progressive double-step duplication is evident when "the second statement revisits the first but at the same time carries the story forward."[4] Second, Markan inclusions as described by Donahue[5] occur when the omniscient narrator inserts a comment after the direct speech of characters in the plot. Fowler depicts the purpose for such stylistic repetitions as "confirmation for the reader of the reliability of the commentary provided by the narrator."[6] Finally, parenthetic repetitions signal to the reader that the bracketed material contains observations worthy of note.[7] Comprehensively, these grammatical repetitions, duplicate expressions, and authorial correspondence all occur within a single pericope. These various types of repetitions serve a literary function to em-

---

1. See Neirynck (*Duality in Mark*, 84–88, 125–26) who calls duality "one of Mark's most characteristic features of style" (49). In addition, Stein (*Mark*, 90) contends that Mark employs double geographical descriptions throughout the gospel (1:28, 38; 4:5; 5:1, 11; 6:3, 45; 11:4; 13:3; 14:54, 66, 68).

2. Fowler, *Let the Reader Understand*, 142.

3. Structural repetitions are a fourth category distinguished by Neirynack (36–37) which include intercalations or Markan sandwiches, frames or frameworks, chiastic repetitions, and chronological linkages like the word "again." These I have described in other chapters.

4. Kelber, *Oral and Written Gospel*, 67–68.

5. Donahue, *Are You the Christ?* 241–43.

6. Fowler, *Loaves and Fishes*, 164.

7. Fowler, *Let the Reader Understand*, 142.

phasize, reinforce, or further the progress of the story. Allusionary repetitions, on the other hand, occur between separate pericopes to create matched episodes and supply a theological purpose. Therefore, one must distinguish Markan duplications and stylistic repetitions from Markan allusionary repetitions.

Allusionary repetitions are correlative or coreferential repetitions. In such examples Mark employs a unique set of words to allude to a different context in order to shine additional light upon the meaning of the present context. Mark is renowned for his intertextuality whereby he alludes to OT texts to enlighten the meaning of a narrative. Unlike Matthew, who directly quotes an OT reference with an introductory formula, Mark only employs similar terminology as when the voice from heaven at Jesus' baptism reminds the reader of both Psalm 2 and Isaiah 42. This same phenomenon occurs within the text of Mark so that we can describe allusionary repetitions as intratextual repetitions.

In this chapter we will demonstrate through extensive examples that Mark is purposely employing these intratextual repetitions to address the important issue of Christology. First-century Judaism expected a Messiah of power and conquest who would reign forever (John 12:24) and re-establish Israel as the center of the earth. The difficult task of the church involved transforming a symbol of shame and degradation, i.e., the cross, and proving that it was God's intended way to deliver Israel. Mark attempts to accomplish this feat through allusionary repetitions whereby an experience of the exaltation of Jesus the Messiah with authority and power is closely paralleled with another text about the passion and death of Jesus the Messiah. Just as NT authors employ promise and fulfillment to indicate how Jesus fulfilled an OT text, so Mark uses intratextual repetitions to demonstrate that the same person who manifests divine splendor and miracle-working authority will also be asked to suffer and voluntarily surrender his life.[8] In addition to Christology, Mark applies this technique on a few occasions to the disciples. Here Mark employs allusionary repetitions to make plain that the disciples who are endowed with power and authority will also be asked to take up their cross and suffer along with Jesus.

With the rise of an emphasis upon the orality of the gospels, some scholars have questioned whether the hearers would pick up repetitions that are strung throughout the gospel. Räisänen, for instance, asserts, "Nor can Mark have expected them to turn to his book over and over again in order to find the alleged connection between sentences in different parts of the gospel, as modern critics are able to do in a culture in which the book has quite a different place from that which it had in antiquity."[9] However, in the ancient world these unique repetitions would stand out just as dramatically to the ear in a group recitation of the gospel as they do to the eye in an individual's reading of the work.

---

8. See Lindar, *New Testament Apologetic*, 75–137 and 253–55 for an exposition of this passion apologetic.

9. Räisänen, *Messianic Secret*, 22–23.

4.2 The Occurrence of Matched Episodes

To establish the presence of Markan allusionary repetitions, we will first describe the most obvious examples that involve the paralleling of entire incidents. Matched episodes are spatially separate scenes that allude to each other through the use of identical vocabulary or theologically loaded terminology.[10] Then we will enumerate other possible Markan repetitions such as loaded vocabulary and imagery, allusions to OT texts, and the recollection of characters in the narrative.

The early church faced the formidable task of altering the cultural view of crucifixion from a stumbling block (σκάνδαλον 1 Cor 1:23; Gal 5:11) and a sign of shame (αἰσχύνη Heb 12:2) for Jews and foolishness (μωπρίαν 1 Cor 1:23) for Gentiles[11] into a method of atonement and a legitimate religious symbol of sacrificial love. To accomplish this task the first disciples quote scriptures like the Suffering Servant songs of Isaiah and the righteous suffering laments (Pss 22; 69 etc.), which the gospel writers include in their crucifixion narratives (Mark 15:24, 27, 34, 36; 14:27 quoting Zech 13:7). Paul reflects upon the seemingly foolish wisdom of God (1 Cor 1:25), whereby Christ through the cross becomes a curse (Gal 3:13) in order to ransom believers (Mark 10:45; 14:24) as an atoning sacrifice (Rom 3:25; 1 John 2:2; Heb 9:5) from death, sin, the law, and eternal punishment. In the Book of Hebrews Jesus' death fulfils the OT system of sacrifices by becoming the once-for-all sacrifice (7:27; 9:26, 28; 10:10, 14). But the crowning blow of the Christian apology centers upon the vindication of Jesus through his resurrection. Mark, however, does not recite resurrection appearances nor reflect theologically upon Jesus' death,[12] but instead employs one unique method to defend a suffering Messiah. Through allusionary repetitions Mark equates a glorious Messiah with a Suffering Servant of God.

4.2a Preparation for the Triumphal Entry and the Last Supper (11:1–6; 14:13–16)

1 <u>ἀποστέλλει δύο τῶν μαθητῶν αὐτοῦ</u>	13 <u>ἀποστέλλει δύο τῶν μαθητῶν αὐτοῦ</u>
2 <u>καὶ λέγει αὐτοῖς</u>	<u>καὶ λέγει αὐτοῖς</u>
<u>ὑπάγετε εἰς τὴν</u> κώμην . . .	<u>ὑπάγετε εἰς τὴν</u> πόλιν
<u>καὶ</u> . . . εὑρήσετε πῶλον δεδεμένον	<u>καὶ</u> ἀπαντήσει ὑμῖν
ἐφ' ὃν οὐδεὶς οὔπω <u>ἀνθρώπων</u> ἐκάθισεν·	<u>ἄνθρωπος</u>

---

10. As distinguished from Markan frames, matched episodes have no structural significance for the gospel.

11. For example, Minucius Felix in his dialogue *Octavius* calls Christianity a sick delusion (11:9) because "To say that their ceremonies centre on a man put to death for his crime and on the fatal wood of the cross is to assign to these abandoned wretches sanctuaries which are appropriate to them and the kind of worship they deserve" (9:4).

12. The use of ransom theology in Mark 10:45 is the only exception.

3 εἴπατε	14 εἴπατε
ὁ κύριος . . .	ὁ διδάσκαλος . . .
4 καὶ ἀπῆλθον καὶ εὗρον	16 καὶ ἐξῆλθον . . . καὶ εὗρον
6 καθὼς εἶπεν ὁ Ἰησοῦς	καθὼς εἶπεν αὐτοῖς[A]

A. Similar charts are reproduced in Taylor, *St. Mark*, 536 and Evans, *Mark 8:27—16:20*, 370.

Eleven identical words in consecutive order indicate that Mark is tying these two passages closely together.[13] In each case Jesus sends two of his disciples into a village or city with specific instructions about a colt upon which no man has ridden or about a man carrying a jar of water. Jesus authoritatively borrows both a donkey for transportation and an upper room for a Passover-type meal. In each case a surprising signal notifies the disciples of unusual circumstances.[14] Whereas pilgrims normally parade into Jerusalem on foot at Passover, now the disciples confiscate a donkey so that Jesus employs a means of transportation nowhere mentioned previously in his ministry. Likewise, in an overcrowded city Jesus reports that a man carrying a jar of water will prominently stand out from the masses, probably since customarily women transported water on their heads in jars while men used skin bottles.[15] Then when the disciples specifically mention "the Lord" (11:3) or "the Teacher" (14:14), everything transpires exactly as Jesus has prognosticated. Remarkably, the owner of the donkey as well as the landlord of the upper room offer what was requested without objection. Is this just an instance of Mark's repetitious style or does the writer have a theological purpose in mind?

In Mark's gospel the triumphal entry is Jesus' first and climatic trip to Jerusalem. To introduce Jesus as the coming Messiah, one would expect Mark to emphasize Jesus' appearance as the Davidic king. However, in 11:1–10 Mark only spends one half of a verse (7c) concentrating on Jesus' kingly arrival at the head of the pilgrim enthusiasts, fulfilling the prophecy of Zecharia 9:9.[16] Interestingly, Mark places his attention upon the preparations for the symbolic action (11:1–7b) and not upon Jesus' entry itself. As Gary Charles exclaims, "Mark spends more time describing the preparations for Jesus' entry to Jerusalem (11:1–7) than the entrance itself (11:8–10), more time talking about a colt than talking about the intentions of the one who will ride it."[17] Jesus intricately prepares every detail of his arrival into Jerusalem, even including the possible

---

13. See Witherington, *Mark*, 370.

14. See Boring, *Mark*, 315; Marcus, *Mark 8–16*, 778.

15. See Donahue and Harrington, 393; Marcus, *Mark 8–16*, 945; Stein, *Mark*, 647; Taylor, *St. Mark*, 537, a suggestion which apparently traces back to Lagrange. Since sometimes male slaves carried jars of water on their heads and Deut 29:10–11 as well as Josh 9:21–27 speak of men carrying water jars, Boring adds, "What is surprising is that the man will meet them, as though looking for them" (*Mark*, 388).

16. The next verses (8–10) focus on the crowd's reaction of spreading cloaks and branches on the road and shouting "Hosanna" rather than upon Jesus himself.

17. Blount and Charles, *Preaching Mark*, 187.

objections that the owner of the colt might raise. All the preparations occur precisely as Jesus predicted, even down to the specification that the colt has never been ridden and stands outside on the street tied at a doorway. Why this elaborate description of preparations and then only a quick narration of the entry? Would an able narrator not reverse this emphasis?

Some dismiss these seemingly peripheral details as another example of Markan clumsiness, but I have become convinced that Mark's plan displays literary and theological brilliance. By concentrating on Jesus' preparations, Mark ties the triumphal entry and the Last Supper closely together.[18] In each scene Jesus is depicted with great authority so that he controls the circumstances of everyday life. In both incidents Jesus' foreknowledge is prominent, the titles "Lord" and "Teacher" become formulaic responses, and the fulfillment of the incidents "just as he said" depict Jesus as authoritative and God's planning as indisputable.[19]

Fowler contends that "The most obvious rhetorical use of repetition is to drive home a point by a succession of hammer blows."[20] These eleven words in a row serve as Markan hammer blows to convince the reader that God has prepared for the death of the Messiah with the same purpose and intensity that he planned the entry of Jesus in triumph. Mark employs identical vocabulary to balance Jesus' exaltation with his humiliation. Just as Jesus receives the form of ovation befitting a king in his entry (2 Kgs 9:13), so the title "king of the Jews" will not be given him until his suffering and death on the cross (15:2, 9, 12, 18, 26, 32). Remarkably, Jesus plans his passion as the Suffering Servant with the same detail and foreknowledge as his coming as the Son of David.[21]

Structurally, Mark parallels his presentation of Christology in the Galilean events and the Jerusalem ministry. In the Galilean section Mark narrates Jesus' miracles and recites Jesus' authoritative parables (Mark 1–8) before he includes the discipleship catechism (8:22—10:52), where Jesus predicts his suffering. Likewise in the Jerusalem ministry, the gospel recounts Jesus' powerful symbolic actions and his convincing arguments that outwit and replace his Jewish opponents (Mark 11–13) before the passion narrative in chapters 14–15. Within these two sections of the Jerusalem ministry, Mark parallels the wording of the triumphal entry with the passion preparation for the Last Supper. The Mount of Olives (11:1) becomes the location where the joyous acclaim "Hosanna in the highest" (11:10) rings out like a prayer.[22] Likewise,

---

18. Burkill concludes that Mark "appears to be acting in accordance with a transcendent scheme which has already been drawn up even to the minutest detail" ("Strain on the Secret," 34).

19. Robbins, "Last Meal," 24.

20. Fowler, *Let the Reader Understand*, 140.

21. Robbins declares that "Mark 14:12–16 portrays Jesus' sovereignty over the passion events, as the preparation for entry into Jerusalem (11:1–6) depicts his authority over the Jewish Temple and its cult" ("Last Meal," 28).

22. From Ps 148:1 Burkill ("Strain on the Secret," 31) demonstrates that "Hosanna in the highest" means "Save us from heaven."

the preparations for the supper lead to the Mount of Olives (14:26), where Jesus prays while he is deeply distressed and troubled (14:33). Instead of referring to these stories as doublets,[23] we prefer to see them as a prominent example of a Markan allusionary repetition correlating glory and passion.[24]

Therefore, Mark employs a variety of techniques to demonstrate that the expected Son of David Messiah must suffer and die. Already at Jesus' baptism Mark alludes to OT verses (Ps 2:7 and Isa 42:1) which combine to confirm Jesus' identity as a Suffering Servant Messiah. A Markan sandwich begins the passion narrative, demonstrating that while enemies inside (Judas) and outside (the Jewish leaders) plot Jesus' demise, God triumphs through a lowly woman anointing Jesus for burial. Later at the Last Supper and trip to Gethsemane Jesus offers ten prophetic words that all come true during the passion narrative.[25] Then at Gethsemane Jesus faithfully prepares for his hour of trial while the disciples sleep on three successive occasions, just as at the Jewish trial Jesus confesses his true identity while Peter three times denies Jesus. Finally, in the crucifixion narrative Mark alludes to OT texts that fulfill his passion[26] and employs irony where Jesus' mockers speak the truth without intention.[27] But in between these sections, Mark constructs an allusionary repetition so that the beginning of the Last Supper narrative repeats the introduction to the triumphal entry to indicate that the same one who arrived as Messiah-king comes now as Suffering Servant.

4.2b The Wording of the Miraculous Feedings (6:41; 8:6–7; 14:22–23)

6:41	καὶ λαβὼν τοὺς πέντε ἄρτους . . .	Taking the five loaves
	εὐλόγησεν καὶ κατέκλασεν τοὺς ἄρτους	he gave thanks and broke the loaves
	καὶ ἐδίδου τοῖς μαθηταῖς [αὐτοῦ]	and gave them to his disciples.
8:6–7	καὶ λαβὼν τοὺς ἑπτὰ ἄρτους	When he had taken the seven loaves
	εὐχαριστήσας ἔκλασεν	and given thanks, he broke them
	καὶ ἐδίδου τοῖς μαθηταῖς . . .	and gave them to his disciples.
	καὶ εὐλογήσας αὐτὰ εἶπεν . . .	Giving thanks for them also, he said . . .

---

23. Evans, *Mark 8:27—16:20*, 370.

24. Collins (*Mark*, 646) believes that 14:13 is modeled on 1 Sam 10:1–10 where Samuel pours oil on Saul's head like the woman anointed Jesus (14:3–9) and then prophecies a series of events in Saul's life just as Jesus predicts what will come true in Mark 14:13. But the wording diverges and the Markan emphasis upon preparation for suffering is completely missing in 1 Samuel. Pesch (*Markusevangelium*, 2:340) argues that both 14:13–16 and 11:1–6 derive from a pre-Markan passion narrative, but see Collins (646, n. 5) for scholars who contend both passages are Markan.

25. Mark 14:13–15 fulfilled at 14:16; 14:18, 20 at 14:44; 14:21a at 14:27; 14:21b assumed but specified in Matt 27:5; 14:22–24 at 15:24–37; 14:25 at 15:36; 14:27 at 14:50; 14:28 at 16:7; 14:30 at 14:66–72; 14:41 at 14:43ff.

26. 15:24 = Ps 22:18; 15:27 = Isa 53:2; Ps 22:16; 15:29 = Ps 22:7; 15:29–32 = Wis 2:17–20; 15:33 = Amos 8:9–10; 15:34 = Ps 22:1; 15:36 = Ps 69:22

27. See Appendix 2 for a plethora of examples.

14:22–23	λαβὼν ἄρτον εὐλογήσας	Jesus took bread and when he had given thanks
	ἔκλασεν καὶ ἔδωκεν αὐτοῖς . . .	he broke it and gave it to his disciples.
	καὶ λαβὼν ποτήριον	Then he took the cup
	εὐχαριστήσας ἔδωκεν αὐτοῖς	and when he had given thanks, he gave it to them.

In chapter 7 we will demonstrate how Mark employs the similarities between the miraculous feedings of the five thousand and four thousand to emphasize that the gospel is intended both for Jews and Gentiles.[28] Here we will answer the question why Mark inserts a third parallel in the formula of the Last Supper. We will argue that through an allusionary repetition Mark addresses the struggle of his first-century audience to accept a crucified Messiah.

Admittedly, differences exist between the miraculous feedings and the Last Supper formulary. Whereas the disciples distribute the bread to the crowd in the feedings, they receive the bread at the Last Supper. No miracles occur in the distribution of the bread to the disciples in the upper room. More importantly, the Last Supper narrative includes a cup of wine whereas the miracle stories mention fish as the added element beyond bread. From this data Collins concludes, "Since the gestures are intelligible as common practices related to ordinary Jewish meals, the significance of the similarities should not be pressed."[29] But why would Mark highlight ordinary meal practices in his gospel?[30] In addition, the fact that Jesus' multiplication of fish is not mentioned in 8:19–20 further indicates that Mark's emphasis centers upon the bread which is then alluded to in the Last Supper. The addition of the cup in the Last Supper parallels the addition of the fish in the miracle feedings. Furthermore, Robbins points out, "When the disciples ask Jesus if they should go away to prepare the Passover, they are mimicking their action in the Feeding of the four thousand when they asked Jesus if they should go away to buy food for the crowd (6:37)."[31] Finally, the underlined Greek wording in the heading of this section demonstrates dramatically the similarities that

---

28. See section 7.6 below.

29. Collins, *Mark*, 655.

30. Meals contain theological significance in the gospels. For instance, the meal in Mark 2:15–17 demonstrates the inclusion of the marginalized in the eschatological banquet of the kingdom just as in the wedding feast of 2:18–20 is eschatological in nature. The reference to food in 7:19 substantiates Jesus' fulfillment of the kosher food laws as 7:24–30 previews table fellowship between Jews and Gentiles. The mentioning of baptism along with the cup in 10:38–40 seems to preview the sacraments. The inability to satisfy Jesus' hunger in 11:12–14 indicates the barrenness of Israel. The woman's pouring out expensive perfume on Jesus' head during a meal (14:3) prepares for Jesus pouring out himself in death and burial. Jesus' future drinking of the fruit of the vine in the kingdom of God (14:25) occurs according to Mark when Jesus drinks the cup at his crucifixion (15:36). John's appetite of locusts (1:6) proves he is a prophet (2 Kgs 1:8). All of these instances contain theological significance.

31. Robbins, "Last Meal," 26 is referring to Mark 14:12.

Mark has created between these accounts.³² The taking, blessing, breaking, and giving of the bread all appear in the same order in each narrative. In fact, "the words of Jesus in the story of the last supper offer the key with which to decode this system of connotative meanings."³³

But how do we make sense of this repetition? What is its purpose? A prominent conjecture holds that all three passages mirror the Eucharist celebration of the early church.³⁴ Since the cup accompanies talk of baptism in 10:38–40, one could argue that this passage refers to the Eucharist as one of the two sacraments of the church. If Mark has eucharistic overtones here, the feedings as well might contain sacramental implications. However, the primary connotation of both baptism and the cup in 10:38–40 is martyrdom, as indicated by Jesus' prediction that both James and John will sacrifice their lives. Although it is possible that the miraculous feedings were rehearsed in the context of the early Christian cult meal, a much more plausible scenario suggests that a pre-Markan oral passion narrative was recited at the Lord's Supper.³⁵ The miraculous feedings were employed for totally different purposes by the early church, as indicated by their placement in the miracle catenae.

Although the wording is similar, the actions of Jesus are different. The two feedings demonstrate Jesus' ability to deliver people from a disaster through a miracle, whereas in the Last Supper and cross narratives Jesus willingly and purposefully succumbs to the disaster. Yet this is precisely Mark's point. Both Jesus' powerful acts and his willingness to suffer contain the same outcome: the world is fed. Therefore Mark wants to emphasize again these two crucial elements in his Christology, i.e., that Israel needs both a miracle working Messiah and a Suffering Servant Messiah. The wording of the Communion formula alludes back to the terminology in the miraculous feedings to indicate that Jesus can only be understood when his power and passion are set side by side.

Discipleship plays an important role in both the feedings and the Last Supper as well. With regard to the feeding of the five thousand, the disciples "do not understand about the loaves because their hearts are hardened" (6:52). Likewise, after the feeding of the four thousand Jesus warns the disciples about the leaven of the Pharisees (8:15) because they have become blind, deaf, ignorant, and hard-hearted (8:17–21). In the same way, at the Last Supper Peter is warned about his upcoming denials (14:29–31) and the rest of the disciples about their apostasy (14:27) and the presence of a betrayer

---

32. See also Camery-Hoggatt, *Irony in Mark's Gospel*, 201, n. 87.

33. Van Iersel, "Reader of Mark," 83.

34. See Robbins ("Last Meal," 21, n. 1) and Fowler (*Loaves and Fishes*, 224, n. 83) for articles and commentaries that support Eucharistic overtones. Robbins' evidence includes: 1) Did 9:3–4 uses the word κλάσμα, a word found in the gospels only in the feeding of the multitudes; 2) catacomb art regularly portrays the Eucharist with the figure of the feeding of the multitude; and 3) the motif of fish is reduced in both Matthew and Luke so that they have interpreted the feedings in a Eucharistic way. See also Quesnell, *Mind of Mark*, 275–76.

35. See chapter 2 above, the end of section 2.8.

in their midst (14:18–21). Discipleship failure holds the accounts together as well as Christology. As Fowler maintains, "when we take care to read the account of the last meal of Jesus and his disciples in light of the previous meals in Mark, we are struck by the recurrence of the dominant theme of discipleship failure."[36]

How does discipleship failure fit in with an emphasis upon the suffering of Jesus in the Last Supper? Here Best explains, "Food is a regular and easily understood metaphor for teaching, and the central element of Jesus' teaching in the Gospel is teaching about the passion and the discipleship which should issue from an understanding of it."[37] After the miracle catenae Jesus thoroughly rebukes the disciples because of their inability to comprehend the meaning of his miracles (8:17–21). Mark employs the misunderstanding of the disciples to call attention to the fact that miracles alone cannot reveal the identity of Jesus; only in the breaking of bread in his passion can Jesus' true identity be perceived. Therefore, "this final meal completes the drama of the Feeding Stories."[38]

Through the literary device of an allusionary repetition Mark displays a proper Christology where, similar to Paul's teaching, the disciples must know Jesus both in the "power of his resurrection and the fellowship of sharing in his sufferings, becoming like him in his death" (Phil 3:10). Through this repetition Mark offers a relevant message for the early church based upon the events of Jesus' life. In the Neronic persecution and as they face the upcoming massacre in Jerusalem, the disciples need to know that the real multiplication and feeding of the entire world does not occur through a rescue miracle but through the cross.

4.2c Times for the Master's Coming (13:35 Fulfilled Initially in 14:17; 14:32–57; 14:72; 15:1)

At the conclusion of the eschatological discourse, Mark includes a call to watch followed by the specific times when prayer and alertness are required. The times picture the four watches of the night in the Roman chronological sequence:[39] evening, midnight, when the cock crows, and dawn. Lightfoot reflects upon this sequence: "The question has often been asked why it seems to be assumed in 13.35 that the coming of the Lord of the house will take place at night, and not by day?" Then he answers this quagmire with his own rhetorical question, "Is it possible that there is here a tacit

---

36. Fowler, *Loaves and Fishes*, 135. See the three arguments of Fowler against a Eucharistic interpretation on pages 139–41.

37. Best, "Miracles in Mark," 549.

38. This is the thesis of Robbins, "Last Meal," 21.

39. Traditionally, Jews marked off the night into three watches (Luke 12:38; Jud 7:19; Jub 49:10, 12). Mark's choice could be explained as an adaptation to Roman Christians who need to be ready to suffer persecution.

reference to the events of that supreme night before the passion?"[40] Since these time designations are located by Mark immediately preceding his passion narrative, we will argue that Mark employs these eschatological time markers as the division of the passion narrative.[41] The implied message states that whereas the disciples are ready and actively waiting for an eschatological victorious Jesus, they are totally unprepared for Jesus in his passion.

These four time delimiters become the four divisions of the passion narrative before Mark moves from these night watches to the hourly designations at the crucifixion: third hour, sixth hour, ninth hour (15:25, 33, 34). Evening occurs in 14:17–31 with the Last Supper; the Gethsemane prayer and the arrest happen at midnight (14:32–51);[42] the Jewish interrogation and Peter's denials take place when the rooster crows (14:52–72); and the trial before Pilate occurs at dawn, as evidenced by the time designation in 15:1. Now it must be conceded that the exact terminology is not employed in each case. Mark does not designate that the prayer vigil and arrest occur at midnight, but it is surely implied as the watch between evening (14:17) and the cock crowing (14:68[?], 72).[43] Furthermore, since the Jewish leaders intend to arrest Jesus secretly (14:1) without the pilgrims at the feast inciting a riot (14:2), what better time to attempt an arrest than at midnight?

Jesus' warning to watch and not sleep (13:34–37) must not only be applied to his eschatological arrival but primarily to the behavior of the disciples throughout the passion narrative. In the first watch during the evening supper after dark[44] Jesus

---

40. Lightfoot, *St. Mark*, 53. Lightfoot changed his mind from 1935 when he wrote that in Mark 13 "there is no reference to the impending passion" (*History and Interpretation*, 94) to 1950 where he becomes the chief advocate that the four time references of 13:35 parallel four time references in the passion narrative.

41. For support see Myers, *Binding the Strong Man*, 347. In addition, Geddert argues that the Parable of the Doorkeeper adjoining this passage in 13:34 never gets entirely told because Mark portrays the real parable from 14:17—15:15: "That the focus shifts from a long journey to a single night is well explained by the fact that, although a long absence is in view on the primary level, Mark knows he intends to portray at a more subtle level the one crucial paradigmatic eschatologically-significant night during which one kept watch faithfully while the others all failed at their posts. That there is a shift from servants (plural) to a single servant (and specifically a door keeper), is explained by the fact that in the final Day and Hour there will be many servants, with Jesus playing the role of the master, but in the impending passion he will be portrayed as a servant, and specifically as a faithful doorkeeper" (*Watchwords*, 92–93).

42. Gray explains that "The three times Jesus prays and then visits the disciples who are sleeping would seem to make up an hour each of the three-hour watch of midnight" (*Temple in the Gospel*, 165, n. 40) so that Judas then arrives right at midnight.

43. Geddert hypothesizes that Mark "may not have wanted to 'over-identify' with the midnight hour lest the reader mistake the Gethsemane experience itself, and not the whole passion, for 'The Hour' of eschatological fulfillment" (*Watchwords*, 133). Furthermore, Mark employs the noun ἀλεκτοροφωνίας at 13:35 but the verbal expression "the cock crew" (ἀλέκτωρ ἐφώνησεν) at 14:72.

44. According to Exod 12:8; Lev 23:5; and Jub 49:1 the Passover lamb was to be eaten at night which would imply that the supper was eaten near the end of the evening watch. For rabbinic reflections on these scriptures, see Finegan, *Handbook of Biblical Chronology*, #605 and #20.

predicts the unfaithfulness of the disciples. Judas will betray him (14:18–21), Peter will deny him (14:29–31a), and the other disciples' promise of faithfulness will remain empty words (14:31b) since they will all fall away (14:27). Then in the second watch, the disciples sleep in the garden of Gethsemane (14:37–42) while only Jesus is awake praying. At Jesus' arrest all the disciples flee (14:50) while one young man would rather lose his clothes than lose his life (14:51). Then in the third watch Peter follows from a distance, but in the end proves himself an unworthy disciple since he denies Jesus on three consecutive occasions (14:66–72). While Jesus is offering the good confession before the Jewish law court (14:61–62), Peter is calling down curses and falsely swearing (14:71).[45] Finally, the disciples are completely absent when Jesus is condemned before Pilate and suffers forsakenness at the crucifixion.

This application of the time delimiters in 13:35 to the passion narrative is also reinforced through the repetition of common themes and vocabulary encountered in the eschatological discourse and the passion narrative.[46]

1. The gospel will result in a world mission.

    13:10   "The gospel must first be preached to all nations."

    14:9   "Wherever the gospel is preached throughout the world, what she has done will be told."

2. The three calls to watch for the second coming (13:34, 35, 37) parallel the three calls to watch for Jesus' passion in the garden of Gethsemane (14:36–41) as well as the triple denial by Peter.

3. Jesus was betrayed by one of his own (14:45), and brother will betray brother to death in the future as prophesized in 13:12 (there is a threefold παραδίδωμι in 13:9, 11, 12 and ten occurrences of this term in Mark 14–15).

4. The trial of Jesus will usher into a trial for the disciples.

    14:53–72 Peter denies the Lord in his suffering.

    13:9–13 The disciples will be faced with suffering where they will be tempted to deny the Lord.

5. False messiahs will appear.

    13:21–23 False christs are coming before the end.

    14:61, 64 The Sanhedrin believes that Jesus is a false Christ.

6. There will be signs of darkness in the heavens.

    13:24   The sun will be darkened and the moon will not give its light.

    15:33   Darkness covers the whole land at Jesus' crucifixion.

---

45. See section 2.7 above.

46. For a helpful diagram of parallels between Mark 13 and Mark 14–15 see Achtemeier, Green, and Thompson, *Introducing the New Testament*, 139.

The Theological Intentions of Mark's Literary Devices

7. Onlookers will see the coming of the Son of Man.

   13:26   "Men will see the Son of Man coming in clouds with great power and glory."

   14:62   "You will see the Son of Man sitting at the right hand of the Mighty One and coming on the clouds of heaven."

8. The temple destruction is prominent in both narratives.

   13:2   "Not one stone here will be left on another; everyone will be thrown down."

   15:38   "The curtain of the temple was torn in two from top to bottom."

The eschatological discourse, therefore, is employed by Mark as a paraenetic call to the readers to watch for Jesus' passion and follow him in his suffering. Mark is not just interested in composing an eschatological calendar of future events.[47] He is calling the readers to a discipleship of the cross, a following of the forsaken one. As Geddert explains, "It is by means of cross-referencing between Mark 13 and the passion narrative that we see most clearly how the passion of Jesus becomes a model for discipleship in the post-resurrection age."[48] Thus Mark parallels the expected times of Christ's second coming with the periods of Jesus' passion to reinforce two themes in his gospel: a crucified Messiah and a discipleship of the cross. This is the purpose of Markan allusionary repetitions throughout the gospel.

4.2d The Threefold Call to Watch (13:32–37; 14:32–42)

13:32–37	14:32–42
32 No one knows the hour	35 Jesus prays that the hour might pass
34 First mention of γρηγορέω The one at the door must keep watch	37 Jesus' first rebuke of the disciples οὐκ ἴσχυσας μίαν ὥραν γρηγορῆσαι;
35 Second mention of γρηγορεῖτε Command to keep watch because one does not know when the master returns	38 Command to keep watch γρηγορεῖτε καὶ προσεύχεσθε ἵνα μὴ ἔλθητε εἰς πειρασμόν 40 Second rebuke to the sleeping disciples
35b Four watches of the night when the master may return	The prayers in Gethsemane occur in the second watch: after evening (14:17) and before the cock crows (14:68?, 72)

---

47. Geddert explains that Mark 13 is "an eschatology highly infused with Mark's passion theology . . ., not an eschatology on the lookout for signs and apocalyptic phenomena" (*Watchwords*, 106).

48. Ibid., 189.

36 If the master comes (ἐλθών), don't let him find you (εὕρῃ) sleeping (καθεύδοντας)	40 When Jesus came back (ἐλθών), he found them (εὗρεν) sleeping (καθεύδοντας)
37 Third occurrence: γρηγορεῖτε	41 Jesus returns the third time and finds them sleeping

In the last section we have displayed how the entire passion narrative alludes to the times of the Master's coming. Now we want to specifically analyze the connections of the prayer vigil in Gethsemane with the three calls to watch in the parable of the doorkeeper (13:32–37). We will demonstrate the similar flow of material, the eschatological nature of the narratives, the reappearance of vocabulary (especially the threefold repetition of γρηγορέω), Mark's unique teaching on the Holy Spirit, and the mutual warning against sleeping. Then we will discuss how Mark employs these two passages as an allusionary repetition.

As seen above, the flow of the material is particularly revealing with the three calls to watch in 13:32–37 paralleling the three failures to watch in 14:32–42.[49] At the outset both passages talk about hours (13:32; 14:35). Mark 13 is obviously eschatological, but in the Gethsemane narrative as well "the term has an eschatological connotation as the fulfillment of Jesus' prophecies in 8:31; 9:31; 10:33–34."[50] Therefore both passages can be conceived of as eschatological even though one speaks of Jesus' exaltation and the other of his passion. In addition, Kelber argues that the eschatological dimension of Jesus' passion is confirmed by the ending of the Gethsemane passage, where the coming of the betrayer is expressed with the term ἤγγικεν just as the coming of the kingdom in 1:15 employs ἤγγικεν. Therefore, "the resumption of this watching-sleeping theme in 14:32–42 casts an eschatological light on the conduct of the disciples at Gethsemane" (13:33–37).[51]

Vocabulary from the parable of the doorkeeper reappears in the prayer vigil in Gethsemane.[52] The term βλέπετε plays an important role in the structure of the eschatological discourse, serving both as an inclusio (13:5, 23) and as the midpoint of a chiasm (13:9).[53] Mark repeats this exhortation in preparing for the parable of

---

49. Against this line of thinking Collins claims, "The contexts and rhetorical force of the two passages, however, are quite different. The parable refers to a time when Jesus is absent and the disciples must 'stay awake' or be watchful in order to be prepared when he returns as the heavenly and glorious Son of Man. Here Jesus is present in all his humanity, distressed and anxious" (*Mark*, 677). However, Collins does not see any connection with the hours of Mark 13:35 and does not recognize the use of allusionary repetitions by Mark which draw together Jesus' glory and suffering.

50. Ibid., 678.

51. Kelber, "Hour," 45, 48–49.

52. The fact that many manuscripts (א A C L W Θ Ψ) add "and pray" to "watch" in 13:33 in order to imitate 14:38 demonstrates that these two passages were connected in early centuries. See Collins, *Mark*, 681.

53. See section 3.10 above.

the doorkeeper (13:33), but then suddenly the term βλέπετε is replaced by γρηγορέω. βλέπω does not appear after Mark 13, nor γρηγορέω before it. Therefore, the threefold repetition of this term γρηγορέω is significant.[54] The threefold failure of the disciples to watch in Gethsemane (14:37, 40, 41) stands as a fitting counterpart to the threefold injunction to the identical action in the eschatological discourse (13:34, 35, 37).[55] In fact, all three occurrences of this verb in Mark 13 function as imperatives, with the ἵνα clause in 13:34 interpreted not as a purpose clause but as an imperatival ἵνα: "tell the one at the door, 'keep watch.'" Mark wants to parallel watching for the eschatological coming of the Messiah in glory with watching for Jesus in his passion. However, although the disciples seem able to watch for Jesus' coming in glory in chapter 13, they fail to watch for his passion in chapter 14. This too becomes a summons to the readers to continue faithfully in their calling and learn to carry the cross. The emphasis upon the readers is illustrated by the ending of Mark 13:37 "What I say to you, I say to everyone: Watch!"

Mark's special doctrine of the Holy Spirit also comes into focus in both the center of the eschatological discourse and in the disciples' failure to watch at Gethsemane. The Holy Spirit for Mark is never identified as the indwelling presence of God, like Paul, or as an empowering divine force, like Luke. Instead Mark always connects the Holy Spirit with trials and the testing of persecution. After Jesus' baptism the Holy Spirit drives Jesus into the wilderness to be tested (1:12). In the eschatological discourse the Holy Spirit reappears as the one who will sustain the disciples with an appropriate testimony during times of persecution (13:11). Then during Jesus' struggle in Gethsemane the disciples cannot watch for Jesus' passion because their flesh is weak, although the Spirit is willing (14:38). Lane correctly argues that "the 'willing spirit' which stands in opposition to the weak flesh is not a better part of the human constitution but God's Spirit who strives against human weakness. The expression is borrowed from Ps 51:12 where it stands parallel with God's holy Spirit."[56] Just as the Holy Spirit drove Jesus into the wilderness, likewise the Holy Spirit will lead the

---

54. For a discussion of this issue by several commentators see the masters dissertation from Calvin Theological Seminary by Zachary King, "Ethical Admonition of Watchfulness," 136, n. 9.

55. Although Brown (*Death of the Messiah*, 141) argues for a chiasm in Mark as in Luke, a tripartite structure fits the passage better. In times of distress, it was customary in Jewish literature to repeat a prayer in triplicate (2 Cor 12:8; Dan 6:10, 13). The tripartite structure fits with the threefold denial of Peter, the triple attempt by Pilate to release Jesus, and the three hours mentioned in the crucifixion. Dowd (*Prayer, Power, and Problem*, 152) envisions two sections with a threefold repetition in each so that in 14:32–36 there are three reports of movements each followed by a report of Jesus' speech while in 14:37–42 Jesus returns from prayer three times and finds the disciples sleeping on three occasions. As an alternative, one might argue that the threefold structure comes from an allusion to the single poem of Ps 41:6a, 12a; 42:5a LXX (42:6a, 12a; 43:5a MT) since the question ἵνα τί περίλυπος εἶ, ψυχή is similar in wording to Mark 14:34 περίλυπός ἐστιν ἡ ψυχή μου ἕως θανάτου. However, at the time of Jesus these were separate psalms as today. Furthermore the expression "until death" is closer to Jonah 4:9.

56. Lane, *Mark*, 520.

readers through the desert of their trials so they are able to bear the cross in contrast to Jesus' disciples in Gethsemane who follow the flesh rather than the Spirit.

Finally, Jesus' return to the disciples who are sleeping (14:37–38, 40–41) is exactly what he had warned would happen in the *parousia* parable (13:36): the master will come suddenly and find his disciples sleeping. In fact the parable of the doorkeeper and Jesus' preparation in Gethsemane are the only two pericopes in Mark where sleeping is a vice (see 4:27, 38; 5:39). If Mark is deliberately using the passion narrative to help define what it means to watch, then watching (γρηγορέω) involves both waiting expectantly for Christ's coming in glory as well as a willingness to alertly follow Jesus during periods of extreme suffering.

The climax of Mark's eschatological teaching is the ethical exhortation "to watch," and the content of watching is then explained in the passion narrative. "Watching" means for the disciples to "go through their passion as Jesus went through his."[57] Like Jesus the disciples must pray without lapses into sleeping, offer themselves to the Father's perfect will whatever this entails, and confess the identity of the Messiah in difficult circumstances. Therefore these passages display another example of an allusionary repetition[58] where Mark demonstrates that a complete Christology proclaims both Jesus' exaltation and humiliation and a sufficient discipleship entails a readiness for Jesus' imminent return as well as an expectant discipleship of the cross.

4.2e Eschatological Splitting / Heavenly Confession / Title of Beloved Son (1:10–11; 9:7; 15:38–39; 12:6)

1:10–11

εἶδεν σχιζομένους τοὺς οὐρανοὺς καὶ τὸ πνεῦμα ὡς περιστερὰν καταβαῖνον εἰς αὐτόν· καὶ φωνὴ ἐγένετο ἐκ τῶν οὐρανῶν· σὺ εἶ ὁ υἱός μου ὁ ἀγαπητός, ἐν σοὶ εὐδόκησα.

---

57. Geddert, *Watchwords*, 195. Now it should be admitted that not every commentator agrees with this analysis. Gundry (*Mark*, 855–56) is confident that 1) "Watch" has no metaphorical significance; it is rather a command to warn Jesus about the arrival of Judas and his mob; and 2) the disciples' sleeping and not watching is only the unfortunate effect of a hearty Passover meal and plenty of wine. Gundry, however, refuses to accept any symbolism in Mark as is evident in the first words of his commentary.

58. There are also close ties between Jesus' transfiguration glory and his passion preparation here in Gethsemane: 1) Peter, James, and John accompany Jesus on both occasions (14:33; 9:2); 2) Jesus addresses God as "Abba Father" (14:36) and at the transfiguration the phrase "my beloved Son" (9:7) is employed; 3) the reaction of the disciples is similarly expressed: "for he (i.e., Peter) did not know what to say" (9:6) and "they did not know what they should answer him" (14:40); 4) in Matthew Jesus falls on his face just as the disciples fall on their faces at the transfiguration (17:6) and "while he was still speaking" is shared by 17:5 and 26:47; and 5) at the transfiguration in Luke 9:32 the disciples are sleepy as in Gethsemane. If these connections are present, then the theme is exactly the same. Just as the disciples wanted to stay on the glorious mountain at the transfiguration rather than facing the demons below in the valley, so here the disciples attempt to avoid following Jesus in his passion.

(he saw heaven being torn open and the Spirit descending on him like a dove. 11 And a voice came from heaven: "You are my Son, whom I love; with you I am well pleased.")

9:7

καὶ ἐγένετο νεφέλη ἐπισκιάζουσα αὐτοῖς, καὶ ἐγένετο φωνὴ ἐκ τῆς νεφέλης· οὗτός ἐστιν ὁ υἱός μου ὁ ἀγαπητός, ἀκούετε αὐτοῦ.

(Then a cloud appeared and enveloped them, and a voice came from the cloud: "This is my Son, whom I love. Listen to him!")

15:38-39

Καὶ τὸ καταπέτασμα τοῦ ναοῦ ἐσχίσθη εἰς δύο ἀπ' ἄνωθεν ἕως κάτω. 39 Ἰδὼν δὲ ὁ κεντυρίων ὁ παρεστηκὼς ἐξ ἐναντίας αὐτοῦ ὅτι οὕτως ἐξέπνευσεν εἶπεν· ἀληθῶς οὗτος ὁ ἄνθρωπος υἱὸς θεοῦ ἦν.

(The curtain of the temple was torn in two from top to bottom. 39 And when the centurion, who stood there in front of Jesus, heard his cry and saw how he died, he said, "Surely this man was the Son of God!")

A whole cluster of similar motifs emerge at Jesus' baptism (1:9–11) and death (15:36–39) in the Gospel of Mark.[59] Through an inclusio Mark connects the beginning and end of Jesus' public ministry.[60] Three significant elements include the unusual use of the term σχίζω, the arrival of the Spirit (τὸ πνεῦμα 1:10) at Jesus' baptism and the departure of Jesus' breath (ἐξέπνευσεν 15:37, 39) at his death, and the voice from heaven paralleling the cry of the centurion with reference to Jesus as the Son of God. We will discuss the significance of these matching motifs in that order to prove how Jesus' baptism and death belong together.[61]

Grammatically, the chief connection focuses upon the unusual term σχίζω, which is employed for both the splitting of the heavens at Jesus' baptism (1:10) and the tearing of the temple curtain at Jesus' death (15:38). Normally this term occurs in everyday situations of splitting wood (Gen 22:3; Eccl 10:9; 1 Sam 6:14), tearing clothes (Luke 5:36; John 19:4; Isa 36:22; 37:1; Josephus *Ant.* 8:207), the ripping of a net (John 21:11), the splitting of a rock (Isa 48:21), or the tearing apart of people through a

---

59. See Motyer, "Rending of the Veil," 155.

60. Collins, *Mark*, 762.

61. Stein (*Mark*, 719) is one of the few who offers resistance to the parallels between Jesus' baptism and his death. He concludes, "But the analogy is not entirely convincing, for a true analogy would involve either (1) the crowd at Jesus' baptism responding to the splitting of the heavens and making the confession of 1:11 and the centurion responding to the splitting of the temple curtain and making the confession in 15:39, or (2) a voice coming out of the sanctuary through the split curtain confessing Jesus' sonship, just as God through the split heavens confesses Jesus' sonship at his baptism." This analysis, however, is asking far too much specificity in the narrating of historical events.

social division (Acts 14:4; 23:7; Ignatius *Phld.* 3:3).⁶² However, it is uniquely utilized in eschatological settings such as when the Mount of Olives will be split in the last days (Zech 14:4) and when divine revelations split the dome of heaven (*Jos. Asen.* 14:3). Messianic figures also used this term to broadcast a divine epiphany, as when Theudas proclaimed he would tear the Jordan River to retake the land from Roman occupation (Josephus *Ant.* 20:97) similar to the dividing of the sea in Exodus 14:21. Therefore Mark portrays both Jesus' glorious baptism and his tragic death as eschatological events. Whereas all three Synoptic Gospels employ σχίζω for the tearing of the temple curtain (Mark 15:38; Matt 27:51; Luke 23:45), at Jesus' baptism Matthew 3:16 and Luke 3:21 use the more familiar term ἀνοίγω and thus drop the inclusio. Matthew and Luke probably want to tie Jesus' baptism closely to Isaiah 64:1: "Oh, that you would rend the heavens and come down, that the mountains would tremble before you!" (LXX 63:17 ἀνοίξῃς τὸν οὐρανόν). Consequently, "it is likely that Mark formulated the tradition about Jesus' baptism in his own words and chose to use the verb ("to split")."⁶³ Mark employs the more rare vocabulary to construct an allusionary repetition so that the death of Jesus is represented as a divine eschatological occasion just as the splitting of the heavens at Jesus' baptism.

A controversy rages over which temple curtain was split.⁶⁴ If the outer curtain is intended, a nice parallel results between the appearance of the curtain as a panorama of the heavens (Josephus *J.W.* 5:212) and the tearing of the heavens at Jesus' baptism.⁶⁵ Since the temple curtain reached eighty feet in height, the centurion could then observe it, especially if Golgotha was located on the Mount of Olives.⁶⁶ In addition, Jackson claims that the association of the Mount of Olives with an anti-temple theme (11:1, 8–11, 15–19, 27–28; 13:2–4; 14:26, 32, 43–49) as well as the fact that "Mark makes sure the reader knows the darkness is at an end (15.33–34) before he introduces the centurion and his sighting" argues for the outer curtain.⁶⁷

---

62. In addition, Wis 5:11 describes the piercing of the air by a bird and Sus 1:55 mentions the cutting of a person in two.

63. Collins, *Mark*, 762.

64. For advocates of both positions see Jackson, "Death of Jesus," 36, n. 23. In addition, Donahue, *Are You the Christ?* 202–3; Dowd, *Reading Mark*, 162; Gundry, *Mark*, 950; Jackson, "Death of Jesus," 24, 27; Juel, *Messiah and Temple*, 140–42; Michel, "ναός," *TDNT* 4:885, n. 21; Motyer, "Rending of the Veil," 155–57; and Ulansey, "Heavenly Veil Torn," 124 support the outer veil while Chronis, "Torn Veil," 110, n. 67; Collins, *Mark*, 760; Evans, *Mark 8:8:27—16:20*, 510; Marcus, *Mark 8–16*, 1056; Maurer, σχίζω, σχίσμα, *TDNT* 7: 961; Malbon, *Narrative Space*, 108; Taylor, *St. Mark*, 596 (for older scholars) support the inner curtain.

65. Ulansey states that "the symbolic parallel is so striking that Mark must have consciously intended it" ("Heavenly Veil Torn," 124–25). However, the heavens were represented on both veils. See Gray, *Temple in the Gospel*, 190 and 191, n. 128.

66. Martin (*Secrets of Golgotha*, 12–19, 58–64) places it on the Mount of Olives, but Taylor ("Golgotha: A Reconsideration," 184–86) disputes this claim and identifies instead a quarry 200 meters south of the traditional site. Cf. Brown, *Death*, 2: 938–39.

67. Jackson, "Death of Jesus in Mark," 24.

However, τὸ καταπέτασμα is the normal term used in the LXX (Exod 26:31–37) for the inner veil, whereas τὸ κάλυμμα is the usual title for the entrance to the holy place (Exod 27:16).[68] Furthermore, the gospel writers designate the location of the crucifixion as "The Place of the Skull" rather than the Mount of Olives, and it is "unlikely that a site in view of the temple would have been chosen for crucifixions, because of the sacred character of the temple mount."[69] Geographically, "The temple was on the eastern edge of the city, facing east. Golgotha was outside the city to the west."[70] Still, there could be a connection between the inner sanctuary and Jesus' baptism since according to Josephus' description of the tabernacle (*Ant.* 3.6.4) the holy of holies was an imitation of heaven as well. Thus the tearing of the inner veil would symbolize the rending of the heavens.

The coming of the Spirit at Jesus' baptism and the departure of Jesus' breath at his death tie these two events together as well.[71] Certainly the resemblance between τὸ πνεῦμα (1:10) and ἐξέπνευσεν (15:37, 39) evidences a wordplay on the term "spirit."[72] However, we must understand the relationship between Jesus' baptism and death correctly. Jackson innovatively interprets Jesus' death as an experience of divine power, with Gundry and Evans following his lead. They proclaim that "The power of Jesus is displayed in his death audibly in the loud shout of v. 37, but it is displayed even more impressively and more tangible in the tearing of the καταπέτασμα τοῦ ναοῦ, 'veil of the temple.'"[73] Jesus' shout is seen as so powerful that it actually tears the temple curtain, a view that Collins characterizes as a "strange hypothesis" and "bizarre."[74] She points out that the word ἐκπνέω is simply a euphemistic way of saying that someone died.[75] Therefore, the forsaken cry of Jesus in 15:34 as well as the mockery (15:26, 29–32, 36) and Jesus' inability to carry his own cross (15:21) indicate that Jesus suffers humiliation, forsakenness, and extreme human weakness.

---

68. However, there are exceptions (Exod 40:5 vs. 40:19; Ep. Aristeas 86; Philo *Vit. Mos.* 2:148; *Gig.*1:270). See Gray (*Temple in the Gospel*, 188–89) for five arguments supporting the inner curtain including the use of terms in the LXX.

69. Collins (*Mark*, 740, n. 88) refers to Ber. 9:5; t. Ber. 61b; Mid. 2:4. See also Marcus, *Mark 8–16*, 1059.

70. Collins, Mark, 760. Marcus remarks that the vision of the centurion "would have had to penetrate intervening objects such as the city wall" (*Mark 8–16*, 1057).

71. See Jackson, "Death of Jesus," 27. Motyer ("Rending of the Veil," 155–57) envisions a Markan Pentecost since the Spirit came upon Jesus at baptism, and at his death he gives his spirit.

72. Shiner, "Ambiguous Pronouncement," 20. Matt 27:50 and Luke 23:46 both repeat the term τὸ πνεῦμα.

73. Evans, *Mark 8:27—16:20*, 508–9. Cf. Jackson, "Death of Jesus," 27 and Gundry, *Mark*, 949–50.

74. Collins: "The idea that a strong wind came forth from Jesus directed specifically and only at the veil of the temple is bizarre" (*Mark*, 763).

75. Jackson ("Death of Jesus," 26) claims that this euphemistic language is only a classical Greek idiom and not employed in Koine Greek. However, Taylor captures the intent of the vocabulary when he remarks, "From a sense of something unusual in the death, all the Evangelists avoid verbs like ἀποθνήσκω and τελευτάω" (*St. Mark*, 596). The special vocabulary of Mark carries the sense of "intense spiritual suffering" as Taylor maintains.

For Mark the loud shout in 15:37 continues Jesus' intense suffering by referring back to his forsaken cry in 15:34, whereas 15:38 and 39 begin God's vindication. The loud cry of 15:37 (φωνὴν μεγάλην) repeats the expression φωνῇ μεγάλῃ in 15:34 referring to Jesus' forsakenness. Then Jesus' suffering is followed by God's vindication since the term ἐξέπνευσεν (15:37) reoccurs in 15:39, and "those standing near" (τινες τῶν παρεστηκότων) in 15:35 parallels the centurion standing near (ὁ παρεστηκὼς ἐξ ἐναντίας αὐτοῦ) in 15:39. These examples of Markan duplicity tie the passion of Jesus to his vindication but do not eliminate Jesus' intense agony. Instead, "both the passive ἐσχίσθη and the somewhat redundant phrase in 15:38 "in two from top to bottom" (εἰς δύο ἀπ' ἄνωθεν ἕως κάτω) suggest that Mark is taking pains to describe the veil's rending as God's own action."[76] God vindicates Jesus through the tearing of the temple veil and the centurion's confession. But in Mark's gospel the centurion sees only Jesus' death, not earthquakes (as in Matt 27:54) or the tearing of the temple veil since the inner curtain is alluded to here.[77]

The flow of Mark 15:37–39 is not easily discerned. Those commentators who interpret Jesus' death as a powerful christological act of glory envision a causal connection so that Jesus' last breath (15:37) causes the tearing (15:38) and the tearing causes the centurion's confession (15:39). Thus Gundry argues for portent theology throughout his commentary so that Mark "makes the passion itself a success story."[78] He insists that the mystique of the oriental foreign language in 15:34 carries the connotation of a power so superhuman that Jesus' death produces a wind strong enough to rend the veil of the temple. In addition, "The use of a reed with a sponge attached to its tip may dignify Jesus by putting him at a height otherwise impossible to reach."[79] However, against Gundry, signs and miracles do not produce faith in Mark's gospel so such a conception of Jesus' death is far from Markan theology.[80] An overview of the gospel confirms Mark's emphasis upon Jesus' passion.[81] Jesus' death then must be read as the story of a martyr being faithful while feeling forsaken, the exact situation in which the readers of Mark find themselves. Mark is paralleling through allusionary language the powerful experience of divine glory at Jesus' baptism with the suffering

---

76. See Chronis, "Torn Veil," 109.

77. Luke 23:47 confirms this view when he states that the centurion merely saw what had happened, which must refer to Jesus' death in 23:46 and not the rending of the temple veil in 23:45 before Jesus' death. The ISV translates Mark 15:39, "When the centurion who stood facing Jesus saw how he had cried out and breathed his last," following the majority of manuscripts which demonstrates that many interpreters connected the centurion's confession with Jesus' death cry and not the tearing of the temple curtain.

78. Gundry, *Mark*, 3. Cf. Jackson, "Death of Jesus," 34, n. 9 for supporters.

79. Gundry, *Mark*, 948.

80. Boring states, "All this is the polar opposite of Mark's own view of the relation of signs and faith" (*Mark*, 433, n. 136).

81. See the long list of evidence given in Chronis, "Torn Veil," 99–100.

of Jesus at the cross. Both are divine epiphanies, placing a Suffering Servant Christology alongside Son of David messianic expectations.[82]

The third way in which Mark alludes back to Jesus' baptism in the narrative of Jesus' death is through a voice that proclaims Jesus as God's Son. In reality, Mark positions three pericopes in sequence to develop the theme of Jesus' identity: baptism, transfiguration, death.[83] Not only is Jesus confessed as the Son in each, but an Elijah reference further connects the passages. Mark pictures John the Baptizer like Elijah immediately preceding the baptism of Jesus (1:6 and 2 Kgs 1:8), specifically identifies him as Elijah immediately following the transfiguration (9:11–13), and the crowd questions whether Elijah will come (15:35–36) right before Jesus' death and the centurion's confession.[84] But in each incident Jesus captures the center of attention as the greater one. In the baptism of Jesus John the Baptizer surrenders the stage to the more powerful one (1:7) just as Elijah prepared the way for Elisha to retake the land of Canaan. In the transfiguration Elijah appears in the epiphany (9:4), but immediately following the voice from heaven the disciples only see Jesus (9:8), so that as they descend the mountain Elijah is identified as John the Baptizer but Jesus as the Son of Man (9:12–13). Finally, Elijah does not appear at the cross (15:35–36) because John the Baptizer has already prepared the way for the Messiah. Therefore, the perceptive reader discovers that the Elijah motif pervades all three narratives.

The three incidents expand the audience who experience the significance of Jesus as the Son of God. At the baptism the voice from heaven is aimed at Jesus himself ("You are my Son") so that his identity is revealed only to Jesus and the reader.[85] At the transfiguration the *bath qol* (9:7) addresses the inner group of disciples (9:2), who now realize Jesus' heavenly identity but are forbidden to reveal it to others (9:9–10). The additional clause "listen to him" (ἀκούετε αὐτοῦ) alludes to Deuteronomy 18:15, 18–19, where God asserts that he will raise up a prophet like Moses who will speak God's words and Israel must listen to him. Finally, 15:39 stands out clearly as the culmination of this crucial Markan motif of the revelation and recognition of Jesus'

---

82. Just as Jesus' baptism refers to Messianic Psalm 2, so Ps 18:4–19 could be alluded to in Jesus' death. See Collins, *Mark*, 761 and "From Noble Death," 497–98.

83. Matera states that "the centurion's confession is a moment of revelation similar to and related to the theophanies at Jesus' baptism and transfiguration" ("Prologue as Interpretive Key," 301). See Ulansey, "Heavenly Veil Torn," 123, n. 1 for authors who see a connection.

84. See Motyer, "Rending of the Veil," 156.

85. Matthew, Luke, and the Gospel of the Ebionites all miss the significance of Mark's sequence. Matt 3:17 changes the voice to the third person so that a heavenly revelation demonstrates that Jesus is greater than John (3:14–15) to answer the Jewish accusation that the one who baptizes is greater than the person baptized. Luke 23:47 alters the centurion's confession so that the title Son of God is omitted. The Gospel of the Ebionites contains two voices from heaven at Jesus' baptism, one in the second person and one for the crowd in the third person.

identity.[86] Not only is the identical title employed,[87] but on this occasion a Gentile reveals Jesus' identity so that now the gospel message reaches the entire world. At Jesus' death the prophet like Moses is given to the Gentiles, and the restriction to not spread the news is lifted since at Jesus' death the Messianic Secret is overturned. Although some object that no *bath qol* resounds at Jesus' death, the centurion's unexpected confession substitutes for God's voice and acts as a sign of divine vindication.

Two objections have been raised against this exegesis. Some interpreters paint the centurion as a negative character who continues the theme of mockery in the Markan crucifixion narrative.[88] In this view the centurion simply continues this sequence of taunts alongside the other ironic statements at the foot of the cross:

15:26; cf. 15:2, 9	King of the Jews
15:31	Savior
15:32	Christ, the king of Israel
15:36	The one connected with the eschatological Elijah
15:39	A son of a god

Therefore, the centurion functions as a mocker who ironically speaks the truth like the other scoffers in the story.

Earl Johnson offers the best arguments in favor of this thesis. Grammatically, Johnson contends that if 15:39 paralleled the baptism and transfiguration events, then the title "Son of God" would not lack the article. Here he calls attention to the exceptions to Colwell's rule in order to argue that the wording υἱὸς θεοῦ is indefinite.[89] However, the articular noun right before this phrase (οὗτος ὁ ἄνθρωπος) makes it highly unlikely that Mark would repeat the article in order to establish a definite noun.

Johnson then proceeds to the imperfect verb in the sentence and contends, "In Mark 15.39 it would be exceptional if Mark transmitted a Christological statement in the imperfect, since he consistently places confessional statements in the present

---

86. For authors who see Mark 15:39 as the key to the gospel see Johnson, "Is Mark 15.39 the Key," 17, n. 3. Taylor (*St. Mark*, 597) envisions the confession as proclaiming the deity of Jesus in a full Christian sense.

87. The specific wording θεοῦ in "Son of God" is omitted at Jesus' baptism and transfiguration since God is the speaker.

88. Cf. Blount and Charles, *Preaching Mark*, 242; Goodacre, *Case Against Q*, 160, n. 28; Johnson, "Is Mark 15.39 the Key?" 14–16; Juel, *Master of Surprise*, 74, n. 7. Marcus concludes that these arguments are not decisive since 1) the disclosure of the Messianic Secret is consonant with Markan Christology; 2) the story places the centurion alongside the women after Jesus' death, not alongside the mockers before that event; and 3) "the centurion's confession is one of three architectonic acclamations of Jesus as Son of God, which are similar in form and seem to structure the whole Gospel" (*Mark 8–16*, 1059). Gray (*Temple in the Gospel*, 194) adds as well that the structure of 15:39 accentuates the "seeing" of the centurion which is contrasted with the mockers who demand to see in 15:32, 36 but fail to truly see.

89. Johnson ("Is Mark 15.39 the Key," 4–6) versus Colwell ("Definite Rule," 12–21). See also Davis, "Mark's Christological Paradox," 11–12 for arguments against Johnson.

tense (1.11, 24; 2.28; 3.11; 8.29; 9.7; 12.35; 14.61f)."[90] But since the death of Jesus has already occurred, a past tense is natural. As Kingsbury explains, "Of course the centurion having just seen Jesus die says that Jesus 'was' the Son of god. But in the resurrection God overturns this 'was' so that it becomes 'is.'"[91] Johnson himself admits that 15:39 closely parallels 11:32, where John the Baptizer is entitled a prophet in the imperfect tense (προφήτης ἦν) after his death.[92] Therefore the use of the imperfect tense is not awkward.

Finally, Johnson considers the cultural background of a Roman centurion and argues that Mark's church would never expect a Roman soldier to comprehend the meaning of Jesus' death. In fact, the readers would assume that a centurion shared "the common negative Roman opinion of those sentenced to die on a cross."[93] Therefore, at the very most the centurion must have thought Jesus was heroic or a demigod.[94] Otherwise Mark becomes "an inept storyteller" who portrays the centurion as "a simple puppet of the Christian kerygma and does violence to his independence as a character."[95] However, if one gives prominence to Mark's literary devices, it becomes apparent that the minor characters serve as the heroes of the story. Blind Bartimaeus functions as the paradigm disciple who sees clearly and follows along the way behind Jesus toward his crucifixion. Simon of Cyrene replaces Simon Peter as the one who carries the cross. In contrast to Judas Iscariot, who plots Jesus' death (14:19), an unnamed woman anoints Jesus for his burial and becomes world famous (14:9). Here too the centurion replaces the disciples at the cross and offers the ultimate Christian confession that Jesus is the Son of God, the title in which Mark inaugurates his gospel at 1:1. Because the inclusion of Gentiles into the Christian church is a prominent agenda of Mark, he portrays the centurion as a prototypical Gentile convert. Finally, the build-up in Mark's gospel regarding the revelation of Jesus' identity from baptism to transfiguration to death argues for a positive affirmation by the centurion.

A second alternative view pictures the centurion's confession positively but visualizes more than three confessions of Jesus as Son of God in Mark. Jackson adds 14:61–62 and 12:6–8 since in these passages Jesus is given the titles "Son of the Blessed One" (14:61) and "the beloved son (12:6).[96] Before the Sanhedrin Jesus openly confesses that he is both Messiah and Son of God with his answer "I am," since now his passion is beginning and the secret of his identity can be disclosed. In the parable of

---

90. Johnson, "Is Mark 15.39 the Key," 7.
91. Kingsbury, *Christology*, 134.
92. Johnson, "Is Mark 15.39 the Key," 7.
93. Johnson, "Is Mark 15.39 the Key," 14. Johnson (13) points out that a Roman soldier's allegiance to the emperor was expected to be absolute and that such a confession would make him guilty of treason, an unlikely scenario.
94. Gould (*St. Mark*, 295) holds the classic interpretation of this view.
95. See Jackson's description of this problem, "Death of Jesus," 18.
96. Jackson, "Death of Jesus," 21.

the tenants Jesus is allegorically identified as the beloved son, which is the identical title placed upon Jesus at his baptism and transfiguration. Jackson notes that the word "see" is employed in each setting: 1) at his baptism Jesus sees the heavens torn; 2) in 9:2, 4 the disciples see Jesus transfigured as well as the figures of Elijah and Moses; 3) in the parable of the tenants the stone which the builders rejected becomes marvelous in our eyes (12:10–11); 4) in 14:62 Jesus promises the Jewish leaders that they will see the Son of Man sitting at the right hand of power and coming on the clouds of heaven; and 5) the centurion sees how Jesus died and offers a christological confession.

Although Jackson offers some interesting exegetical discoveries, in the end both 14:61–62 and 12:6–8 should be categorized as satellite confirmations instead of divine revelations. As Chronis asserts, "one can detect no genuine perception of Jesus' identity. It is only in the depths of his passion that Jesus' full identity becomes manifest."[97] At 12:12 the Jewish leadership realizes that Jesus has categorized them as the wicked tenants, but still they plot to arrest him. Likewise, at 14:63–65 the high priest tears his clothes and denounces Jesus as a blasphemer while all present condemn him as worthy of death. Instead of receiving a divine revelation they ridicule Jesus, spit upon him, strike him with their fists, and with distain ask him to prophesy. Therefore, these are not epiphanies at all and certainly not on the same caliber as the baptism, transfiguration, and death of Jesus.

Instead, 15:39 must be seen as "the punch line of the whole Gospel narrative, the thesis which Mark has ingeniously withheld until this final scene, but which now meets us as Mark's own faith."[98] The centurion focuses upon the crucified Jesus before him and identifies him with the title that has been employed by God himself in the voice from heaven at his baptism and transfiguration. This vindication after Jesus' death is paralleled with an emphasis on Jesus as the righteous sufferer of Psalm 69 at the center of a chiasm that encompasses Jesus' death narrative.[99]

a		15:33	Darkness at the crucifixion as the judgment of God.
	b	15:34	Jesus' cry of dereliction.
	c	15:35	The call for Elijah as a misunderstanding by the Jewish leaders.
	d	15:36a	An offer of wine from Psalm 69 with Jesus as the righteous sufferer.
	c	15:36b	A continuation of the mockery about Elijah by the Jewish leaders.
	b	15:37	Jesus' death cry.

---

97. Chronis, "Torn Veil," 101.

98. Boring, *Truly Human / Truly Divine*, 75. Cf. Davis, "Mark's Christological Paradox," 4.

99. Brower, "Elijah in the Markan Passion Narratives," 89–90. This supplies evidence that the loud cry of 15:37 is the same as the cry of dereliction in 15:34. In addition, Brower (89) identifies the cry of dereliction in 15:34 with Ps 22:1 and the death cry in 15:37 with Ps 22:15 ("my tongue sticks to the roof of my mouth") so that a righteous sufferer motif underlies both of these verses. However, Ps 22:15 is more evident in the cry "I thirst" in John 19:28.

| a | 15:38 | The tearing of the temple veil as the judgment of God upon Israel. |

Therefore, righteous suffering and divine vindication display the double aspects of Christology that Mark continually emphasizes.

What then is the purpose for these similar representations at the baptism, transfiguration, and death of Jesus? In the baptism and transfiguration, which occur in the Galilean portion of Mark, Jesus exaltation is prominent. He receives the power of the Holy Spirit to embark upon a miracle ministry and later Moses and Elijah, symbolizing the law and the prophets, witness to Jesus' greatness. But then at his death Mark alludes back to these passages to demonstrate that the same person is also the one who follows God to the cross and receives vindication for his faithfulness in suffering. Jesus is the beloved son both when heavenly epiphanies appear and also when he is cast out of the vineyard and killed at the cross.[100] This is another example of an allusionary repetition whereby Mark attempts to parallel an exalted Christ with a Suffering Servant Messiah.

Consequently, the narrative emphasizes "a martyrological motif"[101] which becomes paradigmatic for the Christian community. As Senior points out,

> Mark's death scene redefines what a 'Christian death' must look like. To die in faith need not mean peaceful symmetry, or pious decorum. The Marcan Jesus struggles in death, crying out to God in a piercing lament, and breathing his last with a scream. Yet the God of Jesus is present even—and especially—in these moments when human dignity seems shredded.[102]

This revelation of Jesus' veritable identity in the midst of his passion speaks pointedly to a community that must follow a crucified Lord in order to be vindicated as he was. The hour of crucifixion is paradoxically the hour of coronation for Lord and disciples alike. Therefore, this allusionary repetition in Mark emphasizes the double theme of a crucified Lord and a community that must follow a discipleship of the cross.

4.3 The Matching of Loaded Terminology

Besides matched episodes, Mark also uses peculiar memorable expressions to link together passages that speak about an exalted Messiah with other pericopes that emphasize Jesus' suffering and crucifixion. We will concentrate on the best examples first, although once the reader discerns this Markan pattern other possible allusionary repetitions divulge themselves.

---

100. Baptism, transfiguration, and 12:6 are the only places in Mark where the word beloved (ἀγαπητός) is employed.

101. Pohee, "Cry of the Centurion," 91 supported by Shiner, "Ambiguous Pronouncement," 14ff.

102. Senior, *Passion of Jesus*, 147.

4.3a The Right and Left Hand of Jesus (10:40, 37; 15:27) and Cupbearer vs. Cup of Suffering (10:38; 14:23, 36)

Mark 10:37 εἷς σου <u>ἐκ δεξιῶν καὶ εἷς ἐξ ἀριστερῶν</u> καθίσωμεν ἐν τῇ δόξῃ σου
(Let one of us sit at your right and the other at your left in your glory)

Mark 10:40 καθίσαι <u>ἐκ δεξιῶν</u> μου ἢ <u>ἐξ εὐωνύμων</u>

Mark 15:27 <u>ἕνα ἐκ δεξιῶν</u> καὶ <u>ἕνα ἐξ εὐωνύμων</u> αὐτοῦ

Luke 23:33 ὃν μὲν <u>ἐκ δεξιῶν</u> ὃν δὲ <u>ἐξ ἀριστερῶν</u>
(at Jesus' crucifixion, one on his right hand and one on his left)

The highest honor for a citizen was to sit at the right hand of the ruler. In fact, "a person of high rank who puts someone on his right hand gives him equal honor with himself and recognizes him as of equal dignity."[103] Thus, based upon Psalm 110:1 Jesus is described in the New Testament as sitting at the right hand of God.[104] Therefore, when James and John request to sit at Jesus' right and left in his glory they are asking for prominence, status, and eminence.

However, for Mark honorary distinction arrives through taking one's cross and imitating Jesus. Therefore Mark inserts a corresponding saying into the crucifixion narrative about position on Jesus' right and left. Ironically, two thieves rather than these two disciples are placed at Jesus' right and left as he is enthroned upon the cross. These two sayings allude to each other so that glory at the right hand is achieved through martyrdom on the cross. This regular theme in Mark is witnessed as well in Peter's request for the erection of three tabernacles in the glorious splendor of the Mount of Transfiguration, when the appropriate response requires a journey down the mountain toward the crucifixion and the valley controlled by demons (9:17–18).

It is noteworthy that the request of James and John is structured by Mark as the third misunderstanding of the passion predictions (10:33–34). This triadic formula indicates that the disciples' misapprehension is complete. Therefore, the disciples forfeit intimacy with Jesus by their absence at the cross, where anonymous insurrectionists take their place at Jesus' right and left. As Collins notes, "Jesus hangs on a cross with a placard announcing his kingship, but James and John are not with him. Because of their fear of suffering and death, they have abandoned him and the places of honor are filled by men who are unworthy."[105] Through this misunderstanding Mark is calling his community to learn from the disciples' mistakes and willingly drink the cup of Jesus' suffering and be martyred with his baptism.[106]

---

103. Zodhiates, *Complete Word Study Dictionary*, G 1188.

104. Acts 2:34; 5:31; 7:56; Rom 8:34; Eph 1:20; Col 3:1; Heb 1:3, 13; 8:1; 10:12; 12:2; 1 Pet 3:22.

105. Collins, *Mark*, 748.

106. Collins does not apply it to Nero's persecution, but more generally: "It is likely that the evangelist constructed this scene in order to address analogous tensions in early Christian communities" (*Mark*, 498).

The Theological Intentions of Mark's Literary Devices

The imagery of the cup plays a role at the Last Supper and in Jesus' passion in Gethsemane as well.

10:38   δύνασθε πιεῖν τὸ ποτήριον ὃ ἐγὼ πίνω
(Can you drink the cup I drink?)

14:23   καὶ λαβὼν ποτήριον εὐχαριστήσας ἔδωκεν αὐτοῖς, καὶ ἔπιον ἐξ αὐτοῦ πάντες.
(Then he took the cup, gave thanks and offered it to them, and they all drank from it.)

14:36   παρ ένεγκε τὸ ποτήριον τοῦτο ἀπ' ἐμοῦ· ἀλλ' οὐ τί ἐγὼ θέλω ἀλλὰ τί σύ.
(Take this cup from me. Yet not what I will, but what you will.)

In 10:38 the cup carries the connotation of the station of cupbearer who functions as the wine taster at the king's table.[107] The cupbearer of the king served an honorable position in the ancient world since he enjoyed personal access to the presence of the sovereign.[108] Therefore, James and John imagined that drinking the cup in the presence of Jesus would entail personal honor. But Jesus is speaking about the cup of his suffering and his baptism by the fire of martyrdom (Luke 12:50). The symbolic overtones of the cup in 10:38 match its use at the Last Supper (14:23) and the arrest in the garden of Gethsemane (14:36), demonstrating a Markan allusionary repetition. Mark parallels the honor of a cupbearer with the sacrifice of Jesus offering his body and blood to demonstrate that Jesus will achieve glory through the cross, whose imitation will bring honor to the disciple.

Before we accept these references as an allusionary repetition, one objection must be addressed. How can we account for the change of vocabulary from 10:37 to 10:40 so that in the former instance the wording between this event and the crucifixion is not exact (εἷς ἐξ ἀριστερῶν vs. ἕνα ἐξ εὐωνύμων)? Collins maintains that "a different, but synonymous, word was chosen here simply in the interests of a pleasingly varied style."[109] This seems true since Luke 23:33 alters the wording of Mark 15:27 as well. But it should be recognized that when James and John ask to sit at his left hand the term ἀριστερός is employed, while when Jesus' repeats the statement and applies it to those who drink the cup of his suffering and are baptized with his passion, then the term employed at the crucifixion (εὐώνυμος) is substituted. Therefore, Mark changes the vocabulary to have the all-knowing Jesus connect his logion with the experience of the cross.[110] The two sayings are intimately connected through matched terminology and again parallel the two themes of Jesus' glory and suffering.

---

107. Camery-Hoggatt, *Irony in Mark's Gospel*, 162.

108. Remember the narrative of the chief cupbearer in Genesis 41 and Nehemiah's access to King Artaxerxes in Neh 1:11—2:6.

109. Collins, *Mark*, 498.

110. Matthew consistently uses εὐώνυμος in 20:21, 23 and then again in 27:38 to make the allusion more dramatic.

4.3b Drinking the Cup in the Kingdom (14:25; 15:36)

14:25 I tell you the truth, I will not drink again of the fruit of the vine [γενήματος τῆς ἀμπέλου] until that day when I drink it (πίνω) anew in the kingdom of God.

15:36 One man ran, filled a sponge with wine vinegar [ὄξους], put it on a stick, and offered it to Jesus to drink [ἐπότιζεν].

[15:23 Then they offered him wine mixed with myrrh [ἐσμυρνισμένον οἶνον], but he did not take it [ἔλαβεν].]

In the upper room after Jesus and his disciples drink the Last Supper cup (14:23–24), Jesus reports that the kingdom of God will arrive before he drinks wine again. In Jewish eschatology wine functioned as a symbol for the future culmination of the fullness of time, as evident in Isaiah 25:6–8; 2 *Baruch* 29:5–8; 1 *Enoch* 62:13–16; and 1QSa [28a] 2:17–19. As De Jonge demonstrates by quoting a multitude of scriptures, "The eschatological nature of our logion is underscored by the use of the word καινός."[111] Therefore, the disciples expected this promise to be fulfilled in the glory of the messianic banquet (Matt 8:11–12; Luke 13:28–29).

Jesus' parallel statement in Luke 22:18 creates an eschatological fervor that is even more apparent and dramatic. Since the kingdom of God is so immanent that Jesus will not drink of the fruit of the vine before it arrives, immediately a dispute breaks out among the disciples concerning who is the greatest (Luke 22:24). Then Jesus confers upon them a kingdom promising that they will eat and drink at his kingdom table and sit on thrones judging the twelve tribes of Israel (22:29–30). When Jesus questions their readiness, the disciples report that they have two swords with which they are ready to fight so the Son of David can defeat his enemies (22:38). The expectation of the disciples is greatness, honor, exaltation, and victory.

However, Mark envisions this eschatological drinking of wine anew in the kingdom as occurring on the cross.[112] Interestingly Mark's "until that day when I drink it new in the kingdom of God" differs from the Lukan phraseology "until the kingdom of God comes" (22:18) which is likely more original.[113] Mark specifies Jesus' participation in the future banquet, not the entire disciple band as one would expect. The reason for this alteration resides in Mark's intention to tie the coming of the kingdom of God to the day of Jesus' death. Added evidence derives from another enigma in the Markan saying which De Jonge enumerates: "It remains remarkable, then, that our logion presupposes Jesus' vindication after his death and his participation in the joy of the future kingdom without mentioning his *parousia* or assigning to him a central

---

111. DeJonge, "Mark 14:25," 129.

112. See Meier, *Marginal Jew*, 2:306.

113. Meier argues against Schlosser's view that Luke provides an independent witness to the authenticity of this saying, but concedes that "Schlosser may be right that the ending of the saying is more reliably preserved in Luke" (*Marginal Jew*, 2:305).

role in the final breakthrough of God's sovereign rule."[114] Could the reason be that Mark does not want to highlight a future messianic banquet but Jesus' ingestion of wine already on the cross? This would mean that again Mark is employing the literary device of an allusionary repetition to display a Christology that includes both Jesus' glory and his suffering.

To support this hypothesis, we must explain how Matthew and Mark employ the two cups of wine in the passion narrative. Matthew ties both drinks to Psalm 68:22 LXX (69:21 MT) by adding the word "gall" (οἶνον μετὰ χολῆς) in 27:34 (cf. Mark 15:23), so that Psalm 68:22a is fulfilled in the first drink and 68:22b in the second.[115] In Mark, however, the two offerings of wine function differently. Jesus refuses the first drink provided at the beginning of his crucifixion (15:23) because it is mixed with myrrh and thus functions as a narcotic that would anesthetize Jesus from suffering.[116] The second offer comes instead at the time of Jesus' death (the ninth hour of 15:34) and is described as wine vinegar instead of wine mixed with myrrh. This sour wine vinegar "relieved thirst more effectively than water and, being cheaper than regular wine, it was a favorite beverage of the lower ranks of society and of those in moderate circumstances."[117] Kingsbury correctly observes that "The idea is to refresh Jesus so that he will live long enough for all to see whether Elijah will in fact come 'to take him down' (15:36)."[118] On the historical level this offer represents an attempt to keep Jesus alive for further sport and mockery,[119] but on the reader's level an allusion to Ps 69:21 emerges. Therefore Jesus fulfills Psalm 22 in 15:34 and Psalm 69 in 15:36 so that Mark's final portrayal of Jesus before his death is as the righteous sufferer portrayed in Scripture.

Admittedly, the vocabulary diverges between Mark 14:25 and 15:26 with different terms for "wine" and "drink." However, the reason is clarified in Mark's intention to allude to Psalm 69 (ἐπότισάν με ὄξος) and the image of a suffering righteous one, which results in the usage of ὄξος and ποτίζω instead of γενήματος τῆς ἀμπέλου and πίνω. Mark wants to portray Jesus as both the eschatological messenger and the Suffering Servant Messiah, so he arranges this literarily through an allusionary repetition.

Others object that the narrative does not specifically designate that Jesus drank the cup offered him.[120] They argue that Jesus did not participate because he refused to

---

114. DeJonge, "Mark 14:25," 134.

115. Ps 68:22 LXX καὶ ἔδωκαν εἰς τὸ βρῶμά μου χολὴν καὶ εἰς τὴν δίψαν μου ἐπότισάν με ὄξος.

116. Prov. 31:6 explains, "Give beer to those who are perishing, wine to those who are in anguish; let them drink and forget their poverty and remember their misery no more." In the Talmud tractate Sanh. 43a this narcotic is given to the dying "to numb their senses."

117. BDAG, 715.

118. Kingsbury, Christology, 130.

119. See Evans, Mark 8:27—16:20, 501; Marcus, Mark 8–16, 1056; and the list in Stein, Mark, 716-17 for an emphasis upon mockery. Luke 23:36–37 includes this event in the mockery by the soldiers.

120. See Witherington, Mark, 399. France (Mark, 655) suggests that the imperfect tense might perhaps be read as conative, implying that the attempt was unsuccessful.

dull the pain as in 15:23 or because he repudiated any participation in the mockery,[121] or even because of his vow to abstain from wine until the coming of kingdom (14:25).[122] But 15:23 specifically states that Jesus did not drink the first offer, and certainly the reader would have expected a similar statement if an identical response by Jesus was intended later. Furthermore, the parallel in John 19:30a specifies that Jesus received the drink (ἔλαβεν τὸ ὄξος) when it was lifted to his lips. The corresponding saying "It is finished" (John 19:30b) could then be interpreted to mean that the kingdom of God has arrived in Jesus' death.

Strong evidence for an allusionary repetition here derives from the fact that Mark pictures the kingdom of God arriving in Jesus' death in various ways. Jesus is ironically proclaimed King of the Jews by the notice on the cross (15:26) and by the mocking of the teachers of the law (King of Israel 15:32). Particularly important is Mark's description of Joseph of Arimathea as waiting for the kingdom of God (15:43) when he responds boldly at Jesus' death with the kingdom action of identifying himself with Jesus in his burial.[123] Furthermore, when James and John request to sit at his right and left hand in the kingdom (10:35–38) Jesus replies that this is reserved for those who are baptized with his baptism and drink his cup, which occurs at his death with the two thieves at his right and left. Finally, the allusions to Jesus' suffering in Psalm 22 (22:1 = Mark 15:34; 22:7 = Mark 15:29, 31; 22:18= Mark 15:24) need to be coupled with the triumphant ending of vindication in this same psalm. The conclusion of Psalm 22 proclaims a reversal of humiliation through the worship by the Gentiles (22:27 with Mark 15:39), the establishment of God's kingdom (22:28 with Mark 15:43), a possible allusion to resurrection (22:29 with Mark 16:6), and the proclamation to future generations (22:30–31 with Mark 16:7).[124] Therefore, the kingdom of God is manifested in Jesus' personal suffering and death.

If we follow the motif of the kingdom of God throughout Mark's gospel,[125] the corresponding theme of Jesus' death always appears. Jesus' primary message is the arrival of the kingdom (1:15), and his supreme act is the crucifixion and resurrection, which inaugurate the kingdom of God. The mystery of the kingdom (4:11) entails that it arrives in the midst of struggle, suffering, and controversy, which is finally evident at the cross. As demonstrated by the chiasm in the parable of the seed growing secretly, the kingdom of God (4:26) occurs when God uses the sickle to reap the ripe

---

121. See Evans, *Mark 8:27—16:20*, 508.

122. See Marcus, *Mark 8-16*, 1049.

123. Dowd (*Reading Mark*, 164) understands the "waiting" to mean that he missed the significance of the cross, but the minor characters like Bartimaeus, the woman who places all her money in the temple treasury, the woman who lavishes the expensive nard on Jesus, Simon of Cyrene, and the centurion all function as positive models in Mark.

124. See Marcus, *Way of the Lord*, 180–82.

125. The expression "kingdom of God" is employed 14 times in Mark: 1:15; 4:11, 26, 30; 9:1, 47; 10:14–15, 23–25; 12:34; 14:25; 15:43.

grain (4:29), which could serve as a metaphor for Jesus' death.[126] In the parable of the mustard seed (4:30–32) the kingdom of God is pictured as a tree where all the birds of the heaven perch in its shade. This allusion to the Gentiles joining Israel is epitomized by the confession of the Gentile centurion at the cross. The promise that some will not taste death until they see the kingdom of God come with power (9:1) is placed climatically after Jesus' call to take up the cross (8:34) since the kingdom and the cross are intricately tied together. Mark links the plucking out of one's eye to enter the kingdom (9:47) to the salting with fire (9:49), which functions as a metaphor for enduring the eschatological woes of persecution, which Jesus accomplishes on the cross. The irony that only little children can enter the kingdom (10:14–15) and not the rich (10:23–25) compares with the surprising truth that only death will bring life as evidenced in the cross. Jesus' approval of the scribe as "not far from the kingdom of God" (12:34) derives from his confession that love surpasses burnt offerings and sacrifices. At Jesus' death the veil of the temple is torn as a sign of the future destruction of the sacrificial system which will occur in the kingdom of God. Likewise, the drinking of the wine vinegar at his death alludes to the arrival of the kingdom when Jesus drinks of the fruit of the vine predicted at the Last Supper (14:25).[127]

The fact that additional predictions[128] at the Last Supper find fulfillment in the narrative itself offers additional proof for an allusionary repetition between 14:25 and 15:36. The statement that the betrayer will eat from the same bowl as Jesus (14:18, 20) proves true when Judas leads the soldiers at Jesus' arrest (14:44). Jesus prediction that "the Son of Man will go just as it is written about him" (14:21a) is applied to Jesus' death by the quote from Zechariah 13:7, "I will strike the shepherd and the sheep will be scattered" (14:27). Similarly, at the arrest all the disciples flee (14:50) and are completely invisible at the crucifixion. The prediction that Jesus will go ahead of them into Galilee after the resurrection (14:28) is picked up by Mark in 16:7. Finally, Jesus' prophecy about Peter's triple denial before the rooster crows twice (14:30) is fulfilled in the narrative of 14:66–72. Therefore, one would expect the prediction of Jesus not drinking again of the fruit of the vine until the kingdom arrives to be fulfilled also within the bounds of the story itself. In that case the cup Jesus will drink in the kingdom (14:25) is none other than the cup that Jesus drinks on the cross at his death (15:36). Mark has created an allusionary repetition equating a glorious Christ with a suffering Messiah.

---

126. See chapter 5 below, the footnote in section 5.1 which describes the parallelism in the chiasm.

127. The drinking of the wine vinegar at the cross is connected with the call for Elijah. Also the third cup in the Passover Seder is entitled the cup of Elijah. It would be interesting to research if there is any connection between this Seder cup and the call for Elijah in the crucifixion narrative when the wine is offered Jesus. Regretfully, it is extremely difficult to determine the dating of the Passover Seder.

128. Jeremias (*Eucharistic Words*, 210) contends the Jesus is taking a Nazarite vow of abstinence to not participate with the disciples, but this proposal is soundly disputed by DeJonge ("Mark 14:25," 128) who demonstrates that it is a prediction.

4.3c Suffering and Exalted Son of Man Sayings

In Mark the reader encounters both a suffering (8:31; 9:9, 12, 31; 10:33, 45; 14:21, 41) and exalted (8:38; 13:26; 14:62) Son of Man. Interestingly, the suffering Son of Man is absent in the Q tradition and occurs elsewhere only where Matthew and Luke borrow from Mark or edit his material (Matt 26:2; Luke 22:22; 24:7). Mark alone therefore offers a unique combination of a suffering and exalted Son of Man. As Lightfoot explains,

> The distinctive feature in the N.T. use of the term is the combination of the term . . . with necessary suffering and death; and nowhere is this combination more strongly emphasized than in the last half of this Gospel. Between 8.27 and 16.8 the term occurs in twelve contexts, in nine of which it is connected with service, suffering, and death, and only in three with a future coming in power and glory.[129]

In fact, there appears to be a development in Mark's gospel from an earthly Son of Man in 2:10 and 2:28, to a dominance of the suffering Son of Man in the discipleship catechism, to a climax in the passion narrative, which emphasizes the exalted Son of Man of Daniel 7:13 coming in the clouds with great glory (13:26; 14:62) alongside a Son of Man who will be delivered up to death (14:21, 41).[130]

Why would Mark include both of these images of the Son of Man? The reason again involves his desire to employ allusionary repetitions to demonstrate that God intended the Messiah to suffer as well as be glorified. This conception of the Son of Man then has consequences for the vocation of the true disciple as well. Mark employs the concept of the Son of Man "to teach his disciples to understand both the true nature of his messiahship as including suffering and glory, and the true nature of Christian discipleship as the way to glory through suffering."[131] This is the purpose of Mark's allusionary repetitions.

4.3d Jesus Going Before His Disciples and the Motif of Fear (10:32; 16:7–8 and 14:28)

10:32   ἀναβαίνοντες εἰς Ἱεροσόλυμα, καὶ ἦν προάγων αὐτοὺς ὁ Ἰησοῦς, καὶ ἐθαμβοῦντο, οἱ δὲ ἀκολουθοῦντες ἐφοβοῦντο.

(They were on their way up to Jerusalem, with Jesus leading the way, and the disciples were astonished, while those who followed were afraid.)

---

129. Lightfoot, *Gospel Message*, 42.

130. Scholars express this sequence in various ways. Kirchevel says "Mark 1–6 portrays Jesus as the authoritative 'Son of Man' perceived in Psalm 8. In Mark 8–14 there are nine 'Son of Man' passages that portray Jesus as the Suffering Servant of the Lord perceived in Isa 52:13—53:12, even following the sequence of that passage" ("'Son of Man' Passages," 181). Perrin entitles "2:10 and 2:28, the Son of man's authority on earth; 8:31, the Son of man's necessary suffering; and 8:38, the Son of man's apocalyptic authority" ("Creative Use," 357–65). However, each view recognizes the purposeful combination of both suffering and exalted Son of Man sayings.

131. Perrin, "Creative Use," 357.

16:7-8   προάγει ὑμᾶς εἰς τὴν Γαλιλαίαν· . . . εἶχεν γὰρ αὐτὰς τρόμος καὶ ἔκστασις· καὶ οὐδενὶ οὐδὲν εἶπαν· ἐφοβοῦντο γάρ.

(He is <u>going ahead</u> of you <u>into Galilee</u> . . . Trembling and bewildered, . . . They said nothing to anyone, because they <u>were afraid</u>.)

[14:28   ἀλλὰ μετὰ τὸ ἐγερθῆναί με <u>προάξω</u> ὑμᾶς <u>εἰς τὴν Γαλιλαίαν</u>.]

(But after I have risen, I will <u>go ahead</u> of you <u>into Galilee</u>.)

Mark employs similar vocabulary to emphasize on two occasions that Jesus precedes the disciples on their journey to Jerusalem and then to Galilee. In each case the followers of Jesus are described as "afraid".[132] In particular, Mark accentuates the disciples' reaction through a double description of their negative response in each case. In 10:32 both amazement and fear are underscored, and in 16:8 the women are described as "trembling and bewildered" on the one hand and "afraid" on the other. The cause of fear in 10:32 is explained by the passion prediction, which immediately follows the event, while the reason for fear in 16:8 is explained by the crucifixion, which immediately precedes it. In each case Jesus is leading the disciples into situations of possible suffering, which produce a reaction of fear and discipleship failure.

However, the situations are also contrasting since Jesus is preceding (προάγων) them to the cross in Jerusalem at 10:32 while he is preceding (προάγει) them into Galilee in the glory of his resurrection at 16:7-8. Thus Mark intends to parallel a description of Jesus on his way to the cross with another description anticipating Jesus in his resplendent glory to indicate both the true identity of the Christ as well as the type of Messiah whom the community must purpose to follow.

Some might dispute this claim by pointing to the fact that the term προάγω is employed twice more in Mark without any obvious use as an allusionary repetition. However, these two examples do not employ the distinguishing characteristics found in 10:32 and 16:7-8 and display other purposes. The word προάγω in 11:9 is closely linked with "those who followed" like a hendiadys (οἱ προάγοντες καὶ οἱ ἀκολουθοῦντες), so that two groups of pilgrims entering Jerusalem along with Jesus take center stage. Similarly, in 6:45 two infinitive expressions are intricately linked (ἐμβῆναι εἰς τὸ πλοῖον καὶ προάγειν εἰς τὸ πέραν, to get into the boat and to go to the other side) to describe the journey of the disciples across the sea without Jesus. This distinctive grammatical usage sets these passages apart from the ones we are considering as allusionary repetitions. More importantly, the emphasis in those passages is upon the disciples' separation from Jesus, not their following him in both cross and resurrection. Finally, only in 10:32 and 16:7-8 (14:9) is Jesus preceding the disciples. This description results in an emphasis upon both Christology and the implications for discipleship. Jesus will go before the disciples into Galilee just as he went before them into Jerusalem, so that they must follow Jesus in his glorious resurrection but also in the abandonment of the

---

132. See sections 5.2c2 and 5.2c3 for arguments that these passages are also Markan surprises. The fact that they contain both a narrative surprise and an allusionary repetition indicates their significance for understanding the gospel.

cross. The fact that Matthew omits Mark 10:32 and Luke ignores both of these verses indicates their significance to Mark's situation and his purpose for writing. Mark is creating an allusionary repetition.

4.3e Eyes/Ears without Seeing/Hearing (4:12; 8:18)

In this case the repetition of vocabulary is tied to the larger context so that the parallel structure of 4:1–20 and 8:1–21 must be explained. What are the connections?

1. The feeding of the four thousand (8:1–10) corresponds to the parable of the sower (4:1–9) so that this miracle becomes a riddle which must be interpreted allegorically like a Markan parable.[133]

2. Just as Jesus retires with his disciples by themselves (4:10 κατὰ μόνας) to explain the parable, so the community enters the boat, which similarly becomes the house of instruction (8:10, 13).

3. "No sign will be given to this generation" (8:11–13) parallels the withholding of revelation from those outside (4:11–12) in the parable discourse.

4. The admonition to the disciples because of their lack of understanding the miracle (8:14–18) parallels the rebuke for not fathoming the parable (4:13).

5. An OT Scripture (Isa 6:9–10) is first quoted (4:12) and then alluded to (8:18)[134] as a warning against not understanding parables in 4:12 and against misunderstanding miracles in 8:18. Observe the similar expressions and flow of content:

4:12	ἵνα βλέποντες βλέπωσιν καὶ μὴ ἴδωσιν, καὶ ἀκούοντες ἀκούωσιν καὶ μὴ συνιῶσιν, μήποτε ἐπιστρέψωσιν καὶ ἀφεθῇ αὐτοῖς.	they may be ever seeing but never perceiving and ever hearing but never understanding otherwise they might turn and be forgiven.
8:18	ὀφθαλμοὺς ἔχοντες οὐ βλέπετε καὶ ὦτα ἔχοντες οὐκ ἀκούετε; καὶ οὐ μνημονεύετε	Do you have eyes but fail to see? and ears but fail to hear? And don't you remember?

6. The discussion about the meaning of the feeding miracles as an allegorical riddle (8:19–20) corresponds to the interpretation of the parable as an allegory (4:14–20).

7. The sea conversation concludes with a call for ears to hear (8:18, 21) just as the teaching after the interpretation of the parable calls for considering carefully what you hear (4:23–24a; see the inclusio around the parable in 4:3, 9 as well).

---

133. See section 9.3 below describing how Markan miracle stories act like parables.

134. The quotation is by memory as evidenced by the rotating of clauses from the LXX and the omission of 6:10a as well as the wording of the μήποτε clause. The use of Isa 6:9–10 to explain the unbelief in a suffering Messiah is demonstrated by its use in John 12:40; Acts 28:26–27, and Rom 11:8.

Misunderstanding stands out as a major theme in Mark. Mark parallels the parable discourse with his conclusion to the miracle catenae to warn the disciples against not understanding the parables (4:13) as well as not correctly seeing the implications of the miracle stories.[135] Neither Jesus' powerful teaching nor his miraculous works can display his complete identity. This picture of Jesus must be complemented by a Suffering Servant crucified Messiah. Therefore, in the discipleship catechism of 8:27—10:52 Mark continues the theme of misunderstanding. After each of the passion predictions of 8:31; 9:31; and 10:33–34 the disciples choose a Messiah of glory instead of the description Jesus has propounded. Peter prefers Satan's alternative of a Messiah who refuses to suffer (8:32–33). The disciples corporately argue about who will participate in Jesus' greatness rather than become servants (9:33–34). Finally, James and John desire exaltation at the Messiah's right and left rather than a baptism and cup of martyrdom (10:35–38). Mark employs these misunderstandings as allusionary repetitions to correct the eyesight and hearing of his audience so that they recognize and follow Jesus both in his exaltation and his humiliation. This explains the similar flow of material in the parable discourse and Mark's conclusion to the miracle catenae.

4.3f Destroying and Building the Temple (14:58; 15:29)

Jesus' prediction that he will destroy the temple and build another in three days arises in two different contexts in Mark's gospel. During the Jewish trial false witnesses reiterate Jesus' message:

14:58 ἐγὼ <u>καταλύσω</u> <u>τὸν ναὸν</u> τοῦτον τὸν χειροποίητον καὶ διὰ <u>τριῶν</u> <u>ἡμερῶν</u> ἄλλον ἀχειροποίητον <u>οἰκοδομήσω</u>.

(I will <u>destroy</u> this man-made <u>temple</u> and in <u>three days</u> will <u>build</u> another, not made by man.)

Again at the cross those who pass by hurl insults at Jesus, saying:

15:29 οὐὰ ὁ <u>καταλύων</u> <u>τὸν ναὸν</u> καὶ <u>οἰκοδομῶν</u> ἐν <u>τρισὶν</u> <u>ἡμέραις</u>.

(So! You who are going to <u>destroy</u> the <u>temple</u> and <u>build</u> it in <u>three days</u>).

At the Jewish trial Mark combines this accusation with titles highlighting a powerful and glorious Messiah. The Jewish high priest accuses Jesus of assuming he is "the Messiah, the Son of the Blessed One" (14:61) and Jesus responds as the exalted Son of Man of Daniel 7 (14:62). The second accusation, however, occurs at the cross, where Jesus is depicted as a suffering righteous one and far from the traditional picture of a conquering Son of David Messiah. Ironically, at the cross Jesus begins his three-day

---

135. Cf. Donahue, *Are you the Christ?* 83. The verb συνίημι is used by Mark about misunderstanding parables (4:12), in the logion about the cleansing of foods (7:14), as well as in the miracle of the loaves (6:52) and the understanding of the entire miracle catenae (8:17, 21), all passages of Markan redaction.

journey where he will become the new temple of Israel. The two passages together portray a full Markan Christology.

The interconnectedness of these two texts is further evidenced by the fact that when Jesus prophesies the destruction of the physical temple he employs a different term (13:1, 3 ἱερόν not ναός). Instead of speaking about the temple, these two texts mention the sanctuary. Furthermore, although one would expect a repetition of this accusation at the trial before Pilate where Jesus was accused of being a radical revolutionary, instead Mark reintroduces the accusation at Jesus' death. Again Mark's message is that God intended the Messiah to accomplish his mission through suffering. Repetition of loaded terminology becomes a Markan literary device to express his full Christology.

4.3g From a Distance (ἀπὸ μακρόθεν) with Jesus' Miracles (5:6; 8:3; 11:13) and Passion (14:54; 15:40)

The veracity of some of these proposed allusionary repetitions at the end of this list of matching terminology is less certain. But it is interesting how Mark employs the phrase ἀπὸ μακρόθεν both with powerful miracles and with Jesus' passion. In 5:6 the demoniac captivated by a legion of evil spirits observes Jesus *from a distance* before he bows down before him, extols him as Son of the Most High God, and finally receives a dramatic deliverance. In 8:3 the Gentile crowd arrives *from a distance* to experience Jesus' astonishing miracle of feeding four thousand people from a small lunch. Then in 11:13 Jesus notices the fig tree *from a distance* before a nature miracle occurs. On the other hand, Mark employs this identical phrase on two occasions in the passion narrative, where Jesus' suffering rather than his miracle working is emphasized. Peter follows Jesus *from a distance* into the house of the high priest to behold Jesus' interrogation. Similarly, the women watch the crucifixion of Jesus *from a distance*.

Should these descriptions in the passion narrative be taken positively or negatively? Based upon the earlier descriptions of acts of power, Danove argues that "the frames evoked by 'from a distance' impose a positive valuation on the women."[136] Certainly Mark introduces the women positively since they follow Jesus all the way from Galilee (15:41) and are present at the crucifixion (15:40) while the disciples are conspicuously not in attendance. But then the women are reintroduced in 16:1, and now they flee just as the disciples deserted Jesus in the garden and neglect to spread the gospel message because of fear. Therefore, the expression "from a distance" likely prefigures a hesitant group of women whose fear of the consequences of following a crucified Christ takes priority over their former discipleship.[137] This interpretation

---

136. Danove, "Characterization and Narrative Function," 379.

137. Marcus explains that this is "a note of editorial reserve, since it portrays them as unable or unwilling to come to Jesus' aid in his hour of distress, perhaps out of fear of being associated with a condemned criminal" and thus "paves the way for the end of the Gospel, in which they will flee in

is supported by the contrast between Joseph of Arimathea, who boldly buries Jesus because he is expecting the kingdom of God (15:43), and the women, who cannot accomplish their task of anointing Jesus for his burial (16:1) and afterwards neglect to share the gospel because of fear.

Likewise, this phrase ἀπὸ μακρόθεν gives a "qualified" valuation to Peter. Mark 14:54 describes Peter as "following," but he is following "from a distance," which offers a mixed message. Although Peter is more inquisitive than the rest of the disciples, he is unwilling to adhere to Jesus all the way through Jesus' suffering and abandonment.[138] Mark is using this unique phrase to call his community to follow Jesus not only from a distance but to identify themselves with his suffering even if martyrdom is a possible consequence. Therefore, the use of the expression "from a distance" with miracles parallels its use in the passion narrative to call for a discipleship that follows not only a miracle-working Messiah of power but also the crucified Son of God. Mark has created an allusionary repetition.

4.3h The Accusations of Blasphemy (2:7; 14:64)[139]

2:7 τί οὗτος οὕτως λαλεῖ; βλασφημεῖ· τίς δύναται ἀφιέναι ἁμαρτίας εἰ μὴ εἷς ὁ θεός;
(Why does this fellow talk like that? He's blaspheming! Who can forgive sins but God alone?)

14:64 ἠκούσατε τῆς βλασφημίας· τί ὑμῖν φαίνεται;
(You have heard the blasphemy. What do you think? And don't you remember?)

The accusations of blasphemy in the healing of the paralytic (2:1–12) and the Jewish trial (14:55–65) possess a number of interesting repetitions. Prominent of course is the accusation itself. In the Galilean controversy in 2:6 Jesus reads the thoughts of the teachers of the law who accuse him of blasphemy in response to his granting forgiveness of sins to the paralytic. Only God can forgive sins.[140] Likewise, in Jerusalem the high priest accuses Jesus of blasphemy when he represents himself as God's most eminent emissary—the Messiah, the Son of God, and the Son of Man of Daniel 7:13 (14:61–62)—and the one who will destroy the temple and rebuilt it (14:58) by his silence.[141] Both of the accusations point to Jesus' unique authority and personal identity.

---

terror from the site of Jesus' resurrection" (*Mark 8–16*, 1068).

138. See Brown, *Death*, 624.

139. The noun "blasphemy" is used in 3:28 and 7:22 and the verb in 3:28–29; 15:29, but only the two references discussed in this section are accusations that Jesus blasphemed and therefore constitute a separate class. Cf. Anderson, "Trial of Jesus," 117 and Collins, "Charge of Blasphemy," 166.

140. In 2 Sam 12:13 Nathan the prophet offered God's forgiveness to David, but since the accusation of blasphemy is leveled against Jesus here, he must be going beyond the priestly or prophetic prerogative to announce God's forgiveness. Cf. Boring, *Mark*, 76–77.

141. Collins explains, "The intent of destroying the current sanctuary would no doubt have appeared blasphemous to some, especially to the chief priests who administered it. Since it was God's

Therefore Jesus is accused of "inappropriately acting as God's agent or even arrogating divine power to himself"[142] in both references according to Mark.

Second, the scribes sitting and silently judging (2:6 καθήμενοι καὶ διαλογιζόμενοι) suggest something like a tribunal deliberating Jesus' guilt or innocence. In the second accusation at the Jewish trial this jury becomes specifically the entire Sanhedrin. As Anderson observes, "What was begun in 2:7 reaches its climax in 14:64."[143] Third, the title "Son of Man" is integral to both narratives (2:10; 14:62) and specifically offers a defense for Jesus' authority to assert seemingly blasphemous declarations. Fourth, the issue of Jesus' prophetic identity, implicit in 2:1–12, where he knows the thoughts of his opponents, becomes explicit in the trial, where his passion predictions begin to be fulfilled (14:65). Finally, just as the five controversy dialogues of 2:1—3:6 conclude with a plot to kill Jesus (ὅπως αὐτὸν ἀπολέσωσιν), so all of the Sanhedrin agrees that Jesus' words and actions are worthy of death (κατέκριναν αὐτὸν ἔνοχον εἶναι θανάτου). These interconnections would cause any reader of the gospel to parallel these texts.

In summary, the accusations of blasphemy stand out at two prominent locations in the Gospel of Mark. One accusation is placed in Jesus' word-and-deed ministry in Galilee while the other is located in the passion narrative in Jerusalem. Since Jesus performs a miracle in 2:12a, everyone in the crowd is amazed and they praise God, exclaiming, "We have never seen anything like this" (2:12b). However, in 14:63 the high priest tears his clothes in horror because the Sanhedrin never wants to witness anything like this again. The first accusation of blasphemy is tied to Jesus' greatness as a healer; the second is connected with his suffering. Accusations against Jesus, therefore, are directed at his claims to glory but become as well the cause of his passion. These are the two themes emphasized in every one of Mark's allusionary repetitions.

4.4 Possible Matching Terminology

The following examples are questionable, but introduce the reader to the struggle in discerning Markan allusionary repetitions.

---

house, the intention of destroying it would be viewed as an attack on Godself" ("Charge of Blasphemy," 167).

142. Collins ("Charge of Blasphemy," 167) who gives examples from Philo. The claim to be the Messiah or Son of God was not considered blasphemous (see Brown, *Death*, 1:534–36; Sanders, *Jewish Law*, 67–80 vs. the authors quoted by Evans, "In What Sense 'Blasphemy'?" 407, n. 1). Therefore, Gundry (*Mark*, 915–18) thinks Jesus spoke the Tetragrammaton in 14:62 which is blasphemy according to Sanh. 7:5 (see Evans, "In What Sense 'Blasphemy'?" 412–13 for a discussion). Marcus is certainly on the right track when he envisions a "claim to commeasurability with God" ("Mark 14:61," 141) (see also O'Neill, "Charge of Blasphemy," 77). The combination of Ps 110:1 and Dan 7:13 can be interpreted as blasphemous (Evans, "In What Sense 'Blasphemy'" 414; contra Juel, *Messiah and Temple*, 104–6) "because in that saying Jesus predicts that he will be enthroned beside God and will return to be manifest with divine glory" (Collins, 169). For a study on the theme of blasphemy in second temple Judaism, see Bock, *Blasphemy and Exaltation in Judaism*.

143. Anderson, "Trial of Jesus," 118.

The Theological Intentions of Mark's Literary Devices

Mark describes Jesus' cry of dereliction (15:34) and the death cry (15:37) as loud cries from the cross (φωνῇ μεγάλῃ). This phrase is employed previously only to describe the screams of demoniacs (1:26; 5:7), when Jesus demonstrates his power through mighty works.[144] This could be an allusionary repetition indicating that Jesus' power does not just result in miracles but also in the sacrificial giving of himself in martyrdom.

Both 9:23 and 14:36 employ the phrase "all things are possible." First Mark states πάντα δυνατὰ τῷ πιστεύοντι when Jesus performs a task too difficult for the disciples by casting the demons out of the epileptic boy demonstrating his incomparable power. Then Mark repeats the expression ἀββα ὁ πατήρ, πάντα δυνατά σοι when confronted with the cup of death in Gethsemane. Mark appears to be proving that although it was possible for Jesus to avoid death this was the specific plan of God. All things are possible when Jesus performs acts of power but all things are possible as well through Jesus' death on the cross. The loaded terminology links the passages together.

The expression "the disciples did not know how to answer Jesus" is a clause repeated when Jesus reveals his glory at the transfiguration (9:6) but also appears at Jesus' passion in Gethsemane (14:40).

9:6	οὐ γὰρ ᾔδει τί ἀποκριθῇ
	(Peter did not know what to answer.)
14:40	καὶ οὐκ ᾔδεισαν τί ἀποκριθῶσιν αὐτῷ
	(They did not know what to answer him.)

In each case select disciples are involved; Mark records Peter's response in 9:6 and the reaction of Peter, James, and John at 14:40. The disciples misunderstand the message of Jesus when they fail to acknowledge Jesus as both the messianic Son of God (9:6) and the Suffering Servant Son of Man (14:40). These identical themes and repeated phraseology raise the possibility of the presence of an allusionary repetition.

The expression "one hundredfold" associated with the fruitful successful ground in the parable of the sower at 4:8, 20 could be an allusionary repetition with the "hundred times as much" in 10:30, when the disciples leave home, kindred, and work in order to pursue a missionary career. Even though the Greek expressions are not identical (4:8, 20 καὶ ἓν ἑκατόν; 10:30a ἑκατονταπλασίονα), the imagery of a hundredfold multiplication is very memorable. Furthermore, the mentioning of persecution (10:30b διωγμῶν) is a specifically Markan emphasis[145] and could refer back to the warning about the rocky ground (4:17), where because of trouble and persecution (θλίψεως ἢ διωγμοῦ) the disciples fall away. Success brings one hundredfold results, but so does a

---

144. Danker ("Demonic Secret," 48–69) ties these passages together by contending that an evil spirit came out of Jesus with a loud cry as he died and impressed the centurion, but Jesus' connection with the demonic forces is never described in this way by Mark.

145. See Taylor (*St. Mark*, 434) for authors who see it as Markan redaction and an expansion by the early church.

discipleship of the cross. These passages need to be read together, and therefore raise the suspicion of the presence of a Markan allusionary repetition.

Through the expression "gospel" Mark alludes to both a suffering and exalted Messiah as well as a discipleship of glory and the cross. Mark uniquely presents his concept of the gospel both in terms of an exalted message of Jesus' Galilean miracle ministry and proclamation of the kingdom of God (1:14–15) as well as connecting it with the proclamation of his burial and death, as evidenced by the promise to the woman who prepared Jesus for burial (14:9) that her story would be proclaimed along with the gospel. In 1:14 Jesus journeys into Galilee preaching the good news (κηρύσσων τὸ εὐαγγέλιον τοῦ θεοῦ) and begins his miracle ministry, which instantly grabs the attention of the entire area. Likewise, when Jesus journeys to Jerusalem he is anointed for burial as part of the proclamation of the gospel to the whole world (κηρυχθῇ τὸ εὐαγγέλιον εἰς ὅλον τὸν κόσμον). Through unique terminology Mark parallels these events to connect the good news both with Jesus' power and with his death. In addition, the eschatological discourse connects the disciples' proclamation of the gospel with Christ's return in his exalted state (13:10 εἰς πάντα τὰ ἔθνη πρῶτον δεῖ κηρυχθῆναι τὸ εὐαγγέλιον), employing similar vocabulary as 14:9. However, on two other occasions Mark connects the term "gospel" with the loss of one's life for the gospel (8:35) or the loss of one's family, home, and vocation for the sake of the gospel (10:29). Here a discipleship awaiting the reward of a triumphant returning king is paralleled with the discipleship of the cross. These are the common themes of all allusionary repetitions.

The term ἐκθαμβέω (to be overwhelmed) surfaces in contrasting contexts that produce a memorable allusion to one another. At the resurrection of Jesus (16:5) the women see the angel dressed in a white robe and are overwhelmed with excitement. Similarly, yet in a more indirect hidden manner, Mark 9:15 expresses the excitement of encountering a heavenly figure since Jesus is coming down the mount of transfiguration just as Moses descended Mount Sinai in dazzling glory (Exod 34:29). Surprisingly, Mark also employs this term in the garden of Gethsemane at 14:33, where Jesus is "deeply distressed and troubled" (ἐκθαμβεῖσθαι καὶ ἀδημονεῖν). Since ἐκθαμβέω means "to be moved to a relatively intense emotional state because of something causing great surprise or perplexity,"[146] we must ask, "What does Mark portray as 'the intense emotional state'?" In 16:5 and 9:15 the exhilaration of resurrection and glorification stand prominent, but in 14:33 the intense experience comprises Jesus' upcoming death. In fact, the following verse states that Jesus' "soul is overwhelmed with sorrow to the point of death" (14:34). Therefore, in all likelihood Mark uses this term to link these passages together to display a proper Christology.[147] Again the two themes central to all of Mark's allusionary repetitions are remarkably present.

---

146. BDAG, 303.

147. Further backing for this conclusion emanates from Mark's use of the root word θαμβέω which is applied in 1:27 to Jesus' power in casting out demons but is employed in 10:32 when Jesus is going up to Jerusalem to die. But Mark 10:24, when the disciples are amazed at Jesus' statement "how

Finally, particular imagery such as the picturesque references to a fig tree (11:12–14, 20–21; 13:28–31) or the images of a shepherd (6:34; 14:27) could provide allusionary repetitions. As we have demonstrated in chapter 2, the cursing of the fig tree serves as a parabolic lesson about the temple and Jewish worship. This is complemented by the parable of the fig tree, where 13:28 begins with these words, "Now learn this lesson from the fig tree." Each contains an allegorical interpretation, with the fig tree in chapter 11 representing the temple establishment while the fig tree in chapter 13 symbolizes that the eschatological age of Jesus' return is near. The eschatological statement "it is not the season for figs" in 11:13 parallels "the summer is near" in 13:28. Each narrative speaks about the leaves of the fig tree, but in 11:13 the leaves must be understood negatively to mean a lack of fruit whereas in 13:28 "its twigs get tender and its leaves come out" describes the awaited eschatological age of summer. Therefore, Mark repeats the image of the fig tree with two different connotations.[148] On the one hand the fig tree represents the glorious eschatological age, while on the other hand it symbolizes the temple establishment, which will be replaced by Jesus who will build a new temple not constructed with hands through his crucifixion and resurrection. The repeated themes of an allusionary repetition appear again.

Likewise, Mark applies the image of a shepherd both to Jesus' greatness in authoritative teaching and miracles as well as to his passion. Before the miracle of the feeding of the five thousand, 6:34 reports that Jesus had compassion upon the crowds because they were like sheep without a shepherd (ὅτι ἦσαν ὡς πρόβατα μὴ ἔχοντα ποιμένα). Specifically, Mark refers to Jesus' teaching ministry (ἤρξατο διδάσκειν αὐτοὺς πολλά) so that Jesus shepherds his flock through authoritative teaching and compassionate miracles. Then in 14:27 Jesus quotes Zechariah 13:7: "I will strike the shepherd, and the sheep will be scattered" (πατάξω τὸν ποιμένα, καὶ τὰ πρόβατα διασκορπισθήσονται). Here all the disciples will be scandalized by Jesus' passion since they will lose their shepherd. Therefore, Mark employs the imagery of shepherding in both a context of Jesus' power as well as his degradation in death. This allusionary repetition teaches Mark's readers a proper Christology.

Both verses trace back to the Old Testament as well. The description of Israel as sheep without a shepherd derives from such passages as Numbers 27:17; 1 Kings 22:17; 2 Chronicles 18:16; Ezekiel 34:5; and Zechariah 10:2. Although the LXX wording of the Zechariah listing employs ἴασις instead of ποιμήν, the plethora of Zechariah 9–14 texts in the gospels[149] makes an allusion to 10:2 appealing ("Therefore the people wander like sheep oppressed for lack of a shepherd"). The fact that the LXX version states "they were not healed" could have caused Mark to include the saying before a

---

hard it is for a rich man to enter the kingdom of God," does not appear to function as an allusionary repetition.

148. See Williams, *Gospel Against Parable*, 84.

149. See Moo, *Old Testament in the Gospel*, 173–224 and Evans, "Jesus and Zechariah's Messianic Hope," 380–81.

miracle like the feeding of the five thousand. Then Mark 6:34 and 11:7 both contain allusions to the second part Zechariah (10:2 and 9:9) referring to Jesus as the Son of David Messiah-shepherd. However, Mark 14:27 derives from the third part of Zechariah, which emphasizes the passion of the shepherd (Zech 13:7).[150] Thus, through the imagery of a shepherd Mark reveals both the exaltation and humiliation of Christ from the Old Testament. This similar imagery leads us to a discussion of the matching OT texts that Mark employs.

4.5 The Matching of Old Testament Texts

In this section we will demonstrate how Mark employs OT texts to convince his audience of a proper Christology and discipleship. Mark employs allusions to Zechariah 9:9 and Psalm 118:25–26 to describe Jesus' triumphal entry into Jerusalem.[151] In addition Mark produces a second allusion to Psalm 118:22–23 to prooftext Jesus' abandonment by the religious leaders as well as a reference to Zechariah 13:7 to preview Jesus' rejection by his own disciples. The shepherd imagery in the Zechariah texts parallels the kingly metaphors in Psalm 118. Just as at Jesus' baptism a messianic psalm (Ps 2:7) is employed alongside an allusion to the servant songs of Isaiah (42:1) to confirm Jesus' identity as a Suffering Servant Messiah, so the references to Zechariah and Psalm 118 display a combined Christology of a Son of David who becomes a struck-down shepherd and a rejected stone. Mark also applies these texts to the disciples. In one case the sheep will all be scattered and in the other text the master of the vineyard will kill the wicked tenants and give the vineyard to faithful disciples. Therefore, the texts describe both the struggles of the leader and the following of the community, that is, Christology and discipleship.

4.5a Zechariah 9:9 in Mark 11:7 and Zechariah 13:7 in Mark 14:27

Mark's triumphal entry narrative (11:1–10) does not quote Zechariah 9:9 as Matthew and John later do. However, as Lindars maintains, "it is hardly possible to suppose that it is not in the background of thought."[152] When Jesus parades into Jerusalem, the crowds anticipate the return of the kingdom of David (11:10). With the introduction of the title "Son of David" in the immediate preceding pericope (10:47–48), Mark wants to emphasize a royal Messiah theme in the first part of the Jerusalem ministry. Then in the passion narrative Zechariah 13:7 is quoted. In Mark 14:27 the main alteration from the Hebrew, Targum, Peshitta, and almost all Septuagint texts is the employment

---

150. Matthew adds to this trend by quoting Zech 11:12–13 in 27:9–10, and John 19:37 cites Zech 12:10.

151. McWhirter argues that "Mark uses the word 'come' to link Zech 9:9 and Ps 118:25–26" together ("Messianic Exegesis," 86). We will concentrate on parallels of theme.

152. Lindars, *New Testament Apologetic*, 122.

of the first-person singular, "I will strike the shepherd, and the sheep will be scattered." Mark wants a word directly from God so that Jesus' suffering is uniquely orchestrated by a sovereign God.[153] The Markan material flows from a Son of David Christology to a suffering Jesus just as the context in Zechariah extends from the entry of a king to a passion theme, as indicated by a comparison of Zechariah 13:7 with 12:10.[154]

Mark employs these references to Zechariah as an allusionary repetition to reinforce his own brand of Christology. Significantly, the Mount of Olives is both the locale for the triumphal entry (11:1) but also the place of the beginning of Jesus' passion (14:26). Whereas Jewish expectations centered upon the Mount of Olives as the place for political deliverance, Marcus points out that

> Instead of seeing the arrival of the kingdom of God in the appearance of a triumphant Messiah figure on the Mount of Olives, a miraculous deliverance of Jerusalem from the Gentile armies that surround it, and a reactification of the Temple through its cleansing from pagan influence, Mark would see the arrival of the kingdom of God, paradoxically, in the deliverance of Jesus to his Jewish enemies on the Mount of Olives, his humiliating death at the hands of Gentiles in Jerusalem, and the proleptic act of Temple destruction that accompanies that death (see 15.38).[155]

Certainly this alteration would speak powerfully to the Jewish community to prove that the Scripture itself demonstrates that the Davidic Messiah must suffer.

4.5b Psalm 118:25–26 in Mark 11:9–10 and Psalm 118:22–23 in Mark 12:10–11

Similar to Zechariah, Mark employs references to Psalm 118 that portray the Messiah both as a Son of David and a suffering righteous one.[156] Significantly, 118:22–23, quoted in Mark 12:10–11, is taken from virtually the same point in the psalm as the citation of 118:26 in Mark 11:9–10. First Mark portrays the triumphal celebration described in Psalm 118:26, including the cry of "Hosanna," the descriptive expression "who comes in the name of the Lord," and the pilgrim procession waving branches to exhibit how the Messiah arrives triumphantly in Jerusalem. Then Mark inserts the parable of the tenants, where the beloved son is murdered, concluding with a quote

---

153. In the MT the subject of the imperative is "the sword of the Lord" which is virtually God himself: "'Awake, O sword, against my shepherd, against the man who is close to me!' declares the Lord Almighty. 'Strike the shepherd, and the sheep will be scattered, and I will turn my hand against the little ones.'" See Lindars, *New Testament Apologetic*, 131 and Dowd, *Prayer, Power, and Problem*, 134.

154. France, *Mark*, 575.

155. Marcus, *Way of the Lord*, 161.

156. Lindars demonstrates how in the early church Psalm 118 "began by being a Resurrection text, and was quickly drawn into the region of the Passion apologetic" (*New Testament Apologetic*, 254). See also Perrin, "Creative Use," 359.

from Psalm 118:22–23 which portrays Jesus' vindication so that "the stone the builders rejected has become the capstone." From this Stephen Smith rightly concludes that "these two quotations, in effect, present the entire passion story in cameo form: Jesus enters Jerusalem as the Lord's vice regent, bringing in the kingdom of David; he is rejected by the Jewish leaders, but is raised to prominence by God."[157]

Mark's quoting of Psalm 118 on two occasions demonstrates that the Son of David to whom the people cry "Hosanna! Blessed is he who comes in the name of the Lord!" (Mark 11:9) is the same person whom the tenants of the vineyard kill. Therefore, Jesus' speech in Mark 11 concludes with the citation of Psalm 117:23 LXX: "this was the Lord's doing and it is marvelous in our eyes." Thus Mark employs two allusions to Psalm 118 to demonstrate that both Jesus' suffering and his exaltation are marvelous. In the similar use of Psalm 118 and Zechariah 9–14, Mark employs the literary device of an allusionary repetition to speak to the struggle of the Jewish nation to accept a suffering Messiah.

4.6 The Matching of Characters

We have illustrated how Mark uses matching episodes, peculiar loaded terminology, and allusions to OT texts in order to develop his Christology and view of discipleship. Finally, Mark develops characters that remind the reader of previous individuals in the narrative.

4.6a The Parallel Descriptions of John the Baptizer and Jesus

First of all, the identities of John and Jesus are vitally connected.[158] In a pericope that concentrates on John's identity, Jesus is pictured like John the Baptist, Elijah, or one of the prophets of long ago (6:14–16). Similarly, in a passage that centers on Jesus' identity, Jesus is again conjectured as John the Baptist, Elijah, or one of the prophets (8:28). Thus Mark discusses the identity of Jesus both in a passage about John's death and in an episode where Jesus introduces his death with a passion prediction. Specifically, the figure of Elijah ties John and Jesus together. With clarity Jesus proclaims after the transfiguration (9:13) that John the Baptist is the true eschatological Elijah even though the Jewish leaders have not recognized him. Then the figure of Elijah appears again in the mockery of the Jewish leaders who believe that Jesus is calling for Elijah to

---

157. Smith, "Literary Structure of Mark 11:1—12:40," 115. See McWhirter, "Messianic Exegesis," 77.

158. Every gospel as well as the Q material tie John and Jesus together. Matthew has John, Jesus, and the disciples all preaching the kingdom (3:2; 4:17; 10:7). Luke identifies them as cousins (1:36) and develops a parallel narrative of the births foretold (Luke 1:5–25, 26–38) and the births narrated (Luke 1:57–66; 2:1–20). The fourth gospel narrates a parallel baptism ministry of John and Jesus (3:22—4:3). In the Q tradition John's disciples come to Jesus to determine the connection between Jesus and John (Luke 7:31–35).

save the afflicted and rescue the perishing at the cross (15:35).[159] However, ironically Elijah has already arrived in the person of John the Baptist, and Jesus must endure the cross just as John fulfilled his place as a martyr. Therefore, at the transfiguration Elijah is identified with splendor and glory whereas at the cross he is connected with suffering and passion.[160] Mark carefully employs references to Elijah as an allusionary repetition to display Jesus both as the exalted and crucified one.

Second, Mark uses the character of John the Baptizer to foreshadow future events in the life of Jesus.[161] In 6:16 Herod believes that Jesus is John the Baptizer raised from the dead, thus emphasizing the triumph and glory of these two figures. But then Mark introduces a series of similarities that highlight the passion of John. Like Jesus, John is arrested (6:17 / 14:46; 15:1) and faces a conniving plot to take his life (6:19 / 14:1). Then Herod like Pilate hesitates to execute the person in question but in the end bows to pressure and murders John (6:26–27) just like Pilate crucifies Jesus after several protests (15:9–10, 15). But Herodias like the chief priests finally gets her way through scheming and manipulation (6:19, 24 / 15:11). Although the authorities fear both John and Jesus (6:20 / 11:18, 32; 12:12; 14:2), in the end an innocent man (6:26 / 15:10, 14–15) is executed by the civil authorities under false pretenses. Afterwards the disciples arrive to bury the bodies and lay them in a tomb (6:29 / 15:45–46).

Third, 9:9–13 underscores the fact that the deaths of both John and Jesus have been foretold by the Scriptures. Especially crucial to Markan apologetic is the contention that these events occurred "as it is written." First Mark reveals that "it is written that the Son of Man must suffer much and be rejected" (9:12) and then that "Elijah has come, and they have done to him everything they wished, just as it is written about him" (9:13). Therefore, Mark proves from an undisclosed reference to Scripture that the deaths of both John and Jesus have been predetermined by God. Later in the passion narrative Mark returns to this theme in the case of Jesus: "The Son of Man will go just as it is written about him" (14:21).

Finally, Mark applies the term $\pi\alpha\rho\alpha\delta\acute{\iota}\delta\omega\mu\iota$ (deliver, betray) both to John the Baptizer and Jesus. In 1:14 Mark employs the term to describe John's imprisonment, which initiates the ministry of Jesus. However, the majority of references to $\pi\alpha\rho\alpha\delta\acute{\iota}\delta\omega\mu\iota$ apply to Jesus' passion, beginning with the predictions in 9:31 and 10:33 and culminating in the passion narrative when Judas betrays Jesus. Therefore, both figures suffer tragic deaths followed by rumors of resurrection. Mark employs this material as allusionary repetitions to prove that God intended a suffering Messiah who would then be vindicated. Thus a suffering and triumphant Messiah again supply the two themes for an allusionary repetition.

---

159. Jewish traditions narrating Elijah's coming to aid the afflicted include: b 'Abod Zar. 17b; Ta'an 21a; Pesiq Rab. Kah. 18:5; Gen. Rab. 33:3 (Gen 8:1).

160. Broadhead, *Teaching with Authority*, 181. For the use of the Elijah motif to tie together Jesus' baptism, transfiguration, and death see 4.2e above.

161. See section 2.4 above and Wolff, "Zur Bedeutung Johannes," 857–65.

4.6b An Inner Circle (Peter, James, and John) See Jesus' Glory and Passion (5:37; 9:2; 13:3; 14:33)

The inner circle of Jesus' disciples (Peter, James, and John) are awarded the privileged position of viewing Jesus' glory. First they witness Jesus' power over death in the house of Jairus, the synagogue ruler (5:37). Then this special trio (9:2) observes Jesus in his heavenly state with a dazzling transfigured appearance. Finally, along with Andrew (13:3), Jesus reveals to them the inside information of God's special plan for the future when Jesus will be exalted as the Son of Man and appear on the clouds of heaven. With each episode the revelation of Jesus' true identity deepens in its magnificence from resurrection, to heavenly session, to the glory of the *parousia*. But finally this inner circle alone witnesses the same Jesus "deeply distressed and troubled" (14:33) and "overwhelmed with sorrow to the point of death" (14:34). Through this repetition of characters Mark attempts to communicate to his readers that the true followers of Jesus will know and follow him both in his glorious splendor and his crucified humility.[162]

Interestingly, the disciples fail to respond appropriately either to Jesus' heavenly revelation on the mountain or to his anguish in the garden of despair. Because the disciples do not know how to respond to the transfiguration (9:6 οὐ γὰρ ᾔδει τί ἀποκριθῇ), they decide to inappropriately build tabernacles and remain in heavenly worship, where a following of Jesus toward the cross is the required path. Then in 14:40 the insiders fall asleep and do not know how to respond appropriately (καὶ οὐκ ᾔδεισαν τί ἀποκριθῶσιν αὐτῷ) by faithfully watching for Jesus' passion and crucifixion.[163] These incidents provide negative models to warn the readers toward a more appropriate confession and lifestyle. Mark is calling his audience to become a part of the inner circle of believers and to comprehend what Peter, James, and John have failed to grasp, namely that the true glory of Jesus is revealed in his passion. These incidents provide an allusionary repetition to reveal the mystery of a crucified Son of God and the corresponding willingness of the community to experience both humiliation and exaltation in following this Jesus.

4.6c Two Characters with the Name of Simon

The minor characters become the heroes in Mark's narrative since he treats the disciples negatively as a foil to help his community deal with persecution.[164] When Bartimaeus's eyes are opened he follows Jesus along the way to Jerusalem and the cross (10:52) whereas the sons of Zebedee distracted by the pull of status cannot sit at Jesus' right and left hand in the kingdom (10:37). A woman faithfully prepares for Jesus'

---

162. See Boring, *Mark*, 397.
163. Luke 9:32 and 22:45–46 tie each of the incidents together by the theme of sleeping.
164. Marshall, *Faith as a Theme*, 111.

burial by anointing him with expensive ointment (14:3–8) while Judas plots to betray Jesus for money (14:10–11). All the disciples desert Jesus (14:50) so that three women replace the inner circle of Jesus' disciples at the cross (15:40). Of all those standing near the cross (15:35 τῶν παρεστηκότων, 39 ὁ παρεστηκώς), only a Gentile centurion professes Jesus as the Son of God. Similarly, Simon of Cyrene replaces Simon Peter as the one who faithfully carries the cross (15:21 vs. 8:34).

Although Simon Peter stands out as the predominant disciple in the Gospels, his inability to follow Jesus to the cross is highlighted by Mark. After Jesus corrects Peter in 8:33, he issues the call to pick up one's cross and follow him (8:34). Later, leaving the upper room Peter vows insistently, "Even if I have to die with you, I will never disown you" (14:31). Although first-time readers expect this leading character to both listen obediently to Jesus' correction and to fulfill his vow of loyalty, instead a stranger called Simon ends up carrying Jesus' cross. Since Simon Peter deserts his calling and denies Jesus on three occasions, Simon of Cyrene replaces him as the most prominent disciple in the crucifixion narrative.[165]

This replacement of Simon Peter by Simon of Cyrene enables Mark to emphasize discipleship. In the fourth gospel Jesus carries his own cross (John 19:17), emphasizing Jesus' strong inner desire to drink the cup of suffering (John 18:11; 19:28; 10:18; 19:11), but in Mark the theme of discipleship takes prominence in the narrative.[166] The similar expressions in Mark 8:34b (ἀράτω τὸν σταυρὸν αὐτοῦ) and 15:21 (ἵνα ἄρῃ τὸν σταυρὸν αὐτοῦ) indicate the intricate connection between Jesus' discipleship instruction and the action of Simon of Cyrene.[167] Peter, a Jewish insider, cannot follow Jesus' instruction to carry the cross, but Simon of Cyrene, whose children have Gentile names[168] (Alexander and Rufus), fulfills Jesus' instruction on discipleship.[169] Mark develops this allusionary repetition so that his readers will identify with the minor characters in the passion narrative and follow Jesus when self-denial and martyrdom are necessary.

---

165. Myers (*Binding the Strong Man*, 385) envisions a vocabulary connection between Jesus "passing along" (παράγων 1:16) and calling Peter to follow and a certain man from Cyrene passing by (παράγοντά 15:21) on his way from the country, but in the first case the word describes Jesus while on the second occasion Simon is in view.

166. Against Gundry who thinks "it is to dignify Jesus that Mark notes the taking up of Jesus' cross by Simon" (*Mark*, 944).

167. Luke 23:26 elaborates on this connection by adding that Simon walked behind Jesus (τὸν σταυρὸν φέρειν ὄπισθεν τοῦ Ἰησοῦ) like the required disciple of Mark 8:34a (ὀπίσω μου ἀκολουθεῖν).

168. Myers (*Binding the Strong Man*, 385), but Collins (*Mark*, 736) points out that Alexander was common among Jews as well as Gentiles. Josephus (*Against Apion* 2:44) reports that Jews settled in the cities of Libya around 300 BC at the order of Ptolemy I Soter. But the fact that the crucifixion narrative begins with Simon of Cyrene (15:21) and concludes with a Roman centurion (15:39) argues in favor of two Gentiles.

169. Cf. Boring, *Mark*, 427.

4.6d A Young Man Flees Jesus' Passion (14:51–52) and a Young Man Announces Jesus' Resurrection (16:5–7)

14:51 <u>νεανίσκος</u> τις συνηκολούθει αὐτῷ <u>περιβεβλημένος</u> σινδόνα

(A young man, wearing nothing but a linen garment, was following Jesus.)

16:5 <u>νεανίσκον</u> καθήμενον ἐν τοῖς δεξιοῖς <u>περιβεβλημένον</u> στολὴν λευκήν

(They saw a young man dressed in a white robe sitting on the right side.)

Plagued by a multitude of diverse interpretations regarding the identity of this young man, several commentators have surrendered their exegetical skills and decided that the "range of competing and sometimes conflicting interpretations result in a lack of confidence."[170] However, if these two texts are viewed as an allusionary repetition, maybe this particular approach will offer a new slant on the evidence. We will describe the similarities and differences between these two contexts, explain the divergent interpretations, and offer a conclusion why Mark portrays these two texts similarly.

Only Mark's gospel narrates the flight of the young man dressed in a linen cloth and then describes a young man appearing in a white robe during the resurrection account. In the earlier "gospel streaker"[171] narrative a young man flees naked and deserts Jesus in his time of passion. In the resurrection narrative an angelic-like young man appears totally transformed and announces that the crucified one is now risen. Here the young man is described as sitting on the exalted right side of Jesus' tomb clothed in heavenly garb rather than pictured as running away and losing his garment. Whereas fear functions as the motive behind the flight of the young man in the middle of the night (similar to the women fleeing in 16:8), now the newly introduced young man arrives in the morning Easter light proclaiming a message not to be alarmed (μὴ ἐκθαμβεῖσθε 16:6).

A majority of commentators differentiate these two young men as unconnected figures in radically diverse narratives. Attempts at historical reconstruction variously identify the young man in flight as James, the brother of Jesus (Epiphanius, Theophylact), John, the son of Zebedee (Ambrose, John Chrysostom), an autobiographical nugget of Mark,[172] or simply a Passover pilgrim,[173] while the white-robed young man normally appears as an angelic messenger.

---

170. France, *Mark*, 596. See Edwards, *Mark*, 440.

171. This title comes from Lincoln, "Promise and Failure," 288.

172. Lane, *Mark*, 527; Rawlinson, *Mark*, 215; van Iersel, *Mark*, 504. Zahn (*Introduction to the New Testament*, 2:494 = *Einleitung*, 2:245) compares it to an artist's self-portrait in an inconspicuous corner of a busy painting. Johnson ("Who is the Beloved Disciple?" 158) reenacts a scenario how Mark was present at the last supper in his mother's house where the upper room was located and later after going to bed, traveled outdoors to investigate Jesus' arrest.

173. France calls him a "curiosity seeker in the neighborhood" (*Mark*, 595); Theissen envisions one who had "run afoul of the police" and needed "protective anonymity" (*Gospels in Context*, 185).

The Theological Intentions of Mark's Literary Devices

The autobiographical interpretation for the gospel streaker should receive more attention. Opponents contend that it is too hypothetical,[174] of modern origin rather than an ancient interpretation,[175] and that "an eyewitness would not forgo mentioning his eyewitness status and hence an opportunity to authenticate his testimony (contrast John 19:35; 21:24)."[176] But an alternative interpretation of the data suggests that the gospel writers prefer to remain anonymous. The writer of the first gospel identifies himself only by changing the name of a disciple from Levi to Matthew (Matt 10:3) and by describing a kingdom scribe (Matt 13:52). Likewise, Luke and John place themselves in the background by subtly employing "we passages" (Acts 16:10–17; 20:5–15; 21:1–18; 27:1–28:16; 11:28) or by entitling the leading follower of Jesus as the anonymous "beloved disciple." Furthermore, Mark in particular is notoriously cryptic in his narrative details in order to speak at two levels at once, so that non-symbolic interpretations of the incident "insult the literary integrity of the gospel,"[177] Finally, we know from Acts 13:13 and 15:37–38 that Mark struggled with discipleship and fled from Paul's missionary team in Pamphylia, which engendered a major conflict when Barnabas wanted to include John Mark in the return journey.[178] Later Paul was apparently reconciled with Mark, as evidenced by Philemon 24 and Colossians 4:10. Therefore, we encounter in Mark's own life an example of discipleship failure followed by restoration and transformation. Mark's struggle with discipleship is uniquely paralleled in the description of the young man fleeing in the garden when Jesus faced death. This autobiographical interpretation explains the omission by Matthew and Luke as well since they do not wish to embarrass the author of their source.[179] Therefore historically, Mark 14:51–52 records a secret reference to Mark himself while the young man in the resurrection narrative functions as a heavenly angelic messenger.

Substantial evidence supports an identification of the young man with an angel in the resurrection narrative. Angels are regularly labeled young men[180] and are frequently adorned in white robes. Matthew, the earliest commentator on Mark, interprets the term as applying to angels (28:5). Similarly, Luke employs the corresponding word ἄνδρες (24:4), which he later identifies as angels (24:23). Furthermore, the

---

174. Taylor, *St. Mark*, 562.

175. Brooks, *Mark*, 238.

176. Marcus, *Mark 8–16*, 1125.

177. Myers, *Binding the Strong Man*, 368–69.

178. Grammatically, the terms ἀποχωρέω (Acts 13:13) and φεύγω (Mark 14:52, 50) function as synonyms. Louw and Nida (*Greek-English Lexicon*, 1:188) place this term in the word group "leave, depart, flee, escape." Note as well the similarity between ἀφέντες in Mark 14:50 and ἀποστάντα in Acts 15:38.

179. A suggestion by Brown (*Death*, 299) which he does not follow. Matthew and Luke consistently remove negative observations about the disciples.

180. Tob 5:5, 7, 10; 2 Mac 3:26, 33; Gospel of Peter 9:36–37; Josephus *Ant.* 5:277 and 279 include two angelic visitors; Herm Vis 3,1,6 speaks of six young men who are later identified as angels at 3,4,1. See Collins (*Mark*, 795, n. 222) for various versions of Dan 8:15–16 where a young man is identified with Gabriel.

young man clairvoyantly recognizes the motivation of the women for coming to the tomb and thus possesses special knowledge like a heavenly figure. He plays the role of interpreting visions and heavenly experiences like the angel in Acts 1:10–11. In addition, angels frequently respond with the disclaimer, "Do not fear," whereas "awe, fear, or being overwhelmed is a typical reaction ascribed to human beings in accounts of epiphanies of heavenly beings"[181] Finally, Collins suggests that "if the young man here were identical with the young man of chapter 14, he would be introduced as ὁ νεανίσκος ('the young man,' that is, the one mentioned earlier) and not simply as νεανίσκος ('a young man')."[182] On the other hand, the fleeing young man is certainly not an angel since angels regularly perform positive functions, are never described as losing their clothes, and must be distinguished from the other characters in the narrative who are human (Jesus, Judas, disciples, soldiers). Therefore, these two figures at the very least must be distinguished.[183]

However, the two figures could be tied together in a metaphorical manner. Symbolic interpretations connect the two passages thematically through a variety of approaches. Some highlight the motif of baptism as dying and rising with Christ, so that the first appearance of the young man (14:51) stands for dying with Christ while the second appearance (16:5) signifies rising with Christ.[184] In the early church Christian initiates were stripped of their clothes as they entered naked into the water to be baptized but emerged clothed with a white garment. This transformation could be visualized in the conversion from a young man who flees naked to a youth who appears dressed in a white robe. The linen garment the young man leaves behind is then employed to wrap the body of Jesus in 15:46 so that the young man is baptized into Jesus' death and transformed to life. This passage of Mark would then be used liturgically to initiate catechumens during a yearly Easter Eve celebration. Against those who argue for a late liturgical practice, advocates call attention to how Paul combines clothing and baptismal metaphors (Gal 3:27). Finally, just as Mark 14:51 employs a compound verb, to "follow with" (συνηκολούθει), Paul uses similar terms in contexts about baptism, including the compound verbs "being crucified with" (συσταυρόω Rom 6:6; Gal 2:19), "buried with" (συνθάπτω Rom 6:4; Col 2:12), and "raised with Christ" (συνεγείρω (Col 2:12; 3:1; Eph 2:6).

However, this symbolic baptismal interpretation must be rejected. All scholars agree that baptism is not emphasized by Mark.[185] On one occasion (10:39) Mark re-

---

181. Collins, *Mark*, 796, n. 223 contains a plethora of examples.

182. Ibid., 795.

183. Those who see a proof from Scripture through a reference here to Amos 2:16 (Lane, *Mark*, 527 rejected by Schweizer, *Mark*, 317) and then to Amos 8:9 at Mark 15:33 also disregard any connection to the young man in the resurrection narrative. See Collins, *Mark*, 694–95.

184. Scroggs and Groff, "Baptism in Mark," 540. See also Standaert, *Marc*, 496–626.

185. Scroggs and Groff ("Baptism in Mark," 536–37) argue for a reference to baptism at Mark 10:38 but a reference to martyrdom is prominent. Furthermore, the type of baptismal practice envisioned by advocates of this symbolic interpretation only begins in the second half of the second

lates baptism to Jesus' death but never to sitting at Christ's right hand in glory, which an allusion to the young man in the resurrection narrative requires.[186] If an allusion to Pauline terminology is implied, then the terms "putting off" (ἀποτίθημι Rom 13:12; Eph 4:22; Col 3:8) and "putting on" (ἐνδύω Gal 3:27; Rom 13:14; Eph 4:24; Col 3:10, 12) would certainly be present. But the most significant piece of evidence against this interpretation is the fact that the nakedness of the young man is not a positive symbol related to incorporation into Christ's death. Jewish culture considered nakedness shameful and would not use such imagery to communicate a theological truth. In a word, there is no evidence that the young man is baptized before he appears in the resurrection narrative.

An alternative christological interpretation of these episodes states, "Though neither young man is Jesus himself, together they represent him in his death, burial, and resurrection."[187] With regard to vocabulary, Mann asserts that the term συνηκολούθει (14:51) naturally ties the young man with Christ, similar to the women in Luke 23:49 and the three special disciples in Mark 5:37.[188] In addition, both Jesus (14:46, 49 ἐκράτησαν αὐτόν) and the young man (14:51 κρατοῦσιν αὐτόν) are seized by soldiers. The nakedness of the young man then previews the nakedness of Jesus on the cross, where soldiers barter for his garments. Gundry even concludes that "The young man's having on a linen cloth anticipates the linen cloth in which Jesus will be buried (15:46)."[189] In this scenario the young man's successful escape compares with the successful escape of Jesus from death. Just as the young man flees naked by leaving his linen cloth (14:51 σινδόνα) behind, so Jesus is wrapped in a linen cloth (15:46 σινδόνι) from which he escapes by resurrection.[190] Thus "the young man mimics Jesus'

---

century.

186. Fleddermann, "Flight," 417.

187. Gundry, *Mark*, 862.

188. Mann, *Mark*, 599. Cf. Gundry, *Mark*, 882.

189. Gundry argues that "The repetition of 'linen cloth' within both 14:51–52 and 15:46 and the anarthrousness of the first occurrence and the arthrousness of the second in each passage underscore this anticipation" (*Mark*, 862). Against this interpretation, Mark 15:46 states that Joseph bought a garment, not that he found it in the Garden of Gethsemane. Furthermore, only in Luke 24:12 (strips of linen, ὀθόνια) and John 20:5–7 (strips of linen, ὀθόνια, and a burial cloth, σουδάριον) does Jesus leave a garment in the tomb where variant terms are employed as well. So the young man's disposal of the garment cannot be compared to abandoning the resurrection garment since this is not a part of Mark's narrative. Instead, Jackson contrasts the young man with Bartimaeus' joyful shedding of his garment (10:50) that "issues in an enthusiastic discipleship that implicitly accepts the passion by following the way of the cross" ("Why the Youth Shed His Cloak," 288) versus the abortive attempt at discipleship of the cross by the naked youth. This latter interpretation makes much more sense.

190. Kelber, *Passion in Mark*, 174. Some connect this Christological interpretation with Joseph typology so that just as Joseph left behind his clothes in the struggle of temptation (Gen 39:12), so Jesus leaves his clothes behind, but is later united with his brothers. However, Joseph is not used as a type elsewhere in Mark (Gundry, *Mark*, 881; Fleddermann, "Flight," 415) and exact vocabulary is missing (τῶν ἱματίων vs. σινδόνα).

escape from death and almost comically exposes the failure of the plot to kill Jesus."[191] In favor of this proposal Gundry observes that nakedness is employed as a precursive to resurrection in 1 Corinthians 15:37; 2 Corinthians 5:3; and 1 Clement 24:1–5.[192] At the resurrection the young man is dressed in a white robe (Mark 16:5 στολὴν λευκήν), just as at the transfiguration Jesus shines dazzlingly white (9:3 τὰ ἱμάτια αὐτοῦ ἐγένετο στίλβοντα λευκὰ λίαν), anticipating his resurrection. In 16:5 the young man positions himself at the right side of the tomb and Jesus sits at the right hand of God (12:36; 14:62).[193] Just as the young man flees the scene of Jesus' arrest (14:52), so the women who discover Jesus' empty tomb flee the scene of his resurrection (16:8).[194]

The problem with this interpretation lies in the fact that it makes the naked fleeing young man into a heroic figure. For instance, Gundry asserts that the imperfect tense (συνηκολούθει) indicates that the young man is not fleeing with the eleven but instead is following Jesus in his passion.[195] He distinguishes the young man from the rest of the disciples in the garden of Gethsemane since "the disciples are said to have deserted Jesus when they fled (ἀφέντες αὐτὸν) but the young man is not said to have deserted him when he fled."[196] Therefore 14:51–52 should not be connected with the previous section since the word "all" is used with regard to the disciples in the previous verse (14:23, 27, 50) to finish this motif. However, the close contextual connection (1:50–52) and the identical vocabulary (ἔφυγον 14:50; ἔφυγεν 14:52) argue against this exegesis. The characters are portrayed similarly, not contrasted. The young man flees naked in utter disgrace, just as the disciples are disgraced because they sleep when Jesus prepares for his death, flee when he is arrested, deny him at his Jewish trial, and desert him at his crucifixion. Collins correctly asserts that "the young man is best interpreted as one whose flight and abandonment of his linen cloth contrast dramatically with Jesus' obedience in submitting to being arrested, stripped, and crucified."[197] Therefore, Mark portrays the young man as an inadequate disciple rather than as a symbol of Jesus. This corresponds with Mark's emphasis throughout his gospel upon failed discipleship.[198] Certainly this emphasis was immediately relevant to many in Mark's community who had abandoned their faith during Nero's persecution. Instead of leaving all to follow Jesus, they like the young man have left all to flee from Jesus.

After reviewing these interpretive proposals, we will now offer our explanation for the similarities between these two passages. Even though 16:5 designates an angel,

---

191. Kelber, *Passion in Mark*, 175.

192. Gundry, *Mark*, 862.

193. See Scroggs and Groff, "Baptism in Mark," 535.

194. Gundry, *Mark*, 863.

195. Ibid., 862.

196. Ibid., 881. Furthermore, "the details of the young man's linen cloth and nakedness do not link up with the flight of the disciples."

197. Collins, *Mark*, 695.

198. This is supported among others by Fleddermann, "Flight," 417 and Kermode, *Genesis of Secrecy*, 63.

Mark employs the title "young man" to remind the reader of the young man who fled. Although the figures of the young men must be distinguished, Mark can still use similar descriptions to develop an allusionary repetition.[199] The insights of Andrew Lincoln bear repeating.

> I believe a good argument can be made for deliberate ambiguity on the part of the writer. The reader is meant to think of both. The figure in 14:51 and that in 16:5 are both described in the same threefold way—a young man (νεανίσκος), wearing (περιβεβλημένος), and the description of the garment worn. But a transformation has taken place in regard to this last item. As we saw, in 14:51 the young man was dressed for death—in a shroud. In 16:5 he is dressed as befits the new occasion of resurrection—in a white robe (cf. Rev. 7:9, 13, 14). The figure who failed abysmally in the face of death is now restored as the messenger of resurrection and restoration. . . . Just as his presence in the garden underlined the failure of the disciples, so now his presence at the tomb highlights the imminent restoration of the disciples.[200]

Mark envisions a transformation from shame to shameless proclamation, from nakedness to the white robe of new life, from desertion to accompaniment,[201] and from guilt to forgiveness and renewal as evidenced by the statement to "go and tell Peter" in 16:7.[202] In this case, as Van Iersel asserts, "The scene in the garden narrated in 14.51–52 would then be a literary self-portrait in which the narrator portrays himself as one of the many who have failed by running away at the moment of crisis."[203] This differs dramatically from the baptismal or christological interpretation of the young man in Gethsemane, which portrays a positive experience of discipleship. Then when a young man reappears at the tomb dressed in a white robe, he represents a messenger of the resurrection who shows that all discipleship failure has been forgiven. Therefore, even though the first figure is a portrait of Mark himself while the second is an angel, our author uses both to speak about discipleship. Just as Jesus passes from death to life, so the disciple is transformed from failure to triumph. Therefore Christology and discipleship are always combined in Mark's theology. Usually an allusionary repetition describes the exaltation of the Messiah first and then suggests that the reader must embrace a Suffering Servant Christology as well. Here the young man confronts

---

199. Johnson ("Identity and Significance," 125) contends that these passages serve as a frame around the passion and resurrection narratives, but since the passion narrative begins already at Mark 14, it is better to see these as a Markan allusionary repetition.

200. Lincoln, "Promise and the Failure," 292–93.

201. See Williams, *Gospel against Parable*, 72.

202. The disciples receive the promise of restoration through the reference to Peter in 16:7 who has most recently denied the Lord. The women receive the promise of restoration by the angel's word to travel to Galilee for a resurrection encounter. Finally, if Mary in the final scene (15:40; 16:1) is really Jesus' mother, then we have an additional tipoff that Jesus' family will be restored as well. See chapter 5 above, footnote 95.

203. Van Iersel, *Mark*, 504.

a passion situation negatively in the first scene and then is viewed positively in the resurrection narrative. Mark employs this reversal in order to end his gospel with the proclamation of a vindicated Jesus and to point toward the future successful recovery of the disciples. The good news of the gospel wins out in the final scene, even though Mark employs the cryptic literary device of an allusionary repetition to proclaim a message of victory.

Throughout this chapter we have witnessed how Mark employs characters as well as matched scenes and loaded vocabulary to address two disputes in the early church: 1) that God intended his Messiah to suffer and die, and 2) that Jesus' miracle ministry and resurrection do not promise a triumphant life without struggle, but instead Jesus' passion demands that a discipleship of the cross is required of his followers. Mark accomplishes this through the use of allusionary repetitions.

5

Markan Narrative Surprises

5.1 The Definition of a Markan Narrative Surprise

In this chapter we will argue that Mark purposely intrudes into the narrative an unforeseen element which clashes with traditional expectations in order to offer a theological evaluation for the reader. We will entitle these unanticipated ingredients of the story Markan narrative surprises.

How can the reader discern when Mark employs a narrative surprise? First of all, one should recognize that when Mark employs astonishment vocabulary, it is *not* necessarily a Markan surprise since he is descriptively alerting everyone to the surprise. For instance, the word ἐξίστημι (to amaze, astound) discloses an open surprise after the healing of the paralytic (2:12), the resuscitation of a dead girl (5:42 along with the word ἔκστασις as a duplicate expression), and Jesus' sea-walking epiphany (6:51). Furthermore, Mark employs the term θαμβέω[1] (to be astounded, amazed) to describe the overwhelming wonder of the crowd in 1:27 when Jesus dramatically and effectively casts out a demon. Then in 10:24 Mark records the surprise of the disciples that the wealthy would find it difficult to enter the kingdom of God. Finally, in 10:32 Mark uses θαμβέω to depict Jesus' unexpected action of heading straight to Jerusalem when he had already warned the disciples twice (8:31; 9:31) that trouble awaited him there. Similarly, the familiar Greek word ἐκπλήσσω (to amaze, astound) openly communicates surprise. In two of the same contexts where θαμβέω occurs, the people are amazed how Jesus teaches with authority (1:22), and the disciples' amazement grows when Jesus exclaims that a camel can pass through the eye of a needle faster than a rich person enters the kingdom (10:26). This expression describes as well the hometown crowd's amazement at Jesus' wisdom and power (6:2), the astonishment

---

1. Mark employs the related term ἐκθαμβέω somewhat differently with the best translation being "moved to an intense emotional state" (BDAG) rather than "amazed."

at the deaf mute's ears being opened and his tongue loosened (7:37), and the crowd's admiration of Jesus' teaching (11:18). None of these references fit the category of narrative surprise since Mark openly communicates the surprise to the reader.

Finally, Mark includes descriptions of marveling (θαυμάζω) in his accounts. The healed Gerasene demoniac spreads his story of divine transformation throughout the Decapolis and all marvel (5:20). The people of Nazareth are astonished at Jesus' teaching (6:2), but when they become offended by his words Jesus marvels at their lack of faith (6:6). Apart from miracle stories, Pilate marvels twice in the crucifixion narrative, both that Jesus refuses to defend himself (15:5) and that his death occurs so quickly (15:44). Similarly, Mark employs the related term ἐκθαυμάζω at the conclusion of a controversy dialogue to express amazement at Jesus' answer to the Pharisees and Herodians concerning taxes to Caesar (12:24). The overwhelming majority of these examples function as expected gestures of wonder, traditionally occurring after a miracle or impressive teaching by a renowned leader. On the contrary, a Markan narrative surprise is never openly expressed by the writer.

Markan narrative surprises must be distinguished from the surprising twists characteristic of Jesus' parables as well. Whereas in normal Semitic storytelling the third example completes the narrative,[2] the fourth example of good ground in the parable of the soils (4:3–8) becomes the emphasis. Similarly, in the second seed parable the detail that the soil produces grain all by itself (4:28) reverses normal farming procedures and becomes the point of the parable as well as the middle of the chiasm.[3] In the third seed parable the fact that the smallest seed results in a tree where all the birds of the nations find shelter (4:32) seems contrary to human experience and becomes the surprise and emphasis. Likewise, in the parable of the tenants the

---

2. Kelber remarks that "Folkloristic triads have deeply penetrated the narrative" (*Oral and Written Gospel*, 64). In the gospels note the temptation narrative, three seed parables in Mark 4:1–34; three popular opinions about John the Baptizer (6:14–15) followed by three popular opinions about Jesus (8:27–28), three Markan cycles of passion prediction, misunderstanding, and teaching on discipleship (8:31—9:29; 9:30—10:31; 10:32–52), Jesus' three prayers in the garden, Peter's triad of denials etc.

3.

a			kingdom	"This is what the kingdom of God is like.
	b		planting	A man scatters seed on the ground.
		c1	process	27 Night and day,
		c2		whether he sleeps or gets up,
		c3		the seed sprouts and grows,
			d automatic	though he does not know how.
			d automatic	28 All by itself the soil produces grain—
		c1	process	first the stalk,
		c2		then the head,
		c3		then the full kernel in the head.
	b		reaping	29 As soon as the grain is ripe, he puts the sickle to it,
a			kingdom harvest	because the harvest has come."

Cf. Marcus, *Mark 1–8*, 326.

continual visits of the master's emissaries (12:5b) and the added appearance of the rejected son (12:6) after three trips by the servants to the vineyard creates an abnormal story with surprising twists. These examples could be entitled Jesus' parabolic surprises, but they are *not* surprises created by Markan redaction.

In his ministry techniques Jesus also employs surprising deviations from the Jewish tradition. He concentrates on the marginalized and disenfranchised of Israel whereas the Jewish leaders considered such people unclean. He instructs the disciples to shake off the dust of their feet after leaving unbelieving Jewish villages (6:11) even though this was a procedure when departing from Gentile territory. He seeks out his own disciples rather than waiting until they choose him as their master. He instructs his disciples to "leave the dead to bury their dead" (Matt 8:21–22) whereas Elijah gave Elisha permission to return and bury his father (1 Kgs 19:20–21). In his portrayal of the grace and mercy of God, Jesus suggests that humans should forgive seventy times seven (Matt 18:21–22). Finally, the upside-down kingdom of Jesus undermines traditional commitments to family, so that in reply to "blessed is the one who bore you" he responds, "blessed are those who hear the word of God and keep it" (Luke 11:27–28). Again, these are *not* Markan narrative surprises but merely surprising motifs in the ministry of the historical Jesus.

5.2 The Omission of Normal Elements in a Miracle Story

Markan narrative surprises consist of examples of redaction whereby Mark excludes a conventional element in the narrative or inserts an unexpected twist into the traditional story. In this chapter we will simply enumerate the Markan narrative surprises and offer evidence for their presence. In the next three chapters we will explain the theological meaning and intended content of this literary device.

Narrative surprises are evidenced, first of all, in the omission of normal elements in a miracle story. Kelber clearly delineates the three main essentials in the design of a miracle story along with its auxiliary motifs:[4]

1. Exposition of the healing

    a. Arrival of the healer and a sick person

    b. Staging of the public forum (onlookers)

    c. Explication of the sickness

    d. Request for help

    e. Public scorn or skepticism

---

4. Kelber, *Oral and Written Gospel*, 46. Similarly, an exorcism narrative contains three sections (see Kelber, 52): 1. Confrontation (a. meeting of the exorcist and possessed; b. the demon's warding-off formula; c. the exorcist's rebuke and silencing); 2. Expulsion (a. command to exit; b. the demon's violent exit); 3. Acclamation (a. choral formula; b. propagation of the cure).

2. Performance of the healing

   a. Utterance of a healing formula

   b. Healing gestures

   c. Statement of cure

3. Confirmation of the healing

   a. Admiration/confirmation formula

   b. Dismissal of the healed person

   c. Injunction of secrecy

   d. Propagation of the healer's fame

In the confirmation process Kelber's first element (admiration/confirmation formula) is the most important, and it is better to separate these two and give them prominence. Therefore most authors divide the confirmation of healing into two groupings to emphasize both 1) the proof of the successful accomplishment of the miracle and 2) the impression the miracle creates upon the crowd.[5] The proof for the miracle can be entitled "demonstration" and includes such newly acquired physical powers as serving (Mark 1:31), carrying one's bed (Mark 2:12; John 5:9; Lucian, *Philops.* 11), walking around and following (Mark 5:42; 10:52; Plutarch *Cor.* 13), and eating (Mark 5:43; Luke 24:36f).[6] The impression left upon the crowd we will call "reaction" and includes the two important dimensions of acclaim and awe. This distinction will prove crucial in recognizing which elements in a traditional miracle story are missing in Mark's gospel.

5.2a The Omission of the Positive Response of Amazement in Several Miracle Stories

If we examine Mark's ten healing stories,[7] five nature miracles, and three exorcisms and compare them with the traditional elements of this genre, we discover that Mark

---

5. See Bultmann (*History*, 224–25) and Hedrick ("Miracles in Mark") who entitles the four steps in a healing miracle: problem, deed, demonstration, and reaction. It should be admitted that wonder plays a smaller part in Greco-Roman miracles stories (Dwyer, *Motif of Wonder*, 46) so that we cannot speak of a stereotyped concluding motif (Theissen, *Miracle Stories*, 70), but Mark displays a Jewish background throughout the gospel.

6. Theissen, *Miracle Stories*, 66–67. With nature miracles demonstration occurs through insufficient jars to contain all the oil (2 Kgs 4:6f), extra bread left over (2 Kgs 4:44; Mark 6:43; 8:8), and nets breaking and boats sinking from fish (Luke 5:6–7). With regard to exorcisms the demonstration element includes the destructive violence of the departing demon driving a herd of swine into a lake (5:13), knocking over a beaker full of water (Josephus *Ant.* 8,2,5), overturning a pillar (*Vita Apoll.* 4:20), and visible black smoke (Lucian, *Philops.* 16).

7. The cure of the Syrophoencian's daughter is categorized by Hedrick as an exorcism because such a diagnosis arises out of the passage (7:25, 30), but we follow Kelber who categorizes it as a healing since no details of the exorcism are related.

adheres to the established pattern of genre analysis, except that a reaction of awe and acclaim is not included in the following incidents:[8]

1. The stories located in the discipleship catechism section: the blind man in 8:22–26; blind Bartimaeus in 10:46–52; and the exorcism of the boy with the deaf/mute spirit in 9:14–29.
2. The miracle narratives that employ a Markan sandwich: the woman with the flow of blood in 5:24b–34 and the cursing of the fig tree in 11:12–14, 20–23.
3. The two feedings of the multitude in 6:32–44 and 8:1–9.
4. The deliverance of the Syrophoenician's daughter in 7:24–30.
5. The first healing of Peter's mother-in-law in 1:29–31.

Since the first healing in Mark is "told with an incomparable economy of words,"[9] and because it is immediately followed by the reaction of the entire village, which gathers enthusiastically around Jesus' place of lodging to receive healing (1:32–34), the lack of an amazed reaction in the healing of Peter's mother-in-law does not seem to be significant.

The remaining examples of omission, however, reveal Markan theological emphases. Mark places three healing stories in the discipleship catechism section to transform the miracle stories into discipleship narratives. The two-step healing of the blind man omits the positive reaction of awe since it should be labelled a parabolic miracle, where the required response is not just the recognition of a miracle-working Messiah but also the willingness to follow a Suffering Servant Son of Man, as evidenced by the subsequent passage narrating the incompleteness of Peter's confession (8:31–32). Likewise, the appropriate response of blind Bartimaeus consists of following the way of Jesus' suffering (10:52), which is substituted for a verbal response of amazement. The third incident of the epileptic boy ensues after the three leading disciples aspire to build a tabernacle on transfiguration mountain and linger there in the glory (9:2–8), but Jesus corrects their misunderstanding of discipleship by calling attention to his suffering and death (9:9–13). The exorcism of the epileptic boy then becomes an important element in the teaching of discipleship patterned after Mark's regular sequence of passion prediction, misunderstanding, and teaching on discipleship. The climax of the miracle becomes not a reaction of amazement but a private indoor call to prayer (9:28–29), which for Mark means an entreaty for the presence of Jesus since the disciples are unable to cast out the demon on their own.

---

8. See the helpful charts by Hedrick, "Miracles in Mark," 313. Matthew in his miracle section of chapters 8–9 only sporadically concludes with awe (8:27; 9:7, 33) since he wants to climax his narratives with calls to discipleship. Therefore Matthew organizes this section into three sets of three miracle stories (8:1–17; 8:23—9:8; 9:18–34) followed in each case by a call to discipleship (8:18–22; 9:9–17; 9:35–38).

9. Kelber, *Oral and Written Gospel*, 46–47.

The second category above involves miracles that Mark sandwiches together. In chapter 2 we argued that Mark employs intercalations to transform a miracle passage into an object lesson demonstrating the fulfillment of OT cultic regulations through Jesus' kingdom deeds. In addition to that literary device, Mark uses narrative surprises to reinforce this conclusion. In the cursing of the fig tree as well as the healing of the bleeding woman, Mark eliminates the response of amazement.[10] The healing of the Gentile woman's daughter fits this category as well since Mark transforms this miracle story into a teaching on table fellowship between Jews and Gentiles by omitting the positive response of awe. By stringing four passages together dealing with impurity, Mark demonstrates that Jesus' kingdom words and deeds produce clean hands (7:1–13), clean food (7:14–23), clean people (7:24–30), and clean fluids (7:31–37). Surprisingly, two of Jesus' greatest nature miracles, the miraculous feedings, end with statistics rather than acclaim aimed at Jesus.[11] Later in the narrative the disciples are described as hard-hearted because they fail to understand about the loaves (6:52) as well as blind and deaf and forgetful (8:18), since they cannot recall the significance of the two feedings (8:19–20). The more traditional pattern is narrated by John, who concludes with the confession, "Surely this is the Prophet who is to come into the world" (6:14). Mark purposely abolishes this type of ending. These alterations indicate that Mark is writing at two levels and offering a symbolic interpretation of the feedings. These are what I call Markan narrative surprises.

5.2b Astonishment Comes at the Beginning Rather than the End (9:15)

A second alteration from the genre of miracle story focuses on the placing of positive acclaim and awe at the beginning (9:15) rather than the end of a pericope and replacing it with a teaching on discipleship (9:28–29).[12] We will discuss the purpose of this change in chapter 6,[13] but here it is important to recognize the presence of a Markan literary device which I entitle a narrative surprise. When the observers of the disciples' inability to cast out a demon see Jesus, they are overwhelmed with wonder and run

---

10. In the healing of the bleeding woman, there is no response of awe and amazement from the crowd. She is seen as trembling with fear (5:33 φοβηθεῖσα καὶ τρέμουσα), but only Luke 8:47 adds "in the presence of all the people" to add the crowd to the story. However, those present do express awe at the resurrection of the dead girl (5:42 ἐξέστησαν [εὐθὺς] ἐκστάσει μεγάλῃ), the other half of the intercalation, because of the caliber of the miracle.

11. Here the reaction and astonishment of the people appears to be purposely omitted since it is normally present as at 1:27, 45; 2:12; 4:41; 5:15–17, 20, 42. However, Jesus' greatness is still emphasized by 1) the statement "all ate and were satisfied" (6:42) which is a mark of eschatological plenty; 2) twelve baskets of broken pieces were taken up (6:43) and 3) the large size of the crowd. Cf. Boring, *Mark*, 187; Collins, *Mark*, 326.

12. Therefore most authors see it as redactional including Dwyer who sees every reference to fear as positive awe. For a list see Dwyer, *Motif of Wonder*, 148, n. 20.

13. See section 6.5 below.

to greet him. Some authors[14] link this astonishment to the previous passage by arguing that Jesus' glistening white garments from the transfiguration cause this reaction from the crowd. Gundry, for example, points out that Mark has not specified that his transfiguration glory has dimmed.[15] But why would Jesus command his disciples not to relate their experience (9:9) if his afterglow reveals the glorious event anyway? Instead, Mark constructs a discipleship ending to the deliverance of the demonized boy so that the amazing response is now placed earlier in the narrative. Normally the wonder concludes an exorcism, as evidenced by the first paradigmatic exorcism in 1:21–28, where astonishment is mentioned after Jesus' authoritative teaching (1:22) and his powerful exorcism (1:27).[16] The Markan narrative surprise is that no amazement occurs after the exorcism as it does in the more normal patterning in Luke 9:43, "And they all were amazed at the greatness of God." Therefore, the inclusion of this healing in the discipleship catechism section demonstrates that Mark intends more than just a miracle story.

Gundry speaks against "the form critical tendency to assume that stereotypicality signals earliness whereas non-stereotypicality signals lateness,"[17] but he fails to offer any convincing examples against this form-critical principle. He contends that non-stereotypicality derives from the rawness of early data, but the transmission through the use of various genres demonstrates that the stories were systematized early in the tradition as teaching material. The consistency in the structure of miracle stories as well as controversy dialogues argues against Gundry's conclusion that "The form critical attempt to recapture the oral tradition prior to Mark and prior to whatever written sources he may have used, if any, is foredoomed."[18] The fact that miracle stories (the two catenae found in Mark 4:35—8:10) and controversy dialogues (the two catenae in 2:1—3:6 and 11:27—12:37) have been gathered together in the oral tradition evidences the already established patterns of genre. Therefore, when Mark disrupts this pattern we have a narrative surprise.

---

14. Additional opinions including the suggestion that it was the original conclusion to the healing of the blind man in 8:22–26 can be found in Dwyer, *Motif of Wonder*, 147.

15. Gundry, *Mark*, 487–88. This suggestion would tie Jesus with Moses whose face shines when he comes down from Mount Sinai. Other connections with Moses include six days (Exod 24:16; Mark 9:2), a mountain setting (Exod 24:12; Mark 9:2), three companions (Exod 24:9; Mark 9:2), a changed face (Exod 34:29–30; Matt 17:2; Mark 9:3 has only whitened garments), a cloud (Exod 24:15–16; Mark 9:7), a heavenly voice (Exod 24:16; Mark 9:7), the fear motif (Exod 34:30; Mark 9:6), and the building of tabernacles (Exod 25:9; Mark 9:5). But Gundry (495) denies that Mark built his version of the transfiguration on the story of Moses.

16. Dwyer points out that "The combination of the vanquishing of Satan with the summons to faith recalls . . . the programmatic miracle in 1.21–28" (*Motif of Wonder*, 145).

17. Gundry, *Mark*, 19.

18. Ibid., *Mark*, 18.

5.3 Fear Becomes a Negative Concept Instead of Awe (9:6, 32; 10:32; 16:8)

In addition to excising the response of amazement in certain miracle stories, Mark transforms the traditional ending of awe into a negative response of fear, misunderstanding, and hard-heartedness. We will demonstrate that this occurs in the trips across the sea in the next section, but in this segment we will concentrate on four passages which deal with discipleship. We will explicate how Mark combines the original awe in the situation of Jesus with a negative fear to speak to the struggles of his community.

Three uses of the concept of fear are evident in the gospels. First, fear is an expected response to disturbing circumstances. One among the plethora of vocabulary connections between the bleeding woman and the raising of Jairus' daughter is the presence of fear. The woman is afraid to tell Jesus her true story (5:33) since she fears the consequences. Likewise, Jesus attempts to remove Jairus' fear of the ramifications of his daughter's illness with the conventional reply, "Don't be afraid; just believe" (5:36). The Bible employs this comforting expression μὴ φοβοῦ to quiet someone's panic in the midst of troubling circumstances as well as heavenly figures.[19] Anticipated difficult situations cause fear as well. In 11:18 the Jewish leaders fear Jesus because they view him as a threat to their authority as teachers. Similarly, in 11:32 and 12:12 the temple establishment fears the people because the crowds might respect Jesus over them, resulting in a loss of influence.

Second, in the miracle stories the onlookers are typically filled with a fear better described as awe because of the unbelievable act that Jesus has accomplished. For instance, in the first occurrence of the term (ἐφοβήθησαν), in 4:41, this verb is combined with the noun (φόβον μέγαν) in a typical Semitic cognate expression,[20] which produces a conclusion of verbal praise, "Who is this? Even the wind and the waves obey him!" Awe is the recorded reaction as well when Jesus casts out a legion of demons and totally transforms a human life in 5:1–20.[21] Although Joel Williams contends that the fear is negative because it causes the townspeople to beg Jesus to

---

19. With μὴ φοβοῦ we encounter fear of a heavenly figure (Gen 26:24; 28:13 LXX; Jdg 6:23; Luke 1:13, 30; 5:10; Rev 1:17) and fear of circumstances (Gen 15:1; 21:17; 46:3; Deut 31:6, 8; Ruth 3:11; 1 Sam 4:20; 22:23; 23:17; 28:13; 2 Sam 9:7; 2 Kgs 6:16; 1 Chron 22:13; 28:20; Ps 48:17; Prov 7:1 LXX; Isa 7:4; 10:24; 41:10, 13; 43:1, 5; 44:2; 54:4; Jer 26:28; Lam 3:57; Dan 10:12; Luke 12:32; John 12:15; Acts 18:9; 27:24). Likewise, with μὴ φοβεῖσθε we encounter fear of a heavenly figure (Matt 14:27; 17:7; 28:5, 10; Mark 6:50; Luke 2:10; John 6:20) and fear of circumstances (Gen 43:23; 50:19, 21; Deut 1:21; 20:3; 1 Sam 12:20; 2 Kgs 25:24; 2 Chron 20:15, 17; Isa 13:2; 35:4; 40:9; 51:7; Jer 10:2; Matt 10:28; Luke 12:7).

20. BDF 153.1.

21. The transformations include from a Gentile unbeliever (1) to a missionary to the Decapolis (20); from an unclean legion of evil spirits (2a) to a cleansed whole human being (14); from a home in the tombs of death (2b–3a) to someone who wants to live with Jesus (18); from an anti-social existence (3b) to a return to his family (19); from a wild, self-destructive, insane personality (4–5) to a calm, clothed, and sane life (15).

leave (5:17),[22] they do not discover this information until 5:16 after the fear takes place (5:15). Instead the awe is incited by the presence of the supernatural before the eyewitnesses relate what had happened (5:16) so that the tale of the swine convinced the community that Jesus was a public danger (5:17).[23] The fear should not be interpreted negatively here. Similarly, in 6:50 the disciples see Jesus as a ghostly mysterious figure walking on the waves and are terrified (ταράσσω) at his presence so that Jesus in the traditional fashion assures them not to be afraid (μὴ φοβεῖσθε). As in the Old Testament, fear becomes the immediate response to a heavenly presence, whether divine or angelic.[24] Finally, in 6:20 Herod responds in fear to John the Baptizer, who is described as "a righteous and holy man." Here the typical awe in the presence of God is applied to a godly human being.

A third category comprising four Markan texts (9:6, 32; 10:32; 16:8) presents an unexpected negative fear in the context of powerful epiphanic events.[25] The word ἔκφοβοι is employed in 9:6 as a Markan parenthetic comment after Jesus is transfigured before the disciples into a dazzling white heavenly figure along with the OT personages of Moses and Elijah. The three chief apostles suggest the building of three tabernacles on this holy mountain because they are frightened and do not know what to say. In the next section we will show that Mark transposes the expected fear at a divine visitation into the inappropriate negative response of wanting to remain in the glory of the heavenly mountain.[26] This discipleship misunderstanding reoccurs in 9:31, where the disciples are afraid (9:32) to ask Jesus about his passion prediction because of the possible negative consequences for themselves. Then in 10:32, while Jesus is walking ahead of everyone headed toward Jerusalem and is about to proclaim his third passion prediction (10:33), the disciples are again astonished (ἐθαμβοῦντο) and his other followers are afraid (ἐφοβοῦντο) of these potential events. Thus three times in a row the concept of fear is connected with Jesus' passion instead of his expected glory.

This leads to the last reference of fear in 16:8, the ending of Mark. Although the women have already experienced both the fearful awe of the presence of a heavenly figure in 16:5 and the traditional comfort "do not fear" in 16:6, Mark depicts the women as trembling and bewildered (τρόμος καὶ ἔκστασις) and so afraid that they flee and say nothing to anyone about their experience of glory. Normally ἔκστασις follows

---

22. Williams, "Literary Approaches," 27.

23. See Taylor, *Mark*, 284.

24. The normal human reaction when God appears is fearful awe as in Gen 28:17; Exod 3:6; 34:30.

25. In contrast to those exegetes who discern a consistent positive connotation to fear, Danove ("Characterization and Narrative Function," 392) argues for a dominant negative interpretation of fear, but this opinion fails to appreciate Mark's transmission of the elements of a traditional miracle story.

26. See Kingsbury, *Christology of Mark's Gospel*, 100: "The three exhibit great 'fear' (9:6), which in Mark is the opposite of 'faith' and 'understanding.'"

an experience of a divine manifestation, as in Luke 5:26; Acts 3:10; and Mark 5:42, but here it implies confusion and bewilderment as when Isaac is confused when tricked by Jacob out of Esau's birthright (Gen 27:33). Whereas fear and trembling (τρόμος καὶ φόβος) customarily form a common idiom employed to designate a deep respect for someone's power and authority,[27] here the women do not respond with obedience but rather neglect to share the kerygma. The parallel flight of the disciples and the young man in the garden of Gethsemane (14:50–52) reinforces the negative nature of the fear of the women. Just as the disciples were afraid to follow Jesus in his suffering, so the women are afraid to proclaim the resurrection message because of the possible consequence of following Jesus to the cross.

In these four instances fear is not connected with nervousness and anxiety in the presence of an authority figure or awe following a powerful miracle, but instead fear is closely tied to unbelief or hard-heartedness. Thus fear takes on a negative connotation in Mark when the disciples do not understand and appropriate a theology of the cross. Mark links all four of these references to fear with Jesus' passion, as we shall demonstrate in the following exegetical sections.

5.3a Discipleship Fear in Mark 9:6

Problematically, not everyone agrees with this redactionary interpretation of these four Markan texts. Some authors contend that fear should always be taken positively as wonder.[28] Since the transfiguration narrative is categorized as an epiphany story, theophany, enthronement story, or proleptic vision of the exaltation of Jesus as the kingly Son of Man,[29] then the fear of 9:6 is considered a natural response of wonder and awe. Dwyer offers the following evidence:[30]

1. Visions regularly result in a reaction of awe, as evidenced by Daniel 10:7 and 4 Maccabees 4:10. In fact, the heavenly vision in Acts 10:4 when the angel appears to Cornelius employs similar vocabulary (ἔμφοβος and ἔκφοβοι).

2. "The other place in the New Testament where ἔκφοβος is used, Heb 12.21, is a description of the words of Moses upon seeing the glory of the Lord on Sinai in Deut 9.19."

3. The γάρ-γάρ sequence occurs here and in Mark 11:18; 16:8 which all include reactions of wonder.

---

27. Gen 9:2; Exod 15:16; Deut 2:25; 11:23; Isa 19:16; Ps 2:11; 1 Cor 2:3; 2 Cor 7:15; Phil 2:12; Eph 6:5.

28. Dwyer, *Motif of Wonder*; Evans, *Mark 8:27—16:20*; Gundry, *Mark*; Heil, *Transfiguration*; Lane, *Mark*; Magness, *Sense and Absence*; Stonehouse, *Witness*.

29. For the supporters of these various terms for the genre of the story see Dwyer, *Motif of Wonder*, 140.

30. Dwyer, *Motif of Wonder*, 141–43.

4. "The focus on Jesus brings wonder in a way consistent with what has been seen up to now in the gospel."

Gundry adds that the disciples' awe functions as the fulfillment of seeing the kingdom of God arrive in power in 9:1 so that Mark emphasizes the overpowering glory of God's rule.[31] Consistent with his contention that Mark is exclusively concerned with Christology, Gundry asserts that Peter's proposal for three tabernacles places Moses and Elijah on a par with Jesus, resulting in Mark's comment that Peter did not know what he was saying. Jesus is superior.

The first two arguments above could fittingly apply to Matthew's rendition of the transfiguration but not to Mark's. Matthew 17:6 relocates the mentioning of fear to its normal location at the end of an epiphany narrative, where it retains its original meaning of awe in response to the voice from heaven.[32] Therefore Matthew's structure becomes epiphany (17:2–3), the positive response of building three tabernacles (17:4), epiphany (17:5), and the positive response of awe (17:6–7). Mark, on the other hand, inserts a negative response of the disciples (9:5–6) between two epiphanies (9:2–4, 7). In Matthew the recognition of Jesus in combination with Moses and Elijah (as the law and the prophets) is deserving of three tabernacles, and the voice from heaven causes the disciples to fall on their faces in worship and awe. Matthew, then, alters his Markan source to conform it to the prevalent oral tradition of the story, where fear is positive.[33] In fact, in several significant passages Matthew returns to the established oral tradition where Mark has altered and redacted this tradition.[34]

In response to Dwyer's third argument in favor of a response of awe in Mark 9:6, the γάρ-γάρ sequences in Mark are quite divergent. Whereas 11:18 contrasts a positive awe of the crowd with a negative response of the Jewish leaders, the actions of the disciples in 9:6 and the women in 16:8 must be interpreted either entirely negatively or exclusively positively. In 11:18 one γάρ clause applies to the Jewish leaders and the other to the crowd, whereas 9:6 has a consistent audience of the disciples and 16:8 applies both clauses to the women. In addition, the γάρ clauses in 16:8 refer to divergent actions, the first to the women's flight and the second to the women's silence. There is no established pattern as Dwyer maintains.

Regarding Dwyer's fourth argument above, I find it very confusing why he includes the transfiguration in the first part of Mark's gospel when really it functions as an integral part of the discipleship catechism. Since Mark places the transfiguration

---

31. Gundry, *Mark*, 460. Likewise Evans contends that Jesus' "glorification is so impressive that even his closest associates are unable to assess it properly" (*Mark 8:27—16:20*, 37). Cf. also Kazmierski, *Jesus, Son of God*, 126.

32. Hagner, *Matthew*, 494.

33. Stein calls attention to the "agreement between Matthew and Luke which may indicate that they know another tradition independent of Mark which they have incorporated into their accounts" ("Transfiguration," 95).

34. For a series of instances where Matthew follows an older oral tradition, see chapter 2 above, note 194.

narrative after Peter's misunderstanding of Jesus' passion (8:31–33), he wants Peter's comments in 9:5 to serve as a second misunderstanding of Jesus' messiahship. Therefore, Peter's reaction of fear fits a context centered upon a recognition of Jesus' passion and not just his triumphant messianic glory as in the previous miracle section (4:35—8:21).

Against Gundry's contention that Peter's proposal for three tabernacles reduces Jesus' glory, Mark already distinguishes Jesus from Moses and Elijah in 9:2b–3 by calling attention to Jesus' unique glorious appearance.[35] Furthermore, Mark has demonstrated that both Herod (6:15) and the disciples (8:27–30) are incorrect in positing that Jesus should be identified with Elijah. Finally, the subject is taken up directly in the very next passage when John the Baptizer and not Jesus is identified with Elijah (9:13). Therefore, the superiority of Jesus to Elijah and Moses is not the subject matter of the transfiguration.[36] Mark is not criticizing the erection of three tabernacles instead of only one for Jesus, but instead is disparaging contentment in the glory of the heavenly mountain when a journey down the mountain to the cross is necessary.

Certainly Christology stands out as a major focus of the transfiguration story. Only Jesus, of course, is transfigured; likewise the voice from heaven affirms only Jesus as the Son of God. But in light of this strong christological focus, the placement of the redactional 9:6 creates an unusual emphasis upon the conduct of the disciples.[37] Mark's comment functions like an intrusion into the narrative and therefore constitutes a Markan surprise.[38] But the perceptive reader sees here Mark's regular combination of the two themes of Christology and discipleship.

Therefore Mark alters the traditional meaning of fear as awe by interpreting the disciples' response negatively.[39] As Best argues, "Mark has not neglected the original christological setting of the pericope in the tradition but has added another dimension—discipleship—and this in keeping with his whole train of thought in 8:27—10:45."[40] Literarily, Mark is creating a second series of narratives in the first cycle of

---

35. See Thrall, "Elijah and Moses," 305–17.

36. The Gospel of Mark is unique at this point. When Matthew restructures the passage into two epiphanies followed in each case by a positive response, he is calling attention to the unique identity of Jesus when Moses and Elijah disappear. Marcus points out as well that "Later renditions of the transfiguration narrative go further along this same Christocentric road by omitting all references to Moses and Elijah (2 Pet 1:16–18; Acts of Peter 20; Acts of Thomas 143; Acts of John 90)" (*Mark 8–16*, 639).

37. Dwyer (*Motif of Wonder*, 142 and n. 205) concedes that there is widespread agreement that 9:6 is redactional but refuses to admit a negative view of the disciples. Instead, he states that "The redactional operation in the transfiguration encourages the readers to proceed to obedient faith and discipleship." But even Dwyer who advocates an epiphanic view of fear agrees that "The entire pericope of the transfiguration must in fact be viewed as portraying an original Christological setting with the added dimension of discipleship" (138).

38. In a note Nineham (*St. Mark*, 233) even employs italics in his translation of this verse to call attention to the unusual emphasis upon disciples in a passage primarily about Christology.

39. Marcus (*Mark 8–16*, 641) compares 9:6 and 16:8.

40. Best, *Disciples and Discipleship*, 58. See also "Markan Redaction," 50 and Lightfoot, *Gospel Message of Mark*, 44.

passion prediction, misunderstanding, and teaching on discipleship. Just as Peter's profession of Jesus as Messiah (8:29b) produced a passion prediction (8:31) followed by Peter's misunderstanding (8:32b–33) and a lesson on discipleship (8:34–39), so the epiphany of splendor (9:2–4) along with the voice identifying Jesus as God's son (9:7) results in Peter's misunderstanding (9:5–6) followed by a teaching on discipleship on the way down the mountain (9:9–13). The misunderstanding is positioned at the center of the passage to assign it special prominence. Mark's structure inserts a discipleship misunderstanding between two epiphany revelations to call attention to its presence. The omniscient narrator rebukes Peter ("He did not know what to say, they were so frightened") just as Jesus rebuked Peter for his earlier misunderstanding (8:33a). Thus Peter opens his mouth impetuously on two successive occasions so that he does not "have in mind the things of God, but the things of men" (8:33b). To build tabernacles on the mountain and remain in the heavenly glory is a misguided venture. Therefore, Peter and his fellow disciples are now instructed to listen to God's Son, who will inform them about his passion on the way down the mountain.[41]

Additional evidence for a negative interpretation of fear ensues from a comparison of the Greek of Mark 9:6 (οὐ γὰρ ᾔδει τί ἀποκριθῇ) with the vocabulary describing Jesus' agony in the garden of Gethsemane.[42] The similar expression in 14:40, "they did not know what to say to him" (καὶ οὐκ ᾔδεισαν τί ἀποκριθῶσιν αὐτῷ), occurs likewise in a context about discipleship, where the disciples have no excuse for their sleeping instead of preparing for Jesus' passion. Both of these verses contain Markan redaction, awakening attentive readers to the possibility that they as well misunderstand Jesus' true identity and the implications for discipleship.

Therefore, Mark contrasts the glory of the transfiguration with the agony of the crucifixion to which Jesus' journey must lead. While the transfiguration focuses upon the heavenly light belonging to Jesus (9:2–3), his awaited crucifixion will bring supernatural darkness (15:33). At the transfiguration Jesus' clothes become gloriously luminous, betokening messianic power (9:2–3), while at the crucifixion his clothes are stripped off (15:24). The two OT saints who accompany Jesus at the transfiguration (Moses and Elijah) become two criminals who rail against him at his death (15:32). Instead of the powerful presence of Elijah, the intervention of Elijah at the crucifixion fails to occur (15:35–36). Whereas Peter reflects that "It is good for us to be here" at the transfiguration (9:5), the disciples' absence at the crucifixion proves that sadly it is not a good thing for them to be with Jesus at his death. Instead of proposals for building three tents to memorialize the event (9:5), Peter denies that he has any memory of Jesus on three occasions during the Jewish trial (14:54, 66–72). A voice from heaven

---

41. Stein (*Mark*, 413) following Edwards (*Mark*, 268) contends that the call to "hear him" is a rebuke referring backwards to Peter's misunderstanding in 8:31–33, but more likely it refers forward to what Jesus will tell the disciples on the way down the mountain. The teaching part of the cycle is the climax. Cf. Marcus, *Mark 8–16*, 639 and Nineham, *St. Mark*, 236–37.

42. See Kazmeirski, *Jesus, Son of God*, 107.

honors Jesus at the transfiguration (9:7), but at the crucifixion Jesus is abandoned (15:34).[43] Therefore, the content of the Markan surprise in the transfiguration narrative is that the Messiah must suffer—a truth that Peter and the disciples cannot fathom.

5.3b The Addition of Fear to Passion Passages in Mark 9:32 and 10:32

In turning to 9:32 and 10:32 we discover that the fear in these passages likewise is connected with Jesus' passion. In 9:32 the disciples are afraid to ask Jesus about the implications of his passion prediction for themselves. Normally knowledge removes fear, but in this case the disciples are afraid to discover the meaning of Jesus' words. This surprising and unexpected development reveals a Markan narrative shock. Fear resulting from a prediction of Jesus' passion has replaced the more normal awe of Jesus' mighty deeds. The following context proves that their fear must involve a trepidation of suffering and the cross. Immediately after this "question anxiety" in 9:32 the disciples misunderstand Jesus' teaching on self-denial (9:33–34), which is then followed by a teaching on discipleship (9:34–50) aimed at preparing the disciples for a time when they will be salted with the fire of persecution (9:49). Evans correctly explains the two related dimensions of their anxiety: "their fear that Jesus will underscore yet again the certainty of his death" is combined with the fact that "their master may eventuate, even require the death of the disciples."[44] Their fear, then, involves the two themes of a suffering Messiah and a discipleship of the cross.

Mark 10:32 carries on this same theme. The disciples' fear to inquire about Jesus' passion prediction in 9:32 must be equated with the response of fear when Jesus leads the parade into Jerusalem at 10:32. Here the Twelve stand astonished while the other followers appear fearful. Although a contrast between the two groups cannot be proven since both exhibit a similar reaction of astonishment and fear, the two sets of devotees should still be distinguished.[45] Those who followed are probably the women[46] since Mark describes them in a parallel manner to the Twelve in 15:40—16:8 and mentions that they had come up with Jesus to Jerusalem (15:41). Therefore both the disciples and the women respond negatively to Jesus' forthcoming passion in Jerusalem. In both 9:32 and 10:32 the negative response of fear is attached to Jesus' passion predictions. Since the disciples are not ready to follow their leader to the cross

---

43. This material comes from Davies and Allison, *Matthew*, 2:706–7 and Marcus, *Mark 8–16*, 641.

44. Evans, *Mark 8:27—16:20*, 58. However with Mark 10:32, Evans changes his tune and inconsistently states that "The fear here should be understood in the OT sense of awe that overwhelms humans in the presence of the divine."

45. Dwyer (*Motif of Wonder*, 159–60) offers extensive argumentation for only one group, but the presence of one or two groups does not make any difference for interpretation if the two sub-groups are not contrasted.

46. Taylor, *Mark*, 437; Cranfield, *St. Mark*, 335.

in Jerusalem, they misconstrue each of Jesus' prognostications. After 9:32 the disciples argue about who is the greatest and after 10:32 James and John aspire to sit in glory at Jesus' right and left in the kingdom. Just as the apprehension to discuss Jesus' passion prediction in 9:32 indicates "Jesus' essential loneliness on the way to Jerusalem,"[47] so the fear engendered when Jesus leads them toward Jerusalem in 10:32 signifies their refusal to participate with Jesus in his sufferings.[48] On both occasions their fear and astonishment is negative and connected with Jesus' passion.

To support this conclusion we must now argue against those interpreters who refuse to accept this emphasis upon discipleship failure at 9:32 and 10:32 but instead focus solely on Christology. They interpret the fear in 9:32 as a positive holy respect inspired by Jesus based upon the emphatic position of the "him" before the infinitive (αὐτὸν ἐπερωτῆσαι).[49] However, to demonstrate an emphasis upon αὐτὸν the pronoun must precede both verb and infinitive, as in 8:32, or the term must be continuously repeated, as in the five occurrences in 15:20.[50] In his typical fashion Gundry interprets the disciples' lack of understanding as a foil that magnifies Jesus' foreknowledge and awesomeness. He contends that Jesus' destination is not Jerusalem and his awaited passion, but instead Capernaum (9:33), where he instructs his disciples in the sermon of 9:35–50.[51] However, Peter's confession stands as the turning point in Mark's gospel, and from this northernmost point in Jesus' ministry at Philip's Caesarea (8:27) the entire narrative is geared toward Jerusalem. The threefold literary structure of passion prediction, misunderstanding, and teaching on discipleship confirms Mark's emphasis upon Jesus' passion in the middle of his gospel. Similar to Gundry, Dwyer interprets the fear as an awesome holy terror that has attended the mighty works of Jesus and will demonstrate the saving and ruling power of God in Jesus' passion.[52] This view, however, does not match Jesus' cry of desolation from the cross, nor does it envision the consequences of Mark placing 9:32 right between Jesus' passion prediction and the disciples' misunderstanding of his logion. These critics underestimate Mark's clever writing skills and how he employs surprises to apply the Jesus' tradition to his community's struggles.

At 10:32 as well several authors interpret the amazement and fear of the disciples in a positive manner as awe of Jesus. Lane, for example, contends that

---

47. Lane, *Mark*, 337.

48. Marcus (*Mark 8–16*, 744) remarks that the verb "going before" (προάγω) occurs in Josephus' descriptions of the militant activities of first-century Jewish revolutionary figures (War 2:259; 7:438) so that the followers might be fearful of a holy war against Rome, but this information could also fit with a fear that they would be put to death for following Jesus.

49. Dwyer, *Motif of Wonder*, 150; Stein, *Mark*, 440.

50. This pronoun precedes an infinitive in Mark 1:45; 5:3, 4; 6:19; 7:18; 9:32; 12:12 whereas it follows the infinitive in 2:15; 3:21; 5:17; 15:18, 36.

51. Gundry, *Mark*, 504–5.

52. Dwyer, *Motif of Wonder*, 151.

What awakens amazement and terror in the disciples who follow is not the recognition that the road leads to Jerusalem nor an awareness of what will be accomplished there, but Jesus himself. The power of the Lord, who holds in his hands his own destiny as well as that of the people of God, is manifested for Mark and his readers in the awe and dread which characterize those around him.[53]

Lane argues that Jesus preceded his disciples in the parade toward Jerusalem as a demonstration of a "powerful Savior who leads his people with purpose and direction."[54] In this view the use of similar vocabulary (προάγω) anticipates the action of the risen Lord promised in 14:28, who will go before them in resurrection glory into Galilee (16:7). But as we have argued in chapter 4, this is an instance of a Markan allusionary repetition, a literary device that Mark employs to demonstrate that the same Jesus who is exalted in glory (14:28; 16:7) also leads the way to the cross (10:32).[55] Although a rabbi leading his band was a common rabbinic custom,[56] Mark transforms this gesture into a theological concept whereby he calls the Christian community to learn from the mistakes of the disciples and not to be afraid to follow Jesus to the cross.

Dwyer argues for awe instead of fear of martyrdom by employing the hermeneutical principle of clearer passages providing the key for interpreting more difficult episodes.[57] Certainly the majority of references to fear in Mark intend a connotation of awe, but four passages (9:6, 32; 10:32; 16:8) provide a unique category of "fear statements" in the second half of the gospel.[58] These passages are all redactional as even Dwyer admits.[59] Therefore they serve a unique function in Mark and cannot be categorized with the traditional use of amazement and fear after miracle stories. When these passages are seen as instances of Mark's distinctive literary device of narrative surprise, it becomes clear why Matthew and Luke omit the "puzzling references" about fear in Mark 10:32 and 16:8 (9:32 in Matthew) while they insert them into a different spot in the narrative at 9:6 and 9:15.

---

53. Lane, *Mark*, 374 quotes Georg Bertram, θάμβος, *TDNT*, 3:6 without acknowledgement.

54. Lane, *Mark*, 374. See also Gundry, *Mark*, 570–71; Evans, *Mark 8:27—16:20*, 108; and Lightfoot, *Gospel Message of Mark*, 44.

55. See section 4.3d above.

56. Gerhard Kittel, ἀκολουθέω, *TDNT*, 1:213.

57 Attempted emendations prove that Mark 10:32 is a difficult passage and not entirely clear. C. C. Torrey (*Our Translated Gospels*, 151–53) and C. H. Turner (*New Commentary on Holy Scripture*, 51–52) assume that originally Jesus was the person experiencing amazing distress while the Western text omits the fact that those who followed him were afraid (see Lane, *Mark*, 373, n. 60).

58. Best explains, "Mark may not be wholly consistent in the way he speaks of the amazement and fear of the disciples but we need to remember that he is not 'historicizing' the disciples but using them in order to instruct his own church" (*Following Jesus*, 120–21).

59. Dwyer, *Motif of Wonder*. For 9:7 see p. 142 and n. 205; for 9:32, p. 151 and n. 25; for 10:32, p. 160 and n. 60; for 16:8, p. 193 and n. 179. This is also true for the different word used in 9:15 as seen on p. 148, n. 20.

Therefore, the disciples' fear must be understood as an indication of a lack of faith and understanding. The first mention of Jerusalem in Jesus' trip southward (10:32) elicits the fear that Jerusalem will again become the place that rejects the prophets and "thus the place of suffering for those who are true to the way of Jesus."[60] As Best concludes, "they are afraid as they follow because the end for them may be the same."[61] Likewise, an emphasis upon discipleship is evidenced by Jesus' subsequent removal of the Twelve for private instruction in 9:33.[62] Also, in 10:35–40 the disciples learn that they must be willing to be baptized with Jesus' baptism of suffering and drink his cup of passion. Already in 10:32 they are afraid of this prospect. This emphasis makes it likely that the fear of suffering with Jesus becomes the paradigmatic lesson for Mark's community. As Cranfield comments, this portrayal is likely to have been intended as a comfort to Christians in Rome, who at the time of Mark's publication were experiencing a similar fearful and uncertain future.[63] Therefore this Markan surprise calls attention to the twin themes of a crucified Messiah and a discipleship of the cross.

5.3c The Surprising Ending of Mark in 16:8

Finally we arrive at the end of Mark's gospel and the last reference to fear. We will demonstrate the close relationship to 9:6, 32; and 10:32, which all occur in the second half of Mark's gospel where he emphasizes following a suffering Son of Man rather than a miracle-working Messiah. Since this passage is notoriously difficult to interpret, we will provide a lengthy systematization of the various approaches to the conclusion of Mark and then offer evidence that this is a typical Markan narrative surprise.

The *harmonizing ending* of Mark 16:9–20 was popular in Germany until the influence of Wellhausen, who in 1903 convinced exegetes on the continent that Mark intended to conclude the gospel at 16:8. The removal of 16:9–20 to an appendix became the dominant sentiment in the English-speaking world in the second half of the twentieth century after the commentary by Lightfoot *The Gospel Message of St. Mark* in 1950.[64] Today the longer ending is still advocated by William Farmer, Maurice Robinson, and David Alan Black among others.[65] However, its absence in the oldest texts, the witness of the church fathers (Clement of Alexandria, Origen, Jerome, and Euse-

---

60. McKinnis, "Analysis of Mark X 32–34," 85.

61. Best, *Following Jesus*, 120. See also Luz, "Secrecy Motif," 84.

62. Jesus frequently withdraws with his disciples to a house which becomes later the house church used for instruction (οἶκός 3:20; 5:38?; 7:17; 9:28; οἰκία 7:24; 9:33; 10:10; 14:3).

63. Cranfield, *St. Mark*, 335.

64. Julius Wellhausen, *Das Evangelium Marci* quoted in Hooker, *St. Mark*, 391. Lightfoot, *Gospel Message of Mark*, 82. He follows Knox ("End of St. Mark's Gospel," 13ff.) in advocating 16:8 as the original ending.

65. See William P. Farmer, *Last Twelve Verses of Mark*; Robinson and Piermont, *New Testament in the Original Greek*, and Black, *Perspectives on the Ending*. For views of scholars who support the longer ending see Cox, *History and Critique of Scholarship*, chapter 3.

bius) that it was missing in a majority of manuscripts, the conflation of accounts from the other canonical gospels, the change of subject between 16:8 and 16:9, the rhetorical tone and style of the Greek, the diversity of expressions between the gospel and the addition, and the non-Markan vocabulary all prove that 16:9–20 is a later addition.[66] The best explanation for its addition is the compilation of the gospels into a four-set edition in the early second century.[67] The editor wanted Mark to end with identical dramatic resurrection appearances and a missionary commission as the other gospels and so constructed a harmony of their accounts.[68]

Because of the abrupt ending of 16:8 interpreters have advocated a *lost ending*. As the twenty-first century begins, this thesis is gaining rapid prominence in the evangelical community through the commentaries of Gundry, Evans, Witherington, France, Stein, and N.T. Wright.[69] Several tentative explanations have been put forward. Possibly Mark was arrested and put to death or left Rome during the persecution and did not finish the gospel.[70] Several authors discern the lost ending in Matthew 28 so that there is a positive reconciliation with the disciples and a proclamation to the whole world of the gospel of the resurrected Christ.[71] However, the presence of specifically

---

66. κόσμον ἅπαντα (16:15) vs. ὅλον τὸν κόσμον (8:36; 14:9); παρακολουθήσεται (16:17) and ἐπακολουθούντων (16:20) vs. κολουθέω in the rest of Mark; ἐκεῖνος functions as a pronoun in 16:10, 13, 20 whereas it is always employed as an adjective elsewhere in Mark; adverbial participles in the genitive, dative, and accusative in 16:10, 12, 14; non-Markan vocabulary includes πορεύομαι only in Mark 16:10, 12, 15 whereas Mark uses compounds (never the aorist); πενθέω 16:10; θεάομαι 16:11, 14; ἀπιστέω 16:11, 16; ἕτερος 16:12; μορφῇ 16:12; ὕστερον 16:14; ἕνδεκα, the eleven 16:14; ἀναλαμβάνω 16:19; συνεργέω 16:20; βεβαιόω 16:20. For an employment of this information in a different direction see Maurice Robinson's essay in *Perspectives on the Ending*, 60–61.

67. Hengel (*Four Gospels*, 134) dates the addition to Mark at 120 CE since it employs all four gospels. The longer ending was known by Tatian and Irenaeus and displays similarities with *Epistula Apostolorum*. See Hengel, *Studies in Mark*, 168, n. 47 for details.

68. See Evans, *Mark 8:27—16:20*, 546–47 for a comparison of the accounts in Greek.

69. Support comes as well from Alford, Branscomb, Burkitt who wanted a grave accent on γάρ, Bultmann, Cullmann, Dodd, Elliot, Goodspeed, Gregory, Griesbach, Hengel, Metzger, Moule, Moffatt, Osborne, Plummer, Rawlinson, Schlatter, Schnewind, Streeter, Swinburne, Taylor, Trompf, Turner, Westcott and Hort who ended their text with a colon followed by asterisks rather than a full stop, etc. See Croy, *Mutilation of Mark's Gospel*, 174–77. For scholars who support 16:8 as the ending see Kümmel, *Introduction*, 100, n. 72.

70. Instead of an unfinished document others postulate intentional pruning or accidental loss. Bultmann suggests a polemical reason: "It would be more understandable if this lost end had been in strong contradiction to the later Easter legend" (*History*, 285, n. 2), so that the conclusion would have been a source of embarrassment for those wishing to give pre-eminence to Peter (called "ecclesiastical politics" by Trompf, "First Resurrection Appearance," 325). Gundry explains the accidental loss with these ponderings, "The last segment of a scroll becomes the innermost section so that it is subjected to the most stress by being rolled up the most tightly, and deteriorative dampness may have been trapped in it when the scroll was rolled up" (*Mark*, 1017). But Daniel Wallace in his essay in *Perspectives on the Ending* objects, "if the Gospel was written on a roll, then the most protected section would be the end" (35).

71. For supporters of this view see Boring, *Mark*, 452, n. 5. For instance, Witherington (*Mark*, 46, n. 131) states that Matthew contains a redaction of Mark's lost ending in Matt 28:9–10, 16–20 although "Luke knows nothing of this Markan ending but rather supplies other traditions in Luke

Matthean vocabulary, the positive addition of "and great joy" to fear, the specific omission of Peter, the vagueness of the narrative at the exact point where the authentic text of Mark now ends, and the Matthean themes in the Galilean appearance (28:16–20) argue against a recovery of the lost ending from Matthew. There are too many arbitrary assumptions in such a theory and "a loss resulting from a leaf breaking off would hardly have gone unremedied."[72]

The unsatisfactory nature of the terse ending in Mark certainly makes a lost ending attractive. Many scholars contend that Mark's conclusion is grammatically unsatisfactory since a book cannot end with γάρ. However, examples have been unearthed in Plotinus' 32nd treatise (*Ennead* 5:5 τελειότερον γάρ), and the 12th tractate of Musonius Rufus (γνωρίμων γάρ), as well as in the conclusion of a model letter (Demetrius, *Formae Epistolicae*, nr. 21 ὀφείλω γάρ), the end of a story about Aesopus and Xanthos (*Vita Aesopi* 1:67 οὐκ ἔχεις γάρ), the end of a preface of the third book of Polyaenus' *Strategemata* (πρόδηλον γάρ), and the end of a section of Plato's *Protagoras* (328d νέοι γάρ).[73] In particular, Genesis 18:15 parallels Mark 16:8 with regard to vocabulary since Sarah denies that she laughed because she was afraid (ἐφοβήθη γάρ), just as the women did not say anything because they were afraid (ἐφοβοῦντο γάρ). Similarly, Genesis 45:3 contains thematic parallels to the ending of Mark when Joseph's brothers are thrown into confusion (ἐταράχθησαν γάρ) and unable to answer because they pictured Joseph as dead. Therefore van der Horst's conclusion seems reasonable: "common sense alone could argue that, if a sentence or a paragraph can end with γάρ, a book can too."[74] At the very minimum, the best conclusion is to postulate that Mark's ending with γάρ does not offer conclusive evidence either for or against an ending at 16:8.

Gundry argues that ἐφοβοῦντο γάρ starts a sentence rather than ends one since only 10 percent of Mark's γάρ clauses (6 out of 66) conclude pericopes and Mark does not normally end passages on a note of fear.[75] But Gundry admits that 4:41; 9:32; 11:18;[76] and 12:12 conclude passages with the theme of fear, and more importantly

---

24" (49).

72. Kümmel, *Introduction*, 100. Marcus argues that "textual mutilation generally results from decades or even centuries of wear and tear, whereas in the present case we would have to posit a loss that occurred within a decade or so of composition, before Matthew and Luke had gotten their hands on Mark's work" (*Mark 8–16*, 1091).

73. See van der Hoerst, "Can a Book End with GAR?" 121–24. Cox (*History and Critique*, 149–57, 223–28) unearths more than 1500 examples of sentences ending in γάρ. Croy (*Mutilation of Mark's Gospel*, 48) contends that sentences ending in γάρ are much less common in narrative, but Iverson ("Further Word," 86–88) provides data which demonstrates that this conclusion must be adjusted since Croy does "not provide the full interpretative framework." He discovers 16 examples of sentences ending with γάρ in literary genre similar to the gospels between the 3rd century BCE and the 2nd century CE.

74. Van der Hoerst, "Can a Book End with GAR?" 124.

75. Gundry, *Mark*, 1011, #9 and #8.

76. Although a direct object is included in the similar double γάρ sequence in 11:18 (ἐφοβοῦντο

the Markan narrative surprises we have uncovered so far use fear to end a sentence (9:6; 10:32). In addition, several narrative surprises either finish the passage (6:52) or the sentence (9:6) with a γάρ clause like 16:8. Gundry (#6) contends that 16:8 begins a new paragraph since it parallels 16:5 (εἰσελθοῦσαι εἰς τὸ μνημεῖον . . . ἐξελθοῦσαι ἀπὸ τοῦ μνημείου),[77] but each of the γάρ statements offers a reason for the previous statement ("they fled" and "they did not say anything to anyone," each followed by a γάρ clause), so that the final γάρ is a conclusion rather than a beginning.[78] Therefore Mark's ending is indeed grammatically satisfactory.

Mark's ending appears literarily unsatisfactory, leaving the reader asking, "What happened next?" For example, 14:28 and 16:7 refer to a meeting of the disciples and Peter with the resurrected Jesus, which never happens, whereas the other predictions within the gospel are fulfilled, including "the seeing of God's kingdom as having come with power at the Transfiguration, the finding of a colt, some disciples being met by a man carrying a jar of water, the showing of the Upper Room, the betrayal of Jesus by one of the Twelve, the scattering of the rest of the Twelve, the denials of Jesus by Peter, and, of course, the Passion (including numerous details predicted by Jesus) and the Resurrection."[79] However, in order to call attention to the cross Mark does not narrate any fulfillments that would occur after the resurrection, including 1) the downfall of the betrayer (14:21); 2) fasting after the bridegroom is taken away (2:20); 3) the baptism of the Holy Spirit (1:8); 4) the disciples as fishers of people (1:17); 5) the disciples' healing ministry through prayer (9:28–29); 6) the proclamation of the woman's anointing of Jesus (14:9); and 7) James and John experiencing the baptism of suffering and the drink of martyrdom (10:39).[80] Therefore, the omission of the women's communication of the angel's message to the disciples and the narration of Peter's renewal fits Mark's policy.

Mark's ending appears theological unsatisfactory since witnesses to the resurrection are missing, unlike the other gospels as well as evidenced in the apostles preaching (1 Cor 15:5ff; Acts 1:22; 2:32; 3:15; 10:41; 13:31).[81] However, the conclusion makes perfect sense if we postulate that Mark does not narrate any resurrection appearances since the community is living existentially in a similar situation to the first disciples, who know Jesus is risen but are only experiencing the aloneness and alienation of Nero's persecution. This explains why Mark consistently paints Jesus' family (3:21, 31–32) as well as both the male and female disciples (14:50; 16:8) as outsiders since he

---

γὰρ αὐτόν), this example occurs in the first γάρ clause and does not conclude the sentence.

77. However, the entering and the leaving of the tomb certainly tie the story together as an appropriate beginning and conclusion so exegetes should not emphasize that a new paragraph begins in 16:8. See also 3:1 and 3:6.

78. Boomershine and Bartholomew, "Narrative Technique," 221–22.

79. Gundry, *Mark*, 1009.

80. Cf. Best, *Gospel as Story*, 120.

81. Gundry, *Mark*, 1012, #12; and Cranfield, *St. Mark*, 471.

wants to theologically provide a foil for his community, which is likewise struggling with following a crucified Jesus. Literarily, Mark offers an open ending whereby the readers can go back to Galilee where the narrative begins and relive the gospel story without the mistakes of the disciples. Instead of including resurrection appearances, Mark demonstrates Jesus' heavenly glory through such narratives as the transfiguration.[82] Thus Jesus is risen, but the witnesses to the resurrection are missing since Mark wants his readers to become these witnesses in the midst of their faith struggles (13:9–13).

Mark's conclusion appears stylistically unsatisfactory. If Mark entitles his work a gospel or good news, would he end with words of human failure, incomprehension, disobedience, and negative fear? If the purpose of 1:1 is christological ("the gospel of Jesus Christ, the Son of God"), how would the purpose of 16:8 be anthropological by focusing on the women's failure and disobedience? In fact, advocates of this position argue that Mark would have violated the rules of ancient storytelling if he ended such a glorious section on a negative note.[83] Since ancient biographies always end positively even if the main character dies,[84] supporters of a lost ending insist that an abrupt open ending would be completely at odds with the requirements of storytelling in the ancient world.[85] However, compared with the other gospels, Mark's opening is likewise characteristically abrupt and brief. As Magness explains, "Thus the suspended ending and the sparse but powerful prologue to the Gospel complement and balance one another."[86] Morna Hooker compares the Markan ending with other biblical literature which evidences untidy, open-ended conclusions leaving the reader unsatisfied.[87] Likewise, Magness in chapters 3–5 discusses ancient, Old Testament, and New Testament literature to demonstrate that open endings were not uncommon, as evidenced for instance by the Book of Jonah, Jesus' parable of the prodigal son, and

---

82. See Collins, *Mark*, 403.

83. Bruce, "End of the Second Gospel," 169–70; Knox, "End of St. Mark's Gospel," 13–14.

84. See Witherington, *Mark*, 43–44. For example, Plutarch writes a biography of Julius Caesar where the gods avenge his wrongful death through the appearance of a comet and Cassius kills himself with the very same dagger which he had used against Caesar (*Caes.* 69:2–5). In Josephus' autobiography he is finally vindicated by the emperor and God.

85. For support for this opinion see Knox, "End of St. Mark's Gospel," 22–23; Witherington *Mark*, 44; and France, *Mark*, 671–72. Against such an opinion see Petersen, "When is the End not the End?" 153; and Williams, "Literary Approaches," 25.

86. Magness, *Sense and Absence*, 91. For an attempted dismissal of Magness' conclusions on suspended endings see Croy, *Mutilation*, 91–96.

87. Hooker, *Endings*, 7–10. She concludes (82) that all of the gospels and Acts have suspended endings. Bilezikian (*Liberated Gospel*, 134) calls attention to the open-endedness of Greek tragedy.

the ending of Acts.⁸⁸ Therefore we must presume that "Mark's conclusion would have fit into the literary conventions of *his* day."⁸⁹

Mark's ending appears thematically unsatisfactory because motifs such as the Messianic Secret and the disciples' ignorance and misunderstandings are not resolved. Regarding the Messianic Secret, France reports that since Mark begins his story on an overt note of faith in Jesus he "is not likely to leave any room for doubt about its reality at the end."⁹⁰ Then regarding the disciples he adds, "For Mark's story to have finished with ten of the Twelve as deserters, one a traitor, and Peter blasphemously dissociating himself from Jesus would have undone all that Mark has tried to do."⁹¹ In addition, Witherington is especially concerned about the portrayal of women in Mark's gospel. He states that "Mark has carefully built the case for the women to be valid witnesses to the death, burial, empty tomb, and Easter message. He cannot have wished to undermine this case by finishing with "they fled in terror, saying nothing to anyone."⁹² However, the structure of Mark offers evidence in a contrary direction. As we establish in Appendix 4, Mark organizes the gospel into five cycles of discipleship where Jesus' followers start each section positively but because of rejection, misunderstanding, and unbelief end each section on a negative note.⁹³ Similarly Mark concludes each of the trips across the sea with a negative evaluation of the disciples (4:40; 6:52; 8:17–21). Therefore, Mark consistently leaves a negative final picture of the Twelve, Jesus' family, and the women disciples, although this portrayal does not eliminate the possibility of discipleship renewal and restoration.

Mark provides hints that the disciples will be reinstated just as he provides hope for his readers who have forsaken their initial commitment to follow Jesus (13:9–13). The juxtaposition of a promised future in 16:7 with a present failure in 16:8 offers optimism for the future.⁹⁴ The angel's command to tell Peter specifically previews a future reconciliation for the disciples. Jesus' family is given a positive interpretation by mentioning Mary (the mother of Jesus⁹⁵) as one of the women who cares for Jesus'

---

88. However, Magness wrongly arrives at a positive epiphanic estimation of the women's fear through an emphasis upon an inclusio in 1:1 and 16:8 (pp. 88–89). He should take into account the whole structure of the Gospel of Mark where each discipleship section ends with a negative response.

89. Wallace (*Perspectives on the Ending*, 34) has attempted to overcome the two accusations of subtlety and modernity.

90. France, *Mark*, 672.

91. Ibid., 676.

92. Witherington, *Mark*, 416–17.

93. See the conclusion of Appendix 4 as well as the description and evaluation of outline 12.

94. Cf. Myers, *Binding*, 368.

95. Similar descriptions in 7:3 (Ἰακώβου καὶ Ἰωσῆτος) and 15:40, 47; 16:1 (Ἰακώβου τοῦ μικροῦ καὶ Ἰωσῆτος) as well as the identical change of spelling by Matthew in both passages (Ἰωσὴφ 13:55; 27:56) makes an identification with Jesus' mother probable. For support see Ambrose, *De Virginitate* 3:14; Boring, *Mark*, 437; Gundry, *Mark*, 977; Crossan, "Mark and the Relatives," 105–10; and Schmid, *Markus*, 304. According to Trompf ("First Resurrection Appearance," 310, n. 3) James was entitled the younger since he succeeded to the older James, the inner circle disciple and leader of the church

crucified body. This "intentionally but subtly designed" reintroduction of Jesus' family into the narrative[96] indicates that "the final references to Mary the mother of James and Joses have in all probability theological significance."[97] Likewise, instead of a young man fleeing at the betrayal we now encounter a young man in radiant dress at the resurrection so that desertion becomes accompaniment.[98] Finally, the women's fear, flight, and failure to proclaim the gospel will be transformed when the future trip to Galilee proves Jesus' resurrection. Therefore Mark's conclusion fits his purpose.

In summary, the basic problem with the lost ending approach is that "Hypotheses of accidental loss or intentional pruning lack conviction."[99] Understood correctly, all of Mark's themes come to conclusion in the cross. The Messianic Secret is not resolved directly through a resurrection appearance and missionary commission, but instead the cross is called attention to since at Jesus' death the centurion proclaims Jesus as the Son of God and no one commands him to keep silent. The eerie silence of the women indicates that they are still living in the fear of following Jesus to the cross just as the male disciples, who have likewise fled (14:50) in the midst of suffering. Therefore we must look elsewhere for an explanation of Mark's ending to the gospel.

A third perspective on the ending of Mark is the *epiphanic view*.[100] A representative translation of 16:8 is offered by Gundry: "The women flee away trembling, astonished, and awestruck beyond words because of the power of Jesus' resurrection."[101] Similarly, Jesus' death is interpreted as a majestically spectacular event. Evans explains that a "stunning and awesome shout of Jesus brings the death scene to a close," an astounding manifestation of divine power whose force "actually tears the temple veil."[102] Therefore each of the elements of flight, silence, and fear are interpreted positively.[103] Flight and overwhelming awe, then, become a response to a confrontation

---

(Acts 12:2, 17). Questions regarding this interpretation include: 1) why does Mark not name all the sons like Judas and Simon?; 2) why not call her the mother of Jesus like earlier in 3:21, 31–35?; 3) why place her second to Mary Magdalene?; 4) would not the fact that about half of the Jewish women in Palestine in the Second Temple and Mishnaic periods bore the name Mary exclude her? See Marcus, *Mark 8–16*, 1060. But Mark purposely does not call her the mother of Jesus to provide a foil for the church. This is similar to the restraint that John's gospel employs (19:26; 2:4) so that the beloved disciple and the mother of Jesus become a symbol of the church (Brown, *Gospel According to John*, 926). Other opinions identify her as the wife of Clopas (John 19:25) or the mother of James, son of Alphaeus (Mark 3:18).

96. Boring, *Mark*, 437.

97. Trompf, "First Resurrection Appearance," 311.

98. See section 4.6d above and Williams, *Gospel against Parable*, 72.

99. Wedderburn, *Beyond Resurrection*, 136.

100. The main supporters of this view include Catchpole, Collins, Dwyer, Evans, France, Gnilka, Gundry, Lane, Moule, Lightfoot, Magness, Malbon, Meye, Pesch, Stonehouse, and Witherington. For more supporters see Williams, "Literary Approaches," 26, n. 23 and Lincoln, "Promise and Failure," 286, n. 8. Many such as Gundry combine this approach with the lost ending view.

101. Gundry, *Mark*, 14.

102. Evans, *Mark 8:27—16:20*, 510, 509.

103. Dwyer, *Motif of Wonder*, 188.

with the supernatural. Similarly, the women running straight back to the disciples without speaking to anyone indicates quick obedience rather than a failure to report the message.[104]

We will attempt to counter each of these arguments. The grammatical argument states that if the final sentence is understood as an act of unfaithfulness by the women, then one would expect the adversative δέ and not καί.[105] However, this information is misleading since Mark introduces Jesus' rebukes with "and" in 2:17, 25; 3:4, 12, 23; 6:4; 8:17, 21; 10:23; 14:30, 37, 41. Similarly, the negative responses of unfaithfulness by the Pharisees (2:16; 11:18; 3:6[106]), Jesus' family (3:21 with a γάρ clause like 16:8), Judas (14:10), and the disciples sleeping in the garden of Gethsemane (14:37, 40, 41) all begin with καί. Especially important is the parallel use of καί in the final appearance of the disciples, who flee just as the women (14:50 καὶ ἀφέντες αὐτὸν ἔφυγον πάντες; 16:8a καὶ ἐξελθοῦσαι ἔφυγον ἀπὸ τοῦ μνημείου). Both incidents must be seen as instances of unfaithfulness. Finally, Markan variety and interchangeability are demonstrated in the unfaithful activity of Peter, where καί is employed three times when Peter and the disciples sleep in the garden (14:37, 40, 41) while δέ is used for Peter's three denials in the Jewish trial (14:68, 70, 71). Therefore, the employment of καί rather than δέ at 16:8 is insignificant.

The genre argument states that the resurrection, like other traditional miracle narratives, concludes with a reaction of fear and awe (1:27; 2:12; 4:41; 5:15, 20, 42; 6:51; 7:37). Mark would then consistently follow the use of the concept of "fear" in Jewish and Greco-Roman sources as well as early Christian apocryphal literature.[107] However, this traditional usage causes Mark's references to fear as a lack of faith to stand out in prominent contrast.[108] They function as Markan narrative surprises. Even authors like Dwyer concede that 16:8 is "the most puzzling of all the places where the motif of wonder occurs in Mark."[109] The circumstances of Mark's audience have caused him to redact the traditional use of fear and awe, thus adjusting its meaning.

The intertextuality or historical precedent argument concentrates on earlier texts inside and outside of Mark that shine light upon this passage. If one takes *1 Enoch*

---

104. Moule, "St. Mark XVI.8 Once More," 58–59. Geddert counters this view, "If Mark really meant that the women were overawed by the divine messenger and hastened to obey his command, speaking to no one except the disciples, he certainly made his point badly" (*Watchwords*, 163).

105. Gundry, *Mark*, 1010, #3. Holding ("Did the Gospel End at 16:8?" 1) calls attention to 1:45; 7:36; 10:14, 22, 48; 15:23, 37.

106. Mark 3:6 and 16:8, in fact, begin with the same first two words (3:6 καὶ ἐξελθόντες; 16:8 καὶ ἐξελθοῦσαι) and the entering and leaving in 3:1, 6 (εἰσῆλθεν, ἐξελθόντες) coordinate with the entering and leaving of the women in 16:5, 8 (εἰσελθοῦσαι, ἐξελθοῦσαι).

107. Dwyer, *Motif of Wonder*, 194.

108. Speaking specifically about the contrast between the beginning and end of Mark's gospel, Williams states, "In Mark's Gospel fear is a negative reaction that often comes from a lack of trust and understanding or an unwillingness to suffer" ("Literary Approaches," 27).

109. Dwyer, *Motif of Wonder*, 185.

106:4;[110] Daniel 10:7; and Mark 5:14 as parallels, then flight from the presence of the supernatural would likely be the theme of Mark 16:8 as well. However, Mark 14:50 rather than 5:14 is the closer parallel to 16:8. There the disciples flee because they are afraid of Jesus' anticipated passion; likewise, the women in 16:8 flee since they are unwilling to suffer. At first sight Daniel 10:7 appears to be a good prooftext, but in the Old Greek Daniel's comrades "run" (ἀπέδρασαν ἐν σπουδῇ) rather than "flee" (ἔφυγον ἐν φόβῳ), as found in Theodotion's translation. Furthermore, the running and hiding by Daniel's comrades does not carry a positive connotation; they miss God's revelation because of their lack of intimacy and trust in God. Finally, this cowardly interpretation of fear and flight has historical precedence as well since it occurs in such passages as Judges 7:3 and Deuteronomy 20:8, where the fearful are not required to fight in an upcoming battle.

Epiphanic experiences likewise are occasions in the Bible where a temporary silence results from a divine encounter, with supporters of this view calling attention to 1 Samuel 3:15; Isaiah 6:5; Daniel 7:28; Ezekiel 3:26–27; and 2 Corinthians 12:4.[111] However as Marcus points out, in the ending of Mark "the implication does not seem to be that the women are unable to speak but that they choose not to do so."[112] Furthermore, every one of the parallels in Mark where fear results from a divine manifestation gives rise not to stunned silence but to speech.[113] In Ezekiel 3:26–27 God himself makes the tongue of Ezekiel stick to the roof of his mouth, but Mark 16:8 calls attention to the women's action of silence, not God's divine compulsion. Unlike 2 Corinthians 12:4, the women disciples are certainly permitted and not forbidden to impart the resurrection proclamation of the angel. In 1 Samuel 3:15 Samuel is afraid to tell Eli the vision because of the negative consequences upon his family, just as the women are afraid to relate the resurrection proclamation because of the possible negative consequences of persecution. Therefore the epiphanic positive interpretation of Mark 16:8 does not fit Mark's theology.

Finally, Mark 1:44 (μηδενὶ μηδὲν εἴπῃς) is frequently enlisted as the closest parallel to the silence of the women in 16:8 (οὐδενὶ οὐδὲν εἶπαν). "Not saying anything to anyone" is interpreted "with the sense of speaking to no one at all except the appropriate party," thus suggesting "that the women were to be silent to the general public, but

---

110. In 1 En. 106:4 Lamech is afraid of his grandson Noah and flees to his son Methuselah because Noah resembles the sons of the God of heaven with his glorious countenance and his eyes like the rays of the sun (106:5).

111. Dwyer, *Motif of Wonder*, 189. But several of these texts are questionable. In Isa 6:5 the epiphany does not result in silence but unclean lips. The wording of Dan. 7:28 diverges too much to be an applicable parallel (he kept the word in his heart). In Luke 1:20 Zechariah is speechless after an angelic epiphany, but the experience is interpreted negatively as a punishment for unbelief, not as overwhelming awe.

112. Marcus, *Mark 8–16*, 1082 and 1087. As an alternative Marcus rightly surmises that "perhaps the explanation for the motif is to be sought on the level of the Markan community, where fear of persecution is creating a temptation to squelch the gospel message."

113. Cotes, "Women, Silence, and Fear," 153 refers to Mark 4:41; 5:16–17; 5:33; 6:49 etc.

to communicate with the disciples."[114] However, Williams counters this claim by noting that "the silence of the women stands in contrast to the widespread proclamation of the healed leper."[115] Whereas Jesus commands the leper not to speak, he proclaims the gospel message to all; on the other hand, the women say nothing to anyone when the expected response is a sharing of the good news. The combination of flight, fear, and silence must be contrasted with the appropriate reaction to Jesus' resurrection, which would be the anticipation of Jesus' presence, great joy, and proclamation as in Matthew 28:8–9. These details require a negative interpretation of Mark 16:8.

The contextual argument for the epiphanic view reasons that a consistent use of fear in 16:4–5, 8 is the natural reading of the text. Lane argues that "The prior use of the words expressing terror and amazement in verses 5–6 has prepared for the forceful language of verse 8 and confirms that the cause of the women's fear is the presence and action of God at the tomb of Jesus."[116] Since the women are treated positively in the preceding passages as committed followers from Galilee, sympathetic observers of Jesus' death and burial, and insiders to the resurrection message, it would be inconceivable to suddenly portray them as disobedient cowards. However, the contrast in the immediate context between the young man's command to proclaim Jesus' resurrection ("go tell") and the women's noncompliance ("they say nothing") reads more naturally "as an act of fearful disobedience than as an attempt at hurried obedience."[117] Furthermore, the entire outline of Mark's gospel argues in favor of a negative response of misunderstanding and hardness of heart on the part of the women. As Danova explains, "The story of the women re-presents significant elements of the characterization of the (male) disciples of Jesus and establishes narrative grounds for aligning the women with the disciples, from their earlier positive presentation to their final negative valuation."[118] As a conclusion to both the miracle Galilean ministry of Jesus (1:1—8:21) and the passion narrative, Mark develops an intensifying spiral whereby the followers of Jesus begin positively but, faced with adversity, become blind and deaf (8:17–18a), dense (8:18b, 21), hard-hearted (8:17), and cowardly (14:50–52; 16:8) at the end of each section. Thus Mark presents the women positively with regard to their trip from Galilee and their presence at the cross, but negatively when they flee in silence from fear. This Markan pattern takes precedence over the connections with the response of awe in 16:5.

The christological argument states that Mark would not emphasize a lack of discipleship at the conclusion of his gospel when the theme of Christology dominates

---

114. Holding, "Did the Gospel End at 16:8?" 1.

115. Williams, "Literary Approaches," 27.

116. Lane, *Mark*, 590.

117. Williams, "Literary Approaches," 27. Lincoln retorts, "It would be hard to make the women's disobedience and failure any clearer" ("Promise and Failure," 289).

118. Danova ("Characterization and Narrative Function," 375) is referring to the close connection with 14:50.

The Theological Intentions of Mark's Literary Devices

throughout. Stein remarks that "It is hard to imagine that a Gospel that begins with a bold, straightforward 'The beginning of the Gospel of Jesus Christ, the Son of God' (1:1) would end with a negative response of fear and fright by the women in 16:8."[119] Therefore, the epiphanic ending to Mark contends that "the silence and fear of the women are an indirect Christological affirmation."[120] But if one observes that every section of the Gospel of Mark emphasizes Jesus' passion and the cross designed for the disciple, then an ending that points back to the cross rather than stressing the resurrection is consistent Markan theology. An emphasis upon Jesus' passion and its consequences for discipleship saturate all the loci of Markan theology.

1. *Theology*: The voice from heaven at Jesus' baptism and transfiguration indicates God's plan for a Suffering Servant Messiah, a message that the disciples fail to understand. Jesus' one word from the cross in Mark, "My God, my God, why have you forsaken me?," calls attention to Jesus' faithfulness in the face of a feeling of abandonment, which the disciples must also imitate.

2. *Christology*: Each genre of teaching (controversy dialogue, parable, miracle, prophetic action, eschatological teaching, resurrection narrative) demonstrates that the Messiah must suffer, but still the disciples misunderstand.

3. *Pneumatology*: The Holy Spirit is not connected with powerful acts as in Luke or with an indwelling presence as in Paul, but rather with the faithful facing of trials. The Holy Spirit drives Jesus into the wilderness to be tested, where he confronts wild beasts (1:12–13). When the disciples face the wild beasts in arrests and trials, the Holy Spirit will tell them what to say so that worry is eliminated (13:11).

4. *Soteriology*: Atonement comes through the ransom of Jesus (10:45). The most lengthy section of the parable of the sower (4:5–6, 16–17) teaches that the Word of God falls on rocky ground, which will entail persecution and the cross for the believer.

5. *Ecclesiology*: The family of God does not consist of those of blood descent (3:21, 31–32) or the religious leaders (3:22–30), but of those who do God's will ,which implies following Jesus to cross and resurrection. Thus, the lot of the disciple includes facing a time where "brother will betray brother to death and a father his child" (13:12), and the disciples will be flogged in the synagogues (13:9).

6. *The Kingdom of God*: The already-but-not-yet nature of the kingdom implies that both for Jesus and the disciples the gospel proclaims both cross and resurrection. Therefore as Geddert proclaims, "A major element of the secrecy surrounds the fact that the kingdom advances through the suffering and persecution God's

---

119. Stein, "Ending of Mark," 90. On page 95 he contends that the main character is not the women, the disciples, or the angelic messenger, but Jesus, so the expected ending of Mark would center on Jesus.

120. Lane, *Mark*, 591.

representatives are called on to experience."[121]

7. *The Sacraments*: Baptism and the cup of Communion are applied to suffering when Jesus says that "you will drink the cup I drink and be baptized with the baptism I am baptized with" (10:39).

8. *Spiritual Devotion*: Spiritual disciplines like prayer, faith, forgiveness, (11:22–25) and love (12:33) replace the temple ceremonies like sacrifice since the temple mount is thrown into the sea (11:23) through the cross (15:37–38).

9. *Eschatology*: The center of the eschatological discourse (13:9–13) concentrates on suffering, and Mark uses 13:35 to structure the entire passion narrative to indicate that the disciples are not ready to follow a crucified Messiah.

Finally, the early interpretations argument contends that Matthew's understanding of Mark should be normative because of its proximity to the writing of the first gospel. Therefore the fear of the women should be interpreted as awe because of Matthew's explanation μετὰ φόβου καὶ χαρᾶς μεγάλης ("with fear and great joy" 28:8). Likewise, the women's flight should not be understood negatively because Matthew replaces ἔφυγον with ἔδραμον, running to tell the good news. However, a better explanation for these significant changes highlights Matthew's habit of restoring the oral tradition when Markan redaction is obvious.[122] As Juel points out, "Slight changes in wording yield a very different sense; 'They left quickly with fear and great joy' is worlds away from 'They fled . . . for they were afraid.'"[123] Instead of just considering Matthew, we should also investigate the longer ending attached to Mark. As Childs explains, "The longer ending, in addition, functions as a commentary on the first eight verses and plainly rules out interpreting the astonishment and awe of the women in a positive fashion."[124] The lack of faith mentioned in 16:11, 13 and Jesus' rebuke in 16:14 "for their lack of faith and their stubborn refusal to believe" demonstrate that these portrayals are a continuation of a negative interpretation of the women in 16:8.

Therefore the women were not "temporarily struck dumb with awe before the numinous" or overcome with a "stunned silence before the transcendent."[125] Instead, the women respond with silence in the period after the resurrection, a time when secrecy is no longer appropriate (9:9). Flight is the exact response of the unfaithful disciples, and the women's fear is comparable to the negative response of Jesus' followers in Mark 9:6, 32 and 10:32.[126]

---

121. Geddert, *Watchwords*, 201.

122. For a series of instances where Matthew follows an older oral tradition, see chapter 2 above, note 194..

123. Juel, *Master of Surprise*, 116.

124. Childs, *New Testament as Canon*, 95.

125. Lincoln ("Promise and Failure," 286 and 287) argues against these conclusions.

126. Geddert (*Watchwords*, 170) admirably explains the meaning of Mark 16:8.

A fourth approach to the finale of Mark considers 16:8 a *heroic ending* with the women as champions. For instance, Fiorenza explains,

> Though the twelve have forsaken Jesus, betrayed and denied him, the women disciples, by contrast, are found under the cross, risking their own lives and safety. That they are well aware of the danger of being arrested and executed as followers of apolitical insurrectionist crucified by the Romans is indicated in the remark that the women "were looking from afar. They are thus characterized as Jesus' true "relatives."[127]

But this description does not consider 16:8. All exegetes agree that the women disciples are given an exemplary role when they are introduced as loyal followers who travel with Jesus from Galilee (15:41), witness his death (15:40), and observe his burial (15:47; 16:1). Fiorenza recognizes that this positive interpretation "seems prohibited by 16:8," but she entitles this only a "first glance" at the text. In reality, the women do not flee "from the angel and the resurrection news but from the tomb" which is empty.[128] Through such subtleties several feminist exegetes attempt to describe the women without any negative connotations.[129]

Certainly Mark consistently portrays women positively up to 16:8,[130] but the final picture parallels the male disciples.[131] Thus the three women disciples replace the inner group of male disciples, who are unable to support Jesus in Gethsemane in his preparation for the cross. Mark establishes a pattern. In the first scene the women leave their homes in Galilee to follow Jesus (15:41) just as the disciples leave their

---

127. Fiorenza, *In Memory of Her*, 320.

128. Fiorenza, *In Memory of Her*, 321, 322. She admits a fear of being arrested for being close to Jesus' tomb but fails to see its implications for unsatisfactory discipleship. Instead she emphasizes that "despite fear and flight the good news of the resurrection is carried on" (322).

129. Other feministic interpretations recognize the negative ending of Mark, but want to defend the women so that they are understood rather than condemned. Phillips asserts that "a liberating reading of the women's failure will investigate how social structures among the disciples contribute to the women's silence from fear" ("Failure of the Women," 225). She contends that the women "do not know that Jesus would not be there but in Galilee because they were not members of the group privileged to learn his plans." Furthermore, the young man deserves some blame since he gives orders, even though he has no clear relationship with the women. That is, "he acts from male privilege which creates no trust or relationship between him and the women that might lead to their acting on what he says." Such blaming misses the point of failed discipleship. Cotes ("Women, Silence, and Fear," 155–59) argues that the women respond fearfully to the command that they should speak in public because of the typical cultural expectations that demand silence in the public arena, but Phillips (230, n. 26) argues against this suggestion.

130. This includes Peter's mother in law, the menstruating woman and the dead girl, the Syrophoenician woman, the widow who places her all in the temple coffers, and the woman who anoints Jesus for his burial. Danove ("Characterization and Narrative Function," 391) contends that the frame between trembling in 5:33 and amazement in 5:42 confirms a negative valuation of the women, i.e., the bleeding woman and dead girl. But Mark employs the sandwich technique here for a different purpose. See section 2.3 above.

131. Juel explains, "The faithful women have the opportunity to do what the men could not. And they fail. They flee, just as the men—because they are afraid" (*Master of Surprise*, 116).

nets and family (1:16–20).¹³² The male disciples learn of Jesus' passion in the three predictions and commemorate Jesus' death symbolically in the Last Supper just as the women watch Jesus' death from a distance (15:40a) and desire to anoint him for his burial (14:8). Similarly, just as the male disciples in their final appearance are unable to watch during Jesus' preparation for passion and flee at his arrest in Gethsemane, so the women disciples flee in fear in the closing scene.¹³³ Finally, just as Peter fails to witness to Jesus during his trial, so the women say nothing to anyone because they fear what Peter did, suffering the same fate as Jesus. A heroic ending does not explain this dynamic and must be rejected.

We have already evaluated in chapter 1 a fifth approach to the ending of Mark, a *polemical apologetic* against the disciples.¹³⁴ In this view "Mark 16:8b is the evangelist's final thrust in his vendetta against the disciples and his commitment to discredit them completely," so that "the silence of the women robs the disciples of their apostolic credentials."¹³⁵ In this explanation Mark employs these false disciples as a foil for the Jerusalem church, who proclaim a *theios-aner* Christology. Although several scholars support Weeden's hypothesis,¹³⁶ this interpretation conflicts with the promise of the angel to the women in 16:7 and the entire history of the church, which stands dependent upon the ministry of the apostles and the women. Mark envisions the future ministry of the disciples after the resurrection positively, as evidenced by their call to be fishers of people (1:17), their authority to preach and cast out demons (3:14–15; 6:7, 12–13), their orders to share the transfiguration story only after Jesus' resurrection (9:9), the assurance that James and John will imitate Jesus in the pattern of his death (10:39), and the expectation that the women will see the resurrected Jesus (16:7). In addition, as Boomershine points out, "The polemical interpretation of the ending carries with it the correlate conclusion that the characterization of the women earlier in the gospel is highly negative."¹³⁷ Therefore, the ending of the gospel is not a polemic against the women themselves but only against their response of flight and silence; instead the women as well as Jesus' family and the disciples become the heroes of the church (Acts 1:13–14).¹³⁸

---

132. Mark's narrative does not employ the word "disciple" for the women, but uses the terms "followed, served, and came up from Galilee with" (ἠκολούθουν; διηκόνουν; συναναβᾶσαι).

133. This pattern can explain the strange repetition of the three women disciples as well (15:40, 47; 16:1). Mark calls attention to them in their successful beginning following from Galilee (15:40), in their closeness to Jesus' suffering through their identification with his burial (15:47), and in the experience of the resurrection where they falter in the absence of Jesus (16:1). Interestingly the inner circle of Peter, James, and John are also mentioned three times: 5:37; 9:2; 14:33.

134. See section 1.2 above.

135. Weeden, *Traditions in Conflict*, 117.

136. See Crossan, Kelber, and Tyson.

137. Boomershine, "Mark 16:8," 233.

138. For five clear additional arguments against this polemical approach see Croy, *Mutilation*, 103–4.

A sixth approach proposes an *eschatological ending* to the gospel, with the *parousia* occurring in Galilee.[139] Marxsen explains that "since Mark 16:7 refers to a future *parousia* in Galilee, the evangelist must conclude with the disciples not finding Jesus but beginning a search."[140] Certainly the rumor of a resurrection would incite eschatological expectations. As Lane states, "It is probable that the fear experienced at the transfiguration and at the empty tomb was an anticipation of judgment. A devout Jew would understand the announcement that the resurrection had begun to signify that the end was at hand."[141] However, an eschatological excitement at Easter cannot be equated with a *parousia* in Galilee. Mark clearly distinguishes between Jesus' resurrection from the dead (5:42; 8:31; 9:9–10, 27, 31; 10:34; 14:58) and the coming of the Son of Man in the last days (8:38; 10:29–31; 13:5ff; 14:62). As Trompf maintains, "To blur this distinction leaves one with the burden of explaining away why Mark understood the 'Messianic Secret' to cease applying after Jesus was risen from the dead (ix. 9) and why the gospel was to be preached to all nations before the Son of Man came."[142] Other explanations of the ending of Mark provide a consistency with the rest of his gospel.

A second group of scholars promotes the alternative view that Galilee becomes the mission headquarters for the Gentile mission.[143] The shepherd/sheep imagery connected with Jesus' initial prediction (14:27) supports a leadership metaphor, not a *parousia* reference.[144] However, since Acts does not confirm Galilee as the origin of the Gentile mission, a less specific conclusion is preferable. Therefore a third proposal of discipleship renewal envisions Mark's purpose most clearly. "At the meeting in Galilee, Jesus will regroup and restore his disciples."[145] Mark 16:7 is a call to return to where the gospel started in Galilee and relive the story, this time not committing the identical mistakes of the disciples but instead heeding the call to a discipleship of the cross.[146]

Juel disagrees with this claim of discipleship renewal and posits a *dialectical ending*. He quips, "If the unresolved ending offers promise, it is surely not because we are encouraged to believe that we can do better than the disciples or the women."[147] Instead the ending raises questions and causes the readers to thoughtfully reflect upon

---

139. Support comes from Conzelmann, Grant, Hamilton, Kelber, Lightfoot, Lohmeyer, Marxsen, Perrin, and Ramsey. See Weeden, *Traditions in Conflict*, 46, n. 41 and 111, n. 13 for the participants in this debate.

140. Marxsen, *Mark the Evangelist*, 116.

141. Lane, *Mark*, 590.

142. Trompf, "First Resurrection Appearance," 318.

143. C. F. Evans ("I Will Go before You," 3–18) follows the lead of Hoskyns ("*Adversaria Exegetica*," 147–55). For an evaluation see Fuller, *Formation of the Resurrection Narratives*, 59–62.

144. Cf. C. F. Evans, *Resurrection*, 81.

145. Williams, "Literary Approaches," 29.

146. See Miller, *Women in Mark's Gospel*, 184 and the writings of Best and Geddert.

147. Juel, *Master of Surprise*, 121.

their own indifference to the gospel. Juel believes that "The ending produces a tension between disappointment and promise, blindness and insight, concealment and openness, silence and proclamation so that one can only live by promises and be satisfied with questions of meaning." Juel's contention is partly based upon his conviction that the problem facing Mark's audience is not persecution and struggle but overconfidence and indifference.[148]

Similarly, Kermode supports an *enigmatic elusive ending* so that Mark's conclusion compares to a Kafka parable which raises thoughtful questions but offers no satisfying answer.[149] However, these two hypotheses sound conspicuously modern rather than ancient in their orientation. Furthermore, the exegetical details point toward an identification of the gospel with a persecution tract and not an address to those who are content with the way things are.[150] This approach fails to take account of the relevance of 13:9–13 to the ending of Mark's gospel.[151] The followers of Jesus will be delivered up to councils, governors, and kings. Family members will betray their own physical kin to death so that everyone will hate the Christians. An enigmatic dialectical ending would not speak authoritatively to such a situation.

Instead of the seven options described above, the ending of the gospel functions as a *Markan narrative surprise* and serves as a *pastoral exhortation*[152] which speaks existentially to Mark's community. The surprise of 16:8 is evidenced in seeming literary contradictions, mixed messages of genre, and conceptual dissonance through the awkward placing together of divergent themes. Mark creates the expectation of a meeting between the disciples and Jesus through the young man's words in 16:7 and then cancels this expectation with the silence of the women in 16:8.[153] The conclusion functions as a "mysterious anti-climax" since it fails "to resolve the tensions in the story and to provide some sense of closure that seems appropriate to 'good news' about Jesus Christ."[154] The strange grammatical ending to the gospel provokes Iverson to ask, "If Mark's intent was to shock his readers contextually (i.e. without a resurrection appearance), why not add a stylistic punch with an unusual concluding γάρ statement?"[155] Even authors who support an alternative view realize the surprising nature of the ending. For instance, France states, "The note of panic is in itself a surprising way for Mark to continue the story, and still more to conclude his whole work. But much more inexplicable is his comment that the women, who have just

---

148. Ibid., 141, 145.

149. Kermode, *Genesis of Secrecy*.

150. See section 6.8 below, "A Possible Scenario Depicting Mark's Community."

151. Wright states that the women are afraid to proclaim the message "for the reasons mentioned in 13:9–11" (*Markan Intercalations*, 206).

152. For evidence for the ending as a pastoral exhortation see section 6.7 below.

153. Williams, "Literary Approaches," 30–31.

154. Juel, *Master of Surprise*, 107, 111.

155. Iverson, "Further Word," 93.

been given a message of supreme importance to deliver, remained silent."[156] Mark awkwardly places together promise and disobedience, anticipation and fear in successive verses (16:7–8). By combining 16:7 and 16:8 into one document Mark's gospel seems to be written both to encourage and to challenge Jesus' fallible followers.[157] We will investigate Mark's purpose in employing this literary device in the next chapter on Markan mirroring. Now we only want to establish the presence of a Markan narrative surprise employed for pastoral reasons.

5.4 An Additional Theme of Misunderstanding Inserted in the Trips across the Sea (Mark 4:40; 6:52)

Markan narrative surprises transform the normal elements of miracle stories. So far we have discussed the omission of the positive response of amazement, the placing of astonishment near the beginning of a vignette rather than as its concluding element, and the transposition of fear into a negative concept instead of epiphanic awe. Finally, we will reveal how Mark attaches the theme of misunderstanding and hardness of heart to the normal response of awe in the trips across the sea.

In order to link together his miracle section (4:35—8:21), Mark narrates three trips across the sea (4:35–41; 6:45–52; 8:13–16) with an increasing emphasis upon misunderstanding and hardness of heart on the part of the disciples (4:40 before the ending of 4:41; 7:52 concluding a pericope; and the lengthier more dramatic addition of 8:17–21). This triad in the miracle section parallels the three passion predictions (8:31; 9:31; 10:32–34) and discipleship misunderstandings (8:32–33; 9:32–34; 10:35–40) in the discipleship catechism which follows. But there the third climatic section consists of discipleship teaching (8:34–38; 9:35–50; 10:41–45) which should remedy the disciples' intensifying misunderstanding and prepare them for Jesus' passion.

The misunderstandings after dynamic miracles fit the pattern of Markan narrative surprises. However, the presence of misunderstanding does not completely obscure the genre of miracle story in the first trip across the sea (4:35–41). The reader still encounters the typical elements of an "introduction of the scene (vv. 35–36); the need (v. 37); the cry for help (v. 38c); the rescue with a miracle-working word (v. 39ab); the demonstration of the miracle (v. 39c); wonder (v. 41a); and acclamation (v. 41bc)."[158] But notice in this sequence the total omission of verse 40, "Why are you so afraid? Do you still have no faith?" The connection of fear and unbelief after the miracle itself finds no place in the structure of a traditional miracle story. This short surprising intrusion into the narrative finds a home before the final acclamation ("Who is this? Even the wind and the waves obey him!") in order to introduce this

---

156. France, *Mark*, 683. Similarly O'Collins, "Fearful Silence," 489.

157. See Williams, "Literary Approaches," 35.

158. Dwyer, *Motif of Wonder*, 110 following Pesch, *Markusevangelium*, 1:269–70. Specifically, the story is a rescue epiphany.

theme without emphasizing it. An intensification of this motif then follows in the last two sea journeys. Therefore, Mark sets two seemingly contradictory themes next to each other—amazement at a mighty miracle and lack of faith as evidenced in hardness of heart—to create surprise and consternation in the readers so that they will read further to perceive how this incongruity is resolved.

Dwyer, however, explains this seeming paradox through the alternative solution of a pattern of intensification of wonder. According to this theory the fear of circumstances in the first crossing intensifies to trepidation in the presence of the divine and finally to an overwhelming sense of awe in the conclusion of the miracle section. Specifically, "in 4.35–41 there is an initial cowardice (the question τί δειλοί ἐστε) at the storm which is rebuked, and then a greater awe follows (4.41)."[159] Likewise, in the sea-walking trip the disciples' initial fear at the sight of a phantom (6:49–50a) is comforted (6:50b) and then a greater awe follows (6:51). This pattern is established already in 5:35–43, where Jairus' implicit fear from the news of his daughter's death brings comfort from Jesus' words (5:36) and results in a greater wonder when Jesus raises his daughter from death (5:42). Dwyer then reads this pattern into the ending of Mark as well so that the reaction of alarm at the young man (16:5 ἐξεθαμβήθησαν), which is soon comforted (μὴ ἐκθαμβεῖσθε), is followed by a greater and more lasting intensification of the wonder in 16:8 (τρόμος καὶ ἔκστασις; ἐφοβοῦντο).[160]

But if intensification of awe is Mark's purpose, why does he end with hardheartedness in 6:52 as well as 8:17–21 and fear and silence in 16:8b? Furthermore, why the interruption of this pattern in 4:40 by the motif of unbelief? Instead this "remarkable consistency"[161] can only be assumed when some exegetical details are omitted. Dwyer connects 4:40 with the question of the disciples (4:38b "Teacher, Don't you care if we drown?") and not the miracle,[162] but then 4:40 should follow directly after 4:38.[163] Is Mark just a sloppy writer who cannot communicate his intentions? No! The distance from 4:38 must be interpreted as purposeful. Fear functions as an expression of the disciples' condition of non-perception.[164] Mark is inserting the theme of unbelief into

---

159. Dwyer, *Motif of Wonder*, 192. There is an intensity of vocabulary (λίαν [ἐκ περισσοῦ] ἐν ἑαυτοῖς ἐξίσταντο λίαν). See Dwyer, 128, n. 153 for a discussion of the textual problem.

160. Dwyer states that "The appearance of Jesus in Galilee is a more awesome and more appropriate wonder than the appearance of the angel and "sums up all the other acts in the gospel" (*Motif of Wonder*, 192). On page 195 he goes so far as to comment that "The motif of wonder there underscores the event in a way which may make an appearance perhaps unnecessary."

161. Ibid., 194.

162. Ibid., 111. Dwyer contends as well that a γάρ clause is necessary in 4:41 rather than a καὶ beginning to make the statement negative, but a γάρ clause would serve as an explanation for 4:40 whereas Mark intends the two verses to stand in tension and therefore employs "and."

163. On the other hand, Gundry states that "fear relates more naturally to their own following question than to his preceding questions; thus, the fear consists of reverential awe before his power rather than of shock at his implicit rebuke" (*Mark*, 244). But again this makes Mark a clumsy writer.

164. Cf. Kingsbury, *Conflict in Mark*, 98.

the sea-calming story just as he concludes with hardness of heart in the sea-walking journey at 6:52.

But why does Mark not finish off both the sea-calming trip and the sea-walking narrative with unbelief? Authors supportive of a consistent positive interpretation argue that Mark would have placed 4:40 last if he understood the disciples' faithlessness as the emphasis.[165] However, the switch from penultimate in 4:40 to ultimate in 6:52 demonstrates an intensification of emphasis, not of awe but of misunderstanding. Therefore Gundry is correct about 4:35–41 that "Failure on the part of the disciples falls far short of forming the main point of the story,"[166] but Mark introduces the theme here to prepare for the unbelief of the disciples in the following journeys as well as the disciples' misunderstanding with regard to the passion predictions in the discipleship catechism.

The sea-walking narrative (6:45–52) concludes with hardness of heart.[167] Dwyer, however, contends that γάρ is not always employed to introduce an explanation of the preceding phrase but refers to the entire pericope.[168] Through this interpretation the disciples' struggle with faith is connected with their failure to recognize Jesus during the storm rather than a failure connected with the bread miracle.[169] But Boomershine provides a more satisfactory analysis of 6:52: "Narrative comments introduced by γάρ are almost always used to explain confusing or surprising events which have been reported in the previous sentence (e.g., 1:16, 22; 2:15; 3:21; 5:8, 28, 42; 6:17, 18, 20, 31, 48; 9:6, 34; 10:22; 11:13; 14:2, 40, 56; 15:10; 16:4, 8)."[170] Therefore 6:51b–52 must be interpreted as a negative fear while the preceding verses (6:49–50) function as a response of awe to a divine epiphany.[171]

Several authors, on the other hand, interpret the response of the disciples after these two journeys as totally negative.[172] Then not only 4:40 but also the final question in 4:41, "Who then is this, that even wind and sea obey him?," must be viewed as a statement made in unbelief. In a similar vein, Fowler envisions a "triple negative commentary in Mark 6:51b–52—the disciples were 'utterly astounded,' 'they did

---

165. Gundry, *Mark*, 247.

166. Ibid., 244.

167. For a demonstration of the close relationship of the two sea-rescue epiphanies through a schematic comparison of 4:35–41 and 6:45–52 see Heil, *Jesus Walking*, 127–29.

168. Dwyer quotes Bird's famous article on γάρ clauses ("Some γάρ Clauses," 186) who cites 1:16–17; 5:42; 10:45; and 11:13 as examples where γάρ does not explain the previous sentence. But Bird's point is that these are allusive γάρ clauses indicating symbolism.

169. Dwyer, *Motif of Wonder*, 132, n. 174 following Tagawa, *Miracles*, 115 and Magness, *Sense and Absence*, 97.

170. Boomershine, "Narrative Technique," 215. Mark 10:45 as well is arguably a response at the end of a pericope to the surprise that the disciples must become slaves (10:44).

171. Mark 6:51b was in all likelihood the original ending of the miracle story concluding in awe, but Mark transforms it into a negative fear through the addition of 6:52.

172. Kelber, *Kingdom of God*, 50. See also Tyson, "Blindness," 262 and Kertelge, *Wunder*, 100. In this case 4:40 would function as Mark's conclusion, not as an insertion before 4:41.

not understand,' 'their hearts were hardened.'"[173] I would agree that the γάρ clause in 6:52 now transforms the response of utter astonishment in 6:51b into a negative response, but the customary form of a miracle story makes it likely that originally ἐξίσταντο connoted a positive response in the oral tradition. Similarly, 4:41 expresses epiphanic fear, but 4:40 conveys faithless fear.[174] Through this procedure Mark is purposely introducing tension into the narrative. In both sea crossings Mark adds a cautionary element (4:40; 6:52) that complicates the situations of awe following great wonders. This ambivalent response[175] of the disciples entails that although Jesus is a miracle working Messiah, this title does not express a full-orbed Christology. The awe acknowledges Jesus as the Messiah, but the fear demonstrates the insufficiency of this confession, just as Peter's insight in 8:29 acknowledges Jesus as the promised Son of David, whereas his misunderstanding in 8:31 demonstrates that an additional confession of Jesus as the Suffering Servant is necessary. This twofold response of the disciples to the miracle stories prepares for Peter's ambivalent reaction to the identity of Jesus. The unusual twists and contrasting information in these trips across the sea make them parabolic and preparatory to what is ahead in Mark's gospel.

What is the purpose of this conflictual material? In the next chapter, on Markan mirroring, we will consider the specific content of the Markan surprise.[176] For the present, we only want to confirm that Mark employs this literary device. The presence of a Markan surprise at 6:52 is reinforced by the complementary surprises within the story of the sea-walking trip. After a surprising ending to the feeding of the five thousand, which omits the conventional acclaim after a powerful miracle, Jesus uncharacteristically compels (ἠνάγκασεν) his disciples to journey without him across the sea. Astoundingly, Jesus possesses the physical acumen to see his disciples (6:48) struggling in the middle of the Sea of Galilee in spite of the great distance and the blackness of a night darkened by a storm.[177] Several details of the narrative portray Jesus as God, which would produce utter amazement to any Jew.[178] Jesus' actions of traversing the waters (Job 9:8) and stilling the sea (Ps 89:9; 107:28–29) remind the community of exploits only Yahweh can perform. From the disciples' vantage point Jesus intends to leave them alone by "passing by" (6:48c), but in reality this terminol-

---

173. Fowler, *Let the Reader Understand*, 240.

174. Broadhead, *Teaching with Authority*, 94 and Lincoln, "Promise and Failure," 285–87.

175. Boomershine and Bartholomew put it this way, "The narrative comment at the end of this story has the ambiguous impact of explaining a surprising response on the part of the disciples with a comment which in turn raises further questions. It is directly parallel in its form and function to the comments in 16:8" ("Narrative Technique," 216).

176. See section 6.3.

177. Only Mark mentions that Jesus saw (ἰδὼν) the disciples. Heil denies any significance to this comment since it "is not reflected upon in the narrative" (*Jesus Walking*, 69, n. 92). But Mark's comment establishes the god-like knowledge of Jesus similar to 6:48b and c and 50b. Cf. Pesch, *Markusevangelium*, 1:360.

178. See Latourelle, *Miracles of Jesus*, 141

ogy alludes to the manifestation of a divine epiphany (Exod 33:19, 22; 34:6; 1 Kgs 19:11). Likewise, Jesus' response ἐγώ εἰμι in 6:50 employs an OT formula of God's self-revelation (Exod 3:14; Isa 43:1–3, 10–11). Finally, it is bewildering that the disciples leave for Bethsaida (6:45) but arrive in Gennesaret (6:53). These surprising narrative details confirm that the disciples' hardness of heart after the calming of the storm in 6:52 is another Markan surprise.

Whereas with miracle stories "fear" traditionally means awe, in Mark the concept of φοβέομαι has become very complicated because he is attempting to speak at two levels. Because of the literary device of a Markan surprise, fear must be understand not only positively as wonder (4:41; 6:51; 16:5) as in the tradition, but also in the same contexts (4:40; 6:52; 16:8) as taking on a negative connotation introduced by Mark himself. Wonder at Jesus' miracles is incomplete until an understanding of Jesus' passion is included in discipleship. Although originally in the Jesus tradition fear is the expected response of awe to divine epiphanies, Mark connects fear with a lack of faith (4:40), incomplete discipleship (9:6; 16:8), and an insufficient understanding of Jesus' identity (6:52; 9:32; 10:32).

5.5 Surprising Twists in the Narrative

In addition to his surprising transformations of the genre of miracle story, Mark also inserts unexpected twists into the drama of the narrative. We will explicate eight examples in this section.

In Jesus' very first sermon in the synagogue, the sacred place of Jewish worship, an evil spirit manifests itself and offers spiritual resistance to Jesus. Certainly the reader would expect the presence of demons in Gentile territories like the Decapolis (5:1–2), Tyre (7:24–25) or the region of Caesarea Philippi (tying 9:17 with 8:27), in waterless desert wastelands (Matt 12:43; Luke 8:29; 11:24; Rev 18:2), or in the abyss (Rev 9:1; 11:7; 20:1, 3; Luke 8:31), but on Jesus' first day of ministry demons surprisingly appear in the synagogue.[179] This incident evidences the pollution and contamination of the Promised Land. Since the land is in exile, Canaan must be retaken as in the time of Joshua (LXX Jesus). Therefore, Jesus travels "throughout Galilee, preaching in their synagogues and driving out demons" (1:39). Even the worship centers are captivated by Satan's presence so that Israel must be cleansed by a baptism of repentance (1:4–5) and re-established through kingdom preaching and signs (1:15). What message does Mark intend to preach through this narrative surprise? In chapter 7 we will investigate how through mirroring Mark demonstrates that both Jews and Gentiles are included in God's kingdom by means of exorcisms in Jewish as well as Gentile territory.[180]

---

179. It is so surprising that Boring concludes "It is historically unlikely that a demoniac would be present in the synagogue service" (*Mark*, 63, n. 7).

180. See section 7.4 below.

Suffice it here to say that through the literary device of a narrative surprise Mark is offering a symbolic message.

A second narrative surprise occurs in the healing of the leper in 1:40–45. Normally only confrontations with Satan necessitate an exorcist's rebuke and the silencing of the spirit within the person delivered, but in 1:43–44 after the healing of a leper Jesus issues a strong warning as to a demon (ἐξέβαλεν) and a command to silence. Jesus' compassion for the leper (1:41) quickly turns to snorting like a disturbed horse (1:43). Despite the kingdom implications of this great miracle, the leper is surprisingly forbidden to tell anyone that Jesus cleansed him. Finally, an additional surprise follows close on its heels when the leper disobeys Jesus, the ultimate authority figure in the gospel, and spreads the news of Jesus' fame freely throughout the entire area anyway (1:45). In the process it appears that the cleansed leper refuses to visit the priest for confirmation as Moses commanded. One surprise after another structures the narrative. Therefore Mark employs two literary devices in this passage, a frame and a surprise, to offer a theological meaning to this event.

What are the implications of this Markan surprise? We will observe in chapter 7 that the surprise of disobeying Jesus and spreading his fame occurs likewise in Gentile territory at 7:36. Similarly, the other commands to silence after miracles occur in 5:43 in Jewish territory, where Jairus is a synagogue ruler, and in 8:26 at Bethsaida, which is Gentile territory as evidenced by the reference to Greeks in John 12:20–21. Jesus' gospel of the kingdom incorporates both Jews and Gentiles. Then in chapter 8 we will exhibit how both a Markan frame around the five Jewish controversies of 2:1—3:6 and the surprise that Jesus touches a leper together reveal that the OT impurity legislation is now fulfilled because of Jesus' kingdom action. In addition to the christological emphasis present in a miracle story, we discover Jesus' defense of the Christian contention that Gentiles are a part of God's community and that now the OT Jewish purity rites have a new interpretation.[181]

We encounter a third narrative surprise in 7:24–30, where a Gentile woman wins a face-to-face confrontation against the authoritative wisdom of Jesus. In other narratives the onlookers stand amazed at Jesus' argumentative skills (12:17) and dare not confront him (12:34). Here, however, all of Jesus' plans and intentions surrender to the will of this Gentile woman who challenges him head on. First, Jesus' desire to remain incognito is overturned (7:24), and then his refusal to bestow bread to anyone but Jewish children is reversed (7:27–28). By implication the narrative transforms a Gentile "dog" into a participant at the family table.[182] The regulation that "it is not right to take the children's bread and toss it to their dogs" is eliminated. Since this is the only exorcism where the healing is described in the perfect tense (7:29 ἐξελήλυθεν)

---

181. See sections 7.5 and 8.7 below.

182. For cultural connotations included in the term "dog" see Cotter, *Christ of the Miracle Stories*, 152–53.

rather than the aorist (1:25, 26; 5:13; 9:25, 26, 29), even the grammar applauds the faith of this Gentile woman.[183]

The parenthetical statement at 7:26, "And the woman was a Greek, a Syrophoenician by birth," reinterprets a healing narrative into a Jew/Gentile dialogue. The request and bestowal of healing (7:26, 29–30) surround the more profound dialogue at the center of the pericope advocating a new Jew/Gentile relationship (7:27–28). Kelber notes that "the focus of interest falls entirely on the auxiliary motif of request" so that the story could be entitled "The Two Requests Parable."[184] The request for healing of her daughter is accompanied by the more prominent application for table fellowship between Jews and Gentiles. Therefore, Mark transforms a miracle story into an allegorical riddle where the dogs represent Gentiles, children denote Jews, and bread symbolizes table fellowship. Jesus' legislation that "it is not right to take the children's bread and toss it to their dogs" impersonates the typical Jewish response to a Gentile. This uncharacteristic response of Jesus, as evidenced by the preceding passage where Jesus teaches that only inward character issues make one unclean (7:20–23), offers further support that this passage is a Markan narrative surprise. The conclusion there that all food is kosher (7:19b) parallels the new situation of table fellowship between Jews and Gentiles. Therefore, the narrative surprise involves the switch in Jesus' attitude toward the woman from apparent racist insensitivity and public insult to acclaim and admiration.[185] In the end the Gentile's faith surprisingly calls forth an entirely new relationship between Jews and Gentiles.

A fourth narrative surprise occurs in the wording of the feeding of the four thousand. After witnessing the feeding of a multitude of five thousand in 6:34–44, the disciples pose a strange question in 8:4: "But where in this remote place can anyone get enough bread to feed them?" Already in the nineteenth century Gould labeled this detail a "psychological impossibility"[186] since feeding four thousand would not be more difficult that supplying the needs of five thousand. In addition, the structural similarities between the two feeding narratives is overwhelmingly unnatural for two separate historical events.

Large size of the crowd	6:34a	8:1
Jesus' compassion	6:34b	8:2a
Length of time since their last meal	6:35a	8:2b
Jesus calls the disciples to get involved.	6:35b	8:2c
The crowd cannot be sent away to get food.	6:36	8:3
The disciples cannot solve the problem.	6:37	8:4
Jesus' question: How many loaves do you have?	6:38a	8:5a

---

183. See ibid., 157.
184. Kelber, *Oral and Written Gospel*, 48.
185. Bailey, *Jesus through Middle Eastern Eyes*, 217.
186. Gould, *St. Mark*, 142.

The disciples' answer	6:38b	8:5b
Jesus instructs the people to sit down.	6:39a	8:6a
A prayer using the terms "bless" or "give thanks"	6:41a	8:6b
Jesus breaks the bread.	6:41b	8:6c
Jesus gives the bread to the disciples for distribution.	6:41c	8:6d
The same process with the fish is repeated.	6:41d	8:7
The people eat and are satisfied.	6:42a	8:8a
The amount left over	6:43	8:8b
The specific number of people fed	6:44	8:9
They leave by boat for another place.	6:45	8:10

To explain this phenomenon Fowler reports that "The most common critical strategy has been to claim that the stupidity displayed in 8:4 is the accidental by-product of the flesh-and-blood author's careless use of two different versions of the same story."[187] But is this merely the awkward product of an incompetent editor?

Instead of the common source-critical solution, Fowler employs literary criticism and entitles this an instance of dramatic irony: "The author develops a strong ironic tension between the two feeding stories by having the disciples show their lack of understanding not once but twice." The purpose of this irony is to "get the reader to see certain things the author's way, by covert, indirect means."[188] I call this phenomenon another instance of a narrative surprise.[189] In either case, the first step in interpreting such a device is that "the reader is required to reject the literal meaning."[190] The disciples' response is not just a case of simple amnesia.[191] Through this device Mark is calling attention to the obtuseness of the disciples concerning an important theme in his gospel. The repetition of the theme of hardness of heart in 6:52 and then again at the end of this section in 8:17–21 confirms this hypothesis.

What is Mark's purpose in employing this surprising repetition? As we have demonstrated in chapter 4, the Markan repetition between the two feedings and the Last Supper points to Jesus as both the glorious wonder-worker and the crucified Christ whom the disciples are not able to follow. Now we enjoy the additional evidence of a narrative surprise. In chapter 7 we will demonstrate how this further indicates that both Jews and Gentiles will eat at the messianic feast.[192] Again Mark employs literary devices to speak to problems in the Christian community, including the following of a crucified Messiah and the inclusion of Gentiles in table fellowship.

187. Fowler, *Loaves and Fishes*, 217.
188. Ibid., 11. See page 217 as well.
189. Fowler (*Let the Reader Understand*, 141) also labels it a surprise.
190. Fowler, *Loaves and Fishes*, 94 following Booth, *Rhetoric of Irony*, 10.
191. Also regarding 8:19–20 Hugh Anderson proposes that such "a lapse of memory so shortly after two amazing miracles of feeding is inconceivable" (*Gospel of Mark*, 202).
192. See section 7.6 below.

A fifth surprising twist in the narrative occurs in the continual amnesia of the disciples in 8:14: "The disciples had forgotten to bring bread." But then suddenly Mark seems to backtrack and negate this fact by stating "except for one loaf" (εἰ μὴ ἕνα ἄρτον). Again, is Mark just a bungling incompetent author? No! This Markan surprise reveals a theological point that Mark is emphasizing.[193]

Grassi believes that the one loaf represents the united community of Jews and Gentiles based upon his interpretation of the leaven of the Pharisees and Herod (8:15). This leaven of the Pharisees "may be their separatist teaching about table fellowship which made it impossible for Jews and Greeks to share one bread. The same may be true of Herod and his followers who kept Jews and Gentiles secluded from one another in separate communities and cities."[194] However, since the Pharisees are demanding a sign like the feeding of the multitudes, the leaven of the Pharisees in this context is the demand for miracles just as Herod is captivated by Jesus' miracles (6:14; Luke 23:8 "perform a sign"). As we have demonstrated in the last chapter on Markan allusionary repetitions, instead of a miracle feeding Mark proclaims that the true nourishment comes through the breaking of Jesus' body at the Last Supper and on the cross. Therefore, the one loaf of bread that the disciples are ignoring in the sea conversation (8:14) is Jesus in the power of his passion.[195] As Donfried explains, "What the disciples should already have perceived and understood in Mark 6 and 8 by way of anticipation is now made clear in 14,22ff. The bread symbolizes Jesus as the body, as the one who becomes a ransom for many by means of his death."[196] Through the sea conversation the disciples are warned that they can become outsiders by treating miracles as the needed leaven. Although the disciples are insiders because of their special calling (1:16–20), special relationship with Jesus (3:13–14, 34–35), special instructions (4:11–12), and special mission (6:7–12), they become outsiders because they do not understand (8:17, 21) or remember (8:18), and their hearts are hardened (8:17) like the opponents of 3:5. The surprise therefore involves the double theme of Jesus' passion and the disciples' inability to see that Jesus will supply their needs for the discipleship journey when they follow him in his passion rather than look for miracle signs. Instead of demanding that God keep performing mighty deeds whenever they want them, the disciples as well as the readers must accept the sufficiency of the cross.

---

193. Stock states that "the translation 'no bread' is nonsensical when it has just been stated that they had one loaf with them in the boat" (*Call to Discipleship*, 127). See also Beck, "Reclaiming a Biblical Text," 53.

194. Grassi, *Loaves and Fishes*, 43. Boucher (*Mysterious Parable*, 81) combines a Christological with a Jew/Gentile interpretation: "Jesus is the one bread which is broken and given to both Jews and Gentiles (8:14–21)."

195. Boring (*Mark*, 226) points out that Jesus is specifically identified with the bread in 14:22 in a context where unleavened bread is important.

196. Donfried, "Feeding Narratives," 102.

For our sixth example Wenham summarizes the surprising difficulties in interpreting the parable of the doorkeeper in 13:34–36 and fitting it into Mark's context.[197]

1. The parable begins as a normal comparison with a man leaving on a journey, but we never hear what happened to the servants or the watchman since 13:35 suddenly begins a hortatory application.

2. The reader is left with the impression that the journey will be extensive and prolonged, but the watching appears to be over after a single night.

3. In 13:34a the focus is first on the master's servants in the plural but immediately narrows to the doorkeeper in the singular in 13:34b so that the other servants are treated as irrelevant.

4. Grammatical oddities include the use of ἐξουσίαν (authority) in 13:34 with servants and the difficulty of connecting two participles (13:34 ἀφείς; δούς) with καί to an indicative verb (ἐνετείλατο).

To explain these surprises, Wenham offers the traditional solution of a combination of various parables,[198] but Geddert points out that this explains "'how it happened' not 'why it was done.'"[199] Geddert then proceeds to offer a solution that appropriately fits the parable into the context of the passion narrative and a Markan theology of the cross:

> That the parable never really gets told is well explained by the fact that he intends to portray the real 'parable' from 14.17—15.15. That the focus shifts from a long journey to a single night is well explained by the fact that, although a long absence is in view on the primary level, Mark knows he intends to portray at a more subtle level the one crucial paradigmatic eschatologically-significant night during which one kept watch faithfully while the others all failed at their posts. That there is a shift from servants (plural) to a single servant (and specifically a door keeper), is explained by the fact that in the final Day and Hour there will be many servants, with Jesus playing the role of the master, but in the impending passion he will be portrayed as a servant, and specifically as a faithful doorkeeper.[200]

Thus Mark uses the parable to prepare for the passion narrative, as evidenced as well by the time designations in 13:35. In all likelihood the community's struggles with readiness to suffer also play an important role. Traditionally, Jews marked off the night

---

197. Wenham, *Rediscovery of Jesus' Eschatological Discourse*, 18. For a summary see Geddert, *Watchwords*, 92–93.

198. Mark employs the Parable of the Talents (Matt 25:13–15) and then switches over to the Parable of the Watchman (Luke 12:36–38).

199. Geddert, *Watchwords*, 94.

200. Ibid., 93.

into three watches (Luke 12:38), but Mark's employment of four watches (13:35) can be explained as an application to the suffering of Christians under Nero in Rome.[201]

With regard to our seventh narrative surprise, we have already observed in chapter 2 that Mark employs an intercalation to link the cursing of the fig tree with the "cleansing" or "reform" of the temple and thus transforms the passage into a symbolic action of the "destruction" of the temple. Here we will highlight Mark's use of a narrative surprise in two prominent descriptions: 1) Jesus curses a fig tree even though it is not the season for figs (11:13); and 2) the tree withers from its roots rather than the normal procedure of wilting leaves (11:21). Collins further remarks that "It is odd that Jesus is depicted as hungry, since the narrative context implies that he had enjoyed hospitality in Bethany. Finally, it is odd that the disciples are not portrayed as hungry as well."[202] The best explanation for these surprising details is Mark's addition of a symbolic interpretation to the narrative.[203]

Broadhead notes that "The simple information—'for it was not the season for figs'—creates a deconstructive break in the logic of the narrative."[204] From this conclusion some exegetes attempt to solve this dilemma by emending the grammar, denoting it a gloss, or repunctuating the saying with a question mark.[205] On the other hand, Gundry adopts a literal horticultural interpretation so that Jesus is seeking edible buds rather than fruit.[206] France posits a simple hope on Jesus' part that the fruit was further advanced than normal at this time of year.[207] The eschatological messianic explanation envisions Jesus' expectation of a continuous harvest which would signal the end of the age and the presence of the Messiah.[208] But if this verse is another example of a Markan narrative surprise, then "The unexpected and incongruous character of Jesus' action in looking for figs at a season when no fruit could be found would stimulate curiosity and point beyond the incident to its deeper significance."[209]

What is this deeper symbolic significance? The solution must be linked with the second surprise whereby the fig tree wastes away from its roots. Whereas Jeremiah had prophesized that the leaves of the fig tree of Israel would wither (8:13), now the

---

201. See section 6.8 below, "A Possible Scenario Depicting Mark's Community."

202. Collins, *Mark*, 525.

203. Cranfield explains that "an element of the unexpected and incongruous, which would stimulate curiosity, was a characteristic feature of the symbolic actions of the Old Testament prophets (e.g. Jer. xiii.1f, xix. 1f.)" (*St. Mark*, 354). See also Gray, *Temple in the Gospel*, 41.

204. Broadhead, *Teaching with Authority*, 169.

205. See Evans, *Mark 8:27—16:20*, 155–56 for examples.

206. Gundry, *Mark*, 673. Cf. Witherington, *Mark*, 352.

207. France, *Mark*, 440. Pliny the Elder (*Naturalis Historia* 16:49) notes that the fig tree stands out as a tree that produces fruit before leaves. Hunzinger (*TDNT* 7:753) suggests that the fig tree produces two crops, one from late May into June and a larger harvest from the end of August into October.

208. See Derrett, "Figtrees," 253–54; Hiers, "Not the Season for Figs," 395–97; and Telford, *Barren Temple*, 196.

209. Lane, *Mark*, 400. Cf. Blomberg, "Miracles as Parables," 332 and Broadhead, *Teaching with Authority*, 173.

destruction is more pervasive so that Jesus' action symbolizes the rejection of Jewish leaders and the ruin of the temple. It is not the season for figs because the temple establishment is not producing fruit but instead has withered from its roots. Therefore, desiring fruit from the tree metaphorically signifies Jesus' desire for the righteous fruit of Israel.[210] However, it is not the season for fruit since the time of the temple is over and its cult and ritual have been suspended. These surprises fit perfectly with a categorization of the narrative as a prophetic action. In chapter 8 we will demonstrate how Mark employs these narrative surprises to demonstrate that the temple has been destroyed in Jesus' death and has become rebuilt in the person of Jesus and his new community.

A final surprising twist in the narrative focuses on 12:28–34. Previously the Pharisees and the teachers of the law have in every case been portrayed negatively.[211] But in 12:34 Jesus surprisingly praises a member of the religious establishment and proclaims that he is "not far from the kingdom of God." Since this detail protrudes strikingly from Mark's canvass, we must suspect a narrative surprise pointing the reader toward a deeper theological message. Therefore, Loader concludes that "The scribe mouths an important truth which justifies the abandonment of the temple as a sacrificial system."[212] Jesus specifically mentions the kingdom because through his proclamation of the kingdom the OT ceremonial laws and institutions are fulfilled. This is the content of the Markan narrative surprise. In chapter 8 we will explain how this passage fits a Markan pattern of providing the reader a hermeneutic to reinterpret the OT purity legislation.[213]

5.6 The Synoptic Alterations of Later Gospel Writers

The presence of narrative surprises becomes especially prominent when we investigate how the later gospel writers transformed texts because of the difficulty in understanding Mark's subtle literary techniques.[214] All but one of the previous examples are altered in some format.

In Jesus' first sermon the forces of darkness surprisingly manifest their abode in the synagogue (1:23), the center of Jewish religious worship and education. This confirms for Mark the message of John the Baptizer that all must experience a baptism of repentance since the land of Israel stands in spiritual exile. Later Mark narrates exorcisms in Gentile territory, employing similar vocabulary to substantiate a ministry

---

210. Ernst, *Markus*, 325; Giesen, "Der verdotted Feigenbaum," 103; Goppelt, *TDNT* 6:20.

211. Mark 1:22; 2:6, 16; 3:22; 7:1, 5; 8:31; 9:14; 10:33; 11:18, 27; 12:38; 14:1, 53; 15:1, 31. Mark 9:11 and 12:35 can be interpreted as neutral. See Stein, *Mark*, 87.

212. Loader, *Jesus' Attitude*, 101.

213. See section 8.5 below.

214. Achtemeier states "A combination of noting Marcan emphases and Matthean and Lucan changes is an instructive way of determining where Mark's intention ... lay" ("He Taught," 472).

to Gentiles as well. Matthew skips over this incident and so misses Mark's vocabulary ties with the exorcism in the Decapolis (5:1–20). For Matthew the Gentile mission begins after the resurrection (10:5; 15:24), but for Mark Jesus' actions already begin the incorporation of Gentiles into the new Israel through the retaking of the entire land of Canaan.

With regard to the leper who Jesus compassionately heals (Mark 1:41) but then abruptly evicts from his presence like a demon (1:43), both Matthew (8:1–4) and Luke (5:12–16) omit the mention of Jesus' compassion as well as his eviction with a snort. Matthew alone drops the leper's disobedience of Jesus through his proclamation of the good news. Therefore, both Matthew and Luke simplify the narrative and miss Mark's application to Jewish cleanliness rites, whereby Jesus rather than the Jewish leaders becomes the authority who removes the impurity out of leprosy.[215]

It is surprising that only in one case (3:21) does Mark alter the traditional use of ἐξίστημι as amazement and astonishment to "losing one's mind,"[216] thus treating Jesus' family as outsiders (3:31–32). This narrative surprise becomes Mark's method to address those in his community where brother has betrayed brother to death and children have rebelled against their parents and had them put to death (13:12). Matthew and Luke do not employ this literary mirroring and therefore expunge Mark 3:21 and the intercalation so that blood relationships are not appraised negatively. Luke 8:19–21 in fact positions Jesus' encounter with his family after the parable of the sower so that they become positive examples of those who bear abundant fruit by hearing and doing God's word. This alteration by the other evangelists calls attention to the uniqueness of Mark's pericope.

Matthew 8:27 removes the lack of the disciples' faith in Mark 4:40 so that only a marveling response to the sea calming miracle remains: "What sort of man is this, that even the winds and sea obey him?" Instead, Jesus categorizes his disciples as men of little faith (ὀλιγόπιστοι) immediately following their complaint that they are about to perish (Matt 8:25). This adjustment in the flow of the narrative separates the disciple's fear (δειλοί) and lack of faith from the miracle itself. Luke 8:25 maintains the lack of faith emphasis after the miracle but combines the response of fear with marveling (ἐθαύμασαν) instead of lack of faith so that now the disciples' response of fear is entirely positive. Thus the Markan surprise is lost in both cases.

Similarly, in the sea-walking journey Matthew (14:33) removes the hard-heartedness of the disciples specified in Mark 6:52. In addition, Matthew appends the anecdote of Peter walking on the water and his deficient faith (14:31) so that the missing element is specified as miracle faith. In fact, at several points Matthew emphasizes the need for miracle faith (14:28; 17:20; 21:21–22; the use of ὀλιγόπιστος at 6:30; 8:26; 14:31; 16:8). Mark, however, lies on the opposite end of the theological spectrum by

---

215. See section 8.7 below.

216. We have not dealt with this Markan surprise in this chapter since we have exegeted this passage while discussing Markan frames in section 3.5 above.

emphasizing that an experience of the cross must accompany resurrection faith, just as a miracle-working Messiah is insufficient Christology if not accompanied by a Suffering Servant Son of God. Mark assigns a negative response to the disciples (6:52) after the miracle itself to bring this theme to the foreground.

Although Matthew sandwiches together the episodes of the menstruating woman and the deceased girl as in Mark 5:21–43, he does not mention that the father is a ruler of the synagogue (5:22, 38) or that the age of the girl is twelve years (5:42). Through these omissions Matthew misses Mark's application of these stories to Jewish ceremonial legislation. Only Mark employs this intercalation to override the traditional Jewish interpretation of the OT regarding uncleanness through contact with bloody discharges or dead corpses.[217] In addition, Matthew 9:26 concludes the pericope like a traditional miracle story, "the report of this went through all the district," removing the Messianic Secret. Through this procedure Mark's theme of the insufficiency of a miracle-working Jesus is not reproduced.

Matthew's transformation of Mark 7:24–30 centers upon the insertion of Jesus' primary focus of ministry to "the lost sheep of Israel" (Matt 15:24; 10:6). Through this detail Matthew demonstrates that Jesus fulfilled God's end-time call to minister to Israel so that their rejection of the Messiah (Matt 21:28—23:39) results in the opening of Israel to Gentiles as well (28:19–20). Mark, on the other hand, desires to emphasize that Jesus himself offers table fellowship to Gentiles just as he transforms eating rituals so that all foods are kosher (Mark 7:19b).

The sole Markan narrative surprise that is not changed by the later gospel writers is the "psychological impossibility" of the disciples' question after the feeding of the four thousand in Mark 8:4. The replication in Matthew 15:33 might lead to the conclusion that these so-called Markan surprises are just a modern invention, were it not for the totally different reflection that the other gospels offer on the feedings. Matthew eliminates Mark's comment about the feeding of the five thousand in Mark 6:52, "for they did not understand about the loaves," and alters it into the positive confession of faith, "Truly you are the Son of God" (Matt 15:33). Similarly, following the feeding of the four thousand the disciples finally understand that the yeast Jesus warned against was the teaching of the Pharisees and Sadducees (Matt 16:12). Mark's pericope concludes only with misunderstanding (8:17–21). Matthew completely overlooks Mark's employment of a narrative surprise whereby he warns his obtuse and obdurate audience against seeking miracles instead of following to the cross.

In the third gospel Mark's yeast of the Pharisees pericope (Mark 8:15 at Luke 12:1b) follows a Lukan insertion (11:53—12:1a) into a Q sequence of material. We can discern that the crowd of many thousands (Luke 12:1a) recalls Luke's omitted narrative of the feeding of the four thousand (Mark 8:1–9) since Luke inserts precisely at this point "there is nothing hidden that will not be known" (Luke 12:2), which reminds one of Mark 8:17–21. However, Luke transforms the obtuseness and obduracy

---

217. See section 8.6 below.

of the disciples into revelatory insight (Luke 12:2–3). In addition, the leaven of the Pharisees becomes hypocrisy rather than the seeking of miracles as in Mark. Therefore, Luke as well as Matthew overlooks the Markan surprise which emphasizes the misunderstanding of the disciples.

The sea conversation trip (Mark 8:14) occurs within this same context concluding in an interrogation of the disciples through a sequence of ten questions which reveal their misunderstanding of the miracles Jesus has performed (8:17–21). But Matthew 16:5 excises the phrase "have one loaf" from Mark 8:14 so that the disciples simply forgot to take any bread. As a result the surprising tension between having one loaf but not bringing any bread along for the trip is no longer noticeable. Furthermore, whereas Mark 8:17–21 is cryptic,[218] Matthew's version is clear and to the point as Countryman explains: "There is no stray loaf, dragged like a red herring across the path. Jesus does not rail at his disciples, and his reference to the two feedings concentrates on their miraculous quality, not on their statistics."[219] In Mark 8:19–20 the disciples recall the number of baskets filled with leftover food, twelve and seven, but they are baffled concerning Jesus' meaning. Instead, in Matthew 16:9 the disciples do not answer Jesus' questions because they have no memory of the incidents. Absentminded forgetfulness replaces hardhearted blindness. This explains Matthew's duplicate narration of the disciples' dilemma about obtaining food in the desert at both 14:15–17 and 15:33. Matthew understands their forgetfulness literally, whereas Mark places a metaphorical meaning on the incident. Matthew and Luke's consistency in altering the passages about bread indicates that Mark is employing a narrative surprise, whereas the other gospel writers want to clarify or interpret the accounts with a more transparent meaning.

Only Mark recites the two-step healing of the blind man (8:22–26), which follows immediately after Jesus' interrogation of the disciples' sightlessness. Matthew seems uncomfortable with both the lack of instantaneousness of the healing (compare Matt 21:19–20 with Mark 11:21) as well as the employment of spit (Mark 7:43; 8:23). But Mark employs both of these features metaphorically so that the two-stage healing becomes a parable for the appropriate christological confession needed from Peter (8:27–34).[220] The use of spit recalls the healing of the deaf-mute in a similar fashion, where the context of Mark 7 with consecutive passages about clean hands (7:1–13), clean food (7:14–23), clean people (7:24–30), and clean fluids (7:31–37) indicates that Mark is championing a new reading of the OT whereby Jesus provides purity through his healing ministry rather than through certain ceremonial rites.[221] The surprising

---

218 Marcus states, "even in a puzzling work such as Mark, our passage is singularly cryptic" (*Mark*, 512).

219. Countryman, "How Many Baskets Full?" 644.

220. See section 3.8 above.

221. See section 8.8 below.

alteration from a miracle story to a discipleship parable and its use as a frame reveal that Mark is adding a secondary metaphorical meaning.

With regard to the healing of Bartimaeus,[222] Mark concludes the pericope (10:46–52) with the climax, "he followed Jesus along the way," an emphasis upon a discipleship of the cross.[223] Luke, on the other hand, maintains the genre of miracle story by a concluding acclamation where all the people glorify God (18:43). Both Luke 18:43 and Matthew 20:34 delete the metaphor of the way (ὁδός), which Mark employs to bond together the discipleship catechism with an inclusio (Mark 8:27; 10:52). Therefore, only in Mark do the literary devices of a narrative surprise and a frame work together to provide a theological message centering on Jesus' passion and a discipleship of the cross.

The identical conclusion holds for the remaining narrative surprises in the discipleship catechism. We have discovered how Matthew transforms Mark's transfiguration narrative with the misunderstanding at the center by positioning a positive response by the disciples (Matt 17:4) after the epiphany of Jesus' shining face (17:2) and a worshipful prostration of awe (17:6) following the voice from the cloud (17:5). Luke rewrites the escapade as the beginning of Jesus' exodus from this earth (Luke 9:31), culminating in the ascension which is the hinge of Luke-Acts. More importantly, Luke transposes the fear of the three disciples to their entry into the cloud (Luke 9:34) instead of connecting it with their wrong response of wanting to stay in the glory of this mountaintop experience (Mark 9:5–6). Therefore, both Matthew and Luke miss the Markan surprise. Luke eliminates Jesus' conversation with his disciples about his passion on the journey down the mountain as well (Mark 9:11–13) so that their fear of the passion is completely overlooked. Therefore, Mark's intention of paralleling the yearning of the disciples to remain on the mountain with the authorial community's craving for a miracle epiphany instead of a discipleship of the cross is not communicated.

In the healing of the epileptic boy (9:14–29), Mark's transfer of the crowd's amazement to the beginning of the narrative is eliminated by Matthew 17:14 whereas

---

222. The name Bartimaeus seemingly emanates from a compound word, half Aramaic (*bar*) and half Greek (Τιμαῖος), and is therefore another Markan surprise that signifies he is speaking theologically. The name of the father, Timaeus, precedes the son, Bartimaeus whereas in all comparable cases in Mark (1:19; 2:14; 3:17, 18; 10:35) the opposite order occurs so that the name of the father attracts more than the usual attention. Therefore, Mark is deliberately constructing a Greek-Aramaic wordplay, inverting the Aramaic אמט ('unclean') into the Greek "highly prized." Cf. Collins, *Mark*, 509; van Iersel, *Mark*, 340; and Mack, *Mark and Christian Origins*, 297, n. 2. In addition, Hilgert ("Son of Timaeus," 191), Tolbert (*Sowing the Gospel*, 189, n. 21), and van Iersel (*Mark*, 342) think that Mark is alluding to *Timaeus*, one of the principal dialogues of Plato, to capture the theme of Gentiles, but I doubt if a Greco-Hellenistic background is important to Mark. Its placement directly before the triumphal entry into Jerusalem along with the address of Jesus as "Son of David" (10:47, 48) emphasizes the Jewish nature of the passage.

223. Collins asserts, "Although Bartimaeus had not heard that teaching as a character in the narrative, the audiences know that 'to follow Jesus on the way' means to follow him to suffering and death" (*Mark*, 511).

Luke 9:43 transfers it back to its natural placement at the conclusion of the healing. Mark's narrative consummates on prayer (9:29), which is understood by Mark as the discipleship activity of calling the presence of Jesus into any situation.[224] However, Matthew highlights a different aspect of prayer, namely the expectation of divine miracles through faith, and so concludes with a rebuke against insufficient faith (17:20a) followed by an encouragement toward mountain-moving faith so that "nothing will be impossible for you" (17:20b).[225] Luke, on the other hand, ends the pericope like a conventional miracle story with "and all were astonished at the greatness of God" (9:43). Thus both Matthew and Luke in different ways lose the surprising discipleship emphasis in Mark.

Instead of following Mark's attachment of a fear statement to Jesus' second passion prediction (9:32), Matthew reports that the disciples are "filled with grief" (17:23). Therefore, Matthew includes a natural response of distress over Jesus' upcoming death rather than the Markan motif of misunderstanding the importance of Jesus' death and blindness to the implications of following Jesus. Likewise, Matthew transforms the disciple's desire for greatness into a question (18:1). In this way Matthew consistently presents the disciples in a positive light as possessing an intelligent grasp of Jesus' teaching so that in Matthew 13 the verb συνίημι (comprehend) is employed six times (13:13, 14, 15, 19, 23, 51), climaxing in the disciples' understanding of the parables, whereas Mark uses the term in his parable discourse only in 4:12. Luke, on the other hand, emphasizes divine concealment (9:45 "It was hidden from them so that they did not grasp it") so that God's action is emphasized rather than discipleship failure. Likewise with regard to Mark 10:32, Matthew (20:17) completely obliterates Mark's attachment of fear and amazement to Jesus' third passion prediction. Again Luke inserts the motif of divine concealment (18:34), which removes a discipleship emphasis. Therefore, each later evangelist overlooks the Markan surprise at 9:32 and 10:32.

In the cursing of the fig tree narrative Matthew again erases the two Markan surprises. He disregards the phrase "it was not the season for figs" (Mark 11:13 vs. Matt 21:19a), and the withering happens instantly (Matt 21:19b) so that the process of shriveling "from its roots up" (NLB) is likewise ignored. Through these transformations the story becomes easier to understand, but it loses its symbolic overtones. Luke and John, on the other hand, exclude the story altogether. Matthew's omission of these surprises as well as the intercalation indicates that he is not linking the temple action and the cursing of the fig tree together and thus overlooks Mark's theological interpretation.

Of all the controversy dialogues in the gospels, only in Mark 12:28–34 is the opponent complimented.[226] In fact, he is not far from the kingdom of God (12:34).

---

224. See section 6.5 below.

225. Many texts include Mark 9:29 at Matt 17:21 (also the NKJV and ISV), but Codex Vaticanus and the original hand of Codex Sinaiticus support its exclusion (as well as internal evidence).

226. Mark 12:17b does report that the Pharisees and Herodians are amazed at Jesus' answer, but

However, in Matthew 22:35 and Luke 10:25 the teacher of the law receives a negative connotation by asking a question to test Jesus so that any applause is expunged. Matthew even hints at a conspiracy by the Pharisees (22:34) so that the scribe becomes their prosecutor who will outwit Jesus with his arguments. Mark's rationale for the scribe's closeness to the kingdom of God reveals his special intention for including this passage in his gospel. According to the scribe, the teaching of the law (only in Mark) concludes that to love God and one's neighbor "is more important than all burnt offerings and sacrifices" (12:33). Through this narrative surprise Mark is again offering a reinterpretation of the OT ceremonial law and replacing sacrifices with love.[227] This is a singular emphasis of Mark through the employment of a narrative surprise.

Matthew, Mark, and Luke roughly parallel each other for most of the eschatological discourse (Matt 24:1–36; Mark 13:1–32; Luke 21:5–33) and then suddenly diverge and go their separate ways. As Wenham explains, "Mark has a short semi-parabolic section of exhortation to wakefulness (13:33–37); Luke too has a section of exhortation, but it is quite different from Mark's (Luke 21:34–36); Matthew has a much longer conclusion consisting largely of parables (24:42—25:30)."[228] Why would the other gospels suddenly abandon their source? Mark links the eschatological discourse with the passion narrative so that the times when the doorkeeper needs to be ready for the master become the hours of the passion narrative. Mark's audience is not ready to welcome Jesus in his passion, as evidenced by the parallel between the threefold call to watch at 13:34, 35, 37 and the three times the disciples are caught sleeping in the garden of Gethsemane (14:37, 40, 41). Matthew and Luke instead follow the accepted tradition which calls the church to watch for Jesus' return in glory, so that the *parousia* is highlighted four times in Matthew (24:3, 27, 37, 39). In addition, both Matthew and Luke omit Mark's parable of the doorkeeper (13:34–36) because of the unique Markan elements that tie it to his passion narrative. Therefore, they neglect to include Mark's link between readiness for watching for the eschatological coming and a lack of readiness for watching for Jesus' passion.

In Mark 16 we are assured by the young man that Jesus is risen, but surprisingly no resurrection narratives are recorded. Again unexpectedly the women neglect to proclaim what the angel asked because they are afraid. Mark omits the resurrection encounters with Jesus in order to climax his narrative with the cross because his community needs to hear this pastoral exhortation. On the other hand, Matthew and Luke write their gospels after the struggles of Nero's persecution and the fall of Jerusalem and want to focus on the victory of Christianity. Therefore, they alter Mark's ending and narrate resurrection appearances as well as Jesus' mission commission to the apostles.

---

they are introduced as conspiring to trap Jesus in 12:13.

227. See section 8.5 below.

228. Wenham, *Rediscovery of Jesus' Eschatological Discourse*, 15.

In summary, Matthew and Luke do not employ the literary devices we have described in the last few chapters but instead alter the narratives. This consistency in redaction establishes in a backwards manner that these narrative surprises are a specific Markan literary device. These narrative surprises function as a signal for unique Markan theological emphases through symbolism, double-talk, and mirroring. Therefore, we cannot follow the logic of Trocme, who concludes that "the point is thus settled: the author of Mark was a clumsy writer unworthy of mention in any history of literature."[229] Nor can we agree with the conclusions of Gundry, who denies all symbolism in the Markan narratives.[230] We have established Mark's employment of four literary devices: intercalation, frame, allusionary repetition, and narrative surprise. In the next three chapters we will investigate how Mark employs these techniques to mirror his community's experience in Jesus' words and deeds and thus to shine light from the Jesus tradition onto the situation of his own community. We will observe how Mark speaks to situations where the Christian community experienced the absence of Jesus in their life and ministry (chapter 6). Then we will probe how Mark employs these literary devices to address the question of Gentile involvement in the community (chapter 7). Finally, we will describe how Mark employs what we entitle Jewish ceremonial ritual mirroring in order to aid his community in reading the OT legislation with a new hermeneutic whereby Jesus' kingdom words and deeds fulfill the old covenant purity laws and thus make them inoperative (chapter 8).

---

229. Trocmé, *Formation of Mark*, 72.
230. See Gundry, *Mark*, 1.

6

Markan Temporal Mirroring

6.1 A Summary of the Abuses of Mirroring

So far we have identified examples of the literary devices of intercalation, frame, allusionary repetition, and narrative surprise. In the remaining chapters we will demonstrate how Mark employs these literary devices for mirroring the experience of the Christian community. In this chapter we will illustrate how Mark employs the absence of Jesus in various narratives to speak powerfully to a community that felt the absence of Jesus in their life experience.

Attempts to describe Mark's community from the text of the gospel must of course proceed with caution. Mirroring can be misused and abused. A fabricated community can be invented to match data from the text. Just as in polemical writings it is difficult to discern the beliefs of the opponents since we overhear only one partner in the conversation, so in attempting to discern the situation behind narratives we can easily fall into the pitfalls of circularity, undue selectivity, and over-interpretation.[1] This is evident, for instance, in some of Incigneri's arguments for a Roman provenance in the Gospel of Mark, even though I agree with his final conclusion. He contends that the strong man of Mark 3:27 is "an accurate description of Vespasian, who took power by force, held Rome to ransom by stopping the Egyptian grain supply and, with the help of his son, holds on the reigns [sic] of power tightly." Or again, that Mark's readers would remember Titus and Domitian, the two who shared the emperor's glory at the recent triumph over Jerusalem, as they read of the two coregents on the right and on the left of Jesus as he was crucified, implying the criminal nature of the Roman rulers.[2] To avoid this pitfall we have identified the presence of specific Markan

---

1. See Barclay, "Mirror-Reading a Polemical Letter," 73–93.
2. See Incigneri, *Gospel to the Romans*, 187, 184, 221–22. He thinks that the two sons of Zebedee in their desire to sit at the right and left hand in the kingdom represent Titus and Domitian.

literary devices before diagnosing the content of the symbolism that is mirrored in the accounts.

Bauckham has argued that no distinctive communities stand behind the various gospel writers, but that "the gospels were written for broad circulation and a general Christian audience with their implied readership not specific but indefinite."[3] Although Bauckham has offered a correction to the extreme employment of *Sitz im Leben* in developing complicated and imaginative community scenarios, the conclusion of Dunn better fits the facts: "Evangelists wrote out of their more local experience primarily with a view to a much larger circle of churches."[4] Therefore, Bauckham is correct that the target audience of the evangelists is broad but incorrect that the source for the Jesus tradition was not local.

A second danger of mirroring concerns the implication that the historicity of events is undermined. Lemico claims that mirroring forces one to accept the view that the evangelists did not maintain the distinction between their own post-Easter beliefs and those of Jesus.[5] Certainly some writers such as Marxsen have fallen into this error when they claim that the evangelists are only concerned about who Jesus is and not about who Jesus was. In addition, various authors complain that mirroring undermines prophecy so that Mark 13 becomes completely *vaticinium ex eventu*, with nothing derived from the historical Jesus. However, we have argued that Mark employs literary devices to speak at two levels and that the genre of gospel is by definition preached history or kerygmatic biography. Therefore, Mark employs the Jesus tradition to speak to his situation with its own challenges and problems, but without necessarily undercutting the historicity of the events.

Extreme examples have conferred a negative connotation upon mirroring. Jesus' chosen disciples become errant commentators who represent misinformed views of Christ.[6] Authors use Jerusalem/Galilee mirroring to posit a return of Jesus in Galilee. Jerusalem has been read as the Jewish mother church who stands opposed to a Gentile group led by Mark and Paul. Although a contrast between Jerusalem and Galilee exists,[7] the divergent descriptions are not so dramatic as to demand a different theology of Galilee and Jerusalem, as Ricki Watts has demonstrated.[8] Therefore,

---

3. Bauckham, *Gospels for All Christians*, 1.

4. Dunn, *Jesus Remembered*, 252.

5. Lemico ("Intention of the Evangelist," 188–89) follows Moule (*Phenomenon*, 108, 110–12) who emphasizes that Mark does not contain later emphases like an exalted Christology, the disciples' incorporation into the body of Christ, the redemptive significance of Jesus' death, appropriation of its benefits, and a doctrine of the Holy Spirit.

6. Malbon points out that "Kelber further darkens the prevailing view of Jerusalem with arguments that the family and the failed disciples of the Marcan Jesus join the Jerusalem authorities in opposing him" ("Galilee and Jerusalem," 245). See section 1.2 above.

7. See the chart of van Iersel, *Mark*, 78. Malbon concludes, "Structural analysis confirms the proposition of redaction criticism that the distinction between Galilee and Judea is pivotal for the Marcan Gospel" ("Galilee and Jerusalem," 252).

8. Watts, *Isaiah's New Exodus*, 133.

neither Lohmeyer's contention that Galilee represents a Son of Man eschatology while Jerusalem depicts a nationalistic messianic hope,[9] nor Lightfoot's conclusion that Galilee is "the hallowed land of his eschatological coming,"[10] nor Marxsen's proposal that Galilee becomes "the center for the Marcan community"[11] capture the heart of Markan theology. Rather the continual reappearance of four central themes in Mark's use of intercalations, frames, allusionary repetitions, and narrative surprises must lead the interpreter to view the Galilee/Jerusalem contrast as a means to emphasize the passion of Jesus.[12] Jerusalem should be understood theologically as a place of rejection and death, the origin of the Jewish obduracy toward Jesus (3:22; 7:1; 10:33; 11:18), and the reason for God's judgment upon the Jewish rulers (3:6; 7:6, 8; 9:31; 10:33; 12:12; 13:2; 14:41; 15:38) because they bear the guilt for the crucifixion (2:6–8; 3:6; 7:7f, 13; 12:13ff, 28ff; 14:1f, 55). In the process the temple in Jerusalem functions as the negative axis of power, the origin of Jesus' opponents (3:22; 7:1), and therefore the place of confrontation (10:32f; 11:1, 15). Galilee on the other hand becomes the symbolic place of discipleship renewal and the true beginning point for the reader to learn a discipleship of the cross so as to avoid imitating the mistakes of Jesus' disciples. Thus Galilee is a device to move the narrative along as well as a device to move the readers along.[13]

Although mirroring can be misused, Mark employs literary devices as clues to his use of temporal mirroring, the geographical mirroring of Jewish and Gentile lands, and Jewish ceremonial mirroring to teach his audience how to interpret the OT purity laws. In this chapter we will explore temporal mirroring. Mark retells the stories of Jesus to speak existentially about a sense of the absence of Jesus within his community.[14] This has occurred through four prominent developments within the Christian church, including the loss of leadership with the deaths of the apostles like Peter and Paul, the sudden temporary cessation in the frequency of miracles, the struggles with the acceptance of a discipleship of the cross in the midst of Nero's persecution, and the potential loss of Jerusalem as the headquarters for the church. The absence of Jesus in the gospel narratives mirrors the feeling of an absence of Jesus in the Christian community. Six stories in particular center on this theme: the three sea trips with Jesus sleeping (4:35–41), praying on a mountain (6:45–52), and journeying without bread

---

9. See Lohmeyer, *Galiläa und Jerusalem*. For a history of interpretation on this issue see Stemberger, "Galilee: Land of Salvation?" 410–14.

10. Lightfoot, *Locality and Doctrine*, 74.

11. Marxen, *Mark*, 55–56. Stemberger, "Galilee?" 421–25 is persuasive in his doubts that an organized Christian community existed in Galilee when Mark penned his gospel.

12. See our discussion at the end of section 1.7 above.

13. Malbon confirms that "Galilee forms a framework for the narrative action, ordering movements in space" ("Galilee and Jerusalem," 253).

14. Weeden (*Traditions in Conflict*, 115, 134) pictures this absence as the real absence of Jesus, but see Best (*Following Jesus*, chapter 31) who rightly envisions Mark as attempting to demonstrate that Jesus is present in sufferings.

(8:13–21), as well as the inability of the disciples to cast out demons without Jesus' presence (9:17–19), the night journey of the absentee homeowner (13:34–36), and the culminating surprise ending of Mark where Jesus can only be seen in Galilee (16:7–8). We must conclude with Kelber that "The absence of Jesus is thus a presiding feature in the Mkan Gospel."[15] We will argue that Jesus' absence must be related to the time and circumstances of the gospel's composition.

6.2 The Sea-Calming Journey with Jesus' Sleeping (4:35–41)

Although Mark records six boat trips (4:35; 5:21; 6:32, 45; 8:10, 13), as Malbon explains, "Three voyages on the sea, however, are narratively elaborated and dramatize both teaching and healing."[16] As we shall see, each of these focuses on the absence of Jesus in some fashion. Mark has written the sea journey narratives in such a way that they can be read at more than one level. The sea calming of 4:35–41 functions primarily as a rescue narrative that proclaims the coming of the kingdom of God. As Latourella explains, "If we leave aside v. 40 with its reproach of the frightened disciples, we find the classic literary structure of a miracle story."[17] Since scholars who discern a hymnic configuration differ with regard to its line arrangement,[18] the more appropriate structure follows the three scenes of a traditional miracle story. This is supported by the repetition of the term μέγας so that there is a great storm (4:37), a great calm (4:39), and a great fear (4:41)[19] corresponding to the problem, the performance of a wonder, and the reaction in a miracle story.

The problem is delineated through the three descriptions of the tempest, Jesus' slumber, and the panic of the disciples. The obvious dilemma consists of a furious squall where mammoth waves nearly swamp the boat (4:37). The deeper crisis involves the seeming absence of Jesus, who is sleeping in the stern (4:38a). The resulting quandary centers on the disciples' reaction of abandonment, culminating in their question, "Teacher, don't you care if we drown?" The miracle section consists of three parts as well. Jesus rebukes the wind like a demon (compare 4:39 with 1:25)[20] and speaks a transforming word to the waves ("Quiet! Be still!"), with the result that the

---

15. Kelber, *Passion of Mark*, 164.

16. Malbon, *Narrative Space*, 77.

17. Latourelle, *Miracles of Jesus*, 103.

18. Lohmeyer (*Markus*, 89) envisions a six verse ballad with a 2,2,3 / 2,2,3 line arrangement, Pesch (*Markusevangelium*, 1:269) sees five strophes with three lines each, and Schille ("Die Seesturmerzählung Marcus 4 35–41," 34) pictures a hymnic structure of four strophes with three lines each (4:37, 38, 39, 41a). Cf. Guelich, *Mark 1—8:26*, 262.

19. See Marcus, *Mark 1–8*, 336.

20. Jesus speaks identical words to the sea as to the demon in Capernaum: 1:25 ἐπετίμησεν αὐτῷ; . . . Φιμώθητι and 4:39 ἐπετίμησεν τῷ ἀνέμῳ; . . . πεφίμωσο. Although Burkill entitles the pericope, "the exorcism of a storm demon" ("Mark 3:7–12," 413) the genre is more specifically a rescue narrative.

sea turns completely calm. Finally, the traditional elements of response comprise the amazing awe of the disciples (4:41a) and the resulting admiration propagating the healer's fame: "Who is this? Even the wind and the waves obey him!"

Problematically, Mark inserts a surprising response in 4:40 recording the total lack of faith of the disciples. As Guelich comments,

> We are again surprised by Jesus' unexpected rebuke of the disciples after calming the sea but prior to their response. This surprise element stands out the more when the disciples react in 4:41 in consternation. These breaks in the expected flow of the narrative most likely hold an important key for understanding the story's message.[21]

The collision with the traditional elements of a miracle story becomes so dramatic that Matthew alters the order of the narrative and adjoins this lack of faith to the problem section of the miracle story (8:26a) before the calming of the sea rather than in the response to the miracle. Thus Mark tempers the normal miracle ecstasy.

What is the purpose of this Markan surprise? The disciples display a lack of faith as they are faced with the apparent absence of Jesus. Jesus is sleeping in the stern (πρύμνα), a term related to the word "steersman" (πρυμνήτης), so that it feels like no one is steering the boat.[22] The absence of Jesus is reinforced by the unique wording of the disciples' question when they wake up Jesus: "don't you care if we drown?"[23] On the other hand, both Matthew ("Save us! We're going to drown!") and Luke ("We're going to drown") omit any sense of abandonment in the disciples' response to Jesus' sleeping. For Mark, however, the theme of abandonment in the alleged absence of Jesus stands central to the story. Another striking feature involves the disciples' address of Jesus as teacher (διδάσκαλε) rather than lord (κύριε) or master (ἐπιστάτα) as in Matthew 8:25 and Luke 8:24.[24] Therefore, the miracle story becomes for Mark a teaching parable on how to deal with an existential awareness of the absence of God. Boring becomes more specific, stating that the question "'Don't you care that we're about to die?' extends the story into the Markan reader's present, reflecting the anguished prayers of Christians in the time of Nero's rampage against Christians in Rome in 64 C.E. and the terrors faced by Christians in Palestine and Syria during the Jewish revolt."[25] At the end of this chapter we will arrive at the identical conclusion.

---

21. Guelich, *Mark 1—8:26*, 262–63. See our analysis of the narrative surprise in section 5.4 above.

22. Cf. Waetjen, *Reordering of Power*, 112.

23. Gundry contends that "The construction οὐ plus the indicative implies that the disciples do not doubt that Jesus cares" (*Mark*, 239), but one cannot assume from this grammatical structure that the disciples know Jesus' concern, but only that Jesus believes they should. For a parallel see the question in 14:37 where Jesus thinks the disciples should be able to watch with him, but they fall asleep.

24. Boring explains, "They address him as 'Teacher'—odd for a storm-and-exorcism story, where 'master' or 'Lord' would be more fitting—a clue that Mark recasts the miracle story in terms of discipleship" (*Mark*, 146).

25. Boring, *Mark*, 146.

The Theological Intentions of Mark's Literary Devices

The genre of miracle story centers the theme upon Christology, but the apprehension and panic of the disciples emphasizes a negative response to Jesus' apparent absence. Jesus' sleep feels like desertion so that the disciples question Jesus' attentive concern for them and respond with cowardly fear (4:40 δειλοί) even after Jesus is raised up (διεγερθείς) from his sleep and the sea is calmed. Through these Markan intrusions into the miracle story "Jesus finds the disciples harder to calm than the lake."[26] In fact, "Jesus' ability to still the wind and waves produces uncontrollable surges of fear rather than calm."[27] These feelings of the disciples mirror the situation of Mark's community. Jesus asleep in the stern of a boat while the storm rages outside (4:35–41) reminds the community of the storm of persecution they are experiencing with Jesus seemingly asleep. Even though Jesus is resurrected from his sleep, Mark's audience is cowardly questioning the sovereign care of their savior. In the midst of this situation, Mark wants to remind his hearers that Jesus is ready to wake up and authoritatively say, "Peace, Be still."[28] Therefore, the sea-calming narrative captures both Christology and discipleship.[29] Here discipleship is still a subplot since Mark does not place the disciples' lack of understanding (4:40) as the climatic conclusion to the narrative.[30] However, this will change in the sea-walking passage, where Mark consigns the theme of discipleship misunderstanding to the end (6:52).

Scholars who deny a parabolic meaning to the story emphasize that Jesus' siesta is merely the recouping of energy after an exhausting day. Interpreters who emphasize Markan Christology point out that "Jesus sleeps the sleep of utter calm. Mark is not interested in Jesus' being tired, but in his having nothing to fear from a sea storm."[31] An emphasis upon Christology is certainly central to the narrative, as witnessed by the authority with which Jesus rebukes the chaotic powers of nature, the ties with the book of Jonah where Jesus appears as the greater than Jonah,[32] and the acclaim given in the ending at 4:41. However, the unique discipleship motif in Mark cannot be denied. The increasing emphasis upon the unbelief and hard-heartedness of the

---

26. Geddert, *Watchwords*, 75.

27. Johnson, "Mark viii. 22–26," 379.

28. See Nineham, *St. Mark*, 147.

29. Thimmes notes that the narrative begins with the disciples: "Mark employs a clever maneuver and uses the disciples to generate the initial action in the narrative, "they took him" (v. 36)" (*Sea-Storm Type Scenes*, 136).

30. Schenke (*Wundererzählungen des Markusevangeliums*, 40–43) argues that since 4:40 is a Markan insertion, it must be the point of the story at the Markan level, but certainly Mark would have placed it last if he intended discipleship as the main point in this first trip across the sea.

31. Gundry, *Mark*, 239. He points to the emphatic αὐτὸς to contrast the calmness of Jesus' sleep with the raging of the sea. Batto ("Sleeping God," 153–77) calls attention to the psalms, but Ps 44:23–24; 35:23; and 59:4 emphasize a sense of desperation on Israel's part when God is perceived as sleeping as well as the experience of salvation when he awakes from sleep (78:65).

32. See Guelich, *Mark 1—8:26*, 271; van Iersel, *Mark*, 196; and Marcus, *Mark 1-8*, 337–38. For extensive Greek parallels between the LXX Jonah account and Mark see Cotter, *Christ of the Miracle Stories*, 221–23.

disciples in the other sea crossings (6:52 and 8:17–21) indicates that Mark wants to intensify this theme as he proceeds through the miracle stories. Therefore, although δειλοί is only encountered in 4:40, we must assume that it is Markan redaction because of the similarities with the following sea crossings. Interestingly, as Marcus notes, "the call not to be afraid and to have faith is reminiscent of the language of martyrdom (cf. John 14:27; 2 Tim 1:7, and especially Rev 21:8 which conjoins *deilos* and *apistos*, 'cowardly' and 'faithless.')."[33] This, of course, fits perfectly with the possible *Sitz im Leben* we are advocating for Mark's community.[34] We will now demonstrate from the other two sea crossings that the absence of Jesus is the central mirroring motif.

6.3 The Sea-Walking Journey with Jesus Praying on a Mountain (6:45–52)

In this section we will demonstrate how Mark mirrors the seeming absence of Jesus from the community through the themes of Christology and discipleship. The sea-walking journey contains the main features of a miracle rescue narrative. The groundwork for the wonder describes the problem in three ways (6:45–48b). The unbearable contrary winds with the disciples straining at the oars (6:48a) calls attention to the grueling physical circumstances. The fourth watch of the night (6:48b) indicates that the disciples have struggled for hours without making any progress on their journey. Most importantly Jesus' followers are separated from their master, who forces them into the boat in order to pray by himself on the mountainside. Jesus' absence receives increasing stress by placing the forced separation first in the narrative and then attaching increased details (6:45–47 vs. 6:48a–b) describing the disciples stranded in the middle of the lake while Jesus prays alone on the mountain. The miracle portrays an epiphany where Jesus reveals his divine glory and rescues his disciples (6:48c–50). Jesus arrives unexpectedly by walking on the waves, climbs into the boat to accompany his comrades again, and causes the blustery weather to cease by his presence. In response Jesus' followers are completely amazed (6:51).

As a miracle story the Christology of the narrative stands out prominently especially through the surprises in the story. Dramatically, Mark portrays Jesus as the glorified Christ praying on a high mountain as from heaven for his church struggling amidst the chaotic circumstances of life.[35] Even though the darkness of midnight is intensified by the presence of a storm, Jesus amazingly sees the disciples (6:48). Only

---

33. Marcus, *Mark 1–8*, 337.

34. Schenke (*Wundererzählungen des Markusevangeliums*, 77–78) offers a different twist to mirroring by contending that the sleeping of Jesus represents a delay of the second coming whereas the calming of the storm looks forward to the deliverance at the *parousia*. However, there is no hint of a delay in this narrative or in the sea crossings at Mark 6:45–52 and 8:13–21.

35. Malbon explains that "the mountain in Mark, as in the Hebrew Scriptures, is the place where heaven and earth meet" (*Narrative Space*, 80).

God possesses this gift of vision[36] to locate a small boat at night in the middle of a lake which is thirteen miles long and eight miles wide.[37] Jesus then unpredictably transverses the water, which subtly alludes to Job 9:8, "God alone stretches out the heavens and treads on the waves of the sea."[38] As witnessed by other OT references, God alone rescues people from the storms of the sea (Ps 107:23–32; Jonah 1:1–16; Wis 14:2–4).

Then as Jesus draws near to his disciples, Mark reports that "He was about to pass by them" (6:48c). Again Mark employs allusions to the Old Testament to designate the divine character of Jesus. The phrase "pass by" has become a technical term for a divine epiphany, as witnessed by the revelations to Moses (33:19, 22; 34:6) and Elijah (1 Kgs 19:11–13) on Mount Sinai.[39] Gundry points out that "as in the theophanies of Exodus 33–34 and 1 Kings 19, this theophany includes divine speech."[40] Then when the disciples posit the presence of a ghost, Jesus sovereignly proclaims, ἐγώ εἰμι. Although this term normally means nothing more than "it's me," the additional theophanic elements in the story suggest the divine self-identification formula in Exodus 3.[41] Even the misidentification of Jesus by the disciples as a ghost calls attention to a divine epiphany since Job 9:11 again states, "When he passes me, I cannot see him; when he goes by, I cannot perceive him."

Finally, Marcus discerns a simple fivefold chiastic structure to the passage which again calls attention in the center to the unique character of Jesus as he rescues his disciples.[42]

a   Jesus forces the disciples to get into the boat.
   b   Jesus sees the disciples struggling to cross the sea in the storm.
     c   In the fourth watch Jesus comes walking on the sea to them.
   b'   The disciples see Jesus and are disturbed.
a'   Jesus gets into the boat.

However, Mark transforms this story into a discipleship narrative by the addition of several narrative surprises. Even though previously in Mark Jesus huddles with his disciples after noteworthy events (4:10; 6:30–32), here Jesus forces (ἠνάγκασεν) his

---

36. Cf. Pss 10:14; 14:2; 94:7–9; Gen 16:13; Deut 26:7. In Mark 2:5 and 5:32 Jesus has supernatural insight as well.

37. Josephus (*War* 3:506) reports that the lake is 40 stadia wide and 140 stadia long. In John 6:19 the boat is 25–30 stadia from land.

38. See also Ps 77:19; Isa 43:16; 51:9–10; Hab 3:15; Sir 24:5–6.

39. Heil, *Jesus Walking on the Sea*, 70. Malbon ("Jesus of Mark," 367, n. 14) points out that none of the four other Markan usages of παρέρχομαι (13:30, 31(2); 14:35) has such a meaning, but the sea walking pericope is filled with other references to the Old Testament.

40. Gundry, *Mark*, 336.

41. Cf. Hooker, *Message of Mark*, 44; Thimmes, *Sea-Storm Type Scenes*, 160.

42. Marcus, *Mark 1–8*, 429. Meier (*Marginal Jew*, 2:907) reports that 64 words precede this center statement and 64 words follow it.

disciples into the boat to determine how they will function in his absence. At the beginning (6:45) and conclusion (6:52) of the sea-walking narrative the disciples become front and center in the narrative. Even more dramatically than in the sea-calming narrative with the addition of the disciples' lack of faith at 4:40, the sea-walking episode concludes with the misunderstanding and hard-heartedness of Jesus' followers. Instead of the previous narrative of the feeding of the five thousand concluding with amazement and applause, Mark merely recites the number of people fed to confirm the miracle (6:34). Therefore, the sea journey becomes the response to the feeding, as evidenced by the return to this incident in 6:52: "for they had not understood about the loaves; their hearts were hardened." The theme of discipleship ties the two narratives closely together.

The teaching nature of this episode is confirmed by the use of the imagery of a boat in previous Markan usage as well as in the Jewish tradition and the early church. Previously in the parables section the boat served as a pulpit (4:1–2) to teach the crowd, but in the miracle catenae the boat becomes a picture of the learning community, both here and in the previous sea journey in 4:36–38. Tertullian offered the understanding of the church fathers when he explained, "That little ship presented a figure of the Church, in that she is disquieted in the sea, that is, in the world, by the waves, that is, by persecutions and temptations."[43] We see already in the Testament of Naphtali 6 that a boat represented Israel before it became a symbol of the church.[44] For instance, 6:2 reads, "And behold, there came a ship sailing by, without sailors or pilot; and there was written upon the ship, The Ship of Jacob."[45] This emphasis upon the discipleship community becomes equally significant as the Christology in the passage.

Through this double emphasis upon Christology and discipleship the absence of Jesus from his chosen comrades becomes the leading motif. The repetition of this theme in 6:45–47 is striking.[46] First Mark reports that Jesus forces the disciples into the boat (6:45a). Then he mentions that Jesus leaves them (ἀποταξάμενος αὐτοῖς), where the plural is likely meant by Mark to refer to the disciples (τοὺς μαθητὰς) and not the crowd (τὸν ὄχλον).[47] Finally, Mark specifies that Jesus is all alone (6:47b μόνος) on

---

43. Tertullian, *On Baptism*, 12 quoted in Richardson, *Miracle Stories*, 93. For many similar citations from the church fathers see Trench, *Notes on the Miracles*, 152–60, 295–308.

44. See Heil (*Jesus Walking*, 19, n. 16) for evidence that no literary dependence can be established between these documents.

45. Charles, *Apocrypha and Pseudepigrapha*, 2:338. See the application of Testament of Naphtali 6 to Mark 6:45–52 in Deppe, *All Roads Lead to the Text*, 290.

46. Henderson states, "Mark further underscores Jesus' absence from the disciples by taking two more verses to set the scene" ("Concerning the Loaves," 17).

47. See Guelich, *Mark 1—8:26*, 349. Instead of the pronoun, Matt 14:23 specifies τοὺς ὄχλους with a parallel plural in 14:22. Thus Matthew assumes a clumsy Greek expression on Mark's part, but this could be another subtle way for Mark to emphasize a journey without Jesus. Marcus (*Mark 1–8*, 428) believes that evidence for leaving the crowd comes from the parallel in 4:36 (ἀφέντες τὸν ὄχλον), but this would parallel 6:45 (ἀπολύει τὸν ὄχλον), not 6:46 (ἀποταξάμενος αὐτοῖς). Cf. Louw and Nida,

the land. The absence of Jesus from the disciples completely dominates these verses. Certainly the imagery of Jesus praying on the mountain reminded the Christian community of the ascended Jesus, who was now in heaven praying for the church while they struggled below.

The community's struggles are called to attention in several ways. The surprising use of the term βασανιζομένους (6:48a "straining at the oars") confirms the tormented nature of the community.[48] Mark employs this term only one other time: when a legion of tormenting demons oppress a helpless human being (5:7). But the Book of Revelation (9:5; 11:10; 12:2; 14:10; 20:10) with its vivid descriptions of cataclysmic destruction employs this term most frequently in the New Testament,[49] while in the second century this word is regularly deployed to describe martyrdom.[50] Origen also understood the contrary winds as the adverse circumstances of the community: "The Savior thus compelled the disciples to enter into the boat of testing and to go before him to the other side, so to learn victoriously to pass through difficulties."[51] In addition, several OT passages (Exod 14:29; 15:8; Neh 9:11) portray the middle of the sea (6:47) as an abyss of intense danger. Finally, Mark employs the term προάγειν (6:45) to demonstrate that Jesus forces his disciples to proceed alone before him in order to learn to carry out their master's mission without him. Since Jesus usually goes before the disciples (10:32; 14:28; 16:7), this again calls attention to the community.[52] The disciples need to learn to face the difficulties of their journey of discipleship without Jesus' constant presence.

In the midst of this struggle to arrive at home on the other side of the sea, Jesus intends to pass by the disciples (ἤθελεν παρελθεῖν αὐτούς) as he walks on the waves. How would Mark's readers initially understand such a statement? Certainly the natural literal meaning would imply that Jesus is ignoring the plight of the boat community and is journeying to a safehaven without his followers. Therefore it expresses the disciples' mistaken impression of what Jesus was about to do.[53] This sense of abandonment parallels the disciples' cry of despair in the sea-calming journey (4:38): "Teacher, don't you care if we drown?" Their lack of faith (4:40) is likewise paralleled

---

Greek-English Lexicon,15.43. However, it must be admitted that Mark can refer to the crowd with a plural personal pronoun as Henderson (*Christology and Discipleship*, 215) demonstrates in 2:13; 3:9,32; 4:1–2; 6:34; 7:14; 8:2–3; 9:15; 15:8. Therefore, αὐτοῖς could refer to both the disciples and the crowd.

48. The term ἐλαύνω itself can also mean to persecute (Wis 16:18) but not when connected with the sea.

49. The noun is employed at Rev 9:5; 14:11; 18:7, 10, 15 as well.

50. Martyrdom of Polycarp 2:2. See also 2 Mac 7:13; Josephus *Ant.* 16:232.

51. Commentary on Matthew 11:5, in Roberts et al., *Ante-Nicene Fathers*, 10:435.

52. Markus (*Way of the Lord*, 42–43) interprets this statement negatively as if the disciples are attempting to get prominence over Jesus, but this is simply Mark's way to call attention to discipleship.

53. Along with Taylor "it is best to conclude that ἤθελεν is used as a quasi-auxiliary: 'He was going to pass by them'" (*St. Mark*, 329).

but intensified so that now the final word of the pericope centers on the hardheartedness of the community (6:52).[54]

Of course, the passing by of Jesus has been interpreted in other ways.[55] Some authors parallel the "going before" (προάγειν) in 6:45 with the "passing by" in 6:48 (παρελθεῖν) so that the disciples take the lead in 6:45 only to get into trouble whereas Jesus regains his rightful position in 6:48.[56] They point to the calling narratives (1:17, 18, 20; 2:14, 15) and journeys on route (5:37; 6:1; 8:34; 10:32; 14:54) where Jesus walks in front while his disciples follow behind. If the theme here were Jesus' leadership, then the parallel would be valid, but the prominent motif is the separation of Jesus from his disciples. The "passing by" is not intended as an image of Jesus regaining leadership, but rather of continuing his journey alone. Since the sending out of the disciples in 6:7–12, Jesus is allowing them to take the initiative while he plays the role of supervisor. Mark organizes the gospel into a progression of deepening discipleship, which begins with only passive following (from the call in 1:16–20 to the rejection by the Jewish leaders in 3:6), proceeds into an equipping level where the disciples receive Jesus' authority (from the appointment of the Twelve to the rejection by his own people in 6:1–6), and now becomes a reproduction level where the disciples take over under Jesus' supervision (from the sending out of the Twelve in 6:7–12 through the disciples' hard-heartedness in 8:17–21). Jesus is testing their leadership, as seen in 6:37 ("you give them something to eat") as well as in 6:45 with Jesus' sending the disciples ahead without him. So Mark is not polemicizing against their seizure of the leadership role from Jesus, but supplying a test whether they can lead without Jesus' presence or whether they will feel abandoned and experience discipleship failure.

However, the disciples' initial sense of abandonment is replaced by the true meaning of "passing by" as a divine epiphany. The OT narratives about Moses and Elijah hold the correct interpretation of this phrase "passing by."[57] As Henderson points out, "In the case of both Moses and Elijah, God orchestrates a 'passing by' precisely at the point of the character's deepest desperation: Moses has just weathered the golden calf episode, and Elijah has reached a point of despondency when he cries,

---

54. For a list of eight similarities between the sea calming and sea walking trips see Marcus, *Mark 1–8*, 428. Note especially the repetition of the phrase "the winds ceased" in 6:51 and 4:39 which implies the same circumstances.

55. For instance, Snoy ("Marc 6,48," 357–60) thinks that this is a part of the Messianic Secret whereby Jesus is withdrawing in order to safeguard his divine transcendence. Cf. van Iersel, "ΠΑΡΕΛΘΕΙΝ," 1068–69.

56. Henderson, "Concerning the Loaves," 47; Marcus, *Way of the Lord*, 43, n. 115; van Iersel "ΠΑΡΕΛΘΕΙΝ," 1074–76. However, van Iersel seems to argue against this position when on page 1074 he states, "Both at Gennesaret (6,53) and afterwards at Bethsaida (8,22) Jesus and his disciples arrive together." According to his interpretation, Jesus would arrive ahead of his disciples.

57. Fleddermann ("And He Wanted," 391) points out that "pass by" can also mean "to rescue from disaster" and "to save" and contends that Amos 7:8 and 8:2 are much closer to Mark 6:48, but these are judgment oracles ("I will not pass by them anymore"), although Fleddermann sees judgment only at Amos 5:16–17.

'I alone am left, and they are seeking my life, to take it away' (1 Kgs 19.10)."[58] Instead of abandonment, Jesus is coming with a powerful epiphany of his divine presence. Although the disciples struggle in the midst of the perceived absence of Jesus, Jesus fivefold action manifests the reality of God's divine presence. First, Jesus prays on the heavenly mountain for his community in this time of testing. Then with divine sight he sees them from a distance, comes to them as God walking on the water, and passes them by in a divine epiphany reciting the name of Yahweh over them.[59] Since the disciples' identification of Jesus as a ghost resembles the resurrection narratives,[60] Mark proclaims a positive message of a divine deliverance to a community that thinks their only reality is the absence of Jesus.

If, as Best suggests, "the two stories about storms at sea (4.35–41; 6.45–52) are best understood as the way in which Jesus rescues the community in its time of persecution,"[61] is it possible to determine which situation in the early church is mirrored here? Loisy offers a detailed allegory whereby the forced parting by Jesus from his disciples symbolizes his death, the ascent up the mountain to pray corresponds to his resurrection and ascension, and his arrival traversing the water represents his future coming upon the clouds at the fourth watch or end of time.[62] This history of salvation approach is much too detailed in its allegory. If the gospel kerygma is referenced at all, the feeding of the five thousand proclaims Jesus' death, as paralleled in the Last Supper narrative, and the sea-walking pictures his resurrection.[63] More importantly, the parallel between Jesus asleep in the sea-calming and Jesus praying on a mountain in the sea-walking points to Jesus' absence and the community's reaction in such situations. The fourth watch of the night illustrates the length of the community's struggle with the ostensible absence of Jesus as well as the eschatological distress

---

58. Henderson, "Concerning the Loaves," 20–21.

59. See Richardson, *Miracle Stories*, 92.

60. Madden (*Jesus Walking*) offers the most thorough analysis of Mark 6:45–52 as a displaced resurrection narrative, but it is better to discern the church's preaching of the death and resurrection of Jesus in the feeding of the five thousand where Jesus breaks the bread followed by an epiphany of his glory here. Marcus (*Mark 1–8*, 433) includes a handy list of ten similarities with the resurrection stories in Luke and Matthew.

61. Best, *Mark as Story*, 53.

62. Loisy, *Marc*, 201–2 in Boucher, *Mysterious Parable*, 72–73. Best leaves open the possibility of a couple of interpretations: "This may be conceived both as a present coming of the risen Lord in every emergency and also as his once-for-all coming in the *Parousia* to bring final deliverance" (*Temptation and the Passion*, 105). Aus (*Walking on the Sea*, 117–19, 122) hypothesizes that the sea walking mirrors Gaius Caligula who thought of himself as divine, lord of both land and sea, and completed the seeming impossible feat of building a bridge over the bay between Baiae and Puteoli just west of modern Naples. Caligula was like Antiochus Epiphanes who thought "in his arrogance that he could sail on the land and walk on the sea" (2 Mac 5:21). Mark would then be demonstrating that only Jesus as Messiah could walk on the sea. This interpretation overlooks the prominence of the absence of Jesus motif throughout Mark's gospel.

63. Boucher states that "The passion-resurrection foreshadowing provides the most satisfactory explanation available for the joining of these two miracles in Mark" (*Mysterious Parable*, 75).

of the end times.⁶⁴ Since Mark employs πρωΐ for the fourth watch of the night in 13:35, the OT imagery whereby the help of God comes in the morning (Exod 14:24; Ps 46:5; 88:13; 130:6; Isa 17:14; *Jos. Asen.* 14:1–2) also points to the coming resurrection of Jesus (Mark 16:2 λίαν πρωΐ).⁶⁵ The problem of Jesus' absence will be overcome.

The mirroring of the absence of God best applies to the Roman church. As Rawlinson explains, "To the Roman Church, thus bereft of its leaders and confronted by a hostile Government, it must have indeed appeared that the wind was contrary and progress difficult and slow."⁶⁶ Similarly, the sea-calming narrative offers a special word of encouragement to Mark's first readers. As Richardson proclaims, "It might seem to the faint-hearted that the Lord was asleep and indifferent to their peril; but in truth He is present in the Church and will arise and cast out the demon of the storm."⁶⁷ To recognize the presence of Jesus, the disciples must understand the loaves (6:52). They must realize that the feeding of the nations does not happen through bread miracles but through Jesus feeding both Jews and Gentiles at the cross. Jesus forces the disciples into the boat to face the storm so that they will see the presence of Jesus in times of apparent forsakenness and not only in mighty miracles of deliverance like the feeding of the five thousand. Then Mark will add the sea-conversation trip (8:13–21) at the end of the second feeding narrative (8:1–9) to demonstrate that the desire for signs does not guarantee the presence of Jesus. Confronted with an existential awareness of the absence of Jesus during Nero's persecutions, the community must have its eyes opened to see the presence of God in the sufferings of Jesus and in their own discipleship of the cross.

6.4 The Sea Conversation Journey Seemingly without Bread (8:13–21)

Mark includes a third trip across the sea, which serves as a discussion platform for the meaning of the loaves, which the disciples do not understand at the conclusion of the sea-walking trip (6:52). Immediately following the two sets of miracle catenae (4:35—8:9), which begin with a trip across the sea and conclude with a miraculous feeding, Mark adds a rebuke by Jesus aimed at the Pharisees, who seek miraculous signs (8:11–12). Then Mark inserts a third sea trip, which centers on a conversation about bread instead of a miracle story (8:13). Here Jesus warns against the leaven of the Pharisees and Herod, which, based on the sign seeking of the Pharisees, must be a warning about demanding miracles. Instead the disciples must recognize that they

---

64. Similar to Qumran 1QH 3:6, 12–18; 6:22–25; 7:45; and Luke 21:25 ("On the earth, nations will be in anguish and perplexity at the roaring and tossing of the sea").

65. Cf. Dwyer, *Motif of Wonder*, 129; Marcus, *Mark 1–8*, 423. This imagery could reflect as well the experience of the Red Sea where the last watch of the night (Exod 14:24) becomes the demise of the Egyptians but new life for Israel.

66. Rawlinson, *St. Mark*, 88.

67. Richardson, *Miracle Stories*, 92.

have sufficient bread in the boat without a sign. The surprising element in the story, as we discerned in chapter 5, is that the disciples did not bring any bread with them but there was still one loaf in the boat. This loaf must be Jesus himself.[68] The two previous sea journeys center on the absence of Jesus while this final sea conversation becomes a test to see if the disciples are aware of the presence of Jesus even when the necessities of life are absent. Can the disciples believe in the manifest presence of Jesus even when the sea is roaring and Jesus is sleeping in the stern, even when Jesus is absent praying on the mountain and the contrary winds will not allow the disciples to reach their destination, and even when there is no bread for the journey? The leaven of the Pharisees and Herod, understood as the demand for signs, is not needed to bring the presence of Jesus. There is always a loaf in the boat.

The narrative concludes with an extensive seven-to-tenfold rebuke by Jesus of the disciples (8:17–21).[69] The incomprehension of the disciples grows with each sea journey, so that in the sea-calming trip their lack of faith is inserted in 4:40 but the amazement and acclaim of 4:41 takes prominence. The sea-walking journey likewise highlights Christology, but the conclusion now converges on the disciples' hardness of heart (6:52). In the sea-conversation journey discipleship failure becomes the focal point. This failure centers on two important themes in Mark's redaction: 1) the passion of Jesus and the attendant discipleship of the cross and 2) the inclusion of Gentiles in God's plan. As we shall see in chapter 7, the questions about the leftover baskets (8:19 twelve κοφίνους; 8:20 seven σπυρίδων) of bread symbolize Jesus' salvific feeding of both Jews and Gentiles.[70] But Mark primarily emphasizes the fact that Jesus is not absent in the midst of struggles and maltreatment. Just because God does not work any miraculous signs to rescue his people from their extreme circumstances does not mean that Jesus is absent. The disciples remain blind to the fact that the miracle of the loaves really points to the multiplication that will occur through Jesus' passion.[71]

The following context confirms our findings. Jesus and the disciples finally arrive at Bethsaida (8:22), which has been their desired destination since the beginning of the sea-walking journey (6:45). Therefore, the misunderstanding of the loaves by the disciples (6:52) is beginning to be solved. The blind man then receives his sight, but a two-step process is necessary. This process is symbolically explained in the following narrative regarding Peter's confession of faith. Peter will not see the identity of Jesus

---

68. Bread symbolism for Jesus (Klostermann, Grundmann, Pesch, Gnilka, van Iersel etc.) is traceable to Johannes Weiss. Cf. Hebert, "History in the Feeding," 65–72. Gundry (*Mark*, 408), of course, chooses a literal interpretation so that the one loaf cannot satisfy since it is less food than the five or seven loaves. Likewise, for him the reproach against the leaven of the Pharisees means that "Jesus does not want them to buy additional loaves from the Pharisees and the supporters of Herod." Gundry claims that the obscurity of the passage indicates what little concern Mark has for the disciples' dullness, but the intensification of this theme in the sea journeys proves the opposite is true.

69. See the end of section 3.7 above.

70. See 7.6 below.

71. Here Mark uses the literary device of an allusionary repetition as seen in section 4.2b above.

clearly (8:32) until he confesses Jesus both as the miracle-working powerful Messiah (8:29) and as the suffering Son of Man (8:31) and understands the implications of the cross for discipleship (8:34). The disciples will misunderstand the miraculous feedings and not experience the presence of Jesus until they visualize the kingdom of God arriving in the cross. The little word οὔπω (not yet) must not be ignored. In Mark 4:40 Jesus asks, "Do you not yet have faith?" and at 8:17, "Do you not yet see?" and at 8:21, "Do you not yet understand?" Throughout the miracle stories (almost as an inclusio) the "not yet" points ahead to the discipleship catechism of 8:22—10:52, where Jesus will teach his disciples his true identity as a Suffering Servant Messiah and their concomitant identity as cross followers. Through this sea conversation Mark speaks powerfully to a community that feels the abandonment and separation of Jesus in the midst of persecution, the loss of their heroic leadership, and the immanent destruction of their home base of Jerusalem. Even when they lack the necessities of life, there is always a loaf with them, present in the boat which is the church.

Therefore, this entire narrative concluding the miracle catenae could be entitled "a parable in action" since Mark has constructed it with the identical structure to the paradigmatic parable, the parable of the sower and its interpretation.[72] This precise repetition of motifs demonstrates that these miracles function as riddles for Mark which mirror the situation of his audience.[73] Mark retells these three journeys from the Jesus tradition to speak to a church struggling existentially with a sense of the absence of God.

6.5 The Disciples' Inability to Cast Out Demons without Jesus (9:14–29)

A fourth narrative mirroring the perceived absence of Jesus in the community occurs while Jesus is transfigured on a mountain. The imagery is similar to 6:46, where Jesus is praying on a heavenly-type mountain while the disciples cannot complete their task of arriving on the opposite shore. Here the disciples in the valley cannot cast out the demons without Jesus (9:17–19), who appears in a glorified state on the mountain. These circumstances mirror the post-resurrection church, which is struggling with the demons of persecution while Jesus is exalted in heaven. What will it take for the disciples to cast these demons out without Jesus standing beside them? We have to wait until Jesus' instruction at the very end of the narrative to discover the solution to the absence of Jesus.

Christopher Marshall has composed a structure of this narrative with four scenes differentiated by Jesus' varying conversation partners.[74]

---

72. For seven points of comparison see section 4.3e above.
73. See section 9.3 below.
74. This chart is constructed from material in Marshall, *Faith as a Theme*, 114.

Scenes and verses	Characters	Question	Declaration by Jesus
Scene 1: 9:14–20	Jesus and the crowd	What are you arguing with them about?	"You unbelieving generation, how long shall I stay with you?"
Scene 2: 9:21–24	Jesus and the father	How long has he been like this?	"Everything is possible for one who believes."
Scene 3: 9:25–27	Jesus and the demon		"You deaf and mute spirit, I command you, come out of him and never enter him again."
Scene 4: 9:28–29	Jesus and the disciples	Why couldn't we drive it out?	"This kind can come out only by prayer."

However, although this structure identifies the scenes and characters in the dialogue, it does not accentuate the primary emphases of Mark. It is important to notice that the role of the disciples forms an inclusio around the entire narrative when their inability (9:14) to expel the demon (9:18) is answered in 9:29.[75] As Kelber explains, "The story of the exorcism of the Epileptic Boy has been enveloped by the Markan theme of discipleship failure."[76] Therefore, equal attention is not placed on each audience as Marshall's diagram seems to promote.

Elements of a typical exorcism narrative are evident in the confrontation between the exorcist and the possessed (9:20–22), which leads to a miraculous expulsion (9:25–27). However, the normal concluding element of acclamation by the one healed or an expressed awe by the crowd is entirely missing.[77] Instead the expected awe appears to have been surprisingly moved to the beginning of the narrative (9:15), with dialogue inserted between the traditional elements of an exorcism.[78] Struck by the pattern of dialogue in the narrative, Latourelle envisions three scenes with dialogue concluding each section:[79]

1. Jesus confronts the teachers of the law arguing with his disciples (14–15), followed by a dialogue between Jesus and the father as a member of the crowd (17–18).

2. Jesus battles with the demon (19–20), followed by a second dialogue between Jesus and the father (21–24).

3. Jesus expulses the demon (25–27), followed by a dialogue between Jesus and his disciples (28–29).

---

75. Cf. France, *Mark*, 361; Meier, *Marginal Jew*, 2:654–55; Myers, *Binding the Strong Man*, 255.
76. Kelber, *Oral and Written Gospel*, 53–54.
77. Boring, *Mark*, 275.
78. See evidence for a Markan surprise in section 5.2b above.
79. Latourelle, *Miracles of Jesus*, 150.

This discovery reveals that the genre is complicated by the faith struggle of the father as well as the discipleship failures in the absence of Jesus.[80] In fact, they are tied together. The inability to drive out the demon (9:18) leads directly to Jesus' scathing condemnation of this unbelieving generation (9:19a). This impassioned outburst of Jesus concerning the unbelieving generation centers on the disciples, since news of their failure occasions the cry. This continues the Markan theme of the faithlessness of the disciples when Jesus is absent, as evidenced by Jesus' next question (9:19b), "How long shall I stay with you?" Likewise, in the second dialogue with the father, Jesus asks (9:23), "if you can?," specifying surprise that anyone would doubt Jesus' power when he is physically present at that very moment. Finally, the concluding dialogue with the disciples centers on prayer (9:29) which, as we shall see, Mark defines as the manifest presence of Jesus. Therefore, the absence of Jesus is crucial to understanding the narrative.

Gundry argues for an emphasis upon Christology alone. The disciples' inability to cast out the demon becomes "a foil against which Jesus' ability to perform the exorcism will stand out in powerful contrast."[81] The christological accents in the story include "the crowd's amazement at the sight of Jesus, his magnetism, the detailing of the demoniac's symptoms to enhance the exorcism once it occurs, the highlighting of the question concerning Jesus' ability over against the disciples' proven inability, and the detailing of evidence that the spirit has gone out once Jesus commands it to do so."[82] Gundry contends that the crowd's amazement (9:15) is caused by the glistening white garments of Jesus' transfiguration since Mark has not indicated that Jesus' splendor has dimmed. But nothing in the narrative gives the reader any reason to believe that the crowd had any inkling of what has happened on the mountain. In fact, as Stein points out, "the command to silence in 9:9 would be pointless if Jesus still radiated the glory of the transfiguration."[83] Instead, the omission of fearful amazement after the exorcism creates the suspicion that Mark has moved this element to the beginning of the narrative.[84] Therefore, Christology alone does not explain all the elements in the text.

Mark consistently combines the themes of Christology and discipleship, with the latter as the normal concluding element in the narrative.[85] The healing of the epileptic

---

80. Betz states that the "main focus of the story is not upon the boy's healing but upon the father and his conversion" so that it "'flips over' into a 'conversion story,' another literary genre" ("Early Christian Miracle Story," 79). We contend that the material surrounding the miracle story reveals Mark's intention of emphasizing a discipleship narrative struggling with the absence of Jesus.

81. Gundry, *Mark*, 487.

82. Ibid., 502.

83. Stein, *Mark*, 432.

84. See Boring, *Mark*, 273.

85. This includes the three sea journeys with the theme of lack of faith, hard-heartedness, and misunderstanding near the end of each pericope. The healing of Bartimaeus concludes with "following along the way" (10:52b). The two step healing of the blind man in 8:22–26 leads into the proper

is no exception. Jesus' victory over the problems of muteness (9:17), seizures (18), demon possession (20), unbelief (19, 24), and apparent death (26) emphasizes the uniqueness of the character of Jesus. However, the omission of the normal amazement and acclaim formulas and the insertion of the element of awe at the beginning provide narrative surprises that point to the additional element of discipleship failure. Luke 9:43 even reconstructs the traditional genre ending of astonishment, whereas Mark has substituted a teaching on discipleship. More convincing yet is the switch to a private indoor location (Mark 9:28) where the disciples ask Jesus a question, which is a standard Markan reference for discipleship teaching.[86] In addition, the narrative displays elements of a controversy dialogue beginning with an argument and concluding with a pronouncement saying, indicating that the primary purpose is teaching.[87] Finally, the exorcism is placed in the discipleship catechism section of Mark instead of with the rest of the miracle stories. The two additional healings of the blind men (8:22–26; 10:46–52) in this same section also concentrate on discipleship.[88] Therefore the exorcism here is submerged by material on discipleship.[89]

Mark concludes the narrative with the statement that "this kind can only come out by prayer,"[90] as the solution to the inability of the disciples to overcome the demons without the presence of Jesus. It is striking that Jesus' recommended means of

---

Christological designation (8:27–33) and the affiliated discipleship commitment of taking up one's cross and following Jesus (8:34). Finally, the two miraculous feedings omit the amazement and acclaim elements of a miracle story because Mark will demonstrate that the disciples fail to understand the meaning of the feedings (6:52; 8:17–21).

86 See Cotter, *Christ of the Miracle Stories*, 174, n. 17 for secondary support. Jesus and the disciples frequently withdraw to a house representing the house church to receive teaching applied to them alone (κατὰ μόνας 4:10; κατ' ἰδίαν 4:34; 6:31, 32; 9:2, 28; 13:3). See the boat excursions after the miraculous feedings as well. Withdrawal is connected to miracle stories (5:37, 40b; 6:31–32; 7:24, 33; 8:23; 9:2, 28, 30–31), parables (4:10, 34; 7:17), and other instruction (10:10; 13:3) demonstrating the teaching implications of each.

87. The father also addresses Jesus as teacher (9:17). Most of the five traditional elements of controversy dialogues within the gospels can be discerned here: 1) controversy (9:14, 16); 2) the question from the crowd is replaced by an explanation of the father of what happened (17–18); 3) return questions by Jesus (19, 21, 23a); 4) a pronouncement saying (either 23b "Everything is possible for him who believes" or 29 "This kind can only come out by prayer"); and 5) acclaim which comes through the difficult exorcism raising a corpse which proves that everything is possible or acclaim is replaced by the disciples' question and Jesus' instruction which teaches them how to solve the problem. See Riesenfeld, "Composition of Mark," 72–73 who employs the term "apophthegm."

88. An emphasis upon discipleship (along with Christology) might be discerned as well in the parallels with Moses. Hobbs ("Gospel of Mark," 45–46) quoted by Swartley ("Structural Function of the Term," 86, n. 37) points to the encounter with idolatrous Israel in the golden calf incident as a sequel to the disciples' experience of not casting out a demon in the valley beside the mountain of transfiguration.

89. Cf. Best, *Following Jesus*, 68 and Boring, *Mark*, 272.

90. The International Standard Version adds "fasting" to this text, but in doing so misses Mark's emphasis upon prayer as the presence of God or Jesus. The increasing emphasis on the necessity of fasting in the early church as well as the reference to a future fasting in Mark 2:20 argue against its authenticity.

deliverance, namely prayer, is not employed in the story itself.[91] We could even entitle this a Markan surprise since Jesus "lays down a rule for exorcism that he himself is not described as fulfilling."[92] This indicates that Mark has a special theology of prayer. Prayer for Mark is calling forth the presence of Jesus into troubling situations.[93] This emphasis corresponds with the lengthiest teaching on prayer in Mark, which is placed after the cursing of the fig tree and temple cessation action. Since the temple mount is thrown into the sea, the community needs a new presence of God and acts of piety that are appropriate with a new temple made without hands. These worship practices that manifest the presence of God are prayer, faith, and forgiveness (11:22–25). Therefore prayer for Mark is calling Jesus into the present moment and recognizing his invisible presence. Prayer is the opposite of the absence of God.

Most authors miss the connection between prayer and the seeming absence of Jesus in the community. Some explain prayer with the traditional general meaning of petition or supplication, as an alternative to exorcistic praxis,[94] or as the verbalization of faith which expresses an unconditional commitment to the divine will through a dialogue with God.[95] Others define prayer as a manifestation of miracle-working power so that "prayer serves as a vehicle by means of which the God who can do the impossible meets the needs of the Christian community."[96] However, whereas Matthew and Luke stress Jesus' healing power, Mark's focus is not upon miraculous faith but upon the key role of faithful discipleship in the absence of the presence of God. Certainly faith is involved in prayer. Marshall calls attention to the importance of faith in the narrative through 1) the explicit denunciation by Jesus of faithlessness (9:19), 2) an affirmation of the omnipotence available to those who believe (23), 3) a paradoxical confession by the petitioner of unbelieving belief (24), and 4) a saying that implicitly links faith and prayer (29).[97] But Mark's emphasis is not like Matthew's, on supernatural faith; Matthew enhances the theme of faith by appending sayings

---

91. See Collins, *Mark*, 439 and note 115 for opposing views.

92. Marcus, *Mark 8–16*, 665.

93. Prayer is the solution to casting out the demon (9:29) because that is the means by which the community keeps Jesus present in every difficult situation. See Marcus, *Mark 8–16*, 658. In Mark Jesus teaches about prayer (9:29; 11:17, 22–25; 12:40; 13:18; 14:38), models prayer (1:35; 6:46; 14:32–42; 15:34), and blesses food through prayer (6:41; 8:6; 14:22).

94. Koch, *Die Bedeutung der Wundererzählungen*, 122–23.

95. See Marshall, *Faith as a Theme*, 171 and Williams, *Other Followers*, 141 and n. 4 for scholarly support.

96. Dowd, *Prayer, Power*, 129. Cf. Evans, *Mark*, 191. Dowd is more nuanced in her definition of prayer at the end of the book when she concludes that "prayer in the Markan community is not understood one-dimensionally as a vehicle for power with no other purpose.... Prayer is the context for the community's experiences of power, and prayer is the context for the community's experiences of suffering and martyrdom" (164).

97. Marshall, *Faith as a Theme*, 110. On page 115 he ties the theme of faith to a possible structure of the passage: "The first scene climaxes in a lament over unbelief; the second climaxes in a confession of unbelieving belief; the third concretely demonstrates faith at work; whilst the fourth scene relates faith to the practice of prayer."

about moving mountains through mustard seed faith (17:20). Instead, in Mark faith is demanded as an indication of the presence of God. That is why both faith and prayer replace the temple in Mark 11:22–24.

Consistent with the previous pericopes we have investigated, Mark is encouraging the disciples in the midst of a perceived situation of the absence of Jesus. As Twelftree explains, "Mark may be inferring that the disciples are not yet ready for Jesus' absence (cf. 9:19). This is analogous to the situation of Mark's readers."[98] Mark is speaking at two levels. This coheres with the definition of the genre of gospel as kerygmatic history or preached biography. In all likelihood, this passage mirrors the church's experience with Roman harassment and maltreatment. The inability of the disciples to cast out the demons reflects the community's failure to overcome the wild beasts that they face in Nero's persecution. The "how long" questions of Jesus (9:19) echo OT laments over the faithlessness of Israel[99] and thus the lack of faith within Mark's community.

The previous and following contexts tie this passage to suffering. Immediately before the struggle with demons, Jesus offers passion instruction on his descent down the mountain (9:9–13). Then, following the call to prayer, Mark narrates the third passion prediction, where Jesus will be taken from his disciples (9:31). This substantiates our claim that the passage involves the absence of Jesus in the midst of struggles against the demonic powers of this world, which are persecuting the church. Jesus' response that "this kind only come out by prayer" (9:29) calls the community to recognize the presence of Christ in prayer. Jesus will surprise them with his presence as he did at 9:15 after coming down from the heavenly mountain. Through prayer the disciples can overcome even situations of death, similar to the demonic boy who rises from the position of a corpse.[100] Nothing is impossible with faith (9:23) through prayer (9:29), even overcoming a sense of the absence of God.

6.6 The Night Absence of the Master of the House (13:34–36)

Parables as well as miracle stories express the theme of the absence of God. We noticed the narrative surprises in the parable of the doorkeeper (Mark 13:34–36) in the last chapter and concluded that Mark is speaking metaphorically and theologically to his community.[101] What is the message? Again the first line of the parable, "It is like a man going away," reveals that Mark is interested in the response of his audience to

---

98. Twelftree, *Jesus: Miracle Worker*, 89. Marcus rightly explains this as the merging of two narrative planes that contributed to literary incongruities so that "Thus, in the post-Easter period, physical contact with Jesus is no longer possible, but prayer is" (*Mark 8–16*, 665).

99. Marshall (*Faith as a Theme*, 117, n. 1) refers to Num 14:27; Isa 6:11; cf. Deut 32:5, 20; Isa 65:2; Jer 5:21f; Ezek 12:2.

100. Mark employs technical terms associated with Christian kerygma like dead body νεκρός, death ἀπέθανεν, lift up ἤγειρεν, and arise ἀνέστη (9:26–27).

101. See section 5.5f. above.

the absence of Jesus. Jesus' threefold call is to watch (13:34, 35, 37) in the absence of the master.

Since this parable concludes the eschatological discourse, one would expect the watching to relate to the return of Jesus, which is the emphasis in the Matthean version with its repetition of the term *parousia* (24:3, 27, 37, 39). However, an expected long journey from heaven is transformed into a short journey of one night, which as Lightfoot explains must be "a tacit reference to the events of that supreme night before the passion."[102] Therefore, the four times of return spoken about in Mark 13:35 ("in the evening, or at midnight, or when the rooster crows, or at dawn") become for Mark the four stages of Jesus' passion (14:17–31; 14:32–51; 14:52–72; 15:1–20).[103] In each of these four scenes Jesus is watching for the arrival of his passion while the disciples are totally unprepared. While Jesus predicts the betrayal, desertion, and denial of the disciples at the last Supper, they vehemently but mistakenly pledge their loyalty. Instead of watching in the garden of Gethsemane the disciples sleep. When the cock crows Peter denies his master three times just as predicted. Finally, when dawn arrives the disciples are nowhere to be found and remain completely absent during Jesus' Roman trial and crucifixion. Ironically, the disciples seem ready to watch for Jesus in his transcendent glory but totally abandon him in his suffering. Therefore faithful watching in the midst of Jesus' absence applies to the night of Jesus' suffering as well as to the glorified Son of Man's return on the clouds with great power and glory (13:26).

The uniqueness of this theme to Mark is witnessed by the fact that both Matthew and Luke omit the parable of the doorkeeper from the eschatological discourse.[104] But for Mark the parable is central since it both introduces the theme of the absence of Jesus (13:34a) and previews the structure of the passion narrative (13:35b). Discipleship failure in the absence of Jesus stands central to the purpose of Mark's gospel. We have already witnessed how Jesus is praying alone on the mountain while the boat community struggles at sea and how the disciples are incapable of fighting the demonic forces below while Jesus is transfigured above. Then in the garden of Gethsemane Jesus removes himself from his disciples (14:33) and distances himself from the three innermost followers (14:34). While alone, the disciples are unable to watch but can only sleep. Even though Peter, James, and John had witnessed Jesus' defeat of death with Jairus' daughter (5:35–43) and were present at the epiphanic transfiguration scene (9:2–8) when Jesus promised that they would not taste death until seeing Jesus in glory (9:1), they are unable to accompany Jesus in his suffering. When Jesus confronts their inability to watch, the omniscient narrator explains that "they did not know what to say to him" (14:40b). These words recall Peter's fumbling response on

---

102. Lightfoot, *Gospel Message of Mark*, 53. Cf. Geddert, *Watchwords*, 93.

103. See section 4.2c above.

104. Matthew includes a similar motif with the Parable of the Talents in 25:14–30 while Luke chooses a parallel parable from Q as a description of the kingdom in Luke 12:38–40 with 12:41 constructed from Mark 13:37.

the mount of transfiguration: "he did not know what to say" (9:6).[105] In each case the disciples misunderstand the necessity of Jesus' passion and are unprepared to experience the fellowship of his sufferings. Therefore, the threefold call to watch for Jesus in his glory (13:34, 35, 37) contrasts starkly with the threefold sleeping of the disciples in Jesus' passion (14:37, 40a, 41).[106]

In contrast with the disciples' inability to support Jesus in his passion, Jesus himself experiences the presence of God. Jesus addresses God with the intimate name *Abba* (14:36) so that communion with God through prayer prepares Jesus to face his trials. Dowd points out that the narrative consists of two sections (14:32–36, 37–42) each with three parts,[107] with prayer standing at the center, first in indirect discourse (14:35b) and then in direct discourse (14:36). As we discovered in the previous section, prayer for Mark is practicing the presence of God. Therefore in place of the absence of fellowship between Jesus and his disciples, Jesus calls forth the presence of God into his sufferings through prayer even though he is "deeply distressed and troubled" (14:33). Thus Mark structures the *Abba* prayer chiastically (a-b-b'-a'), with the outside couplet expressing trust in God's benevolence while the inward pairing conveys confidence in the power of God:

a		14:36a	Address: "*Abba* Father"
	b	14:36b	Formula of omnipotence: "Everything is possible for you."
	b'	14:36c	Petition: "Take this cup from me."
a'		14:36d	Submission: "Not my will, but yours be done."[A]

A. Dowd, *Prayer, Power*, 111 and 156, n. 20.

Jesus' submission to God's will and his faithful persistence in the midst of deeply distressing emotions and troubling circumstances become a model for Mark's struggling community.[108]

Jesus' crucifixion likewise offers an exemplary approach of dealing with forsakenness in the absence of God.[109] Jesus endures the shame of the soldiers gambling for his clothes (15:24) and the insults of the people passing by (15:29–30), including both the religious leaders (15:31–32a) and those with whom he was crucified (15:32b). Although he had commissioned the Twelve to be with him (3:14 ἵνα ὦσιν μετ' αὐτοῦ),

---

105. 14:40 καὶ οὐκ ᾔδεισαν τί ἀποκριθῶσιν αὐτῷ; 9:6 οὐ γὰρ ᾔδει τί ἀποκριθῇ. Luke ties these two passages together by reporting that the sleepiness of the disciples causes their misunderstanding at the transfiguration as well (9:32).

106. See section 4.2d above.

107. Dowd, *Prayer, Power*, 152. Mark 14:32–36 contains three reports of movements, each followed by a report of Jesus' speech. In Mark 14:37–42 Jesus returns from prayer three times and finds the disciples sleeping.

108. Kelber explains, "On the threshold of his own passion Jesus deals in exemplary fashion with the Christians' crisis of the cross, because the kind of testing he undergoes at Gethsemane may be the very one Christians are exposed to in the Mkan setting" (*Passion in Mark*, 59).

109. Cf. Kelber, *Passion in Mark*, 165 and Geddert, *Watchwords*, 188.

now in his crucifixion Jesus ends up alone. More importantly, the one saying from the cross that Mark employs quotes Psalm 22:1, "My God, my God, why have you forsaken me?" Jesus utters this lament at the climatic ninth hour (15:34) to reinforce Mark's theme of the absence of God's presence. Although Jesus experiences the forsakenness of God, he persists faithfully in his messianic ministry. As a result the kingdom of God arrives in the cross.[110]

Thus Mark's community must not visualize their sufferings as the absence of Jesus but as an opportunity to proclaim the coming of the kingdom of God. Achtemeier appropriately applies this data to the first readers' experience: "Clearly, the suffering of Jesus, and the concomitant suffering of his followers, was a major point for Mark, perhaps even the reason why he wrote his Gospel in the first place."[111] Apparently the community fails to discern the kingdom of God in their sufferings for Jesus. As we shall see later in this chapter, several narrative details suggest a mirroring of the experience of Nero's persecution in Rome. But whatever circumstances are engendering Mark's gospel proclamation of Jesus' life and death, an awareness of the absence of Jesus is central to that reconstruction.

6.7 A Post-Resurrection Journey Following a Crucified "Abandoned" Jesus (16:7–8)

In the last chapter we argued for an interpretation of the ending of the gospel as a Markan narrative surprise serving as a pastoral exhortation. But the content and purpose of this pastoral exhortation can be interpreted in a number of ways. By concluding with discipleship failure is Mark offering a polemic against a *theologia gloriae*? Or is he using reverse psychology to elicit an alternative response to that of the disciples? Or is Mark employing an open ironic ending which the reader must complete? Finally, if Mark is employing one of these techniques, what response is he educing from his audience?

6.7a A Polemic Against a *Theologia Gloriae*

As a prominent advocate of this position, Stock proclaims,

> Perhaps we can sum the whole thing up by saying that Mark wanted to exclude a *theologia gloriae*. Since he alludes to resurrection appearances, Mark knew of them but chose not to describe any. It was his purpose to place Christology so solidly within the context of the Passion that it would be impossible to separate resurrection from suffering.[112]

---

110. See section 4.3b above.
111. Achtemeier, "He Taught Them," 470.
112. Stock, *Call to Discipleship*, 207. See also Lindemann, "Osterbotschaft des Markus," 314–17.

The Theological Intentions of Mark's Literary Devices

Stock contends that Mark establishes his defense against a theology of glory in two stages. First, he breaks off the Messianic Secret on Good Friday instead of Easter Sunday. Then Mark substitutes the silence of the women and a future reunion between Jesus and his disciples in place of resurrection appearances. Stock posits such a dramatic contrast between passion and glory that he believes that "The stronger epiphany and revelation appeared in Mark's source, the heavier the counterweight in Mark's presentation."[113] Therefore, since the reader would expect the strongest *theologia gloriae* in the resurrection narrative, Mark does just the opposite.

Certainly Mark underscores the cross of Jesus, but in the process he balances a *theologia gloriae* with a *theologia crucis*. Evidence for a balance rather than a polemic against a *theologia gloriae* includes the following:

1. The first half of the Galilean ministry concentrates on Jesus' miracles (especially 4:35—8:21) whereas the second half predicts Jesus' passion (the discipleship catechism of 8:27—10:52). Likewise, the beginning of the Jerusalem ministry focuses on Jesus as the Son of David Messiah (Mark 11–12) whereas Jesus' time in Jerusalem concludes with a passion narrative (Mark 14–15).

2. Mark employs the title "Son of God" when Jesus displays his glory (1:11; 9:7) and his passion (15:39).

3. Mark presents both a suffering Son of Man and an eschatological Son of Man.[114]

4. The passion predictions (8:31; 9:31; 10:33) conclude with a prophecy of the resurrection.

5. The mystery of the kingdom of God (4:10) means for Mark that the kingdom is both already (*theologia gloriae*) and not yet (*theologia crucis*).[115]

6. The four eschatological time periods when the glorious Son of Man might come (13:35) are paralleled by the four divisions of Jesus' passion (14:17–31, 32–51, 52–72; 15:1ff).

7. Fear is both awe at Jesus' miraculous glory and a negative fear at the prospect of following Jesus to the cross (9:6, 32; 10:32; 16:8).

8. The Mount of Olives is the place for Jesus' kingly (11:1) and eschatological glory (13:3) as well as his profound suffering (14:26ff).

Therefore, Mark does not hold a negative opinion about miracles, resurrection, and Jesus' glory. As Wedderburn explains, Mark merely "avoids closing with a different

---

113. Stock, *Call to Discipleship*, 208.

114. Mark begins with the Son of Man as an undefined human being (2:10, 28), offers clear premonitions of a suffering Son of Man in the middle (8:31; 9:9, 12, 31; 10:33, 45), and concludes his gospel with the future enthronement of the Son of Man (13:26; 14:62).

115. See Ladd, *Theology of the New Testament*, 91–92.

Jesus who would distract from this suffering one."[116] Just as Jesus' ministry begins with a voice from heaven (1:11) proclaiming Jesus' identity as both Son of David Messiah (Ps. 2:7) and Suffering Servant (Isa 42:1), so Jesus' ministry concludes with both the centurion's proclamation that Jesus is the Son of God at his crucifixion and an angel's message that he is miraculously risen.

6.7b An Example of Reverse Psychology

By accentuating the women's flight, fear, and forgotten mission, Mark could be employing the technique of reverse psychology to promote the opposite behavior.[117] Fowler maintains that the disciples "serve the useful purpose of furnishing the reader with a vivid, memorable, and instructive antithesis to faithful discipleship." Therefore, if Mark's story achieves its objective, "the reader will be more faithful than they and their failure will not have been utterly in vain."[118] This is certainly not an unprecedented literary procedure. Boomershine, for example, offers parallels from the prophetic literature of Judaism, explaining that "as the prophets of Israel knew well, there are two major ways of appealing for righteous behavior: positive sanctions for right actions and negative sanctions for wrong actions."[119] Since each group from the original 120 disciples (the Twelve, women, and Jesus' family) are treated negatively, this explanation of reverse psychology makes perfect sense. But the purpose for the ending can be described in other terms as well.

6.7c An Open Existential Ending which the Reader Must Complete

"Mark's ending disturbs us, because it seems so inconclusive. We long to complete the book—and that of course, is precisely what Mark wants us to do," explains Morna Hooker.[120] The ending is left open since "only the reader can write the ending of this narrative."[121]

Opponents of this theory contend that open endings are a modern invention retrojected back into the first century. They point out that such theories about Mark's ending did not become popular until the movements of narrative and reader-response criticism took hold of gospel scholarship at the end of the twentieth century. Others

---

116. Wedderburn, *Beyond Resurrection*, 143.

117. For scholars who envision this technique see the list in Williams, "Literary Approaches," 32, n. 42. Lincoln entitles this technique the "*kalte Dusche*" effect ("Promise and Failure," 289).

118. Fowler, *Loaves and Fishes*, 147. Witherington (*Mark*, 62) objects that this ending would be cold comfort for Christians under fire, but with 16:7 and 16:8 placed together there is comfort as well as challenge. Cf. Lincoln, "Promise and Failure," 295–96.

119. Boomershine, "Mk 16:8," 238.

120. Hooker, *Endings*, 23.

121. Fowler, *Let the Reader Understand*, 154.

oppose this literary proposal since it has the potential of undermining the historicity of the original events. They argue that Mark is telling the story of people within the text, not of the community in front of the text.

But we have argued throughout that Mark employs narrative surprises to speak at two levels, both the historical and the metaphorical. Mark aims Jesus' historical message at his own community in its later historical setting. The ending of Mark brings the narrative surprises encountered throughout the gospel to its intended goal. Mark's various motifs come together. The community's struggle with the ostensible absence of Jesus causes Mark to purposely keep the resurrection appearances in the future.[122] The discipleship failures in his time cause Mark to underscore the failures of Jesus' disciples, his family, and the women. Their negative portrayal leaves the reader with a decision. As Williams states, "Those who read or hear Mark's Gospel now have the opportunity to take on the role of the perfect disciple."[123] At the story level, the author gives a negative picture of the disciples, "so that at the discourse level the narratee can observe their mistakes and inadequacies and learn to behave differently."[124] The reader must decide to travel to Galilee and begin again the journey of discipleship without making the same mistakes which the disciples, Jesus' family, and the women committed.[125] The reader who makes this journey will understand the necessity of Jesus' passion as well as the disciples' call to take up their cross.

By ending abruptly Mark makes his gospel stand still at 16:8 since this moment in time mirrors the experience of his community. As Hooker perceptively comments, "if the ending of his book is suspended, that is perhaps because the story is still being told in the lives of believers."[126] Just as the gospel concludes between the resurrection occurrence and the experience of its effects in the appearances of Jesus, so Mark's community finds itself in a similar situation, where they believe in Jesus' resurrection but are for the present not experiencing the miraculous effects of Jesus' glory but only the reality of the cross through persecution. Therefore, Mark's gospel was written to promote a discipleship of the cross, not to evangelize unbelievers. Through an open ending Mark mirrors existentially the situation of his readers and through reverse psychology he challenges this audience.

A pastoral exhortation involves both challenges and encouragement.[127] The negative responses that the women must overcome include flight, fear, and the refusal to proclaim the gospel message. Therefore instead of flight from possible insult, mock-

---

122. Collins asserts, "The decision not to narrate them, however, does have the effect of emphasizing the absence of Jesus in the time of the author and audiences" (*Mark*, 797).

123. Williams, "Literary Approaches," 32.

124. Fowler, *Let the Reader Understand*, 260.

125. See Geddert, *Watchwords*, 195 and Dyer, *Prophecy on the Mount*, 207.

126. Hooker, *Endings*, 27. See also Geddert, *Watchwords*, 172.

127. For an emphasis upon both warning and the promise of restoration see Williams, "Literary Approaches," 33–35 and Lincoln, "Promise and Failure," 283–300.

ery, imprisonment, and death, the community must embrace an abandoned crucified Christ. Whereas both the men and women disciples experienced failure in following Jesus, Mark's ending encourages the community to persevere despite failure and disobedience.[128] Instead of allowing fear of following a crucified Messiah to silence one's proclamation, the community is encouraged and challenged to overcome their fear of witnessing.[129] Therefore, one could say that an indirect apostolic commission ends the gospel since Mark narrates this negative example as a call for the more appropriate response to go and tell. Similarly, the specific command to tell Peter (16:7) must speak about restoration after denial.[130] The situation of betrayal within the community described in 13:12 demonstrates that this encouragement would speak existentially to Mark's community. Since the Christian movement spread with unprecedented growth and fervor, we know that the silence of the women was temporary.[131] This must mean that Mark was not just speaking historically but was proclaiming a message to his readers. An ending so stark and abrupt can only represent an author's deliberate rhetorical strategy.

What situation is Mark mirroring in the narrative? Since Mark 13 describes the two prominent features of the period between the resurrection and the *parousia* as missionary proclamation (13:9–10) and suffering discipleship in the midst of persecution (13:9, 11–13, 19–20), the fear, silence, and fleeing described in 16:8 must involve precisely these items. As Boomershine explains, "The character of Mark's ending would suggest that his listeners faced a situation in which proclamation of the gospel carried extreme risks and was associated with fear."[132] The most likely scenario compares the fear of the woman to share the message of Jesus' resurrection (16:8) with the community's fear of persecution if they testify to Jesus' name. Mark's church recognizes itself in this scene. The women are afraid to proclaim the message for the reasons mentioned in 13:9–11: They will be delivered up to councils, governors, and kings; family members will betray other family members to death so that everyone will hate the Christians. But just as Jesus will soon meet his disciples in Galilee in resurrection victory, so the seeming absence of Jesus in the fiery persecution will not last long. Mark's ending, therefore, is both appropriate and powerful because of Mark's technique of mirroring.

---

128. Cf. Lincoln, "Promise and Failure," 297.

129. Cf. Boomershine, "Mark 16:8," 237 and Rhoads and Michie, *Mark as Story*, 61–62.

130. Collins explains, "The implication is that his failure is not permanent. He will have opportunities in the future to deny himself, to take up his cross, to follow Jesus, and to show that he is not ashamed of Jesus and his words (8:34–38). The same applies to the other disciples who abandoned Jesus at the time of his arrest (14:50)" (*Mark*, 797).

131. See Cranfield, *St. Mark*, 469; Painter, *Mark's Gospel*, 210; and Boring, *Mark*, 301.

132. Boomershine, "Mark 16:8," 238.

6.8 A Possible Scenario Depicting Mark's Community

Each of the incidents we have examined depicts discipleship failure tied to the absence of Jesus. Jesus is sleeping at the stern (4:38), removed on a mountain praying (6:46), not acknowledged as the sustaining bread of life (8:14), transfigured on a mountain (9:3, 19), the absentee owner of the house (13:34), and the abandoned crucified one who will meet them again in Galilee (15:35; 16:7). Instead of faithfulness in times of struggle, the alternative activities of the disciples involve despairing questions (4:38), faithlessness which must be rebuked (4:40), misunderstanding and hardness of heart (6:52; 8:17, 21), the inability of this unbelieving generation (9:19) to continue the ministry of Jesus without his physical presence (9:18b), sleeping instead of watching (14:37, 40, 41), abandoning Jesus in his hour of trial (14:50–52), and fearful flight and silence (16:8). A contrast so stark and abrupt can only represent an author's deliberate rhetorical strategy. Mark must be mirroring a situation in his community.

Any depiction describing the scenario of this community must of course remain tentative. Our sources and methods never enable us to be certain about the situation of the community behind the text.[133] However, the hypothesis that Mark is involved with a community in Rome still reeling from the effects of Nero's persecution and hearing regularly about the Roman military attack on Jerusalem is supported by three sets of data: 1) the apparent absence of God during this time is visible in the loss of apostolic leadership; 2) the temporary cessation of rescue miracles; and 3) the experience of persecution. First, we know that Peter and Paul died around this time (*1 Clem* 5:3–7) and were likely killed in Nero's persecution.[134] This loss of apostolic leadership certainly caused trauma in the community and spurred the testimony of a written witness like Mark's gospel. In addition, the siege of Jerusalem by Roman troops threatened the loss of apostolic leadership there, so a situation of intense struggle is anticipated.

Second, whereas previously God performed amazing miracles of deliverance to set free Peter from prison and the sword (Acts 12:1–10) and to release Paul from the confines of the jail in Philippi to powerfully preach the gospel (Acts 16:22–30), now the miracles cease and the community's leaders pass on. No longer can epiphanic miracles be expected in every dire situation; the community must learn the miraculous power of a discipleship of the cross. This fits hand and glove the situation portrayed in the Gospel of Mark, where Jesus as the powerful Messiah performs mighty miracles in the first half of the gospel but his identity is incomplete without a narration of the passion. Likewise, Mark's portrayal of the disciples demonstrates that miracles alone

---

133. Frequently historical conclusions warranted by the evidence are very limited as demonstrated in the warning by Wisse ("Historical Method," 35–42).

134. See Brown, *Antioch and Rome*, 97. Finegan (*Handbook of Biblical Chronology*, 388) places the deaths of Peter and Paul as late as 67 CE with evidence from Eusebius (pp. 379–80) and Jerome (p. 385). However, Nero was absent from Rome from September, 66 to March, 68 so that it is more likely that their deaths occurred before his travels.

do not produce an appropriate response. Repeatedly Mark describes the disciples as misunderstanding and hard-hearted after miracles (4:40; 6:52; 8:17–21; 9:6); they must have their eyes opened (8:22–26; 10:46–52) to the road of suffering and to the necessity of taking up one's cross. Thus Mark's theology of miracles can be explained by a need in the church during Nero's persecution and the fall of Jerusalem to minimize the sign nature of Jesus' ministry (the leaven of the Pharisees and Herod in 8:15) and highlight the discipleship of the cross (as seen in the discipleship catechism at the center of Mark's gospel). The omission of resurrection appearances thus calls attention back to Jesus' crucifixion. Mark fine-tunes all the details of the narrative to highlight a discipleship of the cross, which is demanded in the midst of Nero's persecution and the Roman attack on Jerusalem.

Third, the evidence for persecution in the gospel harmonizes best with the most well-known example of brutalizing mistreatment at the time of the writing of the gospels, i.e., Nero's oppression of Christians. Certainly persecution does not dominate the gospel,[135] but from the reference in 13:19 ("those will be days of distress unequaled from the beginning, when God created the world, until now) unparalleled suffering is occurring. The following references from every strata of the gospel confirm a background of persecution:[136]

1. The wild beasts faced by Jesus in the wilderness testing can apply to Mark's audience, as Lane argues, "The detail, recorded only by Mark, that in the wilderness Jesus was with the wild beasts (Ch. 1:13) was filled with special significance for those called to enter the arena where they stood helpless in the presence of wild beasts."[137]

2. The reference in 2:18–19 predicting a time to fast after the bridegroom is taken away implies a period of distress to which Mark is addressing his gospel.

3. In the application of the parable of the sower (4:17)[138] to the disciples (4:10) instead of the crowd (4:1–2), the reference to a persecution where many fall away from the faith fits the time of Nero. An emphasis upon the rocky soil is dem-

---

135. Cf. Best, *Mark as Story*, 53.

136. However, Juel (*Master*, 145) and Ourisman argue that "The narrative was addressed not to an impoverished and persecuted congregation but to an indifferent and unperceptive congregation. The implied reader is not poor and suffering but comfortable and complacent" (*From Gospel to Sermon*, 33). Johnson adds that "The message is mainly one of warning against smugness and self-assurance. He seems to be saying, 'If you think you are an insider, you may not be'" (*Writings*, 161, 169). However, a better explanation is that Nero's persecution caused the insiders to become outsiders as evidenced in Mark 13:12.

137. Lane, *Mark*, 15. Evidence for use of this term for martyrdom in the arena at Rome comes from Ignatius of Antioch (Rom 4:1).

138. "The word πρόσκαιροί in 4:17 is a rare word with martyrological connotations referring to those who, when confronted with a choice between martyrdom for the kingdom of God and apostasy for the sake of the things of this age, chose the latter." See Marcus, *Mystery*, 66, n. 187 who cites 4 Mac 15:2, 8, 23; 2 Cor 4:17–18; Heb 11:25; Diog 10:8.

onstrated by the more extensive discussion of this seed in 4:5–6 since the seed along the path receives thirteen words and the seed among the thorns seventeen words, whereas Mark employs thirty-three words to describe the rocky soil which depicts persecution.

4. Martyrdom dominates the main characters in the gospel. John the Baptizer is only mentioned four times after he has baptized Jesus, and three of them are tragic (imprisonment at 1:14; martyrdom at 6:14–29; his role as the forerunner of a martyred Messiah at 9:11–15). Likewise, not only Jesus (9:31; 10:33; 15:15) but also the disciples (13:9, 11–12) will be delivered over to martyrdom.

5. Out of the entire sayings tradition Mark chooses logia that center on discipleship, such as denying oneself, taking up one's cross, and following Jesus (see 8:34–38 attached to Peter's confession).

6. The unique text in 9:49, "You will be salted with fire," implies a time of testing where the disciples will become the salted sacrifice.[139]

7. Mark adds "with persecutions" to the traditional saying of 10:29–30 to contemporize the text, as evidenced by its omission from Matthew 19:29 and Luke 18:30.[140] Furthermore, the promise of new and more extensive family relationships offers consolation to persons experiencing the pain of alienation and estrangement from their natural families as predicted in 13:12.

8. Jesus' prediction in 10:39 that James and John will drink the cup and be baptized in suffering becomes a call to discipleship for the entire community.

9. Following the cursing of the fig tree, Mark inserts statements about faith, prayer, and forgiveness. Marcus explains that "In the Markan situation, 11:23–25 would probably be heard as a counterbalance to the doubt, despair, and bitterness prevailing within a community racked by war and persecution, in which family members are betraying each other to death and Christians are being hated by 'all' (cf. 13:12–13)."[141]

10. Mark sandwiches together Jesus' trial and Peter's denials. Through this literary device Mark allows Jesus to make the "good confession" as a model for Christians under duress, whereas Peter becomes a negative example of those who crumble under pressure. In this way Jesus' trial becomes a narrative of the trials of

---

139. Fire is frequently a metaphor for persecution (1 Pet 1:7; 4:12; Rev 3:18). Salted with fire means to become a sacrifice that must be placed in the fire with a background in Lev 2:13. For commentators who support a reference to persecution see Stein, *Mark*, 450.

140. See Witherington *Mark*, 285 and Graham, "Passion Prediction," 21.

141. Marcus, *Mark 8–16*, 795. Incigneri contends that forgiveness is included because Mark is extending forgiveness to those who have denied the Christian faith since "Mark hoped to convince those who would exclude the lapsed that it does not matter how grave the sin has been, and that betrayal is as bad, and as forgivable, as denial" (*Gospel to the Romans*, 346).

Christians in Mark's own time.[142]

11. Bammel adds that "If Mark's Gospel was written for Rome, then the reference to 'envy' in 15.10 may be another piece of evidence of the martyrological substructure of the Gospel."[143] The Jews persecute Jesus because of envy; Paul and Peter are killed at Rome because of envy (1 Clem 5:2–5); likewise envy becomes the reason for Nero's persecution of the church of Rome as well.[144]

12. Since Mark repeatedly connects Christology and discipleship, he would naturally include an application to the community with the depiction of the sufferings of Jesus. Significantly, Mark highlights the intense mocking at Jesus' death on three separate occasions (14:65; 15:16–20a, 29–32).[145] The fact that Jesus is mocked both at the Jewish trial (14:65) and the Roman trial (15:16–20a) could parallel the anticipated persecution of the disciples by both Jews and Gentiles described in 13:9. The mockery of Christians in Rome during Nero's persecution is evidenced by the depictions given by Roman writers about the mockery bestowed on the Christians at their deaths in the arena. In such a situation it is understandable why Mark would end his gospel with fleeing women who are afraid to share the good news.

The best-known persecution that fits the time of Mark's gospel is Nero's torture of Christians, with Tacitus (15:44) reporting that the Christians were "substituted as scapegoats and punished with the utmost refinements of cruelty."[146] If the audience of Mark's gospel was struggling with flight, regret, fear, and silence, this picture fits with the future to which Jesus calls his followers in Mark 13:9–13.[147] In addition, Tacitus (Annals 15:44) reports the Christians' unfaithfulness and betrayal of one another under the Roman persecution.[148] These breakdowns in faith and community parallel the discipleship failures narrated in Mark's gospel, where "brother betrays brother to

---

142. Boring, Mark, 410. Regarding Mark 14:67 Boring thinks that "The charge that he is with 'the Nazarene' is similar to the later charge of belonging to the 'sect of the Nazarenes' (Acts 24:5)" so that Peter "belongs to a suspect group; the charge is 'ecclesiological' rather than 'christological,' though in Mark's mind the two are inseparable" ((415–16). The trials of Christians also involved an attempt to make followers curse Jesus (Pliny, Letters, 10,96,5) as Peter did (Mark 14:71).

143. Bammel, Trial of Jesus, 98. He suggests Phil 1:15 as further evidence if the epistle emanates from Rome.

144. Tacitus 15:44 reports that in the capital Christianity had recently become in vogue, so Nero apparently resorted to ridicule and accusation out of envy.

145. Marcus contends that "Mark 15:16–32, therefore, is best viewed as a unified, three-part passage on the mockery of Jesus' kingship" (Mark 8–16, 1045).

146. "Dressed in animal skins they were torn to pieces by dogs, or crucified, or made into torches to be ignited after dark as substitutes for daylight."

147. Mitchell, Beyond Fear and Silence, 85.

148. Tacitus IV, Loeb Classical Library, 283–84: "First, then, the confessed numbers of the sect were arrested, next, on their disclosures, vast numbers were convicted, not so much on the count of arson as for hatred of the human race." Cf. also Pliny, Epistles 10,96,5–6.

death" (13:12).¹⁴⁹ Furthermore, as Incigneri points out, "The story of Peter's apostasy would be a strong motive to accept and forgive those leaders and ordinary Christians who betrayed others under the horrors inflicted by Nero."¹⁵⁰ Finally, the unique Markan passage of 9:50b exhorts the persecuted community of 9:49 to "Have salt in yourselves, and be at peace with each other." Mark stresses this covenant of salt since members of his community have broken their loyalty bonds by betraying each other (13:12) during Nero's persecution.¹⁵¹

However, many prominent scholars today employ the data from Mark 13 to argue for a provenance in greater Palestine or Syria instead of Rome.¹⁵² Kee contends that "the practices having to do with agriculture, housing, employment, and landownership and taxation" argue for a rural district of Syria-Palestine.¹⁵³ However, Van Iersel counters this thesis with the more natural explanation that "the local colour of the story requires no specific explanation when it agrees with that of the place where the story is set."¹⁵⁴ Theissen has produced some very thoughtful studies upon specific cultural designations in Mark's gospel. He argues that the use of "a Greek" as a cultural designation (7:31) derives from an oriental perspective rather than a Roman point of view, that the association of Idumeans with Syrophoenicians by the Roman Juvenal (*Sat.* 8:159) makes Mark's coupling of "a Greek" with a "a Syrophoenician" appear non-Roman, and that the appearance of a Cyrenian in Mark 15:21 matches the presence of Cyrenians in the church at Antioch, Syria (Acts 11:20).¹⁵⁵ However, Hengel offers counterevidence that the oldest examples of the expression "Syrophoenician" occur in Roman writers in the Latin of the second and first centuries BCE and that this term distinguished the Phoenicians of Syria from those of Libya, a distinction not needed for an audience in Syria.¹⁵⁶ Furthermore, Gundry's counterarguments which emphasize the presence of Rufus in the church at Rome (Rom 16:13) cancel out any connection with Syria.¹⁵⁷ Finally, Mark's knowledge of greater Syria does not appear

---

149. Black, "Was Mark a Roman Gospel?" 39.

150. Incigneri, *Gospel to the Romans*, 322.

151. Collins (*Mark*, 607) believes that the events predicted in 13:12 are apocalyptic commonplaces as evidenced by 1 En 100:2; 2 Esdr 5:9; 6:24; Sib Or 2:154–76 or inspired by Micah 7:6, but the fact that Matthew places this material in the mission discourse of chapter 10 demonstrates that it was expected to occur within the church's mission experience similar to Nero's persecution.

152. This would not include Galilee since as Collins explains, "A problem with locating the composition of Mark in Galilee is that there probably was no major Christian community there in the earliest period" (*Mark*, 101). See Stemberger, "Galilee—Land of Salvation?" 421–25.

153. Kee, *Community of the New Age*, 102.

154. Van Iersel, *Mark*, 36.

155. Theissen, "Lokal- und Sozialkolorit," 222–23 and *Gospels in Context*, 245, 247.

156. Hengel, *Studies in Mark*, 29.

157. Gundry, *Mark*, 1045.

very accurate since he rehearses a journey of Jesus from Tyre to the Decapolis that travels the roundabout journey north to Sidon (7:31).[158]

Marcus ties the provenance very closely with the details of Mark 13, asserting that "the instruction to Judean Christians to flee to the hills upon the appearance of the abomination of desolation (13:14–15) reflects the Markan community's history," so that the hills concerned are those on the eastern edge of the Jordan Valley in the Decapolis region, where two stories in Mark originate (5:1–20; 7:31–37).[159] Boring as well asserts that "Chapter 13 points to a community directly affected by the Jewish revolt in Palestine. The readers are themselves in the situation of crisis brought about by the war (13:14, 37)."[160] But the details of Mark 13 do not necessarily require a close geographical connection. The constant flow of envoys between the Roman army in Jerusalem and the capital brought regular news about the events in the east. Peppard points out that "The movements, successes, and failures of the Roman military were among the most trafficked bits of information available in the Empire."[161] Reports of revolts reached Rome speedily as evidenced by Josephus' description of an uprising among the Germans during this time period: "for as soon as ever the news of their revolt was come to Rome, and Caesar Domitian was made acquainted with it, he made no delay even at that his age, when he was exceeding young, but undertook this weighty affair" (War 7:85).[162] Thus the evidence on both sides cancel each other out.

However, the theme of persecution against Christians is very difficult to locate in greater Syria and fits best with a Roman origin. In addition, the weight of the external witnesses tips the scale in Rome's favor since the church fathers favor a provenance in Italy.[163] Although this evidence is frequently discounted, the second-century commentators stand a lot closer to the events than scholars from the twenty-first century.

---

158. Collins (*Mark*, 369) counters with the weak argument that people's knowledge of geography was lacking because of the paucity of maps and atlases and that Mark constructed this roundabout itinerary deliberately.

159. This corresponds to the report of Eusebius (*Church History* 3,5,3) and Epiphanius (*Panarion* 29,7,7–8). Marcus does specify a disclaimer, "To be sure, a Syrian provenance is not a mathematical certainty, and most of the exegesis would work just as well if the setting were Rome" (*Mark 1–8*, 36).

160. Boring, *Mark*, 17.

161. Peppard, *Son of God*, 88.

162. News during the revolt traveled fast according to ancient standards. War. 1:80 states, "But, in a little time, news came that Antigonus was slain in a subterraneous place." War 6:153–54 reports that news of the death of Simon son of Gioras reached Rome quickly. Concerning Vespasian, War 4:618 asserts, "Now fame carried this news abroad more suddenly than one could have thought, that he was emperor over the east." Communication was constant among the cities of the empire as evidenced by the message Vespasian received from Rome while dwelling at Caesarea (War 4:588) and the message from Rome to Alexandria found in War 4:656. However, War 4:352 could be employed against this thesis. The quotes are from Josephus and Whiston, *Works of Josephus*.

163. Irenaeus, *Against Heresies* 3,1,1; Eus. H.E. 5,8,2–4; Anti-Marcionite prologues; Clement of Alexandra in *H.E.* 6,14,5–7.

Similarly a Roman calendar is evident[164] as well as non-Palestinian divorce practices where a wife can initiate the proceedings (10:12).[165]

The numerous Latinisms in Mark link it closely with a Roman environment as well.[166] Kelber objects that

> Upon analysis, the Latin loan-words in Mark fall exclusively into the category of military and economic terms. This reflects the situation not of Rome, but of an occupied country, because it is there that the imperial power imposes its military might and economic structure most tangibly upon the people. Roman origin of the gospel would have resulted in a penetration of Latinisms into the domestic, social and religious language of the gospel.[167]

However, transpositions of well-known Latin idioms into non-Greek word combinations, as well as the significant number of examples where Mark employs Latin sentence structure instead of Greek word order, prove that the influence of Latin upon Mark's text is greater than Kelber admits.[168] Therefore, we favor the conclusion of van Iersel that "The chance of such an influence was much greater in Rome than in an arbitrary part of Galilee or Syria."[169]

Finally, a relationship with other literature from Rome adds evidence to this thesis. For instance just as Mark 7:19 declares all foods clean, so Paul's Epistle to the Romans states, "in the Lord Jesus I am fully convinced that no food is unclean" (14:14).[170] Black calls attention to contact points between the Epistle to the Romans and the Gospel of Mark with regard to issues of ethnicity, social background, economic and social standing, religious organization, political turbulence, Jewish/Gentile relations, and interaction with the empire on such matters as taxes to Caesar.[171] Furthermore, Peter is repeatedly yoked with Rome by the church fathers (Papias, Irenaeus, Clement,

---

164. Traditionally Jews marked off the night into three watches (Luke 12:38), but Mark's adaptation of his source to Roman readers is detected in his employment of four watches in Mark 13:35 as well as 6:48.

165. Marcus (*Mark 8–16*, 707) considers exceptions but concludes, "To be sure, the categorical nature of Josephus' assertion that Salome and Herodias, in divorcing their husbands, were not following their country's law, is weighty" (*Ant.* 15:259–60; 18:136).

166. See the thorough and well-organized discussion by van Iersel, *Mark*, 33–34.

167. Kelber, *Kingdom*, 129, n. 1. Cf. Cadbury, *Making of Luke-Acts*, 88–89.

168. See the list of examples compiled by van Iersel, *Mark*, 33–34. In addition, Hengel (*Studies*, 29) and Witherington (*Mark*, 21) report that the Latin *quadrans* (Mark 12:42) was not circulated in the East.

169. Van Iersel, *Mark*, 35.

170. See Brown (*Antioch and Rome*, 198–99) for several other similar texts. Boring's evidence (*Mark*, 17–18) that the gospel is totally unlike Paul's epistle to the Romans is based upon unproven interpretations and genre differences.

171. Black, "Was Mark a Roman Gospel?" 36–37.

Origen, Eusebius, Epiphanius, Jerome), and in 1 Peter 5:13 Mark resides with Peter in Rome.[172]

Certainly, on the issue of provenance "we are deprived of the hard, corroborative evidence that is a historian's bread and butter."[173] Yet with Cranfield we can conclude that "the arguments in favour of Rome are not conclusive, but they are much stronger than those put forward in any other place."[174] Therefore, a provenance in Rome has strong evidence in its favor, and even stronger if we consider how the issue of the absence of Jesus in the Gospel of Mark relates intricately with Nero's persecution of Christians at Rome.

---

172. See Richard Bauckham's chapter "Papias on Mark and Matthew," in *Jesus and the Eyewitnesses*. Even if 1 Peter is pseudonymous, this reference indicates that the early church associated Peter and Mark together in Rome.

173. Black, "Was Mark a Roman Gospel?" 39.

174. Cranfield, *St. Mark*, 8–9, n. 4.

7

Geographical Mirroring: Jewish and Gentile Territory

In chapters 2–5 we detected examples of the Markan literary devices of intercalation, frame, allusionary repetition, and narrative surprise and investigated how Mark employs them to highlight theological themes. In the last chapter we explored how Mark employs a series of passages which emphasize the seeming absence of Jesus in order to mirror the struggles which the early church is facing and to demonstrate how Jesus is present as a Suffering Servant Messiah who will lead his people in the midst of struggle through being cruciformed to Jesus. In this chapter we will investigate how Mark foresees the inclusion of Gentiles into the covenant community. First, we will review how Mark describes the Gentile mission both as Jesus did with an eschatological approach and as the other gospel writers did by employing the additional history of salvation or *heilsgeschichtlich* approach. Then we will concentrate on Mark's unique means of already placing the inclusion of the Gentiles into the ministry of Jesus through 1) the sequence of the miracle catenae, which typologically mirror the conquest of the land of Canaan (which now includes Gentiles), and 2) geographical mirroring by locating the two miraculous feedings on Jewish and Gentile territory. Historically, the early Christian church did not recognize this reality until the vision of Peter and the reception of the Holy Spirit by Cornelius and his clan (Acts 10), but Mark attempts to demonstrate that Jesus was welcoming Gentiles already through the use of the literary devices of typology and geographical mirroring.[1]

---

1. Of course, the real problem in the early Church was not the Gentile mission as such since Gentiles were already accepted into the community as proselytes, but rather the terms on which the Gentiles could become members of a predominantly Jewish Church, namely circumcision. But circumcision itself is not an issue raised in the ministry of Jesus.

Geographical Mirroring: Jewish and Gentile Territory

7.1 Jesus and the Gentile Mission

Jesus' relationship to Gentiles has been hotly disputed.[2] The universalist interpretation regards Jesus as the first missionary to the Gentiles with his openness to marginalized people and his trips into Gentile territory.[3] Following this view, Schnabel proclaims that "His (Jesus') encounters with Gentiles indicated, sometimes quite clearly, that the gospel of the kingdom of God establishes a new covenant community which encompasses Jews and Gentles alike."[4] The particularist view, on the other hand, claims that Jesus completely restricted his mission to Israel (Matt 10:5b–6; 15:24).[5] Because first-century Christianity does not invoke sayings of Jesus to defend the Gentile mission, the outpouring of the Holy Spirit upon all people groups and a rereading of the Septuagint in light of the belief that the eschaton had dawned in Christ's death and resurrection must have inspired the Gentile mission, not Jesus' teaching.

The more nuanced *Heilsgeschichtlich* position states that Jesus anticipated a universal mission after his resurrection (see Mark 13:10; 14:9; Matt 28:19) but limited his ministry to Jews during his lifetime (Matt 10:5b–6).[6] According to this position Jesus connects the obduracy of Israel with the future inclusion of the Gentiles (Mark 11:15–17; 12:1–9; Matt 8:11; 10:15f; 11:21–24; 12:38–42), so that the rejection during Jesus' particularist ministry leads to the universal ministry of Jesus' disciples in salvation history. The Gentile mission therefore belongs to the period between resurrection and *parousia* so that we can entitle this position the "periods of salvation history approach."

Jeremias' eschatological interpretation has gained the most scholarly support.[7] According to this position Jesus "maintained a positive hope for the Gentiles, but

---

2. See the four attempted solutions in Hahn (*Mission*, 26–29), the three conceptions of a particularist and universalist approach in Schnabel ("Jesus and the Beginnings," 38–39), and the history of explanations in Wilson (*Gentiles*, 21–28). We differentiate five positions: 1) the universalist; 2) the particularist; 3) the restoration of Israel view which posits realized eschatology; 4) the *Heilsgeschichtlich* periods of salvation history position; and 5) the end of the age eschatological approach.

3. Cf. Spitta (*Jesus und die Heidenmission*, 72–75, 109–16) and the summary in Wilson (*Gentiles*, 21) as well as the advocates mentioned by Bird (*Jesus and the Origins*, 21–23) and Schnabel ("Jesus and the Beginnings," 39, n. 12). For instance, on numerous occasions Jesus seems to be oblivious to and even consciously rejects the regulations concerning clean versus unclean (cf. Mark 1:41–42; 2:14–17; 5:25–34, 40–42; 7:1–23; etc) which could include Gentiles.

4. Schnabel, "Jesus and the Beginnings," 58.

5. For quotes from advocates of this position, see Bird, *Jesus and the Origins*, 18.

6. Wilson (*Gentiles*, 22) places in this category Beasley-Murray (*Jesus and the Future*, 197–98) and Bosch (*Die Heidenmission*, 157). Schnabel ("Jesus and the Beginnings," 38, n. 10) adds Meinertz (*Jesus und die Heidenmission*, 84ff, 114f, 159f). For objections to this view see Wilson, *Gentiles*, 24–25.

7. Terminology is confusing. Wilson (*Gentiles*, 25) entitles Jeremias' approach both eschatological and *heilsgeschichtlich* (24) while Bird (*Jesus and the Origins*, 174) calls it a salvation history approach. We distinguish three salvation history approaches: 1) realized eschatology in the time of Jesus through the restoration of Israel; 2) periods of salvation history (*heilsgeschichtlich*); and 3) the future end time eschatological view so that Jeremias' view would correspond with the last one.

believed that this hope would be fulfilled in the apocalyptic events of the Endtime."[8] Jesus preached that the kingdom was at hand and therefore the flocking of the Gentiles to Israel was imminent as based upon the OT promises.[9] This view claims that originally Mark 13:10 referred to an apocalyptic proclamation when the Gentiles would flock to Zion in the last days, but that Mark reinterpreted this saying to apply it to a historical mission by the disciples.

Recently Michael Bird has emphasized that Jesus' mission centered on the restoration of Israel inclusive of Gentile involvement, thus a realized eschatology occurring within the time frame of Jesus' earthly ministry itself. He envisions the following elements in a Jewish restoration eschatology: 1) the re-establishment of the twelve tribes; 2) the advent of a messianic figure(s) to defeat Israel's enemies; 3) a new or purified temple; 4) abundant prosperity with the return of Yahweh to Zion; and 5) the subjugation or admission of the Gentiles.[10] Bird therefore opposes Jeremias' view by proclaiming that "Jesus expected the restoration of Israel to result in Gentiles participating in the kingdom not merely in the future but even in the present as a foretaste of that restoration."[11] However, since the inclusion of Gentiles would be subsequent to the restoration of Israel, it appears anachronistic to parallel them together in the ministry of Jesus, although a foundation for a later Gentile mission was established in the teaching and activities of Jesus.

In spite of Bird's efforts to the contrary, it seems highly unlikely that Jesus embarked on any mission effort aimed at Gentiles during his lifetime.[12] Wilson even contends that "there is no evidence that Jesus either foresaw or intended there to be a mission to the Gentiles such as actually took place in the early Church."[13] He argues that such a mission is indirectly excluded by Matthew 10:23b, which assumes that the Son of Man will come before the end of the disciples' operation in Israel. More significantly, Jeremias points out that "it remains a striking fact that we have no support for the view that the early church embarked upon the Gentile mission immediately after the resurrection."[14] The Gentile mission was started by the Hellenistic members of the primitive community, followed by Paul and Barnabas, who never personally heard

---

8. Wilson, *Gentiles*, 28. See also Jeremias, *Jesus' Promise to the Nations*, 22–23; Lohmeyer, *Markus*, 272–73, 295–96; and Meyer, *Aims of Jesus*, 167–68. For six criticisms of Jeremias' position, see Bird, *Jesus and the Origins*, 15–18.

9. Boring (*Mark*, 213) refers to the following traditional texts: Isa 2:2–3; Mic 4:1–2; Isa 19:25; 25:6–8; 54:15 LXX; Dan 7:14; Amos 9:12; Zech 9:10; Sib Or 3:716–27, 772–75; T Benj 8:2; 1 En 10:21; 48:5; 90:33; 2 Bar 68:5.

10. Bird, *Jesus and the Origins*, 27.

11. Ibid., 174. See page 175 for his exegetical arguments.

12. See Hengel, *Between Jesus and Paul*, 62–64.

13. Wilson, *Gentiles*, 18. However, Bird (*Jesus and the Origins*, 10) rightly refutes much of the evidence of Wilson's three main arguments.

14. Jeremias, *Jesus' Promise to the Nations*, 25. Cf. also Wilson, *Gentiles*, 27.

a commission to the nations from Jesus.[15] Therefore, Jesus held the traditional eschatological understanding that "Gentiles would not participate in salvation until the final inbreaking of the kingdom of God."[16] Consequently, Wilson assumes that behind Mark 13:10 and 14:9 lie genuine words of Jesus which refer to a future apocalyptic proclamation to the Gentiles in the last days.[17] Hence the placement of a missionary commission at the conclusion of the gospels (Luke 24:47; Matt 28:18–20) implies that only with the death and resurrection of Jesus has the eschatological hour arrived. Only in a post-resurrection setting does Jesus send his disciples to the nations.

Even though Jesus never embarked upon an intentional Gentile mission, all of the gospel writers narrate episodes of contact with Gentiles through which a future historical mission to the nations is anticipated. Therefore, the only appropriate solution is to posit that Jesus responded to Gentiles on exceptional occasions with considerable reluctance when Gentiles initiated the action.[18] For instance, the centurion explicitly requests Jesus' presence to heal his servant (Luke 7:3; Matt 8:5) and the Greeks avidly pursue Jesus' disciple Philip (John 12:20–21) before Jesus proclaims that his hour has arrived. Similarly, when the Syrophoenician woman encounters Jesus, he is purposely seeking solitude from any contact in Gentile territory (Mark 7:24).[19] Jesus' negative response to the woman, "first let the children eat all they want" (7:27a), expresses the traditional understanding that Gentiles will not enter into the blessings of Israel until the end time. However, the woman's surprising response of faith points to the fact that this future time is approaching. Finally, this healing along with that of the centurion's servant (Matt 8:13; Luke 7:10) occurs at a distance so that Jesus himself does not keep close contact with Gentiles.

---

15. Therefore, according to this view the early church initially understood the Great Commission as a mandate to spread the news to all Jews throughout the nations.

16. Wilson, *Gentiles*, 28. The traditional negative Jewish view of Gentiles is displayed in the gospels as well. Jeremias (*Jesus' Promise*, 42) demonstrates that they are "far from God, they are concerned only with their material needs (Matt 6.32 parallels Luke 12.30); their benevolence extends only to their compatriots (Matt 1.47); their rulers are despots (Mark 10.42); their prayer is a vain repetition (Matt 6.7); even when they are God's instruments (Luke 21.24; Mark 10.33), they use their power destructively."

17. Wilson, *Gentiles*, 26. OT texts expressing the Gentiles joining Israel in the last days through an eschatological pilgrimage can be found in Jeremias (*Jesus' Promise*, 58–59; extra-canonical literature on 61) as well as in Wilson, (*Gentiles*, 2).

18. See Wilson, *Gentiles*, 18. Luke 13:16; 19:9 confirm that Jesus aimed his ministry at children of Abraham.

19. Other interpretations of Jesus' withdrawal include flight to escape the hostility of Herod Antipas (but Luke 13:31–33 is against this) and because the Galilean ministry had failed so Jesus reconsiders the nature of his work. See Taylor, *St. Mark*, 636. However, the additional incident when Jesus encounters a Gentile Gerasene demoniac follows a sea journey where Jesus also seeks a secluded means of teaching his disciples as in Mark 6:31–32.

7.2 The Gentile Mission as Understood by the Gospel Writers

The Gospel of Mark continues Jesus' expectation of an end time eschatological inclusion of the Gentiles within Israel, but interprets that expectation within a history of salvation viewpoint so that Jesus' death becomes that eschatological event. Because Mark connects Jesus' death with the coming of the kingdom of God,[20] the references in 10:45 to "the Son of Man giving his life as a ransom for many" and in 14:24 to "the blood of the covenant which is poured out for many" should be understood eschatologically to apply to Jesus' death and therefore include Gentiles.[21] In addition, the reference to the Gentiles in the temple cleansing from Isaiah 56:7 (Mark 11:17, "My house will be called a house of prayer for all nations") carries an eschatological connotation as Jeremias teaches:

> The eschatological moment has arrived; the profaned sanctuary is to be cleansed; God is coming to his Temple. This is the point where the restoration of Israel begins, to be completed when the nations throng to worship in God's House whose gates stand open day and night.[22]

The Messiah's first act on his arrival at the sanctuary in Jerusalem is to symbolically transform the temple into a place for universal worship as expected in the new age.[23] Jesus' temple action therefore emphasizes the presence of God for the Gentiles just as the splitting of the temple curtain at Jesus' death (15:38) allows God's presence to fill the entire earth and the centurion's confession of faith anticipates the coming Gentile mission.[24] Mark calls attention to the subsequent results that will occur for the Gentiles when Israel is restored but applies them to Jesus' eschatological death.

Finally, Mark highlights the eschatological motif of the Gentile mission by transmitting Jesus' parables. In Mark 4:32 the picture of the kingdom of God as a tree where all the birds of the heaven perch in its shade functions as an allusion to the Gentiles joining Israel in the new age (Dan 4:9, 18; Ezek 17:23; 31:6; *1 En.* 90:30; *Midrash* Ps 104:13).[25] Similarly, the removal of the wicked tenants and the transfer of the vineyard to others (12:9) in the parable of the tenants speaks of the eschatological offer of salvation for the Gentiles, although the original meaning in the *Sitz im Leben Jesu* primarily concerns the poor and disenfranchised of Israel.[26] Interestingly, Boobyer

---

20. See section 4.3b above.
21. Cf. Hahn, *Mission*, 118.
22. Jeremias, *Jesus' Promise*, 66.
23. See Lightfoot, *St. Mark*, 64.
24. The names of Simon of Cyrene's sons in 15:31, Alexander and Rufus, are also probably Gentile names and the two Gentiles, Simon and the centurion, could provide an inclusio around the crucifixion narrative.
25. Jeremias, *Jesus' Promise*, 68–69.
26. Cf. Jeremias, *Parables of Jesus*, 76. Wilson states that the reference to both a beloved son and the "others" as Gentiles "enhances the connection which Mark sees between the death of Jesus and the admission of the Gentiles" (*Gentiles*, 29).

calls special attention to Mark's linking of the giving of the vineyard to others with a quote from Psalm 118 that "it is marvelous in our eyes." He contends that this marvel "will surely have meant for him that it was marvelous in the eyes of the members of the Gentile Christian church for whom Mark compiled his gospel."[27]

Not only does Mark continue Jesus' eschatological emphasis of an end-time mission to the Gentiles, but he also anticipates a new church stage in salvation history where the Gentile mission will be enacted. Since Mark does not include resurrection narratives where Jesus pronounces a mission commission, Jesus accomplishes this prophetically in Mark. Just as the three passion predictions of Jesus (8:31; 9:31; 10:33) and every prophecy in the upper room (14:18, 20, 25, 27, 28, 30, 41) come true in the passion narrative, in the same way Jesus offers prophecies about the Gentile mission after his resurrection which will come true (13:10; 14:9). In the eschatological discourse (13:10) Jesus proclaims that "the gospel must first be preached to all nations." The importance of this passage is demonstrated by the fact that Mark has inserted the missionary commission at the very center of a chiasm.[28] If this verse refers to Gentiles (εἰς πάντα τὰ ἔθνη), as evidenced by 13:8 (ἔθνος ἐπ' ἔθνος), then 14:9 implies Gentiles as well (εἰς ὅλον τὸν κόσμον) since the preaching of the gospel is again emphasized ("wherever the gospel is preached throughout the world, what she has done will also be told, in memory of her").[29] Therefore, Jesus does not engage in a Gentile mission in Mark but predicts and commissions a future universal mission to the nations as a new era in salvation history.[30]

---

27. Boobyer, "Galilee and Galileans," 342.

28. The center (13:9–13) of the five-fold chiasm found in Mark 13:5–23 focuses on persecution at the beginning (9) and end (12–13) with the preaching to the nations in the power of the Spirit at the very middle (10–11).

29. Kilpatrick ("Gentile Mission in Mark," 149) believes that these texts did not originally contemplate a Gentile mission by linguistically connecting 10a with 9 and 10b with 11 with a full stop after ἔθνη so that preaching is the occasion for the arrest. But convincing objections against this thesis are given in Wilson (*Gentiles*, 23–24) and Bird (*Jesus and the Origins*, 168, n. 265).

30. Jeremias (*Jesus' Promise*, 23) attempts to fit Mark 13:10 and 14:9 into the *Sitz im Leben Jesu* through an eschatological understanding of the Gentiles instead of a history of salvation perspective with distinct periods of time. He insists that Mark 14:9, "the proclamation to all the world" will not take place historically but by God's angel at the last day. A similar interpretation is then given to the closely-related saying in Mark 13:10. Jeremias attempts to get behind the Markan text to the world of Jesus who closely ties together eschatology and the flocking of the Gentiles to Zion in an OT manner. However, Mark does not picture a movement of centripetal evangelism toward Zion as the appointed center for the gathering of the nations. Instead, the gospel anticipates a centrifugal mission that extends to all the nations of the world. On the other hand, Wilson contends that Mark 13:10 is clearly an editorial insertion since "It uses the language of early Christian preaching—πάντα τὰ ἔθνη, κηρύσσειν, εὐαγγέλιον—and is therefore a *vaticinium ex eventu* from the missionary period of the Church" (*Gentiles*, 19). Marcus supports this position by adding, "This verse interrupts the natural connection between the prophecy of persecution in 13:9 and the instruction about how to respond to this persecution in 13:11" (*Mark 8–16*, 884). The best explanation for these difficulties and differences of interpretation is that Mark transforms an eschatological view of a Gentile mission into a history of salvation approach.

The other gospel writers follow Mark in emphasizing Jesus' eschatological message but then constructing the Gentile mission into history of salvation periods as well. However, each gospel develops this *Heilsgeschichtlich* approach in their own unique manner. Matthew is prominent among the gospel writers in employing the technique of promise and fulfillment to advocate a missionary activity among the Gentiles.[31] The magi symbolizing the Gentile nations of the last times bring their wealth to Israel and worship the Messiah (2:11), fulfilling Isaiah 60:3–6, 11 (cf. Ps 72:15, 17; Num 24:17). In fact, some Gentiles have already previewed this occurrence by joining the messianic line of Israel, as witnessed by the four women in Jesus' genealogy: Tamar, Rahab, Ruth, and Bathsheba, the wife of Uriah the Hittite.[32] Furthermore, Jesus resides in "Galilee of the Gentiles" so that a great light is dawning among a people living in darkness (Matt 4:15–16; Isa 9:1–2).[33] Through the faith of a Gentile centurion[34] (8:1–10, 13) Matthew envisions that the eschatological feast following a pilgrimage of the nations to Israel will soon occur (Matt 8:11–12 vs. Luke 13:19, which is unconnected with Luke 7:1–10).[35] Finally, Jeremias contends that the future mission to the Gentiles is visible in Matthew's interpretations of the parables of the tares and the net, where the field is the world in a universal sense in 13:38 and "all kinds of fish" in 13:47 is allegorized to refer to the peoples of the world.[36] In this unique gospel material Matthew imitates Jesus' emphasis upon the eschatological inclusion of the Gentiles through promise and fulfillment.

In distinction from these specifically Matthean references emphasizing the fulfillment of OT promises, Jeremias treats the specification of a mission to only the lost sheep of the house of Israel in Matthew 10:5b–6 and 15:24 as authentic Jesus material. His grounds include the following: 1) the passages are full of Aramaisms; 2) Jesus completely avoids the Hellenistic cities of Galilee, including Sepphoris, only four miles from Nazareth, and Tiberias, only three and a half miles from Magdala; 3) the healings of Gentiles occur at a distance in the climax of the pericopes (Matt 8:13;

---

31. See Jeremias, *Jesus' Promise*, 34 and Clark, "Gentile Bias in Matthew," 165–72.

32. However, since they are compared with Mary who is accused of impure sexual activity, the reason for their inclusion in the genealogy must be similar and therefore their nationality is only of secondary importance. Furthermore, their inclusion in Israel is not given eschatological significance since they are merely proselytes.

33. Sim ("Matthew and the Gentiles," 20) thinks that the formula quotation in 12:18–19 also speaks about the Gentiles.

34. Allison (in Davies and Allison, *Matthew*, 2:27–28; *Jewish Tradition in Q*, 176–91; and *Jesus of Nazareth*, 141–44) contends that Jesus was speaking of Diaspora Jews, but the inclusion within the healing of a Gentile as well as the lack of evidence that Jesus treats Diaspora Jews as distinct from Palestinian Jews rules such a conclusion doubtful. See Meier (*Marginal Jew*, 2:315) and Jeremias (*New Testament Theology*, 246) for opposition to Allison.

35. See Wilson (*Gentiles*, 3, notes 5 and 6) for those who see a present event in the life of Jesus. But as Wilson (4) demonstrates, it refers "clearly to a future apocalyptic event" demonstrated by "the presence of the patriarchs, the irrevocable judgement on the sons of the kingdom, the future tenses of the verbs, and the traditional apocalyptic themes of the Messianic banquet and the outer darkness."

36. Jeremias (*Jesus' Promise*, 35) discovers 36 examples of Matthean redaction in 13:36–43.

15:28); and 4) Jesus' purpose in invading foreign territory is not to pursue missionary activities but for concealment.[37] The difficulty in deciding whether this saying traces back to Jesus is witnessed by the fact that Wilson first offers five reasons for the unauthentic nature of these verses and then immediately disputes each of these five sets of evidence.[38]

The truth of the statement that Jesus concentrated his ministry upon the lost sheep of Israel should not be disputed, but it is suspicious that these particular sayings stand uniquely in Matthew whereas the Q (Luke 10:1–3) and Markan contexts (7:24–30) lack these words. Jeremias contends that they are absent from the other gospels because of the particularist qualities which Luke and Mark do not share,[39] but Matthew includes a similar openness to Jesus' ministry to Gentiles in most other passages as witnessed above. A better explanation proposes that these verses match Matthew's apologetic purposes, which stand central to his gospel.[40] Matthew employs traditional material that was utilized in his community against the accusations of the Pharisaic synagogue.[41] The synagogue apparently contended that if Jesus is the promised Messiah then God must have rejected his people since the entire Jewish nation failed to accept Jesus' messiahship. Matthew, on the other hand, attempts to

---

37. Ibid., 32–35.

38. See Wilson, *Gentiles*, 14–15.

39. Jeremias, *Jesus' Promise*, 27.

40. The apologetic in the birth narrative centers on the accusations that Jesus was born out of wedlock (1:20–23) and hailed from Nazareth, not Bethlehem (2:4–8). In Jesus' baptism the polemic is against the contention that John the Baptist is greater than Jesus since he baptized him (3:14) as well as the assertion that Jesus would not submit to baptism unless he was a sinner who needed repentance (3:15, 17). In the center of the gospel Jesus is pictured as the paradigmatic Israelite who walks the journey from Egypt to the promised land and is thus greater than Moses. Matthew's apologetic also provides a structure for Matthew 21–23 with Psalm 118 fulfilled in the beginning, center, and conclusion of this section. This OT psalm predicts that Jesus will arrive as the Son of David (Ps 118:26 in Matt 21:9), be killed as the stone which the builders rejected (Ps 118:22 in Matt 21:42) and return in the name of the Lord as the eschatological blessed one (Ps 118:26 in Matt 23:39). In the crucifixion Matthew polemicizes against the accusation that Jesus was not yet dead when taken from the cross (Matt 27:36). Finally, in the resurrection narrative Matthew includes material negating the claim that the disciples stole Jesus' body and proclaimed that he was risen (28:12–15).

41. The traditional nature of Matt 10:5–6 is demonstrated by the absence of Matthean vocabulary since εἰς ὁδὸν is not characteristic of Matthean redaction and τὰ πρόβατα τὰ ἀπολωλότα οἴκου Ἰσραήλ is the only occurrence of an attributive between a noun and its qualifying genitive in the gospel. See Davies and Allison, *Matthew*, 2:168–69, 550–51. Where does this traditional material originate from? Hahn (*Mission*, 32, notes 1 and 55 but especially note 5) agrees that these sayings are additions to the context but thinks that Matthew took this material from a primitive Palestinian source so that it is not traceable to free editorial revision. Meier (*Marginal Jew*, 3:544) and Sanders (*Jesus and Judaism*, 220) propose that the saying emanated from circles of Palestinian Christianity that rejected the Gentile mission, but no early Christian group opposed the Gentile movement, only the terms of entry into the church. See Bird, *Jesus and the Origins*, 53–55. According to Kennard ("Reconciliation *Tendenz* in Matthew," 159–63), Matthew's desire to please two different Christian factions accounts for the inclusion of 10:5–6 and 28:19, but the battle in Matthew is between the church and the synagogue, not intra-ecclesiastical warfare. Therefore, traditional Jewish-Christian apologetic against the accusations of the synagogue is a better hypothesis.

demonstrate that Jesus' mission was directed entirely at Israel so that the unbelieving Jews are without excuse. God did not reject Israel, but Israel rejected God's Messiah so that subsequently the Gentile mission resulted. There is therefore no excuse for the non-Christian Jews since Jesus' entire ministry was geared toward them. If Israel had received Jesus as Messiah, the Son of Man would have brought to fruition the kingdom of God after the disciples proclaimed Jesus' message to the towns of Israel (Matt 10:23), but now because the nation rejected Jesus the message must be brought to all the nations (Matt 28:19) before the Son of Man arrives. The Matthean apologetic thus leads to the conclusion that a new era of salvation history is beginning with the Gentile mission.

Luke employs the Matthean technique of promise and fulfillment as well in order to insert an emphasis upon the eschatological inclusion of the Gentiles. In the birth narrative (Luke 2:32), Simeon prophesizes that Jesus will be "a light for revelation to the Gentiles and for glory to your people Israel," which is a direct allusion to Isaiah 49:6 (cf. 42:6). At 3:6 Luke extends the quote of Isaiah 40:3–4 to include "all people will see God's salvation" (vs. Mark 1:3).[42] Luke 3:38 traces Jesus' genealogy back to Adam, instead of Abraham as in Matthew, so that Jesus' mission is aimed at all humankind. More importantly, Luke 4:26–27 recalls the Gentile contact of Elijah and Elisha with the widow at Zaraphath and Naaman the Syrian to anticipate that the gospel message will be received by Gentiles.[43] Furthermore, the designation of seventy-two or seventy in Luke 10:1 likely echoes the LXX table of nations in Genesis 10:2–31.[44] Finally, the missionary commission in Luke 24 is "firmly embedded in the scheme of prophecy and fulfillment."[45]

Whereas Matthew adds the particularist ministry of Jesus to Israel at 10:5b–6 and 15:24 to emphasize that a new period of salvation history has begun with the church age, Luke instead attaches the Book of Acts and develops remarkable literary parallels between the two volumes. Luke ties Jesus' life into the history of the Roman Empire by employing Caesar's edict to bring Jesus to Bethlehem and by ending the story of Paul's missionary journeys in Rome, the capital of the Gentile world. Literarily, this creates

---

42. Cadbury (*Making of Luke-Acts*, 254) argues that Luke was interested in "the salvation of God" rather than "all flesh" since he omits "for all nations" at 19:46 (Mark 11:17). But the destruction of the temple in Luke's time better explains the omission in 19:46.

43. Lukan redaction is demonstrated in the programmatic nature of this passage summarizing the life and ministry of Jesus through Luke's most typical themes: universalism, the Holy Spirit, the Jews' rejection of the gospel, prophecy and fulfillment, eschatology, Elijah typology, and the poor and needy. See Wilson, *Gentiles*, 40.

44. However, for arguments and supporters of a background in Num 11:16–17, 24–25 see Wilson (*Gentiles*, 45–47) who supports the view that "the mission of the Seventy is clearly to Israel" (47). We contend that the mission is to the mixed people groups of the land of Canaan since passages concerning the Samaritans surround this pericope (9:51–56 and 10:25–37). Since Luke narrates a mission of the twelve (9:1–6) followed by a mission of the seventy (10:1–20), an allusion to his formula "to the Jew first, but also to the Gentile" could be present meaning the Samaritans here.

45. Wilson, *Gentiles*, 48.

an inclusio around Luke-Acts (Luke 2:1; 3:1 and the appeal to the emperor in Acts 28) which displays that Jesus' ministry to Israel in the gospel continues in a second stage in the Book of Acts (1:1) which culminates in the statement that the Gentiles will receive the gospel message (28:28). Already at Jesus' birth, the angels proclaim "good news of great joy for all the people" (2:10), which will only be realized in the Book of Acts. Since the two terms "the bringing of good news" (εὐαγγελίζομαι) and the title "Savior" (σωτήρ 2:11) are employed regularly in the kerygma in Acts as well, Gentile readers are also in the mind of Luke here in the gospel.[46] Therefore, the message of Jesus is not restricted to the obscure surroundings of Galilee but is central to events occurring in the Graeco-Roman world. As Wilson states, "Luke synchronises [sic] salvation history with general world history," thus hinting at the universal significance of the gospel message.[47]

A reversal of geography in Luke and Acts also alters the destination of the gospel from Jewish Jerusalem to Gentile Rome. The mission to the Gentiles in the second volume is already anticipated by the three rejections of Jesus at the beginning of his Galilean ministry (4:28–29), the travel narrative beginning in Samaria (9:51–53), and Jesus' entry into Jerusalem (19:41–42), so that a reversal takes place in the Book of Acts, where the gospel is accepted in Jerusalem, Samaria, and the ends of the earth. Likewise, Luke parallels his emphasis upon the marginalized in the gospel with the centrality of the Gentiles in Acts. Significantly, Luke introduces Gentile centurions at the center and conclusion of each volume to call attention to the faith of Gentiles. At the center of the gospel in 7:1–10 the centurion who possesses greater faith than any Israelite becomes the equivalent to the first Gentile convert, Cornelius (Acts 10).[48] The centurion who proclaims Jesus innocent at his climatic death (Luke 23:47) corresponds to the centurions who save the innocent Paul, the apostle to the Gentiles, from the mobs (Acts 22:26; 23:23) and death at sea (Acts 27:43). Finally, Luke hints at the evangelistic procedure of "to the Jew first but also to the Gentile" (Acts 13:46, Antioch; 18:6, Corinth; 19:9, Ephesus) with the parable of the great banquet, where after the original invitation has been rejected by the Jewish leaders, Jesus extends the guest list to the marginalized in 14:21 and then the further distant Gentiles in 14:23 ("Go out to the roads and country lanes and make them come in").[49] Therefore, both Luke and Matthew emphasize the eschatological arrival of the Gentile mission through promise and fulfillment, but they employ different methods to demonstrate that salvation his-

---

46. Since Luke 2:31, "in the sight of all people," refers both to Jews and Gentiles, likewise 2:10 includes Gentiles even though the singular is employed. The singular λαός normally applies to Jews, but in Acts 15:14; 18:10 Gentiles are included in the new people of God.

47. Wilson, *Gentiles*, 38.

48. See Wilson (*Gentiles*, 31) who thinks that Luke adds specific details to enhance the parallel with the narrative of Cornelius (compare Matt 8:1–10 without acts of charity).

49. The consensus among commentators holds that the double invitations to those who were originally uninvited includes in the second group the Gentiles according to Luke's analysis. See the discussion in Bird, *Jesus and the Origins*, 81–83.

tory has entered a new era with the mission to the Gentiles, i.e., the Lukan addition of a second volume versus the Matthean addition that Jesus himself only ministered to the lost sheep of Israel.

The Gospel of John employs two procedures that foresee a new period of salvation history with the Gentiles. First of all, John employs prophetic anticipation as Mark does in 13:10 and 14:9 by having Jesus state in John 10:16, "I have other sheep that are not of this sheep pen," so that both Jews and Gentiles become one flock. Then in 12:20–23 John employs Jesus' actions along with his words to likewise anticipate a mission to the Gentiles. The Greeks come seeking Jesus, and Jesus replies that "The hour has come for the Son of Man to be glorified," implying that only after his death and resurrection will the gospel be extended to the Gentiles.

Second, John employs similar literary techniques to what we will discover in Mark, i.e., typology and geographical mirroring, to insert the Gentile mission into the narrative. By calling special attention to the first two signs that occur in Cana (2:11; 4:54), John is demonstrating Jesus' retaking of the entire land of Canaan in chapters 2–4.[50] Within this section John mirrors the historical growth of the mission of the church as evidenced in the Book of Acts.[51] Similar to Acts 1:8, where the gospel is proclaimed in Jerusalem, Judea, Samaria, and to the ends of the earth, the fourth gospel calls for a faith response from the Jews (John 2:18) and the Jewish leaders (3:1) in Jerusalem (2:13), from John the Baptizer and his disciples in Judea (3:22), from the woman and citizens of Samaria (4:4), and from the Gentiles in Galilee (4:43). First the Jews come to Jesus in Nathaniel, the true Israelite in whom there is no guile, followed by the Jewish religious leaders and their need to be born again (3:1–21). Then Jesus' mission grows to include John's disciples (3:22–36), the Samaritans (4:4–42), and finally the Gentiles from the land of Palestine, as demonstrated by the title given to Jesus preceding the passage (4:42 "savior of the world") and the reception by the royal official's entire household (4:53) similar to the household baptisms in Acts 11:14; 16:15, 31.[52] Therefore, John's use of literary devices compares most closely with Mark's.

In summary, the gospels contain both an eschatological view of the Gentile mission as emphasized in Jesus' proclamation as well as a history of salvation approach to the Gentile mission which speaks clearly to their own time and place. Matthew and

---

50. Through a play on words Cana probably becomes a symbol for Canaan possibly alluding to Isa 11:11 where "in that day the Lord will extend his hand yet a second time to recover (תונקל) the remnant which is left of his people.... He will raise a banner for the nations and gather the exiles of Israel." See Hanhart, "Structure of John 1:35—4:54," 43, n. 3. However, the city is spelled Κανά while the land is spelled Χαναάν (Acts 7:11 and 13:19) so that the similar pronunciation is emphasized for the ear and not the eye.

51. Cf. Barrett, "Parallels between Acts and John," 164, 168. Although most of Hanhart's essay ("Structure of John 1:35—4:54") is eisegesis, there is truth to his statement that "Whereas Luke wrote a companion volume to his Gospel showing a connection between Jesus' ministry and 'acts' of his apostles, John wrote as it were a Gospel and Acts in one" (46).

52. For evidence that the royal official was a Gentile see A. H. Mead, "βασιλικὸς in John 4:46–53," 69–72.

Geographical Mirroring: Jewish and Gentile Territory

Luke in particular employ the technique of promise and fulfillment to proclaim an eschatological expectation of a mission to the Gentiles. As we have seen, each Synoptic Gospel develops the history of salvation approach differently, with Mark (and John) employing prophetic prediction (13:10; 14:9), Matthew contrasting Jesus' particularism to Israel (10:5b-6; 15:24) with the Great Commission to the nations (28:19), and Luke adding a second volume to historicize Jesus' eschatological emphasis. Therefore, all the gospel writers have seen the eschatological expectations of Jesus fulfilled in the early church. However, as we shall now demonstrate, Mark also employs two unique literary devices to allude to the importance of the Gentile mission: 1) Promised Land typology and 2) geographical mirroring.

7.3 The Problem of Markan Geography

We have not yet discussed the journeys of Jesus into Gentile territory in the miracle section of Mark 4:35—8:26. What significance does this play for Mark's conception of the role of Gentiles in the church? In this section we will argue that Mark employs two literary devices for theological purposes. First of all, Mark utilizes the typology of the retaking of the Promised Land to indicate that the land of Canaan is polluted and unclean and therefore needs to be reconquered as the kingdom of God. Specifically, Mark employs two miracle catenae that begin with a sea journey and conclude with a miraculous feeding to typologically describe Israel's journey across the Jordan River to celebrate an eschatological feast in the Promised Land. Second, Mark portrays the miraculous feedings on Jewish and Gentile territory so that the geographical designations demonstrate that the mission of Jesus is intended for both Jew and Gentile. We entitle this literary device geographical mirroring.

But to prove this thesis we need to demonstrate that Markan geographical details are trustworthy or at least that they provide a meaningful pattern. Fowler reports that Mark evidences little concern for geographical exactitude and "when scrutinized, the geographical references associated with the boat trips are either vague, inaccurate, or contradictory."[53] On the contrary, we will argue that Mark has specific theological reasons for his geographical descriptions.

It appears contradictory that in the sea journey at 6:45 Jesus heads toward Bethsaida but arrives instead in Gennesaret (6:53). However, Mark has purposely altered the series of miracle stories in the oral tradition and located the second touch healing in Bethsaida later in the book (8:22–26) to symbolically prepare for Peter's incomplete confession of faith (8:29) and serve as a frame around the discipleship catechism with another healing of a blind man (10:46–52). Jesus travels to the Jewish destination Gennesaret rather than the Gentile destination Bethsaida in order that Mark can insert a controversy dialogue and parable about Jewish cleanliness rites (7:1–23 clean

---

53. Fowler, *Loaves and Fishes*, 58.

hands and kosher food) before miracle stories that involve unclean people (7:24–30) and impure fluids (7:31–37).[54] Thus Mark's redactional purposes account for the unexpected change in place designations.

Other place descriptions seem inaccurate and unreliable. In 5:1 the geography is so confused that various manuscripts posit that Mark mentions the Gerasenes, Gadarenes, or Gergesenes. However, this textual problem does not change the unanimous opinion that this area is the Gentile territory of the Decapolis (5:20). Mark 7:31 implies that Jesus traveled through Sidon on a journey from Type to the Sea of Galilee, which causes interpreters to conclude that the author exhibits little knowledge of the geography of Palestine. On the other hand, Wefald explains that "if 'returned' is not understood as 'immediately and directly returning' but as beginning a long roundabout way of eventually returning to Galilee by circling through Sidon . . . , then Jesus' journey can be understood as not being confusing, but as staying in Gentile territory exclusively for its duration."[55] So Mark's geography is inexact, but the Jewish or Gentile nature of the landscape can be easily identified.

The basic problem is that the geographical references are vague. For instance, what does it mean to cross the sea? Is it a westward or eastward journey or just a short excursion along one of the shorelines? Can we pinpoint what is Jewish and what is Gentile territory from Mark's descriptions? Fowler complains that "Mark never bothers to tell us explicitly on what side of the Sea of Galilee events take place."[56] As a consequence some conclude that the localizations "all function merely to provide artificial background scenery for the episodes in the narrative" and do not link geographical locales with ethnic groups.[57] On the other hand, Wefald positively declares, "While not crystal clear in exact detail, geographical references that are somewhat fuzzy could still communicate political and cultural information very distinctly."[58]

We will attempt to demonstrate that Mark offers transparent narrative signals for discerning Jewish versus Gentile locales. The first sea trip to Gerasa (5:1) is clearly within the Decapolis (5:20) and therefore Gentile territory as witnessed by the unclean pigs (5:11–13) and the dwelling among tombs (5:5).[59] The return journey results in an encounter with the ruler of a synagogue (5:22) and patients who suffer from maladies that result in ceremonial uncleanness (bleeding and death). Combined with the

---

54. See section 3.7 above.
55. Wefald, "Separate Gentile Mission," 12, n. 27.
56. Fowler, *Loaves and Fishes*, 60.
57. Ibid., 66.
58. Wefald, "Separate Gentile Mission," 8 versus Fowler, *Loaves and Fishes*, 60.
59. Some authors call attention to the address "Son of the Most High God" (5:7) as well and compare it with Gen 14:18; Num 24:16, and Isa 14:14. See the authors mentioned by Watts, *Isaiah's New Exodus*, 164, n. 141. Koch ("Inhaltliche Gliederung," 151–53) attempts to show that Jesus is clearly active in Gentile territory only in 7:24–30. But Koch (164, n. 60) is mistaken when he contends that the Sea of Galilee lies precisely in the middle of the region of Galilee so that the Decapolis should be considered entirely Jewish terrain.

number twelve (5:25, 42) which holds the passage together as a Markan sandwich and alludes to stories that have direct relevance to the twelve tribes, these details witness to the Jewish nature of the incident.

In the second journey, Jesus' company embarks on a boat trip to a solitary place (6:32–34) which is still within Jewish borders as evidenced by Jesus' characterization of the audience as sheep without a shepherd (6:34; Israel in Num 27:17; 1 Kgs 22:17; Ezek 34:5) as well as the twelve baskets of bread left over (6:42). Mark regularly employs the phrase εἰς τὸ πέραν (4:32 & 5:1; 5:21; 6:45; 8:13) to indicate a journey to a shore of the Sea of Galilee that stands opposite of the Jewish or Gentile territory where Jesus began. Since this phrase is not employed in 6:32, the trip is entirely within Jewish terrain.[60] Therefore, with Jewish territory assured, Mark employs the general destination "a solitary place."

In order to continue the sea journey after the feeding of the five thousand, Jesus' disciples trek toward Bethsaida (6:45). Since Bethsaida is located on the eastern shore of the Jordan, they are headed toward what now has become Gentile territory.[61] However, Mark interrupts this objective so that he can insert incidents that involve the Jewish purity rites of washing hands and eating kosher food. Therefore, Mark alters the destination to Gennesaret (6:53), where Jewish cleanliness issues constitute an important debate. Then in 7:24 Jesus undertakes a land journey to Tyre (7:24), followed by a trip through Sidon, past the Sea of Galilee, and into the Decapolis (7:31), so that all the events in 7:24—8:9 take place in Gentile territory. This has special significance for the feeding of the four thousand, whose Gentile audience is further reinforced by the fact that the crowd comes from afar (8:3) and the miracle results in seven baskets left over, symbolizing as we shall see the seven Gentile nations of the land of Canaan (Deut 7:1; Acts 13:19).

Finally, Mark inserts a third sea journey, which he employs to summarize the theological implications of the miracle catenae. First Jesus travels by sea to Jewish terrain in 8:10[62] so that Mark can include a dialogue with the Pharisees about demanding signs. This speedy conversation (8:11–12) escorts the narrative to another sea adventure (8:13) toward Gentile territory and the destination of Bethsaida (8:22).

---

60. Kelber (*Kingdom*, 58, 61) incorrectly perceives both the terms διαπεράω (to cross over) and πέραν (the other side) as linguistic signals of a full west-east or east-west crossing of the lake and not simply a side trip. Therefore, the summary healing statement in 6:53–56 is seen as a reference to activity among the Gentiles illustrating that "the kingdom has arrived in full on the eastern shore." Furthermore since neither word appears at 8:10, Kelber insists that the voyage to Dalmanutha is merely a side trip on the east coast. As a result Kelber must envision 8:13 as a voyage from east to west even though the landing is Bethsaida. Therefore, this presupposition leads to wrong conclusions and distorts Mark's geographical program as witnessed by the audiences whom Mark addresses. See also Petersen, "Composition of Mark 4:1—8:26," 199.

61. When Matthew omits the destination Bethsaida but still states that Jesus went to the other side (14:22), he misses the Jew/Gentile distinction in geography since Jesus remains in Jewish territory (14:24).

62. The Matt 15:39 reference to Magdala offers the best commentary on Dalmanutha.

By land Jesus finally reaches the northernmost city of the ancient land of Canaan, Caesarea Philippi (8:27), where Peter's confession changes his destination toward Jerusalem. This analysis of the three sea trips demonstrates that Mark pays special attention to Jewish versus Gentile geography throughout this miracle section (unlike what Fowler and others advocate).[63]

7.4 Mark's Employment of Typology to Designate the Gentile Mission

In this section we will argue that Mark employs Jesus' journeys into Gentile territory to recall the OT typology of the retaking of the land. The sea journeys that begin each miracle catena have as their destination Gentile regions. The sea-calming voyage (4:35–41) takes Jesus into the Decapolis, and the original destination of the sea-walking trip is the city of Bethsaida (6:45), which lies just east of the Jordan River. In both sea journeys the chaos of the sea miraculously turns to calm, enabling the disciples to arrive at the other shore. In 6:48–49 Jesus even walks on the lake as if it is dry ground. This is reminiscent of Joshua's miraculously crossing the Jordan River on dry ground before beginning the conquest of Canaan.

The boat trips result in a cleansing of the land through Jesus' exorcisms. In the first trip Jesus purifies the Decapolis through the casting out of a legion of evil spirits (5:9). Since the term "legion" was employed of an army battalion whose Roman Palestinian force, the *Legio Decima Fretensis*, used a wild hog as their emblem, the exorcism denotes more than just a personal deliverance. The death of the two thousand pigs in the sea (5:11–13) purges the land of its pollution (Lev 11:7; Deut 14:8).[64] Mark pictures Jesus' ministry as a conquest of this Gentile territory so that the gospel is preached and the land becomes holy again (5:20).

The second journey to Tyre and Sidon likewise begins with an exorcism, that of the daughter of the Syrophoenician woman. Through this deliverance and the unexpected faith of the Gentile woman Jesus cleanses the impure Gentile "dogs" (7:27–28)

---

63. See Malbon (*Narrative Space*, 26–27, 40) and Wefald ("Separate Gentile Mission," 13) for clear narrative signals to the reader for discerning a Jewish versus Gentile locale.

64. Myers (*Say to This Mountain*, 59) and Horsley (*Hearing the Whole Story*, chapter 6) prefer a political interpretation where legion represents the Roman empire. Arguments in favor of this position include: 1) the name of the demon is a Roman army term; 2) "swear to God that you won't torture me" (5:7) implies that the man has been tortured by a Roman legion; 3) Jesus dismisses the demons similar to the dismissal of troops; 4) the pigs charge down the hill like an army; 5) the incident recalls the drowning of the Egyptian army in the sea with whom Israel was held captive; 6) a wild hog was the emblem of the *Legio Decima Fretensis*, a section of the Roman military forces stationed in Galilee during the war of 66–70; and 7) the inhabitants are fearful of reprisal by the Romans. However, this modern political interpretation arose out of cultural situations within twentieth century colonization. A reconquest of the land fits the facts better since the ties with the first exorcism in the synagogue (1:21–28) demonstrate that Jewish territory is also polluted. Furthermore, Jesus entering into negotiations with the demons does not seem like an appropriate technique against an oppressive army. Finally, the accusation that Jesus is possessed by a demon (3:22) certainly does not indicate that he sided with the Romans.

so that table fellowship between Jew and Gentile can result. Mark sequences the narratives to address important issues dividing Jews and Gentiles. Through the insertion of 7:1–23 into the miracle catenae Mark creates a progression of stories dealing with impure hands, food, people, and fluids. Jesus' teaching and miracles usher in the kingdom of God and as a result ceremonial uncleanness is removed.

The third journey northward climaxes in Caesarea Philippi (8:27), although the excursion does not end until the return to Galilee in 9:30. In this case Jesus performs the exorcism at the end of the trip after his transfiguration into divine glory on a high mountain (9:2). While the majority of the disciples in the valley below are unable to cast out the demon (9:9, 14) and thus retake the Promised Land, Jesus resurrects this seemingly dead demoniac boy to new life (9:26–27) and teaches his disciples that he is always with them through prayer to cast out the demons (9:29). The highpoint of the trip, however, narrates Peter's confession (8:29) so that Jesus is proclaimed as Messiah in Gentile territory. Since now Jesus has retaken the entire land of Canaan, including Gentile territories, he immediately turns toward Jerusalem and his upcoming passion (8:31), where his messiahship will culminate.

In each particular Gentile region Jesus opens eyes and ears to the truth of the gospel and tongues are loosed to proclaim the kingdom of God. In the Decapolis the demoniac becomes the first missionary to the Gentiles (5:20) after a rejection of Jesus by its original inhabitants (5:17). Later in the Decapolis Jesus places his fingers into a deaf man's ears and touches his tongue with spit to open his ears to the gospel and his tongue to proclaiming the good news so that the people of the region cannot stop talking about Jesus (7:31–37). In Tyre the Gentile woman's faith opens the reader's eyes to the new implication of table fellowship between Jews and Gentiles (7:28–29). In Gentile Bethsaida the physical eyes of the blind man receives sight (8:22–26) to prepare for Jesus' open proclamation (8:32) of his suffering and death and the demands of a discipleship of the cross (8:34).

Why are the Decapolis, Bethsaida, Tyre and Sidon, and Caesarea Philippi chosen? In addition to historical reasons, these locales function as the former boundaries of the land of Canaan. The Decapolis represents the territory which at one time belonged to the tribes of Israel beyond the Jordan but has become the ten Gentile cities. Bethsaida is the first town east of the Jordan and so in the present time functions as the entrance into Gentile territory.[65] Since according to Genesis 10:19 Sidon was the northern border of Canaan, Matthew's transformation of the Syrophoenician woman described in Mark 7:26 into a Canaanite (15:22) suggests that the retaking of the land of Canaan is central to Jesus' kingdom ministry.[66] The fourth gospel employs a simi-

---

65. Remember that in John 12:20–21 the Greeks come to Philip who is from Gentile Bethsaida to indicate that Jesus' hour and the time of the Gentile mission is near.

66. Jesus is changing the negative conception of Canaanites by demonstrating that they are also a part of the retaking of the land of Canaan in the last days. But other scholars discover other reasons for Matthew's change such as a word play on Χαναναία / κυνάρια, translation variants from the Aramaic kěna'ănîtā,' or an OT reference to Gen 9:25 about slaves connoting the woman's subordination

lar literary device when the first two signs occur at Cana (John 2:13; 4:54) so that the retaking of Canaan (a play on the pronunciation of words) involves the arrival of the eschatological age (2:1–12) with a new temple (2:13–22) and the resulting conversion of the Jewish leaders (2:23—3:21), the disciples of the Baptist (3:22–36), the Samaritans (4:1–42), and the Gentiles in the land (4:43–54).

Finally, Mark's specific reference to the region around Caesarea Philippi "is a very appropriate place since, according to rabbinical statements, it is on the boundary between the Holy Land and Gentile territory."[67] With the source of the Jordan River situated here, Caesarea Philippi marks an appropriate beginning of Canaan. Josephus reports that Galilee reaches all the way to Sidon (*Ant.* 8,2,3) and to the sources of the Jordan (*Ant.* 5,1,24) which of course is Caesarea Philippi.[68] Therefore, Avi-Yonah reports that "The Hasmonean leader, Alexander Jannaeus (103–76 BCE) realized the almost complete unification of the Holy Land for the first time since King David" when he extended the state "to encompass Carmel and its coast, the Jordan Valley up to the sources of Dan and Paneas, and nearly the whole of the Transjordan mountains."[69] Each one of these locations in some manner calls attention to the retaking of the entire land of Canaan. Therefore, Mark pictures Jesus visiting the northern and eastern borders of Canaan just as people visited Jesus from Idumea (3:8), the southern border of the Promised Land.

In addition, Mark ties the first exorcism in Gentile territory (5:1–20) with the initial exorcism by Jesus in Jewish territory (1:21–28 in the synagogue) through a parallel structure,[70] so that both Jewish and Gentile territory constitute the Promised Land in the time of Jesus.

	Capernaum	Gerasa
A. The conflict	Have you come to destroy us? (1:24) = demons in Jewish territory	They begged him not to expel them from the country (5:10) = demons on Gentile land
B. The demoniac's challenge	What do you want with us? (1:24 Τί ἡμῖν καὶ σοί;)	What do you want with me? (5:7 Τί ἐμοὶ καὶ σοί;)
C. The address	Jesus, Holy One of God (1:24 Ἰησοῦ Ναζαρηνέ ὁ ἅγιος τοῦ θεοῦ) = Jewish title	Son of the Most High God (5:7 Ἰησοῦ υἱὲ τοῦ θεοῦ τοῦ ὑψίστου) = Hellenistic title

---

to Jews. See Davies and Allison, *Matthew*, 2: 547.

67. Schweizer, *Good News Mark*, 171.

68. This is quoted in Sternberger, "Galilee—Land of Salvation?" 416–17. Malbon (*Narrative Space*, 181, n. 55) muses that Caesarea Philippi is an appropriate setting for a religious question (8:27) since it is famed for an ancient pagan shrine in a cave dedicated by the Greeks to Pan and the Nymphs. However, we would place the emphasis upon the border of Canaan.

69. Avi-Yonah, *History of Israel*, 140. Caesarea Philippi was known from its older more famous name, Paneas. This was the northern border whereas the southern border included Idumea which was conquered earlier by John Hyrcanus "obliging them to adopt Judaism" (137). People visit Jesus from this southern border of Idumea at Mark 3:8 to receive the message of the kingdom of God.

70. See Myers, *Say to this Mountain*, 58 and Wefald, "Separate Gentile Mission," 13–14.

D. Jesus' command	Come out of him! (1:25 φιμώθητι καὶ ἔξελθε ἐξ αὐτοῦ)	Come out of the man! (5:8 ἔξελθε τὸ πνεῦμα τὸ ἀκάθαρτον ἐκ τοῦ ἀνθρώπου)
E. The demon's defeat	The unclean spirit . . . went out of him (1:26 τὸ πνεῦμα τὸ ἀκάθαρτον . . . ἐξῆλθεν)	The unclean spirits came out (5:13 ἐξελθόντα τὰ πνεύματα τὰ ἀκάθαρτα)
F. The crowd's reaction	They were astonished (1:27 ἐθαμβήθησαν ἅπαντες)	They were afraid (5:15 ἐφοβήθησαν) and amazed (5:20 πάντες ἐθαύμαζον)
G. The spread of Jesus' fame	Jesus' fame spreads throughout the region of Galilee = Jewish land (1:28)	His preaching results in the amazement of the Decapolis = Gentile territory (5:20)

What is Mark's purpose in this exact replication of material? Again the retaking of the land is being described. First the Jewish synagogue must be purified through exorcism (1:23-28). Then the surrounding Gentile lands, including the Decapolis (5:1-20; 7:31—8:9), Tyre and Sidon (7:24-30), and the region around Caesarea Philippi (8:27—9:29), must be exorcised so that the renewed Promised Land includes both Jews and Gentiles.[71] Just as Jesus leaves the wilderness and crosses the Jordan River to retake Jewish territory, so he calms the sea and walks on water like dry ground to retake Gentile territory. Wefald even finds it significant that the first three exorcisms occur upon Jewish territory (1:21-28, 32-34, 39; 3:11-12) while the latter three transpire during Jesus' journeys through Gentile territory (5:1-20; 7:24-30 and 9:14-29).[72] Thus Jewish land must be purged first.

In order to prove that Mark was advocating a retaking of the land, we must demonstrate that the land was in exile. N.T. Wright argues for Israel's exile by pointing to unfulfilled OT prophecies about the return of the Shekinah glory to the temple (Isa 52:7-10; Ezek 43:1-7).[73] The empty holy of holies demonstrates as well the incompleteness of Israel's restoration.[74] In 2 Maccabees 2:5-8, Jeremiah rebukes those who are attempting to locate the cave where the prophet hid the ark of the covenant and altar of incense since "the place shall remain unknown until God gathers his people together again and shows his mercy. Then the Lord will disclose these things, and the

---

71. Boring says, "Israel is no longer exclusively the Holy Land—the Christ-event exorcizes Gentile territory; analogous to 7:19, Jesus proleptically makes all lands clean" (*Mark*, 152). Cf. LaVerdiere, *Beginning*, 1:130.

72. Wefald, "Separate Gentile Mission," 13.

73. Wright, *New Testament*, 269-70.

74. Similarly the Talmud (b. Yoma 21b) describes five items missing from the Second Temple, namely the ark, the fire from heaven, the Shekinah, the Holy Spirit, and the Urim and Thummim. For other descriptions of missing elements see Yoma 52b; Rabba Songs 8,9,3 on 8:8; and Rabba Numbers 15:10 on 8:2. Some scholars dispute whether the missing presence of God in the Second Temple was a widely held view because of Joel 4:17; Ps 135:21; Matt 23:21; 11QT 29:7-10; War 6:299; m. Sukkah 5:4 and the conclusion of Yoma 21b which says, "They were present, but they were not as helpful [as before]." See Davies, "Presence of God," 32-36. We will demonstrate why the first view is correct.

glory of the Lord and the cloud will appear." Thus the promises of the return of God's presence to dwell in the midst of Israel would only occur in the future.[75] Therefore, the land remained unclean and in exile when Jesus' ministry began.

The contention that divine revelation has stopped points as well to a situation of continual exile. During the intertestamental period 1 Maccabees 9:27 explains that "there was great distress in Israel, such as had not been since the time that prophets ceased to appear among them."[76] In fact, the altar of burnt offering is said to be dismantled until a prophet will arise (1 Mac 4:46), and Simon Maccabeus is both governor and high priest because a trustworthy prophet has not yet arisen (1 Mac 14:41). Although limited occurrences of prophecy still occur,[77] Josephus explains that no exact succession of prophets has existed since the time of Artaxerxes (*Ag. Ap.* 1:8); instead the prophets are sleeping (2 *Bar.* 85:3). Without the presence of God's appointed servants the land remains defiled and still in exile.

Convincing evidence derives as well from the self-conception of Israel, who visualized themselves as slaves in their own land (Neh 9:36–37; CD 1:3–11). Wright points out specific texts which describe Israel's exile, including Baruch 3:8 ("See, we are today in our exile where you have scattered us") and 2 Maccabees 1:27 ("Gather together our scattered people, set free those who are slaves among the Gentiles"). However, since these texts could refer to the tribes who were still expected to return to Canaan, we need to distinguish carefully between the exile of Jews in the dispersion and an exile in the land of Palestine.[78] This oversight in the works of N. T. Wright and Craig Evans makes several of their arguments suspect, but does not necessarily negate their conclusion.[79] Since Israel at the time of Jesus still remained in the thrall of foreigners, Canaan itself is pictured as polluted and impure.

---

75. See Clements, *God and Temple*, 134.

76. Dan 3:38 LXX states "In our day we have no ruler or prophet or leader" (Prayer of Azariah 15). Seder Olam Rabba 6 clarifies, "Until [Alexander of Macedon] the prophets prophesied in the holy spirit, from now on turn your ear and hear the words of the sages." But Baba Bathra 12a states, "from the destruction of the temple." Cf. Orton, *Understanding Scribe*, 194–95, n. 61.

77. Josephus reports of John Hyrcanus that he possessed the three greatest privileges: the rule of the nation, the office of High Priest, and the gift of prophecy (*War* 1:68f; *Ant.* 13:282f, 299f, 322). Josephus who prophesied himself that Vespasian would become the emperor (*War* 3:400–402; Suetonius, *Div. Vesp.* 5:6; Cassius Dio, *Hist. Rom.* 66:1,4) reportedly experienced nightly dreams in which God foretold the impending fate of the Jews and the destinies of the Roman sovereigns (*War* 3:351). Likewise he witnessed a series of spectacular omens, portents, and prophecies (*War* 6:288–315) that the temple would be destroyed. Philo alludes to prophesy continuing in his time (*Quis Rerum Divinarum Heres* 259–62), and John 11:51 assigns this gift to the high priest.

78. Since these documents are written in the second century BCE and later, Evans ("Jesus and the Continuing Exile," 82–83 and 305, n. 12) argues that this is not a reference to the Assyrian exile of the northern tribes of Israel.

79. See Bryan, *Jesus and Israel's Traditions*, 12–20. His arguments against Wright's lack of clarity include 1) "texts in which exile language occurs are rare" (13); 2) "many Jews continued to live outside the land and the regathering of these Jews was an anticipated part of restoration" (13); 3) "It is at least ironic that he has chosen a term which connotes removal from the Land to describe the situation of Jews living in the Land" (12); 4) Wright has equated bondage and exile, two concepts that can be

The need for a retaking of the land is also demonstrated by observing the symbolic actions of prophetic revolutionary movements in the first century. Josephus wrote about an Egyptian Jew (cf. Acts 21:38) who after trekking into the wilderness to show Israel the signals of liberty (*War* 2,13,4), he proceeded to the Mount of Olives and proposed to force an entrance into Jerusalem to set himself up as leader of an exiled people. Using typological language, he proclaimed that "the walls of Jerusalem would fall down; and he promised that he would procure them an entrance into the city through those walls, when they were fallen down."[80] Similarly, the prophetic action of Theudas (cf. Acts 5:36) demonstrated that many considered the land so polluted that a new division of the Jordan River and conquest of the land was needed as in the time of Joshua.[81] The similarities between Theudas' revolt and Joshua's conquest include the circuitous route through the wilderness,[82] the division of the Jordan River, and the walls of Jerusalem falling down similar to the earlier Jericho.[83] Therefore, as Evans maintains, "A new conquest of the Promised Land presupposes the assumption that the people really do not possess the land."[84] The promised land remains in exile and needs to be retaken.

Similarly, sectarian Judaism witnesses to the pollution of the temple and the land, as evidenced by the retreat of the Essenes out of Jerusalem into the desert. They picture themselves as the captives of Israel who left the land of Judah to dwell in the land of Damascus (CD 6:4–5).[85] The Dead Sea Scrolls exhibit an exile theology with the true remnant of Israel awaiting the redemption of the land from captivity.[86] However, the eschatological battle between the sons of light and the sons of darkness is approaching "when the exiled sons of light return from the desert of the nations to camp in the desert of Jerusalem" (1QM 1:3). Merely entitling the Promised Land "the wilderness of Jerusalem" indicates the exilic state that is imagined. Therefore, the continuing exile

---

separated (14); 5) Jews would not have considered themselves in exile during Hasmonean times, but only after the entrance of Pompey so the entire Second Temple period is not a time of unremitting exile (15–16); 6) Wright has omitted the partially realized eschatology that is evident in works of the Second Temple period (16); 7) "the continued absence of many Jews from the Land did not so much create a pervasive sense of ongoing exile as indicate that the time was not yet" (18); 8) "a continued sense of exile is inferred from a continued hope of restoration" (19).

80 Josephus *Ant.* 20,8,6.

81. Josephus *Ant.* 20,5,1. This occurred in 45–46 CE. See Evans, "Jesus and the Continuing Exile," 78–80.

82. Amos 2:10 "I led you around in the desert forty years" employs similar vocabulary in the LXX (περιήγαγον ὑμᾶς ἐν τῇ ἐρήμῳ) as in Josephus, *War* 2:259 (προῆγον εἰς τὴν ἐρημίαν).

83. Evans calls attention to the fact that "Taking up possessions heightens the parallel, for the ancient Israelites carried their possessions across the Jordan to the Promised Land" ("Jesus and the Continuing Exile," 81). *Ant.* 20:97 employs τὰς κτήσεις.

84. Evans, "Jesus and the Continuing Exile," 82.

85. Cf. Abegg, "Exile and the Dead Sea Scrolls," 115–23.

86. Evans ("Jesus and the Continuing Exile," 85 and 305. n. 18) refers to Garnet (*Salvation and Atonement*).

of the land must be assigned to the theology of sectarian Judaism and not necessarily to the entire population of Palestine.[87] As Bauckham articulates, "an expectation of the restoration of Israel was widespread in late Second Temple Judaism" but "specific Jewish groups, such as the Qumran community, had additional reasons for deploring the status quo and hoping for change, such as belief that the priestly ministry in the temple was so corrupt and misguided as to be invalid."[88]

Finally, the most important witness to the pollution of the land is the ministry of John the Baptizer, a story that is oozing with typology. Before the conquest of the land the Israelites found themselves in the desert, the exact location where the Baptist's ministry transpires. John purposely chooses the wilderness as his locus of ministry to indicate that the Promised Land is again saturated with ungodliness, moral pollution, and subjugation so that another conquest is required. According to Luke 3:7 John compares the inhabitants of the land to a brood of vipers whose destination is the coming wrath unless they are purged. Therefore, John's message centers on repentance (Mark 1:4), which was an indispensable prerequisite for Israel's restoration.[89] Those who come to John confess their sins (1:5) since the sacrificial system of the temple establishment is bankrupt.

Through persuasive preaching John compels the covenant people to participate in the ceremony of baptism. Although many envision a background in the ceremonial lustrations of Qumran[90] or the teaching of Leviticus,[91] Jewish proselyte baptism provides a more meaningful backdrop.[92] The protest from the crowd, "We have Abra-

---

87. But some scholars even deny that Diaspora Jews of the Greco-Roman period viewed their situation outside the land as exile. See Scott, "Exile and Self-Understanding," 174.

88. Bauckham, "Restoration of Israel," in Scott, *Restoration*, 435.

89. Cf. Sanders, *Jesus and Judaism*, 106ff.

90. Witherington ("John the Baptist," 384–85) lists six similarities between John and Qumran. See Scobie (*John the Baptist*, 103–10) who envisions an initiatory lustration at 1 QS 2:25—3:12 (105–6). However, the differences with Qumran stand out: John's rite was 1) an initiatory ritual (although disputed by Taylor, *Immerser*, 69) that was 2) unrepeatable (although questioned by Taylor, *Immerser*, 70–71), and 3) focused on moral impurity rather than ceremonial uncleanness so that 4) no probationary period is required.

91. See Collins, *Mark*, 138–40. However, the term "bathe" (יָחַר) is not employed in the Old Testament but instead "to dip" (לבט), and more importantly, an OT background does not explain why the Pharisees would oppose John's baptism by asserting "we have Abraham as our father" or why John would state that he could raise from these stones sons of Abraham (Matt 3:9; Luke 3:8).

92. Jeremias (*Infant Baptism*, 24–37) contains four basic arguments in favor of an early date for proselyte baptism which are succinctly summarized by Webb (*John the Baptizer*, 123) while Derwood Smith ("Proselyte Baptism," 24–37) offers arguments for a late date. Jeremias contends that "1 Cor. 10:1–2 shows us that this doctrine of the baptism of the desert generation, which is of fundamental importance for proselyte baptism, was already familiar to Paul, the pupil of the Hillelite Gamaliel I" (32). I take the reference in Pesaḥ 8:8 and Eduyyot 5:2 referring to a dispute between Hillel and Shammai whether a new proselyte may immerse himself and eat the Passover meal as an indication that proselyte baptism predates John. On the other hand, Sanders (*Judaism*, 73–74) believes that the issue is impurity rather than initiation with a disagreement between the Shammaites who required only a sunset for semen-impurity versus the Hillelites who demanded a week for corpse-uncleanness

ham as our father" (Matt 3:9; Luke 3:8), reveals that Jews could not initially imagine undergoing a ceremony that was aimed at Gentiles. The rejection of John's message by the Jewish leaders (cf. also Mark 11:29-33) adds evidence to the controversial nature of his baptism. These protectors of the institutions of Judaism are surely attempting to preserve temple sacrifice as the place where forgiveness of sins occurs[93] and defend the unique heritage of Israel over against the Gentiles. Their refusal to repent indicates an unwillingness to accept John's proposal and the assumption of sectarian Judaism that the land was in exile and needed restoration. Thus John the Baptizer prepares the way of the Lord by proclaiming through word ("repent!") and deed (proselyte baptism) that the entire land and all the people are unclean.

The typology of Elijah substantiates this opinion. Mark begins his gospel with a quote from Malachi 3:1 about a messenger who is identified as Elijah in Malachi 4:5. John's clothing of camel's hair and his leather belt further remind the reader of Elijah in 2 Kings 1:8.[94] In addition, John's triple reference to fire in Matthew 3:7-12 / Luke 3:7-9, 16-17 (the unfruitful tree is burnt; a baptism of fire; and the burning of chaff) recalls the fire that Elijah calls down from heaven (1 Kgs 18:38)[95] during the reign of Ahab and Jezebel, when the land lay polluted by the worship of foreign gods (16:31-33; 18:18) and false prophets ruled the people (18:19, 22, 40). A similar situation of impurity must be postulated during the time of John the Baptizer. This is confirmed by the special name "John" that the angel of the Lord assigned to Zechariah (Luke 1:13) and the commotion it caused among his relatives (1:59-62). The surnames Johanan and Jonas were used interchangeably at this time in Israel's history, as evidenced by the description of Peter as "Bar-Jonah" in Matthew 16:17 and "Son of John" in John 1:42.[96] The theological significance of this nomenclature entails that

---

(cf. also Webb, *John the Baptizer*, 126-27). However, the change in Yebam 46a from the Jerusalem Talmud which speaks about proselyte participation in the Passover to the Babylonian Talmud which talks about the initiation rite of proselyte baptism implies that the rabbis understood Pesaḥ 8:8 to apply to initiation. A description of proselyte baptism is found in b. Yebam. 46a-48b; cf. Sifre Num. 15:14. For a list of supporters, see Taylor, *Immerser*, 64-65, n. 29 and Webb, *John the Baptizer*, 123, n. 93. Doubts about an early dating emanate from the failure of both Philo and Josephus to mention the necessity of immersion when they speak about proselytes so that the first certain reference comes from Epictetus (*Dissertationes* 2,9,19f) from approximately 108 CE. Those who favor an early second century date (90-130 CE) call attention to a debate between Eliezer ben Hyrcanus who seems to have advocated the traditional view that a male who had been circumcised but not immersed was a proper proselyte and Joshua ben Hananiah who promoted the view that one who had been immersed but not yet circumcised was still a proper proselyte. See Taylor, *Immerser*, 67.

93. For an understanding of John's baptism as an attack on the temple cult, see Becker (*Jesus of Nazareth*, 33-34) and Webb (*John the Baptizer*, 203-5). Scobie (*John the Baptist*, 107) thinks that Qumran utilized an initiatory lustration that took the place of temple sacrifices and mediated forgiveness of sins.

94. Mark 9:12-13 par.; Luke 1:17; and Matt 11:14 further confirm such an identity.

95. See also the fire from heaven in 2 Kgs 1:9-12 immediately after the description of Elijah's clothing.

96. The textual problems in John 1:42 and 21:15-17 also demonstrate the interchangeability of these names. In the LXX it is a variant of יוחנן ($Ἰωάν[ν]ης$), e.g., 4 Kgs 25:23.

just as Jonah went to the Gentiles at Nineveh with a message of destruction, so John accosts the Jews treating them like Gentiles since the land is in exile. Therefore, John's radical solution to the captivity of Israel causes a stir throughout the entire Jewish community and accounts for the notoriety of John in the tradition.

Finally, the Elijah typology in the Baptist narrative recalls Elijah's consummate journey from the Promised Land, across the Jordan in a reverse direction, and into the wilderness (2 Kgs 2:1–12). Then, after Elijah's exodus to heaven, Elisha takes over Elijah's ministry in the wilderness and retraces his exact steps into Canaan (2 Kgs 2:13–25) since the land must still be retaken.[97] Likewise, Jesus travels to the wilderness to replace John, but only begins his ministry when he returns to the land of Canaan (Mark 1:14). By identifying John as Elijah, Stek points out that "Jesus was offering a subtle self-disclosure as the Elisha / Joshua—His Semitic name—who would complete John's ministry."[98] Thus John and Jesus together solve the problem of Canaan's exile.

This process matches the development found in Isaiah 40, another typological element of the narrative. This chapter begins with the voice of one calling for a road through the wilderness back to the Promised Land (40:3–4). Then Isaiah proclaims the coming of the sovereign Lord in power (40:10a), who will enter the land and bring the gospel (good tidings) to Jerusalem and the towns of Judah (40:9) through the arm of his rule and reign (40:10b). The early church saw this as Jesus' proclamation of the kingdom of God preceded by John's voice in the wilderness. Thus the typology of Moses/Joshua; Elijah/Elisha; and Second Isaiah 40–55 / Third Isaiah 56–66 gets repeated in the ministries of John the Baptizer and Jesus. Therefore, Joshua, Elijah, Second Isaiah, and John the Baptist deliver Israel from exile while Joshua, Elisha, Third Isaiah, and Jesus bring God's people into the Promised Land.

Therefore, the exile of Canaan nears its end with the arrival of Jesus. Although Jesus continues John's message of judgment, Mark 1:14–15 recites what is new in the ministry of Jesus. First of all, "the time is now" (1:15a) so that Jesus alters the future eschatology of the Baptizer into an eschatology in the process of being realized. Second, "the realm [the kingdom of God] is here" (1:15b) so that Jesus enters the land instead of remaining in the wilderness. Finally, "the news is good" (1:15c) so that Jesus begins to proclaim the gospel rather than a message of judgment. After his reception of the Holy Spirit, Jesus travels throughout the entire land of Canaan among both Jewish and Gentile territories to proclaim that the exile is over and the promises of the new covenant are being manifest.

---

97. Samaria (2 Kgs 1:1); Bethel (2:2); Jericho (2:4); Jordan (2:6); wilderness; Jordan (2:14); Jericho (2:18); Bethel (2:23); Samaria (2:25).

98. Stek, "Elijah," 67. See also Brown, "Jesus and Elijah," 85–104.

7.5 The Typology of the Pre-Markan Miracle Catenae: An Emphasis upon the Exodus and the Retaking of the Land

We have just demonstrated how Mark employs the journeys into Gentile territory to represent the retaking of the land of Canaan, which now includes Gentiles. We discover a similar typology in the double miracle catenae (4:35—8:9), which begin with a crossing of the sea followed by several miraculous deeds and conclude with a miraculous feeding.[99] Certainly this flow of material would remind any reader of God's dealings with Israel in the Old Testament. In the exodus, the crossing of the Red Sea on dry ground through a divine act of rescue (Exod 14) is followed by several miraculous divine actions like the sweetening of the bitter waters of Marah and the gift of an oasis at Elim with twelve springs and seventy palm trees (Exod 15) and is concluded with an incredible feast of manna in the wilderness (Exod 16). Likewise, the typology in Mark's gospel begins in each catena with a deliverance through the sea, then evidences God's mighty miracles and concludes with an eschatological feast. Would this sequence allude solely to the typology of the exodus from Egypt or would the retaking of the land of Canaan also play a vital role in the symbolism? In this section we will first demonstrate how most scholars only call attention to the exodus motif, and then we will argue that an equal emphasis upon the conquest of the land is necessary to provide a suitable typological background for the Gospel of Mark.

The common parlance among scholars in speaking about the restoration of Israel under John the Baptist and Jesus is exodus language. However, this terminology expresses only a half-truth; the preferable typological vocabulary should include conquest lingo or the retaking of the land as well. It is commonplace, for instance, to compare Jesus' trips over the sea to Moses' crossing of the Red Sea, where a divine rescue occurs in each case. Stegner calls attention to the fact that Mark's sea-walking narrative contains thirty-two words that are also found in the Septuagint of Exodus 14.[100] Specifically, Israel questions God's concern (Exod 14:11, "Was it because there were no graves in Egypt that you brought us to the desert to die?") just as the disciples mistrust Jesus' care for their well-being (Mark 4:38, "Teacher, don't you care if we drown?"). In the first trip the disciples exhibit a similar fear as the Israelites (Exod 14:10; Mark 4:41), and the hardened hearts of the disciples in the second trip (Mark 6:52) could provide a comparison to Pharaoh's hardening (Exod 14:4, 8, 17).[101] With regard to the sea-walking trip, Henderson adds that "Mark appears to continue his

---

99. See section 3.7 above for a chart of the miracle catenae.

100. Stegner ("Jesus' Walking on the Water," 217–20) bases his entire interpretation on a background from Exodus 14. See also Malbon, *Narrative Space*, 78. Gundry calls attention to differences: "But there the danger came from enemies. Here it comes from a storm. There the wind enabled a crossing. Here it threatens a crossing. The crossing was by foot. Here it is by boat. There the waters engulfed enemies. Here it engulfs no one" (*Mark*, 243). But these minor historical details miss the symbolism.

101. Malbon, *Narrative Space*, 85. The Egyptians meet their demise in the sea during the morning watch (Exod 14:24) just as Jesus passes by the disciples at the fourth watch of the night (6:48).

depiction of a New Exodus in the passage's reference to the 'mountain' as Jesus' destination for prayer"[102] since the most direct interactions between Yahweh and Moses occur on a mountain. However, the drying up of the Jordan River under Joshua (3:15–16) captures the identical theme and occurs in the renewal under Elijah and Elisha as well (2 Kgs 2:8, 14). Therefore, both the exodus and the retaking of the land must be seen as the background for the interpretation of the gospel events.

Similarly, the events occurring in the wilderness are normally associated by scholars with the exodus from Egypt rather than Israel's arrival in the Land of Promise. For instance, Exodus typology is regularly employed to depict Jesus' miraculous feedings of the five thousand and four thousand.[103] However, the comparable events to the miraculous feeding with manna (Exod 16) occur in the land of Canaan in the narratives of Joshua and Elisha as well. After crossing the Jordan River on dry ground, Israel through the leadership of Joshua celebrates the Passover meal, where Israel eats from the milk and honey of the land after the manna stops (Josh 5:10–12). Similarly, after Elisha crosses the Jordan on dry ground (2 Kgs 2:14), God performs a feeding miracle where a hundred men are fed from twenty loaves (2 Kgs 4:42–44). Although these parallels receive minute attention when Jesus' feedings are discussed in the secondary literature, they picture more closely the milk and honey promises of the land of Canaan than a temporary deliverance from hunger when food was scarce in the wilderness. Finally, the abundance of food left over alludes to 2 Kings 4:43 and denotes the eschatological feast of God dwelling with his people as in the gift of rest in the land (as we shall see).

Likewise, the exorcisms of Jesus in foreign territory like the Decapolis are usually linked with the exodus, not the conquest of Canaan. As Wefald explains,

> It is difficult not to see allusions to the Exodus. As Pharaoh's legions are his military, the pigs possessed by the demons' Legion rushed (very unpiglike) in formation as military legions. . . . Pharaoh's legions drowned (Exod 14.28) as did the pigs (Mark 5.13); the Egyptians were being led by demons (heathen gods), as the pigs were led by demons (Mark 5.6–13). The result of the Exodus, the crossing of the Red Sea, was to manifest the glory of God to the Gentiles (Exod 14.4; esp. Isa 66.19); the result of the Gerasene account is that the demoniac-become-missionary manifested among the Gentiles the glory of what Jesus had done (Mark 5.20).[104]

---

102. Henderson, *Christology and Discipleship*, 210.

103. See Kee, *Community of the New Age*, 112. Watts states that "the number of Exodus parallels suggests that it is predominant" (*Isaiah's New Exodus*, 179). However, his references on page 178 to a sheep without a shepherd (Num 27:16ff) and the division into hundreds and fifties (Exod 18:21) can just as easily refer to a leader who will guide them into the promised land and an army that is prepared for the conquest.

104. Wefald, "Separate Gentile Mission," 15.

However, the primary OT allusion centers on Isaiah 65:1–5, where Israel already lives in the Promised Land. In Isaiah's context Canaan must be purified (65:2–3) since the land is polluted by a people who "sit among the graves" and "eat the flesh of pigs" (65:4). Now in Mark 5 Jesus is casting the legion of demons out of the man who lives among the tombs in a land overrun with unclean swine. In Isaiah the cities in the Promised Land have become a desert as demonstrated by the immediately preceding passage: "Your sacred cities have become a desert; even Zion is a desert, Jerusalem a desolation" (64:10). The typology places Israel again in the desert so that a new conquest of the land is necessary. The exodus language and symbolism is certainly present, but the retaking of the land should be given equal attention.[105]

Steven Bryan shares my viewpoint that the conquest has "not received the attention it deserves from contemporary scholars."[106] As an example he illustrates how the so-called sign prophets of the first century are regularly identified with the exodus whereas the promised signs relate more properly to the conquest.[107] Scholars consistently associate the imagery of liberation and freedom with the exodus, but texts like Psalm 44:2–4 concentrate on God's conquest of the land, demonstrating that "it was not only the Exodus but also the Conquest which could stimulate aspirations of freedom."[108] Jesus' movement out of the desert (Mark 1:14) and his choice of twelve disciples (3:14–19) emphasize the resettlement of the land, not an exodus out of Egypt. Finally, the OT assurance that God would give over the peoples of the land into Israel's jurisdiction (Neh 9:24) becomes reality in Jesus' ministry throughout the Jewish and Gentile parts of the land of Canaan. Therefore, a balanced presentation envisions an entire movement from exodus to conquest as the background of Mark's gospel. To his credit Watts argues that Isaiah's new exodus schema involves three stages:

A. Yahweh's deliverance of his exiled people from the power of the nations and their idols

B. The journey along the "Way" in which Yahweh leads his people from their captivity among the nations

C. Arrival in Jerusalem, the place of his presence, where Yahweh is enthroned in a gloriously restored Zion[109]

In this scheme the wilderness is pictured both as the place where God brought the Israelites after their deliverance from Egypt and the location where God prepared Israel for the conquest.

---

105. See Reid, "Jesus," 114 for a discussion.
106. Bryan, *Jesus and Israel's Traditions*, 27.
107. Ibid., 14.
108. Ibid., 28.
109. Watts, *Isaiah's New Exodus*, 135. However, he entitles this entire process merely a New Exodus whereas the restoration or Conquest should also be emphasized.

This double emphasis upon both exodus and conquest plays an important role in the OT narratives as well as the Gospel of Mark. In the initial conquest of the land in the Joshua narrative the description casts the eye of the reader back to the exodus since the monument of twelve stones is to remind Israel that "the Lord your God dried up the waters of the Jordan for you until you crossed over, as the Lord your God did to the Red Sea which he dried up for us until we crossed over" (Josh 4:23).[110] The pattern of sea crossing, mighty miracles, and feeding narrative is repeated in the exodus, conquest, and Jesus' ministry. The miracles immediately following the crossing of the sea in the conquest, such as the rolling away of the reproach of Egypt by the circumcision at Gilgal (Josh 5:9) and the falling of Jericho's walls (Josh 2, 6), both correspond to a series of mighty deeds in the Exodus narratives as well as to the middle section of Jesus' miracle catenae.[111] Finally, Israel celebrates the feast of the Passover (Josh 5:10–12) so that the manna stops and now Israel eats the milk and honey of the land. This event parallels both the feeding with manna and quails in Exodus 16 and the two miraculous feasts at the denouement of Mark's miracle catenae.

A second typological parallel to Jesus' actions is developed in the Elijah/Elisha cycle, which likewise rehearses both a new exodus and the retaking of the land. First, Elijah purifies the land from the worship of Baal through fire (1 Kgs 18) just as Israel is delivered from the gods of Egypt. Then Elisha begins the conquest of the land with a divine desiccation of the Jordan River (2 Kgs 2:13–14), which reminds one of the miraculous crossing of the Red Sea as well as providing a paradigm for Jesus' baptism through the Jordan River followed by his miracle ministry in Galilee. Immediately following this entrance into the land, the narrative records mighty acts of God such as the healing of the springs at Jericho (2 Kgs 2:19–22), the defeat of Moab through a divine mirage of bloody water (3:15–23), the sustaining flow of the widow's oil (4:1–7), the Shunammite's son restored (4:8–37), and the deliverance from poison food (4:38–41), all culminating in a multiplication of bread (4:42–44). The purifying of the waters at Jericho reminds one of Moses' similar action at Marah (Exod 15:23; 2 Kgs 2:19), and at the same time the use of salt (which normally produces unproductive land) evokes the restoration of the city of Jericho, which had been destroyed when Israel entered the land, so that the curse is now removed. These mighty acts of God remind readers of the events following the exodus, the crossing of the Jordan River, and Jesus' baptism. These restoration miracles culminate in a final food miracle where twenty loaves from Baal Shalishah feed one hundred hungry people (2 Kgs 4:42–44). Marcus develops a chart to compare the similarities between the feedings in 2 Kings 4:42–44 and the Gospel of Mark.[112]

---

110. See Bryan, *Jesus and Israel's Traditions*, 31.

111. This includes the sweetening of the bitter waters of Marah (15:22–26) and the gift of the twelve springs and seventy palm trees at Elim (15:27) in Exodus and Jesus healings before the feedings of both the five thousand and four thousand.

112. Marcus, *Mark*, 415–16. See also Collins (*Mark*, 320) who mentions verbal similarities.

	2 Kings	Mark
1	Elisha takes bread and ears of grain.	Jesus takes bread and fish.
2	Elisha commands, "Give to the men that they may eat."	Jesus commands, "Give them something to eat."
3	The servant asks skeptically how to feed a hundred men.	The disciples ask skeptically how to feed the crowd.
4	Elisha repeats the command.	Jesus commands the disciples to seat the people.
5	The servant sets food before the people.	The disciples distribute food to the people.
6	People eat and food is left over.	People eat and food is left over.

Again the cycle from crossing the river to a miraculous eschatological feast becomes a paradigm for the exodus/conquest motif in the ministry of Jesus.[113]

A third typological parallel is developed in Isaiah 40–55, where scholars continually allude to the exodus but seldom emphasize the retaking of the land. Certainly Second Isaiah emphasizes the exodus since the rescue from captivity in Babylon is specifically compared with the deliverance from Egypt (43:16–17; 44:27; 50:2b; 51:9-10; 63:11–14). For instance, 51:10 recites the mighty exodus work of the Lord, who "dried up the sea, the waters of the great deep, who made the depths of the sea a way for the redeemed to pass over" (51:10).[114] But the climax of 51:11 concentrates on the restoration of Israel in the land when "the ransomed of the Lord shall return and come to Zion with singing" (ESV).[115] Similarly, in 44:27 the Lord reminds his people of the exodus ("Be dry; I will dry up your rivers") but only when predicting the rebuilding of Jerusalem (44:26, 28). Likewise, 63:11–14 recalls the days of Moses but concludes with the statement that "they were given rest by the Spirit of the Lord," which highlights the work of Joshua. Therefore, God's redemption involves three actions: 1) an exodus from exile (48:20; 52:11–12) through the destruction of Babylon (41:25; 43:14; 45:1–3; 47:1–15; 48:14); 2) salvation in the wilderness (40:3–5; 41:18–19; 42:15–16;

---

113. Although there are remarkable parallels between the OT and gospel narratives from crossing to feast, some details do not fit exactly: 1) miracles occur in Exodus 17–18 so that the feeding (Exod 16) is not necessarily the final element; 2) in Joshua the feeding occurs before the miraculous defeat of Jericho; and 3) in 2 Kings Elisha's miracles continue after the feeding at Baal Shalishah.

114. Motyer states, "Four elements in these verses point to the exodus as the past event referred to: (i) the *making of a road in the depths* echoes the Red Sea experience; (ii) the *redeemed*, when it refers to a past experience, describes those who came out of Egypt; (iii) the only historical event which prefigures eschatological redemption is the exodus (Ezek 20:33f); (iv) *Rahab* is used as a code-name for Egypt" (*Isaiah*, 408). However, Baltzer explains that 35:10 "may also be a reference to the crossing of the Jordan and the entry into the promised land" since Josh 4:21–24 is a renewal of the Red Sea miracle (*Deutero-Isaiah*, 357). In addition he points out that "the strong arm of 51:9 recalls Deut 4:34; 5:15; 7:19; 11:2; 26:8" which "always refers to the divine act of redemption in the exodus."

115. This emphasis in Isa 51:11 surprises many exegetes so that they contend that this was an addition from Isa 35:10. Westermann (*Isaiah 40–66*, 253) places Isa 51:11 after 52:2. Oswald concludes that "This verse is problematic because its connection to the preceding cry is not clear" and because it repeats 35:10 (*Book of Isaiah*, 343). However, both the exodus and the conquest are themes of Isaiah 40–66.

43:19–21; 44:3–4; 49:9–12; 51:3); and the culmination is 3) the return to the land (49:6a; 49:8; 51:1). Similar to the three steps in Mark's miracle catenae, Isaiah 40–66 speaks about a drying up of the waters (this time in the desert) followed by a series of mighty miracles where the Lord will tend his flock again like a shepherd (40:10–11) and anoint Cyrus as a Messianic deliverer (45:1). Finally, these miracles will result in a remarriage to divorced Israel in the land (54:1, 5–8) so that Jerusalem will become a gilded city of precious stones (54:11–12). This renewal in the land will culminate with a feast of the richest of fare to which everyone is invited (55:1–2). Again this typology brings to mind the familiar sequence of Jesus' miracle catenae in Mark's gospel.

The community at Qumran and the Dead Sea Scrolls offer a final example. At Qumran the exodus served as the primary ideological motivation for their flight into the wilderness. But this only prepared for an eschatological restoration so that a new conquest lies on the horizon of their immediate future (4Q171 2:26—3:2; 4Q161 5 and 6:15–20; 4Q434 2:2–3; 1QM 1:2–3; CD 8:14–16; 19:26b–29a).[116] Their present experience in the wilderness is thus conceived of as a time of affliction prior to their inheritance of the land. The movement from John the Baptist in the wilderness to Jesus' messianic ministry in the land parallels the anticipated experiences of the Qumran community.

In the New Testament John the Baptizer's ministry of fiery purification (like Elijah's) takes place in the wilderness in preparation for Jesus' crossing of the Jordan River in baptism and his retaking of the land as God's kingdom. The structuring of the material with this theological agenda assumes that Israel has turned from God as in the time of Ahab and Jezebel and needs cleansing. But now God's messianic prophet has arrived to purify the land and restore God's kingdom to Israel. The series of narratives intimately ties together the stories of Moses/Joshua; Elijah/Elisha; and John the Baptizer/Jesus into a typological pattern of deliverance through the water to a sumptuous feast of promised restoration, which as we shall see is celebrated in both Jewish and Gentile territory. Just as the exodus from Babylon culminated in the retaking of the land, so John's baptism through the Jordan River culminates in the reconquest of the land through Jesus. Therefore, the exodus is the primary typological metaphor in John the Baptizer's ministry, but the retaking of the land becomes front and center in Jesus' miracles.

7.6 Mark's Employment of Geographical Mirroring to Designate the Gentile Mission in the Two Miraculous Feedings (6:35–44; 8:1–9)

In the last section we have described the first purpose for these miracle catenae, i.e., the retaking of the Promised Land. But the special quality of this land consists in its makeup of both Jewish and Gentile territory. The Sea of Galilee then functions "to

---

116. For a quotation of these passages, see Abegg, "Exile and Dead Sea Scrolls," 124–25.

GEOGRAPHICAL MIRRORING: JEWISH AND GENTILE TERRITORY

'bridge' the deeply alienated worlds of Jew and gentile."[117] In a series of boat trips the Markan Jesus opens the frontier toward Gentile land, connecting it with Jewish land. We have contended in chapter 6 that the theme of the seeming absence of Jesus is first and foremost in these sea journeys. Mark wants to help his community deal with the persecution they are facing by exhorting them to not make the same mistakes the disciples committed in the sea trips but instead to experience the presence of Jesus in the midst of struggles. In addition, the parallel Jewish and Gentile missions are evident in the geographical mirroring that pervades the miracle catenae and surfaces especially in the two feeding narratives. Therefore, the church's acceptance of a Gentile mission functions as an important secondary theme in this material. Mark wants to demonstrate that Jesus himself was pushing his followers to include a Gentile mission in their discipleship.

The various miracles in the chiastic structured miracle catenae occur in both Jewish and Gentile territory.[118]

a		4:35–41	Jesus calms the *water*	6:45–56	Jesus walks on *water*
			To *Gentile territory*		Leaves for Bethsaida (6:45), *Gentile land*, but arrives at Gennesaret (6:53), Jewish land
	b	5:1–20	Decapolis exorcism	8:22–26	Healing the blind man
			Gentile territory: pigs		*Gentile territory*: Bethsaida (see John 12:20–21)
		c 5:25–34	Unclean bleeding woman	7:24–30	Syrophoenician woman's daughter
			Jewish territory: reference to 12		*Gentile territory*: Tyre
	b'	5:21–23,35–43	Jairus' dead daughter	7:31–36	Decapolis healing of the deaf/mute
			Jewish territory: reference to 12		*Gentile territory*: Decapolis
a'		6:34–44	*Feeding* of the five thousand	8:1–10	*Feeding* of the four thousand
			Jewish territory: reference to 12		*Gentile territory*: reference to 7 (see Acts 13:19)

The miracle sequence begins with Jesus headed to the Gentile Decapolis, where he confronts a legion of demons. With a background in Isaiah 65:1–5, Wefald proposes that "the Gerasene demoniac is to be understood as the Gentile of Isaiah"[119] since both sit among the tombs (Isa 65:4a; Mark 5:5;), spend the nights in secret places (65:4b; 5:5), live among pigs (65:4c; 5:11), and say something equivalent to "keep away; don't come near me" (65:5a; 5:7). Since Paul applies Isaiah 65:1–2 to the inclusion of Gentiles in Romans 10:20–21, the exegetical parallels between the two passages

---

117. Myers, *Binding the Strong Man*, 189. Cf. van Iersel, *Mark*, 279.

118. For a more complete description with arguments see section 3.7 above.

119. Wefald, "Separate Gentile Mission," 15. This passage whose original application was to Jews who have fallen into Gentile practices now because a message of hope and inclusion for the Gentiles.

prove convincing. Thus this exorcism revokes the barrier of the Gentiles' uncleanness so that an authorized mission to the Gentiles by Jesus can proceed through this first missionary to the Gentiles (Mark 5:20).

The healings of the deaf-mute and the blind man with saliva take place in the Gentile territory of the Decapolis and Bethsaida as well. Although spittle (7:33; 8:23) functioned as a popular healing technique in the Hellenistic world, to the reader acquainted with the Old Testament this description would brand both men as marginal and unclean. In spite of the fact that Jesus' mission was not aimed at Gentiles, he heals these two so that the mute can speak clearly (7:35 ἐλάλει ὀρθῶς) and the blind man can see clearly (8:25 ἐνέβλεπεν τηλαυγῶς). These two incidents, which originally were coordinated in the chiasm, proclaim that through Jesus Gentiles can now see and hear clearly the gospel message as well as proclaim it to others (7:36).[120]

In Jesus' encounter with the Syrophoencian woman, the phrase "Let the children first be fed" (Mark 7:27) sounds suspiciously similar to the mission policy of the early church, "to the Jew first, but also to the Greek" (Acts 3:26; 13:46; Rom 1:16; 2:9). The parallels with the Q story of the centurion (Matt 8:5–13; Luke 7:1–10) suggest that the standard justification for Gentile inclusion is highlighted, namely that through faith the barrier between Jew and Gentile is abolished so that the Gentiles are welcomed into the people of God.[121] Therefore as Wilson concludes, "whereas for Jesus this incident was a proleptic sign of the future participation of the Gentles in the kingdom of God, for Mark it has become part of the justification for the Church's Gentile mission."[122] Mark endeavors to demonstrate that the inclusion of Gentiles is "not due simply to some arbitrary church decision" but was "Jesus's doing from the start!"[123] In the two miracle catenae, the Jewish bleeding woman and the unclean Gentile woman are positioned at the center of each chiasm to emphasize that salvation and purity are extended both to an unclean Jewish daughter (Mark 5:34) and a Gentile who has a daughter with an unclean spirit (7:25).

The theme of the Gentile mission stands out most prominently in the two miraculous feedings to which we now turn. But in order to prove this thesis, we will have to explore the various scholarly interpretations to determine whether the purpose of these two feedings is primarily historical, christological, eschatological, sacramental, metaphorical, or polemical.[124]

---

120. In addition, the Messianic Secret is ignored here in Gentile territory (7:36–37) as well as earlier in Jewish land (1:43–45) possibly demonstrating that the gospel is for both Jew and Gentile.

121. Cf. Fuller, *Interpreting the Miracles*, 59. Table fellowship is included in both passages with the crumbs from the table paralleling the feast with Abraham, Isaac, and Jacob in the kingdom of God.

122. Wilson, *Gentiles*, 30. Strangely, Achtemeier places the Syrophoenician woman in Jewish territory since, "if Jesus himself is on foreign soil, then he himself is not in fact limiting the 'bread' to the 'children'" ("Isolation of a Pre-Markan Miracle Catenae," 287). But the point of Mark 7:24 is that Jesus is in hiding on retreat to avoid contact with foreigners.

123. Stein, *Mark*, 355.

124. Mack (*Myth of Innocence*, 222–24, 230–33) offers an additional social-science alternative

Geographical Mirroring: Jewish and Gentile Territory

Literalists believe that the two accounts merely specify two different historical happenings.[125] In this case repetition highlights the importance of a particular lesson for the church, as when Luke twice repeats the economic commitments of the early community (Acts 2:42–46; 4:32–35) and Paul employs two scripture quotations (Exod 16:18 and Ps 112:9 in 2 Cor 8:15; 9:9) to encourage the sharing of resources. The christological interpretation recalls the impressive kingdom acts of Jesus' miracles to proclaim Jesus as lord over nature when the winds and waves obey him, lord over the spiritual forces when the legion of demons are drowned, lord over disease and death in the various healings, lord over human conflict in the controversies about purity issues, lord over all peoples through contact with the Syrophoenician woman, and lord over human need by twice miraculously supplying food for the destitute. The eschatological interpretation asserts that the two feedings recall Moses supplying manna and quails for Israel in the wilderness (Exod 16 and Num 11) and Elijah and Elisha multiplying food in times of distress (1 Kgs 17:7–16; 2 Kgs 4:42–44) to indicate their fulfillment in the new messianic age. The sacramental interpretation calls attention to the ties between the two feedings and the Last Supper, where the bread and fish become the bread and wine of Holy Communion. The metaphorical interpretation states that the locations of the miracles emphasize that Jesus welcomes both Jews and Gentiles into table fellowship through his kingdom actions. Finally, the polemical view offers a corollary to the metaphorical view by insisting that Jesus is rebuking the disciples for their inability to comprehend the importance of a Gentile mission.[126]

In order to decide between these options we must investigate the possible symbolism in the two feeding miracles. We will argue that the feeding narratives themselves highlight the inclusion of Jews as well as Gentiles in the eschatological feast, which is beginning already in the ministry of Jesus. However, Mark's additional commentary

---

that the catenae describe the origins of a congregation in process of formation just as the crossing of the Red Sea and the feeding in the wilderness established Israel before the taking of the land. However, he argues against himself when he admits that even though Jesus' miracles are occasions for the crowds, they do not form a congregation (230) and when he asserts that "miracles do not result in a collection of followers distinguished from the crowd" (231). In fact the leaders do not even understand the miracles.

125. Others, of course, contend that the two narratives are duplicates of one event which became confused in the tradition so that later Christians thought they were separate accounts. Cf. Quesnell, *Mind of Mark*, 36 38.

126. These scholars emphasize the disciples' resistance to the Gentile mission rather than their acceptance of it. Kelber (*Kingdom*, 57–58) thinks that the community's resistance to the Gentile mission is mirrored in the exegetical data that Jesus must force the disciples into the boat to travel toward the Gentile Bethsaida (6:45) whereas they finish their journey in the Jewish territory of Gennesaret (6:53). In addition, Malbon ("Jesus of Mark," 372) suggests that the disciples' inability to understand about the loaves (6:52) is interpreted as their resistance to a Gentile mission and an unwillingness to move beyond their own religious tradition. Likewise, Rau ("Markusevangelium," 2122–24) interprets Jesus' intention to "pass by" (6:48) as Jesus' desire to lead the Markan community into a mission in non-Jewish areas which is checked by the disciples' fear. However, we have argued already in chapter 1 that there is not a polemic against the disciples in Mark but that their experiences become a teaching lesson for the church.

in 8:10–21 brings Christology to the forefront, but not in the traditional sense of the greatness of the miracle worker. Instead, the disciples do not understand the loaves because they have not accepted the discipleship consequences of a Suffering Servant Messiah, which Mark develops in the following discipleship catechism (8:27—10:52). Therefore, Mark combines an original eschatological and metaphorical interpretation in the oral tradition with a christological emphasis, although he continues to underscore the Jewish/Gentile nature of the community as evidenced in 8:19–20.

Therefore, the feeding of the five thousand represents salvation for the Jews. Evidence for this conclusion includes the following details, which separately do not seem compelling but together suggest the reasonable hypothesis that this first feeding is aimed specifically at Jews.

1. The twelve baskets left over provide a standard representation for Judaism as in the choosing of the twelve disciples.

Although many scholars consider this only a minor detail affirming the greatness of Jesus' miracle, all agree that Jesus ministered to Jewish people in this miracle. Some contend that both the twelve and seven baskets left over symbolize that the "bread of life is inexhaustible,"[127] but this does not explain why Mark would narrate the miraculous feedings twice. The more appropriate solution is proposed by Wefald: "Twelve instantly symbolized the twelve tribes of Israel, the whole of Israel."[128] When Mark develops the intercalation between the bleeding woman and the dead girl, he employs the number twelve to tie together these two narratives which occur on Jewish territory and involve Jewish purity rites.[129] The identical reasoning applies here.

2. The wicker baskets (6:43; 8:19 κόφινος) were distinctively Jewish food containers.[130]

We will discuss this claim in detail when we consider the symbolism in the feeding of the four thousand. Simply put, Mark employs two terms for baskets (κόφινος vs. σπυρίς) to distinguish a Jewish crowd from a Gentile audience.

3. Mark describes the crowd as sheep without a shepherd (6:34) since this terminology functions as a common designation for the covenant people.[131]

Whereas in the feeding of the four thousand Jesus' compassion is aimed more generally at the crowd from far away (8:2 ἐπὶ τὸν ὄχλον vs. 6:34 upon the πρόβατα), the familiar description "sheep without a shepherd" employed in Numbers 27:17; 1 Kgs 22:17; 2 Chr 18:16; Ezek 34:5; Jdt 11:19 (cf. Isa 40:11; Jer 31:10; Zech 13:7; 2 Bar. 2:52) indicates that the feeding of the five thousand deals with Israel. Thus divergent vocabulary calls attention to a different understanding of the audience.

---

127. See Hebert, "History in the Feeding," 71.

128. Wefald, "Separate Gentile Mission," 22.

129. For a more detailed description of Mark's use of the number 12, see section 8.5 below.

130. Supporters include Rawlinson, *St. Mark*, 87; Richardson, *Miracle Stories*, 91–92; and "Feeding of the Five Thousand," 146.

131. See Boucher, *Mysterious Parable*, 69; Collins, *Mark*, 319; and Masuda, "Good News of the Miracle," 205.

4. The division into groups of fifty and one hundred (only at Mark 6:40) reminds the reader of the tribal encampments of Israel in the Sinai peninsula (Exod 18:24–26) after the feeding in Exodus 16.

These divisions were also employed at Qumran (1QSa 1:14f; CD 13:1; 1QS 2:21; 1QM 4:2) in their self-identification as the new Israel. Thus Jesus would be the leader of the new Israel since he provides bread for the people like Moses. On the other hand, Hebert offers an alternative suggestion that these sizes reflect the believers in first-century churches. These "scattered Christian congregations, tempted to feel lonely, each a tiny handful of people amid a vast pagan population, must see themselves as members of the universal Church of Christ."[132] However, these numbers do not suggest a tiny group of people, and this ecclesiastical proposal does not explain the relevance of this data to the feeding of the five thousand. Therefore again Mark is calling attention to the Jewish nature of the community.

5. The green grass of Mark 6:39 could refer to the time of the spring Jewish Passover feast since John 6:4 reports that the feeding of the five thousand occurs during the time of Passover.

Green grass in the desert signified spring in Palestine, which was also the time of the Passover. The parallel narrative in John's gospel applies Jesus' bread to Moses' manna miracle, which was one of the most noteworthy events in Israel's history. Significantly, the end of the miracle of manna is associated with the Passover in Joshua 5:10–12 as well. Finally, since the feeding of the four thousand neglects to mention the green grass, no connection with a Jewish feast is assumed, opening the possibility of Gentile imagery.

However, other interpretations of this datum are equally possible, such as Friedrich's conclusion that the green grass symbolizes the eschatological blooming of the desert or van Iersel's supposition that Psalm 23 may be in the author's mind.[133] It is very difficult to decide here between a symbolic interpretation or a descriptive historical detail.[134] Since the green grass paints a realistic picture, a historical reminiscence seems the best solution. Either way, a Jewish audience should be assumed.

6. The feeding of the five thousand envisions an assembly of only men, in keeping with the Jewish requirement that counted only males as properly constituting a congregation (6:44 πεντακισχίλιοι ἄνδρες vs. 8:9 ὡς τετρακισχίλιοι).

Is it significant that Mark omits the term "males" in the feeding of the four thousand? Against such a supposition Matthew adds ἄνδρες at 15:38 to Mark's narrative of the four thousand and in each case (Matt 14:21; 15:38) qualifies the number by the statement "besides women and children." If Mark has purposely referred solely to

---

132. Hebert, "History in the Feeding," 70.

133. Friedrich, "Die beiden Erzählungen," 18–19; Hebert, "History in the Feeding," 70; and van Iersel, "Die wunderbare Speisung," 188.

134. Gundry (*Mark*, 331) consistently rules out symbolism.

males in the feeding of the five thousand,[135] then the only justifiable conclusion would be that Matthew does not follow Mark in his Jew/Gentile symbolism. Standing alone, this detail cannot substantiate an emphasis upon a Jewish audience.

7. In Mark 6:41 Jesus speaks a typical Jewish blessing (εὐλόγησεν) over the food whereas in 8:6 a Gentile blessing is preserved (εὐχαριστήσας).

The problem with such an interpretation is that 14:23 utilizes εὐχαριστήσας, where the audience is all Jews, while 8:7 employs εὐλογήσας for the fish in the feeding of the four thousand. In addition, both of these words trace back to a singular term in both Hebrew and Aramaic.[136] Finally, Turner points out Mark's style of using near-synonyms in close proximity for no apparent reason except variety.[137] Grassi argues that the use of both forms with the bread and fish in the miracle as well as at the Last Supper with the bread and cup (14:22–23) suggests a bringing together of both Jewish and Gentile practices.[138] However, if Mark is attempting to separate the Jewish and Gentile feedings through the use of two separate narratives, it would be confusing to suddenly employ these terms together. Therefore this argument is not valid.

8. The five loaves through which Jesus feeds the people are the five books of Moses.[139]

Again such a supposition is very doubtful. Since Mark refers to the book of Moses in the singular (ἐν τῇ βίβλῳ Μωϋσέως) in 12:26, he would not allude to five books here. Instead, the reference is merely traditional and historical.

The exegetical material favoring an application to Gentiles in the feeding of the four thousand includes both strong and weak arguments. However, the inclusion of

---

135. The term ἀνήρ is only used by Mark of Herod (6:20) and husbands (10:2, 12).

136. Cf. Hebert, "History in the Feeding," 69.

137. Turner, "Style of Mark's Eucharistic Words," 108–11. Cf. Masuda ("Good News of the Miracle," 202) for evidence of alteration in inscriptions.

138. Grassi, *Loaves and Fishes*, 42.

139. Grassi, *Loaves and Fishes*, 33. This view traces back at least to Hilary of Poitiers ("On Matthew 14:10," 258:20–22). For a second interpretation, Wefald hypothesizes that "the five initial loaves could possibly represent the five tribes of Israel still then in existence (the seven northern tribes having disappeared with the Assyrian deportations and never returned). Starting with what Israel is, five tribes, five loaves of bread, Jesus is able to feed all of Israel and fully restores Israel to twelve tribes, twelve baskets of bread" ("Separate Gentile Mission," 23). However, the theory that only seven northern tribes were lost in the Assyrian deportations does not seem to be a well-known view in ancient times. For a third interpretation, Drury ("Mark," 14–17) employs Mark 2:23–28 about David's actions in 1 Sam 21:3 whereby the normal twelve loaves (Lev 24:6) are reduced to seven after David takes five. As David's son, Jesus also takes five loaves in the first feeding, but as David's Lord (Mark 12:35–37), Jesus miraculously restores them to a full twelve with the leftovers. Then in the second feeding Jesus employs the remaining seven. For a fourth interpretation, Masuda ("Good News of the Miracle," 205) asserts that the seven loaves in the second narrative derive from the total of loaves and fish in the first story (5 + 2 = 7) and that the total loaves employed in both equals twelve which symbolizes fullness. However, only the baskets left over have significance for Mark since these are the two questions that Jesus addresses to the disciples in 8:19–20. Mark does not utilize arithmetic.

a second narrative almost identical to the first[140] requires a literary rationale, and the supposition of a Gentile audience fits the exegetical evidence hand in glove.

1. Whereas the feeding of the five thousand occurs at a solitary place (6:32), the geography of Mark 8 is more specific since the preceding healing takes place in the Decapolis.

The time reference in 8:1 is very general ("during those days") so some assume that the author is separating the upcoming incident from its context. However, the specific place reference in 8:10 to the Jewish region of Dalmanutha where Jesus encounters Pharisees argues for a sea journey from a Gentile location. Therefore the Feeding of the four thousand would continue the geography of the Decapolis found earlier in 7:31.

Stein contends that the omission of the phrase εἰς τὸ πέραν at 8:10 entails a location on the same side of the Sea of Galilee,[141] but if in the last geographic reference at 7:31 Jesus heals the deaf-mute in the Decapolis then the following trip is from Gentile to Jewish territory to confront the Pharisees in the region of Dalmanutha. In addition, Stein argues that this previous healing of the deaf-mute also occurs in Jewish territory since the phrase εἰς τὴν θάλασσαν τῆς Γαλιλαίας at 7:31 is the normal expression employed by Mark for the intended destination.[142] However, Mark's style is to place last in a list the immediate locale for what follows as in 10:1 and 11:1.[143] Therefore, the emphasis falls upon what happens within the Decapolis. In addition, the Sea of Galilee also serves as the shoreline for Gentile landscape, so that when this body of water is linked with the Decapolis as in 7:31 (ἀνὰ μέσον τῶν ὁρίων Δεκαπόλεως) Gentile terrain is certainly presumed. Stein also employs the grammatical argument that when Mark uses the order of participle + πάλιν + verb the term "again" modifies the participle (2:1; 5:21; 7:14; 10:32), whereas πάλιν modifies the verb when the order of πάλιν + participle + verb is employed (7:31; 14:39, 40).[144] Presuming for a moment the veracity of this grammatical argument, then Jesus would be again returning to the Sea of Galilee where he called his disciples (1:16), but since the identical phrase εἰς τὴν θάλασσαν is employed of Gentile territory in 5:13, this could as well refer to a second trip to the

---

140. For the striking parallels see section 5.5d above.

141. See Stein, *Mark*, 358.

142. Stein points out that εἰς with ἦλθεν refers to Jesus' destination in 1:14, 29, 39; 5:1; 6:53; 8:10; 9:33; 14:16 and with the historical present at 3:20; 5:38; 6:1; 8:22; 10:1, 46; 11:15, 27; 14:32. Stein (361) also contends that the Aramaic word εφφαθα ("be opened" 7:34) proves that Jewish territory is in view as at 5:41, but the use of a foreign word in a healing narrative frequently connotes power and authority.

143. Guelich, *Mark*, 392.

144. Stein, *Mark*, 358–59. However, it is doubtful if "again" refers to the participle in 10:32 since Mark does not say that Jesus has taken aside the twelve using the verb παραλαμβάνω before this, whereas this is the third passion prediction explaining what would happen to Jesus. Stein does not mention 8:1, but although the order is πάλιν, participle, verb, the repeated event is narrated in the participle, namely a second feeding before a large crowd.

Decapolis, where Jesus had already visited in 5:1–20.¹⁴⁵ However, this grammatical argument is not valid for 7:31 since then Jesus would be passing through Sidon again (ἦλθεν διὰ Σιδῶνος), but there is no previous event that occurs in Sidon in Jesus' ministry. Instead, the πάλιν must modify the participle in 7:31 so that Jesus returns from the region of Tyre just as he had entered it in 7:24. Finally, Stein appeals to Matthew's redaction of this passage (15:29), where Jesus travels to a mountain in Jewish territory near the Sea of Galilee (with no mention of the Decapolis) as he did after the feeding of the five thousand (Matt 14:23).¹⁴⁶ However, Matthew ignores all mission efforts to Gentiles in his Markan source since the Matthean Jesus envisions himself only sent to the lost sheep of the house of Israel (15:24).¹⁴⁷ Therefore, Gentile territory is assumed in the Markan context.

2. The order of the feedings is important since this portrays the salvation of Gentiles after the restoration of Israel.

This mission sequence appears consistently in the New Testament as evidenced in Paul (Rom 1:16; 2:9), the history of the early church (Acts 13:46; 3:26; 18:6), the Gospel of Luke (9:1; 10:1) with the two mission journeys of the Twelve and the Seventy (72), and Matthew's clarification that Jesus came for the lost sheep of Israel (10:6 15:24) but later also for the Gentiles (28:20). Thus a reference in the Gospel of Mark to a Gentile feeding following a Jewish miracle would not be unexpected since it corresponds with the theology of the church.

3. Since Mark employs bread as a symbol throughout the miracle section of his gospel,¹⁴⁸ it is likely that the bread in the feeding of the four thousand also contains an additional metaphorical meaning.

Bread is the subject matter when Jesus discusses the Jewish ceremonial cleansing rites in 7:1–23. The controversy about eating bread (ἄρτος 7:2, 5) without washed hands culminates in Jesus' proverb in 7:15, which Mark applies allegorically, concluding that Jesus declared all foods (βρώματα) clean (7:19b). If Jesus employed bread here to speak about issues related specifically to Israel, likewise the feeding of the five thousand in Mark 6 involves Jewish issues, especially with the cryptic reference in 6:52 that the disciples did not understand about the loaves (ἄρτοις). Similarly, in

---

145. In addition, the phrase in Mark 1:16 is παρὰ τὴν θάλασσαν, and Jesus returns there in 2:13 (πάλιν) so that a reference in 7:31 is unnecessary.

146. Stein, *Mark*, 358.

147. For instance, the conclusion to the exorcism of the Gerasene demoniac in Matthew depicts the inhabitants pleading for Jesus to leave Gentile territory (8:33) so that a mission to the Decapolis by the healed man is omitted completely (Mark 5:19–20). Whereas the Q material of Luke 10 envisions a mission by the 70 which would entail a corresponding mission to the 70 nations of the world, Matthew omits Luke 10:17 where the 70 return and has Jesus instruct his disciples not to go to the Gentiles (10:5–6), even though in the context Matt 9:37–38 = Luke 10:2 and Matt 10:9–15 = Luke 10:4–12. Therefore, one would expect the Feeding of the four thousand not to occur on Gentile territory in Matthew.

148. See section 1.5 above.

the narrative of the Syrophoenician woman (7:24–30) bread is pictured as the special presence of God for the Jews. However, through the woman's confession of faith bread is distributed to the Gentiles as well. Consequently, this symbolism carries over to the feeding of the four thousand in 8:1–9. Finally, in his reflections upon Jesus' miracles in 8:11–21 Mark speaks about one loaf (8:14 ἄρτον), which entails that through Jesus, the one loaf, the new Israel comprises both Jews and Gentiles.[149] This is reinforced by references to both the twelve baskets left over at the feeding of the five thousand and the seven at the feeding of the four thousand in 8:19–20, so that both Jews and Gentiles now come into Mark's purview at the conclusion to the miracle catenae. Thus Mark continuously gives the bread a symbolic interpretation throughout this section on Jesus' miracles.

4. It is possible that Mark employs the chronological reference "in those days" (8:1 Ἐν ἐκείναις ταῖς ἡμέραις) to designate the eschatological time when the Gentiles will be incorporated into Israel.

Since this phrase is employed eschatologically in the OT prophetic books (Jer 31:33; Joel 3:1; Zech 8:23) as well as twice in Mark's eschatological discourse (13:17, 24), "in those days" could refer here to the eschatological event of the Gentiles joining Israel.[150] The use of this phrase in Mark 1:9 could confirm this view since 1:10 refers to the tearing of the heavens at Jesus' baptism which indicates that the eschatological revelation of the last days has begun.[151]

5. Whereas the feeding of the five thousand emphasizes the initiative of the disciples (6:35–37), Jesus takes charge (8:2–3) in the Feeding of the four thousand to allow Mark to clarify that Jesus is the author of the ministry to the Gentiles.

This noticeable difference in the strikingly similar accounts could be significant since Mark has emphatically stressed the ministry of the disciples beginning with their mission outreach in 6:7–13. Therefore, Mark highlights the disciples' faith and problem-solving initiative in the feeding of the five thousand and the sea-walking adventure, where the disciples battle the storm without Jesus. In the first feeding the disciples perceive the problem and report to Jesus that the hungry people should be dismissed to purchase food because of the late hour and desolate location (6:35–36), but Jesus insists that they themselves give the people something to eat (6:37). On the other hand, in the second feeding Jesus has compassion for the people and decides not to send anyone home hungry since they could collapse on the way (8:2–3). This

---

149. If the seven basketfuls of pieces left over are symbolic, could it also be possible that the seven loaves combined with the five loaves employed by Jesus to feed the five thousand introduces a new 12 tribes of Israel that is fed with both multiplications? For an interpretation that the one loaf is Jews and Gentiles together see Kelber (*Mark's Story*, 40), Beck ("Reclaiming a Biblical Text," 52, 54), Best (*Following Jesus*, 21), Boring (*Mark*, 226–27), Boucher (*Mysterious Parable*, 81), and Stock (*Call to Discipleship*, 127). We prefer the interpretation that the one loaf is Jesus himself.

150. See Markus, *Mark 1–8*, 163, 487.

151. See also Marcus (*Mark 1–8*, 169) and Jeremias (*New Testament Theology*, 69–70) who see a paradise motif here.

contrasting description in similar narratives implies that Jesus initiates the Gentile mission just as he is responsible in Mark for proclaiming all foods clean (7:19b), two issues of supreme importance for Gentiles.

6. The seven baskets left over represent the seven nations of Canaan that Israel conquered (Acts 13:19; Deut 7:1).

The early church employed the imagery of seven and seventy for the nations. The seventy or seventy-two table of nations in Genesis 10 was probably employed in Luke 10 to indicate a ministry to the world broader than the mission of the twelve tribes in Luke 9:1–6.[152] While subjugating the land of Canaan, Israel conquered seven nations (Deut 7:1). This number is then employed by Paul in his sermon at Pisidian Antioch (Acts 13:19) to present the gospel both to the "People of Israel and you Gentiles who worship God" (13:16). Earlier in Acts the seven deacons are appointed in addition to the twelve apostles to lead the Hellenistic community associated with the dispersion. The apostles remain in Jerusalem (Acts 8:1) but the seven deacons and especially Philip extend the gospel to the Samaritans (8:4–25) and Ethiopians (8:26–40). Finally, as Boring explains, "The translation of the Bible into Greek was called the 'Seventy,' suggesting it was for all nations."[153] Therefore, seven or seventy refers to the broader community beyond Israel.

7. The number four thousand (8:9) represents the nations of the world just as there are four corners of the earth and four directions of the compass.

Gundry counters that the qualification ὡς (about, approximately) with four thousand rules out a symbolic meaning because "at the level of symbolism there is no need for approximations."[154] For instance, number symbolism is frequently diagnosed in the fourth gospel (2:6, 19; 5:5; 21:11) but when ὡς is employed (1:39; 4:6; 6:10, 19; 19:14, 39; 21:8), the presence of symbolism is extremely doubtful. Furthermore, the similar number reference in Mark 5:13 (about two thousand pigs) does not fit the size of a Roman legion and therefore contains no symbolic meaning. In addition Marcus points out that the number four thousand exhibits absolutely no metaphorical significance in 1 Samuel 4:2; 1 Chronicles 23:5; and Acts 21:38.[155] Nevertheless, it is possible that the derivative number four could represent the nations since it commonly de-

---

152. However, the numbers seven and seventy also symbolize fullness so that the 70 or 72 leaders anointed by the Holy Spirit in Num 11:24, 26 represent all Israel. For 70 see Gen 46:27; Exod 1:5; 15:27 (both 12 and 70); 24:1, 9; Jud 8:30ff; 1 Sam 6:19; 2 Kgs 10:1ff; Isa 23:15–17; Jer 25:11–12; Ezek 8:11; Dan 9:24. Regarding seven, the Old Testament speaks about the creation in seven days, seven of every animal that enter the ark, the sevens in Pharaoh's dreams in Genesis 41, seven day feasts, and seven times around Jericho. The fullness of Israel could include the total dispersion or both Jews and Gentile converts together including especially ministry to the Samaritans evidenced by their presence both before (9:51–56) and after (10:25–37) the mission to the 70.

153. Boring, *Mark*, 221. See also the seven Noachide commandments for Gentiles (t. Abod. Zar. 8:4; b. Sanh. 56ab).

154. Gundry, *Mark*, 397.

155. Marcus, *Mark 1–8*, 490.

GEOGRAPHICAL MIRRORING: JEWISH AND GENTILE TERRITORY

scribes the four corners of the earth (Matt 8:11–12), the four winds (Mark 13:27), and the four directions of the compass (Rev 7:1). However, since Mark only calls attention to the number of baskets left over (8:19–20), the number of people (five thousand or four thousand) is probably of little significance to Mark.[156]

8. Many perceive a symbolic reason for the remark that some have come from a distance (8:3 ἀπὸ μακρόθεν) since non-Jewish nations in the OT are described as "far-away" (Deut 28:49; 29:22; 1 Kgs 8:41, etc.) whereas Israel is "near" (Ps 148:14).[157]

In opposition, Stein remarks that Mark 8:3 would have specified "from Tyre and Sidon and throughout the Decapolis" if he had a Gentile audience in mind,[158] but the Markan narrative assumes a continuation of geography from 7:31. In addition, Gundry retorts that "from afar" in 11:13; 14:54; 15:40 has nothing to do with Gentileness, and Mark specifies that only "some" came from a distance thus destroying a general characteristic of the crowd as Gentile. As an alternative he proposes that "from afar" is a characteristically Marcan allusion to Jesus' magnetism.[159] However, an attraction to Jesus is not accentuated in any of the other usages of this term "from a distance," including 5:6. As a result every passage has its own unique emphasis. Since this vocabulary stands uniquely in the feeding of the four thousand, a Gentile theme takes precedence over other interpretations. Furthermore, the NT distinction between those who are near and those far off (Eph 2:11–13, 17; Acts 2:39; 22:21) is regularly applied to the relationship between Jews and Gentiles, so that the wording "from afar" in the feeding of the four thousand likely speaks typologically of Gentiles.

---

156. Proposals for symbolic numbers are varied and extremely hypothetical. Wefald ("Separate Gentile Mission," 23) conjectures that five thousand symbolizes both the four corners of the world plus Palestinian Jews. Danker ("Mark 8:3," 215–16) compares the four thousand to the Gibeonites (= Hivites in Josh 9:7 as one of the seven nations) who pretend to come from a distance and escape through a ruse involving loaves of bread which was revealed after three days (like the three days in the feeding of the four thousand at 8:2). He supposes that "The apparent triviality of these words in an otherwise highly compressed narrative vanishes when it is realized that Mark may be echoing either Josh 9:6 or Isa 60:4 or both." Therefore, Jesus' compassion and inclusion in a messianic banquet replaces the OT slavery by Jesus' counterpart, Joshua (Josh 9:21–22). In opposition Gundry (*Mark*, 396) observes that the Gibeonites are not without bread. Regarding other numbers, Wefald observes that the seven loaves at the beginning and seven baskets at the conclusion indicate that Gentiles are "not absorbed into the twelve restored tribes of Israel but stand in their own place within the new people of God which Jesus is inaugurating" (24). Grassi observes about 8:2 that "The 'three days' are mysterious, perhaps a proleptic hint that the Gentile apostolate only takes place after Jesus' death." Others tie the three days to Joshua 9 where the non-Jewish Gibeonites come from afar (9:6), make a covenant of bread with Israel, and only at the end of *three days* (9:16) does Joshua find out they are really neighbors" (*Loaves and Fishes*, 42). Countryman ("How Many Baskets Full?" 650–51) believes the declining numbers in the second narrative reflects the declining of Jesus' miraculous power as he approaches the suffering of the cross. But see Wefald ("Separate Gentile Mission," 16–17, n. 35) for evidence against this thesis. All of these are examples of over-interpretation.

157. Cf. Marcus, *Mark 1–8*, 487.
158. Stein, *Mark*, 368.
159. Gundry, *Mark*, 396. Cf. Stein, *Mark*, 368–69.

9. Whereas the wicker baskets used in the feeding of the five thousand (6:43; 8:19 κόφινοι) exhibit Jewish connotations, the larger hampers (8:8, 20 σπυρίδαι) in the feeding of the four thousand regularly appear in writings describing the Greco-Roman world.[160]

Evidence for this distinction derives primarily from two references in Juvenal's *Satires* (3:14; 6:542), wherein he depicts a Jew using a κόφινος.[161] According to Zodhiates' research, the Jews carried their food in these wicker baskets while traveling in Gentile countries to avoid defilement.[162] An influential opponent to this interpretation, Hort, concedes that "no passages have been found in Greek literature where the words are used synonymously"; nevertheless, he contends that "the distinction appears to lie in the material, consistency, and use."[163] Whereas κόφινος consists of a stiff wicker basket that was used with products from the soil, σπυρίς describes a flexible mat-basket that was regularly employed by fishermen. Hort highlights the additional benediction upon the fish in the second feeding (8:7) insisting that "The change is too marked to be accidental; and it affords an additional reason for believing that the baskets of the second miracle are the implements of the fisherman, not of the tiller of the soil."[164] However, the feeding of the five thousand contains three references to fish (6:41a, 41b, 43) while the second feeding only one so that fish seem to receive more attention in the first miracle. In opposition to a Jew/Gentile distinction Hort calls attention to Psalm 80:7 LXX (81:6), where the earth basket of Egyptian laborers is labeled κόφινος.[165] However, the clause "their hands were set free from the basket" is referring to Jewish slaves in Egypt, who probably used their own baskets since they must gather their own straw (Exod 5:7–18). Therefore Hort's alternative theory cannot be substantiated. Gundry argues that Christian Jews used a σπυρίς in Paul's escape over the wall in Acts 9:25,[166] but this occurs in Gentile territory, where Gentile implements would be employed. Fowler disputes a Jew/Gentile distinction by referring to the writings of Josephus (*War* 3:95), where κόφινος specifies the equipment of a Roman infantryman and therefore not a Jewish basket.[167] However as a Jewish author,

---

160. For support for this thesis see the lexicons (under κόφινος) of Moulton and Milligan; Liddell, Scott, and Jones; and *BAGD* (but not *BDAG*). However, Louw and Nida (*Greek-English Lexicon*, 2nd ed., 1:70) deny that NT contexts and extra-biblical usage distinguishes these terms. For commentary support for this distinction see Hooker, *St. Mark*, 188 and Twelftree, *Jesus: Miracle Worker*, 81.

161. 3:14 *Iūdaeis, quōrum cophinŭs faenŭmquĕ sŭpellex*; 6:542 *cophino faenoque relicto . . . Iūdaea tremens*.

162. Spiros Zodhiates, *Complete Word Study Dictionary*, G2894.

163. Hort, "A Note," 567.

164. Ibid., 570.

165. Ibid., 568. Also Gen 40:16, a bread basket of Pharoah's baker, where Aquila substitutes κόφινος for κανᾶ.

166. Gundry, *Mark*, 398. Hort believes that a fishing basket is employed in Acts 9:25 since in 2 Cor 11:33 Paul uses the term σαργάνη which "was woven of rushes and intended to receive fish" ("A Note," 571).

167. Fowler, *Loaves and Fishes*, 211, n. 117.

Josephus would employ Jewish terminology for his descriptions. Yet this example is the hardest to dismiss since Roman soldiers are specifically the subject matter. Therefore, the evidence is ambivalent and one should proceed with caution in emphasizing the Jew/Gentile usage of these terms. However, since the geographical locations vary between Jewish and Gentile lands and there is consistency of vocabulary in all the accounts of the different feedings as well as in Mark's later comments upon the specific miracles (8:19-20), a Jew/Gentile distinction is certainly attractive.[168]

10. The resisting of a Gentile mission by Jesus' followers explains Mark's emphasis upon the misunderstanding of the disciples throughout the miracle section (4:40; 6:52; 8:14-21).

Wefald observes that the Jewish disciples resist the second (Gentile) feeding (8:4) but not the first (Jewish) feeding. In fact, "The disciples never questioned Jesus about how one could feed the Jews in the first feeding of 6.30-44, but in fact they volunteered to go and buy bread for that Jewish crowd, something which they do not volunteer in the second feeding of 8.1-10."[169] With regard to the word order of the disciples' question in 8:4, Wefald contends that the term τούτους precedes the verb and subject in an irregular manner to emphasize the distain of the disciples for the Gentile crowd. He reasons that this emphasis upon τούτους is coupled with the description "from far away" by its close proximity (8:3b) and thus refers to Gentiles in contrast to 6:34, where Mark refers to the crowd as sheep and thus people whom Jesus' disciples would recognize as their own countrymen. However, Wefald mistakenly interprets the question beginning with πόθεν as an interrogative of cause ("How?") whereas the more natural translation is an interrogative of locale ("Where?").[170] There is therefore no contrast with the earlier feeding since at 6:36 the disciples are similarly attempting to discover surrounding villages where they could buy food. Furthermore, Jesus speaks more harshly with the disciples in the first feeding when he demands in 6:37, "You give them something to eat." Therefore, the disciples' question stems not from their resistance to Gentiles but from their inability to act without Jesus. Finally, the disciples' lack of understanding in Mark always highlights their inability to understand the passion of Jesus, as evidenced here by the similarity with the Last Supper narrative.[171] Therefore, although we should posit a Jew/Gentile distinction in the two miraculous feedings, Jesus is not subtly rebuking the disciples for their lack of concern with Gentiles but instead for their faulty perception of the purpose, definition, and significance of miracles. Thus the polemical view for explaining the two feedings

---

168. See Horn, "Use of the Greek New Testament," 301. He also argues that the Gentile baskets were bigger, and therefore the leftovers were greater for the multitudes of Gentiles in the world.

169. Wefald, "Separate Gentile Mission," 20.

170. *BDAG*, 838. With regard to English translations, the NASV, NIV, NET, NAB, NJB, and ISV have "where" while the NKJV, RSV, NRSV, ESV, NLT use "how." But "how" is not necessarily understood as Wefald understands the question.

171. See the Markan repetition explained above in section 4.2b.

presents inadequate explanations of the exegetical data since Mark emphasizes Jesus' desire to feed the Gentiles and not any repulsion against Gentiles by the disciples.

Prominent interpreters from differing traditions with divergent presuppositions have offered their support for the attractiveness and sufficiency of the symbolic view of the two miraculous feedings.[172] But the prominence of Jew/Gentile geographical mirroring does not necessarily eliminate a christological, eschatological, or even eucharistic interpretation of the feeding narratives. This question can only be solved by investigating Mark's commentary on the miracle catenae in 8:10–21.[173] In the feeding of the four thousand itself (8:1–9) a christological emphasis is evident in Jesus' multiplication of a small boy's lunch into a feast for the entire multitude. But what type of Christology is Mark promoting? Whereas the Pharisee's request a sign (8:11), Mark points out that the disciples already have a loaf of bread in the boat, namely Jesus (8:14). Jesus warns the disciples to beware of the leaven of the Pharisees and Herod (8:15), who seek a physical miracle and do not perceive the real feeding miracle in Jesus' death. Disciples become hard-hearted outsiders devoid of understanding (8:17–21) if they do not perceive that Jesus is the bread that must be broken for the world. As Donfried explains, "What the disciples should already have perceived and understood in Mark 6 and 8 by way of anticipation is now made clear in 14,22ff. The bread symbolized Jesus as the body, as the one who becomes a ransom for many by means of his death."[174] To clarify this truth Mark follows the miracle section with a discipleship catechism predicting Jesus' death, the misunderstanding by the disciples, and teachings on the discipleship of the cross. Since understanding the true character of a suffering Messiah is the theme of the Markan controversy dialogues, parables, eschatological discourse, and passion narrative, it must be Mark's main point in the miracle section as well.

An eschatological interpretation is not entirely excluded either. The miracle catenae, which begin with a trip across water as on dry ground like Moses, Joshua, and Elisha and conclude with a miraculous feast like manna in the wilderness, the Passover after the manna stops in the land of Canaan, and Elisha's miraculous feast as he brings salvation to the land all point toward the future eschatological banquet. Therefore, the two miraculous feedings in Mark recall the two manna feedings in the wilderness (Exod 16 and Num 11) to indicate their fulfillment in the new messianic age.[175] Just as the memory of manna in the wilderness recalls the theme of obduracy

---

172. See Kelber, *Oral and Written*, 126; Twelftree, *Jesus Miracle Worker*, 81–82; Kingsbury, *Conflict in Mark*, 100; Broadhead, *Teaching with Authority*, 136; Richardson, *Miracle Stories*, 97–98; and Boucher, *Mysterious Parable*, 78 and n. 51 for a list of additional scholars.

173. This concluding section added by Mark draws together the themes in the miracle stories. See Fowler, *Loaves and Fishes*, 109; Quesnell, *Mind of Mark*, 125.

174. Donfried, "Feeding Narratives," 102.

175. Farrer (*Study in Mark*, 291) thinks that the fish are analogous to the quails, as the bread represents manna. The question, "How could so many be fed with so few resources?" (6:37) could be a resonance to the similar question in Num 11:21–22, "Would they have enough if all the fish in the sea

(Ps 78:17–32; Ps 105:40; Neh 9:15–17), so Mark's commentary after the feeding of the four thousand centers on the hard-heartedness and lack of understanding of the disciples. Therefore, we may rightly assume both an eschatological feast as well as table fellowship between Jews and Gentiles since the gathering of the Gentiles was believed to occur at the future banquet.[176] However, the eschatological nature of the feedings is now in the background since Mark does not directly pick up this theme in his commentary on the miracle catenae in 8:10–21.

Many authors highlight a eucharistic emphasis in the miraculous feedings by calling attention to the four eucharistic terms that Jesus employs: "took bread," "blessed" or "gave thanks," "broke it," and "gave it to them."[177] These four phrases occur in this exact order in the six accounts of the multitude feedings throughout the gospels (except John 6:11, which omits the breaking), in the three narratives of the Last Supper in the Synoptic Gospels, in Paul's description in 1 Corinthians 11:23–26, and in the meal at Emmaus in Luke 24.[178] Since the theme of remembering was central to the celebration of the Eucharist in the early church (Luke 22:19; 1 Cor 11:24–25), Jesus' question in Mark 8:18, "Do you remember?," reminds one of "Do this in remembrance of me."[179]

However, the specific content of this eucharistic view varies all the way from pointing to Jesus' death to an emphasis upon the sacraments. Certainly the disciples' total inability to understand the feedings directs the reader toward the Last Supper, as we have demonstrated in chapter 4.[180] But the sacraments themselves are never Mark's focus. When he speaks about baptism and the cup (10:38–39) Mark refers to Jesus' death and the subsequent martyrdom of the apostles.[181] Although Hebert employs 1 Corinthians 10:17 ("Because there is one loaf, we, who are many, are one body, for we all partake of the one loaf") to argue for a sacramental reference at Mark 8:14,[182] the one loaf in the boat is Jesus, not the Eucharist. Likewise, in Mark's commentary immediately following the feeding of the four thousand, he does not transmit Jesus' formula of distribution but the amount of baskets left over (8:19–20). Christology and discipleship become the primary application of the feedings, not the Christian meal.

---

were caught for them?" according to Boucher (*Mysterious Parable*, 70).

176. See Camery-Hoggatt, *Irony in Mark's Gospel*, 146.

177. See especially Catholic authors: Achtemeier, "Origin and Function," especially 207–9, 214–19; Grassi, "Eucharist in the Gospel," 595–608; Quesnell, *Mind of Mark*, 193–208; Stock, *Call to Discipleship*, 126ff.; and van Iersel, "Die wunderbare Speisungi," 171ff as well as John 6:52–58.

178. See Hebert, "History in the Feeding," 69.

179. The formula for the Lord's Supper employs the noun while Mark uses the verb, but this is the only occurrence of this word in Mark's gospel.

180. See section 4.2b above.

181. Sacraments are not important at other points since in Mark 1:8 John baptizes with water but Jesus baptizes with the Holy Spirit producing a Christological emphasis and the washing in Mark 7:4 is ritual, not sacramental.

182. Hiebert, "History in the Feeding," 71.

However, a correct understanding of the eucharistic interpretation where the bread symbolizes Jesus himself and the elements themselves are moved to the background[183] fits hand and glove with a Jew/Gentile geographical mirroring. As Stock explains, "The passage may be taken as an early expression of open table fellowship for followers of Jesus of both Jewish and Gentile origin. The one bread is more than adequate for all of their needs."[184] But "the absence of wine, the use of fish,[185] and the fact that Mark has not conformed this story to that of the Last Supper (cf. 6:41 and 14:22) argue against a thorough Eucharistic interpretation of this feeding."[186] In addition, the gathering of leftovers plays no role in the Lord's Supper even though Mark's accounts of the feedings and his reflection upon them emphasize the leftover bread.

Therefore, the passion of Jesus is always the central theme Mark wants to emphasize, also in Mark 8:10–21. Jesus first travels to Jewish territory (8:10) where the Pharisees demand a miracle (8:11–12). Then Jesus enters a boat again (8:13) headed for Gentile territory (8:22) where the journey becomes a sea conversation about bread. The disciples must turn away from the leaven of the Pharisees and Herod and its demand for a sign (8:15) since Jesus as the bread is always with them (8:14).[187] However, the disciples do not understand the loaves (6:52) because they (and Mark's readers) want a Messiah who provides mighty signs rather than a multiplication that comes through death. Therefore, Mark inserts the healing of the blind man in the next pericope (8:22–26) to open the eyes of the disciples to the power of a Messiah who must suffer (8:31) alongside the expected Son of David Messiah (8:29).

In addition, Mark preserves the secondary theme of a Jew/Gentile geographical mirroring from the tradition in 8:19–20.[188] Therefore, the theme of bread, which runs throughout the entire miracle section, receives a double application in the life of Mark's community. Mark concludes his miracle catenae with a tenfold rebuke (8:17–21) because the disciples misunderstand the personhood of the miracle worker (8:11–18) and the inclusion of the Gentiles in table fellowship with Jews (7:24–30; 8:19–20), as evidenced by the geographical mirroring of the two feeding narratives. Mark retells the story of Jesus to persuade his community to follow a crucified Messiah instead of pursuing the leaven of the Pharisees. In addition, Mark narrates both

---

183. Quesnell (*Message of Mark*, 257) has a more general "eucharistic" interpretation which includes the aspects of the Eucharist itself as well as the recollection of the passion and death of the Lord, the expectation of an eschatological banquet, the union of Jew and Gentile, the message of salvation, and faith as a way of life.

184. Stock, *Call to Discipleship*, 127.

185. Richardson ("Feeding," 147) points out that fish played an important role in early Christian eucharistic symbolism (frescoes in the catacombs), but this material is much later than the New Testament.

186. Twelftree, *Jesus: Miracle Worker*, 76–77.

187. Best explains correctly the symbolism: "Jews and Gentiles are then united in the one loaf (8:14–21), namely Jesus who alone is necessary and is sufficient for both" (*Following*, 218).

188. Geddert points out that "to focus on Gentiles as if it were Mark's central concern is to mistake a part for the whole" (*Watchwords*, 128–29).

miraculous feedings so that the community will accept Jesus' plan to have both Jews and Gentiles participate in table fellowship. These two themes, a crucified Messiah and developing a community of both Jews and Gentiles, become the two themes that Mark emphasizes.

Since Jewish conceptions of purity kept Jew and Gentile apart, Mark must also address the matter of OT cleanliness rites. Consequently, Mark must teach the Gentiles how to interpret the OT purity legislation in the new covenant of Jesus. Just as Mark employed geographical mirroring to address Jew/Gentile relations, so he will employ Jewish ceremonial ritual mirroring to tackle the issue of the normativity of the ceremonial law. We now turn to a discussion of these concerns.

8

Jewish Ceremonial Ritual Mirroring

8.1 Two Contrary Views Regarding Mark's Attitude toward OT Purity Laws

We have argued that Mark employs literary devices for theological reasons to demonstrate that 1) Jesus' kingdom words and deeds prove that the Messiah must suffer death, 2) the disciples must take up their cross and follow him, 3) Gentiles are included in the new covenant community, and 4) the Jewish purity rites have now been fulfilled so that the Old Testament must be read in a new manner. This chapter will focus on the last of these propositions. We will begin with the clearest example in 7:19b, where Mark comments upon Jesus' "parable" (7:15) about defilement, demonstrating that "In saying this, Jesus declared all foods clean." Here Mark openly reveals his agenda that Jesus has transformed all Jewish purity rites. Following an examination of food laws, we will turn to other important issues such as Sabbath observance, the temple and sacrifices, touching unclean fluids and dead bodies, and the treatment of lepers.

We will argue that Mark offers an authoritative rationale for the Gentile church's cessation of Jewish ceremonial rituals by demonstrating that Jesus' kingdom words and deeds have fulfilled these OT regulations. Problematically, some scholars envision a positive evaluation of Jewish rituals by Mark. Loader, for instance, contends that "Mark is not portraying the new as a total replacement of the old," so that "when the Law becomes an issue, Mark emphasizes continuity."[1] These authors argue that Mark is defending Jesus' loyalty to the law by demonstrating that all charges by the Jewish leaders that Jesus acts contrary to the Torah are without foundation.[2] The

---

1. Loader, *Jesus' Attitude*, 55.

2. Ibid., 31. "On Mark's understanding, then, in none of the five instances does Jesus act contrary to Torah" (37).

prominent example concerns Jesus sending the leper to the Jewish authorities for confirmation of his healing (1:45), which prepares the way for five controversy dialogues where Mark defends Jesus against accusations of blasphemy (2:1–12), defilement from sinners (2:13–17), lack of ceremonial piety (2:18–22), and breaking the Sabbath (2:23–28; 3:1–6). According to this position, Jesus is portrayed by Mark as "a Torah-observant Jesus concerned about boundaries."[3]

This premise of a Torah-observant Markan Jesus controls the manner in which specific passages are interpreted. Loader supports the Western text reading of Mark 1:41 which "portrayed Jesus as angry because he had been approached by a leper, who was thus transgressing Torah,"[4] resulting in Jesus becoming unclean. Therefore Mark is careful to point out that the disciples in 7:3, 5 have not violated the Torah but only the tradition of the elders.[5] Loader believes as well that Jesus' question aimed at the bleeding woman in 5:30, "Who touched my clothes?," comes close to an angry response which his disciples seek to assuage.[6] Jesus is disgusted when people fail to abide by the OT ceremonial law.

Other authors support Loader's contention. Marcus calls attention to the Sabbath observance described in 1:32–34 whereby "the godly folk of Capernaum wait patiently for the sun to go down and the Sabbath to end before bringing their ill and afflicted ones to the new healer who has arisen in their midst."[7] Although the exorcism in the synagogue and the healing of Simon's mother-in-law take place on the Sabbath, these authors point out that Mark is careful to narrate that Jesus did not initiate the first event and the other healing took place privately inside a house. Likewise, Booth contends that "Mark uses the allusion to Jesus' tassel, κρασπέδον (6:56), immediately prior to the conflict over purity in 7:1–23, as a way of asserting Jesus' adherence to Torah."[8] Finally, the Markan Jesus portrays a conservative approach to Gentiles so that confronted with the inquiry of the Syrophoenican woman, Jesus retorts, "it is not right to take the children's bread and toss it to the dogs" (7:27).

Loader attempts as well to demonstrate that Mark has no interest in purity issues and therefore refuses to alter the normativity of the OT regulations.[9] For example, in the exorcism at Gerasa Mark declines to pay any special attention to the contaminated

---

3. Ibid., 25, n. 40.

4. Loader, "Challenged at the Boundaries," 57. Loader (61) argues that Matt 8:7 should be a question of protest, ἐγὼ ἐλθὼν θεραπεύσω αὐτόν, indicating Jesus' hesitancy of contact with a Gentile in a similar encounter in the Q tradition. However, the response by the centurion, "I do not deserve it" does not fit well with this question and the Lukan account does not contain these words.

5. Rudolph, "Jesus and the Food Laws," 294.

6. Loader, "Challenged at the Boundaries," 58.

7. Marcus, *Mark 1–8*, 200.

8. Booth, *Jesus and the Laws*, 31.

9. See Loader's conclusion (*Jesus' Attitude*, 134) that silence indicates irrelevance for Mark. On the other hand, we will argue that Mark employs literary devices to state his conclusions in an indirect manner.

cemetery or the unclean pigs (5:3, 5, 11–13). Although the intercalation of two women (5:21–43) bristles with issues of purity, "it is all the more striking that Mark shows so little interest."[10] Finally, "Mark is silent about what constitutes Sabbath observance for his community."[11] Therefore, Mark continues to advocate Mosaic teaching on the ceremonial law according to Loader.

Other scholars oppose this understanding of Mark's gospel, with Neyrey offering an extensive list of examples where the Markan Jesus did not observe the Jewish ceremonial regulations so important to the Judaism of his day.[12]

1. Jesus purposefully came in contact with unclean people: he voluntarily touched a leper (1:41) and took a corpse by the hand (5:41).

2. Jesus was touched by a menstruating woman,[13] a traditionally unclean person (5:24–28).

3. Jesus called a public sinner to be an intimate: to Levi sitting in his tax booth he said, "Follow me!" (2:13–14).

4. Jesus travelled extensively in Gentile territory, thus crossing boundaries he ought not to cross and exposing himself to pollution on every side. He regularly crossed the Sea of Galilee into non-kosher territory (4:35–42); he toured the "region of Tyre and went through Sidon to the Sea of Galilee, through the region of the Decapolis" (7:31).

5. While traveling on a journey through Gentile territory, Jesus had commerce with unclean people such as the Syrophoenician woman (7:24–30).

6. Jesus regularly was in contact with the possessed, the blind, the lame, and the deaf—all figures who are unclean in some way according to Leviticus 21:16–24.

7. Jesus broke one of the strictest purity laws in Israel as he disregarded all dietary restrictions: "Thus he declared all foods 'clean'" (7:19b).

8. Contrary to all purity rules, Jesus shared meals with unclean sinners: "He sat at table in Levi's house and many tax collectors and sinners were sitting with Jesus" (2:15).

9. Jesus' disciples also did not have regard for the surface of the body; they did not wash their hands before eating, showing unconcern for what passed through their mouths: "The Pharisees saw that some of his disciples ate with hands defiled, that is, unwashed" (7:2).

---

10. Loader, *Jesus' Attitude*, 61. Loader states, "Mark was probably aware of the purity issues in these stories, but they were no longer his concern" (65).

11. Ibid., 132.

12. These 15 examples are taken directly from Neyrey, "Idea of Purity," 107.

13. I employ menstruating and bleeding as synonyms in this passage although in the OT impurity laws *niddah* refers to menstruating women and *zabah* to women with a vaginal bleeding outside the period of menstruation which is really the situation in Mark 5.

10. In what must have been shocking to Mark's ancient audience, Jesus applied his own spittle to the eyes of a blind man (8:23) and to the tongue of a dumb person (7:33), showing disregard for bodily orifices and bodily emissions.

11. In the mass feedings in 6:37–44 and 8:1–10, Jesus showed no concern for the purity of the folk with whom he ate or for any of the rituals to be practiced prior to eating.

12. Jesus' disciples plucked grain on the Sabbath, "doing what is not lawful to do on the Sabbath" (2:24). Jesus himself healed on the Sabbath (3:1–6).

13. Jesus thoroughly disrupted the temple system. He halted worshippers from their holy rites by chasing away those who facilitated the payment of temple tithes and the offering of gifts (11:15). It is even said that he "would not allow anyone to carry anything through the temple" (11:16), which may refer to Jesus' supposed interruption of the carrying of sacrificial vessels and offerings from the people's court into the altar area.

14. Jesus' negative attitude to temple space is clarified when it is linked with a later statement that love of God and neighbor is "worth more than all whole burnt offerings" (12:33).

15. Jesus' enemies perceive him as speaking against the holy place (14:58; 15:29), a perception with which Mark apparently agreed (see 13:2). Since the temple is the chief expression of the purity system of first-century Judaism, Jesus' "pollution" of the temple (11:15–19) and his prediction of its destruction (13:1–2) should surface as the major charges against him by the temple elite in Jerusalem (14:58; 15:29). From their perspective, in showing such contempt for its chief symbol, Jesus was rejecting the whole system.

So two contrary views have been expressed regarding Mark's attitude toward OT purity laws. Which is correct? We agree with Loader that Mark does not repeatedly specify in an upfront manner that OT purity laws are cancelled. The historical Jesus maintained a conservative view of the law. However, Mark employs literary devices to indicate to the reader that by implication the OT ceremonial regulations have been fulfilled in the kingdom of God through Jesus' words and actions. Therefore, Mark demonstrates that the Gentile church's reading of the Old Testament is already inherent in the teaching and miracles of Jesus.

8.2 The Ceremonial Purity of All Unclean Food (7:14–23)

In this section we will distinguish three differing standpoints in the early church on the importance of kosher foods for the Christian life. We will argue that both Paul and Mark arrive at the identical conclusion that only the ethical commands of the law are normative for both Jewish and Gentile Christians. This innovative reading of the Old

Testament is clarified by Mark by his editorial comment in 7:19b and will offer a clue to discover the same new reading of the law for other ceremonial activities that are now fulfilled through Jesus' kingdom words and actions.

Since on one occasion (7:19b) Mark attaches an editorial comment to Jesus' teaching, this statement most clearly reveals Mark's attitude toward OT ceremonial legislation. In fact, this is the one place where Loader admits that the Markan Jesus is expressing discontinuity with Judaism.

> While the narrative begins with a dispute over particular Jewish applications of biblical law, effectively it ends up denying the principle of the biblical law itself. Treating external items as unclean is depicted as absurd. In the same spirit food laws are held up to ridicule: the food does nothing more than pass through the stomach and then into the toilet![14]

Loader even concludes that the "purity laws and food laws are not just of lesser importance; they have no status."[15] To determine Mark's position on food laws, we have to first examine three differing positions in early Christianity : 1) the circumcision party and James; 2) the middle stance of Peter, Luke, and Matthew; and 3) the Gentile-affirming position of Paul and then return to the interpretation of 7:15 and 19b.

The circumcision party maintained that Gentiles must be converted to Judaism before becoming adherents to Christianity and thus must be circumcised (Acts 15:1, 5). This minority position in the church[16] advocated a strict interpretation of ceremonial regulations and refused to eat with Gentiles because their dishes were unclean and their meat could have been offered to idols.[17] Peter held this view before

---

14. Loader, *Jesus' Attitude*, 126. Therefore, Loader (124–28) enumerates both continuity and discontinuity between the Markan Jesus and the OT purity laws.

15. Ibid., 128. Loader concludes that the Markan Jesus differentiates within Torah: "Food laws, purity laws concerned with externals, the sacrificial cult—these are no longer accepted as Torah" (132).

16. Sanders contends that "the position that Luke is opposing in Acts 15 is the one that he considers the essential position of Jewish Christians and not merely that of a minority" (*Jews in Luke-Acts*, 123). Thus Sanders views the comment in Acts 21:20 that "thousands of believing Jews are zealous for the law" negatively. However, numerical statements acclaiming the popularity of Christianity are always positive by Luke (Acts 2:41, 47; 4:4; 5:14) and serve as division points in the organization of Acts (6:7; 9:31; 12:24; 16:5; 19:20). Furthermore, Paul displays a unifying attitude toward this group by partaking in a ceremonial purification rite (21:24), whereas he constantly opposes the circumcision party. Therefore, the views of the Pharisaical party (Acts 15:1, 5) must be a minority position.

17. This hard-line approach is exemplified by R. Eliezer ben Hyrcanus (Hul. 2:7), the Essenes whom Josephus reports bathed even after contact with novices like after any contact with Gentiles (War 2:150), and other passages like Jub 22:16 ("Separate thyself from the nations, and eat not with them"); Joseph and Aseneth 7:1 ("Joseph never ate with the Egyptians for this was an abomination to him"); Aristeas 139 (Moses "fenced us round with impregnable ramparts and walls of iron that we might not mingle at all with any of the other nations"); and 3 Mac 3:4 ("but because they worshiped God and conducted themselves by his law, they kept their separateness with respect to foods"). See Bockmuehl, *Jewish Law in Gentile Churches*, 59. The impurity of contact with Gentiles is rightly defended by Alon ("Levitical Uncleanness of Gentiles," 146–89) and Sanders, (*Judaism: Practice and Belief*, 72–76). On the other hand, Bauckham ("James, Peter, and the Gentiles," 96) claims that Gentiles were not considered ritually impure by distinguishing impure and profane, but on 103–4 Bauckham

the divine revelation concerning Cornelius changed his mind, as Acts 10:28 (11:3) specifies: "You are well aware that it is against our law for a Jew to associate with a Gentile or visit him. But God has shown me that I should not call any man impure or unclean." The circumcision party criticized Peter for his change of behavior: "You went into the house of uncircumcised men and ate with them" (11:3). The traditional authority and persuasive power of this position is demonstrated when the Pharisaical party arrives at Antioch and Peter as well as Barnabas revert to not eating with Gentiles (Gal 2:12–13).

The circumcision band at Antioch is reported to have come from James (Gal 2:12a), but Acts 15 reveals that James did not agree with their stance on the circumcision of Gentile Christians.[18] Yet since Paul identifies the circumcision party with James, they must have agreed on the prohibition of table fellowship between Jews and Gentiles. Therefore, James maintained a strict interpretation of the law and would not eat with Gentiles. Chilton argues that "Yakov's perspective here is not that all who believe are Israel (the Pauline definition), but that in addition to Israel God has established a people in his name."[19] Therefore, James envisions two socially distinct and parallel movements: one to the circumcised who keep the entire law of Moses, and one to the Gentiles who maintain the requirements of the apostolic decree (Acts 15:20, 29) as the aliens in the land did in Leviticus 17:8–13.[20] Unlike the circumcision party, James maintains that it is unnecessary for Gentiles to be converted to Judaism and observe circumcision, but like the circumcision party he contends that they have an obligation to obey the requirements that God gave for Gentiles since "Moses has been preached in every city from the earliest times" (Acts 15:21). Thus James initiated the apostolic decree as Luke reports in Acts 15:19: "It is my judgment" (διὸ ἐγὼ κρίνω).[21] James believes that the eschatological fulfillment of Amos 9:11–12 has arrived with the restoration of Israel (9:11) and the streaming of the Gentiles to Israel's faith (9:12).[22] But differing requirements still hold for each, with Jewish Christians observing the entire law whereas Gentile Christians must preserve only the commandments that applied to the resident alien in the Old Testament.[23] Therefore Chilton and

---

concedes that many authors employ the words interchangeably including Mark.

18. Regarding James' leadership, Luke reports that "some went out from us without our authorization and disturbed you, troubling your minds by what they said" (15:24).

19. Chilton, "Brother of Jesus," 37. See Catchpole, "Paul, James, and the Apostolic Decree," 430.

20. See Chilton, "Brother of Jesus," 40; Jervell, *Luke and the People of God*, 144; and Waitz, "Das problem des sogenannten Aposteldekrets," 277.

21. James' speech in cooperation with the elders in Acts 21:17–25 repeats the Apostolic Decree (21:25).

22. In their commentaries on Acts, Longenecker (447), Haenchen (448), Krodel (281), and Conzelmann (117) all contend that it would be impossible for James to have derived his point from the Hebrew text, but the Gentiles' inclusion in Israel is the same in the MT and LXX, although the means of that inclusion (conquest vs. conversion) is different. See Dubis ("Use of Amos 9:11–12," 79 and 72–80) for a discussion of the text of Amos which James quoted in Acts 15.

23. Thus Acts 15:16 refers to a remnant of Jews and 15:17 to a remnant of Gentiles. However,

Neusner are correct when they conclude that "James insisted upon the leadership of the movement from Jerusalem, the continuation of sacrifice in the Temple, the purity of all those (Jews and non-Jews) associated with him, and the separation of Jews and non-Jews at meals."[24]

Since Peter experienced table fellowship with Cornelius (Acts 11:3) and ate with the Gentile believers at Antioch until messengers from Jerusalem arrived, he represents a middle position of eating with Gentiles as long as ceremonial purity is maintained.[25] Already at this time Jews ate with Gentiles, but on such occasions they either brought their own food or ate only vegetables.[26] This is the position of the weaker brother mentioned by Paul in Romans 14:2. As a Jew, Peter refused to eat non-kosher food (Acts 10:14; 11:8);[27] however, the vision from heaven convinced Peter that he must break the tradition of no close contact between Jews and Gentiles. Therefore, Acts 10:15 and 11:9 ("Do not call anything unclean that God has made pure") should not be understood as applying to food by Luke but to people.[28] This is evidenced by the conclusion of Peter that "God has shown me that I should not call any man impure or unclean" (10:28). The four corners of the sheet thus signify that all nations are invited to salvation. The vision is symbolic rather than literal, as demonstrated by Acts 10:34–35: "God does not show favoritism but accepts people from every nation." Therefore, until the circumcision party came to Antioch Peter ate with Gentiles but

---

Braun ("James' Use of Amos," 119–20) argues that "remnant of men" cannot be equated with Gentiles but must be believing Jews since the remnant idea in its soteriological sense is employed exclusively in the Bible with regard to the Jews. But Dubis ("Use of Amos 9:11–12," 98) quotes Isa 60:3–14; Zech 9:7; 14:16 to demonstrate the falsity of Braun's claim. Synthetic parallelism is employed as in the NET Bible translation "so that the rest of humanity may seek the Lord, namely, all the Gentiles I have called to be my own."

24. Chilton and Neusner, *Judaism in the New Testament*, 127.

25. Chilton and Neusner affirm that "Peter is definitely associated in the New Testament with a style of interpretation which is distinct from Paul's and James'" (*Judaism in the New Testament*, 109). Gal 2:14a reports that Peter lived like a Gentile, but this must mean that he freely associated with anyone rather than that he willingly ate non-kosher food. This activity would contrast him with the Judaizers and would account for Paul's accusation in 14b that by withdrawing he was forcing Gentiles to follow Jewish customs by not permitting them to eat non-kosher meat when with Jews. On the other hand, Booth (*Jesus and the Laws of Purity*, 82) thinks that Peter knowingly ate non-kosher food with Gentiles until emissaries arrived from James which would falsely associate Peter with the position of Paul.

26. See Dan 1:3–7; 1 Mac 1:62–63; Ep Aristeas 181–84; Tob 1:11; Jud 12:1–2.

27. As Tomson says, it is "inconceivable that Peter waived the biblical dietary regulations in Caesarea" (*If This Be from Heaven*, 99), and, "Nowhere is it indicated in what follows that at Cornelius' house Peter ate things prohibited by Jewish law. On the contrary, just like the centurion of Capernaum (Luke 7:6), Cornelius himself is full of understanding of the Jewish customs" (232).

28. Pettem rightly concludes, "The vision is thus never interpreted to mean that the category of dietary purity is eliminated, nor even that all animals are declared clean within the sphere of Jewish dietary purity" ("Luke's Great Omission," 43). Peter himself (10:28) as well as the circumcised believers in Jerusalem (11:18) apply the vision to people, not food. But this position appears not to have been universally accepted since Paul's thinking in Rom 14:14, 20 as well as Mark 7:19b seems to apply the vision to food.

did not touch unclean food, but at Antioch Peter experienced a crisis of conscience, which Svartvik explains with remarkable clarity.

> When Peter came to the Gentile Christians in Pauline communities he thought that they were adhering to the terms of the Jerusalem Council and therefore saw no reason not to eat with these fellow-Christians. When he found out that Paul did not regard the Decree as binding, Peter withdrew from fellowship of table in Antioch—thus criticizing the Pauline standpoint. Paul rightly saw this withdrawal as an attack on his mission and therefore vehemently condemns Peter in Gal 2 for a vacillating behaviour.[29]

Thus the practice of eating meat with Gentiles became a difficult and controversial issue for the early church.

Luke accepts this middle position as well since he narrates Peter's encounter with Cornelius but omits Peter's temporary retreat from this position at Antioch recorded in Galatians 2:11–14.[30] In fact, the entire work of Luke-Acts seeks to foster sympathy for the Jewish ceremonial laws. Jesus' family observes the purification rites after the birth of a first-born child (Luke 2:22–24) and travel to the temple at Passover every year (2:41). In Acts Paul is described as a keeper of the ceremonial law (21:24) so that he keeps vows (18:18; 21:26) as well as the regulations of temple observance (21:29). The Lukan Paul always ministers at the synagogue first (13:5 Salamis; 13:14 Antioch of Pisidia; 14:1 Iconium; 17:1–2 Thessalonica; 17:10 Berea; 18:4 Corinth; 18:19 Ephesus) and regularly observes Jewish feasts (27:9 the fast of the Day of Atonement; 20:6 the Feast of Unleavened Bread at Philippi; 20:16 Pentecost; 18:21 Passover [in the Western text and the KJV]). In Acts (23:6; 26:5) Paul still represents himself as a Pharisee whereas in Philippians 3:5 the past tense is employed.[31] Although no references to the content of the apostolic decree occur in Paul's writings, in Acts 15:22, 25 Paul supports the apostolic decree and reads it to every church he visits (15:30; 16:4). Surely this picture of Paul is Lukan apologetic to unite both Gentile and Jewish Christianity under the leadership of Luke's hero, namely Paul.

---

29. Svartvik, *Mark and Mission*, 114.

30. However, several commentators place Luke closer to Paul's position. Jack Sanders (*Jews in Luke-Acts*, 121, 139) and Seifrid ("Jesus and the Law," 43) hold that the vision of Peter in Acts 10 both abrogates dietary purity and justifies the Gentile mission (139), but they fail to offer any solid exegetical arguments. Blomberg ("Law in Luke-Acts," 72) also ties Luke closely with Paul's position of a law-free Christianity by positing a progression of the concept of the law in Luke-Acts, but he fails to emphasize the continuity with the Old Testament. On the one hand, Jervell states dogmatically that according to Luke "Jesus did not alter anything, the law is permanently valid" (*Theology of Acts*, 56). In distinction from these authors we propose that Luke maintained a middle point of view.

31. Therefore Luke contends that false witnesses accuse Paul of advocating that believing Jews no longer circumcise their children (Acts 21:21) and false witnesses charge Stephen with saying that Jesus "will change the customs that Moses handed down to us" (Acts 6:13–14).

Finally, Luke omits Mark 7:1–23 since it reflects an intra-Christian debate between Palestinian and Pauline Christians which he refuses to touch.[32] As Pettim explains, "Luke had to omit the Marcan pericope on dietary law because of his belief in the permanence of God's law for the Jews."[33] All of this data suggests that Luke advocated a middle road of associating with Gentiles while maintaining the eating habits of a Jew. The giving of the Holy Spirit to Gentiles "just as he did to us" (Acts 10:47; 11:17; 15:8) demands table fellowship with Gentiles, but the restrictions demanded in the law of resident aliens (Lev 17–18) must still be maintained. If Pentecost is the eschatological renewal of Israel (Acts 15:16), then Caesarea is the incorporation of Gentiles into that renewal (Acts 15:17).

What about Luke 10:7–8 in the mission of the seventy or seventy-two disciples where they are commanded to "eat whatever is set before you"?[34] Must we assign a more liberal attitude to Luke here, similar to what we will discover in Paul, since the reference to the Gentile cities of Tyre and Sidon (10:13) might imply that Jewish Christians are to eat whatever Gentiles eat? Although reference to these towns could symbolize a future Gentile mission for Luke, the situation in Jesus' time is set in a Jewish Palestinian environment. Understood within a Palestinian ministry context, the text involves how a disciple obtains food and one's attitude toward hospitality, not what types of food are to be eaten. Therefore, the mission of the seventy-two disciples does not refer to a world-wide Gentile mission but must refer to an outreach to the mixed people groups of the land of Canaan, as evidenced by passages concerning the Samaritans both before (9:51–56) and after (10:25–37) this pericope. We must conclude that Luke supports a mediating position that prizes table fellowship with Gentiles but supports purity rituals for Jewish Christians. His acceptance of the apostolic decree evidences a compromising spirit for the sake of unity in the church. Regarding justification Luke uncompromisingly proclaims that through Christ "everyone who believes is justified from everything you could not be justified from by the law of Moses," but with regard to lifestyle issues he supports the apostolic decree as a concession to scrupulous Jewish believers who avoided all meat in environments where they could not be sure that the meat had been prepared in a "kosher" manner.

---

32. The Great Omission in Luke omits Mark 6:45—8:26 between the various titles of Jesus employed by Herod (6:14–15) and the disciples (8:28). Through this procedure Luke removes similar stories like the second journey across the sea and the feeding of the four thousand in order to fit the material on one scroll. But the omission of Mark 7:1–23 fits this polemic chiefly found in Acts of narrating Paul as the hero of both Gentile and Jewish Christianity.

33. Pettim, "Luke's Great Omission," 47. Cf. Collins, Mark, 118.

34. Thomas 14 ties together the sayings from Luke 10:7–8 and Mark 7:15 (Matt 15:11) indicating that they were read together by early Christians. However, Deconick clarifies that Thomas emanates from a later time when the saying is "no longer intended simply to address the question of how a preacher was to obtain food. The question now is whether the preacher must seek only kosher food, a question that arises only where Jews have crossed over the social boundaries that separate them from Gentiles" (*Original Gospel of Thomas*, 89). In Thomas it is "now an injunction from Jesus, lifting the Jewish dietary restrictions altogether and refocusing the discussion on ethical practices."

Matthew as well advocates this middle position since he omits Mark 7:19b ("Jesus declared all foods 'clean'") and eliminates Mark 7:3 ("all the Jews do not eat unless they give their hands a ceremonial washing") since he wants to criticize the tradition of handwashing but maintain kosher food laws for Jewish Christians.[35] In addition, Matthew avoids Mark's unqualified statement in 7:15 by eliminating the word "nothing" so that Jesus' parable now reads, "What goes into a man's mouth does not make him 'unclean'" (Matt 15:11), instead of "Nothing outside a man can make him 'unclean' by going into him." Likewise, Matthew omits the second part of Mark 7:18, "Don't you see that nothing that enters a man from the outside can make him 'unclean'?," and combines 7:18 and 7:19a together to read, "Don't you see that whatever enters the mouth goes into the stomach and then out of the body?" (Matt 15:17). The entire pericope now concerns eating with unwashed hands as indicated by Matthew's concluding addition (15:20), "eating with unwashed hands does not make him 'unclean.'" The inclusio between 15:2 and 15:20 demonstrates that Matthew wants to criticize only the Pharisaic tradition of handwashing but to maintain that food laws are still in place for his Jewish Christian community.[36] Therefore, the middle position advocated by Peter, Luke, Matthew, and Barnabas[37] stated that Jewish Christians could dine with Gentiles on the explicit or implicit understanding that the food they would eat was neither prohibited in the Torah nor tainted with idolatry.

Paul, on the other hand, embodies a third approach to food laws treating them as matters of adiaphora so that one's conscience as well as the peaceful well-being of the community dictates whether food laws should be followed. This position is evidenced by the inclusio around Romans 14:1—15:7, centering on the exhortation to "receive fellow believers" as well as the repetition of the phrase "one another" in 14:13 ("stop passing judgment on one another"); 14:19 ("edification for one another"); and 15:5

---

35. Carlston ("Things that Defile," 75, n. 1) claims the reason for Matthew's omission is the elimination of explanatory parentheses (Mark 14:12; 15:16, 42. Cf. Mark 5:9, 41; 6:17, 19, 45; 7:31, 34; 8:3; 10:1; 14:1; 15:7; 16:1; per contra 15:22), but theological reasons take prominence as can be visualized in the new arrangement of material in Matthew 15.

36. Therefore, Collins concludes, "Matthew has recast the Markan pericope in such a way that the anti-nomistic Markan flavor can no longer be detected" (*Mark*, 117). On the other hand, Carlston claims that "in this context all he does is limit the discussion to the matter of hand-washing (which he explicitly rejects) without taking any particular stand on the necessity of the food laws" ("Things that Defile," 77). He argues that "if Matthew really wished to exclude the kind of laxity represented by his Markan source, it is hard to see why he kept the potentially dangerous parable around which this whole controversy is constructed" since at other places Matthew revises thoroughly (Mark 1:12; 10:18) or removes Markan statements (Mark 3:21; 7:33–36; 8:22–26). But the Matthean revisions mentioned above as well as his approach to the law in other places reveal that "Matthew retains the ceremonial law, but it has undergone a reassessment under Christian motives" as shown in Barth, Bornkamm, and Held (*Tradition and Interpretation*, 91).

37. Cf. Chilton, "Brother of Jesus," 36 and n. 17. Catchpole ("Paul, James, and the Apostolic Decree," 441–42) hypothesizes that the split between Barnabas and Paul which Luke locates immediately after the decision on the Apostolic Decree (Acts 15:36ff) was caused by a disagreement on the relationship between Jews and Gentiles, but Luke makes the issue the presence of John Mark on the missionary journey.

("live in harmony with one another"). As Moo concludes, "His concern is not so much with the 'rights' and 'wrongs' of this particular issue but with the 'peace' and 'mutual edification' of the body of Christ."[38] Paul's general principle states that "nothing is unclean in and of itself" (14:14 ISV).

Similarly, in the midst of a controversy about eating meat offered to idols, Paul concludes in 1 Corinthians 8:8, "we are no worse if we do not eat and no better if we do." Christianity is a matter of the heart where faith resides. Therefore Paul's repeated chorus in his letter to the Galatians that neither circumcision nor uncircumcision counts for anything but faith working through love (Gal 5:6; 6:15; cf. 1 Cor 7:18–19; Rom 3:30) can be applied to food laws as well. As Paul says, "God's kingdom does not consist of food and drink, but of righteousness, peace, and joy produced by the Holy Spirit" (Rom 14:17). Here in Romans Paul considers himself among the "strong" (15:1) liberated Jewish Christians who believe that they are no longer bound by the ritual requirements of the Mosaic law.[39] Therefore the "weak" are mainly Jewish Christians who refrain from certain kinds of foods and observe certain days out of continuing loyalty to the Mosaic law.[40] This pejorative phrase "weak in faith" makes clear where Paul's sympathies lie. As Moos exclaims, "We cannot avoid the impression . . . that Paul would hope that a growth in Christ would help those who were 'weak' become 'strong.'"[41]

Although an apostle of freedom, Paul immediately qualifies his assertion of liberty in both Romans 14:14 and 14:20. The well-being and unity of the body of Christ is more important than a dogmatic stance on ritual purity. Since purity issues such as kosher food and Sabbath observance are disputable matters, Paul behaves like a Jew around Jews but lives like a Gentile among Gentiles (1 Cor 9:20–21). Therefore, Jewish and Gentile Christians should not condemn each other (Rom 14:13) or offend each other (1 Cor 8:13; Rom 14:19–20).

Regarding the apostolic decree of Acts 15,[42] certainly Paul would have left the meeting in a positive frame of mind since the council decided that circumcision should

---

38. Moo, *Romans*, 832.

39. Paul states in Gal 5:3, "I declare to every man who lets himself be circumcised that he is obligated to obey the whole law." From this statement one could conclude that all Jewish Christians need to keep the law according to Paul. But he considers himself, a circumcised Jew, as crucified to the law (Gal 2:19–20), so he is not speaking about mandatory requirements for Jewish Christians.

40. For supporters of this view and five other theories see Moo, *Romans*, 828–29.

41. Moo, *Romans*, 836.

42. The Apostolic Decree (15:29) is included proleptically in 15:20 and retrospectively in 21:25. Regarding the text of the Apostolic Decree, certainly the four-fold text is original. In the Alexandrian text four cultic-centered prohibitions are enumerated with πορνεία understood against the background of Lev 18:6–18. However, in the Western text the three ethical cardinal sins in the Jewish tradition are listed, i.e., idolatry, sexual abuse, and bloodshed accompanied by the silver rule. The dropping of πνικτός in the Western tradition (D, Irenaeus, Ephraem) indicates a similar ethical application of the decree. These would be later attempts to make the command relevant to a Christian community that no longer follows the cultic regulations of Lev 17–18 for Gentiles. See Svartvik (*Mark and Mission*,

not be demanded of Gentile believers. But some of the prescriptions for Gentiles that James sets down were in all likelihood completely ignored by Paul.[43] The only known restrictions that Paul imposes upon non-Jewish believers are ethical and relational in content. In 1 Corinthians 5–7 Paul addresses the issue of sexual immorality or πορνεία and in 1 Corinthians 8–10 the controversy about eating meat offered to idols. His conclusion that Christians can eat anything sold in the meat market is based upon Psalm 24:1 ("The earth is the Lord's, and everything in it") rather than Leviticus 17. Only when relationships can be damaged, as when someone at the dinner objects (1 Cor 10:28), does Paul instruct the Corinthians that they should not eat meat consecrated to gods. Only when ethical conduct or relationships in the church were involved does Paul prohibit these practices. Therefore, the evil Paul speaks about is not εἰδωλόθυτος, eating food to idols, but εἰδωλολάτρης, idolatry (1 Cor 10:7, 14).

Paul completely ignores any of the ceremonial regulations, such as the dietary rules concerning the meat of strangled animals and abstaining from blood.[44] Just as "Circumcision is nothing and uncircumcision is nothing" (1 Cor 7:19a) since they are distinguished from God's commandments (7:19b), so these ceremonies including the eating of kosher meat are nothing to Christians since "food does not bring us near to God; we are no worse if we do not eat, and no better if we do" (8:8).[45] The apostolic decree of James was based upon the directives to alien residents specified in Leviticus 17–18,[46] but for Paul "Christ is the end of the law so that there may be righteousness for everyone who believes" (Rom 10:4; cf. 6:14–15; 7:4). Therefore, in Romans 14:14 Paul appeals to union with Christ as the basis for his beliefs: "As one who is in the Lord Jesus, I am fully convinced that no food is unclean in itself." Here as well as in the controversies regarding Sabbath observance (Rom 14:9) and food laws (14:15), Paul is basing his practices upon the kerygma of Jesus' death and resurrection rather

---

120) for convincing arguments in favor of the Alexandrian text. However, Boman ("Das textkritische Problem," 26–36) argues that the Western text is older.

43. See Jervell, *Theology of Acts*, 4.

44. Hemer (*Book of Acts*, 269) suggests that the decree was employed by Paul only within a limited geographical vicinity, but this distinction appears trivial. The measures Paul accepted would have involved ethical concerns as argued by Borgen ("Catalogues of Vices," 126–41).

45. Tomson, *If This Be from Heaven*, 239. See also Catchpole, "Paul, James, and the Apostolic Decree," 431.

46. Lev 17:8 (meat sacrificed to idols), 10–12 (blood), 13 (strangled meat); 18:6–23 (sexual immorality) with 26 as a summary, "The native-born and the aliens living among you must not do any of these detestable things." See Svartvik, *Mark and Mission*, 126; Fitzmyer, "Jewish People," 194; and Rudolph, "Jesus and the Food Laws," 300 and n. 50 for support for this position. On the other hand, Seifrid ("Jesus and the Law," 49) refuses to tie the decree to Lev 17–18 since the term προσήλυτος, by which a foreigner is designated in Lev 17–18 LXX, would be understood to refer to a full proselyte, not to a sojourner within Israel. But the similar content and order of material demonstrates clearly that Lev 17–18 is the background for the Apostolic Decree. Likewise, Wilson (*Luke and the Law*, 94ff) disputes this position since he thinks Luke was concerned with ethical issues and pagan cults rather than Levitical and OT cultic regulations. For arguments against Wilson, see Franklin (*Luke: Interpreter of Paul*, 47–48).

than appealing to a specific logion of Jesus, as we will see in Mark's case.[47] Therefore, Pauline theology proclaims that "All food is clean" (Rom 14:20; 1 Cor 8:8) since the issue for Paul is faith (Rom 14:1–2, 22–23) working through love (14:15) and leading to peace (14:19, 17).

So far we have elucidated the three positions in the early church with regard to the application of OT food regulations to Christians. Now we will explain where Mark fits into this debate. Mark 7:15 reads that "Nothing outside a man can make him 'unclean' by going into him," and Mark's commentary upon this logion clarifies that "In saying this, Jesus declared all foods 'clean'" (7:19b). Whereas the threefold occurrence of the *bath qol* (Acts 10:16) and the reception of the Holy Spirit by both Jewish and Gentile believers convinced the early church that nothing should interfere with the fellowship of Jewish and Gentile Christians, Mark envisions the authority for such a situation as deriving from Jesus himself.

We will argue that Mark supports Pauline theology on this point of purity issues.[48] Just as Paul refuses to compromise the table fellowship of Jewish and Gentile Christians, Mark places the discussion of food laws immediately before the encounter with the Syrophoenician woman, where table fellowship between Jews and Gentiles becomes the central issue.[49] The similarities with Pauline terminology are striking.

Mark 7:15a	οὐδέν ἐστιν ἔξωθεν τοῦ ἀνθρώπου εἰσπορευόμενον εἰς αὐτὸν ὃ δύναται <u>κοινῶσαι</u> <u>αὐτόν</u>
Romans 14:14	οὐδὲν <u>κοινὸν</u> δι' <u>ἑαυτοῦ</u>
Mark 7:19b	<u>καθαρίζων</u>[A] <u>πάντα τὰ βρώματ</u>α
Romans 14:20	<u>πάντα</u> (<u>βρώματα</u>) μὲν <u>καθαρά</u>

A. For arguments against the textual reading καθαρίζον and the English translations KJV, NKJV, and NEB see Rudolph, "Jesus and the Food Laws," 292, n. 2.

We have concluded above that Paul is not quoting a logion of Jesus in Romans 14. But could Mark be quoting Paul, as Räisänen suggests by demonstrating how the Markan redaction at 7:19b stands strikingly similar to Romans 14:20?[50] The "everything"

---

47. Evidence against a particular saying of Jesus includes 1) Romans 14 does not include the issue of hand-washing; 2) If Paul employed Jesus' saying in this adiaphora section, surely he would have included it as well in his central arguments about the law, foremost in the Galatians debate; and 3) the introductory formula is similar to Pauline convictions expressed in Gal 5:10; Phil 1:25; 2:24; Rom 8:38; 15:14; 2 Thess 3:4; and 2 Tim 1:12. For a list of contemporary authors in favor of and against a quotation of Jesus see Räisänen (*Paul and the Law*, 246, n. 98 and 248).

48. Whereas the older dominant position denied connections between Paul and Mark as evidenced by the writings of Werner (*Der Einfluss paulinischer Theologie*) and Romaniuk ("Problème des Paulinismes," 266–74), more recent scholarship supports a similar theological perspective. See Collins, *Mark*, 356; Marcus, "Mark—Interpreter of Paul," 473–87; Painter, *Mark's Gospel*, 4–6; and Svartvik, *Mark and Mission*, 345–46.

49. Svartvik contends that the "best parallel to the Cornelius episode is, in fact, the story of the foreign woman in Mark 7:24–30" (*Mark and Mission*, 119).

50. Räisänen, "Jesus and the Food Laws," 88. Kazen (*Jesus and Purity Halakhah*, 230) posits that the expression "everything is clean" could be imagined as originating with Jesus if a saying not tied to kosher food like Luke 11:41 is assumed. There is similar vocabulary (πάντα καθαρά), and Jesus

and "nothing" parallel each other. The repetition of the Jewish purity terms κοινόν (3x in Rom 14:14; Mark 7:2, 5) and κοινῶσαι / κοινοῦντα (Mark 7:15, 18, 20, 23) indicates both matching terminology and content. Just as Paul stated that "the kingdom of God is not a matter of eating and drinking" (Rom 14:17), so Mark applies this principle to a kingdom parable of Jesus. Both Paul and Mark turn a discussion of ceremonial law into ethical instruction. Paul at the end of his discussion of eating meat sacrificed to idols climaxes his discussion with four ethical prohibitions to avoid idolatry (Rom 10:7), sexual immorality (10:8), testing Christ (10:9), and grumbling (10:10). Similarly, Mark replaces handwashing halakah and kosher food legislation with twelve ethical vices to be avoided (7:21–22) since they defile the heart. Räisänen points out as well that "The sarcasm in v. 19 is indeed comparable to Paul's outbursts in Gal 5.12 or in Phil 3.2."[51] Finally, the reproach "are you so dull?" (Mark 7:18) addressed to the disciples in the house "suggests that ritual purity is a bone of contention not only between the Markan community and the Pharisees but also within the community itself."[52] In Mark the interlocutors completely disappear in 7:14–23, indicating that discipleship teaching aimed at the community becomes the theme, not a controversy with opponents as in Matthew. Paul addresses a similar situation in Rome, which could have been Mark's home community as well.[53] Therefore, both Paul and Mark advocate the removal of food taboos for the Christian community.

Is this also the view of Jesus when in Mark 7:15 he asserts, "Nothing from the outside can make a person unclean"? Recent interpreters have offered impressive arguments for denying that Jesus nullified the OT food regulations with this statement.

The grammatical argument specifies that Jesus' saying originally meant that "things from the outside will not make someone unclean compared to things that come from within." Dunn contends that in the original Aramaic the "not . . . but" antithesis should not be understood as an "either . . . or" but instead with the force of "more important than," as in Mark 2:17.[54] Jesus' statement offers a relative depreciation of external purity.[55] The situation is similar to Luke 11:38, where the Pharisee is amazed that Jesus has not first bathed himself before the meal. Then Jesus replies,

---

employs the categories of inside and outside (11:40). However, Luke's saying differs from Matt 23:26, and giving alms to the poor is certainly a Lukan emphasis as when Cornelius is proclaimed clean in the vision from heaven (Acts 10:15) after he is described by an angel as an almsgiver (10:2, 4), a word occurring 10 out of 13 times in Luke-Acts.

51. Räisänen, "Jesus and the Food Laws," 90.

52. Marcus, *Mark 1–8*, 458.

53. See Dunn (*Romans 9–16*, 795) and our discussion of a Roman provenance at the end of chapter 6.

54. Dunn, *Jesus, Paul, and the Law*, 51. For support see Bockmuehl (*Jewish Law in Gentile Churches*, 11), Booth (*Jesus and the Laws*, 69–70), Holmén (*Jesus and Jewish Covenant Thinking*, 240–41), Sanders (*Jewish Law*, 28), and Svartvik (*Mark and Mission*, 406).

55. Therefore Rudolph translates Mark 7:15, "There is nothing outside a man which *cultically* defiles him as much as the things coming from within a man *ethically* defile him" ("Jesus and the Food Laws," 298).

"Now then, you Pharisees clean the outside of the cup and dish, but inside you are full of greed and wickedness" (Luke 11:39). The comparable saying in Matthew 23:25–26 adds the priority of inward cleanliness like Mark 7:15 when it declares, "First clean the inside of the cup and dish, and then the outside also will be clean" (Matt 23:26).

The consistency argument then states, "If, however, Jesus said 'not only what goes in defiles, but even more, what comes out,' the law would be maintained and radicalized, but not opposed."[56] This radicalization of the law is consistent with Jesus' proclamation on divorce (Mark 10:5–12) and similar to his deepening and broadening of the law in the six antitheses of Matt 5:21–48. Therefore as Marcus explains, Jesus is "not so different from that of the prophets who railed against their fellow Israelites' preoccupation with external ritual rather than justice."[57] Jesus is opposed to prioritizing ritual purity over moral purity.[58] The fact that Jesus is not accused of abrogating food laws at his trial argues against his abrogation of the OT food laws during his lifetime.

The argument from background states that Jesus' proclamation is "too drastic a denunciation of basic tenets of Judaism to have been countenanced by any Jew other than a complete apostate."[59] Before the Jew/Gentile debate in the early church, the question of consuming unclean food would be tantamount to revoking one's membership among God's holy people.

The contextual argument discerns an inconsistency between Mark 7:1–13 and 14–23 if Jesus annuls OT food laws in the second half of this passage. As Rudolph argues, "It is unlikely that Jesus made this pronouncement on the inviolability of the Torah, rebuked others for neglecting God's commandments (vv. 6–13), and then immediately after declared prominent parts of the Torah abolished (v. 19c)."[60] Jesus would not have appealed to the authority of Moses at one moment (7:10) and then drastically conflict with Moses and the law in the verses following (7:19b). Instead, it is the traditions of the elders (παράδοσιν τῶν πρεσβυτέρων) that disturb Jesus throughout the incident, in particular their washing of hands legislation and their Corban ideology. Therefore, the original ties between 7:1–13 and 14–23 involving the single issue of hand washing are still visible in Mark through the repetition of vocabulary (the root κοιν in 7:2, 5 and 7:15, 20, 23) as well as the fact that 7:15 provides the answer ("nothing from the outside can defile you") to the question in 7:5 ("Why do your disciples eat with unwashed hands?").[61] In addition, the contrast of inside/out-

---

56. Sanders, *Jesus and Judaism*, 260.

57. Marcus, *Mark 1–8*, 153.

58. As Rudolph explains, "Jesus' position may be contrasted with his Pharisaic interlocutors who prioritized ritual purity over moral purity. They were concerned with handwashing while indifferent to the needs of their parents" ("Jesus and the Food Laws," 297).

59. Booth, *Jesus and the Laws*, 90.

60. Rudolph, "Jesus and the Food Laws," 295.

61. Therefore, Lambrecht ("Jesus and the Law," 73) divides Mark 7 into question (1–5) and answer (6–23) and Booth (*Jesus and the Laws*, 61–62) outlines the passage as a single pericope: Introduction

side in 7:14–23 parallels the contrast of lips/heart in 7:6.[62] Finally, the "you also" of 7:18 equates the disciples with the Pharisee-scribes of 7:1–13.[63] Although the original unity of the passage involving unwashed hands is still visible, Mark has created a new discussion on eating non-kosher food.[64] Matthew demonstrates that originally the entire passage centered upon handwashing rituals by employing the normal structure of a controversy dialogue[65] and by concluding the passage with this summary: "eating with unwashed hands does not make him 'unclean.'" Thus "Jesus' teaching from beginning to end is focused on the postbiblical practice[66] of ritual handwashing; the biblical dietary laws are not at issue."[67] Only in Mark does the issue of abolishing food laws come to the surface.

Finally, the non-inclusion of Jesus' statement in the struggles of the early church over Jew/Gentile relationships argues against Jesus himself abrogating the food laws. Carlston reports that "given the early existence of such a radical saying as v. 15, it is startling that no one ever seems to have made use of it in the subsequent turbulent decades."[68] Certainly if Jesus had spoken as plainly as Mark assumes, it would be hard to explain the struggles evidenced in such passages as Acts 10 and Romans 14. If Jesus had taught the acceptability of eating unclean food, Peter would not have been shocked by the vision from heaven. Either the early church was completely ignorant of the saying or, more likely, it was applied to traditions like handwashing and not to the observance of OT food laws. Therefore as Bryan asserts, "the fact that Mark has

---

(1, 2, 5), the Question (5), the Isaiah Reply (6–7), the *Corban* Reply (9–12), the Purity Reply (14–15), a Scene-change (17), the Medical Explanation (18–19), and the Ethical Explanation (20–22).

62. Likewise the vices of 7:21 stem from the Decalogue and could create an intended link with honoring one's parents in 7:10.

63. Mark himself seems to be contrasting the disciples in 7:18 with the crowd in 7:14, but there is no evidence of the crowd's dullness. Therefore, originally the contrast was with the Pharisees, but Mark changes the audience to redactionally move the theme of the passage in a new direction.

64. See Banks, *Jesus and the Law*, 140 and Dunn, "Matthew's Awareness of Markan Redaction," 1349–60.

65. 1) Action initiating the controversy (15:1–2a); 2) question from the opponents (15:2b); 3) Jesus' counter question (15:3); 4) the central saying (15:11); 5) the reaction (15:12–20). Mark 7:6–13 does not include Jesus' counter question and places the quote from Isa 29:13 first.

66. Ritual hand-washing before regular meals was likely a post-biblical, *Haberim*/Pharisaic innovation. Cf. Rudolph, "Jesus and the Food Laws," 294 and n. 14 for support. Regev ("Pure Individualism," 180–81, 188–89) argues that this custom arose before Hasmonean times and was observed not only by the Pharisees but by Jews in Palestine as well as the Diaspora. Therefore, Svartvik is correct in asserting that Jesus' view is "best understood as a rebuff to advocates of an expansive interpretation of the purity laws, i.e., those who ate their ordinary food almost as priestly food—and expected everyone else to do the same" (*Mark and Mission*, 406).

67. Rudolph, "Jesus and the Food Laws," 308. We follow Rudolph in advocating that Jesus did not address the issue of the abolition of food laws, but reject his view that Mark only had Gentile Christians in mind when he inserted Mark 7:19b.

68. Carlston, "Things that Defile," 80. Räisänen concurs, "there is no evidence that anybody, conservative or radical, ever appealed to this saying in the course of the debates over Gentile mission and table fellowship" ("Jesus and the Food Laws," 142–43).

not placed the deduction of 7.19b on Jesus' lips shows that he too was aware that Jesus was not specifically addressing the issue of prohibited food."[69]

Even though I find the above arguments substantial and convincing, some still propose that Jesus does reject Mosaic purity laws. Perrin declares that the radicality of Jesus' statement proves its authenticity since, although "it completely denies a fundamental presupposition of Jewish religion: the distinction between the sacred and the secular," it "is completely coherent with the almost equally radical attitude and behaviour of Jesus in connection with 'tax collectors and sinners.'"[70] Witherington links the removal of food laws with Jesus' proclamation of the kingdom of God: "The coming of the dominion of God has made obsolescent the boundary-defining rules found in the Levitical code."[71] However, Jesus' message of the eschatological inbreaking of the kingdom proclaimed the present reality of future blessings rather than the undoing of the past OT legislation. John Riches supports an abrogation of the ceremonial laws by Jesus since the "substituting of the qualities of forgiveness and love for fixed boundaries is characteristic of Jesus' teaching on a range of topics."[72] Therefore, he posits that "If the phrase 'which entering in' is a Markan addition, then the reference may be extended to include contact with dirt, dead bodies, certain forms of sickness, and the bodily emissions of others."[73] We will argue that this is true for Mark as an implication of Jesus' teaching applied to problems facing the early community, but Jesus himself merely placed a priority on the ethical demands of the law over the ritual legislation.[74] The saying with Mark's interpretation in 7:19b is too radical for Jesus and presupposes a discussion in the early church.[75]

Originally, then, the entire incident involved the Pharisaic tradition of handwashing and its relationship to the purity of food so that Jesus proclaims, "Washing the hands in order to preserve the purity of food is senseless, since foods which go into a man cannot reach and defile the heart."[76] Mark, however, sees more. Mark

---

69. Bryan, *Jesus and Israel's Traditions*, 165.

70. Perrin, *Rediscovering the Teaching of Jesus*, 150.

71. Witherington, *Mark*, 202. Lambrecht concludes that "the historical Jesus was in reality both anti-Halachah and anti-Torah" ("Jesus and the Law," 77). Merkel believes that Mark softens Jesus' requirements: "He also limits the saying, which applies to all the commandments about purity, to the food laws (7:19b), and he diverts attention from the deeper opposition by means of the peremptory, 'parenetically sonorous but theologically inoffensive catalogue of vices'" ("Opposition between Jesus and Judaism," 140).

72. Riches, *Jesus and the Transformation*, 138.

73. Ibid., 137.

74. In the story recited in Papyrus Oxyrhynchus 840 Jesus also gives more weight to inner purity than to outer purification. See Kazen, *Jesus and Purity Halakhah*, 260.

75. Marcus concludes, "The judgment that all foods could be eaten was hammered out by Christians when the entry of growing numbers of Gentiles into their community made a decision on the issue imperative" (*Mark 1–8*, 458).

76. Lambrecht, "Jesus and the Law," 72. Cf. Booth (*Jesus and the Laws of Purity*, 90), Bryan (*Jesus and Israel's Traditions*, 165), Crossley (*Date of Mark's Gospel*, 200), Marcus (*Mark 1–8*, 453), Räisänen

redacts Jesus' saying so that a wisdom proverb is now entitled a parable (7:17), which is explained to the disciples in a typical Markan fashion in a house (which becomes the house church). The first part of the parable (7:15a) is allegorically interpreted as applying to OT food laws in 7:18–19 and the second half of the riddle is introduced with a redundant ἔλεγεν δὲ ὅτι and metaphorically applied to a list of vices (7:20–23) similar to the lists in other early church literature.[77] If the Matthew version is closer to the *Sitz im Leben Jesu*, then Mark transforms one controversy into two with different audiences: 1) 7:1–13 against the Pharisees on the subject of handwashing and 2) a parable to the people (7:14–15) that is explained to the disciples (7:17–23) and thus addresses the church controversy about OT food regulations. As Marcus notes, "This sort of private instruction is often a Markan device for addressing issues that have arisen in the evangelist's own day."[78]

In the broader context Mark structures chapter 7 into four incidents that proclaim Jesus as the agent of cleansing, resulting in clean hands (7:1–13), clean food (7:14–23), clean people (7:24–30), and clean fluids (7:31–37). Mark has inserted 7:1–23 into an already formed miracle sequence at this point[79] to connect it with the next story of the Syrophoenician woman, which also involves cleanliness. Grammatical connections include the tie between the difficult plural at 7:2 (τοὺς ἄρτους) referring back to the feeding story of 6:34ff., which in turn points forward to the Jewish children who must first be fed (7:27 χορτασθῆναι and 6:42 ἐχορτάσθησαν) before the Gentiles eat. The order of events appears to carry with it theological significance so that the offer of the bread of salvation to Jews in the feeding of the five thousand precedes the abolition of divisive Jewish laws in 7:1–23, which in turn leads to the offer of salvation to Gentiles in the story of the Syrophoenician.[80] Therefore, the point of Jesus has been sharpened in the course of its transmission so that all foods are now declared clean since OT cleanliness texts have been fulfilled in Jesus' kingdom words.[81] For Mark, just as dirty hands do not desecrate the entire body, so impure food cannot produce

---

("Jesus and the Food Laws," 90), and Rudolph ("Jesus and the Food Laws," 294) for support that the original logion spoke only about hand-washing. Mark 7:9–13 is not necessarily an addition since 1) the reference to "the commandment of God" in 7:8 prepares for the citations in 7:10; 2) Jesus accuses the questioners not only of abandoning the commandment of God but of nullifying it; and 3) these sections are arguments from both the prophets and the law.

77. See Gal 5:19–21; Col 3:5–8; 1 Pet 3:15. But they are also found in Jewish writings contemporary with Jesus (1QS 4:9–11), and Philo has 150 items in *Sacrifices of Abel and Cain* 32.

78. Marcus, *Mark 1–8*, 458.

79. See section 3.5 above.

80. Initially Booth (*Jesus and the Laws of Purity*, 29) doubts this interpretation since 1) "even the discerning reader may fail to recognize such interwoven themes" and 2) the series is broken by the insertion of the sea walking pericope and summary healing report in 6:45–56, but on further reflection he notes that the sea walking passage concludes with a return to the bread theme. Furthermore, the summary healing report serves as a conclusion to the healing catenae until Mark can return to it. Minimally, the stories are linked together by the bread theme, although the exact order may not be significant.

81. See Dunn, "Jesus and Ritual Purity," 51 and Lohmeyer, *Lord of the Temple*, 31.

defilement. The list of vices in 7:23 indicates that only ethical impurity truly defiles, so that the Markan Jesus, as we shall see, fulfills the impurity legislation against contract with corpse, menstruation, abnormal genital discharges, and scale disease in people and houses.[82] But the question remains, did Mark intend the abrogation of food laws for all Christians or just for Gentile Christians?

Rudolph provides some persuasive arguments for his conclusion that Mark 7:19b should read, "thus he declared all foods clean [for Gentile believers]."[83] First of all, Mark's audience is primarily Gentiles. Dunn finds this especially significant for chapter 7: "It is also clear that this unit is directed towards a Gentile audience: verses 3–4 explain Jewish customs ('all the Jews'!); and most commentators agree that verse 19c ('cleansing all foods') is designed to point out or serve as a reassurance to Gentile believers that the Jewish food laws were not obligatory for them."[84] However, in contradiction to this conclusion, Juel maintains that "Mark presumes an audience that locates itself in Israel's heritage."[85] Certainly Mark's audience must have included a large Jewish component given the Aramaicisms, the expectation of a deep knowledge of the Old Testament,[86] the use of Semitic constructions to address the audience, as well as the details of Jewish rituals that are described, such as impurity from leprosy, corpse contact, and menstruation. A mixed audience of Jews and Gentiles must therefore be assumed.

Rudolph's second argument for the restriction of the abolition of food laws to Gentiles insists that the apostolic decree assumes the continuing validity of the Torah's dietary laws for Jewish believers.[87] Such a debate about what aspects of the OT ritual regulations should apply to Gentiles could only arise if both parties agreed on the lasting significance of the Mosaic law for Jews. Therefore Rudolph is opposed to employing abolition vocabulary (e.g. "revoked," "abrogated," "invalidated") when talking about Jewish Christians.[88] To substantiate this line of thinking, Rudolph reports

---

82. Boucher sees Mark's explanation as a giant leap forward in the history of religious thought: "The saying annuls the whole concept of material or cultic impurity (which regards uncleanness as unholiness) held by so many religions of antiquity, including Judaism. This remarkably original saying, then, represents a great step forward in the history of religion. It removes uncleanness, or unholiness, from the realm of material things and situates it exclusively in the realm of ethics" (*Mysterious Parable*, 67).

83. Rudolph, "Jesus and the Food Laws," 305. The law remains unchanged for Jewish Christians, but "Mark finds in Jesus teaching the basis for Gentile exemption from the Leviticus 11 dietary laws" (307).

84. Dunn, "Jesus and Ritual Purity," 45.

85. Juel, *Master of Surprise*, 145.

86. Van Iersel concludes, "the intended readers either had a Jewish upbringing in a Hellenistic environment, or had regularly heard readings from the Old Testament whether or not at assemblies of the community" (*Mark*, 55).

87. Rudolph ("Jesus and the Food Laws," 300, n. 48) states that both parties in the discussion of Acts 15 agreed that circumcision and Torah obedience remained obligatory for Jewish Jesus believers.

88. Ibid. adds, "Abolition language also fails to account for widespread acceptance of the Apostolic Decree as a ruling that upheld two levels of obligation to the Torah" (306).

that "The prescriptions of the Apostolic Decree enjoyed almost universal assent in the Church until at least the sixth century."[89] But this is an exaggeration. The liberated view, whereby the OT ceremonial regulations are abrogated for Christians (both Jew and Gentile) because of the new covenant in Jesus, won out because it was continually advocated by some from the first century. The theological grounding behind Paul's unwillingness to propagate parts of the apostolic decree appears to lie in the presupposition that the decree divided Christianity into two groups.[90] Paul, on the other hand, promoted both Jewish and Gentile Christians as the new Israel (Gal 6:16).[91] Therefore, an appeal to the apostolic decree does not settle the matter of the continuation of the dietary laws. Rudolph believes that Mark was attempting to construct a theological basis from Leviticus 17–18 for the Acts 15 food laws for Gentiles by exempting them from the dietary laws of Leviticus 11 through the teachings of Jesus.[92] However, the prescriptions for Gentile believers in Acts 15 were not exemptions but additions; in reality there were no requirements for Gentiles regarding any of the ceremonial OT regulations. They were Gentiles, not Jews.

A better argument for an application of Mark 7:19b to only Gentiles would see a parallel progression between the vision of Acts 10 involving Peter's contact with the Gentile Cornelius and the account of the cleansing of food in Mark 7:14–23 coupled with Jesus' contact with the Gentile Syrophoenician woman in 7:24–30. As Boucher reports, "It has been observed that the wisdom saying on what defiles and the miracle of the Syrophoenician woman together are equivalent to Acts 10:1—11:18."[93] Then the proclamation that all foods are clean in Mark 7:19b must be understood metaphorical like Acts 10:15, "Do not call anything impure that God has made clean," with both applying to the cleanliness of people, not food. However, this metaphorical interpretation is stated in Acts 10:28b, 34–35[94] whereas in Mark 7:19b the natural straightforward interpretation requires a literal meaning involving OT food regulations.

Rudolph's third argument employs the similarities between Mark 7:15, 19b and Romans 14:14, 20 to argue that "Mark has taken Pauline *halakhah* (specifically for Gentile Christians) and rooted it in Jesus' teaching in Mark 7."[95] We agree that Paul

---

89. From Bockmuehl, *Jewish Law in Gentile Churches*, 167, n. 94 quoted by Rudolph, "Jesus and the Food Laws," 301.

90. This distinction in the decree is upheld by Jervell, *Luke and the People of God*, 190–91; Rudolph, "Jesus and the Food Laws," 307; Tomson, *If This Be From Heaven*, 234 etc.

91. The 'Israel of God' is an implied contrast to the 'Israel after the flesh' (1 Cor 10:18; cf. Rom 9:6; Gal 3:29, Phil 3:3). J. B. Lightfoot states, "It stands here not for the faithful converts from the circumcision alone, but for the spiritual Israel generally, the whole body of believers whether Jew or Gentile; and thus καὶ is *epexegetic*" (*St. Paul's Epistle*, 224).

92. Rudolph, "Jesus and the Food Laws," 304.

93. Boucher, *Mysterious Parable*, 68 citing Montefiore, *Mark*, 163 who quotes Bacon, *Gospel of Mark*, 147.

94. Also the ἐξαυτῆς of Acts 11:11 ties it closely with Acts 11:9.

95. Rudolph, "Jesus and the Food Laws," 305.

and Mark evidence the identical perspective on OT food laws, but one should not limit Paul's comments to Gentiles because he includes himself (Rom 15:1) as one of the so-called strong brethren whose consciences are not seared when they eat non-kosher food. If Paul is willing to sacrifice his dietary principles for the sake of the faith of others, so should other Jewish Christians be willing to let go of the kosher food requirement.

Therefore, we would contend that Mark 7:15 and 19b pertain to all Christians and that Mark is not applying the legislation to Gentile believers alone.[96] The simplest meaning is that unclean food does not defile, and consequently it may be eaten. As Räisänen concludes, "Mark 7.19 leaves no doubt about the repudiation of all food laws on the *editorial* level."[97] The first argument in favor of an application to all Christians stems from geography. Mark places the conversation of 7:1–23 on Jewish territory whereas he could have waited until after 7:24–30, where Gentiles are accepted by faith through an encounter with Jesus in Tyre. In addition, we will argue later that the ritual regulations of defilement through corpses and menstruation are also fulfilled by Jesus in the intercalation at 5:21–43, which occurs on Jewish territory and must therefore apply to Jewish Christians. Each of the issues of clean hands, food, people, and fluids in 7:1–37 are important discussions within Jewish Christian circles and therefore must apply to them as well.

Second, 7:19b specifically claims that all food is clean, not that all who eat the food are pure (meaning clean) people.[98] Third, Mark follows Paul who likewise does not see two tracks within Christianity but one new Israel. Fourth, both Paul and Mark condemn only ethical and relational sins and would not distinguish between Jews and Gentiles with this emphasis. Finally, simply put, Jews never expected Gentiles to observe the food laws; they were Gentiles. So why would Mark make the point that Jesus declared all foods clean for Gentiles, when they were never expected to keep these ritual laws in the first place? As Bauckham clarifies, "Forbidden animals are impure for Jews, according to Leviticus, but they are not impure for Gentiles, who quite legitimately eat them."[99] Since the OT rules of ritual purity did not apply to Gentiles, naturally they would not apply to Gentile Christians either.

Therefore, Mark reveals an implication of Jesus' kingdom proclamation for all Christians, not just Gentile Christians.[100] As Marcus says, "Not everyone agreed with Paul that the Law was passé—but Mark did."[101] Even though fine exegetes of both

---

96. See Boring, *Mark*, 203–4; Stein, *Mark*, 347.

97. Räisänen, "Jesus and the Food Laws," 132. This view is supported by Hugh Anderson, *Gospel of Mark*, 188; Hooker, *St. Mark*, 179; Markus, *Mark 1-8*, 458.

98. See Booth, *Jesus and the Laws*, 221.

99. Bauckham, "James, Peter, and the Gentiles," 103.

100. Banks is certainly correct that "it remains open for laws to be observed if the individual so desires" (*Jesus and the Law*, 145). Therefore, Jewish Christians could certainly continue to observe the OT food laws as Romans 14 implies as well. But as Christians, it was not necessary.

101. Marcus, *Mark 1-8*, 486.

the gospels and Paul argue that Mark 7:19b "is designed to point out or serve as a reassurance to Gentile believers that the Jewish food laws were not obligatory for them,"[102] we would contend that no Jew ever expected the Gentiles to observe the ceremonial law. Therefore Mark is helping his community read the Old Testament in a new way.[103] Literally, Mark is resolving the purity issue before an extensive "Gentile mission" can be undertaken (7:24—8:10). As Boring points out, "In Mark's view, as God has originally declared some foods to be unclean for Israel, so Jesus is now acting with the authority of God to declare that all foods are clean, thereby breaking down one of the barriers that separated Jewish from Gentiles Christians and facilitating the church's Gentile mission."[104] The importance of Mark 7:19b cannot be minimized; the removal of purity barriers creates a new community that is cleansed by Jesus' kingdom words and miracle actions.

8.3 The New Wine Must Be Placed in New Wineskins (2:21-22)

In the last section we analyzed Mark's editorial comment in 7:19b, which discloses his conclusion that kosher foods are no longer normative for the Christian community but only the ethical virtues and vices that are connected with these ceremonial laws. Mark 2:21-22 supports the claim that Mark envisions Jesus as changing the ritual customs of Israel. Along with a prediction of Jesus' death at 2:20 ("the bridegroom will be taken from them"), this logion on the need for new institutional containers stands at the middle of the chiasm of the controversy dialogues of 2:1—3:6, thus demonstrating its importance.[105] In these five controversy dialogues against the Pharisees Mark defends Jesus' insubordinate activities of forgiving sins by a human agent,[106] table contact with tax collectors and sinners, replacing fasting piety with feasting, and challenging their traditions of Sabbath observance by plucking grain and healing on the day of rest. In summary, the new age which Jesus pictured as a new garment (2:21) and the abundance of wine (2:22) demands new lifestyle priorities. Therefore, this centralized saying speaks to all of the changes Jesus is proclaiming through the arrival of the kingdom of God. Mark demonstrates the importance of this saying by concluding the central section of the chiasm with this parable, by adding a line to Jesus' parallel structure to emphasize newness, and by employing irregular surprising vocabulary to indicate symbolism.

An analysis of the saying itself reveals Semitic parallelism concluding with a line that does not fit its well-knit structure.[107]

---

102. For example, Dunn, "Jesus and Ritual Purity," 45.
103. See Stein, *Mark*, 346.
104. Boring, *Mark*, 203.
105. See our support for Dewey's chiasm in section 3.4 above.
106. The sole authority of God to forgive sins is evidenced at Exod 34:6–7; Isa 43:25; 44:22.
107. See Guelich (*Mark 1—8:26*, 114) who adds that the accent on the new is evidenced by

a	21 "No one sews a piece of unshrunk cloth on an old garment;	(proverb)
b	if he does,	(conditional)
c	the new piece (τὸ πλήρωμα) will pull away from the old,[A]	(reason)
d	making the tear (σχίσμα) worse	(result)
a	22 And no one puts new wine into old wineskins	(proverb)
b	if he does,	(conditional)
c	the wine will burst the skins,	(reason)
d	and both the wine and the wineskins will be ruined.	(result)
	No, he pours new wine into new wineskins."[B]	

[A]. Literally, "the fullness is removed (taken away) from it, the new from the old."

[B]. Maartens ("Mark 2:18–22," 43) contends that 2:22 is a chiasm with this last statement stating a conclusive reaffirmation of the principle in 22a. However, then the reader would expect a chiasm in 2:21 as well.

This last line, which alters a warning into a positive action, becomes the emphasis. Jesus could have added a saying to a perfect parallelism to call attention to its prominence, but more likely it is Markan redaction explaining the consequences of Jesus' saying, similar to 7:19b with regard to food laws. The dissonance of emphasis with the entire controversy dialogue supports this conclusion. Fasting is incompatible with the wedding feast of the kingdom (2:19–20) just as a patch does not fit with an old garment (2:21) and an aged wineskin cannot contain fresh wine (2:22).[108] The disparity is highlighted in three examples, and not in the necessity of new containers.

In addition, this conclusion to the Markan passage is omitted in the Gospel of Thomas 47, which offers seven examples of incompatibility:

1. "Jesus said: It is impossible for a person to mount two horses
2. and to stretch two bows.
3. And it is impossible for a servant to serve two masters.
4. Or else he will honour the one and insult the other.
5. No person drinks old wine and immediately desires to drink new wine.
6. And new wine is not put into old wineskins, so that they do not burst;
7. nor is old wine put into (a) new wineskin, so that it does not spoil it.
8. An old patch is not sewn onto a new garment, because a tear will result."[109]

---

dropping any reference to old wineskins.

108. Carlston points out that "The central emphasis here seems to be not the danger of damage to the old (it is already damaged) or the loss of the new (since the patch as such is worthless), but the incompatibility of the new and the old" (*Parables*, 126).

109 *Evangelium Thomae Copticum*. Coptic, Greek, English, and German (Stuttgart: Deutsche Bibelgesellschaft, 1996), 531.

Therefore, Jesus likely emphasized the incongruity of two items like fasting and a wedding ceremony, whereas Mark goes a step further and proclaims that Jesus instituted new practices for a new community ("new wineskins"). If this is true, then the phrase in 2:21 "the new from the old" is also Markan redaction that contrasts old and new practices, as evidenced by English versions placing it as an explanatory statement set off by hyphens (ISV, NCV) or commas (ASV, NASV, ESV, NET, NJB, NRSV).

The redaction by Matthew and Luke indicates a tendency to soften Mark's conclusion. Matthew pictures himself as a scribe of the kingdom "who brings out of his storeroom new treasures as well as old" (13:52). Therefore, he concludes that "both are preserved" (Matt 9:17), indicating an emphasis upon the continuity between Judaism and Christianity. Luke attaches a saying (5:39) which is placed earlier in Thomas 47[110]: "And no one after drinking old wine wants the new, for he says, 'The old is better.'" This saying is notoriously difficult to interpret.

Most interpret Luke 5:39 as a condemnation by Jesus of the traditionalism of the religious leaders.[111] As Metzger proclaims, "the point is that the prejudiced person does not even wish to try what is new (the gospel), being satisfied that the old (the Law) is good."[112] Judaism prefers the status quo and argues that old wine is better. In this way Luke explains why Judaism has not accepted Jesus' words. Therefore, the saying is interpreted as ironic. As Fitzmyer explains, "On the face of it, the saying would support Jewish rejection of Jesus' preaching. But by its irony the saying carries just the opposite meaning." It is "a wry comment on the effect that clinging to the old has on those who have closed their minds to his message about the new economy of salvation."[113] In support of Judaism's preference for the old, Stein calls attention both to the Pharisees' attitude in Jesus' time and the views of the circumcision party in Luke's time (Acts 11:2–3; 15:1–2,5).[114]

However, Luke 5:39 is better understood not as an ironic wry polemic. First, the categorical subject "no one" is inappropriate for a polemic against the Pharisees. A statement that "some prefer old wine" might serve the purposes of an apologetic, but

---

110. Thomas fails to include Mark's conclusion in 2:22 whereas it would fit well with Gnostic theology: the new wine must be placed in the new wineskin of Gnosticism. So we must assume that the canonical version was unknown to the author since it is at some distance from the wedding saying as well (Thomas 104). In addition, the first two incompatibilities in Thomas are completely missing in the canonical gospel and the omission of the God and Mammon logion in Thomas is strange considering its attitude against commercial activity as witnessed in Thomas 63 and 64. Finally, the explanations attached to the sayings ("lest they burst, lest it spoil, and because a tear would result") are short and to the point compared to the elaborations in the canonical gospels. Therefore, Patterson discerns "the presence of two different tradition-historical streams" (*Gospel of Thomas*, 41–42). See also Montefiore and Turner, *Thomas and the Evangelists*, 64–65.

111. For supporters see Good, "Jesus, Protagonist of the Old," 23, n. 7.

112. Metzger, *Textual Commentary*, 116.

113. Fitzmyer, *Gospel According to Luke I–IX*, 602. Cf. Marshall, *Commentary on Luke*, 228.

114. Stein, *Mark*, 186. Then the textual change to "better" (χρηστότερος) would fit a polemic against the Pharisees who would insist that the old is better, not just good.

the employment of οὐδεὶς parallels the statements in 5:36 and 37 that "no one tears a patch from a new garment and sews it on an old one" and "no one pours new wine into old wineskins." Therefore, these statements must parallel each other in theme which is impossible if 5:39 is understood as a polemic. Second, with an apologetic interpretation the insertion of Luke 5:39 is due to an entirely external cause, the catchword νέον connected with wine.[115] But in the Gospel of Thomas the theme of incompatibility intricately holds all the sayings together. Just as it is impossible to mount two horses, stretch two bows, or serve two masters at the same time, so it is ridiculous to drink old wine and then switch to new wine, or place new wine in old wineskins, or old wine in new wineskins, just as it is unworkable to sow an old patch on a new garment. These seven incompatibilities thrust home one inescapable message. Therefore in Luke the natural expected interpretation would be that "Just as the old patch does not match the new garment and new wine will not survive in old wineskins, so no one desires new wine after drinking old." These three statements about incompatibility compare favorably with the seven statements in Thomas. With reference to the controversy dialogue within the context, these verses would replace the normal reaction of the crowd with a generalizing parable about the incompatibility of old and new. So the inappropriateness of fasting when the bridegroom is present (Luke 5:34) is strengthened by sayings about the incongruity of the old and new (5:36, 38, 39).

But unlike the Gospel of Thomas, Luke includes the statement from Mark that "new wine must be poured into new wineskins" immediately preceding "the old wine is good." Therefore, these two statements are employed by Luke to balance each other. Both the new wine and the old wine are good and must be preserved. This theme matches the addition in Matthew 9:17 of "and both are preserved." Therefore, similar to their theology of food described in the last section, where both Matthew and Luke emphasized continuity with the OT regulations, here they want to preserve both the old and the new wine so that both are commended. Since the Christian scribe trained in kingdom values treasures both the new and the old (Matt 13:52), neither the old nor the new are given precedence. Therefore, the translation of χρηστός in Luke 5:39 should not be translated in the comparative, "is better" (KJV, NKJV, NCV, NIV, TNIV), but in the positive sense, "the old is good also" (ASV, RSV, NRSV, NET, ESV, ISV).[116] This view fits perfectly Lukan (as well as Matthean) theology which emphasizes continuity, so that as Green insists, "He portrays the old garment as in need of repair, while rejecting the ideas that new cloth might provide the needed solution or that the old cloth should simply be cast aside in favor of the new."[117] Through the added explanation "the patch from the new will not match the old" (5:36) and

---

115. See Jeremias, *Parables*, 104.

116. Although Semitic speech contains no comparatives and although Luke sometimes uses the positive degree of an adjective in the sense of a comparative (10:42) or a superlative, the theme throughout this passage rules out a comparative interpretation.

117. Green, *Gospel of Luke*, 250.

the attachment of 5:39 Luke demonstrates his intention "to emphasize the value of the old."[118] Mark, on the other hand, underlines the newness of the kingdom and the fresh wineskins that are required.

In the same way that Matthew omitted Mark 7:19b to revert the passage to speaking about the issue of handwashing, in this pericope Matthew and Luke insert statements so that Jesus' message is clarified. According to Matthew and Luke, Jesus' teaching preserves the old, whereas Mark emphasizes the new wineskins that are required since the new garment contains the fullness (πλήρωμα). Jesus' understanding must be tied to his preaching of the kingdom of God. The bridegroom has arrived (Mark 2:19), and whereas John the Baptist remained in the wilderness practicing asceticism including fasting, Jesus announces the new wine of the time of restoration so that feasting in the Promised Land is the appropriate response.[119] The dirge melody of the Baptizer has been replaced by the joyful dance of Jesus' kingdom message (Matt 11:16–19 / Luke 7:31–35). Jesus compares the incompatibility between his group's feasting and the fasting of John's disciples as well as the followers of the Pharisees to proclaim the arrival of the kingdom of God. But Jesus is not challenging the structures, institutions, and regulations of Judaism.

Before we can move to describe how Mark employed Jesus' teaching, we must evaluate the new Jewish-oriented interpretation of this Lukan passage.[120] Scholars such as David Flusser and Brad Young contend that Jesus' purpose "is to revitalize fresh skins for the best of the old wine."[121] According to this perspective the Pharisees favored innovative oral interpretations of Scripture while Jesus supported only the written teachings of the Torah. Therefore in this context John the Baptist and the Pharisees were calling for additional fast days not recognized by the Jewish Scriptures.[122] Therefore, according to Brad Young, "when we prefer new wine, the message of Jesus is distorted."[123]

Good reports that "Despite Luke's obvious use here of the Markan source, he achieves in our view a reinterpretation which reverses Mark's understanding of the whole passage."[124] Luke would then be closer to the understanding of Jesus while

---

118. Carlston, *Parables*, 63.

119. See Guelich, *Mark 1—8:26*, 115.

120. Kee ("Old Coat," 13–22) offers yet an additional interpretation so that "The point of the parable is that through thoughtless and ill-considered actions there is a danger of loss" (19). In this case there would be no intended contrast between the old and the new since "if the double parable dealt with the old versus the new, we should expect to have the old coat and the new coat, old wine and new wine." But this interpretation demands a new context to the parable and does not accept a contrast between both Jesus and the Pharisees and Jesus and the Baptist's disciples on the issue of the presence of the kingdom. Instead of a kingdom parable, it becomes a discipleship parable.

121. Young, *Jesus the Jewish Theologian*, 159. Cf. Flusser, "Do you Prefer New Wine," 26–31; Good, "Jesus, Protagonist of the Old," 19–36.

122. Young, *Jesus the Jewish Theologian*, 156.

123. Ibid., 160.

124. Good, "Jesus, Protagonist of the Old," 25.

Mark would favor a Pauline interpretation. However, we have seen that Jesus' message emphasizes the incompatibility of the old and new and does not favor one over the other. This Jewish-oriented interpretation therefore misconstrues the emphasis by allowing Luke 5:39 to determine the meaning of the entire passage rather than envisioning a series of sayings on incompatibility. In addition, Luke's passage says nothing positive about old wine skins, and no process of aging of the wine skins is advocated. Finally, the context displays Jesus advocating a new power for the Son of Man to forgive sins (Luke 5:24) and to serve as lord of the Sabbath (6:5). Jesus is innovative in these controversies and not advocating a return to the old.[125]

Mark, however, extends the meaning and application of Jesus' statement so that Jesus' own teaching reinforces the new Christian manner of reading the Old Testament. Mark moves from the theme of incompatibility to the conclusion that new wineskins are needed for the new wine of the kingdom. The surprising vocabulary employed by Mark hints at an additional horizon to the parable. The unusual use of πλήρωμα for patch (rather than repeating ἐπίβλημα) conveys the sense of the fullness of the gospel.[126] In the New Testament this term πλήρωμα is regularly employed theologically to describe the fullness of God (Eph 1:23; 3:19), christologically to exalt Jesus (John 1:16; Col 1:19; 2:9; Eph 4:13), soteriologically to portray the church (Eph 1:23; 3:19), and eschatologically to depict the fullness of time (Gal 4:4; Eph 1:10) and the fullness of the Gentiles (Rom 11:12, 25). One would expect some of these nuances to rub off in the use of πλήρωμα here in the Gospel of Mark.

Second, Mark employs the term "schism" for a tear in the garment. Since this term σχίσμα repeatedly describes divisions between groups in the New Testament (John 7:43; 9:13; 10:19; 1 Cor 1:10; 11:18; 12:25), by implication a division between people groups, for instance Jews and Gentiles, will occur if the new wine is not placed in new wineskins.[127] Combined with the term πλήρωμα, the implied message states that if the fullness of the garment (see Heb 1:10–12; Ps 102: 26–28; Isa 51:6) is not manifested in the people of God, a schism will result.

Third, in the two added statements of Mark to the tradition the term καινός is introduced (2:21b, 22b) alongside νέος (2:22ab new wine). The seemingly redundant "the new from the old" (2:21b) appears to be "redactional reflecting a Markan

---

125. New wine is also mentioned in John 2:1–11 and here the best wine is kept for last and is newly made from the six stone barrels which served the cleansing rites of Judaism. If these passages were related in the early church, they would advocate the superiority of the new Christian movement and not a return to the old.

126. Therefore, Luke 5:36 transforms the sentence to remove the word πλήρωμα. In addition, Maartens believes that "It is further significant that the author uses παλαιόν and not ἀρχαῖον to qualify ἱμάτιον: the word ἀρχαῖον means 'old in point of time.' The contrast which the author draws between the new patch of cloth and the old garment is not a contrast *in point of time* (= ἀρχαῖον) but a contrast *in point of use* (= παλαιόν). The old garment is 'worn out'" ("Mark 2:18–22," 40).

127. Marcus surmises that Mark may be referencing "the futility of trying to mend the schism between Jewish Christians and other Jews" (*Mark 1–8*, 238), but this emphasis plays no role in Mark.

emphasis on the 'new.'"[128] If the old and new are combined (a new patch on an old garment or new wine in old wineskins), the fullness is removed (taken away) from it, the new from the old. Already in Mark 1:27 Jesus employs a new teaching with authority (διδαχὴ καινὴ). Now Jesus has authority to alter the current views of who can forgive sins (2:1–12), when defilement occurs through table fellowship (2:13–17), what forms of piety are appropriate in the kingdom age (2:18–22), and how the Sabbath should be observed (2:23–28; 3:1–5). Finally, Mark's addition to Jesus' parallelism, "the new wine must be placed in new wineskins," provides a generalization summarizing these specifics. Mark expands the meaning so that the parable in 2:19 does not just apply to Jesus' feasting but also to the incompatibility of Judaistic practices with Christianity. This incompatibility becomes highly apparent when it leads to the bridegroom's death (2:20).[129]

Certainly 2:21–22 is first of all an eschatological claim that the day of salvation has arrived, so that John's disciples (2:18) no longer need to emphasize asceticism but enjoy the kingdom blessings. Yahweh is restoring the fortunes of Zion so that according to Zechariah 8:19 the entire fasting schedule will be changed to feasts. The metaphors describe eschatological expectations including the old earth being wrapped up like a garment (Ps 102:26–28; Heb 1:10–12; Isa 51:6; cf. 34:4) and new wine flowing down from the mountaintops (Amos 9:13b). The new age is pictured like new clothes just as Paul admonishes his readers to put on the new nature after removing the old (Eph 4:22–24; Col 3:10, 12; Gal 3:27; Rom 13:14). Similarly, the presence of wine symbolizes the new earth as when Noah plants a vine in the restored earth after the deluge (Gen 9:20) and the spies return with clusters of grapes from the Promised Land (Num 13:23ff). Likewise, extra-biblical apocalyptic literature compares the new age to one vine sprouting a thousand branches, one branch growing a thousand clusters, one cluster producing a thousand grapes, and one grape generating a cor of wine (2 Bar 29:5–6).

Grammatically, the term σχίσμα is related to the expression σχιζομένους in Mark 1:10 and ἐσχίσθη in 15:38. Since those occurrences demand an eschatological meaning tying Jesus' baptism and his death to the fullness of God's eschatological plan, in 2:21–22 there must be a contrast between old and new. If 2:21–22 is categorized as a parable, then we must infuse the Markan definition of parable as an allegorical riddle into the meaning of the saying.[130] The first parable expresses the incompatibility of the old age and the new age. One cannot just patch the old garment since the new will tear away from the old. The fullness (πλήρωμα) will not be present but instead a schism (σχίσμα) will result. Then after the second parable Mark adds the solution. Alternatively, a new wineskin is needed for the new age. The lesson to be drawn from

---

128. Guelich, *Mark 1—8:26*, 114.

129. See Guelich, *Mark 1—8:26*, 115. Mark ties ἀπαρθῇ in 2:20 with αἴρει in 2:21.

130. Luke 5:36 entitles it a parable. For a full blown description of Mark's parables as allegorical riddles see section 9.2 below.

the two failed experiments is that new wine must be placed into fresh wineskins.[131] The two additions to the logion by Mark, "new from the old" in 2:21 and "placing new wine in new wineskins" in 2:22, demonstrate that Mark envisions the need for new structures and considers the new superior to the old.

What are the new wineskins that Mark is advocating?[132] Taylor envisions a change of institutions since "a new message must find a fresh vehicle, if it is not to perish and to destroy existing institutions."[133] Collins makes this suggestion more specific by explaining that "from the point of view of the followers of Jesus after Easter, the saying legitimated the new social formations and religious innovations of the communities founded in his name."[134] Therefore, Mark contrasts the practices of Judaism with the new wineskins of Christianity. Through the imagery of the bursting of old wineskins and the tearing of cloth, the Markan Jesus envisions new wineskins for the traditional Jewish institutions and practices. The age of fulfillment has arrived.

In summary, this Markan emphasis upon the new wine placed in new wineskins demonstrates that a new situation demands new practices.[135] Second, the aim of Mark is to foster a rereading and interpretation of the Hebrew Bible.[136] Mark places these short parables found in 2:21–22 at the middle of the five controversy dialogues in 2:1—3:6 to provide summarizing instruction for how the church is to deal with important Jewish traditions. Mark is employing what we call ceremonial ritual mirroring to parallel the situation of Jesus with the struggles of the early church. Specifically, what practices are in Mark's mind? We will argue in the upcoming sections that these new wineskins include a new temple fulfilled in both Jesus (14:58; 15:29–30, 38) and the community (11:22–25), new sacrifices (12:33), a new view of the Sabbath (2:23–3:6), and a new theology of cleanliness regulations since the prohibitions against defiled food (7:19b) and contact with menstruating women and corpses (5:21–43) as well as lepers (1:40–45) have been fulfilled in Jesus' kingdom pronouncements and miracles.

8.4 The Sabbath Is Made for Humans to Do Good (2:23—3:6)

In this section we will examine the views of Jesus' forbearers on Sabbath observance and compare them with Jesus' stance as evidenced in his controversies with the Jewish leaders in Mark 2:23—3:6. Then, based upon the omission of 2:27 from the other

---

131. Cf. Kanjirakompil, "New Wine," 249.

132. Young argues for a personal renewal interpretation so that Jesus envisioned "a revitalized people—enjoying the best of the old wine" (*Jesus the Jewish Theologian*, 158). But this implies a reading of the Pauline concepts of death to the old life and resurrection of the new into Jesus' statement and assumes the earlier Jewish interpretation we have discarded.

133. Taylor, *Mark*, 212.

134. Collins, *Mark*, 200. France talks about the "incompatibility with the existing forms of religion and society" (*Mark*, 141).

135. See Stein, *Mark*, 135 and Nineham, *St. Mark*, 102.

136. See Hultgren, *Jesus and His Adversaries*, 161.

Synoptic Gospels because of its radical implications, we will conclude that Mark presents the view of Paul that Sabbath observance is a matter of personal preference in Christ. In this way Mark employs the kingdom teachings of Jesus to fulfil the OT ceremonial regulations and offer the Gentiles in particular a new way to read the dictates of the law. This does not entail, however, that Mark misrepresents the time of Jesus since he faithfully presents the response of Jesus' contemporaries to the Sabbath especially in the beginning and conclusion of the gospel.[137]

As N.T. Wright maintains, the Sabbath in the Old Testament "is rooted in the two greatest narratives which shaped ancient Israel: Creation and Exodus."[138] The Decalogue in Exodus 20:11 grounds the Sabbath in the creation story while Deuteronomy 5:15 bases its instruction on the Exodus redemptive deliverance. In addition, the Old Testament contains several specific Sabbath prohibitions (Exod 16:22–30; 34:21; 35:2–3; Num 15:32–3e6; Neh 10:31; 13:15–22; Jer 17:21–22) but these never add up to a comprehensive definition of forbidden work.[139] Therefore only in post-biblical writings does one encounter a fence around the law (Jub 2:29–30; 50:6–13,) which reaches its climax in the thirty-nine prohibited acts specified in the Mishnah (*Sabb.* 7:2). In Jesus' time the Essenes, in reaction to the perceived state of defilement of the temple establishment, constructed a conservative set of halakic case law, which included not assisting a person out of a pit or an animal in giving birth on the Sabbath (CD 10:14—11:18). Likewise, the Pharisees opposed Jesus' healing ministry on the Sabbath (Mark 3:1–6; Luke 13:10–17; 14:1–6; John 7:22–23; 9:13–16), but their perspective appears to be based upon the premise that deeds which prevented death were permitted (*Yom.* 8:6). However, the seriousness of working on the Sabbath is evidenced by a tradition of capital punishment for profaning the Sabbath that extends from Exodus through Jubilees and Qumran into the Mishnah.

In the first mentioning of the Sabbath in Mark (1:21), the issue of breaking the Sabbath is not raised. France offers a double explanation contending that "a command to a demon did not qualify as 'work' in the same way as a physical healing, but also because the question of Jesus orthodoxy in this matter was not yet an issue."[140] Against France's first proposal, Jesus does get in trouble in Luke 13:11 for healing a woman

---

137. In Mark 1:32 the sick gather at Jesus' door to be healed only after the Sabbath sunset. Adela Collins explains that "The fact that the people of Capernaum waited until the sun had gone down to bring the sick and possessed to Jesus implies that either the activity of bringing them or healing them, or perhaps both, is unlawful on the Sabbath" (*Mark*, 175). In 15:42 Jesus' body must be buried before the Sabbath according to Jewish tradition, and in 16:1 the women attempt to finish their task of anointing the body of Jesus only after the conclusion of the Sabbath.

138. Wright, *Scripture and the Authority of God*, 143.

139. France, *Mark*, 143.

140. France, *Mark*, 149. Riesenfeld (*Gospel Tradition*, 118) offers a theological explanation arguing that the mentioning of the Sabbath contains eschatological significance in relation to the overthrow of darkness and the introduction of messianic authority. However, Carson counters this with the simple observation that "no explicit connection between eschatological, messianic authority and the Sabbath is offered in the text itself" ("Jesus and the Sabbath," 59).

crippled by a spirit for eighteen years on the Sabbath. Therefore the second explanation that the question of Jesus' orthodoxy in observing the Sabbath day had not yet arisen captures the intention of Mark.[141] Mark has a different agenda for these opening events of Jesus' ministry. Mark's purpose for binding 1:16–39 together explains the lack of emphasis upon Sabbath breaking in the beginning of his gospel. In Jesus' first ministry campaign Mark attempts to demonstrate the paradigmatic nature of Jesus' ministry by placing together discipleship making (1:16–20), teaching (1:21–22), deliverance ministry (1:23–28), healing (1:29–34), and prayer (1:35–38).[142] These five dimensions of Jesus' ministry serve as an archetype for the mission of the church. Mark will focus on Jesus' relationship to the law, culminating with the issue of the Sabbath in the following controversy dialogues and the frame around them.

Mark 2:22—3:6 recites two controversies involving the Sabbath whose combination must be traditional, as evidenced by the similar procedures of both Matthew and Luke. Matthew maintains the unity of the two controversies about the Sabbath in 12:1–13 even though he employs the other controversies in Mark as calls to discipleship (9:9–16) in his section on miracle stories. Likewise, Luke 13:10–17 and 14:1–6 are clearly tied together since they involve stories about a woman and a man[143] around the two issues of healing and eating habits on the Sabbath, in reverse order from the subject matter of the controversy dialogues in Mark.[144]

To determine the specifics of the conflict in Mark 2:23–28, we must clarify what is forbidden on the Sabbath. The offense in plucking grain on the Sabbath does not involve a stroll longer than a Sabbath day's journey, nor the stealing of food since "the disciples were taking *Peah*, the grain left for the poor on the borders of people's fields,"[145] nor the construction of a roadway[146] since this is an absurd way of constructing a

---

141. Gundry (*Mark*, 87) supported by Boring (*Mark*, 67) and Stein (*Mark*, 95) point out that Sabbath observation does not arise as an issue till 2:23—3:6.

142. See section 3.3 above.

143. Luke pairs men and women together as in the examples of Zechariah and Elizabeth, Simeon and Anna, Priscilla and Aquila, the healing of loved ones of the centurion and the widow of Nain, Simon the Pharisee and the sinful woman, and in the parables of the leaven and the mustard seed, the lost sheep and coin, the widow and the judge, the men and women taken and left (17:34–35), and the sign of Jonah and the Queen of Sheba (11:30–31).

144. Luke probably includes them from a source about ministry to the marginalized so that in 13:10–17 Jesus sides with a woman with an infirmity against the leader of the synagogue and in 14:1–6 with a sick man with dropsy over against the ruler of the Pharisees. In each section the disease is associated with a ritual action so that in 13:10–17 a woman is untied just as it is permissible to untie animals on the Sabbath and in 14:1–4 the man is healed of a water disease just as it is permissible to remove an animal from a well on the Sabbath. The former pericope was moved by Luke to tie it by catchword with the former stories linking the 18 who died at the tower of Siloam (13:4) with the 18 years the woman has been crippled (13:11).

145. Casey, *Solution to the 'Son of Man' Problem*, 122–23. See Lev 19:9–10; 23:22.

146. This is the position favored by Marcus (*Mark 1–8*, 239–40) and Jewett (*Lord's Day*, 37) who follows Bacon, (*Beginnings of Gospel Story*, 30–31).

road.¹⁴⁷ Instead the issue focuses on the transgression of Exodus 34:21, "Six days you shall labor, but on the seventh day you shall rest; even during the plowing season and harvest you must rest."¹⁴⁸ Although it was permissible to pick grain with one's hands according to Deuteronomy 23:25 ("If you enter your neighbor's grainfield, you may pick kernels with your hands, but you must not put a sickle to his standing grain"), the stricter interpretation of the Pharisees prohibited such actions on the Sabbath during the harvest mentioned in Exodus 34:21.¹⁴⁹ The Pharisees defined the plucking action of the disciples as reaping.¹⁵⁰

It is important to demonstrate how Mark 2:23–28 fits together. The Pharisees' challenge in Mark 2:24 ("Look, why are they doing what is unlawful on the Sabbath?") receives two answers from Jesus, each with its own introductory formula. The first saying (2:25–26) is placed in the traditional question form of a controversy dialogue, with 2:27 serving as the pronouncement saying to conclude the conversation. However, as we shall see, 2:28 appears to be the conclusion to a controversy dialogue instead of the more normal reaction of a crowd. Many scholars claim that the repetition of the formula καὶ ἔλεγεν αὐτοῖς in 2:27 implies an addition to the original context.¹⁵¹ However, the five traditional elements of a controversy dialogue bind the entire pericope closely together.

1. Description of a conflict situation (Mark 2:23)
2. Question by Jesus' opponents (2:24)
3. Jesus' return question (often with a quotation from Scripture) (2:25–26)¹⁵²

---

147. Neirynck labels this explanation an "unintelligible action of making a path by plucking the ears of corn" ("Jesus and the Sabbath," 258). Stein adds that one does "not make a road by picking grain but rather by plucking up the stalks or beating them down" (*Mark*, 144). The expression ὁδὸν ποιεῖν can mean just to travel as in Judg 17:8.

148. See France, *Mark*, 145.

149. Philo (*Life of Moses* 2:22) supports this view. Luke's addition of "rubbing them in their hands" (6:1) may be an indication that the disciples follow Deut 23:25 and do not employ a sickle.

150. See Collins, *Mark*, 201; Loader, *Jesus' Attitude*, 33; Kazen, *Jesus and Purity Halakhah*, 58.

151. Bultmann, *History*, 16; Lane, *Mark*, 118–19; Taylor, *St. Mark*, 218. Evidence might include the fact that Mark 2:25–26 centers on a scriptural proof from 1 Sam 21 following the term "Sabbath" placed in the plural at 2:24 whereas 2:27 emphasizes the original intention of the Sabbath for the benefit of humanity with the word "Sabbath" placed in the singular.

152. Some authors (Parrott, "Conflict and Rhetoric," 117; Hultgren, "Formation of the Sabbath Pericope," 41) argue that 2:25–26 was secondarily added by Mark because 1) in the other controversies of 2:1ff the argument is Christological; 2) the Sabbath motif is missing although it is included in the midrash (Yalqut Shim'oni on 1 Sam 21:5 and b. Menahoth 95b); 3) the Pharisees accuse a group (the disciples), while the story focuses on a single individual's (David's) actions; 4) "David was in real need, and the disciples are idly nibbling to satisfy their appetite" (Lindars, *Jesus Son of Man*, 103); 5) the reference tones down the statement of 2:27 by offering a precedent for the breach of Sabbath casuistry; and 6) the formula καὶ λέγει αὐτοῖς is employed again in 2:27. However, these arguments lose their weight if we recognize that 2:25–26 function as Jesus' return question which is a traditional element in a normal Markan controversy dialogue.

4. The pronouncement saying (2:27)

5. Response by the crowd or an additional concluding saying (2:28)

If we investigate how Luke employs Markan and Q material, it becomes clear that the new introduction at 2:27 does not entail that Mark employs different sources at 2:25–26 and 2:27–28. For instance, Luke replicates the eschatological discourse of Mark 13 but inserts an introduction at Luke 21:10 (ἔλεγεν αὐτοῖς) to divide the two questions of 21:7, "when will these things happen?" and "what will be the sign?" Then at 21:29 he repeats this procedure to indicate a switch of genre from eschatological teaching to parable. Likewise, in the continuous Q material in chapter 12 Luke inserts introductory statements to identify a switch in audiences at 12:15, 22, 54 and the alternation to a parable at 12:16 (cf. 11:5). On this subject Hagner points out that an introductory phrase "can equally well mark a new aspect of material being presented at the same occasion."[153] Therefore, we cannot conclude that Mark is placing divergent material together when he includes the introduction καὶ ἔλεγεν αὐτοῖς or καὶ ἔλεγεν right in the middle of a discourse at Mark 2:27–28 (Luke 6:5) as well as Mark 2:11; 4:9, 21, 24, 26, 30; 6:10; 7:9; 9:1. This was a traditional editorial procedure. Therefore the entire passage of Mark 2:23–28 fits well together.

It is notoriously difficult to demonstrate conclusively Jesus' view on such a controversial subject as the Sabbath.[154] Some prefer a radical Jesus. Rordorf contends that Jesus' actions on the Sabbath annulled the fourth commandment, so that with regard to Mark 3:1–6 he argues that "the Sabbath commandment was not merely pushed into the background by the healing activity of Jesus; it was simply annulled."[155] Countering Jeremias, Merkel likewise maintains that "It is not merely a matter of an attack on the Pharisaic Sabbath *halakha*, as Jeremias maintains, since the sayings in Mark 2:27 and 3:4 plainly qualify the absolutely unquestionable commandment to keep the Sabbath holy, whose violation is punishable in the Torah by death."[156] Certainly the early patristic apologists read the literature in this manner since they list breaches of the Sabbath in order to produce a strong case against keeping the Sabbath.[157]

1. David partook of the forbidden showbread on the Sabbath (Matt 12:3).

---

153. Hagner ("Jesus and the Synoptic Sabbath Controversies," 224) includes some additional arguments from Gundry (*Mark*, 143–44).

154. For arguments from various authors against the authenticity of the Sabbath passages in the gospels and a rebuttal of these arguments see Hagner ("Jesus and the Synoptic Sabbath Controversies," 215–33).

155. Rordorf, *Sunday*, 70.

156. Merkel, "Opposition between Jesus and Judaism," 139. See Jeremias (*New Testament Theology*, 209) whose arguable main thesis is that "Jesus lived in the Old Testament. His sayings are incomprehensible unless we recognize this" (205).

157. See Justin Martyr, *Dialogue* 23:3; 27:5; 29:3; Epiphanius, *Adversus Haereses* 30,32,10; Clement of Alexandria, Stromateis 6,16,141,7; 6,16,142,1; Victorinus of Pettau, *De Fabrica Mundi* 6. Additional references are included in the footnotes of Bacchiocchi (*From Sabbath to Sunday*, 27–28).

2. Sacrifices continue on the Sabbath (Matt 12:5).

3. The priests circumcise on the Sabbath (John 7:23).

4. God himself does not interrupt his word on the Sabbath (John 5:17).

5. God himself broke the Sabbath by commanding Joshua and Israel to walk around the walls on seven successive days (Josh 6:4).

6. The Maccabees fought on the Sabbath (1 Mac 2:39–41).

However, we will argue that the NT passages contain no evidence that Jesus either rejected the Sabbath law or questioned that the Sabbath was intended as a day of cessation from work.[158] As Dunn points out, "In these accounts it is not yet an issue as to *whether* the Sabbath needs to be observed; the issue is rather *how* the Sabbath is to be observed."[159] This does not mean, however, that Jesus' understanding of what was not permissible coincided with existing interpretations. Instead of paying attention to halachkic argumentation, Jesus followed broad principles such as doing what is good and beneficial to humans.[160] He regarded Sabbath observance as a beneficial privilege, not a mere legal point as the Pharisees assumed. Thus Jesus identified with the stream of interpretation where Sabbath rest originated for the benefit of workers (Deut 5:14–15) and is presented as a blessing instead of a burden (Isa 58:13).[161] Therefore, Jesus attempted to "liberate the day from the multitude of rabbinical limitations and thereby restore it to its original divine intention."[162] This position which emphases joy and service could be entitled the redemptive function of the Sabbath.

Mark 2:27 is not extraneous to the passage but sounds similar to the Jewish interpretation of the Sabbath in *2 Baruch* 14:18, "And you said that you would make a man for this world as a guardian over your works that it should be known that he was not created for the world, but the world for him." This sentiment coheres as well with the logion assigned to R. Simon b. Menasya (c. 180 CE) in *Mekhilta* on Exodus 31:13–14 and to R. Jonathan b. Joseph in the Talmud, Yoma 85b, "Unto you the Sabbath is delivered, and you are not delivered to the Sabbath."[163] Therefore, Jesus theology of the Sabbath can be compared with some contemporary views within Judaism.[164] However,

---

158. Cf. Guelich, *Mark 1—8:26*, 127.

159. Dunn, "Mark 2:1—3:6," 406.

160. See France, *Mark*, 150 and Guelich, *Mark 1—8:26*, 128.

161. Jeremias supports this conclusion with an argument from the sequence of creation: "The sequence of the creation of man on the sixth day and the ordinance of the day of rest on the seventh shows that it was God's will as creator that the day of rest should serve men and bring them blessing" (*New Testament Theology*, 208).

162. Bacchiocchi, *From Sabbath to Sunday*, 72.

163. For the Hebrew text and supporting literature see Niernyck, "Jesus and Sabbath," 246, n. 67.

164. We cannot go so far as Nineham (*St. Mark*, 116 and n. 1) who thinks that the words of Jesus are meant as a variant of this rabbinic commonplace. But neither can we agree with Beare ("Sabbath Was Made for Man?" 130–36) that Mark 2:27 is wholly inconceivable in any Jewish teacher, including Jesus.

the overwhelming number of rabbinic Sabbath sayings concentrate upon problems of infringement of the Sabbath law or on the justification of possible relaxations dealing with the preservation of human life and thus differ from Jesus' perspective. Jesus contends that "human need and well-being override the prohibition of work on the Sabbath."[165]

How then does Mark 2:27 relate to the subject matter of the following verse, "So the Son of Man is lord even of the Sabbath"? Mark 2:27 consists of antithetic parallelism constructed as a chiasmus (abba):

<u>τὸ σάββατον</u>   διὰ τὸν <u>ἄνθρωπον</u> ἐγένετο
καὶ οὐχ ὁ <u>ἄνθρωπος</u> διὰ <u>τὸ σάββατον</u>

Mark 2:28, however, finishes off the paragraph as a generalizing conclusion connected by the word ὥστε so that the term καὶ in the phrase κύριός . . . καὶ τοῦ σαββάτου indicates that since the Sabbath was made for humans, the representative of all humans, namely the Son of Man, must also be lord of the Sabbath.

Many commentators understand the use of ὥστε here to imply a Markan addition, but the following arguments demonstrate the interconnectedness of 2:27–28.

1. Vocabulary linkage argues for a single section.

Connecting hook words such as οὐκ ἔξεστιν (24, 26), σάββατον (24, 27, 28), and τί ποιεῖν (24, 25) from the question of the Pharisees in 2:24 tie the various verses of 2:23–28 together, and each part has its particular rhetorical function.[166]

2. The structure of Mark fits a traditional controversy dialogue.

Certainly there is a tendency within the transmission tradition to add material as evidenced by the inserted material in the Matthean parallel (12:5–7),[167] but in Mark's case each element plays a role in a traditional controversy dialogue.

3. Parallelism followed by a generalizing conclusion is common Jesus parlance.

Burney claims that a couplet followed by a summarizing comment as in Mark 2:27–28 betrays a genuine form used by Jesus.[168] Prominent examples include Luke 6:43–44a and 6:45 in Jesus' sermon on the plain.[169]

4. The use of ὥστε clauses in independent sentences offer a necessary conclusion.

---

165. Collins, *Mark*, 209.

166. See Dewey, *Markan Public Debate*, 94–96.

167. Supported by Parrott, "Conflict and Rhetoric," 119. Matthew adds 12:5-6 in the identical form of a return question by Jesus since he evidently realized that the 1 Sam 21 incident did not occur on the Sabbath. In addition, Matthew includes both an argument from the law (12:5) and the prophets (12:6 from Hos 6:6). Hicks ("Sabbath Controversy in Matthew," 86–87) supposes that Matthew adds 5–6 because a halakaic question demanded a halakaic response, not just a haggadic argument like Mark 2:25–26.

168. Burney, *Poetry of Our Lord*, 97–99.

169. In addition, a generalizing conclusion is given after several parallel statements in Luke 6:27–30 and 31; 6:32–35 and 36; as well as 37–38a and 38b.

A popular opinion argues that "here, as elsewhere in Mark, such a clause enunciates the conclusion Mark is drawing from what has preceded."[170] Supporters elicit examples such as Mark 15:5 where Pilate is amazed and 2:12 where a miracle precipitates the crowd's reaction, but those are uses of ὥστε with an infinitive and thus not a similar expression. In addition, Fowler contends that ὥστε clauses when employed as independent sentences regularly point out an inside view, not something known to the characters in the story itself.[171] However, Mark 10:8 (Matt 19:6) as well as Matt 12:12; 23:31 are examples of a continuation of Jesus' speech and not a conclusion by the author unknown to the participants of the event.[172] Therefore, one can conclude from these examples that Mark 2:28 is not necessarily a parenthetical remark of the author. The fact that Matt 12:8 replaces ὥστε with γάρ when he omits Mark 2:27 demonstrates that Matthew sees an already establishing connection.

5. An understandable rationale explains the omission of Mark 2:27 by Matthew and Luke.

As we shall see, Matthew and Luke omit Mark 2:27 because of its liberalizing tendencies. On the other hand, the most propounded theory for a Markan addition of 2:28 contends that it was added to narrow the scope of the saying in contrast with 2:27.[173] Jesus as Son of Man replaces the people as the sons of men. But this does not fit the liberalizing tendency of Mark in the other examples illustrated in this chapter. Furthermore, the two verses are closely tied together if Jesus saw himself as the paradigm Son of Man who demonstrates the truth of 2:27. Therefore, it is highly unlikely that a narrowing of the Sabbath legislation would at the same time cause the addition of 2:28 by Mark and the subtraction of 2:27 by Matthew and Luke.

6. The presence of self-identification statements in the other controversy dialogues of Mark 2:1—3:6 argues for the inclusion of 2:28 here.

---

170. Witherington, *Mark*, 132.

171. Fowler, *Let the Reader Understand*, 103–4.

172. Matt 12:12 does change the question of Mark 3:4 into a conclusion but it is not placed at the end of the passage but before the healing as in Mark. The parallel to Matt 23:31 in Luke 11:48 demonstrates that it is not the redacted conclusion of an author but is part of Jesus' discourse since Luke employs a synonym (ἄρα μάρτυρές ἐστε instead of ὥστε μαρτυρεῖτε ἑαυτοῖς).

173. See Parrott ("Conflict and Rhetoric," 119) who finds support in Bultmann, Cranfield, Dewey, Dibelius, Grundmann, Käsemann, and Taylor. In a second opinion, Hultgren (*Jesus and His Adversaries*, 114, n. 65) posits that 2:23–24, 28 were original and 2:27 was added to generalize the Son of Man's authority to all humankind. Then 2:25–26 were inserted to shore up the passage with a scriptural precedent. But we are offering extensive arguments that 27–28 belong together. A third opinion maintains that only an original *chreia*-saying (2:27) was remembered by the church (see Parrott, 127). Then its expansion is explained by the community's need for self-definition with 1) the addition of a setting (2:23–24) featuring an adversarial relationship between Jesus and the Pharisees; 2) the citation of a precedent (2:25–26) which not only continued the adversarial relationship ("have you never read . . . ?") but also established a continuity of ethos between Jesus and David and 3) 2:28 as a demonstration of the authority of the Son of Man who was a figure of significance to Mark's community. But if only 2:27 was original, why would Matthew and Luke omit only this saying.

Jesus' self-designation of himself as the Son of Man in 2:28 corresponds to the former reference in 2:10[174] as well as Jesus' identifications of himself as the great physician (2:17b), the bridegroom (2:20), and the one who has come "to do good" and "to save life" (3:4). Therefore, christological designations are an intricate part of each controversy dialogue. In particular, the presence of καὶ as "also" in the phrase καὶ τοῦ σαββάτου must relate back to 2:10.[175] Therefore, κύριός ἐστιν ("is Lord") corresponds to ἐξουσίαν ἔχει ("has authority"); ὁ υἱὸς τοῦ ἀνθρώπου ("Son of Man") matches 2:10 exactly; and καὶ τοῦ σαββάτου ("also of the Sabbath") corresponds to ἀφιέναι ἁμαρτίας ἐπὶ τῆς γῆς ("to forgive sins on the earth"). From this evidence we conclude along with Gundry, "Thus it seems that Jesus' lordship over the Sabbath is something in addition to his authority to forgive sins (καὶ as "also")."[176] These consistent self-designations indicate one reason why these controversy dialogues were originally connected.

7. "Son of Man" is a self-designation employed only by Jesus in the Synoptic Gospels.

Although it is notoriously difficult to establish the meaning of the term "Son of Man," scholars agree that the early church seldom employed this term to designate Jesus (outside the gospels only in Acts 7:56; Heb 2:6 = Ps 8:5; Rev 1:13; 14:14 = Dan 7:13). The most consistent understanding of the term would then conclude that both 2:27 and 2:28 emanate from Jesus.[177] Certainly as Dunn points out, the "surprising appearance of the two Son of Man sayings so distinct and isolated from the others used by Mark"[178] demonstrates that Mark is employing source material. Therefore Markan redaction is unlikely.

8. A correct understanding of the term "Son of Man" supports the tie between 2:27–28.

---

174. Mark 2:10 has likewise been categorized as a parenthetical remark directed to the reader. But Hare notes that "the Markan anacoluthon is not remedied by placing v. 10 in parentheses; indeed, it is aggravated," and that "neither Matthew nor Luke found Mark's language so intolerable as to demand editorial revision" (*Son of Man Tradition*, 185).

175. Hagner ("Jesus and the Synoptic Sabbath Controversies," 237) supports an emphatic καί as "even of the Sabbath," but the comparison is unclear. In the application of this statement, Hagner seems to apply the "even" to the Son of Man so that he concludes, "this is no ordinary teacher or healer who has the temerity to violate accepted norms of Sabbath activity." Rather than the supreme test of Jesus' lordship over religious practice being the Sabbath, the καί more appropriately refers back to 2:10 as Gundry (*Mark*, 143–44) argues.

176. Gundry, *Mark*, 144. Therefore, it is surprising that the only major English versions to translate καὶ as "also" are the KJV and the NKJV as well as the less well-known Young's Literal Translation and the Darby Bible.

177. Cf. Carson, "Jesus and the Sabbath," 6. Furthermore, both Matthew and Luke take over Mark 2:10a but treat it as a genuine self-designation, not as a Markan editorial comment which they usually drop elsewhere.

178. Dunn, "Mark 2:1—3:6," 398. He is referring to Mark 2:10 and 2:28.

Some argue that the switch from ὁ ἄνθρωπος in 2:27 to ὁ υἱὸς τοῦ ἀνθρώπου in 2:28 reveals that the statements do not belong together.[179] However, if Son of Man is understood as a generic title that Jesus employed as a prophetic messenger chosen by God to represent humankind, then the statements in 2:10 and 2:28 both make sense. Jesus sees himself as the Son of Man in the sense of Psalm 8:5, who (as the new Adam) is crowned with glory and honor and made ruler over the works of God's hands so that everything is placed under his feet.[180] Therefore in 2:10 Jesus functions as God's chosen instrument on earth to demonstrate that the eschatological time has arrived where sins are forgiven.[181] By implication Jesus' followers as human beings representing the Son of Man can forgive sins as well (Matt 18:18; John 20:23). Likewise, regarding Sabbath observance, the Sabbath was made to meet the concrete needs of human beings (2:27), and this representative human being (2:28) stands on the side of all humanity to proclaim that the Sabbath was made for their benefit.[182] Therefore, the disciples of the Son of Man also become lords of the Sabbath in the sense that their needs take precedence over its regulations. This is supported as Guelich contends by a connection with 2:25–26: "What David in view of his calling and position did with and for his own, so Jesus in view of his calling and position could do for his own."[183] The human being is given authority over the Sabbath since Jesus as the paradigmatic Son of Man is lord of all creation.

Since Mark 2:27 and 2:28 belong together, we must account for the reason why both Matthew and Luke (independently) omit only the pronouncement saying of 2:27.[184] Several suggestions are highlighted in exegetical journals:

---

179. The different Greek translations do not support the identical Aramaic phrase. However, this fact also argues against the "universal view" that contends both verses originally spoke about all humans as Son of Man and lord of the Sabbath. See Carson ("Jesus and the Sabbath," 57, n. 106) for supporters of the universal view including Cullmann, Jewett, Rordorf, and Wellhausen.

180. Therefore in the NT epistles the words from Psalm 8 "put everything under his feet" refer to Christ's work (1 Cor 15:27; Eph 1:22; Heb 2:6). In the suffering Son of Man statements Jesus presents himself as the representative of every suffering righteous person spoken about in the personal lament psalms. Furthermore in the eschatological Son of Man statements, Jesus sees himself as the human being who exalts his community to the throne of the Ancient of Days as in Dan 7:13. Finally, Ps 80:17 ("Let your hand rest on the man at your right hand, the son of man you have raised up for yourself") is related to the branch in 80:15 so that Son of Man becomes a messianic title for Jesus so that he represents every royal deliverer in Israel's history.

181. Lindars (*Jesus Son of Man*, 45) illustrates from the Prayer of Nabonidus found at Qumran how an exorcist can receive God's authority to heal an ulcer and forgive sins.

182. Swete explains, "The Sabbath, being made for man's benefit, is subject to the control of the ideal and representative Man, to whom it belongs" (*St. Mark*, 50).

183. Guelich, *Mark 1—6:26*, 128.

184. Mark 2:27, of course, could have been added by Mark (it is missing in Codex D) so that Matthew and Luke have the original saying, but Hultgren argues persuasively that "The saying in 2:28, if originally alone, would have produced material in which Jesus, rather than his disciples, breaks the sabbath law" ("Formation of the Sabbath Pericope," 22).

1. "The play on words is lost in Greek, which may help explain why Matt 12 and Luke 6 have dropped 2:27."[185] Here Guelich is referring to the change in Greek from ὁ ἄνθρωπος to ὁ υἱὸς τοῦ ἀνθρώπου. However, this accounts for why 2:27 could have been separated from 2:28 but does not offer sound reasoning regarding the reason why the specific content of 2:27 was omitted.

2. Since Jubilees 2:31 restricts observance of the Sabbath to Israel, some scholars contend that Mark 2:27 counters this view by extending rabbinic maxims to the Gentile world. Then Matthew and Luke would question that such a procedure was justified.[186] But the issue in question does not concern the relationship of Jews and Gentiles.[187] Furthermore, Luke is very comfortable extending the OT ceremonial regulations involving aliens to the Gentiles as seen in the apostolic decree.

3. "Matthew was aware that the sentiment was used by his opponents (cf. Mek. on Exod 31.14; b. Yoma 85b)."[188] Therefore, Matthew counters his opponents by the omission of this logion in order to demonstrate that only Jesus has authority over the Sabbath. Although Matthew does witness a comprehensive apologetic against accusations from the Pharisaic synagogue, this fails to account for the similar omission in Luke's gospel.

4. Matthew and Luke wanted to heighten the christological element in the passage by eliminating an anthropologically based argument.[189] The prominence of Christology in the early church certainly could account for emphasizing 2:28, but already it stands at the conclusion of the passage in Mark and the omission of 2:27 would not be needed to heighten the Christology.

5. The radical nature of the statement could be misunderstood as a "denigration of the Sabbath."[190] In this case 2:27 would be read as "a literal rejection of all obligation to observe Sabbath restrictions."[191] Since we have demonstrated on other issues of the law how Matthew and Luke maintain a conservative emphasis, this explanation best fits the facts.

---

185. Guelich, *Mark 1—8:26*, 126. But Luke cannot be expected to know the Aramaic background of the sayings of Jesus since he drops all Markan Aramaisms.

186. Mentioned by Bacchiocchi, *From Sabbath to Sunday*, 56, n. 104.

187. See Carson, "Jesus and the Sabbath," 65.

188. Davies and Allison, *Matthew*, 2:315.

189. Neirynck, "Jesus and the Sabbath," 230. Regarding Luke, Carson asserts, "Luke, by leaving out any form of Mark 2:27 and Matthew 12:5–7, jumps from the example of David to the lordship of Christ over the Sabbath, and thus may be saying in effect, 'A greater than David is here'" ("Jesus and the Sabbath," 68).

190. Marcus (*Mark 1–8*, 242), but he emphasizes more the elimination of an anthropologically based argument.

191. Mentioned by France, *Mark*, 146.

The conservative approach of Matthew is demonstrated in his appeal to scriptural references, including the Torah proper (12:5f), the prophets (12:7) as well as the historical books (12:3–4). Mark 2:27 could have been included as an appeal to the creation order since humans were created before the Sabbath, but Matthew does not employ this argument. Why? Matthew was afraid that the principle of the superiority of humans to the Sabbath could be misunderstood as freedom of conscience to choose to ignore the Sabbath rituals altogether. Matthew's conservative view toward the Sabbath is apparent also in 24:20 ("or on the Sabbath" added to Mark 13:18), where even the eschatological woes will not justify traveling more than a Sabbath's day journey.[192] Instead of using Mark 2:27, Matthew substitutes a quotation from Hosea 6:6 ("I desire mercy and not sacrifice") as the pronouncement saying for the conflict.[193] Although the meaning changes little since mercy takes precedence over Sabbath law in Matthew just as human need supersedes ceremonial law in Mark,[194] the significant difference is that now Matthew is quoting Scripture. Mark 2:27 is therefore omitted since it has the potential of advocating a new view of Sabbath observance that might be seen in the synagogue as unfaithful to traditional practice and therefore advocate antinomianism.[195] Writing for a Jewish audience of Christian believers, Matthew takes care to diminish the more radical implications which follow from the Markan form of the tradition.[196]

Luke as well preserves a more conservative view of Sabbath observance than Mark, probably in order to unify the Jewish and Gentile branches of the church.[197] Already we have discovered how Luke omits Mark 7:1–23 and adds a statement of Jesus regarding the advantage of old wine in Luke 5:39. Similarly, through the apostolic decree Luke applies to Gentiles the OT commands for the sojourner required in Leviticus 17–18. Therefore, it would be natural for Luke to also apply to Gentile believers the other expectations of the alien, like keeping the Sabbath (Exod 20:10; 23:12; Deut 5:14). The incidental reference to a Sabbath day's journey in Acts 1:12 suggests the prescriptive nature of this regulation. Therefore, Luke as well omits Mark 2:27 because of a possible misunderstanding advocating an antinomianism that would not emphasize the continuity between the law and the gospel of Jesus Christ.

Now we are ready to explicate Mark's understanding of the Sabbath regulations. Mark climaxes Jesus' teaching on the Sabbath with a self-proclaimed reference to Jesus as "lord of the Sabbath," thus expressing a high Christology whereby Jesus possesses

---

192. For supporters see Bacchiocchi, *From Sabbath to Sunday*, 71, n. 143.

193. Hos 6:6 appears to become the pronouncement saying both here and in Matt 9:10–13.

194. Cf. Hicks, "Sabbath Controversy in Matthew," 84 and Hill, *Gospel of Matthew*, 115.

195. The identical rationale explains the Matthean redaction of Mark 3:1–5 in Matt 12:9–14. Instead of asking a question (Mark 3:4), the Matthean Jesus emphasizes what is lawful (12:12b). Cf. Hill, "On the Use and Meaning," 114.

196. Dunn, "Mark 2:1—3:6," 412. Cf. Kazen, *Jesus and Purity Halakhah*, 58.

197. The motive for Luke's portrayal of Paul as a law abiding Jewish Christian in line with James and the Jerusalem congregation is to unify the Jewish and Gentile church under Paul's leadership.

an authority at least equal to that of the Mosaic law.[198] Since lord of the Sabbath in the Old Testament involves the institution and consecration of the Sabbath (Gen 2:3; Exod 20:8–11; 31:12–17; Lev 23:3), Jesus is performing the tasks designated to God.[199] Likewise, when Mark 2:25–26 and 2:28 are combined, the resulting David/Jesus typology takes on clear messianic overtones.[200] All three Synoptic Gospels agree on this point.

With regard to 2:27, Bacchiocchi correctly observes that Jesus "does not abrogate the original Sabbath commandment, foreseeing the institution of a new day, but rather He strikes off the shackles imposed by the rabbinical Sabbath theology of postexilic Judaism which had exalted the Sabbath above human needs."[201] However, the elimination of Mark 2:27 by both Matthew and Luke demonstrates that they perceive the additional meaning that Mark has attached to this statement. Jesus' meaning that "humanity created in the image of God must be seen as more important than God's gift of the Sabbath"[202] now means that Christians are free to decide as a matter of conscience if they will observe the OT Sabbath regulations. Jesus radicalized the law by reaching to the heart of its intent and inculcating its inner spirit, but Mark applies this new attitude to specific regulations. Therefore, Neirnyck speaks about a "provocative radicalism"[203] and Nineham goes so far to proclaim that "no doubt it was on the basis of it that the early (gentile) Christians felt justified in ceasing to observe the Sabbath and observing Sunday instead."[204] Mark employs Jesus' saying to express the fulfillment of the OT Sabbath regulations. Likewise, regarding the next incident in Mark, Stephen Smith argues that "The action of Jesus in 3,1–5 is a liberating action designed to free the oppressed from the very legal restrictions which the Judaising Christians were intent on perpetuating."[205] Therefore, Mark envisions in Jesus' statement a new way of reading the Old Testament so that mandatory Sabbath observance is not demanded of the Christian community.

Mark's view of Jesus coheres with the views of Paul in his epistles, who considers that Sabbath observance is a matter of personal preference in Christ. As a consequence Paul can state in Romans 14:5 that "One man considers one day more sacred than another; another man considers every day alike. Each one should be fully convinced in his own mind" so long as he "does so to the Lord" (14:6).[206] This roughly corresponds

---

198. See Hooker, *Son of Man in Mark*, 102 and Achtemeier, "He Taught Them," 471.

199. Stein, *Mark*, 149.

200. Guelich, *Mark 1—6:26*, 128.

201. Bacchiocchi, *From Sabbath to Sunday*, 56.

202. Stein, *Mark*, 148.

203. Neirnyck, "Jesus and the Sabbath," 263.

204. Nineham, *St. Mark*, 106.

205. Smith, "Mark 3,1–6," 173. Smith posits that Mark used his narrative in paradigmatic fashion to deal with some of the problems that arose in the church so that "the Marcan Judaisers could be akin to the 'weak' faction in Rom 14–15, and their opponents to the 'strong'" (172, n. 59).

206. Bacchiocchi (*From Sabbath to Sunday*, 364–65) concludes that Rom 14:5 does not speak

to an interpretation of the postulate that "the Sabbath was made for people." A person's needs discerned by the freedom of an individual's conscience determines the binding character of the Sabbath regulations since God created the day of rest for a person's benefit.

Within the five controversy dialogues of 2:1—3:6 and the frame immediately introducing them (1:40-45), the Markan Jesus discusses the sensitive issues of the OT ritual laws. Mark concludes the middle controversy by affirming that fresh wineskins are necessary to preserve the new wine (2:22). This entails a new theology of table fellowship so that Christians no longer become ritually polluted from close contact with sinners (2:15-17)[207] and lepers (1:40-45) or by kingdom celebrations which omit the normal spiritual discipline of fasting (2:18-19).[208] Likewise, the regulations of the Sabbath law are given a new interpretation so that the Pharisee's limitation to actions that spare human life is now altered, so that the Sabbath's purpose is now to provide for human needs (2:27) and the doing of good (3:4) as in Jesus' healing actions. Mark then employs Jesus' logion to offer permission to Christians—Gentiles in particular but also Jews like Paul and Mark—to read the OT regulations in such a manner that offers them freedom to place human need before the strict enforcement of ceremonial regulations. The struggles in the *Sitz im Leben Jesu* therefore mirror controversies in the early church. Here as well as in other places throughout the gospel "Mark appeals directly to the authority of Jesus to justify the liberating activity of his community."[209]

8.5 The New Temple and the New Synagogue / House for the New Israel Along with the Replacement of Sacrifices

In this section we will demonstrate how Mark gives new meaning to the terms Israel, temple, and sacrifice so that a metaphorical meaning replaces a literal connotation. Beginning with Jesus' calling of the Twelve, we will show how Mark pictures Jesus establishing a new Israel and its most prominent institution, a new temple, where God's people now offer new sacrifices. So far we have demonstrated how Markan editorial comments (7:19b), additions to the oral tradition (2:21), and omissions by Matthew

---

about the Sabbath since the context concerns abstinence from foods and the Sabbath is a day of feasting. However, the additional reference in Col 2:16, "Therefore do not let anyone judge you by what you eat or drink . . . or a Sabbath day," is consistent with an interpretation applying Rom 14:5-6 to the Sabbath.

207. Sanders (*Jesus and Judaism*, 209) maintains that Jesus' eating with sinners does not imply ceremonial impurity, but Tohar 7:6 states, "If tax gatherers entered a house, [all that is within it] becomes unclean" as argued by Collins (*Mark*, 192, n. 71). The Pharisees were concerned as well with a sinner touching Jesus in Luke 7:39. Cf. Evans, "Who Touched Me?" 364, n. 27.

208. Mark 2:1-12 fits this pattern as well if we accept the interpretation that the main issue involved in the controversy is the right to declare sins forgiven (divine passive) outside the cult and without reference to the usual means of forgiveness laid down in the law and enacted by the priest. See Lohmeyer, *Lord of the Temple*, 26.

209. Smith, "Mark 3,1-6," 173.

and Luke (2:27) indicate that Mark was speaking about the fulfillment of Jewish ceremonial legislation in the early church. In this section Mark will again employ unusual vocabulary, which the other gospel writers either omit (12:32–33) or interpret differently (11:24-25), and use typology like the number twelve and the temple to mirror in Jesus' lifetime what the early church will proclaim, i.e., a new Israel and a new temple.

The historicity of the twelve disciples is today a bedrock claim based upon a scholarly consensus that Jesus chose twelve disciples to symbolize the twelve tribes of Israel who became "the new people of God in the last days."[210] The changing of Simon's name to Peter in the context of the list of the Twelve (3:13–19) points to the establishment of a new people of Israel just as the alteration in the names of Abraham and Sarah as well as Jacob to Israel initiated a new consciousness in the identity of God's chosen people. If the Twelve "symbolize and anticipate the eschatological restoration of the twelve tribes of Israel,"[211] then the use of the designation "twelve" throughout Mark's gospel must represent Israel and speak to the fulfillment of various aspects of their religious life.

In Mark the designation "twelve" most frequently refers to the twelve disciples themselves (3:14, 16; 4:10; 6:7; 9:35; 10:32; 11:11; 14:10, 17, 20, 43), but twelve becomes significant in two other narratives to represent new developments in the life of Israel.[212] The twelve baskets left over (6:43; 8:19) in the feeding of the five thousand signifies that Jesus' ministry will feed and nourish all of Israel, as we discovered in chapter 7. In addition, through an intercalation Mark links a woman hemorrhaging for twelve years (5:25) with a twelve-year-old corpse (5:42) to mirror Jewish purity requirements from the Old Testament and speak about Jesus' fulfillment of them. Similarly, here Mark mirrors changes in the life of Israel through the use of the number twelve, where the establishment of a new Israel requires a new reading of the Old Testament.

The new Israel contains a new temple as well.[213] We have demonstrated in chapter 2 how Mark through the literary device of an intercalation transforms Jesus' cleansing of the temple into a narrative that proclaims the destruction of the temple.[214] For Mark "the Temple is not 'God's house' (11:17); it is merely the residence of the Jewish lead-

---

210. Bornkamm (*Jesus of Nazareth*, 150) turned the tide against the views of Bultmann (*Theology of the New Testament*, 31). For a list of scholars who deny that the twelve existed during Jesus' lifetime see Meier ("Circle of the Twelve," 635-72, especially 643, n. 22) and Bird (*Jesus and the Origins*, 33, n. 41).

211. Collins, *Mark*, 297.

212. In the OT Israel is represented by twelve loaves of bread (Lev 24:5), twelve pillars (Exod 24:4), twelve stones (Exod 28:21; Josh 4:3, 8, 9, 20; 1 Kgs 18:31), twelve staffs (Num 17:2,6), twelve dishes and twelve animal offerings (Num 7:84, 86, 87), twelve bulls (Ezra 8:35), and twelve pieces of garment (1 Kgs 11:30).

213. The Qumran sectarian community believed that in the new age God would create a new temple that would last forever (11QTa = 11Q19 29:6–10; Jub 1:17, 27, 29; 4Q Florilegium = 4Q174 1:1–7).

214. See section 2.5 above.

ers (14.49)."²¹⁵ In a similar manner Mark transforms the cursing of the fig tree from a dramatic act with a call to miracle faith (Matt 21:21) into a parabolic message to Israel about the demise of Jewish leadership and the destruction of the temple mount as the root of Jewish religious life (Mark 11:12–25).²¹⁶ Since the temple is already symbolically destroyed in Jesus' temple action, it is replaced by both the person of Jesus and the new community.

In place of the temple, in the new Israel Jesus becomes the presence of God among his people: "the stone the builders rejected has become the capstone" (Mark 12:10).²¹⁷ The fate of the temple and that of Jesus are tightly intertwined.²¹⁸ The three-day reconstruction of the new temple becomes the interval of Jesus' death and resurrection (14:58). Likewise, Mark places the rending of the temple curtain (15:38) alongside Jesus' final cry so that it exactly locates the terminus of a defunct system. Furthermore, the quote from Isaiah 56:7 ("My house will be called a house of prayer for all nations" Mark 11:17) combined with the tearing of the temple veil demonstrates that "Mark understands the cleansing of the temple as the abolition in principle of an institution which was restricted entirely to the Jews."²¹⁹ In Acts 22:17–21 Paul is praying in the temple when he receives his revelation of a mission to the Gentiles, but for Mark the Gentile mission is associated already with Jesus' actions destroying the physical temple since the Gentile centurion proclaims Jesus' identity immediately following the tearing of the temple veil. In Acts 6:14 Stephen, who for Luke becomes a paradigm of Jesus, is accused of proclaiming that "Jesus of Nazareth will destroy this place and change the customs Moses handed down to us." But Mark is unique among the Synoptic Gospels in his attempt to illustrate how Jesus himself changed the customs handed down by Moses.

The radicalism of Mark's temple theology is clearly visible in the Matthean and Lukan redaction of Mark's gospel. Unlike the Markan sandwich where the imminent destruction of the temple is interpreted in the light of the cursing of the fig tree (Mark 11:12–14, 20–21), Matthew reports Jesus healing the blind and lame in the temple (21:14) while the children shout "Hosanna" (21:15). Matthew 17:24–27 provides divine support for the temple institution since God miraculously supplies the children of the kingdom with the needed funds to pay the temple tax so as not to give offense.

Likewise, Luke maintains a positive attitude toward the temple as God's abode on earth²²⁰ so that the temple serves as an inclusio around the birth narrative (1:9;

---

215. Trocmé, *Formation of Mark*, 103.

216. Best, "Mark's Preservation of the Tradition," 160.

217. See Edwards, "Markan Sandwiches," 208.

218. Gray states, "the temple theme is so central to Mark's understanding of Jesus that he identifies the end of Jesus with the end of the temple" (*Temple in the Gospel*, 156). See Donahue, *Are you the Christ?* 137; Seeley, "Jesus' Temple Act," 274.

219. Schweizer, *Mark*, 233.

220. Acts 7:47 has been taken to imply a radical opposition against the temple, but see Dahl ("Abraham in Luke-Acts," 145) for arguments against this view.

2:41) as well as the entire gospel (1:9; 24:53). Jesus' ministry begins and ends in the temple so that immediately after his baptism one temptation occurs at the temple (4:9), and only in Luke are Jesus' last teachings in Jerusalem specified as taking place in the temple (21:37). Similarly, the Book of Acts opens with the church worshipping in the temple, and Paul's trial in Jerusalem is preceded by a contested entrance into the temple (Acts 21:26–29) just as Jesus' cleansing of the temple led to his trial (Mark 11:18). Luke, however, completely omits Mark 14:58 (Matt 26:61) and Mark 15:29 (Matt 27:40), which contain accusations and mockery about Jesus' negative attitude toward the temple in the Jewish trial and at the cross.[221] In a similar vein Luke completely eliminates Jesus' violent actions against the temple, such as the overturning of the tables of those selling doves and the closing of the temple by forbidding merchandize to be carried through its courts (Mark 11:15–16 vs. Luke 19:45). On the other hand, Mark describes the temple as "made with hands," an expression associated with a polemic against idolatry in the Old Testament (Isa 21:9; 31:7; 46:6; Lev 26:1 LXX; cf. Acts 7:48).[222] Therefore, at the Markan stage of the narrative χειροποίητος functions as a polemical indictment of the cult of the temple as idolatrous.[223] Whereas in Matthew and Luke the event is characterized as a temple cleansing, Mark describes the temple action as a prophetic act proclaiming the temple's demise.

Not only does Mark replace the temple with Jesus' resurrected body, but the Christian community becomes the location where the spiritual rituals of the former temple occur.[224] When Jesus commands his community to not doubt but believe that this mountain will be cast into the sea (Mark 11:23), the obedient faith of the Christian community removes the temple mount from its place at the center of religious life.[225] When Mark positions teaching about prayer and forgiveness after the temple action (11:24–25), these practices of piety replace the temple ceremonies.[226] As Gray asserts, "Jesus' sayings about faith, prayer, and forgiveness (11:22–25) which point out the key features that once gave the temple its unique identity are, for Mark's readers, features that are embodied by the Christian community."[227] Thus the counterpart of Jesus' negative action in overturning the tables in the temple becomes the positive feat of establishing another table, namely the rite of the Eucharist, at the Last Supper.[228] If Jesus is the chief cornerstone then the community constitutes the building stones.

---

221. Jesus' prediction of the destruction of the temple (Mark 13:2) is included in Luke 21:6, but this, of course, is the future event occurring in 70 CE.

222. Evans, "Jesus' Action," 248.

223. Evans, *Mark*, 446. The alternative, "made without hands" (ἀχειροποίητος) could be a term coined by Mark (Taylor, *Mark*, 566) or invented by an early Christian tradition (Brown, *Death*, I: 439).

224. See Geddert, *Watchwords*, 138.

225. See Smith, "Literary Structure," 123.

226. See Juel, *Messiah and Temple*, 135–36 and Loader, *Jesus' Attitude*, 104.

227. Gray adds, "This is the first hint in Mark's story that there will be a new temple" (*Temple in the Gospel*, 46).

228. Gray explains, "Read in light of Mark's strong antitemple polemic, the Last Supper is clearly

The house church therefore replaces the temple house. In Mark's gospel the new community frequently gathers by itself in a house, which becomes an opaque epigram to replace the synagogue.[229] Jesus and his disciples frequently withdraw to a house, which mirrors the later teaching in the house church (οἶκός 3:20; 5:38?; 7:17; 9:28; οἰκία 7: 24; 9:33; 10:10; 14:3). Through withdrawals from the busyness of ministry the disciples receive teaching applied to them alone (κατὰ μόνας 4:10; κατ' ἰδίαν 4:34; 6:31, 32; 9:2, 28; 13:3). Discipleship withdrawal is connected with almost every genre of literature which Mark employs including, miracle stories (5:37, 40b; 6:31–32; 7:24, 33; 8:23; 9:2, 28, 30–31), parables (4:10, 34; 7:17), controversy dialogues (10:10), and eschatological revelations (13:3), demonstrating the teaching implications of each of these genre. This teaching now occurs in the house church, where Jesus as the new temple dwells.

Interestingly, one of the first Markan surprises in the gospel is that a demon inhabits the synagogue (1:23).[230] Just as in his first synagogue appearance Jesus commands the demon to "be quiet and come out of him" (1:25), Mark employs this term for casting out demons when he cleanses the temple (11:15 ἐκβάλλω). Then immediately after leaving the synagogue, Jesus enters a house (1:29), the house of Simon and Andrew, in order to heal their mother-in-law. Burton Mack goes so far as to declare that the purpose of the healing of Peter's mother-in-law "is to set the contrast quickly between the synagogue where conflict will break out and the 'house' where healing and ministry takes place."[231] Although we doubt that Mark introduces a symbolic narrative within the first chapter of his gospel, certainly as the gospel proceeds the withdrawals into a house begin to symbolize the house church. The synagogue, on the other hand, becomes the place where Jesus is rejected by the Jewish leaders (3:1–6) and well as his own people (6:2ff) and where his disciples will be persecuted (13:9). Therefore, it would not be inappropriate to state that for Mark the house church replaces the synagogue.

A new temple demands new sacrifices as well. The only teacher of the law commended by Jesus concludes that "To love God with all your heart, with all your understanding and with all your strength, and to love your neighbor as yourself is more important than all burnt offerings and sacrifices" (12:33). In return Jesus comments, "You are not far from the kingdom of God" (12:34). What is the meaning of this strange exchange with Jesus' normal enemy?

This evaluative comment by the teacher of the law declares that love trumps sacrifice. Jesus' contemporaries understood the preeminence of love over sacrifice along

---

an alternative cultic action that subverts the need for the temple and its sacrifices" (*Temple in the Gospel*, 161).

229. See Best, *Following Jesus*, 227; Boring, *Mark*, 66; Malbon, *Narrative Space*, 118 and Miller, *Women in Mark's Gospel*, 125.

230. See section 5.5a above.

231. Mack, *Myth of Innocence*, 240.

the lines of the OT prophets.[232] In 1 Samuel 15:22 the prophet proclaims, "To obey is better than sacrifice, and to heed is better than the fat of rams." Isaiah 66:2–3 contrasts a humble and contrite spirit with the offering of sacrifices, while 1:13, 17 compares meaningless offerings and detestable incense with seeking justice and defending the cause of the marginalized.[233] More pointedly Hosea 6:6 contrasts love and sacrifice: "For I desire steadfast love and not sacrifice, the knowledge of God rather than burnt offerings" (NRSV). Possibly Jesus anticipated the termination of atonement sacrifices in the eschatological age similar to *Leviticus Rabbah* 9:7 (from Jer 33:11) which reads, "In the time to come all sacrifices will be annulled, but that of Thanksgiving will not be annulled."[234] More likely, this rabbinical reference evidences a later time, and Jesus was merely comparing the importance of love to sacrifices as he had compared ethical purity to ceremonial righteousness in Mark 7:15.

If this is Jesus' perception, how does Mark understand the scribe's statement about sacrifices? Again Mark inserts more radical content into Jesus' pronouncement. Judaism would have interpreted the love of God in such a way as to include the cult, but for Mark the love command being more important than sacrifices and burnt offerings (12:33) entails the fulfillment of the sacrificial system. According to the traditional Jewish understanding, God forgives sins on the basis of his commanded sacrifices and commissioned priests.[235] But now Mark purposely places this radical comment on the lips of a Jewish teacher of the law to proclaim that love is the only sacrifice now required. This kingdom insight of the scribe indicates that a rereading of the OT prescriptions for sacrifice is necessary. Mark's theology of the kingdom of God compares favorably with Paul's in Romans 14:17, where the kingdom is a matter of righteousness, peace, and joy in the Holy Spirit and does not involve food laws, Sabbath observance, and sacrifices. Just as the temple mount is thrown into the sea in Mark 11:23 and prayer and forgiveness become the new temple piety, so here the love command replaces sacrifices.

The more conservative Matthew and Luke again omit the scribe's application, indicating that this is not a consensus view in early Christianity.[236] Just as Matthew

---

232. See Keerankeri, *Love Command in Mark*, 171.

233. Likewise Ps 40:6 and Jer 6:19–20; 7:21–28 are comparable in theme to 1 Sam 15:22; Ps 51:16–17 with Isa 66:2–3; and Micah 6:6–8 and Amos 5:21–24 to Isa 1:13–17.

234. See Davies, *Torah in the Messianic Age*, 55.

235. Lohmeyer, *Lord of the Temple*, 26.

236. In Luke's comparable dialogue the scribe offers the pronouncement saying (10:27) instead of Jesus, but there is no comparison of the love command with sacrifices. In Acts 21:16 Luke emphasizes that Paul took part in sacrificial worship. Furnish (*Love Command*, 37–38) offers details of Lukan redaction. For a different emphasis in Matthew see Furnish, *Love Command*, 30. Bornkamm ("Das Doppelgebot der Liebe," 92–93) contends that Matthew and Luke knew an older version of this anecdote that lacked Mark 12:32–34 since 1) they both identify the questioner as a νομικός (lawyer) rather than a γραμματεύς (scribe); 2) the purpose of the incident is to test Jesus so that a friendly conversation is not presupposed; and 3) differences include the omission of the Shema and the second dialogical interchange. Collins more properly maintains that, "the agreement against Mark can easily be explained

and Luke omit Mark 2:27 with regard to the Sabbath and 7:19b with regard to food laws, so here the exclusion of 12:33 demonstrates a fear that this verse could be understood in the wrong way and alienate advocates of Jewish Christianity. Jesus vigorously demands a reverential attitude towards the temple and altar in 23:16–22 and speaks positively about sacrificial worship in 5:23–24.[237] Alternatively, Mark places upon the lips of Jesus (12:34) an agreement with the Jewish scribe that the kingdom of God does not primarily involve burnt offerings and sacrifice. Therefore, this passage would have been particularly effective in instructing Gentile readers how to interpret the OT passages about the necessity of sacrifices. Mark's negative attitude toward the physical temple and sacrificial worship indicates the fulfillment of this legislation.

Contrary arguments suggesting that Mark does not advocate the annulment of sacrifices can all be countered. Trocmè concludes that "Mark relates the incident without the slightest reservation regarding the value of these rites"[238] since 1) instead of a negative stance Mark demonstrates an indifference to the sacrificial cult which is nothing unusual to primitive Christianity; 2) the saying takes up the theme of the Hebrew prophets whose indignation was directed against the unworthiness of the people who offered the sacrifices, not the practice itself; 3) Mark demonstrates a positive attitude towards the rules regarding showbread (2:26), the offerings prescribed in Leviticus 14:1–32 for the leper (1:44), and the placement of monetary offerings in the boxes at the temple which contributed toward the sacrificial system (12:41–44); and 4) "there is nothing in the account of the cleansing of the Temple to make one suppose that Jesus was attacking either physically or verbally the cult of sacrifice itself." Instead, Isaiah 56:7, which Jesus partially quotes in Mark 11:17, mentions the burnt offerings and sacrifices that the foreigners will offer when Yahweh invites them into his house of prayer.[239]

Regarding arguments 1 and 4 above, Trocme inconsistently advocates a negative view on the part of Mark toward the physical temple but a positive theology of sacrifice. He contends that while Mark fails to hold out any hope for the temple, he nonetheless visualizes the sacrificial system positively. Since the splendor (13:1–2) and the material organization of the temple (11:15–16) are suspect according to Trocmè,[240] would not this result in a sacrifical system that is suspect as well? Certainly

---

as coincidental, independent editing on the part of Matthew and Luke," and the omissions indicate that "neither may have understood Mark's purpose in portraying the scribe positively, so they both transformed the anecdote into the more common controversy-dialogue and, in the process, shortened Mark's version" (*Mark*, 571).

237. Jeremias, *NT Theology*, 207. The vocabulary of the sacrificial cult is only used rarely by Mark whereas Matthew employs θυσιαστήριον 6 times (none in Mark), προσφέρω 3–4 times in a ritual sense (only Mark 1:44), δῶρόν 9 times (only Mark 7:11 to translate κορβᾶν), and θυσία with two quotes from Hos 6:6.

238. Trocmè, *Formation of Mark*, 102.

239. Ibid., 102–3.

240. Ibid., 104.

the overturning of the tables of those selling doves (11:15) is consistent with a negative attitude toward sacrifice. Furthermore, the quotation from Isaiah 56:7b calls attention to prayer rather than sacrifices as well as the inclusion of Gentiles within the covenant. Therefore, Mark purposely omits the context of this passage (Isa 56:7a) that speaks about burnt offerings and sacrifices.[241] Finally, the unusual length of the scribe's statement (forty-six words), where he even repeats Jesus' words, demonstrates that Mark is calling special attention to this part of the dialogue. Mark's evaluation of sacrifices goes beyond the traditional understanding that sacrifices must be accompanied with the correct heart attitude; for Mark this practice is fulfilled by Jesus' kingdom words.

Regarding argument 2, we have demonstrated how Mark takes a more radical stance than Jesus by consistently advocating a fulfillment agenda to Jewish ceremonies. Since Mark places the radical statement about sacrifices on the lips of a supportive Jewish teacher of the law, Mark is not directing his attack against the unworthiness of the people but against the sacrificial system itself.

Finally regarding argument 3 above, we will argue in a later section of this chapter that Mark 1:44 should be interpreted as a negative attack upon the priesthood, who see themselves as the guaranteers of purity, whereas in reality only Jesus through his kingdom acts of healing can declare someone clean. In addition, 2:26 does not emphasize Jesus' positive attitude toward the regulations regarding showbread but instead highlights the situations of human need that override the ceremonial system. Finally, Jesus' admiration for the widow's contribution to the temple offering functions as a call to radical discipleship for Mark rather than as a defense of temple devotion. In the very next passage (13:2) Jesus predicts the destruction of the temple. Therefore Mark's gospel does not advocate a positive attitude toward sacrifices.

In conclusion, the call and commission of a new Israel by the Markan Jesus (3:14) entails the arrival of the eschatological age with the destruction of the physical temple (11:23; 14:58), an inclusion of the Gentiles (11:17), and an internalization and ethicalization of the sacrificial system evidenced by faith, prayer, forgiveness (11:22, 24–25), and the practice of the love command in the new community (12:33). Mark employs the stories of Jesus to demonstrate how his preaching and kingdom actions establish a new way of reading the OT ceremonial regulations. So far we have discovered how Mark reconstrues the food laws, Sabbath rituals, and the sacrificial system. Now we will summarize how he reinterprets the purity regulations concerning contact with menstruating women, corpses, lepers, and the use of spittle.

---

241. Isa 56:7a says, "Their burnt offerings and sacrifices will be accepted on my altar."

8.6 An Unclean Menstruating Woman and an Unclean Dead Girl (5:21–43)

Since we have already established the unique importance of Mark's use of the literary device of intercalation in chapter 2,[242] here we will merely indicate how those results fit into the theme of this chapter on Jewish ceremonial rituals and their fulfillment in the teaching and kingdom actions of Jesus. We will outline the various proposals suggesting Mark's purpose in constructing an intercalation and conclude that Mark's literary device offers a theological perspective on the cleanliness rites demanded after contact with menstruating women or dead bodies. Just as the Markan sandwich of the cursing of the fig tree circling the temple action demonstrates that the season for a physical temple is over (11:13) and that the fig tree of Israel has withered from its roots (i.e., its temple leadership), so the intercalation of two unclean situations which Jesus heals indicates that the OT legislation regarding menstruating women and touching corpses has been fulfilled.

The theological nature of the other intercalations proves that "the evangelist did not combine the two stories merely to delay Jesus' arrival at Jairus's house so that a sufficiently plausible amount of time could pass."[243] Suspense is created but Mark has more in mind. In place of such an interpretation Collins suggests that the purpose of the sandwich is "to illustrate for Jairus and the audience, what kind of faith or trust Jesus is advocating." In arriving at this conclusion Collins refuses to admit that the number twelve in the narrative carries any symbolic significance.[244] However, we have argued above that a reference to the number twelve as with the twelve disciples reveals that Mark is speaking some symbolic truth about Israel. Here he wants the healing of a hemorrhaging woman with menorrhagia[245] and contact with a dead body to mirror the OT ceremonial regulations, so that the new Israel can discern that cleanliness comes from Jesus and not in maintaining the Jewish rituals. Admittedly, this passage is advocating a response of trust since both women are saved (5:23, 28) through their faith (5:34, 36). But what is the content of the faith? It is a faith in Jesus whereby purity is imparted by his kingdom actions rather than observing the required ceremonial actions.

Since Jesus is the central character in each story, certainly a christological emphasis is prominent as throughout the entire gospel. Cotter narrows this christological emphasis to stress the character of Jesus: "his intense kindness to these women, his sensitivity, and his unfailing benevolence."[246] However, Jesus' character qualities are

---

242. See section 2.3 above.

243. Collins, *Mark*, 284.

244. See Collins, *Mark*, 286; and Schweizer, *Mark*, 120. In section 2.3 above we argued against Christopher Marshall's evidence for an emphasis on faith as the crucial theme.

245. For a medical description of the woman's disease see Derrett, "Mark's Technique," 475–76.

246. Cotter, "Mark's Hero," 78.

seldom mentioned and certainly not consistently emphasized by the gospel writers. For instance, Twelftree explains that "in the first three healing stories Jesus is depicted as being compassionate toward outsiders" but only Mark 1:41 mentions σπλαγχνίζομαι while it is completely omitted by Luke and Matthew in the healing of the leper.[247] Mark 8:2 speaks of compassion before the feeding of the four thousand, but again Luke omits it, although he employs the word uniquely at Luke 7:13 with the widow of Nain. Matthew 14:14; 20:34; and 9:35-36 all speak of the compassion of Jesus in his miracle ministry, although the parallel verse to Matthew 14:14, Mark 6:34, connects Jesus' compassion with teaching. Based upon this inconsistent emphasis upon Jesus' character quality of compassion, Richardson comments that "If we examine the miracle-stories of the Gospels, we find few references to the compassion of Jesus, and we do not receive the impression that those stories have been included in the tradition because of the Evangelists' interest in the motives of the Lord."[248] This evidence rebuts Cotter's conclusion that Mark's purpose is to call attention to Jesus' character. Since the passage highlights the power that emits from Jesus' person (5:30), Jesus' authority is emphasized as in the previous contexts where Jesus is pictured as the lord over nature (4:35-41), demonic forces (5:1-20), as well as disease and death (5:21-43). So Christology is central to Mark, but not the motives of Jesus. Yet Christology does not explain the presence of a Markan sandwich in 5:21-43.

Instead of the literary interpretation emphasizing the production of suspense in the narrative, the teaching-of-faith function, or a christological emphasis, others propose a social interpretation which identifies the two women with the marginalized of society since they are both women and unclean. However, contact with the marginalized and disenfranchised is more a Lukan theme than a Markan topic. The emphasis upon touching in the narrative, a term employed four times in 5:27-31, indicates that the uncleanness of two Jewish characters is Mark's emphasis.[249] The social prejudice raised by the women's impurity traces back primarily to a religious issue. As Wainwright exclaims, "Each of the females who enters this combined story is encountered as a pollutant, outside the boundaries of ritual cleanliness."[250] Mark is

---

247. Twelftree, *Jesus, the Miracle Worker*, 95.

248. Richardson, *Miracle Stories*, 32-33.

249. The purity issue was already recognized by Tertullian in *Marc.* 4:20 (cf. Selvidge, *Woman, Cult, and Miracle Recital*, 20-21) and John Chrysostom in *Hom.* Matt 31:1-2 (cf. Kahl, "Jairus und die verlorenen Töchter Israels," 62, n. 4).

250. Wainwright, "Gospel of Matthew," 650. Levine ("Discharging Responsibility") offers a feisty rebuttal of these claims contending that 1) uncleanness is never mentioned (74), 2) it is not clear that the woman's bleeding is vaginal since nothing is said about the location of the hemorrhage (75); 3) it is not clear that Mark had Levitical legislation in mind (75); 4) the invoking of uncleanness is an overreading of the text (76), and 5) these conclusions are premised on overdrawn stereotypes of Judaism and women (77). However, Levine's contentions are not convincing for an interpretation of Mark (she writes about Matthew) and probably controlled by her polemic against a supersessionist theology (71) and against any tendency to connect women with issues of sexuality. However, she is correct that impurity is not a concern of Matthew since he omits the age of the dead girl and organizes the

not highlighting the characters in the story but rather the issue of how one becomes clean. Just as Mark reforms his audience's view regarding Jewish food laws, Sabbath observance, temple piety, and sacrificial rites, so he advocates a new reading of the Old Testament with regard to contact with menstruating women and corpses. The mention of Jairus as a leader of the synagogue as well as the mirroring use of the number twelve in the narrative introduces purity themes central to Judaism.[251] Through this miracle Jairus as leader of the synagogue should have learned for all of Israel that Jesus supplies purity, not the OT formal rites. By touching a bleeding woman and a dead girl, the Markan Jesus ignores and thereby dismisses purity codes.

Mark chooses phraseology in Jesus' contact with the bleeding woman that mirrors relevant passages in Leviticus (Mark 5:25 with Lev 15:19 and Mark 5:29 with Lev 12:7 LXX).[252] Especially important to the Markan context is Leviticus 15:19, "When a woman has her regular flow of blood, the impurity of her monthly period will last seven days, and anyone who touches her will be unclean till evening."[253] Thus the reader expects the healing of this woman by touch to result in a state of uncleanness for Jesus, but instead the woman becomes clean.[254]

Similarly, the touching of a corpse produces impurity as evidenced by Leviticus 22:4; Numbers 5:2; 6:6, 11; 9:6-7, 10; 19:11-22; 31:19-24.[255] In fact, Tomson makes the case that "the strongest source of impurity is a human corpse" since the wait-

---

healings together in chapters 8–9 in three cycles of triple healings followed by calls to discipleship. So her conclusion that "Matthew does not abrogate the laws of physical purity any more than the dietary regulations" (77) is exegetically supportable. Haber (*They Shall Purify Themselves*, 125–26) demonstrates that this discussion illustrates a debate in feminist hermeneutics. The early feminist interpretation contended that the woman's impurity was fundamental to the interpretation of the narrative (Selvidge, Wainwright), but more recently feminists dismiss it as an issue (D'Angelo, Fonrobert, Kahl, and Levine for Matthew). Haber supports a so-called middle position in which the woman's health is the central issue but where impurity is inextricably connected to her physical condition. Kazen (*Jesus and Purity Halakhah*, 132–33, n. 241) exemplifies how the different interpretations stem from possible anti-Jewish implications of exegesis. Interpretations amenable to a contemporary worldview have hindered an historical recovering of the issues in the text.

251. Cotter contends that "a linkage of the stories to introduce a conflict over Torah is not coherent with this evangelist" since "Mark himself shows that he is quite ignorant of Jewish Scripture and customs" ("Mark's Hero," 56). These conclusions should be refuted since each of the confrontations in Mark 2:1—3:6, for instance, involves conflicts over the law, and Mark is filled with controversy dialogues (see Mack, *Myth of Innocence*, 379–84 for a chart). Cotter is controlled by her minority assumption that Mark is a Gentile, and so she spends the entire essay examining Hellenistic background.

252. See Selvidge (*Woman, Cult, and Miracle*, 48–51) for a lengthy but exaggerated list.

253. Cf. Niddah 7:4; Zabim 5:1, 6; 11Q Temple 45:7–17; 46:16–18; 48:14–17; Josephus *Ant.* 3:261. Repugnance for menstruating women is found in Ezek 36:17; CD 4:12—5:17; 11QTemple 48:15–17; Josephus *Bell* 5:227; Zabim 4:1.

254. Weissenrieder contends that "Jesus was not risking contamination by being touched by the hemorrhaging woman, since the Levitical text in question distinguishes between contamination of people and objects when referring to irregularly menstruating women," but this strict distinction does not hold weight ("Plague of Uncleanness?" 210).

255. The suggestion of Loader (*Jesus' Attitude*, 61, n. 118) that Mark's comment that the girl was only sleeping actually removes any sense of impurity falters at understanding a metaphor literally.

ing period after such a ceremonial impurity is seven days.[256] In fact, this type of contact is entitled the "'father of fathers of impurity' in the rabbinic system, since it contaminated persons and vessels with a seven-day impurity, not only by touch, but even by overshadowing."[257]

In this Markan sandwich three different Greek words are employed to describe this human contact: ἐπιτίθημι in 5:23 and κρατέω (grasping her hand) in 5:41 with regard to the twelve-year-old girl and ἅπτω in 5:27, 28, 30, 31 for the woman sick for twelve years.[258] Mark employs these terms interchangeably throughout his gospel.[259] In miracle stories these terms originally connote a healing technique, but as in the other passages discussed in this chapter Mark uniquely adds the dimension of uncleanness.[260] The touching combined with a symbolic employment of the number twelve to refer to Israel and the reference to a leader of the synagogue reveals that Mark is mirroring the OT legislation concerning uncleanness.[261] The question "Who touched me?" in 5:30 surprises the disciples (5:31) since the crowd is pressing upon Jesus, but the reader who knows that the woman is unclean is surprised additionally by the fact that Jesus allows himself to become unclean. Finally, the issue of impurity is raised with Jesus' order to offer the young girl something to eat. On the surface level this proves that she is physically whole, but for Mark this signifies in addition that she is ritually whole and able to enjoy social contact.[262] In contrast with Mark's emphasis, the issue of impurity is not raised in Luke 7:14 when Jesus touches the coffin[263] of a dead person, since no intercalation is included to tie the event with another issue of impurity. Instead Luke employs the narrative simply as a miracle story proclaiming the greatness of the healer, as is evident by the response of awe and praise (7:16) missing in the Markan account. This is the difference between Mark and Luke.

---

256. Tomson, *If This Be from Heaven*, 95. The seriousness of such uncleanness is magnified by Ohalot 1:1, "A man who touches the corpse is unclean with the uncleanness of seven [days], and a man who touches him is unclean with the uncleanness [that passes at] evening" (Neusner, *Mishnah*, 950).

257. Kazen, *Jesus and Purity Halakhah*, 164–65.

258. For a complete analysis of the words for touching in Mark see section 8.7 below.

259. ἅπτω in 1:41; 3:10; 5:27, 28, 30, 31; 6:56; 7:33; 8:22; ἐπιτίθημι in 5:23; 6:5; 7:32; 8:23, 25; 16:18, and grasping the hand (κρατέω) in 5:41; 1:31; 9:27.

260. Cf. Evans, "Who Touched Me?" 368.

261. The church fathers go too far in their symbolic interpretations so that an anachronistic allegorization results. In their homilies both Jerome and Peter Chrysologus use this passage polemically interpreting the women with the flow of blood and Jairus' daughter as types of the church and the synagogue respectively (Jerome, *Homily* 77 and Chrysologus, *Sermon* 36; see Collins, *Mark*, 106, n. 45 for details).

262. Malina and Rohrbaugh (*Social-Science Commentary*, 209–10) argue that by addressing the woman as a family member ("daughter" 5:34), Jesus demonstrates that the social ostracism caused by her disease has been overcome.

263. "In the rabbinic system, the bier would count as a rinsable vessel, transmitting a seven-day impurity, just like the body (m. Oha 1:1–3)," as Kazen notes (*Jesus and Purity Halakhah*, 176).

Mark places the fulfillment of the OT ritual legislation upon the lips of Jesus.[264] The radicalism of these claims is indicated by the more conservative attitude that Matthew and Luke take toward the law.[265] In omitting the age of the girl as twelve and her father as a leader of the synagogue, Matthew loses a crucial element of the intercalation, demonstrating that he does not perceive the deeper meaning of Mark's text. Similarly, Luke envisions the OT ceremonial regulations continuing for Jewish Christians. Luke 11:44 assumes that the laws of ritual uncleanness regarding dead bodies still apply so that hidden graves do truly defile those in contact with them. Luke 16:17, "It is easier for heaven and earth to disappear than for the least stroke of a pen to drop out of the Law," clearly advocates the continuing significance of the law whereas the parallel in Mathewt 5:18 posits a time when heaven and earth will disappear and everything will be accomplished. For Luke the law was delivered by angels (Acts 7:53) and consisted in "living words" which are perpetually valid (Acts 7:38).

Not only does Luke not repeat specific passages from Mark's text that emphasize discontinuity with the OT legislation, but he chooses alternative narratives that stress continuity with the old. Instead of Mark 7:1–23, which takes a controversy about handwashing and transforms the narrative into a proclamation that all foods are clean, Luke adds an introduction to the woes against the scribes and Pharisees (Luke 11:42–52) where Jesus himself, not the disciples (Mark 7:2), neglects to wash his hands (Luke 11:38). The conclusion of the discussion is not a declaration about OT food laws but rather an exhortation favoring almsgiving, an important Lukan emphasis upon the poor (Luke 11:41, "But give what is inside the dish to the poor, and everything will be clean for you"). Instead of a discussion about kosher foods by Jesus (Mark 7:19b), Luke reports the vision of Peter in Acts 10 and applies the message to the acceptance of Gentiles into the community. Instead of an intercalation between the temple cleansing and the cursing of the fig tree (expected at Luke 19:45), Luke tells the parable of the fig tree (Luke 13:6–8), which omits a declaration of judgment against the temple and Judaism but instead emphasizes a period of grace ("leave it alone for one more year and I'll dig around it and fertilize it"). Instead of the marriage and divorce controversy where Jesus asserts that Moses' command was changed because of their hardness of heart (Mark 10:5), Luke chooses the Q passage (16:18), which does not mention any change from the creation ordinance in the Mosaic legislation. Finally, Luke leaves out Jesus' trip to Tyre and Sidon and the discussion with the Syrophoenician woman (Mark 7:24–30), the healing of the deaf mute in the Decapolis along with the feeding of the four thousand (Mark 7:31—8:9), and the mentioning of the Gentile city of Caesarea Philippi (Mark 8:27) with Peter's confession in order to separate the

---

264. Kazen rightly makes this distinction: "While Mark may intend his readers to see Jesus as giving up Jewish law . . ., it is difficult to imagine the historical Jesus as consciously proclaiming Christian theology through accidentally being touched by an unclean person" (*Jesus and Purity Halakhah*, 133, n. 241).

265. Cf. ibid., 174.

mission to the Jews from that of the Gentiles. In this way the restored Israel is established first, to which then the Gentiles can become attached as evident in the Book of Acts. These separate missions indicate that Jewish Christians must maintain the OT ceremonial regulations, while Gentile Christians only follow the apostolic decree of Acts 15. Through these means Luke maintains a conservative attitude toward the law. This purposeful redaction by Matthew and Luke sharpens our contention that Mark employs an intercalation of the bleeding woman and the dead girl to address the issue of ceremonial purity and the fulfillment of OT regulations. Through this literary device Mark reveals to the reader that he is offering a theological interpretation of the event for the Christian church.

In summary, this intercalation is a multidimensional narrative: 1) a medical healing story where Jesus' power overcomes disease; 2) a resurrection story where the sting of death is taken away for a leader of the synagogue's daughter through faith; 3) a social healing story where a disenfranchised woman is welcomed back into mainline society; but uniquely 4) also a religious story where Jesus' kingdom action demonstrates that he alone brings purity and not the Jewish ceremonial rites of avoidance of hemorrhaging women and corpses.

8.7 An Unclean Leper (1:40–45)

In chapter 3 we demonstrated how this passage along with 3:7–12 serve as a literary frame around the controversy dialogues of 2:1—3:6 to demonstrate to the early church that the kingdom of God is hidden in struggle and conflict. In chapter 5 we concentrated on how Mark employs the literary device of narrative surprises to indicate that he has added theological motifs to an original miracle story. Now we will demonstrate how Mark employs Jewish ceremonial mirroring to clarify that the OT legislation against contact with lepers has been abolished through Jesus' kingdom miracles.

Mark introduces the ceremonial uncleanness caused by leprosy in Jesus' healing of the leper in 1:40–45. Skin diseases resulted in ostracism from social relations.[266] According to Leviticus 13:45–46 the infected leper must live alone outside the camp and call out "unclean, unclean" to avoid any personal contact. Even after Miriam is healed of leprosy, she must remain outside the camp for seven days. Josephus explains that Moses took this uncleanness very seriously so that "such as either touch them, or live under the same roof with them, should be esteemed unclean" (*C. Ap.* 1:281). Therefore Elisha avoids contact with the leper whom he heals in 2 Kings 5:1–14. In fact, touching a leper was the equivalent of contamination by a corpse (Josephus *Ant.* 3:264). Therefore, by touching the leper Jesus recognized that he would be ceremonial unclean as well. Ironically, instead of Jesus becoming unclean the leper is cleansed.

---

266. In addition to the scriptures see 11Q Temple 45:17–18 from the Qumran writings and b. Nid. 64b from rabbinical literature.

Touching produces contamination. Therefore, we must investigate how Mark employs the various terms for touching, grasping, or laying on of hands in his gospel. Mark utilizes the following vocabulary.

A. Laying hands on someone: ἐπιτίθημι

1. Jairus pleads with Jesus to lay hands on his dying daughter (5:23).
2. Jesus places his hands on a few sick people in Nazareth (6:5).
3. People beg Jesus to lay his hands on a deaf-mute (7:32).
4. Jesus places his hands on a blind man along with spitting on his eyes (8:23).

B. Touching: ἅπτω[267]

1. Jesus touches the unclean leper (1:41).
2. Those with diseases were pushing forward to touch Jesus (3:10).
3. The woman with a blood disorder touches Jesus (5:27, 28, 30, 31).
4. The people beg to touch even the edge of Jesus' cloak (6:56).
5. Jesus spits and touches a deaf-mute's tongue (7:33).
6. The people beg Jesus to touch a blind man (8:22).
7. Jesus touches the children in order to bless them (10:13).

C. To use one's hands to establish close contact: κρατέω

1. Jesus takes the hand of Peter's mother-in-law with a fever (1:31).
2. Jesus takes the hand of a dead girl (5:41).
3. Jesus grasps the epileptic by his hand and lifts him to his feet (9:27).
4. In other passages the term is used to seize someone with force (3:21; 12:12; 14:1, 44, 46, 49, 51) or to cling to or observe (7:3, 4, 8; 9:10).

From the examples of general healing procedures above (3:10; 6:5, 56), we can deduce that the concept of touching is primarily connected with the genre of miracle story.[268] So how can one determine if Mark contains an added emphasis upon ceremonial uncleanness? We have argued throughout that Mark employs literary devices like intercalations, frames, and narrative surprises to demonstrate when he is attempting to say something theological beyond the literal level. In the narrative of the healing of the leper Mark employs all of these devices since it is the first time that he mirrors OT ceremonial regulations through a healing narrative. Before this, as in

---

267. Additional references in Luke link touching both with the impurity of contact with a sinner (Luke 7:39) and as a healing technique (7:14; 22:51) while Matthew adds references only to a healing technique (20:34; 17:7 healing fear). Luke employs the term in another sense for lighting a fire or lamp as well (Luke 8:16; 11:33; 15:8; Acts 28:2).

268. The symbolic act of the laying on of hands involves passing on a blessing only in Mark 10:16 (Matt 19:13, 15). Other biblical references include Acts 6:6; 8:17, 19; 9:17; 13:3; 19:6; 1 Tim 5:22.

the healing of Peter's mother-in-law, Mark is merely exhibiting the miracle ministry of Jesus.[269] The following section will provide evidence that Mark intends the story as more than just a healing narrative.

Mark has transformed the healing of the leper into a complicated bundle of diverse motifs. The original miracle story can still be viewed in 1:40–42, 44b–45.[270] The traditional elements include: 1) an account of the sick person's medical history and encounter with the healer (1:40); 2) the details of the therapeutic action (1:41–42); 3) proofs for the success of the therapy (44b); and 4) a response of acclaim and renown from the audience (1:45). The story follows the healing of Peter's mother-in-law in 1:29–34 and bears a similar structure.[271]

Elements in a healing story	1:29–34	1:40–45
1) Description of the illness,	Peter's mother-in-law has a fever.	A man has leprosy
including a request for healing	They told him about her	He says, "If you are willing, you can make me clean."
2) The healing touch,	He grasped her hand and raised her up.	Jesus touched the man. "I am willing; Be clean!"
which accomplishes the cure	The fever left her.	Immediately the leprosy left.
3) Demonstration of the cure	She began serving them.	Go to the priest for confirmation of the healing.
4) The audience's response	The whole town gathered at the door for more healing.	The leper spread the news and people came from everywhere.

However, 1:43–44a interrupts the normal progression of a healing story and ultimately changes the intention of the whole narrative. When the leper approaches in humility ("begged him on his knees") with faith ("you can make me clean"), Jesus

---

269. Concerning Peter's mother-in-law, Wainwright argues that "Jesus' simple action in reaching out and touching her breaks open the boundaries that defined 'clean' and 'unclean,'" since lying in bed and sick with a fever "is a possible pollutant especially if this sickness is connected to her time of ritual uncleanness" ("Gospel of Matthew," 648). However, Jesus first ministry campaign contains paradigmatic examples of his full-orbed ministry including discipleship making, teaching, deliverance, healing, and prayer. For instance, Mark does not call attention to the healing occurring on the Sabbath. The healing of the leper begins Mark's examples of mirroring.

270. Taylor explains, "The Miracle-story proper seems to end with 42, followed perhaps by 45, and 43f has the appearance of a Pronouncement-story on the question of obedience to the Law, a matter of great interest to Jewish-Christian communities" (*Mark*, 185). Cotter (*Christ of the Miracle Stories*, 23) offers in Greek and English what she thinks is the original pre-Markan story.

271. Marcus (*Mark 1–8*, 207) thinks that the healing of the leper could have originally belonged to the Capernaum day section and formed a triad of exorcistic-like healings. Then each may have ended with a section on the spread of the mission: a) 1:21–26: the exorcism of a demon in the synagogue resulting in amazement (1:27) and increased mission (1:28); b) 1:29–31: the fever excised from Peter's mother-in-law with an increased mission in 1:32–39; c) 1:40–42: the cleansing of a leper with the spread of the mission in 1:43–45. But we have argued for Markan frames in 1:14–15, 39 and also around the five controversy dialogues of 2:1—3:6 as seen in section 3.4 above.

gazes with compassion upon him. However, suddenly in 1:43 Jesus is described as ἐμβριμησάμενος, a word which expresses a range of negative sentiments from "storm at, scold, or even be angry at."²⁷² Originally a physical gesture accompanied this attitude, such as "rapid breathing out between the teeth"²⁷³ or a "snort" or "puff" like a disturbed horse,²⁷⁴ so that several exegetes prefer the translation "growling."²⁷⁵ Attached to Jesus' growling is the surprising action of driving the leper away. This term ἐκβάλλω is regularly employed by Mark to describe the casting out of demons (1:32, 39; 3:15, 22, 23; 6:13; 7:26; 9:18, 28, 38).²⁷⁶ How should the reader understand this "unexplainable note of harshness on Jesus' part,"²⁷⁷ this dramatic switch from compassion to growling, from a healing touch to a forceful dismissal?

Uncomfortable with this disturbing change in the narrative, many commentators choose to harmonize these expressions by interpreting both 1:41 and 43 either positively or negatively. Gundry interprets both ἐμβριμησάμενος αὐτῷ and ἐξέβαλεν positively, "not to express displeasure but to emphasize the forcefulness of the thrusting out and of the instructions which accompany it."²⁷⁸ Therefore Jesus is calling attention to the urgent need to sacrifice at the temple and to receive the priest's approval to enter society again.²⁷⁹ But this distorts the natural meaning of these terms and fails to parallel these descriptions with the leper's failure to carry out Jesus' command.

More popular is the substitution of the variant "indignant" (ὀργισθείς) for "moved with compassion" (σπλαγχνισθείς) in 1:41 to provide a consistent negative interpretation.²⁸⁰ Then throughout the passage Jesus is angry that the demonic evil of leprosy has devoured the human community. But the external evidence for ὀργισθείς is very weak with only one uncial and a few early Latin documents favoring it (D a ff2 r1* Ephraem). Furthermore, the Western text when standing along is extremely suspect and "is our most eloquent witness to the fact that the early church could and did alter

---

272. Bonner, "Traces of Thaumaturgic Technique," 178. Upbraiding because of disgust is evident in Mark 14:6 and anger is expressed in the LXX at Lam 2:6; Dan 11:30. For the use of the expression in John 11 see Matthew Black, *Aramaic Approach*, 240–43.

273. Bishop, *Jesus of Palestine*, 89–90.

274. Cf. Guelich, *Mark 1—8:26*, 72 and Rawlinson, *Mark*, 21 who quote Aeschylus, *Thebes*, 461.

275. Kee, "Aretalogy and Gospel," 418, n. 123 which Gundry follows throughout his commentary.

276. Cf. Van der Loos, *Miracles of Jesus*, 486.

277. Guelich, *Mark 1—8:26*, 74.

278. Gundry, *Mark*, 96. Gundry's grammatical arguments on pages 96–97 are more appropriate examples of Markan style rather than evidence for a positive interpretation.

279. Similarly, Stein interprets ἐμβριμησάμενος as being deeply moved similar to John 11:33, 38 so that the leper feels "an urgent need to seek the priest" (*Mark*, 107).

280. The TNIV is the first major English translation to accept this variant and translate the verse "Jesus was indignant," although commentators have favored this interpretation for a long time. Among others see Boring, *Mark*, 70–71; Cave, "Leper, Mark 1:40–45," 246; Cranfield, *Mark*, 92; Guelich, *Mark 1:8–26*, 74; Hooker, *St. Mark*, 79; Lake, "ΕΜΒΡΙΜΗΣΑΜΕΝΟΣ and ΌΡΓΙΣΘΕΙΣ," 197; Lightfoot, *Mark*, 25–26; Nineham, *Mark*, 86; Rawlinson, *Mark*, 21; Schweizer, *Mark*, 58; Taylor, *Mark*, 187; Turner, "Textual Commentary," 157; Wojciechowski, "Touching of the Leper," 114.

the transmitted sayings of Jesus."[281] The prominent expert D. C. Parker concludes that the main characteristic of Codex Bezae "is its lack of definition, its freedom in transmission. It will have been too subject to change and to outside influence to have had a strong influence on other texts."[282] To support the reading "moved with compassion," we can do no better than quote the convincing evidence from Metzger's *Textual Commentary*:

> (1) The character of the external evidence in support of ὀργισθείς is less impressive than the diversity and character of evidence that supports σπλαγχνισθείς.
>
> (2) At least two other passages in Mark, which represent Jesus as angry (3.5) or indignant (10.14), have not prompted over-scrupulous copyists to make corrections.
>
> (3) It is possible that the reading ὀργισθείς either (*a*) was suggested by ἐμβριμησάμενος of ver. 43, or (*b*) arose from confusion between similar words in Aramaic (compare Syriac *ethraḥam*, "he had pity," with *ethra'em*, "he was enraged").[283]

Thus even though many commentators argue that this variant improves the flow of the text, another solution must be discovered. The clue comes when one realizes that the "Western" texts alter the original reading in two ways, either changing "compassionate" to "angry" to coordinate with Jesus' stern rebuke and angry dismissal or eliminating Mark 1:43 while keeping the reading "compassionate." Therefore the best explanation for the textual problems is a scribal attempt to eliminate a fickle Jesus and produce a consistent flow in the narrative. Thus the original reading must be σπλαγχνισθείς (compassionate).

If a textual change is not supported, maybe Mark incorporates two sources into one account. A common hypothesis states that Mark combined the healing account of a leper by touch (1:40–42, 44a, 45) with a parallel exorcism narrative of a spirit of leprosy (1:43, 44b). Marcus, for instance, states that "Mark's desire to emphasize the exorcistic aspect of the cure has apparently gotten the better of his quest for narrative coherence."[284] Then one account described Jesus moved with pity for the

---

281. Parker, *Codex Bezae*, 285. In the Synoptic gospels I researched 75 variants which have the sole support of D and its Latin comrades and none of them are placed in the NA27 text: Matt 3:17 (2x); 4:4; 5:32; 6:8, 10; 9:17, 34; 14:2, 3; 16:11; 23:34; 26:15; 27:1; Mark 1:6, 41; 2:25; 3:6; 6:39; 7:6; 9:42, 43; 10:23; 13:14, 33; 14:1 (2x); 14:21, 61, 65, 70, 71, 72; 15:8, 43; Luke 1:63; 2:4, 39, 42; 3:12; 6:14, 49; 7:14, 26, 44; 8:17, 27, 45; 9:8, 18, 23, 25, 26; 10:5, 22; 11:30, 46, 51; 12:2, 21; 13:20; 16:8, 9; 18:20; 19:24; 20:2, 31, 42; 21:2, 6, 31, 36; 22:24, 42; 24:15.

282. Ibid., 284. Again only D and a few old Latin manuscripts omit the "and" and the double negative.

283. Metzger, *Textual Commentary*, 65. Stahlin, ὀργή, *TDNT* 5:427, n. 326 explains the confusion as an interchange of gutturals (ḥeth and 'ayin; סערתא ethra'em = enraged and סחרתא ethraḥam = he has pity on) at an early stage in the tradition.

284. Marcus, *Mark 1–8*, 209. This theory seems to trace back to Lohmeyer, *Markus*, 44–46.

leper while the other recorded Jesus' "hot indignation against the leprous spirit which had produced the agonized urgency of the man's appeal."[285] In an exorcism context ἐμβριμησάμενος could then be taken as prophetic frenzy or pneumatic excitement.[286] Then 1:44b–45 would be a duplicate response to the healing with the exorcism account ending in the confirmation by the priest as a witness (1:44b) and the healing concluding with the mission witness of the leper so that people come to Jesus from everywhere (1:45).

Although this two-source theory is an attractive solution since the story remains a healing narrative throughout, it pictures Mark as a clumsy editor who cannot even smooth out differences in source material to create a coherent narrative.[287] Even a proponent of this theory such as Nineham admits that "the command to silence has been rather awkwardly combined with the instruction."[288] More seriously, the anger occurs at the wrong point in the story, after the man has been healed.[289] In addition, the object of Jesus' anger has become a person rather than the disease. The resulting grammatical peculiarities argue against this theory as Gundry perceptively points out: "He thrusts out the leper, not the leprosy which would require αὐτήν, 'it,' to agree in gender with λέπρα, 'leprosy,' nor the demon which would require αὐτόν to agree in gender with δαιμόνιον, 'demon.'"[290] Therefore again we can only conclude that another solution must be discovered.

Instead of attempting to reduce the narrative to the interweaving of miracle stories, we should recognize that 1:40–45 is a mixed form combining the miracle genre with Markan redaction similar to a conflict story.[291] Mark is preparing for the controversy dialogues of 2:1—3:6 by placing them within a frame to offer a theological interpretation of their significance. The sudden switch in Jesus' mood to growling irritation in 1:43 is a literary device that we have entitled a Markan narrative surprise. Mark purposely intrudes into the narrative an unforeseen element which clashes with traditional expectations in order to offer a theological evaluation for the reader. Therefore the coherence of the story gives way to Mark's special concerns. For instance, after being eyewitnesses to a powerful stilling of the storm the disciples are surprisingly

---

285. Nineham, *Mark*, 87. Kee thinks that "the verse makes perfect sense if ἐμβριμησάμενος is viewed as an alternate translation of g'r, the technical term for bringing a demon under control, and if what is expelled (αὐτῷ) is the demon that causes the disease rather than the man" ("Aretalogy and Gospel," 418).

286. Theissen, *Miracle Stories*, 57–58; cf. Bonner, "Traces of Thaumaturgic Technique," 171–78.

287. For a discussion whether Mark is just a clumsy writer or whether he purposefully creates "unevenness" by adding his redactive footnotes to the tradition, see section 1.3 above.

288. Nineham, *Mark*, 87.

289. Therefore, Meier concludes that "the expelling of the demon would take place after the man is emphatically said to be cured of the leprosy which makes this solution highly unlikely" (*Marginal Jew*, 749, n. 107).

290. Gundry, *Mark*, 103.

291. Cf. Broadhead, *Teaching with Authority*, 74–75.

fearful and faithless in 4:40. Likewise, in 6:52 Mark alters the traditional ending of awe to Jesus' epiphany of walking on the sea to negative fear and hardening of heart. Both of these changed endings to miracle stories offer a theological evaluation of the purpose of Jesus' miracle ministry, which continues into 8:17–21. In the third crossing of the sea narrative at 8:14 Mark states that the disciples forget to bring bread, but then suddenly changes his mind and states that they have one loaf. This narrative surprise reveals to the reader that Mark is speaking metaphorically and offering a theological perspective of the bread. Likewise, Jesus' negative reaction (ἐμβριμησάμενος) and subsequent act of thrusting the leper out (ἐξέβαλεν) transform a healing story into a conflict narrative at 1:40–45.[292] How does this insight alter our interpretation of this passage?

In a normal healing narrative the authentication from the priest that the leper was healed would provide confirmation to the outside world that a miracle had occurred. Therefore in Matthew's account (8:1–4), which is placed into two chapters of miracle stories and omits Jesus' emotions (both positive and negative), the journey to the priest must be interpreted as confirmation of the leper's healing.[293] But the intrusion of Jesus' anger and the casting out of the leper along with Mark's signature secrecy motif indicate that Mark is redacting the normal genre to prepare for the controversies of 2:1—3:6. The key to unlocking the meaning of this pericope is to realize where Mark positions Jesus' response of disgust in the narrative. The placing of Jesus' anger after the healing of the leper and before his brash dismissal to visit the priestly establishment indicates that Jesus' growling is not aimed at the leper or the demon harassing him or even the grip of evil upon the human condition, but at the Jewish leadership in Jerusalem. As Broadhead maintains, Jesus' negative response "creates a dramatic shift in the focus of the story and foreshadows the growing tension between Jesus and the religious leaders."[294]

After the healing of the leper, two disturbing concerns (ἐμβριμησάμενος) enter the Markan Jesus' mind: 1) will this healing label him as primarily a prophet with miraculous powers (instead of a suffering Messiah, which is Mark's concern) so that the crowds will overwhelm him and he will not have time to disciple his close followers (1:45b)?; and 2) will the priesthood recognize his authority and kingdom healing ministry or will they be distracted by superficial ceremonial regulations like his touch of the leper and consequent impurity and thus remain hard-hearted? Mark then addresses the first concern in 1:44a through the addition of the Messianic Secret and the

---

292. Taylor, *Mark*, 185.

293. Matthew places this healing found in Mark 1:40–45 immediately after the Sermon on the Mount (ahead of the healing of Peter's mother-in-law in Matt 8:14–17 / Mark 1:29–31) since he wants to tie the story with elements in the sermon describing Jesus' attitude toward the law. Matthew ends the passage (8:4) with Jesus fulfilling even the least of the commands of the law like Matt 5:17–19, but at the same time Jesus touches an unclean leper and therefore exemplifies the "but I tell you" of the six antitheses in 5:21–48. This displays a different agenda than Mark.

294. Broadhead, *Teaching with Authority*, 74.

second concern in 1:45a through narrating that the leper never journeyed to the priest but instead proclaimed the prominence of Jesus. The reader must assume here that Jesus is anticipating this meeting between the healed leper and the Jewish inquisitors before he verbally sends the leper away. Jesus knows that his touching of the leper will be seen as a purity violation on the part of the interpreters of Moses in Jerusalem. The issue at hand is whether Jesus and his followers or their Jewish opponents are faithful interpreters of the Mosaic tradition.[295] The additional elements that move the narrative beyond a miracle story point more to Jesus' relationship with the Jewish establishment than his contact with the leper as the purpose of the account.

In summary, the exegetical evidence that Mark transforms this healing narrative into a controversy about Jesus' right to represent Moses in interpreting the law includes the following:

1. Whereas normally Jesus would become unclean through touching a leper, instead the leper is cleansed. In the new kingdom age cleansing occurs through Jesus rather than through sacrifice at the temple and a priestly declaration of purity.[296] In fact, the employment of the term "be cleansed" (καθαρίσθητι) instead of "be healed" indicates that purity issues are central to this narrative.[297]

2. Mark's placing of Jesus' negative response (1:43) after the leper's healing (1:42) but prior to the command to travel to the priest (1:44b) indicates that Jesus' growling displeasure is aimed at the priestly establishment who are inadequately interpreting the law of Moses. This is Mark's consistent message throughout the gospel. Already at 1:4 John the Baptist has conferred God's forgiveness without the temple apparatus of priesthood and sacrifice. In 7:10 Jesus becomes the authoritative interpreter of the fifth commandment given through Moses rather than the Jewish leaders, who use Corban to nullify the Word of God (7:11–13). In 9:4, 5 at the transfiguration Moses is witnessing to Jesus. In 10:2–9 Jesus interprets Moses' command about marriage because the Jewish leadership through their hardness of heart have misunderstood the intention of Moses' legislation about a certificate of divorce.[298] Finally, in 12:19 the Sadducees do not represent Moses since they know neither the scriptures nor the power of God (12:24) even though they argue about the intricacies of levirate marriage. Therefore as Broadhead insists, Mark 1:44 "is a thoroughly negative, prophetic condemnation of the religious leaders of Israel."[299]

---

295. Hooker, *St. Mark*, 24–25.

296. Cf. Broadhead, *Teaching with Authority*, 74.

297. Boring states that "the man asks for 'cleansing' (not 'healing'), which will not only restore him physically but give him his life back by reinstating him in society" (*Mark*, 71).

298. Collins (*Mark*, 468) concludes that when Jesus says, "Therefore what God has joined together, let man not separate" (10:9), he is speaking about Moses in Deut 24:1. She is following Fraade, "Moses and the Commandments," 399–422.

299. Broadhead, "Witness of the Leper," 260.

3. Jesus' strong emotion in 1:43 about a possible upcoming confrontation between the leper and the Jewish priesthood parallels Jesus' foreknowledge of the judgments of the teachers of the law in 2:8 and foreshadows Jesus' anger and deep distress in 3:5 (μετ' ὀργῆς, συλλυπούμενος) over their hardness of heart. Therefore 1:44 "serves as the opening volley in this conflict."[300]

4. Mark constructs a narrative surprise through the contrast between Jesus' compassion in 1:41 and the rebuke and the expulsion of the leper like a demon in 1:43, indicating that he is speaking symbolically. Jesus' casting out of the leper (1:43 ἐξέβαλεν αὐτόν) parallels the Holy Spirit's sovereign driving of Jesus into the wilderness earlier in this chapter (1:12 αὐτὸν ἐκβάλλει).[301] Therefore, Jesus like the Spirit is driving the leper into the desert of trial, where he will be required to testify against the Jewish priesthood in favor of the authority of Jesus to interpret the regulations of Moses.

5. Mark employs the healing of the leper as a frame around five controversy dialogues (2:1—3:6), where Jesus is opposed by the religious leaders. Therefore, this story must be related to controversies with the Jewish establishment. The reference to a plot to kill Jesus occurs suspiciously early in the narrative (3:6) but is easily explainable if Mark intends to demonstrate that already in 1:44 Jesus is replacing the Jewish leadership as the authority in Israel.

6. The cleansed leper does not obey Jesus by journeying to the priest to confirm his purity. Instead he preaches the word (1:45), which means spreading the good news about Jesus and demonstrating that Jesus provides wholeness rather than the priesthood. The leper "is portrayed in post-Easter terms as a missionary of the Christian faith,"[302] meaning that the Christian is no longer obligated to observe the laws respecting the touching of lepers.

7. The grammar in the phrase εἰς μαρτύριον αὐτοῖς (1:44c) can mean to give a testimony against them (dative of disadvantage) as in 6:11 and possibly 13:9. Therefore, the Markan Jesus is testifying against the authority of the Jewish priests since he will replace them as the leader of Israel.

What are the objections to this viewpoint and can they be countered? Although several authors contend that Mark is totally unconscious of the problem of contact with a scale-diseased person,[303] Marcus points out that "the repetition in 'stretched out and touched' and the omission in the Greek of the pronoun 'him' make Jesus' act of touching the sufferer emphatic, and this emphasis is most easily explained by the

---

300. Ibid., 263.

301. The word is connected as well with conflicts between Jesus and the Jewish authorities in 11:15 (the driving out of merchants from the temple) and 12:8 (throwing out the wicked tenants from the vineyard).

302. Boring, *Mark*, 72.

303. For instance, Sariola, *Markus und das Gesetz*, 66–67.

man's impurity."³⁰⁴ The more profound objection is that by sending the leper to the priest Mark is indicating Jesus' support for the Jewish ceremonial regulations. Latourelle, for instance, points out that the visit to the priest is the normal conclusion of a healing story, where an "official attestation of the cure" bears witness to the full reality of a miracle.³⁰⁵ This fulfillment of the requirements of Leviticus 13–14 would then indicate Jesus fidelity to the law so that Moses becomes a witness to Jesus' actions.³⁰⁶ Consequently, Jesus' rebuke would be aimed at the leper and not the priesthood. For example, Loader explains Jesus' reaction as "anger at the man's blatant disregard of the norms of society" which "coheres with Jesus' stern instruction to the man to obey such laws and show himself to the priest."³⁰⁷ In this scenario Mark would be preparing for the controversy dialogues of 2:1—3:6 by presenting Jesus as Torah observant.³⁰⁸ But why would an author introduce controversies with the Jewish leadership by showing that he is not in controversy with the temple establishment, especially after cleansing the synagogue of demons?

Our position becomes more convincing when we view how the other gospel writers handle this pericope. Matthew's commentary on Mark deliberately omits the leper's response to Jesus (1:45) so that Jesus' command itself becomes the climax.³⁰⁹ Therefore, Matthew is attempting to clarify the narrative to demonstrate Jesus' submission to the OT law rather than the leper's disregard for confirming his healing through the priesthood and not offering the sacrifice Moses required.³¹⁰ Matthew purposely ignores the Markan ending because he emphasizes the church's continuity with OT regulations, whereas Mark emphasizes the new wineskins.³¹¹

Likewise, Luke 5:15 overlooks the fact that the leper disobeyed Jesus and "went out and began to talk freely" and instead calls attention to the positive appeal of Jesus' teaching and healing ministry just as a normal healing narrative concludes with the acclaim of the miracle worker.³¹² Luke like Matthew wants to highlight Jesus' obedient response to OT regulations. Luke 17:14 offers a second example where Jesus sends the

---

304. Marcus, *Mark 1–8*, 206.

305. Latourelle, *Miracles of Jesus*, 88. See also Schweizer, *Mark*, 58.

306. See Fuller, *Interpreting the Miracles*, 49–50.

307. Loader, *Jesus' Attitude*, 20. He adds on page 24 that "Mark obviously includes in his value system the need for official acts which enable reintegration of the leper within society."

308. Loader, *Jesus' Attitude*, 26, 28, 37. Boring states that Mark is "showing in advance Jesus' respect for law, temple, and priesthood" (*Mark*, 70), so that this passage is "a preemptive strike of the accusations to come" (72).

309. See Fuller, *Interpreting the Miracles*, 78.

310. The fact that there is no indication that the leper reported to the priest in Mark must lead to the supposition that the leper is surprisingly disobedient to Jesus as supported by Collins (*Mark*, 179), France (*Mark*, 120), Marcus (*Mark 1–8*, 210), Witherington (*Mark*, 104), etc.

311. As readers of all four gospels we should realize that both continuity and discontinuity or newness became important emphases for the Christian church.

312. Luke changes the subject to ὁ λόγος rather than the direct object τὸν λόγον so that "a report went out" which is the standard acclaim after a healing narrative.

healed lepers to the priest, thus demonstrating his faithfulness to the OT law. In fact, in Luke 17:12 the lepers stand at a distance to make their request of Jesus so that no contaminating contact occurs between Jesus and the lepers. However, the omission by Luke and Matthew of Mark's surprising alterations to a healing story indicate that Mark is developing an additional message beyond that of the historical Jesus. Jesus' touching of the leper, his disturbed response following the healing, and the surprise that the leper fails to report to the priest provide evidence that Mark employs the leper pericope for his own purpose to demonstrate that the OT purity laws about lepers have been fulfilled in Jesus' ministry.

This is confirmed if we rightly understand the phrase εἰς μαρτύριον αὐτοῖς in Mark 1:44. Most Bible versions simply translate it literally with the phrase "as a testimony to them." The leper would then be faithfully executing the law by receiving from the priesthood a testimony of his cleanness before entering back into society (Lev 13:2–44). However, αὐτοῖς can be interpreted as a dative of disadvantage ("a testimony against them") similar to the expression in 6:11 so that Jesus' disgust (1:43) is aimed at the priesthood.[313] Loader disagrees with this interpretation by arguing that "This presupposes a level of confrontation for which the narrative has not prepared the hearer."[314] At first glance it appears that Loader is correct that Mark has not prepared the reader for a confrontation with Judaism since the controversies begin in chapter 2. But already at 1:23 the devil has entered the Jewish synagogue, and at 1:22 Jesus' teaching is already contrasted with the teachers of the law. There Jesus' authoritative instruction replaces the synagogue teaching just as the coming of the kingdom to the leper replaces the cultic regulations about leprosy. Furthermore 1:40–45 functions as a frame around the controversy dialogues and therefore introduces the conflicts which will follow. Therefore in Mark the prepositional phrase εἰς μαρτύριον αὐτοῖς should be translated with a dative of disadvantage, as "damning evidence against the priests if they establish that a healing has taken place and accept the cleansing sacrifice but do not recognize the person and the power of the healer."[315]

Broadhead offers 1) grammatical, 2) linguistic, 3) structural, and 4) theological grounds for this thesis.[316] Grammatically, εἰς μαρτύριον αὐτοῖς in the LXX is usually understood in an adversative sense.[317] In controversies with the Jewish leaders Matthew employs μαρτυρεῖτε ἑαυτοῖς negatively, "to testify against themselves" (23:31).[318]

---

313. The fact that this expression can be translated both ways is clearly demonstrated by the diversity in English translations. The identical expression is almost universally translated "testimony to them" in Mark 1:44 but "testimony against them" in 6:11 (KJV; NKJV; NASB: RSV; NRSV; NIV; TNIV; NAB; NET; ESV; ISV).

314. Loader, *Jesus' Attitude*, 22.

315. Van der Loos, *Miracles of Jesus*, 489.

316. Broadhead, "Witness of the Leper," 260–64.

317. Deut 31:19 in A, 26; Josh 24:27; Job 16:9; Hos 2:12; Amos 1:11; Micah 1:2; 7:18; Zeph 3:8 and also the verbal form in Deut 4:26; 30:19; 31:18. See Cave, "Leper: Mark 1:40–45," 249.

318. See also Jas 5:3. For references from the book of Acts and Pauline literature which employ

Linguistically, Mark 6:11 must be interpreted as a witness against unbelieving Jews when the apostles shake off the dust of their feet as a testimony against them. Likewise, Mark 13:9 can be read negatively with the disciples witnessing against their persecutors.[319] Thus, the reading of 1:44 as negative prophetic witness against the priesthood is supported by a detailed and consistent plot structure throughout Mark.

Interpreters dispute whether the plural pronoun "them" (αὐτοῖς) in 1:44 refers to the priest (which is singular) or to the unmentioned audience in 1:45.[320] Originally in the oral tradition, when the story was purely a healing narrative, the testimony could have been to the crowds so that they offer acclaim to the healer.[321] But the plural is employed here to indicate the entire priestly establishment. Mark's surprising insertion of conflict language anticipates a polemic against the entire temple establishment over Jesus' authority to interpret the OT law code. Therefore, the struggle involves who has authority to interpret the OT regulations—the priesthood or Jesus.

Mark is not attempting to demonstrate that Jesus was faithful to the law of Moses by sending the leper to the priests, but revealing that Jesus has the authority to alter the OT legislation.[322] Just as Jesus as the eschatological messenger proclaims forgiveness of sins (2:10) in place of the temple authorities and sacrificial system, so Jesus replaces the priestly establishment as the one who proclaims the lepers clean. As the bridegroom of a new covenant (2:19), Jesus' presence subordinates the call to fast and maintain a distance from the impure to the joy of the eschatological meal, which even tax collectors and sinners attend (2:15). Similarly, the Son of Man is lord of the Sabbath (2:28) so that Jesus overturns the priority of ceremonial purity in favor of doing good on the Sabbath (2:27; 3:4). The narrative concluding the leper's healing (1:44b–45) prepares for this emphasis in the controversy dialogues. The Christian church can now read the Old Testament in a new way.

---

similar expressions to express the conflict between the Christian message and its opponents, see Broadhead, "Witness of the Leper," 262.

319. Mark 1:44; 6:11; and 13:9 all assume conflict with Jewish opposition. Whereas "against" is almost universally employed at Mark 6:11, only the KJV translates "as a testimony against them" in 13:9 even though the context develops a conflict between the disciples and their persecutors. Wallace (*Greek Grammar beyond the Basics*, 144) lists Mark 13:9 as a probable dative of disadvantage. Luke changes Mark 6:11 to ἐπ' αὐτούς (9:5), obviously interpreting the expression negatively, but leaves the dative off in 21:13 (Mark 13:9) so that it is difficult to discern Luke's view.

320. For instance, the RSV translates Luke 5:15 (and Mark 1:44) "for a proof to the people" and the Good News Bible "to prove to everyone that you are cured" (but the ISV has "as proof to the authorities").

321. Among others see Cranfield, *St. Mark*, 95; Klostermann, *Markusevangelium*, 24; Pesch, *Markusevangelium*, 1:146; and Taylor, *Mark*, 190. Luke 5:15 adds the plural "huge crowds" (ὄχλοι πολλοί) to the Markan description (1:45) so that the witness to αὐτοῖς could be understood as a positive confirmation of healing to the people as expected in a healing narrative without the intrusion of a controversy.

322. Budeshine states that the "healing of the leper itself constitutes an appropriation of the rights and powers of the priests and the Law" ("Jesus and the Disciples," 198).

8.8 Unclean Fluids (7:31–37)

This final example of Markan mirroring of Jewish ceremonial regulations is the most difficult to demonstrate and can only be accepted as a corollary of the other examples discussed above. In the healing of the deaf-mute in Mark 7:33 Jesus places his fingers in the man's ears and spits on his tongue. Spittle was employed foremost as a healing ointment in the ancient world. Pliny refers to spittle as a medical remedy ten times throughout his *Natural History*. An interesting parallel to this Markan passage is the comment that saliva can calm mental illness if placed behind the ear with one's finger (28,5,25).[323] Similar to Jesus' healing of the blind man in 8:22–26, Suetonius in his *Life of Vespasian* 7:2–3 narrates that "the god declared that Vespasian would restore the eyes, if he would spit on them."[324] Likewise, the remedy of spittle played a role in the battle between the Egyptian gods Horus and Seth. When Horus' eye became injured, spit was applied to heal his sight.[325] Specifically referring to Jewish background, Van der Los comments that

> In Judaism spittle was regarded as highly medicinal. Eye trouble was healed by spitting on the eye in question, and spittle from a man who had not broken his fast was considered to possess particularly great curative powers. It was very common to spit on the sick parts of the body when pronouncing conjurations, so as to drive out the demon who had ensconced himself in this sick part of the body.[326]

Therefore throughout ancient civilizations saliva was employed as a healing agent.[327]

Mark 7:31–37 is then basically a healing narrative as evidenced by the following:

1. The passage evidences the standard progression of steps in a normal healing narrative:

    a. The problem is reported with a group of people begging Jesus to heal the man as well as the gesture of taking the man aside by himself, demonstrating the difficulty of curing this disease (7:32).

    b. A description of the healing technique (7:33–35) including fingers in the

---

323. See Collins, *Mark*, 370 for references. Other ancient reports of spittle as a healing agent include Galen' report that saliva is a remedy for psoriasis (*On the Natural Faculties* 3:7 § 163) and the inscription at the shrine of Asclepius in Epidaurus which refers to a dog who healed a boy from Aegina with its tongue. See Collins, *Mark*, 371, n. 73.

324. See Collins, *Mark*, 371, n. 74 for the reference and other examples.

325. See Van der Loos, *Miracles of Jesus*, 307, n. 4. For other Egyptian examples see Hull, *Hellenistic Magic*, 76.

326. Van der Loos, *Miracles of Jesus*, 309. The term "bond of the tongue" could imply that a demon has control (see support in Collins, *Mark*, 372) and in Jesus' other healing of a deaf-mute boy, the disease is explicitly ascribed to a demon (9:17, 25).

327. For a discussion whether purity issues were in the foreground or background of Jewish miracle stories, see section 9.6 below.

ears, spitting upon the tongue, a gaze toward heaven, a deep sigh,[328] and the use of a foreign incantation (the Aramaic *Ephphatha*).[329]

    c. A proof or demonstration of the healing through the plain comment of the man and the fact that the more Jesus silences the crowd, the more loudly they declare his praises (7:35b–36).

    d. The amazement of the audience (7:37a) and their acclaim of the healer as evidenced by the crowd's chorus, "He has done everything well" (7:37b).

2. Jesus employs spit to heal both the deaf-mute here and the blind man in 8:22–26, which serves as a parallel narrative.

3. Spit was seen in ancient times as carrying the life-force of the individual.

But in addition to its use in miracle stories, spittle functions as a transmitter of defamation and impurity in Jewish circles. In fact, the Old Testament never advocates saliva as a healing technique. Instead spitting is employed as a means of vilification and mockery,[330] so that in Isaiah 50:6 spitting and mockery become a hendiadys. In the New Testament as well Jesus himself is spat upon as a sign of offense and insult (Matt 26:67; 27:30).

Leviticus 15:8 describes the effects of defiling spit: "If the man with the discharge spits on someone who is clean, that person must wash his clothes and bathe with water, and he will be unclean till evening." Contact with spittle produces similar consequences to that of leprosy as in Numbers 12:14, where Miriam is excluded from the camp because of impurity for seven days even though she has been healed, since "if her father had spit in her face, would she not have been in disgrace for seven days?" Furthermore, an anonymous opinion in the Talmud declares that spittle produces impurity (b. Nid. 55b), so that if saliva splashes on the clothes of a high priest he cannot perform his duties on the Day of Atonement (b. Yoma 47a; Niddah 33b).[331] In particular, people were not to spit on the temple mount or in the house of the Lord since it was equivalent to spitting God in the eye (b. Ber. 62b).[332]

With this background it is logical that Mark presents spittle with a negative connotation implying impurity.[333] In order to mirror OT regulations where spittle

---

328. Collins (*Mark*, 371) interprets the sighing as the drawing in of spiritual power rather than Hull's suggestion that the sighing is an imitation of the restoration of speech and of forcing out the in-dwelling demon (*Hellenistic Magic*, 84 from Menzies, *Earliest Gospel*, 159).

329. However, because these words are translated, they do not function as a secret spell. Cf. Kazen, *Jesus and Purity Halakhah*, 170.

330. See Job 30:10. Through spit those who refused to participate in Levirate marriages were defamed and insulted (Deut 25:9).

331. See further opinions in *b. Eru.* 99a; *Hag.* 23a; *Yoma* 47a.

332. See Preuss, *Biblical and Talmudic Medicine*, 86.

333. It seems that one should assume both a Hellenistic and Jewish background to this passage. Because the healing occurs in the Decapolis presumably among Gentiles, the Hellenistic background of spittle as a healing technique is primarily emphasized. But because Mark inserts 7:1–23 into the

produces impurity, Mark adds this emphasis to a traditional healing narrative as evidenced by the following:

1. The primary evidence centers on Markan redaction, which is evident in the insertion of 7:1–23 into the miracle catenae so that the sequence of topics for discussion becomes impure hands (7:1–13), kosher food (14–23), unclean people (24–30), and finally impure fluids (31–37). Through this insertion Mark's purposes become visible, namely that Jesus altered the food laws, the Jew/Gentile distinction, and the contamination by unclean fluids.

2. Mark consistently applies the dictum "new wine must be placed in new wineskins" to the Jewish ceremonial regulations of the Old Testament, including kosher food, Jew-Gentile relations, the temple and sacrificial system, Sabbath regulations, contact with dead bodies, menstruating women, and lepers, and now contact with impure fluids.

3. Just as Mark employs the parallel healing of the blind man (8:22–26) in a symbolic manner to speak about the blindness of Peter and the rest of the disciples (8:27–33), so he uses the deaf-mute man's healing to speak symbolically about Jewish impurity regulations.

4. Combined with the preceding story of the Gentile Syrophoenician women, "this loosing of deaf ears and silent tongues among the Gentiles provides a sharp contrast to the deafness and blindness exhibited by religious leaders (7:1–13)."[334]

5. If one admits that impurity plays a role in Mark 7:31–37, then we can understand both why Matthew and Luke omit it and why Mark believes it is important to his story. Matthew omits this passage along with the healing of the blind man with spittle (Mark 8:23) because he does not want to ascribe impure methods of healing to Jesus. Luke, on the other hand, excludes a healing that could easily be associated with magic since he repeatedly demonstrates that Christianity is more powerful than magic (Acts 8:18–24; 13:6–12; 16:16–18; 19:13–20; 28:4–6). Therefore, for a Jewish audience the spittle entailed impurity while for a Gentile audience saliva contained the connotation of magic. Mark, on the other hand, desired to demonstrate both the power of Jesus to a Gentile audience and clarify that the Jewish methods of causing impurity no longer applied to Christians because of Jesus' kingdom deeds.

From this data we conclude that Mark has again added a new symbolic dimension to the healing narratives.[335] Mark accomplishes this theological agenda through

---

context and because a rereading of the OT Jewish ceremonies is crucial in discerning the connection between unclean hands, food, people, and fluids (Mark 7:1–37), a Jewish background with saliva as ritually unclean is necessary as well.

334. Broadhead, *Teaching with Authority*, 143.

335. This type of symbolic or allegorical interpretation is completely different from the

intercalations, frames, narrative surprises, allusionary repetitions, and here though Jewish ceremonial mirroring. The Markan Jesus heals with spit to indicate that OT legislation about fluids causing impurity is no longer applicable in the new age because of the kingdom actions of Jesus.

8.9 Conclusions

In this concluding section we will summarize how Mark goes beyond Jesus in his interpretation of the Jewish ceremonial law to speak to the needs of the early church through Jesus' words and deeds. We have consistently observed that Jesus himself complies with Jewish regulations regarding food, purity rites, and Sabbath legislation but continually challenges the Pharisaic interpretations which formalized the law into outward regulations out of touch with human need. Jesus' attack on the Jewish establishment draws upon and intensifies the prophetic heritage in Israel. As a reformer Jesus attempts to penetrate to the heart and intention of the law and uncover its essence. On occasion this entails breaking boundaries of tradition so that as a result he faces opposition from the Jewish establishment. However, Jesus' quotations of Scripture within the controversies indicate that he was loyal to the law and observant of its regulations.

1. In justifying the breaking of the Sabbath for food-consumption purposes, Jesus appealed to the example of David in 1 Samuel 21:7 (Mark 2:25–26).

2. In criticizing Pharisaic divorce laws, Jesus appealed to God's original law in Genesis 1:27 and 2:24 (Mark 10:6, 8).

3. In reforming the temple system, Jesus appealed to traditional prophetic criticisms of Israel's cultic system in Isaiah 56:7 and Jeremiah 7:11 (Mark 11:17).

4. In commenting on the Pharisees' tradition of Corban, Jesus insisted on the primacy of one of the Ten Commandments, "honor your father and mother" (Mark 7:10), as well as Isaiah's critical remarks (Isa 29:13 LXX in Mark 7:6–7).

5. Jesus criticizes the priority given to sacrifices if the commandment to love God

---

allegorization of the fathers as, for instance, the writings of Gregory the Great (Hom. 2:1082) which report that 1) the deaf-mute symbolizes the human race with its physical and spiritual weaknesses; 2) touching the man is Jesus' incarnation; 3) taking the man aside from the crowd represents the spiritual life which is led aside from confused thoughts, disordered actions, and undisciplined talk; 4) the finger in the ears is the words of the Spirit since the finger of God represents the Spirit in Luke; 5) spit symbolizes the impartation of divine wisdom; 6) the groan is Jesus teaching us to sigh with heartfelt regret until the flesh is purged; and 7) the command to silence is allegorized as an indication that humility always comes before glory. See Cahill, *First Commentary*, 65, n. 14 and Collins, *Mark*, 108–9. The popular symbolic interpretation of the 19th century was to picture such gestures as fingers in the ears, spit touching the tongue, and sighs as "symbols of Christ's mercy, of his power, of his grace in awakening faith" (Hull, *Hellenistic Magic*, 73) as expressed in the commentaries of Lindsay, Gould, and Swete. But the Biblical tradition does not mention faith at this point in the narrative of Mark, and these techniques are not preparations for healing.

(Deut 6:4–5) and one's neighbor (Lev 19:18) is not given precedent (Mark 12:30–33).

6. Similar to the Jews of his day, Jesus enjoins the Ten Commandments on the rich young man who asked what was necessary to "inherit eternal life" (10:19).

However, at the same time as Jesus remains true to the Scriptures, he opposes the Pharisees because of their oral traditions.

1. Jesus polemicizes against human traditions (Mark 7:8–9, 13) like Corban and required handwashing before meals (Matt 15:20 is closer to Jesus' point of view than Mark 7:19b).

2. Whereas the Pharisees added 613 oral traditions to the law as a fence around it, Jesus' woes against the Pharisees oppose this increase in formal regulations (Matt 23; Luke 11:37–53).

3. Jesus heals on the Sabbath (Mark 3:1–5; Luke 13:10–17; 14:1–6; John 5:1–18; 9:14) and allows his disciples to pick heads of grain (Mark 2:23–28), which break the boundaries of tradition to demonstrate that human need takes priority over the letter of the law.

4. Jesus' command to leave the dead to bury your dead father (Luke 9:59–60) breaks sacred customs (Gen 25:9; Tob 4:3; 6:14; Aboth 1:2; Ber. 3:1) and a Pharisaic understanding of the fifth commandment.

5. Jesus' statement that fasting is unnecessary in the presence of the bridegroom (Mark 2:19) disregards the Pharisaic requirement of weekly fast days (Did 8:1), but not the biblical requirement to fast on the Day of Atonement.

6. Jesus flouts the separatist policy of the Pharisees (Lev 10:10) by eating with sinners (Mark 2:15–16).

7. Jesus forgiving sins (Mark 2:5) violates the Pharisaic interpretation that only God can forgive sins (Exod 34:6–7; Num 4:18–19; Ps 30:4; Isa 43:25; Micah 7:18 etc.), but demonstrates God's personal pastoral care toward a needy person.

8. Jesus condemns outward piety that establishes one's legalistic righteousness since the heart of the law is justice, mercy, faithfulness, and the love of God (Matt 23:23; Luke 11:42).

9. Jesus criticizes the Pharisees' oath-making since their regulations avoid God's principle of telling the whole truth (Matt 5:33–37; 23:16–22).

Jesus' alternative to the formalism of the Pharisees is essentially a reformist view that attempts to penetrate to the essence or intent of the law.

Mark believes that Jesus Christ has become the standard by which Israel's Scripture is fulfilled and understood correctly. He discerns in Jesus' sayings and kingdom miracles implications for the theology and behavior of the early church. Therefore,

Mark retells the healing narratives and infuses some of Jesus' logia with additional implications that mirror the struggles faced by the early church, specifically the four problems of a crucified messiah, a suffering community, the inclusion of Gentiles, and the reading of the Old Testament without the requirements of kosher food laws, sacrifice, and purity regulations. Therefore we can detect an overlay of Markan radicalism on Jesus' teaching about the law.

Jesus insisted upon a policy of including the marginalized within Israel and therefore redefined the meaning of Israel, but not by including Gentiles within the fold. Mark, however, through the narrative of the Syrophoenician woman demonstrates that faith in Jesus becomes the new entry point into the community for both Jews and Gentiles (7:24–30). Jesus proclaimed that ethical purity was more crucial than ceremonial spotlessness (7:1–23), but Mark insists that Jesus cancelled the food laws (7:19b) by stating that nothing coming from the outside can make anyone unclean (7:15). Jesus spoke in Semitic parallelism about the inability to patch an old garment with an unshrunk cloth or to place new wine in old wineskins, but Mark follows with the application that new wine must be placed in new wineskins (2:22), meaning that new institutions and ceremonies replace the old. Jesus emphasized that the Sabbath should be a positive experience of rest and doing good rather than legalistic restrictions that overlook human need. Mark, however, contends that Jesus' logia and actions imply a freedom of conscience in observing the Sabbath since "the Sabbath was made for man, not man for the Sabbath" (2:27). Human well-being moved Jesus to break the social taboos of touching lepers, menstruating women, and corpses, but Mark inserts new meaning into the healings through intercalations, frames, and narrative surprises so that the OT purity regulations regarding contact with unclean people no longer apply in the new dispensation. Whereas Jesus cleansed the temple, Mark through a sandwich with the cursing of the fig tree asserts that Jesus replaced the temple and initiated new acts of piety corresponding to OT sacrifice (11:23–25). Whereas Jesus placed prominence upon the motive for observing the law, namely love for God and neighbor, Mark has a Jewish scribe declare that the love command is more important than all burnt offerings (12:33), implying that sacrifices are abrogated in the kingdom of God.

Can we legitimately employ abolition vocabulary (e.g., revoked, abrogated, invalidated, replaced, supplanted, superseded) to describe Mark's perspective on OT ceremonial regulations? Yes, to some degree! Christians are not required to observe these OT ceremonial regulations. However, we should nuance this statement by confirming that Mark has in mind especially Gentile Christians. But this does not eliminate Jewish Christians entirely, who, following Paul's instruction, should become like one not possessing the law for the sake of the mission to the Gentiles (1 Cor 9:21). Mark promotes a theology akin to Paul where the OT legal requirements are *adiaphora*. Certainly Jewish Christians can continue to observe ceremonial purity, but these stipulations can never be employed to separate them from fellowship with the Gentiles. The Gentiles, on the other hand, should place communal unity before individual liberty and not offend Jewish Christians by their unlawful actions.

For many today, supersessionist language is anti-Semitic. However, this type of thinking explains historically the development of Christianity as a separate religion. There was much debate over these issues in the first century and diversity of opinion reigned until the temple and its sacrificial system were destroyed and Christianity became primarily a Gentile movement.[336] Rudolph contends that abrogation language is "anachronistic, for it disregards the validity of these laws for Jewish Christians" and therefore "fails to account for the widespread acceptance of the Apostolic Decree as a ruling that upheld two levels of obligation to the Torah."[337] Although this is true regarding Lukan theology, Mark and Paul walk down a different pathway. The purpose of Mark's radicalism is to enable Gentile Christians to read the Old Testament in a new manner. Therefore, Mark transforms Jesus' reformist position into a limited supersessionist view. Fowler writes about Mark that "Like a seaman jettisoning cargo in a storm, Mark undertook a thorough and severe critique of all things Jewish in his Christian heritage."[338] Sandmal adds that "So extreme is this denigration that it appears to suggest a disconnection between Christianity and the Judaism in which it was born."[339] However, it is important to distinguish this position from incipient Christian imperialism which destroys the ethnic particularity of the Jewish followers of Jesus. Sadly, that is what eventually happened in the later history of the church. For Mark the words and actions of Jesus are eschatological experiences that signify the arrival of the new age wherein the regulations of Scripture are fulfilled through the advent of the Messiah.

Many scholars contend that Mark cannot be exegeted in this fashion because he gives no indication of a symbolic interpretation of Jesus' words or miracles. But we have argued that Mark employs the literary devices of intercalation, frames, narrative surprises, allusionary repetitions, and various types of mirroring to unpack the implications of Jesus' words and actions for the problems faced by the early church.[340] In the final chapter we will review these literary devices and the theological issues that Mark addresses through them.

---

336. See Chilton and Neusner, *Judaism in the New Testament*, 111.

337. Rudolph, "Jesus and the Food Laws," 306.

338. Fowler, *Loaves and Fishes*, 182–83.

339. Sandmal, *Judaism and Christian Beginnings*, 351.

340. In addition, Camery-Hoggatt (*Irony in Mark's Gospel*, 180) inserts irony into this list, a topic we have addressed in Appendix 2. He concludes that "Mark's ironies express a crisis of loyalties between Christianity and traditional Judaism, at every point along the way calling into question those institutions and attitudes which oppose the emergence of this new and different expression of piety. A survey of the specific ironies would reveal challenges leveled against the institution of the temple, against an exclusivist posture toward the Gentiles, against any piety which rejects as unworthy the 'people of the land'—including tax-collectors and sinners, and against any brand of messianism which disregards or denies the necessity of suffering." These are the very issues that we have raised in our presentation.

9

Mark's Symbolic Use of Miracle Stories

In this work we have identified the following literary devices in the Gospel of Mark: intercalations, frames, allusionary repetitions, narrative surprises, temporal and geographical mirroring, and Jewish ceremonial mirroring.[1] We have argued that Mark employs these literary devices theologically to reveal to the reader when he adds extra symbolic content to the narratives. The following chart displays the particular literary devices that Mark employs in each miracle story or epiphany.[2]

9.1 Literary Devices Employed in the Markan Miracle Stories

1. 1:21–28	Exorcism in the synagogue	surprise, Jew/Gentile mirroring, ritual mirroring
2. 1:29–31	Peter's mother-in-law	none; used instead as the first miracle story
3. 1:40–45	The cleansing of the leper	frame, surprise, ritual mirroring
4. 2:1–12	The paralytic	none; used instead as the first controversy dialogue
5. 3:1–5	The man with a paralyzed hand	ritual mirroring
6. 4:35–41	Sea calming	frame, surprise, absence mirroring, Jew/Gentile mirroring, repetition

---

1. This is our concluding chapter where we will apply our results to Markan miracle stories. For conclusions about Mark's approach to the law and Jewish ceremonies see the conclusion of chapter 8. For conclusions on introductory matters regarding Mark's gospel turn to the end of chapter 6. For conclusions on Markan redaction of intercalations and an outline of the pre-Markan passion narrative, see the conclusion to chapter 2. For a description of possible oral sources Mark employed for controversy dialogues and miracles, see the ending of chapter 3. Finally, for an outline of the gospel see structure 12 and the ending of Appendix 4.

2. See Appendix 1 for a chart of each literary device, the passages that employ them, and the theological theme associated with each.

The Theological Intentions of Mark's Literary Devices

7. 5:1–20	The Gerasene demoniac	Jew/Gentile mirroring
8. 5:21–43	The bleeding woman and the dead girl	intercalation, surprise, ritual mirroring
9. 6:35–44	Feeding of the five thousand	Jew/Gentile mirroring, repetition
10. 6:45–52	The sea walking	surprise, absence mirroring, Jew/Gentile mirroring, repetition
11. 7:24–30	The Syrophoenician's daughter is healed	surprise, Jew/Gentile mirroring
12. 7:31–37	The healing of the deaf-mute	Jew/Gentile and ritual mirroring
13. 8:1–10	The feeding of the four thousand	surprise, Jew/Gentile mirroring, repetition
14. 8:11–21	The sea conversation	frame, surprise, absence mirroring
15. 8:22–26	Healing of the blind man	frame, surprise
16. 9:2–8	The Transfiguration	surprise
17. 9:14–29	Healing a boy with an evil spirit	surprise, absence mirroring
18. 10:46–52	Healing of blind Bartimaeus	frame, surprise
19. 11:12–14, 20	Cursing of the fig tree	intercalation, surprise, ritual mirroring
20. 16:1–8	The resurrection	surprise, absence mirroring

As evidenced by this extensive list, on many occasions Mark attaches literary devices to the normal genre of miracle story to instill a theological or symbolic emphasis. In fact, many of the miracles become very similar to Mark's concept of a parable. Mark employs parables as allegorical riddles that need explanation.[3] The allegorical application of the parable of the sower (4:3–9) in Mark 4:14–20 becomes the standard method to understand all of the Markan similitudes, as evidenced by his comment, "If you can't understand the meaning of this parable, how will you understand all the other parables?" (4:13 NLB).[4] The Markan phrase "to speak in parables" (12:1; 3:23; 4:2, 11) connotes speaking in allegorical riddles, as evidenced by the fact that only one parable is narrated in Mark 12 even though the plural is employed.[5] In addition, whereas Mark 4:11 employs the singular μυστήριον ("The secret of the kingdom of God has been given to you. But to those on the outside everything is said in parables"; i.e., riddles), Matthew and Luke amend the text to the plural (μυστήρια) since they interpret each type of the four soils as a separate secret. Thus "speaking in parables" becomes a loaded expression for Mark which means more than just telling stories but

---

3. Cf. Beasley-Murray, *Jesus and the Kingdom*, 105; Burkill, "Cryptology of Parables," 33–34; France, *Mark*, 188; Jeremias, *Parables of Jesus*, 16; Kelber, *Kingdom in Mark*, 32ff; Kermode, *Genesis of Secrecy*, 23–24; Marshall, *Faith as a Theme*, 60; Patten, "Form and Function," 255ff; Rhoads and Michie, *Mark as Story*, 55–56; Shiner, "Ambiguous Pronouncement," 18.

4. See Fowler, *Let the Reader Understand*, 183.

5. Matthew, however, understands the phrase as meaning more than one parable and so includes a series of three in Matt 21:28—22:14. Both Matt 12:25 and Luke 11:17 omit the phrase from Mark 3:23 by employing the Q wording instead. Luke 8:4 changes to the singular since he only includes the Parable of the Sower while Matthew recites many parables.

entails instead speaking at two levels. The following lengthy list of Markan parables illustrates the riddle quality of each. From this information we will demonstrate how Mark understands several of the miracles in a similar manner.[6]

9.2 Markan Parables as Allegorical Riddles (Puzzles Needing Interpretation)[7]

1. The parable of the seeds (4:3–9) becomes the paradigm parable which is interpreted as the parable of the soils (4:14–20).

    a. The seed on the path = Satan stealing any productivity.

    b. The rocky ground = trouble and persecution causing a short life of discipleship.

    c. The thorny ground = worries, wealth, and desires choking the word.

    d. The fruitful ground = those who hear the word, accept it, and produce a crop.

2. The parable of the lamp (4:21–22)

    a. The lamp = the parable (especially the Sower Parable which speaks of the Word).

    b. Put under a bowl or bed = hiding the interpretation of the parable and the kingdom.

    c. Put on a lampstand = understanding parables by explaining the riddle of their meaning in church through allegory.

3. The parable of the measure (4:24–25)

    a. The measure = the amount you give to other people will result in others being generous in return (applied to the judgment in Matt 7:2; Luke 6:38).

    b. The interpretation = those who regularly hear parables will receive the explanation.

4. The parable of the seed growing secretly in 4:26–29 (according to Joel Marcus)[8]

    a. Sowing (4:26) = the time of Jesus (nearness of the kingdom 1:14–15; 11:10; 12:34).

---

6. As Geddert reports, "Both the parables and the miracles of Jesus have meanings deeper than whatever appears at the surface of the empirical data" (*Watchwords*, 74).

7. Jesus probably deduced this method from Nathan's parable in 2 Sam 12:1–4 where the ewe lamb represents Bathsheba, the rich man equals David, and the poor man is Uriah.

8. Marcus (*Mystery of the Kingdom*, 198–99) supports allegory, but I am doubtful about his conclusions and believe this is the only parable that Mark does not make into an allegorical riddle. Instead the chiastic structure calls attention to the middle of the parable which emphasizes the automatic growth of the kingdom.

b. Growth (4:27–28) = the time of the church (the hidden presence of the kingdom 4:11; 10:14–15, 23–25) (Marcus does not specifically allegorize blade, ear, and full grain, but they could exhibit the gradual manifestation of the kingdom during the church age[9]).

   c. Reaping (4:29) = the *parousia* (the kingdom coming in power).

5. The parable of the mustard seed (4:30–32)

   a. A small mustard seed = the tiny church community.

   b. Largest of all the garden plants = the miracle growth of the kingdom.

   c. The birds perch in its shade = the Gentiles and nations of the earth will make their home with the church community (Ezek 31:6; 17:23; Dan 4:9, 18).

6. The parable of the unclean man (7:15) spoken to the crowd (7:14), with its application (interpretation) in a house (7:17) to the disciples (7:18–23)

   a. Explication of 7:15a ("nothing outside a man can make him unclean") in 7:18–19 = the solving of the riddle means that Jesus declares all foods clean.

   b. Explication of 7:15b ("what comes out of a man, that makes him unclean") in 7:20–23 = the solving of the riddle means identifying the twelve inner ethical character qualities that cause impurity.

7. The parable of the wicked tenants (12:1–12)

   a. The reference to Isaiah 5:1–2 identifies the vineyard as Israel. But in the context of Jesus' temple speeches, it more specifically becomes a metaphor for the temple.

   b. The tenants = the Jewish leaders.

   c. The servants = the prophets (like Heb 11:32–37).

   d. The slain son = Jesus (killed outside the vineyard in Matt 21:39 and Luke 20:15).

   e. The people to whom the vineyard is given = the church (although others contend it refers to the poor and marginalized in the *Sitz im Leben Jesu*).

8. The parable of the budding fig tree (13:28–29)

   a. This kingdom parable has become an eschatological parable: just as when the leaves sprout you know that summer is near, so when the signs of the kingdom occur you know that Jesus is coming soon.

   b. "The twigs getting tender and the leaves coming out" (13:28) represent "these things happening" (13:29), i.e., the signs of the times mentioned

---

9. Ibid, 194.

earlier in Mark 13.

   c. "Summer" (13:28) is interpreted as "the door" (13:29), applying the riddle to Jesus' glorious return.

9. The parable of the doorkeeper (13:33–36)

   a. The man going away (the owner of the house 13:35) = Jesus.

   b. His house with his servants in charge = the church.

   c. The one at the door to keep watch = the leaders of the church like Mark.

   d. The time of his coming becomes for Mark the hours of Jesus' passion so that the disciples must be ready to follow Jesus to the cross: evening = Mark 14:17–31; midnight = 14:32–14:52; the rooster crows = 14:53–72; dawn = 15:1ff.

   e. Comes suddenly = the *parousia*, so that the disciples are instructed not to be sleeping, which means not becoming lethargic in discipleship.

10. The parable of the strong man (3:27)

    a. The strong man = Satan.

    b. The stronger one who enters his house = Jesus.

    c. The carrying off of his possessions = Jesus' deliverance ministry.

9.3 Miracle Stories Become Acted Parables (Allegorical Riddles)[10]

Just as Mark envisions additional symbolic meaning in Jesus' parables, likewise he adds theological content to most of the miracle stories.[11] Mark's goal is to speak to the four struggles of the early church: 1) a crucified Messiah; 2) a discipleship of the cross; 3) the inclusion of Gentiles into the community; and 4) a new reading of the Old Testament envisioning the fulfillment of Jewish ceremonial rituals. We will provide at least one example of each.

---

10. Note the title of Blomberg's article, "The Miracles as Parables" in *Gospel Perspectives*, volume 6. Donahue employs the entire gospel as a parable in "Jesus as the Parable of God," and *Gospel as Parable*, 194–216. It is important to clarify what we do not mean by allegory. We agree with Boring that "The narrative is not a mystical allegory, but takes place in the everyday world: a road is a road and a boat is a boat. Yet, like the parables that begin in the everyday world and then point beyond themselves without being obvious about it, the narrative as a whole is charged with transcendent potential: 'Let the reader understand' (13:14)" (*Mark*, 38).

11. Some authors argue that miracles, like parables, only have one point—the historical wonder-working of Jesus. All the rest of the details are just to add color and details of reality as when Jesus lays on a cushion (4:38) with other boats in his caravan (4:36). However, we have demonstrated above that Jülicher's definition of parable does not apply to the Gospel of Mark, although it is true for Luke's gospel. The same can be said for many of Mark's miracles.

9.3a. Miracle Stories Illustrating Jesus as a Crucified Messiah with a Corresponding Discipleship of the Cross

9.3a1 The Second Touch Healing of the Blind Man (8:22–26)

Instead of leaving the two-stage healing of the blind man at Bethsaida in the miracle catenae of Mark 4:35—8:9, Mark places this story after Jesus' condemnation of the disciples' blindness (8:17–21) and before Peter's confession of faith to indicate the two-step process necessary to remove the blindness of the disciples. In addition, Mark employs this passage as a frame around the discipleship catechism (8:27—10:52) along with the healing of blind Bartimaeus, which also is transformed into a discipleship narrative.[12] Through this alteration of the order of the material and organizing technique, Mark transforms a miracle story into a symbolic discipleship narrative emphasizing following a crucified Jesus to the cross.

A. The blind man (8:22) represents the disciples, who are blind to the true identity of Jesus (8:28).

B. Jesus leads the blind man outside (8:23), indicating a private conversation about discipleship, just as Jesus takes the disciples off by themselves to the villages around Caesarea Philippi (8:27).

C. The blind man is healed but cannot see clearly so that people look like walking trees (8:24), and Peter makes the positive confession of Jesus' messiahship but then is rebuked by Jesus for his continued half-blindedness (8:29, 33).

D. The blind man needs a second touch (8:25a) just as Peter needs a second insight into Christology to see clearly that Jesus is a Suffering Servant Son of Man (8:31). The second touch becomes the acceptance of the implications of a Suffering Servant Messiah, which is taught throughout the discipleship catechism.

E. The blind man sees everything clearly (8:25b) just as Jesus now speaks plainly (8:32) and enlightens the disciples on the necessity of his journey to the cross (8:31) and their subsequent following in a discipleship of the cross (8:34).

9.3a2 Bartimaeus Following Jesus on the Way (10:46–52)

Through surprises in a healing narrative and a frame with the second touch healing of the blind man, Mark transforms this incident into a discipleship story where Bartimaeus recognizes the true nature of Jesus as both the Son of David and the suffering Messiah. The climatic conclusion highlights following Jesus along the way which entails for Mark a discipleship of the cross.[13]

---

12. See section 3.7.
13. See section 3.8.

A. The unique name Bartimaeus is a strange combination of Aramaic and Greek entailing that the son of the unclean one (the Aramaic) has become a son of honor (the Greek) since he recognizes a Jesus headed for Jerusalem and follows along the way.

B. The incident is not told at the arrival in the town (vs. Luke 18:35) when Jesus passes the gate where beggars usually sit but at Jesus' exit from Jericho (10:46) since Mark wants the reader to concentrate on Jesus' destination of Jerusalem and the newly enlightened beggar's following toward the cross.

C. Bartimaeus addresses Jesus on two occasions as Son of David (10:47–48), which parallels Peter's address of Messiah in the beginning of the discipleship catechism (8:27). But unlike Peter, Bartimaeus follows it with a confession of Jesus as the suffering Son of Man by following along the way (10:52b).

D. The call by Jesus (10:49) and Bartimaeus' gesture of "throwing his cloak aside" (10:50), just as the disciples left their nets to follow Jesus, transforms the narrative from a miracle story to a discipleship genre.

E. Following along the way (10:52b) means more than traveling down the road since it represents the way of discipleship, so that this term begins (8:27) and ends the discipleship catechism. Therefore, for the reader Bartimaeus replaces Peter as the true disciple who exhibits both a christological confession ("Son of David") and the appropriate response of following to the cross.

9.3a3 The Sea-Walking Journey (6:45–52)

The genre of miracle story was traditionally employed to present the wonders of a miracle worker. However, through the use of narrative surprises Mark transforms the trips across the sea to emphasize the additional themes of the absence of Jesus and the misunderstanding by the disciples of the place of miracles in God's plan. Similar to the disciples' struggle on the chaotic sea without Jesus in the boat, the community faces difficult times where it feels like their master has passed them by. But in reality Jesus will come miraculously to their aid. However, the disciples' hearts are hardened because they do not understand the loaves (6:52), i.e., that Jesus' power is manifested in his death where he miraculously feeds his people. The misunderstanding by the disciples grows throughout the three sea journeys (4:40; 6:52: 8:17–21), demonstrating that miracles alone are insufficient to provide for the needs of the community. The disciples must realize that following a crucified Jesus through the storm comes before a share in his resurrection glory. The sea-walking journey illustrates a narrative written at two levels like one of Mark's parables.

A. 6:45 Jesus compelling his disciples to enter the boat means that the difficult experiences the community is experiencing are all planned by God.

B. 6:46   Jesus praying upon a mountain = an absent Jesus in heaven praying for the struggling community similar to the sleeping Jesus of 4:38.

C. 6:48   Jesus sees the disciples struggling even though the middle of the lake is miles away = the divine oversight over the discipleship community in their struggles.

D. 6:47, 51 (4:36–37)   The boat = the community or the church (see the *Testament of Naphtali* 6).

E. 6:48a–b (4:37, 38b)   The storm at sea = chaos and the trials and persecution of the church.

F. 6:48c   Jesus passing by the boat seems on the surface as a lack of divine concern for the community (which mirrors the church's feelings), but at a deeper level Jesus passing by is a divine epiphany similar to those experienced by Moses (Exod 33:22) and Elijah (1 Kgs 19:11).

G. 6:50   "It is I" (ἐγώ εἰμι) = the manifestation of Yahweh through the divine name similar to Exodus 3.

H. 6:52   Fear and the inability to understand about the loaves, lack of faith (4:40) and hard-heartedness (8:17–21) = the failure to understand the symbolic meaning of the feeding of the five thousand, with its relationship to the Last Supper, demonstrating that miraculous provision comes through Jesus' passion and a discipleship of the cross.

9.3b Miracle Stories Illustrating the Inclusion of Gentiles into the Community

9.3b1 The Syrophoenician Woman (7:24–30)[14]

Mark inserts the controversies about unclean hands (7:1–13) and non-kosher food (7:14–23) before this healing. In this manner he transforms a miracle story into a discussion about the inclusion of Gentiles (unclean people) in the covenant community. The Markan surprises in the narrative confirm that the story has become a parable about table fellowship between Jews and Gentiles.[15] The request and bestowal of healing (7:26, 29–30) surround the more profound dialogue at the center of the pericope advocating a new Jew-Gentile relationship (7:27–28). Thus Mark transforms a miracle story into an allegorical riddle where the dogs represent Gentiles, children denote Jews, and bread symbolizes table fellowship. A Gentile's faith surprisingly calls forth an entirely new relationship between Jews and Gentiles.

---

14. Boring states, "That Mark is a two-level drama is nowhere more apparent, or more important in understanding the text, than in his narrative of the Syrophoenician woman's encounter with Jesus" (*Mark*, 206).

15. See section 5.5c.

Mark's Symbolic Use of Miracle Stories

- A. 7:24   Jesus alone in a house with his disciples entails that the reader should expect teaching on discipleship.
- B. 7:25–26   The presence of an evil spirit implies that the land needs to be cleansed or retaken as part of the Promised Land, that is, the Gentile land of Tyre and Sidon, which is the northern boundary of the land of Canaan.[16]
- C. 7:27   The children = the Israelites.
- D. 7:28   The dogs = the Gentiles.
- E. 7:28   The table = table fellowship between Jews and Gentiles through their faith.
- F. 7:27   The bread is not specified, but could be the gospel or more specifically Jesus himself, as in Mark 8:14 and the miraculous feedings of the five thousand and four thousand.

9.3b2 Healings of the Five Thousand and Four Thousand (6:35–44; 8:1–10)

The inclusion of Gentiles is also symbolically illustrated in the miraculous feedings.[17]

- A. The miraculous feeding = Jesus as bread (as seen in 14:22 and the one loaf of 8:14 as well as in Jesus' monologue in the fourth gospel at John 6:32–51).
- B. Twelve baskets left over (6:44; 8:19) = plenty of spiritual food remaining for Israel.
- C. Seven containers remaining (8:8, 20) = plenty left over for the Gentile nations of Canaan (Acts 13:19).
- D. The hardheartedness of the disciples (6:52; 8:17–21) = their inability to see the connection with the last supper since the real feeding miracle happens upon the cross.

9.3c. Miracle Stories Illustrating the Fulfillment of Jewish Ceremonial Rituals

9.3c1 The Cursing of the Fig Tree (11:12–14, 21–25)

Mark employs mostly controversy dialogues to speak to the struggles in the early church concerning the Old Testament purity rites as we demonstrated in chapter 8. However, the two intercalations that involve miracle stories[18] are also used to mirror Jewish institutions and ceremonies to enable the Gentile community to reinterpret the

---

16. See section 7.5.
17. See section 7.6.
18. See sections 2.3 and 2.5.

Old Testament. The cursing of the fig tree provides a theological window into Mark's theology of the temple in the same manner that the healings of the hemorrhaging woman and dead girl through Jesus' touching of unclean people mirror OT purity requirements.

A. The fig tree = Israel, or more specifically the temple, the primary institution of Israel, and the Jewish leadership, which controls the temple establishment.

B. Jesus is hungry (11:12) means that metaphorically Jesus is hungry for the righteous fruit produced by Israel.

C. The fig tree has nothing but leaves (11:13) signifies that Judaism looks fine from the outside but is fruitless in reality.

D. It is not the season for figs (11:13b) means that the time for Israel's fruit as well as the physical temple in Jerusalem is past; instead, it is time for the Christian community to present its produce of faith, prayer, and forgiveness (11:22–25) in a temple not made with hands.

E. The fig tree withered from its roots (11:20) = the withering of the Jewish leadership.

F. The mountain thrown into the sea (11:23) = the temple mount destroyed.

G. Faith, prayer, and forgiveness (11:22–25) = the sacrifices of the new temple made without hands.

9.3c2 The Healings of the Bleeding Woman and Dead Girl (5:21–43)

Mark employs the literary device of an intercalation to link two stories together which speak to Mark's readership about purity rites in Israel. Through Jesus' kingdom actions the menstruating woman and dead girl are healed and made clean indicating that Jesus is fulfilling the OT purity legislation and teaching the Christian community a new way of reading the ceremonial regulations.

A. The number twelve employed in both stories (5:25, 42) means that the narrative centers on Jewish concerns.

B. The bleeding woman mirrors OT purity rites that are required for hemorrhaging women.

C. The dead girl whose father is a leader of the synagogue (5:22) mirrors OT purity rites about contact with a corpse.

D. Healing by touch is first of all a curative technique, but Mark emphasizes the supplementary dimension of impurity through touch to recall OT purity legislation.

E. Jesus' healing of each indicates that in the kingdom age Jesus now provides purity so that the OT ceremonial regulations are now fulfilled.

From these examples we can perceive how Mark employs miracle stories as symbolic actions.[19] These miracle stories function as allegorical riddles similar to Markan parables.[20] Mark parallels the parable collection in 4:1–34 with a miracle collection in 4:35—8:9, which begins with the identical boat (4:36) that Jesus employed as a pulpit to teach the parables (4:1). Then immediately following the miracle catenae at 8:10–21, Mark employs a parallel flow of material to the parable of the sower and its interpretation (4:1–20) so that the explanation for miracles parallels the explanation for parables.[21] Furthermore, the thematic flow of the bread motif throughout the entire miracle catenae indicates that Mark is attempting to produce a cumulative symbolic effect.[22] As Camery-Hoggatt remarks, "All of them have to do with bread, and with defilement, and with the matter of Jewish legal piety . . . and point beyond themselves to a deeper level of significance."[23] But the most important signal that Mark employs to hint at symbolism are the literary devices of intercalations, frames, allusionary repetitions, narrative surprises, and various types of mirroring. The list beginning this chapter indicates the prevalence of these literary strategies within the miracle stories. But which miracles of Mark do not have symbolic significance?

9.4 Growth in the Symbolic Meaning of Miracles Stories in Mark's Narrative

Not all of Mark's miracle stories are used symbolically. Why not? Mark evidences different purposes for compiling the material throughout the gospel. Scholars view this progression of miracle stories in various ways. Glasswell, for example, states that "The first group of miracles in the gospel belong to a part of the gospel concerned with the christological question of Jesus' authority. . . . The nature and necessity of faith is the point of the next group of miracles beginning at 4:35. . . . The last miracle would seem also to have a parabolic meaning concerned with Jesus' authority because of its close connection in Mark with the cleansing of the temple."[24] Van Iersel explains that "The reader of Mark is able to read the first three chapters as a story about Jesus—and is able to remain confined to the *denotative* level of meaning. With chapter 4 the reader comes across a cluster of *signifiers* which indicates that certain passages in this chapter have meanings that cannot be grasped at first."[25] Likewise, Geddert

---

19. Theissen concludes that "Primitive Christian miracle stories are symbolic actions in which a new understanding of existence is opened up" (*Miracle Stories*, 287).

20. Marshall, *Faith as a Theme*, 60.

21. See section 4.3e.

22. See section 1.5.

23. Camery-Hoggatt, *Irony in Mark's Gospel*, 142–43.

24. Glasswell, "Use of Miracles," 156, 157, 159 respectively. See Latourelle (*Miracles of Jesus*, 249) for a different view of the progression emphasizing a change from Jesus' power to his weakness.

25. Van Iersel, "Reader of Mark," 91.

explains that "After 3.6 Jesus presents his teaching almost exclusively in parables with hidden meanings and miracles with hidden implications," while Stock remarks that Mark "moves from the miraculous to the kerygmatic."[26] Although they describe the progression differently, all agree that Mark inserts a more symbolic interpretation of miracles as the gospel progresses, especially when Mark places healing stories in the discipleship catechism of 8:27—10:52 after the miracle catenae have been concluded.

In the beginning ministry campaign of Jesus, Mark only intends to introduce the various aspects of Jesus' messianic ministry, including his kingdom preaching (1:14–15), discipleship calling (1:16–20), authoritative teaching (1:21–22), exorcisms (1:23–28), healing ministry (1:29–34), and prayer times (1:35–39). Here Mark introduces Jesus' theme of the kingdom of God and the authority that Jesus possesses as the harbinger of the kingdom. However, Mark does not bring to the surface possible symbolic images, such as the fact that the healing of Peter's mother in law occurs on the Sabbath[27] or the theme of touch, which is later employed to mirror the touching of impure objects. Just as the twelve disciples are presented first of all as model examples of those who instantly obey and sacrifice vocation and family for the kingdom of God, so the miracles initially are demonstrations of kingdom power. Later the disciples take on the additional overtone of symbolizing those who misunderstand the significance of Jesus ministry just as the miracles will produce misunderstanding and a lack of faith (4:41; 6:52; 8:17–21). Mark's purposes change as the gospel progresses.

9.5 Mark Envisions Additional Theological Meaning in Jesus' Actions

Therefore, as Mark proceeds he adds theological meaning to the miracle stories. However, scholars differ widely on their interpretation of the symbolism, with several authors rejecting all metaphorical explanations because of some outlandish proposals that overemphasize Markan subtlety.[28] But abuses of symbolism should not cause readers to return to the position that Jesus performs miracles only for their evidential value. Against a purely Christological interpretation of the symbolism, Glassford remarks, "The miracles are not appealed to directly as obvious proof of the claims made for Jesus in the work as a whole."[29] As an alternative motive for the miracle stories,

---

26. Geddert, *Watchwords*, 79 and Stock, *Call to Discipleship*, 147.

27. Therefore, Myers (*Say to this Mountain*, 15) reads too much into the narrative when he contends that Jesus' boundary breaking social stance is the emphasis since Peter's mother-in-law is the first woman to appear in Mark's narrative and her serving Jesus (like Mark 10:45) implies she is a prominent disciple of Jesus. Nor is Wainwright on target when she insists that "Jesus' simple action in reaching out and touching her breaks open the boundaries that defined 'clean' and 'unclean'" like the menstruating women later ("Gospel of Matthew," 648). Finally, we cannot accept the symbolic conclusion of Mack that "Its purpose is to set the contrast quickly between the synagogue where conflict will break out and the 'house' where healing and ministry takes place" (*Myth of Innocence*, 240).

28. Notice Gundry's immediate rejection of all symbolism on the first page of his commentary on Mark. We have offered examples that over-interpret the data in section 1.4 above.

29. Glasswell, "Use of Miracles," 154.

Kock points to the miracle authority[30] of Jesus to elicit faith in the reader. But Glasswell rightly replies that "They do not point to faith so much as represent truths about the nature of faith in Jesus."[31]

What is the nature of faith that Mark endeavors to express? Myers proclaims that Jesus emphasizes a boundary-breaking social action type of faith: "there is no case of healing and exorcism in Mark that does not also raise a larger question of social oppression."[32] Blomberg, on the other hand, emphasizes the eschatological dimension of faith: the miracles are "viewed as genuine, symbolic enactments of the dawning new age."[33] Certainly Mark has a multifaceted conception of miracles. He introduces Jesus as a miracle worker in the first chapter, and then in the miracle catenae (4:35—8:21) demonstrates the authority and power of Jesus over every enemy including sickness, hunger, demons, the sea, and death. The miracles become signs of the kingdom to proclaim the realized nature of the reign of God. These kingdom signs then elicit faith in the hearer.

But what is unique about the miracles in Mark? It is not their christological importance or the fact that they produce faith in the audience. At the climax of the miracle catenae after the disciples have witnessed two miraculous feedings and a sea calming and sea walking epiphany, they are still blind, deaf, hard-hearted, and dull of understanding (8:17–21). Apparently miracles cannot offer a complete picture of Jesus' identity. Mighty deeds do not bestow an unambiguous legitimization of Jesus. His identity and mission remain hidden in miracle working and only become comprehensible in his passion (14:62) and crucifixion (15:39).[34] Thus Mark constructs a frame around the discipleship catechism to preach to the community that they need a second touch to follow Jesus on the way to the cross. Mark also employs an allusionary repetition to indicate that the feedings of the five thousand and four thousand point toward the real feeding when Jesus offers himself in his crucified body as acted out in the Last Supper. Again Mark uses an intercalation to demonstrate that the temple is defunct and will only be rebuilt in a temple made without hands through Jesus' death and resurrection. Mark uniquely employs the miracles to call attention to two themes: a suffering Messiah and the concomitant call upon the community to a discipleship of the cross.

The Markan insertions into this miracle section also reinforce these peculiar emphases.[35] Mark inserts the rejection at Nazareth by Jesus' own people (6:1–6a)

---

30. Koch (*Bedeutung der Wundererzählungen*, 180) places the authority of Jesus at the head of ten messages which he contends the miracle stories convey.

31. Glasswell, "Use of Miracles," 154.

32. Myers, *Say to this Mountain*, 14.

33. Blomberg, "Miracles as Parables," 348.

34. See Koch, *Bedeutung der Wundererzählungen*, 185–86.

35. See section 3.7 above, where we demonstrate that Mark breaks up an original miracle catenae by moving the two-stage healing of the blind man to 8:22–26 and inserting material between its component parts at 6:1–31 and 6:53—7:23 to speak to the four themes the early church needed to

into the middle of the miracle catenae to create a new discipleship outline[36] whereby the reader is challenged to a resilient faith that overcomes persecution and rejection. Immediately the third cycle of discipleship begins (6:6b–13), where Jesus' followers take a more active part in Jesus' ministry by duplicating his message and work as they carry out their mission two by two with only spartan provisions. Meanwhile, Mark narrates the death of John the Baptizer through an intercalation that ties the death of John to the beginning of the ministry of the Twelve. Through allusionary repetition as well as intercalation Mark links the ministries and suffering of John the Baptizer, Jesus, and the disciples.[37] These Markan insertions as well as the transfer of the two-stage healing of the blind man to introduce the discipleship catechism at 8:22–26 reinforces Mark's two themes of a suffering Messiah and the call to a discipleship that overcomes rejection.

Mark also employs the geography of the miracle stories as well as the similar composition of the feeding narratives to emphasize that Jesus welcomed Gentiles into the kingdom of God.[38] In chapter 7 we argued that the original purpose of the double string of miracle stories contained in 4:35—8:9 was to proclaim a gospel that brought good news both to Jews and Gentiles. Mark maintains this emphasis in the miracle stories by returning to this theme in 8:19–20, where the twelve baskets from the feeding of the five thousand refer to Israel and the seven containers at the feeding of the four thousand apply to the Gentiles. In addition, at the center of the chiastic structures of the miracle catenae stand both a Jewish (5:25–34) and a Gentile woman (7:31–37) who experience unexpected fellowship as well as healing from Jesus. This message of the inclusion of the Gentiles into the community becomes the third theme that Mark wishes to convey through this symbolic use of miracles.

The other inserted material at 6:53—7:23 introduces the fourth major concern that is unique to Mark's gospel, i.e., the place of OT purity rituals in the life of the Christian church. First of all, Mark composes a new summary of Jesus' healing ministry in 6:53–56 to replace the healing of the blind man, which he moves to 8:22–26 to become a parabolic introduction to the discovery of Jesus' true identity in 8:27–34. This summary alters the geographical location from Gentile territory (Bethsaida 6:45) to the Jewish landscape of Gennesaret (6:53). Now Mark can introduce the Jewish ceremonial rites concerning unclean hands (7:1–13) and impure food (7:14–23) before the miracle stories that speak about unclean people (7:24–30, the Syrophoenician woman) and unclean fluids (7:31–37, the healing of the deaf-mute through spit). Through this procedure Mark proclaims that the requirement of washed hands is just a tradition of men (7:8) and the regulations about kosher food are now cancelled so that all foods are declared clean (7:19b). Jesus' kingdom words (7:15) have the

hear.

36. See the conclusion of Appendix 4.
37. See sections 4.6a and section 2.4.
38. See sections 7.4 and 7.6.

authority to fulfill OT ceremonial regulations. Thus the predominantly Gentile Christian community can read the Old Testament in a new manner through the coming of the eschatological Messiah.

Whereas this theme of the fulfillment of OT ceremonial regulations is addressed head on in 7:19b, in other locations Mark employs the literary devices of intercalation and narrative surprise. Mark sandwiches together the stories of the cursing of the fig tree and the temple action to signify the passing away of the temple establishment. Here Mark also utilizes narrative surprises to indicate the symbolic nature of the story through Jesus desiring fruit when it isn't the season for figs (11:13) and by describing the fig tree's withering from its roots (11:20) rather than through the normal wilting of leaves. Likewise, through interlocking the touch healings of a hemorrhaging woman and a dead girl (5:21–43), Jesus reverses the impurity that is caused by contact with a bleeding women and a corpse to indicate that these OT regulations are fulfilled. In the healing of the leper (1:40–45) Mark employs narrative surprises to demonstrate that Jesus now has the authority to proclaim a person pure rather than the priests.[39] Finally through the surprising answer of a teacher of the law, Mark reveals that burnt offerings and sacrifices are fulfilled by the love command (12:33–34). Therefore, Mark employs these literary devices to assign to Jesus all the answers to the problems that the early church faced. Jesus' miracle ministry and wise kingdom sayings contain the solutions which will solve all the community's problems.

9.6 Examples Favoring a Two-Level Approach to Mark[40]

One needs bifocals to appropriately read the Gospel of Mark. Whereas Jesus cleansed the temple, Mark envisions this prophetic action as an annulment of the physical temple and a replacement of its cultic rituals with faith, love, prayer, and forgiveness (11:22–25; 12:33). In contexts about purity issues Jesus primarily emphasizes the inward motivation of an action rather than conformity to formal restrictive rituals, but Mark himself sees in Jesus' kingdom teaching and miracles the fulfillment and therefore the cessation of various Jewish regulations.[41] For Mark, Jesus' logion in 7:15 does not just call attention to the importance of the inward motivation of the law but annuls the distinctions between kosher and unclean food (7:19b). For Jesus the Messianic Secret was a mission strategy to not create messianic hysteria (John 6:14–15) and to allow sufficient free time to train his disciples (Mark 1:45), but for Mark it becomes a theological tool to emphasize a proper Christology. Finally, Mark envisions

---

39. See section 8.7.
40. Boring asserts that "The narrative throughout is implicitly a two-level drama, which becomes evident in numerous specific scenes" (*Mark*, 7) referring to 4:35–41; 5:35–43; 6:2, 31–44, 45–52; 7:24–30; 8:3; 9:2–8; 10:2–12; 12:18–27; 16:5–8.
41. See the conclusion of section 8.9.

the anointing of Jesus in 14:3–9 not just as a holiday anointing with precious ointment but as a preparation for the Messiah's burial.

Mark overlays the proclamation of the gospel, which normally concentrates on the person and work of the hero Jesus, with the theme of discipleship. Mark constructs the trips across the sea to mirror the life of the community, which feels the absence of Jesus in their struggle with persecution. Mark mirrors the future ministry to the Gentiles in Jesus' trips to Gentile territory. Finally, he mirrors the OT ceremonial legislation in the healings of a leper, bleeding woman, and dead girl.[42] In the *Sitz im Leben Jesu* parables are recited to reveal the kingdom of God, but from the perspective of Mark the parables were told to conceal (4:11–12) and thus explain Jewish unbelief. Whereas the traditional ending of a healing narrative accentuates fear as awe, Mark transforms the awe to a negative fear at significant points when he wants to emphasize the misunderstanding by the disciples (16:8; 9:6, 32; 10:32). The known heroes of the Jesus movement (the Twelve, the family of Jesus, and the women as in Acts 1:13–14) now become negative characters in order to allow those who have apostasized themselves in Mark's community to identify with their discipleship struggles. The fact that Jesus' family members become outsiders (3:31, 34) is "heavy with implications for the disciples' relations with their own kin,"[43] as evidenced by Mark 13:12. In fact Mark 13:9–13 becomes "a passion prediction for Mark's community."[44] In addition, the two miraculous feedings become more than just historical occurrences since, as Kelber points out, "this duplication of traditional material was ideally suited to mirror the bifocal experience of his own (i.e., Mark's) communal life."[45] Finally, the continual misunderstanding by the disciples throughout the gospel addresses the dilemma facing Mark's own audience and their mission in the world. They need the eyes of the gospel to discover anew that Jesus intended to suffer and die and that a discipleship of the cross was Jesus' plan from the very beginning.

Of course, the miracle stories are first of all demonstrations of the authority and power of Jesus. But Mark's gospel contains a "hidden agenda" of other themes which the attentive reader can discern through the literary mechanisms he employs. Mark employs Hellenistic literary forms like controversy dialogues and healing narratives whereby miracles occur through touch, spit, and special formulas.[46] However, the content and background of Mark's gospel is typically Jewish so that the OT Levitical concerns over leprosy, kosher food, menstruation, and corpses are right below the surface of the gospel.

---

42. The last three sentences have been the theses of chapters 6, 7, and 8 above.

43. Barton, *Discipleship and Family Ties*, 107.

44. See the title of Helen Graham's article, "A Passion Prediction for Mark's Community: Mark 13:9–13." Matthew moves this section to the mission discourse at 10:17–22.

45. Kelber, *Kingdom in Mark*, 63. We have argued that they speak both to Jew/Gentile inclusion in the community and to the priority of a discipleship of the cross over an emphasis upon miracles.

46. For the Hellenistic nature of controversy dialogues see the articles in *Semeia* 20 that compare Jewish and Greco-Roman literature. For Hellenistic features in miracle stories see section 8.8.

Therefore two possible scenarios present themselves. One proposal contends that the healings through touch began in the Palestinian culture as purity issues, but later because of the Greco-Roman healing procedures the purity issues faded into the background. Thus Kazen thinks that Mark himself is completely indifferent to purity regulations.[47] The second scenario, which we favor, asserts that the emphasis upon touching began in the Palestinian culture as purity issues then receded into the background based upon Hellenistic methods of reciting miracle stories, but was reclaimed by Mark to address Jew/Gentile conflicts in the early church and to help the Gentile community read the Old Testament in a "Christian" manner. The fact that Mark inserts an aside at 7:19b expressing his theological conclusion that Jesus declared all foods clean indicates that Mark is speaking to problematic ecclesiastical issues.[48] Therefore Mark's preaching of the Jesus tradition to the problems of his community explains why he alludes to OT ceremonies throughout the gospel.

Mark does not bring to the surface the purity issues explicitly. His chief aim as elsewhere involves Christology, but as Boring remarks, "There is no Christology apart from ecclesiology and discipleship."[49] Through literary devices Mark speaks at two levels. At a time when Jewish ceremonial strictness dominated the landscape, Jesus was critical of the Pharisaical purity traditions and emphasized the priority of ethical concerns,[50] which was read as a lenient attitude toward the law by the Pharisees. However, Mark discerns in Jesus' sayings a more radical approach to OT regulations. In order to convey this insight, Mark does not manipulate the words and deeds of Jesus, but instead adds explanations like 7:19b on some occasions but more frequently molds the material through intercalations, frames, narrative surprises, and allusionary repetitions to speak to issues relevant to the early church.[51] Mark employs Jesus' kingdom sayings and kingdom deeds to mirror struggles and issues in the first-century church.

I would categorize Mark as a sophisticated pastor-theologian. Although history is of utmost importance to Mark, he is not involved solely in archivistic activity. As Achtemeier explains, "If his eye was on the past, from which his traditions came, his eye was also on the present, for which he was writing his Gospel."[52] The uniqueness of Mark's theology derives from his endeavor to demonstrate that distinctly Christian

---

47. Kazen, *Jesus and Purity Halakhah*, 197, 105–6, 136, 164, 174.

48. Kazen does not deal with the redaction of Matthew and Mark and so does not reflect upon the differences between the gospel writers which would reveal that these issues of purity were contemporary discussions within the church.

49. Boring, *Mark*, 57.

50. The love command is central to Jesus and fulfills the law and the prophets (Matt 22:40). Jesus contends that the heart of the law is justice, mercy, faithfulness, and the love of God (Matt 23:23; Luke 11:42).

51. Concentrating on the additional literary device of irony, Camery-Hoggatt asserts, "Mark's ironies express a crisis of loyalties between Christianity and traditional Judaism, at every point along the way calling into question those institutions and attitudes which oppose the emergence of this new and different expression of piety" (*Irony in Mark's Gospel*, 180).

52. Achtemeier, "He Taught," 466.

beliefs have their origin in Jesus' kingdom teaching and miracle-working activity. Mark employs literary devices to present theological truths. Like the blind man who needs a second touch, the eyes of Mark's readers must be opened to these added symbolic dimensions of the gospel. Or alternatively one can reject a two-level approach to the Gospel of Mark and contend that interpreters like myself are just dreamers who impose fantastic patterns not intended by the original author. Only you the reader can decide.

Appendix 1

A Summary of Markan Literary Devices

A. Markan Intercalations — Theme

Universally Recognized Markan Sandwiches

1. Accusations against Jesus	3:20–34(35)	Suffering Messiah + discipleship
2. The bleeding woman and dead girl	5:21–43	Jewish regulations
3. The mission of the Twelve and John's death	6:7–30	Suffering Messiah + discipleship
4. The fig tree and the temple action	11:12–26	Jewish regulations
5. Those plotting vs. the woman preparing	14:1–11	Suffering Messiah + discipleship
6. Peter's denial and Jesus' Jewish trial	14:53–72	Suffering Messiah

Possible Single Set of Character Intercalations (Appendix 3)

1. The Purpose of the parables	4:3–20 or 4:1–34	Suffering Messiah + Discipleship
2. Betraying and denying vs. instituting	14:17–31	Suffering Messiah
3. The woman's silent watching versus Joseph's bold action	15:40—16:8	Discipleship

B. Markan Frameworks — Theme

1. The gospel of the suffering Son	1:1, 14–15	Suffering Messiah
2. Successful preaching ministry	1:14–15, 39	Contrast with passion
3. Secrecy frame around controversies	1:40–45; 3:7–12	Suffering Messiah
4. Insider/outsider frame	3:13–19, 33–34	Discipleship
5. Seed parables frame	4:1–2, 33–36	Discipleship

Appendix 1

6. Sea trips frame	4:35–41; 8:13–21	Discipleship
7. Blind men healed frame	8:22–26; 10:46–52	Suffering Messiah + discipleship
8. Royal psalms frame	11:9–11; 12:36 + 13:1	Suffering Messiah
9. Woman's sacrificial action frame	12:41–44; 14:3–9	Discipleship
10. Burial actions frame	14:3–9; 15:47—16:1	Suffering Messiah
11. Success & failure of women disciples	15:40–41; 16:7–8	Discipleship

C. Markan Allusionary Repetitions   Theme

Matched Episodes

1. The planning of the entry	11:1–2; 14:13	Suffering Messiah
2. The wording of the feedings	6:41; 8:6–7; 14:22–23	Suffering Messiah
3. Times for the master's coming	13:35/14:17, 32–57, 72; 15:1	Discipleship
4. The Threefold call to watch	13:33–37; 14:37–42	Suffering Messiah
5. Eschatological splitting / Son of God	1:10–11; 9:7; 15:38–39	Suffering Messiah

Matching of Loaded Terminology

1. The right and left hand of Jesus	10:40, 37; 15:27	Discipleship
Cup-bearer vs. cup of suffering	10:38; 14:23, 36	Suffering Messiah
2. Drinking the cup in the kingdom	14:25; 15:36	Suffering Messiah
3. Suffering Son of Man	8:31; 9:9, 12, 31; 10:33, 45; 14:21, 41	
and exalted Son of Man	8:38; 13:26; 14:62	Suffering Messiah
4. Jesus going before his disciples Connected with the motif of fear	10:32; 16:7–8 and 14:28	Suffering Messiah Discipleship
5. Eyes/ears without seeing/hearing	4:12; 8:18	Suffering Messiah
6. Destroying and building the temple	14:58; 15:29	Suffering Messiah
7. From a distance (ἀπὸ μακρόθεν)	5:6; 8:3; 11:13; 14:54; 15:40	Discipleship
8. The accusation of blasphemy	2:7; 14:64	Suffering Messiah

Possible Matching Terminology

9. Loud cries	1:26; 5:7 and 15:34, 37	Suffering Messiah
10. All things are possible	9:23; 14:26	Suffering Messiah
11. Disciples do not know how to answer	9:6; 14:40	Suffering Messiah
12. Receive one hundredfold	4:8, 20; 10:30	Discipleship
13. Preaching the gospel	1:14; 14:9	Suffering Messiah
14. ἐκθαμβέω; overwhelmed	9:15; 16:5 and 14:33	Suffering Messiah

A Summary of Markan Literary Devices

15. Imagery of the shepherd and the fig tree	6:34; 14:27 11:12–14, 20–21; 13:28–31	Suffering Messiah Suffering Messiah

Matching of Old Testament Texts

1. Repetition of Zechariah	11:7; 14:27	Suffering Messiah
2. Repetition of Psalm 118	11:9; 12:10	Suffering Messiah

Matching of Characters

1. John's and Jesus' identity "as it is written" Elijah at the transfiguration and cross	6:14–16; 8:27–32 9:12–13; 14:21 9:4; 15:35	Suffering Messiah
2. An inner circle (Peter, James, John) see his glory and suffering	5:37; 9:2; 14:33	Suffering Messiah & Discipleship
3. A disciple named Simon	14:66–72; 15:21	Discipleship
4. A young man appearing	15:51–52; 16:5–8	Suffering Messiah

D. Markan Narrative Surprises   Theme

(Demonstrating symbolism)

Criteria Demonstrating the Presence of a Markan Surprise:

1. Does not fit the normal elements of a miracle story

a. Surprise that Jesus' miracles must be kept secret	1:43–44	Suffering Messiah + Jewish regulations
b. Fear becomes a negative concept in the sea journeys	4:40; 6:51–52	Discipleship
c. Feedings do not end in awe but misunderstanding	6:52; 8:19–20	Discipleship
d. Astonishment comes at the beginning rather than end	9:15	Jewish regulations
e. Healings of blind become a parable and calling story	8:22–26; 10:52	Suffering Messiah + Discipleship
f. Fear becomes a negative concept instead of awe	9:6, 32; 10:32	Discipleship
g. A resurrection story ends in fear, flight, and silence	16:8	Discipleship

2. Does not fit the expected drama in a narrative

a. Surprise that a demon would be in the synagogue	1:23	Jew/Gentile
b. The "psychological impossibility" of the disciples' question after the feeding of the 5,000	8:4	Discipleship + Jew/Gentile
c. Not the season for figs but Jesus curses the fig tree	11:13	Jewish regulations
d. The fig tree withers from its roots, not leaves	11:21	Jewish regulations

APPENDIX 1

e. A teacher of the law is not far from the kingdom	12:32–34	Jewish regulations
f. A long journey turns into a single night of watching	13:34–35	Discipleship

3. Does not fit the expected vocabulary

a. Compassion for a leper is turned to rebuke; a healing rather than an exorcism involves silencing	1:41, 43	Jewish regulations
b. Wanting to pass by the boat to immediately entering	6:48	Jewish regulations
c. Change from "dog" to a person of great faith	7:27–29	Jew/Gentile
d. "Forgotten to take any bread" changed to "one loaf"	8:14	Suffering Messiah + discipleship

4. Synoptic alterations: changed by later gospel writers

a. Jesus' own family thinks he is losing his mind	3:21	Discipleship
b. There is no resurrection narrative with Christ appearing to his disciples in Galilee	16:1–6	Suffering Messiah
c. The women neglect to do what the angel asked	16:7–8	Discipleship

E. Markan Temporal Mirroring   Theme

(The absence of Jesus from his disciples mirrors the absence of Jesus from the Christian community.)

1. Jesus asleep in the boat while the storm is raging outside	4:35–41	Discipleship
2. A praying Jesus on the mountain watching his disciples labor against the wind and sea	6:45–52	Discipleship
3. The disciples' inability to cast out the demon without Jesus present	9:17–19	Discipleship
4. The parable of the absentee landlord	13:33–36	Discipleship
5. The sleep of the disciples	14:32–42	Discipleship
6. The fear of the woman to share the message of Jesus' resurrection without Jesus	16:8	Discipleship

F. Geographical Mirroring in the Miracle Stories: Jewish/Gentile Territory   Theme

(The retaking of the land demonstrates an emphasis upon Jew and Gentile.)

1. The boat trips enlarge the conquest of the promised land to Gentile territory (Decapolis, Tyre and Sidon)	5:1ff; 7:31ff	Jew/Gentile
2. The pre-Markan structure of two sets of miracle stories	4:35—8:10	Jew/Gentile
3. At the center of each cycle is the Jewish unclean woman and the Gentile Syrophoenician woman	5:25–34 7:24–30	Jew/Gentile

4. The feedings of the 5,000 and 4,000 demonstrate that the eschatological feast is for Jews and Gentiles	6:34–44; 8:1–10	Jew/Gentile
5. The demon cast out of the synagogue cleanses Judaism and cast out of Decapolis cleanses Gentile territory	1:21–28; 5:1–20	Jew/Gentile
6. The Messianic Secret is ignored in Jewish and Gentile territory demonstrating that the gospel is for both	1:43–45 7:36–37	Jew/Gentile

G. Jewish Ceremonial Ritual Mirroring   Theme

(Jesus fulfills Jewish ceremonial regulations through his kingdom words and actions.)

1. The ceremonial purity of all unclean food	7:1–23	Jewish regulations
2. The new wine must be placed in new wineskins	2:21–22	Jewish regulations
3. The Sabbath is made for humans to do good	2:23—3:6	Jewish regulations
4. The new temple (11:12–26) and the new synagogue/house for the new Israel (3:13–19) with new sacrifices (12:33)		Jewish regulations
5. An unclean menstruating woman and dead girl	5:21–43	Jewish regulations
6. An unclean leper	1:40–45	Jewish regulations
7. Unclean fluids	7:31–37	Jewish regulations

APPENDIX 2

Examples of Irony in Mark's Gospel

Definition: Shipley defines irony as "a device whereby . . . incongruity is introduced in the very structure of the plot, by having the spectators aware of elements in the situation of which one or more of the characters involved are ignorant."[1]

Theological Use: Mark employs irony for Christological purposes, and therefore it is found primarily at the end of the book and related to the passion with Jesus as king.

Social Use: Irony forces the reader to a decision and aids in group-boundary definition by dividing listeners and readers into insiders and outsiders (4[2]).

A. Preparation for Irony in Mark's Gospel[3]

1. The beginning of the gospel about Jesus Christ, the Son of God (1:1): "The insight the reader enjoys from the prologue in 1:1 naturally places him at an advantage over the characters of the story, and at virtually every point he will be called upon to pass judgment on them for their blindness or obtuseness" (93).

2. The voice from heaven at Jesus baptism addresses only Jesus (1:11): "At Jesus baptism the reader and Jesus have been told something which is carefully shielded from the story's characters. The ironic tensions in points of view which are later all developed in one way or another play off this central distinction. The reader and Jesus know that he is Son of God and Messiah; the other characters do not" (98).

---

1. Shipley, *Dictionary of World Literature*, 331.
2. All parenthetic page references are from Camery-Hoggatt, *Irony in Mark's Gospel*.
3. Camery-Hoggatt (*Irony in Mark's Gospel*) admits that this material is not directly ironic. With regard to the temptations he reports that "the double significance here is not quite clear enough for the temptation to be classed as ironic" (98) and that there is nothing directly ironic about 1:16–20 (101).

3. Four men drop everything to follow Jesus without knowing anything about him (1:16–20) whereas later in the story, when they know his message and mission, they all abandon him (14:50) (101).

4. Exorcisms: The readers overhear the disclosures by the demons of Jesus' identity, of which the characters are ignorant. "The result is that Jesus, the demons, and the reader stand together in a kind of occlusion, such that their common knowledge separated them from the remaining characters in the story" (105; cf. 122).

5. The Messianic Secret: "Inasmuch as the reader knows from the very beginning that Jesus is the Christ, the Son of God, there is never any question of a Messianic Secret for the reader of the gospel."[4]

B. Irony Outside the Passion Narrative

1. The Jewish leaders plot to kill Jesus on the Sabbath (3:6) after condemning Jesus for his Sabbath activity (3:4) (119).

2. By opposing Jesus as the one who casts out demons by Beelzebub, the scribes have actually aligned themselves with the demons (124).

3. Miracle stories consistently end with the audience marveling at Jesus' miracles (1:27, 37; 2:12; 4:41; 5:20; 7:37), but instead at Nazareth Jesus marvels at the audience's lack of faith (6:6) (141).

4. Camery-Hoggatt (145) discerns three movements of irony in the intrusion of the death of John the Baptist into the narrative (6:14–29): sarcastic irony, comic irony, and irony of tone.

5. Mark 7:9 is verbal irony mixed with sarcasm: "You have a fine way of setting aside the commands of God in order to observe your own traditions!"[5]

6. The story of the Syrophoenician woman (7:24–30) is "peirastic irony—from πειράζειν —, a verbal challenge intended to test the other's response, so that Jesus is speaking tongue-in-cheek" (150).

7. The irony of the two feedings (6:30–44; 8:1–10) is that their meaning is "something which the disciples cannot possibly have seen," namely "the extension of the eschatological meal to the Gentiles" (152).

8. "Peter, as the representative of the disciples, will declare that Jesus is the Christ and yet entirely misunderstand what that declaration means" (8:27–33), since he is like the twice-touched blind man in 8:22–26 who has "sight, not insight, a flash, but not sustained illumination" (155).

---

4. Fowler, *Loaves and Fishes*, 158.
5. Fowler, *Let the Reader Understand*, 167.

9. Passion predictions: "At the precise moment of Peter's confession the blindness of the disciples becomes explicit" (157). "The plainer are the predictions, the more difficult and obtuse appear the disciples" (158).

10. In 9:36-37 Jesus teaches his disciples about receiving children while he embraces them, yet in the immediate context (10:13-16) when Jesus again takes the children in his arms, the disciples rebuke him.[6]

11. James and John in asking to be at the right and left in the kingdom "have unwittingly asked to take the places of the brigands on the crosses on either side of him" (10:35-41 with 15:27) (162).

12. It is ironic that only a blind man (Bartimaeus) truly sees who Jesus is and follows him (10:46-52) (165).

13. "The conquering Messiah will storm Jerusalem on a colt, his army a mob of pilgrims armed with palm-fronds, their battle-cry an ancient *hallal* which is overcoded with implications they cannot understand" (166).

14. The "cleansing" of the temple turns out to be a destruction because the rulers set out to destroy the cleanser (11:18).

15. 16:8 "The irony is that until now, men and women who were told to say nothing frequently spoke freely, unable to contain the good news. Now the women are given the best news of all and are told to speak, but apparently say nothing!"[7]

C. Irony Throughout Each Mockery of the Passion Narrative

1. Mockery at the Jewish trial:

   a. Jesus is accused of proclaiming the destruction of the temple (14:57-58) when really the Jewish leaders accomplish it by destroying Jesus, the temple (173).

   b. Jesus is accused of law breaking whereas the Jewish leaders break their own laws through false witnesses and the nature of the trial so that "Jesus is vindicated by the reader at precisely the moment that the authorities condemn him and hand him over to Pilate for formal trial and execution" (174).

   c. Mark has the high priest ironically attribute to Jesus the major titles of the gospel (14:61 as in 1:1).

   d. "At the precise time when the court attendants were heaping scorn and derision upon Jesus' claim to be the Messiah, the prophecy that Peter would

---

6. Ibid., 173.
7. Hooker, *Endings*, 16.

deliberately deny him was being fulfilled."[8]

   e. The high priest charges Jesus with blasphemy (14:64) for telling the truth, while practicing blasphemy himself by condemning the Messiah (173).

   f. Jesus is blindfolded and commanded to prophesy (14:65) while the priestly establishment fulfills Jesus' prophesy (10:34).

2. Mockery at the Roman trial:

   a. Pilate and the bystanders ironically call Jesus "king" (15:2, 9, 12, 32) with the address "Hail, king of the Jews" (15:18) similar to the familiar "Ave Caesar" (174).

   b. The authorities release a murderer and kill an innocent man (15:6–14).

   c. The soldiers dress Jesus in a purple robe and a crown of thorns (15:17–19) whereas ironically Jesus really is a king deserving of kneeling allegiance.

3. Mockery on the cross:

   a. "Those who mock Jesus speak the truth but do not mean the truth."[9]

   b. The sign "King of the Jews" (15:26) is true, "his only appropriate coronation" (85).

   c. Jesus' placement between two brigands (15:27) would be understood as part of a royal pageantry since the king has his chief supporters on his right and left (see Philo, *Flaccus* 38).

   d. The mockery of destroying the temple (15:29) happens in the curtain ripping (15:38).

   e. The Jews mock Jesus saying, "save yourself" (15:30) when really Jesus is saving the whole world by dying (176).

   f. The soldiers are gambling for his clothes (15:24) and at the same time fulfilling Scripture (Ps 22:18), a blind spot for the characters but obvious to the reader.

   g. The bystanders see Elijah as an agent of rescue, standing between Jesus and his death, but Elijah has already come not as a rescuer from the cross but as a prophetic sign of Jesus' death (9:12–13).[10]

   h. The cry "My God, my God, why have you forsaken me" has "a literal meaning in the story and another, more profound meaning for those who have ears to hear," that is who know the ending of Psalm 22.[11]

---

8. Lane, *Mark*, 541.
9. Shiner, "Ambiguous Pronouncement," 17.
10. Senior, *Passion in Mark*, 125.
11. Shiner, "Ambiguous Pronouncement," 17.

i. "The execution of the King of the Jews as a criminal occurred at the third hour (v. 35), the time of the morning *Tamid* on behalf of the people. In other words, the crucifixion, far from being the disaster Jesus' opponents wanted, is really the sacrifice of Jesus on behalf of the people."[12]

4. Irony in the rest of the passion narrative:

   a. It is "deeply ironic that the chief priests are depicted preparing for this sacred time (i.e. the Passover) by plotting a murder in stealth" (note Mark 7:21–22, where the same word is found in a list of defiling qualities: 14:1 ἐν δόλῳ; 7:22 δόλος).[13]

   b. A woman anoints Jesus' head (as king) so that he becomes king in his death. The preparation for burial, however, turns out to be good news (14:3–9).

   c. The Jewish leaders practice deceit through including the insider Judas in their plans (14:1–2, 10–11), yet they are the ones deceived.

   d. "Judas calls Jesus 'rabbi' and kisses him, thereby handing him over to death (14:45)."[14]

   e. Peter fabricates a lie ("I don't know this man you are talking about" 14:71) "and yet never were truer words spoken" (172).

   f. The women and Joseph take great pains to bury the one whom no tomb will hold (15:42–47).

---

12. Pobee, "Cry of the Centurion," 95.
13. Barton, "Mark as Narrative," 232.
14. Fowler, *Let the Reader Understand*, 159.

Appendix 3

A List of Possible Markan Intercalations by Various Authors

Author	B. Weiss	Rawlinson	E. Klostermann	Von Dobschutz	Bultmann	Burkill	Nineham
Year	1917	1925	1926	1928	1933	1963	1963
Pages	Fitzpatrick, 51–52	42–43	Fitspatrick, 52–53	193–98	2nd ed., 365	121 n. 10, 242 n. 43	112, 298
Mark 1:1–6							
1:21–27							
1:14–39							
2:1–12							
2:1—3:35							x
3:1–6							
3:20–35	x	x	x	x	x	x	
4:1–20/34	x						
5:21–43	x	x	x	x	x	x	x
6:6–30	x	x	x	x	x	x	x
8:1–21							
8:14–17					x?		
8:27—9:1	x						
9:36–44					x?		
11:12–21	x	x		x		x	x
13:1–23	x				x		
14:1–11	x	x	x	x	x	x	x
14:17–31 or 12–25					x x		
14:53–72	x				x	x?	
15:6–32			x				
15:40—16:8							

APPENDIX 3

Author	Lambrecht	Schweizer	Stein	Kühn	Neirynck	Donahue	Lane
Year	1967	1970	1971	1971	1972	1973	1974
Pages	299–300	116	193	200–202	133	58–59	28
Mark 1:1–6	x?						
1:21–27	x						
1:14–39	x						
2:1–12							
2:1—3:35							
3:1–6							
3:20–35	x	x	x	x	x	x	x
4:1–20/34	x						
5:21–43	x	x	x	x	x	x	x
6:6–30	x	x	x	x	x	x	x
8:1–21							
8:14–17	x?						
8:27—9:1							
9:36–44	x?						
11:12–21		x	x	x	x	x	x
13:1–23	x						
14:1–11	x	x	x	x	x		x
14:17–31 or 12–25	x x						
14:53–72	x	x	x?	x?	x		
15:6–32			x?	x?	x		
15:40—16:8							

Author	Trocmé	Achtemeier	Lefevre	Anderson	Kee	Farla	Harrington
Year	1975	1975	1975	1976	1977	1978	1979
Pages	82 n. 2, 231	31–32, 80, 101–2, 117–18	403–16	38–39, 324–25	54	117–30	43, 70, 83, 217, 227, 235
Mark 1:1–6			x 1:1–13				
1:21–27							
1:14–39							
2:1–12					x		
2:1—3:35							
3:1–6					x		
3:20–35	x	x	x	x	x	x	x
4:1–20/34		x?					
5:21–43	x	x	x	x	x	x	x
6:6–30	x	x	x	x	x	x	x
8:1–21	x						

A List of Possible Markan Intercalations by Various Authors

Passage							
8:14-17							
8:27—9:1							
9:36-44							
11:12-21	x	x	x	x	x		x
13:1-23		x?					
14:1-11	x		x	x		x	x
14:17-31 or 12-25			x				
14:53-72	x	x		x	x	x	x
15:6-32			x		x		x
15:40—16:8							

Author	Kermode	Dewey	Fowler	Rhoads, Michie	Wright	Sergeant	Best
Year	1979	1980	1981	1982	1985	1985	1989
Pages	128-34, 161 n. 2	21	165	51	17	14-19	52
Mark 1:1-6							
1:21-27					x		
1:14-39							
2:1-12	x				x		
2:1—3:35							x
3:1-6	x				x		
3:20-35	x	x	x	x	x	x	
4:1-20/34					x		
5:21-43	x	x	x	x	x	x	x
6:6-30	x	x	x	x	x	x	x
8:1-21							
8:14-17							
8:27—9:1							
9:36-44	x						
11:12-21	x	x	x	x	x	x	x
13:1-23	x?						
14:1-11		x	x		x	x	x
14:17-31 or 12-25						x	
14:53-72	x	x	x	x	x	x	x
15:6-32	x		x		x		

Appendix 3

Author	Edwards	Guelich	Marshall	Gundry	Shepherd	Telford	Marcus
Year	1989	1989	1989	1993	1995	1999	2000
Pages	197–98	169–171	91–92	672	522	25	364
Mark 1:1–6							
1:21–27				x			
1:14–39							
2:1–12							x
2:1—3:35							
3:1–6							
3:20–35	x	x	x	x	x	x	x
4:1–20/34	x					x	
5:21–43	x	x	x	x	x	x	x
6:6–30	x	x	x	x	x	x	x
8:1–21							
8:14–17							
8:27—9:1							
9:36–44		x					
11:12–21	x	x	x	x	x	x	x
13:1–23							
14:1–11	x	x	x	x	x	x	x
14:17–31 or 12–25	x		x			x	
14:53–72	x	x	x	x	x	x	x
15:6–32							

Author	Geddert	Kazen	France	Boring	Collins	Healy	Stein
Year	2001	2002	2002	2006	2007	2008	2008
Pages	416–17	129 n. 224	18–19	157	698 n. 3	342	114 n. 1
Mark 1:1–6				x (4–8)			
1:21–27				x			
1:14–39							
2:1–12				x			
2:1—3:35							
3:1–6							
3:20–35			x	x	x	x	x
4:1–20/34	x			x			
5:21–43	x	x	x	x	x	x	x
6:6–30	x	x	x	x	x	x	x
8:1–21							
8:14–17							
8:27—9:1							

A List of Possible Markan Intercalations by Various Authors

Passage							
9:36–44							
11:12–21	x	x	x	x	x	x	x
13:1–23				x (5–27)			
14:1–11	x	x	x	x	x	x	x
14:17–31 or 12–25				x (18–25)			
14:53–72	x		x	x	x	x	
15:6–32	x (21–26) x (37–39)						
15:40—16:8							

From all this data, six intercalations stand out based upon the overwhelming support of nearly 100 percent of the interpreters. In each case, as the years have progressed the consensus has grown (see 14:53–72 for instance). In addition, the next best-supported candidate (15:6–32) received the votes of less than one third of the exegetes and none since 1985.

How do these six examples stand out? What do they have in common that is missing in the other suggestions? Each sandwich comprises a narrative (versus a teaching) which combines stories of different sets of characters: 1) Jesus' family and the teachers of the law (3:20–35); 2) Jairus and his daughter compared with the menstruating woman (5:21–43); 3) the disciples' mission trip and Herod's treatment of John the Baptizer (6:6–30); 4) the disciples' witness of the withered fig tree and Jesus' conflict with the money changers, chief priests, and teachers of the law over the "temple cleansing" (11:12–21); 5) Judas' pact with the teachers of the law to eliminate Jesus combined with the anointing of the woman at Simon the Leper's house (14:1–11); and 6) Peter's denials to several servants in the courtyard with Jesus' testimony before the Sanhedrin (14:53–72). Likewise, all include the interruption of a narrative with another event which adds drama, irony, and theological meaning to the story.

Several other candidates meet some of these qualifications but fail at other points. In the parables narrative the sequence of seed parables is broken up by other parables, but this is teaching material and not narrative. Specifically, 4:1–34 contains three seed parables (parable of the Sower and interpretation, 4:1–20; parable of the seed growing secretly, 4:26–29; and parable of the mustard seed, 4:30–32) with the parable of the lamp on a stand and the parable of the measure conspicuously placed in the middle (4:21–25). Within this context others discern a second Markan sandwich in 4:1–20, where the parable of the sower (4:1–9) is separated from its interpretation (4:14–20) by a change of location, audience, and talk about the mystery of the kingdom (4:10–13). These two possible intercalations are tied together since the interpretation of the parable of the lamp in verse 22, "For whatever is hidden is meant to be disclosed," solves the mystery of the kingdom from verses 11–12. So the inside sections of each sandwich are interconnected. The one chiasm resolves the other as witnessed in Joanna Dewey's outline of 4:1–34 in chapter three above. Furthermore,

4:1–34 is connected closely with the theme of a suffering Messiah, another characteristic of Markan intercalations. Just as the Messianic Secret will be disclosed when Jesus is crucified and the centurion makes a public proclamation of Jesus as Son of God (15:39), so the mystery of the kingdom is resolved at the cross when the man waiting for the kingdom, Joseph of Arimathea, takes a kingdom action and asks for Jesus' crucified body (15:43). However, these supposed intercalations in Mark 4 lack contrasting characters set in a narrative sequence along with the resultant dramatic irony. Instead, this passage consists of parables and teaching. So I would prefer to categorize 4:1–34 as a Markan framework since it does not obey all the rules of a Markan sandwich.

Mark 15:6–32 is frequently identified as an intercalation since the mocking by soldiers (15:16–20) is interpolated between Jesus' sentence of crucifixion (15:6–15) and the execution itself (15:21–32). Supportive evidence includes the employment of two sets of characters without any character crossover except for Jesus and parallel actions of mocking, which convey similar content. Finally, the triple repetition of the phrase "king of the Jews" (15:9, 18, 26) establishes a *Leitwort* connection, and "a possible dramatized irony exists in the way in which both the religious leaders and the soldiers mock Jesus."[1] However, along with Shepperd we must reject this example since 15:6–32 functions as a single narrative without the usual gap in the story. Furthermore, the phrase "king of the Jews" is not limited to this possible intercalation but is employed continuously throughout the passion narrative. Finally, the mocking of Jesus is not distinctive to this passage but occurs in the Barabbas episode (15:7–11), the taunting by the soldiers (15:17–18), and the triple mockery by the robbers (15:27–30), chief priests (15:31–32), and those standing near the cross (15:35–36). Therefore, because of this continuity in succeeding scenes, this passage cannot be identified as an intercalation. It is preferable to identify the structure as a triad of events (a common Markan pattern) with a narrated response to each scene: 1) trial (15:1–15) and the response of the soldiers (15:16–20); 2) crucifixion (15:21–27) and the response of the spectators (15:29–32); and 3) death (15:33–37) and the response of the centurion and rending of the veil (15:38–39).[2]

Other passages fail the test by narrating only a single set of characters. In 14:17–31 two narratives about the disciples are interspersed with an action of Jesus so that the prediction of tragic abandonment of Jesus by the Twelve through betrayal (14:18–21) and denial (14:27–31) encompasses Jesus' establishment of the new covenant. Irony is present as well since the covenant is broken almost before it is instituted. Important verbal connections in the frame include: 1) the similar denials of the disciples in 14:19 ("Surely not I?") and Peter's denial in 14:31 ("I will never disown you"); and 2) both the betrayal by Judas and the desertion by the other disciples are described as fulfilling

---

1. Shepperd, *Sandwich Stories*, 358.
2. Culpepper, "Passion and Resurrection," 584.

Scripture.³ Finally, the themes of a suffering Messiah and abandoned discipleship are also prominent.⁴ Certainly these are consistent traits of other intercalations.⁵ However, here the characters are identical in each part of the narrative. Therefore, hesitantly, we must disqualify this passage as a Markan sandwich.

Mark 15:40—16:8 narrates three scenes, with the women's progression of discipleship described in the outer narratives and Joseph of Arimathea's bold witnessing to the coming of the kingdom in Jesus' death in the center section. New time designations occur at 15:42 (preparation day) and 16:1 (the Sabbath was over) to support this delineation. Furthermore, the theme of a suffering Messiah (15:41 the women following Jesus to Jerusalem and 15:46 Joseph identifying with Jesus in his death) is front and center as well as a corresponding discipleship (15:43 vs. 16:8).⁶ Finally, the familiar presence of irony is discerned in the fact that a Jewish official exerts more courage and kingdom awareness than any of the disciples (15:43) with regard to Jesus' death and burial. However, as with 14:17–31 no gap in the narrative of 15:40—16:8 actually occurs. Certainly the main characters switch from the women (15:40–41,47) to Joseph of Arimathea (15:42–46), but the repetition of the women's names (15:40, 47; 16:1) as well as Joseph's burial of Jesus and the women's corresponding action of purchasing spices to anoint the dead body indicate that a single narrative is in view, not an intercalation.

Boring supports 1:22–27 as the first Markan intercalation so that this literary device is introduced in the initial ministry of Jesus in Galilee. Support for this conclusion comes from the fact that "Jesus' authoritative new teaching forms the framework and main theme (cf. 22, 27) within which an exorcism story is inserted."⁷ The phrase "teaching with authority" is repeated (1:22 διδάσκων αὐτοὺς ὡς ἐξουσίαν; 1:27 διδαχὴ καινὴ κατ᷂ ἐξουσίαν), and in each case the astonishment of the crowd is noted, although different terms are employed (1:22 ἐξεπλήσσοντο; 1:27 ἐθαμβήθησαν). However, all the other intercalations portray different central characters in the two pericopes as well as a variant plot, whereas 1:22–27 merely repeats vocabulary at the beginning and end of a narrative and occurs throughout in the same location, a synagogue. In addition, the theme of Jesus' authority diverges from the three themes that Mark emphasizes in the other intercalations. Therefore, this passage contains an inclusio rather than a Markan sandwich.

---

3. 14:21 καθὼς γέγραπται περὶ αὐτοῦ; 14:27 ὅτι γέγραπται.

4. Fowler asserts, "The two units in 14:18–21 and 14:27–31 conspire to shroud 14:22–26 with the severest failure of discipleship imaginable: scandalization (14:27), renunciation (14:30), and outright treacherous betrayal (14:18–21)" (*Loaves and Fishes*, 136).

5. France (*Mark*, 573) and Myers (*Binding the Strong Man*, 355) label it an intercalation.

6. Therefore, Edwards ("Marcan Sandwiches," 213) labels this an intercalation since the two characters are contrasted with the women watching the events while Joseph acts.

7. Boring, *Mark*, 63.

Appendix 3

In 2:1–12 a controversy between Jesus and the Jewish leaders about forgiveness of sins interrupts the narrative of Jesus' healing of the paralytic. The chiastic structure[8] and the awkward repetition of "he said to the paralytic" in 2:5 and 2:10 have caused some to label this a Markan sandwich.[9] But the best explanation for the similarities is the combination of two genre, a healing story and a controversy dialogue.[10] Since the healing story is placed around the controversy, it bears some resemblance to an intercalation, but the differences are substantial: 1) the presence of one continuous scene, not two separate stories; 2) an unusual character crossover occurs with the paralytic; 3) no ellipsis moves across the inner story; 4) no action occurs in the outer story that crosses over to the inner story; and 5) no dramatized irony can be clearly identified.[11] Therefore, I employ the term ring composition for this literary device instead of intercalation.[12]

In conclusion, we have narrowed the possible examples of intercalations down to six. Several other examples like 4:1–34; 14:17–31; and 15:40—16:8 follow an A1-B-A2 schema in which the B episode forms an independent unit of material, but the characters in the narrative do not change. One could label these as "single set of character intercalations." Although these passages include an interpolation into a narrative and emphasize the themes of a suffering Messiah who desires a faithful following of discipleship, they do not meet all the requirements contained in the legitimate Markan intercalations.

---

8. Marshall (*Faith*, 83–84) employs this chiasm:

a		2:1–2	Introduction
	b	2:3–5	Spiritual healing
		c 2:6–10a	Controversy about forgiveness
	b'	2:10b–12a	Physical healing
a'		2:12b	Conclusion

9. Cf. Marcus, *Mark 1–8*, 219. Compare Boring (*Mark*, 75) who accepts an intercalation with Stein (*Mark*, 115) who rejects a Markan sandwich.

10. See Camery-Hoggott, *Irony*, 109; Donahue, *Are You the Christ*, 82; Fuller, *Miracles*, 50–51; Kee, *Community*, 55; Taylor, *Mark*, 191–92; Mead, "Healing of the Paralytic," 348–54.

11. See Shepperd, *Sandwich Stories*, 357, for disqualifying criteria.

12. Cf. Dewey, *Markan Public Debate*, 68, 70, where she explains that a ring composition surrounds an interpolation (6–10a). Dewey (68) also employs the term "frame," but I want to save that term for two different narratives that supply bookends to a series of pericopes. The purpose of the ring composition here is to enable the narrator to reinforce the parallelism of forgiveness of sins and physical healing (73). A parallel ring composition appears in the last controversy dialogue of 2:1—3:6 (Mark 3:1, 2–5a, 5b–6).

Appendix 4

Outlines of the Structure of Mark
(Outlines based upon literary devices, geography, genre, and content)

Interpreters outline the Gospel of Mark with a multiplicity of structures. Although almost universal scholarly agreement exists as to the delineation of the individual pericopes or "minimal compositional units," wide disagreement reigns as to how these units fit into a composite structure.[1] Since I have argued that Mark employs the literary device of a framework to develop his theology, I will begin with an outline based upon Markan frames. Then I will examine other structures and critique their strengths and weaknesses. First I will dissect outlines organized according to literary devices like frames, transitions, chiasms, and three-step progressions (structural patterns 1–4). Then I will analyze the commonly accepted outline organized by geography (5). Third, I will investigate structures controlled by genre including gospel preaching, drama, deep structure plot, and rhetorical arguments (6–9). Finally, I will critique outlines based upon content, especially Christology and discipleship (10–12). In conclusion, I will argue that Mark employed a two-step process of redaction of the oral tradition. First he placed frames around the material that was orally collected together by genre, and second he constructed a discipleship scheme where each section begins with a positive response of following but concludes with rejection and discipleship failure in order to speak to the historical struggles of the Christian community.

---

1. See Petersen, "Composition of Mark 4:1—8:26," 186–87. However, in ancient texts Codex A (Alexandrinus) incorporates 48 κεφάλαια while Codex B (Vaticanus) includes 62 division markings.

Appendix 4

Structural Pattern 1: Based on Markan Frames

(Frames around fivefold structures, which frequently employ chiasms)

I. The beginning of the gospel (1:1–15)   Fivefold chiastic structure

Theme: The message and ministry of John and Jesus are paralleled just as their deaths will be paralleled later.

Frame		1:1	The gospel of Jesus Christ
a		1:2–4	John in the wilderness
b		1:5	The baptism of the people by John
c		1:6–8	John refers to the mightier one who will baptize with the Spirit.
b'		1:9–11	The baptism of Jesus by John
a'		1:12–13	Jesus in the wilderness
Frame		1:14–15	The gospel of God

II. The dimensions of Jesus' ministry: first ministry campaign (1:16[14]–39)

Theme: This fivefold summary of Jesus' ministry becomes paradigmatic for the church.

Frame	1:14–15	Preaching in Galilee (εἰς τὴν Γαλιλαίαν κηρύσσων)
1.	1:16–20	Disciple making: Jesus' calling of two sets of brothers
2.	1:21–22	Teaching: teaching with authority
3.	1:23–28	Deliverance: victory over demons
4.	1:29–34	Healing: Jesus' extraordinary healing ministry
5.	1:35–38	Prayer: withdrawal for prayer in a solitary place
Frame	1:39	Preaching in Galilee (κηρύσσων ... εἰς ὅλην τὴν Γαλιλαίαν) Summary of Jesus' word and deed ministry

III. Five controversy dialogues with the Jewish leaders (1:40—3:12)

                                                                                          Fivefold chiastic structure

Theme: Jesus' secret identity as well as the kingdom are manifested in conflict.

Frame: Messianic Secret		1:44–45	Mark introduces the Messianic Secret to conclude the healing of a leper.
a		2:1–12	Forgiving sins: paralytic healed (again in Capernaum)
b		2:13–17	Eating with sinners: call of Levi (again by the sea)
c		2:18–22	Fasting and the new age (the center = crucifixion at 2:20)
b'		2:23–27	Sabbath eating rituals: picking grain on the Sabbath
a'		3:1–6	Sabbath healings: healing of withered hand (again in the synagogue)
Frame: Messianic Secret		3:7–12	Summary statement with the Messianic Secret applied to demons

IV. Insiders and outsiders: Jesus' true family (3:13–35) — Fivefold chiasm

Theme: Those one would expect to be on the inside, like blood relation and religious leaders, turn out to be outsiders.

A.		a	3:13–19	Appointment of the twelve disciples	Markan frame
B.				Accusations by Jesus' family and Jewish leaders	Markan sandwich
	1.	b	3:20–21	Accused by his family: Jesus is out of his mind.	
	2.	c	3:22–30	Accused by the Jewish leaders: Jesus is possessed by a demon.	
	3.	b'	3:31–34	Jesus' family arrives to take him home but they become outsiders.	
C.		a'	3:35	Announcement of membership in Jesus' family	Markan frame

V. Meaning of Jesus' parables (4:1–34) — Two fivefold chiastic structures

Theme: The mystery of the kingdom found in the shorter chiasm is resolved in the larger chiasm through the parables of the lamp and measure.

1			4:1–2	Introduction: teaching parables in a boat	Markan frame

- Many parables (4:2 ἐν παραβολαῖς πολλά; 4:33 παραβολαῖς πολλαῖς)
- Teaching (4:2 ἔλεγεν αὐτοῖς ἐν τῇ διδαχῇ; 4:33 ἐλάλει αὐτοῖς τὸν λόγον)
- A boat (4:1 εἰς πλοῖον; 4:36 ἐν τῷ πλοίῳ)
- Speaking to the crowds (4:1 ὄχλος πλεῖστος) contrasted with speaking to the disciples 4:34 (κατ' ἰδίαν δὲ τοῖς ἰδίοις μαθηταῖς)

2			4:2b–20	Parable material: parable and interpretation
	a		4:2b–9	Parable of the sower
		b	4:10	Question from the disciples about its meaning
			c 4:11–12	Mystery of the kingdom
		b'	4:13	Reproof to the disciples for not understanding
	a'		4:14–20	Interpretation of the parable of the sower
3				Sayings material: Do not let the parable remain a mystery.
	a		4:21, 22	Parable of the lamp and interpretation
		b	4:23	Exhortation to the audience: "He who has ears to hear, let him hear."
		b'	4:24a	Exhortation to the audience: "Consider carefully what you hear."
	a'		4:24b, 25	Parable of the measure and interpretation
2'			4:26–32	Parable material: two kingdom parables
	a		4:26–29	Parable of the seed growing silently
		b	4:30–32	Parable of the mustard seed

Appendix 4

1'   4:33–34   Conclusion: discussion of parables   Markan frame
              and departure in a boat

VI. The miracles of Jesus: three trips over the sea (4:35—8:21)

Theme: The misunderstanding of the disciples intensifies after each trip across the sea (4:40; 6:52; 8:17–21) to prove that the identity of Jesus cannot be fathomed through his miracles, but only in his passion.

A. Sea-calming trip (4:35–41)   Markan frame

B. Fivefold miracle catenae from the oral tradition[2]   Fivefold chiasms

a	4:35–41	Jesus calms the water, leaves for *Gentile territory*	6:45–56	Jesus walks on water, leaves for Bethsaida, *Gentile land* (6:45), but arrives at Gennesaret, *Jewish land* (6:53)
b	5:1–20	Decapolis exorcism (an unclean land is cleansed) *Gentile territory*: pigs	8:22–26	Healing the blind man (two-stage process of healing with spit) *Gentile territory*: Bethsaida (see John 12:20–21)
c	5:25–34	Sick woman (unclean bleeding woman saved) *Jewish territory*: reference to 12	7:24–30	Syrophoenician woman (unclean Gentile woman receives salvation) *Gentile territory*: Tyre
b'	5:21–23, 35–43	Jairus' dead daughter (dead bodies are no longer unclean) *Jewish territory*: reference to 12	7:31–36	Decapolis healing of the deaf-mute (two-stage process of healing with spit) *Gentile territory*: Decapolis
a'	6:34–44	Feeding of the 5,000 with 12 baskets surplus *Jewish territory*: reference to 12	8:1–10	Feeding of the 4,000 with 7 baskets surplus *Gentile territory*: reference to 7 (see Acts 13:19)

C. Markan additions upon the themes of discipleship and purity (6:1—7:37)

   1. Rejection at Nazareth to end a discipleship cycle, and a mission trip to begin one (6:1–29)

   2. Pericopes upon clean hands and clean food (7:1–23) are placed before the healing of the Syrophoenician woman's daughter to connect the healings with the Gentiles becoming clean (7:24–30) and the removal of uncleanness through fluids (7:31–37).

D. Sea conversation trip (8:14–21)   Markan frame

VII. Discipleship teaching: three cycles on following a suffering Messiah (8:22—10:52)

Theme: Discipleship blindness is removed by receiving the discipleship catechism.

---

2. See Achtemeier, "Toward the Isolation of Pre-Markan Miracle Catenae," 265–91.

Outlines of the Structure of Mark

A. The blind man needs a second touch to see clearly (8:22-26) Markan frame

(The blind man represents Peter [and the readers], who will need a second touch in his confession of Jesus as not only Messiah but also suffering servant.)

B. First cycle (8:31—9:29)

  1. Passion prediction (8:31) following Peter's confession of Jesus as Messiah (8:27-30)

  2. Misunderstanding: rebuke of Peter (8:32-33)

  3. Teaching on discipleship (8:34—9:29)

C. Second cycle (9:30—10:31)

  1. Passion prediction (9:30-32)

  2. Misunderstanding: the disciples dispute who is the greatest (9:33-34).

  3. Teaching on discipleship (9:35—10:31)

D. Third cycle (10:32-52)

  1. Passion prediction (10:32-34)

  2. Misunderstanding: the request of James and John for exaltation (10:35-40)

  3. Teaching on discipleship (10:41-52)

E. Blind Bartimaeus is healed and sees clearly to follow Jesus down the road of discipleship toward the cross (10:46-52). Markan frame

VIII. Jesus' triumphant ministry in Jerusalem (11:1—12:40)

Theme: The messianic prophet and teacher has become the new king, temple, and leader of the Jewish nation.

A. Markan frame

  1. Geographical: enter and leave the temple (11:11; 13:1).

  2. Title "Son of David" (10:48; 11:10; 12:35)

  3. Citations of OT royal psalms (11:9-10 = Ps 118; 12:36 = Ps 110)

B. Three prophetic actions aimed at Judaism Fivefold structure

  1. Jesus claims his kingship at Jerusalem in his triumphal entry (11:1-11).

  2. The cursing of the fig tree defines and symbolizes Israel (11:12-14).

  Markan sandwich

  3. The prophetic action against the temple foreshadows its destruction (11:15-19).

  4. The fig tree withers by its roots (11:20-21).

APPENDIX 4

    5. The new way to worship the king through faith, prayer, and forgiveness (11:22–26)

  C. Five controversy dialogues: Jesus as authoritative teacher (11:27—12:40)

a		11:27–12:12	The authority of Jesus and John the Baptizer (chief priests, scribes, and elders turn against Jesus) (Ps 118:22–23 at the beginning)
	1.	11:27–33	Deadlock: each side refuses to answer.
	2.	12:1–12	In the parable of the wicked tenants the Jewish leaders are condemned (Jesus as the only Son).
b		12:13–17	Paying taxes to Caesar: greatest commitment (Pharisees and Herodians against Jesus)
c		12:18–27	Marriage at resurrection (Sadducees against Jesus) (center = resurrection)
b'		12:28–34	Love God and neighbor: greatest commandment (teachers against Jesus)
a'		12:35–44	Jesus' wisdom is triumphant (Son greater than David) (Ps 110:1 at end).
	1.	12:35–37	Jesus' question "Whose son is the Christ?" cannot be answered.
	2.	12:38–40	The teachers of the law are condemned.

IX. The eschatological discourse (Mark 13)

Theme: The way to watch for Jesus' coming in glory is to give all that you have now.

  A. The woman puts everything into the temple treasury (12:41–44).

                                                                                                              Markan frame

  B. Signs of the end of the age (Jesus as the eschatological prophet) (13:1–37)

    1. Double introduction (13:1–4)

      a. Jesus' prediction of the destruction of the temple (observation and prediction) (13:1–2)

      b. The disciples' question about when this will be fulfilled (two questions) (13:3–4)

    2. Signs of the end (13:5–27)

      a. Signs upon the earth (begin and end with βλέπετε) (13:5–23)

                                                                                                  Fivefold chiasm

a		13:5–6	Beware of false messiahs (inclusio with 13:21–23 Βλέπετε)
b		13:7–8	General signs (things heard): beginning of birth pains
c		13:9–13	Persecution (βλέπετε at the beginning, middle, and end; 13:5–23)
b'		13:14–20	Abomination of desolation (things seen): tribulation (θλῖψις)
a'		13:21–23	Beware of false messiahs (inclusio with 13:5–6; βλέπετε)

      b. Signs in the heavens (13:24–27)   Fivefold poetic parallelism

Outlines of the Structure of Mark

>But in those days, following that distress
>a the sun will be darkened,
>a and the moon will not give its light;
>b the stars will fall from the sky,
>b and the heavenly bodies will be shaken.
>c At that time people will see the Son of Man
>c coming in clouds with great power and glory.
>d And he will send his angels
>d and gather his elect
>e from the four winds,
>e from the ends of the earth to the ends of the heavens.

3. Double paraenetic conclusion using parables: a call to watch (13:28–37)

   a. Parable of the fig tree: nearness of Jesus' coming (13:28–31)

   b. Parable of the doorkeeper: suddenness of Jesus' coming (13:32–37)

If references to the *parousia* begin at 13:32 with 13:1–31 about the destruction of Jerusalem, then a chiasm could result:

a		13:24–25		Signs in heaven = the destruction of a major city or country
	b	13:26		The Son of Man ascends to be enthroned with the Ancient of Days.
		c	13:27	Angels gathering the elect = the apostolic mission to the Gentiles (13:10)
	b'	13:28–29		"It is near" = The time has come for the destruction of Jerusalem (like 13:26 "at that time").
a'		13:30–31		Heaven and earth passing away in this generation refers back to 13:24–25.

  3. The woman anoints Jesus with an expensive perfume offering 14:1–9.
                       Markan frame

X. The passion narrative in Jerusalem (14:1—16:1)

Theme: The prophetic anointing of Jesus before his passion and the inability to anoint Jesus at the normal time indicate that the death of Jesus was in God's divine plan.

 A. The woman anoints Jesus' body to prepare for his burial (14:1–9)
                        Markan Frame

 B. The narrative is organized into the watches of the night (previewed in Mark 13:35) and the hours of the crucifixion   Fivefold structure

(The disciples are prepared for Jesus' coming in glory but not his coming in suffering.)

  1. Evening, ὀψὲ (14:17–31) (14:17 "when evening came," ὀψίας γενομένης)

   Discipleship failure: Jesus predicts that the disciples will fall away (14:27) and that Peter will not be ready for Jesus' passion (14:29–30).

2. Midnight, μεσονύκτιον (no mention of midnight, but the disciples sleep) (14:32–51)

   Discipleship failure: Instead of watching the disciples sleep (14:37–38, 40–41).

3. When the rooster crows, ἀλεκτοροφωνίας (14:53–72) (14:72 the cock crows, ἀλέκτωρ ἐφώνησεν; 14:68 some manuscripts)

   Discipleship failure: Peter denies the Lord while Jesus perseveres in the good confession before his enemies.

4. Dawn, πρωΐ (15:1–20) (15:1 πρωΐ; the dawn in 16:2 provides the hope)

   Discipleship failure: The disciples are completely missing in the trial before Pilate.

5. Third hour, sixth hour, ninth hour (15:25, 33, 34) (crucifixion of 15:20–39)

   Discipleship failure: None of the disciples are in fellowship with Jesus in his sufferings on the cross.

C. The inability of the women to anoint Jesus' body (15:47—16:1)

				Markan Frame
XI. The resurrection narrative (16:2–8)				Fivefold chiasm
a		15:40–41	The faithful beginning of the women disciples is described	Markan frame
	b	15:42–46	A forgiven Jewish leader seeking the kingdom of God buries Jesus	
		c	15:47—16:3	The women, not remembering Jesus' prediction of resurrection, attempt to anoint Jesus' body with spices, but he is risen and not there.	
	b'	16:4–6	An angel described like the young man of 14:51–52 makes it appear that a forgiven disciple announces Jesus' resurrection.	
a'		16:7–8	As with the apostles, the women forsake their discipleship commitment and flee in fear without proclaiming the gospel message.	Markan frame

The content of the Gospel of Mark is roughly organized by genre since the oral tradition as well as Mark himself in some cases has collected together similar material from the Jesus tradition, like controversy dialogues (2:1—3:6; 11:27—12:37), parables (4:1–34), miracle stories (4:35—8:21), discipleship teaching (8:31—10:45), prophetic actions (11:1–26), an eschatological discourse (ch. 13), and the passion narrative (chs. 14–15).

Mark then surrounds this material with a framework that, like a picture frame, enables the reader to focus upon the material within the frame from a certain theological perspective (see the designated themes mentioned after each frame above). Several of these frames are more obvious than others. Two healings of blind men encapsulate the discipleship catechism, with the need for a second touch from Jesus (8:22–26) preparing for Peter's confession and his subsequent misunderstanding (8:27–34), while the three cycles of discipleship teaching culminate in the healing of Bartimaeus (10:46–52), who now successfully recognizes Jesus as the Son of David and follows along the way to Jesus' passion. Likewise, the continuous flow of the narrative from 1:45 to 3:7 (skipping 2:1—3:6) indicates that Mark has composed a frame around the controversy dialogues to indicate that the Messianic Secret will only be exposed in conflict. In addition, the two stories of women who offer their all in service of God's kingdom (12:41–44; 14:1–9) surround the eschatological discourse and provide a third example of a prominent Markan frame. Finally, the successful attempt of the woman to anoint Jesus for his burial parallels the unsuccessful undertaking of the women to anoint Jesus in the tomb, thus indicating that all of the material in between has been carefully planned in God's divine scheme. Once these more unmistakable frames have been detected, the reader can surmise that Mark has regularly employed this literary device throughout his gospel. The Markan frame is an extension of the more frequently recognized Markan intercalation or sandwich where the identical story is interrupted (rather than a similar narrative), shining theological light upon the enclosed material. The presence of this frame structure is convincing since it divides the material along the lines of genre and plays a similar role as the Markan sandwich. More significantly, it exposes the themes of Mark, which center upon a Christology that holds together Jesus as Davidic Messiah with Jesus as suffering servant Son of God, which consequently demands a discipleship of the cross.

Although this is a recognized literary feature of Mark, lingering doubts remain in some scholars' minds that Mark employs the frame as a structural device throughout his gospel. Here it must be admitted that Mark frames his material somewhat differently at times. Most often Mark encircles a fivefold structure with a frame, but on other occasions the fivefold outline includes the frame so that a triadic structure is encircled by a frame.[3] Sometimes one element of the frame is employed again in the next frame (the eschatological discourse and passion narrative), while on most occasions the frame is distinct from the surrounding material. Therefore, this different usage or lack of consistency undermines the clarity of this literary device at times.

Second, Mark demolishes the fivefold structuring of material at specific points in the gospel. In the miracle section Mark adds material on purity in 6:53—7:20 so that the following miracles of the healing of the Canaanite woman's daughter and the deaf-mute man with spit are transferred into theological reflection on the Jewish purity rites of clean hands, kosher food, Gentile inclusion in table fellowship, and impurity through fluids. Furthermore, the inclusion of 6:1–20 imports a new structure onto this section where the rejection by Jesus' countrymen in 6:1–6 concludes a section on discipleship while the following mission trip of the disciples initiates a new section.[4] Finally, the

---

3. For a chart of the different usages see the end of chapter 3 on Markan frames.
4. See the concluding outline (12) for an investigation of Mark's motive and purpose.

healing at Bethsaida (8:22–26) is removed from the miracle section and placed as a frame for the discipleship catechism. Therefore a new structure appears, with the three trips across the sea corresponding to the three cycles of discipleship catechism placed at the middle of Mark's gospel. These alterations should make the reader aware that, in addition to the structuring of material by frames, Mark includes other emphases such as the fulfillment of certain Jewish purity rites and a call to persistent discipleship in the face of suffering. However, these irregularities should not cause us to discount the importance of Markan frames in the structuring of the gospel. Instead we must recognize a two-stage redaction by Mark, as will be explained at the conclusion of this appendix.

Structural Pattern 2: Transitions Providing Structure

Since transitional material frequently divides an author's writing, a reader might expect this division in the Gospel of Mark as well. In fact, in the first paragraph of D. A. Carson's interpretation of Mark, he concludes that "this fast-paced narrative is punctuated by six transitional paragraphs or statements, which divide Mark's account into seven basic sections."[5] However, striking differences over the number of transitions in Mark's gospel indicate that this method of dividing the material is not convincing. Furthermore, the sections are divided differently, with Carson choosing for geographical transitions and Perrin for christological and genre transitions.

1. Carson[6]: 1:14–15; 3:7–12; 6:1–6; 8:27–30; 10:46–52; 14:1–2
2. Perrin[7]: 1:14–15, 21–22, 39; 2:13; 3:7–12; 5:21; 6:6b, 12–13, 30–33, 53–56; 10:1
3. Charles Hedrick[8] adds to Perrin's list: 1:5, 28, 32–34, 45; 2:1–2, 15; 4:33–34; 6:1; 9:30–32; 10:32
4. Wilhelm Egger[9]: 1:14–15, 21–22, 32–34, 39, 45; 2:1–2, 13; 3:7–12; 4:1–2; 6:6b, 30–34, 53–56; 10:1

Hedrick notes that these transitions are "not literary summaries in the narrow sense that they catch up in a brief single statement the essence of a broader literary segment that precedes or follows, like good introductory or concluding sentences to paragraphs."[10] He argues from similarities with Philostratus's *The Life of Apollonius of*

---

5. Carson, Moo, and Morris, *Introduction to the New Testament*, 89.
6. Ibid., 89–91.
7. Perrin, *New Testament*, 145–47.
8. Hedrick, "Role of Summary Statements," 289–311.
9. Egger, *Frohbotschaft und Lehre*, 2. Stein (*Mark*, 160) does not see the summaries as structural indicators but identifies summaries at 1:14–15, 28, 32–34, 39; 2:13; 3:7–12; 4:33–34; 6:12–13, 53–56; 9:30–32; 10:1, 30–32.
10. Hedrick, "Summary Statements," 294.

Tyana that Mark's transitions "broaden, expand, and intensify the ministry of Jesus."[11] However, the transitions then serve such different functions that a consistent purpose throughout the transitions of Mark's gospel is impossible to grasp. Because of their different length, function, difficulty to discern, and concentration in the first half of the gospel, transitions do not provide a precise strategy for outlining Mark's gospel.

Carsons' outline using six transitional paragraphs based on geography[12]:

I. Introduction (1:1–13)

    Transitional Markan summary (1:14–15)

II. First major section: the authority of Jesus exhibited in word and deed (1:16—3:6)

    Transitional Markan summary (3:7–12)

III. Second major section: Jesus as Son of God rejected by his own people (3:13—6:6a)

    Transitional Markan summary (6:6b)

IV. Third major section: Jesus as Son of God misunderstood by his disciples (6:7—8:22)

    Transitional giving-of-sight story (8:23–26)

V. Fourth major section: Christology and Christian discipleship in the light of the passion (8:27—10:45)

    Transitional giving-of-sight story (10:46–52)

VI. Fifth major section: the days in Jerusalem prior to the passion (11:1—12:44)

VII. Apocalyptic discourse with introduction (13:1–37)

    A. Introduction to the apocalyptic discourse (13:1–5a)

    B. Apocalyptic discourse (13:5b–37)

VIII. Passion narrative with introduction (14:1—16:8)

    A. Introduction to the passion narrative (14:1–12)

    B. The passion narrative (14:13—16:8)

Structural Pattern 3: Chiastic Structures

Mark employs several fivefold chiastic structures throughout his gospel, as evidenced by our research into Markan frames in chapter 3. However, these all involve shorter passages so that I have become convinced over the years that the presence of macro-chiastic

---

11. Hedrick, "Summary Statements," 311, with examples from Philostratus on 304–9.
12. Carson et al., *Introduction*, 89–91.

structures covering an entire book is dubious.[13] We have outlined criteria for evaluating chiasms in section 3.1, entitled "Structural Techniques in the Gospel of Mark."

With regard to the chiastic structures below, the very general outline by Bas Van Iersel certainly rings true. The way of discipleship section is undoubtedly central to Mark's theology. Furthermore, the frame around this section offers Mark's perspective on miracle stories. Likewise, the shift from Galilee to Jerusalem effectively captures the chronology of the narrative. However, there are additional nuances to Mark's structure which this skeleton structure does not apprehend. Yet when scholars attempt to be more specific than Van Iersel, items in the outline fail to form parallel structures. For instance, one would anticipate that the five controversy dialogues in 2:1—3:6 would fit chiastically with the five pronouncement sayings in 11:27—12:37, but both Humphrey and Scott discern alternative parallels. Furthermore, Scott locates the transfiguration as the central narrative, while the fourth chiasm below posits Peter's confession as the transitional element. In reality, both miss the triadic structure in Mark which unveils the gradual revelation of the Messiah. At Jesus' baptism, God confirms to Jesus personally that he is the suffering servant Messiah. Then at the transfiguration the voice from heaven reveals to Jesus' closest disciples his true identity. Finally, through the centurion's confession of Jesus as Son of God at the crucifixion the Messianic Secret is unveiled to the entire Gentile world. In addition, the threefold trips across the sea and the three cycles of passion prediction, misunderstanding, and teaching on discipleship are also bypassed in these chiastic structures. In a word, macro chiastic outlines miss the subtleties in Mark's structure.

		Van Iersel's Macro-Chiastic Outline[A]	
a		1:2–13	Prologue: the wilderness
	b	1:14–15	Prospective hinge
		c	1:16—8:21	Galilee
			d	8:22–26	Frame: the blind see.
				e	8:27—10:45	The Way
			d'	10:46–52	Frame: the blind see.
		c'	11:1—15:39	Jerusalem
	b'	15:40–41	Retrospective hinge
a'		15:42—16:8	Epilogue: the tomb

A. Van Iersel, *Mark: A Reader-Response Commentary*, 84.

---

13. Authors who perceive a chiastic structure for Matthew include Combrink, "Structure of the Gospel of Matthew," 61–90; Fenton, *Saint Matthew*, 15–16; H. B. Green, "Structure of St. Matthew's Gospel," 47ff.; Gaechter, *Das Matthäus Evanglium*, 17; and Lohr, "Oral Techniques," 403–35. For the Gospel of John see Ellis, *Genius of John*, 14–15.

Outlines of the Structure of Mark

Humphrey's Macro-Chiastic Outline[A]				
a			1:1–15	Opening section: Jesus is identified as Son of God.
		1	1:16–20	Interlude: Jesus' first followers
b			1:21—3:6	First major section: Jesus' ministry occasions opposition.
		2	3:7–19	Interlude: of Jesus, disciples, mission
c			3:20—6:13	Second major section: of response to Jesus, judgment
		3	6:14–29	Interlude: John the Baptist gives his life.
d			6:30—8:21	Third major section: Jesus comes to Israel as its true teacher.
		4	8:22–26	Interlude: healing of the blind man
e			8:27—10:45	Central section: the "secret" wisdom (giving all to all gains all, e.g., Jesus)
		4'	10:46–52	Interlude: healing of the blind man
d'			11:1—12:40	Third last section: Jesus comes to Israel as its lord.
		3'	12:41–44	Interlude: A widow gives all she has.
c'			13:1–37	Second last section: of discipleship, judgment
		2'	14:1–9	Interlude: of Jesus' departure and discipleship
b'			14:10—15:39	Last section: betrayal, rejection, and death of Jesus
		1'	15:40–47	Interlude: Jesus' last followers
a			16:1–8	Climax: Jesus is confirmed as Son of God by his resurrection.

A. Humphrey, "*He is Risen!*" *A New Reading of Mark's Gospel*, 4.

M. P. Scott's Macro-Chiastic Outline Centering Upon Transfiguration[A]			
a		1:2	An angel witnesses to his coming.
b		1:11	You are my Son.
c		2:7	Who can forgive sins? (εἰ μὴ εἷς ὁ θεός)
d		3:29	The guilt of the scribes
e		3:33	Who is my mother?
f		3:35	The primacy of doing God's will
g		4:40	Who is this that the winds obey him?
h		6:3	Jesus is called the son of Mary.
i		8:27	Who do you say that I am?
j		8:31	Prophecy of betrayal, passion, resurrection
k		9:7	This is my Son: listen to him.
j'		9:30	Prophecy of betrayal, passion, resurrection
i'		10:18	Why do you call me good? (εἰ μὴ εἷς ὁ θεός)
h'		10:47	Jesus is called Son of David.
g'		11:28	By what authority do you do these things?
f'		12:30	The primacy of God's commandment to love
e'		12:37	How is the Christ David's son?
d'		12:40	A judgment on the scribes
c'		14:61	Are you the Christ, the Son of the Blessed God?

Appendix 4

b'		15:39	Truly, this man was the Son of God.
a'		16:6	An angel witnesses to his going.

A. M.P. Scott, *Biblical Theology Bulletin* 15 (1985):18-19, 25.

		\multicolumn{2}{l}{Macro-Chiastic Outline Centering upon Peter's Confession as the Turning Point}	
a		1:1, 11	The beginning of the gospel (1:1) with Jesus exalted as the Son at his baptism (1:11)
b		1:14-39	First day of Jesus' ministry
c		2:1—3:6	First set of five controversy dialogues
d		4:1-34	Jesus' parabolic discourse concerning the present kingdom of God
e		4:35—8:21	Three trips across the sea
f		8:27-30	Peter's confession of faith
e'		8:31—10:52	Three passion predictions
d'		Mark 13	Jesus' eschatological discourse concerning the future kingdom
c'		11:27—12:40	Second set of five controversy dialogues
b'		14:12—15:41	Last day of Jesus' ministry
a'		16:1-8	The end of the gospel with Jesus exalted in his resurrection as Son of God

Structural Pattern 4: Three-Step Progression

Lohmeyer

Lohmeyer is famous for his consistent outline of the Gospel of Mark in triads. In total he envisions thirty-six triadic sections divided into six sections organized either by geography or theme.[14]

1. The beginning (1:1—3:6)

    a. The beginning of the gospel (1:1-8, 9-11, 12-13)

    b. Preaching and discipleship (1:14-15, 16-18, 19-20)

    c. The first day in Capernaum (1:21-22, 23-28, 29-31)

    d. Outside Capernaum (1:32-34, 35-39, 40-45)

    e. The controversy with the sinner and tax collector (2:1-12, 12-14, 15-17)

    f. The controversy with fasting and the Sabbath (2:18-22, 23-28; 3:1-6)

2. Around the Sea of Gennesaret (3:7—6:16)

    a. The Twelve (3:7-10, 11-12, 13-19)

    b. Jesus' relation and opponents (3:20-21, 22-30, 31-35)

---

14. Lohmeyer, *Das Evangelium des Markus*, 5*-6*.

c. Parable of the sower (4:3–9, 10–12, 13–20)

d. Explanation of the speech (4:21–35, 26–29, 30–32)

e. Miracles at sea (4:35–41; 5:1–20, 21–43)

f. Rejection and sending (6:1–6, 7–13, 14–16)

g. Death of John the Baptizer (6:17–29) (not a triad)

3. The bread miracles (6:30—8:26)

   a. Miracles at sea (6:30–44, 45–52, 53–56)

   b. Clean and unclean (7:1–13, 14–15, 17–23)

   c. Miracles in Gentile territory (7:24–30, 31–37; 8:1–9)

   d. The incomprehension of the signs (8:10–13, 14–21, 22–26)

4. The way of suffering (8:27—10:52)

   a. The secret of the Son of Man (8:27–29, 30–33, 8:34—9:1)

   b. The revelation of the Son of Man (9:2–8, 9–13, 14–29)

   c. In Galilee (9:30–32, 33–37, 38–50)

   d. In Judea and Perea (10:1–12, 13–16, 17–31)

   e. To Jerusalem (10:32–34, 35–45, 46–52)

5. Jesus' message in Jerusalem (11:1—13:37)

   a. The first day (11:1–6, 7–10, 11)

   b. The second day (11:12–14, 15–17, 18–19)

   c. The third day (11:20–25, 27–33; 12:1–12)

   d. Three controversies (12:13–17, 18–27, 28–34)

   e. Three teachings (12:35–37, 38–40, 41–44)

   f. The apocalyptic teaching (13:5–13, 14–27, 28–37)

6. The passion (14:1—16:8)

   a. Before the feast (14:1–2, 3–9, 10–11)

   b. The Passover evening (14:12–16, 17–21, 22–25)

   c. The night of the arrest (14:26–31, 32–42, 43–52)

   d. The Sanhedrin (14:53–54, 55–65, 66–72)

   e. The morning (15:1–5, 6–15, 16–20)

   f. The crucifixion (15:20–23, 24–27, 29–32)

   g. The death (15:33–37, 38–39, 40–41)

   h. The burial and empty tomb (15:42–46, 47; 16:1–8)

Appendix 4

Some of Lohmeyer's suggestions are ingenious, such as the three-day outline in Jesus' Jerusalem ministry. But problems emerge when Lohmeyer attempts to crunch the whole gospel into a triadic mold. Since he cannot fit the death of John the Baptist into a triadic outline (6:17–29), he assumes that this pericope is not integral to Mark's gospel. However, this intercalation with the mission of the disciples leaves a Markan fingerprint and thus proves its importance to Mark's theology. Furthermore, the division of 7:14–23 into two sections (14–15, 17–23) bifurcates Jesus' parable and interpretation. In addition, his outline of the way of suffering in 8:27—10:52 interrupts the threefold structure of passion prediction, misunderstanding, and teaching of discipleship so crucial to this discipleship catechism. Finally, his six sections include material that is not germane to the title of each section, so that the controversies of 2:1—3:6 become included in "the beginning" of the gospel and the women's role in the burial and resurrection is simply attached to the passion narrative. Finally, important literary devices are bypassed, like the recognition of a Markan frame combining the two-stage healing of the blind man with the Bartimaeus pericope.

Robbins

Based upon the frequent employment of triads in the Gospel of Mark[15] and especially the three cycles of passion prediction, misunderstanding, and teaching on discipleship in the central section of 8:27—10:52,[16] Robbins proposes a three-step rhetorical sequence throughout the gospel. Whereas Lohmeyer attempts to divide the Gospel of Mark by geography (Sea of Gennesaret; Jerusalem), genre (miracles, passion narrative), and content (way of suffering), Robbins more satisfyingly identifies the two major themes of Mark as Christology and discipleship. His outline suggests that the threefold division of each section centers on Christology while the application section following this triad concentrates on discipleship. Each triad of Christology concentrates on a different title or designation of Jesus (italicized below).[17]

Introduction	1:1–13	John the Baptizer prepares the way for Jesus
Section 1	1:14–15, 16–18, 19–20	*Jesus*: proclaiming the gospel of God and summoning
	1:21—3:6	Initial stage of the teacher–disciple relationship
Section 2	3:7–8, 9–12, 13–19	*Son of God*: casting out demons and healing
	3:20—5:43	Special Instruction and Awareness of Special Powers
Section 3	6:1–3, 4–6, 7–13	*The Prophet*: rejection of the wonder-working teacher
	6:14—8:26	Performance of duties within discipleship
Section 4	8:27–30, 31–33, 34—9:1	*The Son of Man*: suffering, death, and resurrection
	9:2—10:45	Struggle over the teacher's value system

---

15. See the 23 examples given by Neirynck, *Duality in Mark*, 110–12.
16. Robbins, "Summons and Outline" 97, 113.
17. Ibid., 113–14.

Outlines of the Structure of Mark

Section 5	10:46–48, 49–52, 11:1–11	*The Son of David*: powerful teaching in Jerusalem
	11:12—12:44	Addressing general issues in public forum
Section 6	13:1–2, 3–4, 5–37	*The Teacher* prepares his disciples for his absence and return as Son of Man
	14:1—15:47	Unwillingness to accept the necessity of the arrest, trial, and death of the Teacher
Conclusion	16:1–8	The resurrection

The problem with Robbins' analysis centers on the fact that he omits many of the Markan triads, in particular the threefold passion prediction of the discipleship catechism, which was the forerunner of his insights. Furthermore, his proposals for a threefold structure are not examples that Neirynck has recognized, nor do they include the more explicit examples of the three seed parables (4:1–34), the three extended trips across the sea (4:35–41; 6:45–53; 8:13–21), the three prophetic actions aimed at Judaism (11:1–26), the threefold failure to watch in Gethsemane (14:32–42), Peter's threefold denial (14:66–72), and the three time designations on Good Friday (15:25, 33, 34). This inconsistency argues against taking Robbins's suggestion seriously.

Structural Pattern 5: Geographical Structure

Certainly Mark has a chronological interest. He prepares the reader for later events, as when the small boat is ready in 3:9 and finally used in 4:1ff. or when Jesus inspects the temple on Sunday (11:11) before cleansing it at 11:15ff. on the next day. Glances backward are employed as in the narration of John the Baptizer's death in 6:17–29 and the allusion to John's baptism at 11:30. Prediction and fulfillment are important themes to Mark which demand a chronological scheme. We see this in the betrayal by Judas (14:18–20 and 15:44–46), the scattering of the disciples (14:27 and 14:50), and the denials of Jesus by Peter (14:30–31 and 15:66–72).

However, if a chronological outline were strictly followed, Jesus' ministry would only comprise one calendar year, climaxing in a single trip to the Passover feast. More importantly, as Wegener points out, this chronological and geographical data "provide transitions from scene to scene but do not group pericopes into longer sequences and therefore are not helpful in determining the overall outline of Mark's narrative."[18] Although a division can be made in the gospel between the Galilean ministry and the Jerusalem ministry,[19] the biographical connections of time and place are very general (καί, πάλιν, ἐκεῖθεν, ἐκείναις ταῖς ἡμέραις) and provide no structural clues to the themes of the gospel. Therefore, as Hawkin maintains, a geographical outline "presses

---

18. Wegener, *Cruciformed*, 87.

19. Therefore, Tolbert (*Sowing the Gospel*, 113–14) has argued for a two-part division of the material that follows the introduction (Mark 1–10 and 11–16). However, Kümmel (*Introduction to the New Testament*, 82–84) argues for five geographical divisions: Galilee (1:14—5:43); travels (6:1—9:50); journey to Jerusalem (chapter 10); Jerusalem (11–13); and passion and resurrection (14–16).

the structure of Mark into moulds which are quite minor in the Gospel."[20] In the outline below we include a reference to all the chronological data, and the table that follows lists support for a Galilee/Jerusalem outline, with the discipleship catechism of 8:22—10:52 as transitional.[21]

I. Judea

    A. Desert region (1:4); Jordan River (1:5)

    B. Galilee (1:14); Sea of Galilee (1:16)

II. A day in Galilee

    A. Capernaum synagogue (1:21); Simon's house (1:29); after sunset (1:32)

    B. Solitary place early in morning (1:35); throughout Galilee (1:39)

III. Again in the same places

    A. Capernaum again after a few days (2:1)

    B. Beside the lake again (2:13); Sabbath in the grain fields (2:23)

    C. Synagogue again (3:1)

IV. Lake journeys

    A. Lake (3:7); mountainside (3:13); house (3:20)

    B. By the lake again (4:1); across the lake to the Gerasenes or Gaderenes (5:1); Decapolis (5:20)

    C. Across the lake (5:21); Nazareth (6:1); village to village (6:6); solitary place (6:32)

    D. Across the lake to Bethsaida (6:45); Gennesaret (6:53); Tyre (7:24)

    E. Through Sidon to the Sea of Galilee into Decapolis (7:31); boat to Dalmanutha (8:10)

    F. In a boat to the other side (8:13); Bethsaida (8:22)

V. Journey to the north outside of Galilee

    A. Villages around Caesarea Philippi (8:27)

    B. Mountain of transfiguration after six days (9:2); house (9:28)

VI. Journey to Jerusalem through Perea

    A. Through Galilee (9:30); house in Capernaum (9:33)

    B. Judea across the Jordan (10:1); on the way (10:17, 32)

    C. Jericho (10:46)

---

20. Hawkin, "Symbolism and Structure," 106.

21. Evidence for a bipartite structure is taken from Boring, *Mark*, 4–5.

Outlines of the Structure of Mark

VII. Passion week in Jerusalem

    A. Sunday: Bethphage and Bethany at the Mount of Olives (11:1); Jerusalem into the temple (11:11)

    B. Monday: Bethany (11:12); Jerusalem to cleanse the temple (11:15)

    C. Tuesday: evening out of the city (11:19); morning return (11:20); Jerusalem in the temple (11:27); where the offerings were placed (12:41); leaving the temple (13:1); Mount of Olives (13:3)

    D. Wednesday: feast of unleavened bread two days away (14:1); Bethany at Simon the leper's (14:3)

    E. Thursday night: first day of unleavened bread (14:12); city in a large upper room (14:15–17); Mount of Olives (14:26); Gethsemane (14:32); before the high priest (14:53)

    F. Friday: Pilate very early in the morning (15:1); Praetorium (palace) (15:16); Golgotha (15:22); third hour (15:25); sixth hour (15:33); ninth hour (15:34); evening of preparation day (15:42)

    G. Saturday night: Sabbath is over (16:1)

    H. Sunday: very early on the first day of the week (16:2); visit to the tomb (16:3)

Evidence for a Bipartite Division by Geography

Part 1 (1:1—8:21)	Part 2 (11:1—16:8)
Galilee	Jerusalem
Calling, sending disciples	No calling or sending disciples
Miraculous ministry	Non-miraculous ministry
Exorcisms	No exorcisms
Success	Rejection
Major central discourse: parables	Major central discourse: apocalyptic
Kingdom parables	No kingdom parables
Mystery of the kingdom	Jesus the king
Purity, Sabbath, synagogue	Temple
Secrecy commands	No secrecy commands
Unhealed blindness to a suffering Messiah	Blindness healed
No valid confession	Valid confession: Jesus, centurion
Key symbols: bread, sea, boat	Key symbols: cup, way, cross

Structural Pattern 6: Kerygma Providing Structure

C. H. Dodd is famous for pointing out the interconnections between Peter's preaching of the gospel in Acts 10:37–41 and the structure of Mark's gospel.[22] The sequence begins with Jesus' baptism and ends with the resurrection, omitting any birth narra-

---

22. Dodd, "Framework of the Gospel Narrative," 396–400.

tive. The description in Acts 10:38 that Jesus "went around doing good and healing all who were under the power of the devil" fits perfectly with the narratives of Mark's gospel. Certainly these similarities prove that Mark is a literaturization of the oral proclamation. However, Nineham points out that "very few pericopae contain internal evidence exact enough to tie them firmly to one particular place in the outline."[23] Furthermore, instead of Mark following the pattern of early Christian preaching, this structure could have been derived by Luke from Mark's gospel itself.[24] Finally, this structure only provides a skeleton and does not capture the intricacies of Mark's gospel. Certainly the primary Markan themes, literary devices, as well as the specifics of Jesus' teaching and miracle ministry are ignored by this skeleton outline.

I. The baptism that John preached (Acts 10:37 = Mark 1:1–8, "Beginning of the gospel")

II. Jesus anointed with the Holy Spirit and power (Acts 10:38a = Mark 1:9–15)

III. Jesus doing good, healing, and casting out demons (Acts 10:38b = Mark 1:16—10:52)

IV. Jesus killed in Jerusalem (Acts 10:39 = Mark 11:1—15:47)

V. God raised Jesus from the dead as witnessed by the disciples (Acts 10:40–41 = Mark 16)

Structural Pattern 7: A Five-Act Hellenistic Drama

(Teaching scenes replace the normal four choruses in Hellenistic drama.)

Has Mark created a drama to be read aloud and acted out before the 85–90 percent of adult males and 95 percent of women in the first-century Mediterranean world who were illiterate?[25] Recent commentators have argued this thesis[26] by investigating indicators within the text (Mark 2:10; 13:14[27]), memory devices such as catchwords and chiasms, and references to exhortations to read the documents aloud (Col 4:16). Silent reading, although not unknown in the ancient world,[28] was not the normal practice, as evidenced by Augustine's surprise that Ambrose read without speaking (*Confessions* 6.3.3). The NRSV even translates ὁ ἀναγινώσκων in Revelation 1:3 as

---

23. Nineham, "Order of Events," 226.

24. Ibid., 229.

25. For a discussion of literacy see Harris, *Ancient Literacy*, 248–84, 328–30.

26. Dewey, "Oral Methods of Structuring Narrative," 32–44; idem, "Mark as Interwoven Tapestry," 221–36; idem, "Mark as Aural Narrative," 45–56; Malbon, *Hearing Mark*; Shiner, *Proclaiming the Gospel*; Stanton, *Gospel for a New People*, 73–75.

27. "Let the reader understand" is interpreted as a note to the actor to be highly demonstrative at this point in the story since historically it applies to present happenings and grammatically calls attention to the solecism "standing where he should not." Best, "Gospel of Mark," 124–32.

28. Cf. Knox, "Silent Reading in Antiquity," 421–35.

"Blessed is the one who reads aloud the words of the prophecy, and blessed are those who hear."[29] Therefore, Achtemeier concludes that acoustic echo is more important than visual repetition and that "methods of organization of thought intended to make that thought accessible will, in ancient writings, be based on sound rather than sight."[30]

Although the gospel writers probably included both readers and hearers in their audience,[31] it is doubtful that Mark composed this work as a five-act Hellenistic play as Mary Ann Beavis proposes.[32] The teaching in Mark is spread throughout the gospel and not just in four long sermons, as evidenced by the fact that Jesus is also teaching at Mark 1:21-22; 2:13; 6:2, 34; 8:31; 11:17; 12:35. Furthermore, the so-called second chorus of teaching about clean and unclean things is really a series of narratives. Finally, this outline concludes the miracle section at 6:52 whereas the two miraculous feedings (6:35-44; 8:1-9) and three sea trips (4:35-41; 6:45-53; 8:13-21) should be tied together.

Act I	1:1—3:35	Narrative: prologue, controversies
	4:1-34	Teaching: parables (see!)
Act II	4:35—6:52	Narrative: miracles
	6:53—7:23	Teaching: clean and unclean
Act III	7:24—9:29	Narrative: revelations
	9:30—10:45	Teaching: discipleship
Act IV	10:46—12:44	Narrative: Jerusalem, controversies
	13:1-37	Teaching: apocalyptic discourse (hear!)
Act V	14:1—16:8	Narrative: passion, empty tomb

Structural Pattern 8: Deep Structure Organization[33]

Based upon the structural analysis of narratives by A. J. Greimas,[34] Ched Myers and Dan Via distinguish five irreducible diachronic elements in Mark's narrative.

1. Mandate
2. Acceptance or rejection of the mandate
3. Confrontation
4. Success or failure in achieving the mandate
5. Consequence or attribution

---

29. In addition, Knowles ("Reading Matthew," 57) points out that the NT contrast (Rom 2:13; Jas 1:22-25) is between hearers and doers of God's word, not readers and doers.
30. Achtemeier, "*Omne verbum sonat*," 18-19.
31. Knowles, "Reading Matthew," 68ff. See also Millard, *Reading and Writing in the Time of Jesus*.
32. Beavis, *Mark's Audience: The Literary and Social Setting of Mark 4:11-12*, 163.
33. Myers, *Binding the Strong Man*, 120-21; Via, *Ethics of Mark's Gospel*, 40ff.
34. Greimas, *Sémantique structural*, 196-97, 205.

Appendix 4

Via claims that "its focus on confrontation is especially applicable to the Markan narrative where conflict is such an important element in the plot."[35] Certainly this analysis uncovers important plot sequences in Mark's gospel, such as Jesus' immediate confrontation with the devil after his baptism as well as the early placement of the conflict dialogues in 2:1—3:6 with Jesus' death already implied at 2:20 and 3:6. Yet because of the inevitable movement away from the text and toward abstraction in structural analysis, the following outlines miss the development of the major themes of Mark like the nature of Jesus' identity, the mystery of the kingdom, the theological interpretation of miracles, and discipleship of the cross.

I. Main plot: Jesus' achievement of his mandate

    A. Beginning of the story

        1. Mandate: Jesus' call at his baptism through the voice from heaven (1:9–11)

        2. Acceptance or rejection of the mandate: Satan's temptations and the beginning of Jesus' ministry (1:12–15)

        3. Confrontation: Jesus' first sermon (1:21–28) and the controversy dialogues of 2:1—3:6

        4. Success or failure: plot to kill Jesus (3:6)

        5. Consequence or attribution: Jesus withdraws and the narrative regenerates with the naming and commissioning of his disciples (3:7–12).

    B. Middle of the story

        1. Mandate: The appointing of a new Israel in the twelve disciples (3:13–19)

        2. Acceptance or rejection of the mandate: Jesus teaches his disciples by themselves in a house (4:10, 34)

        3. Confrontation: Conflicts with the Pharisees (3:20–30), his own family (3:31–35), demon-possessed people (5:1–20), and his people at Nazareth (6:1–6)

        4. Success or failure: Successful mission of the twelve (6:7–13)

        5. Consequence or attribution: Mighty miracles are witnessed (6:30—8:26)

    C. End of the Story

        1. Mandate: Peter's confession and Jesus' decision to go to Jerusalem (8:27–31)

        2. Acceptance or rejection of the mandate: Jesus' acceptance but the disciples' rejection in their triple misunderstanding of the threefold passion prediction (8:32—10:52)

---

35. Via, *Ethics of Mark's Gospel*, 41.

3. Confrontation: Jesus' cleansing of temple, cursing of the fig tree, and the controversy dialogues with the Jewish leaders (Mark 11–12)

4. Success or failure: Jesus' trial and crucifixion (Mark 14–15)

4. Consequence or attribution: Ironically, Jesus' passion is really a success as proven by the resurrection, which provides a new story whose ending is up to the readers.

II. Subplot with the disciples

   A. Mandate: the call to carry on the work of the kingdom (1:17; 3:14; 6:7)

   B. Acceptance or rejection of the mandate: rejected once it is revealed as the way of the cross

   C. Confrontation (6:53; 8:17ff; 8:33 etc.)

   D. Success or failure: failure of the disciples as they scatter (14:50)

   E. Consequence or attribution: The disciples are given another opportunity because of Jesus' resurrection (16:6–7).

III. Subplot with the crowd

   A. Mandate: The crowd acknowledges Jesus' authority (1:22).

   B. Acceptance or rejection of the mandate: They accept Jesus as king at the triumphal entry (11:9–10) but reject Jesus at his trial.

   C. Confrontation: The crowds watch Jesus square off with the Jewish leaders.

   D. Success or failure: the call for the terrorist Barabbas and the execution of Jesus (15:6ff)

   E. Consequence or attribution: The crowd remains under the old order (15:11).

IV. Subplot with the Jewish leaders

   A. Mandate: Jesus asserts his authority over Jewish regulations (2:10, 28).

   B. Acceptance or rejection of the mandate: continual rejection (3:6; 6:26; 11:28; 12:13; 14:1–2)

   C. Confrontation: Jesus' cleansing of temple and the controversy dialogues with Jewish leaders

   D. Success or failure: At the trial the Jewish leaders have a choice what to do with Jesus.

   E. Consequence or attribution: They mock and reject their Messiah (15:29–32).

APPENDIX 4

Structural Pattern 9: Rhetorical Structure[36]

With the rise of narrative criticism, comparisons of the gospels with Greco-Roman rhetoric have become popular. However, the only NT gospel writer that undeniably betrays influence from the classic rhetoricians is Luke.[37] Therefore, the categories of the following outline are doubtful for the Gospel of Mark, which is dominated by a Jewish background. Furthermore, the miracle section in the following outline is broken up and the discipleship catechism is no longer central to the structure.[38] Finally, as Adela Collins maintains, "The main problem with this approach is that 6:14—10:52 is still narration, even if it has more strongly didactic character than the preceding material."[39]

I. *Exordium*: *proemium*: introduction (1:1–13)

 a. Establishes rapport between the speaker and audience

 b. Creates interest in the subject matter

 c. Possibly foreshadows the major topics

II. *Narratio*: *prothesis* (1:14—6:13)

 a. States the proposition (*propositio*)

 b. Provides background information

 c. Provides rationale for the point to be made

 The *partitio* was added later as a separate unit with the enumeration of the opponent's arguments.

III. *Probatio*: *pistis* or *confirmation* (6:14—10:52)

 a. Presentation of arguments

 b. Quotations from supportive authorities

 c. Citation of parallels and examples which the audience would find favorable

IV. *Refutatio* (11:1—15:47)

 a. Refutation of opposing views

V. *Peroratio*: *epilogos* or *conclusion* (16:1–8)

 a. Summary of major points and appeal to the audience's reason

 2. Arousing of emotions in support of the proposition as well as the speaker

---

36. Standaert, *L' Evangile selon Marc: Composition et genre littéraire*, 27–29, 51.
37. Cf. Witherington, *Acts of the Apostles*, 35–49.
38. For additional criticisms of Standaert, see Best, *Mark: Gospel as Story*, 103–4.
39. Collins, *Mark*, 90.

Structural Pattern 10: The Theme of "The Way"

The theme of the way is certainly central to the discipleship catechism of 8:22—10:52. Not only does ὁδός serve as an inclusio in 8:27 and 10:52, but it is employed on seven occasions (8:27; 9:33, 34; 10:17, 32, 46, 52) in this central section. In fact, this term is associated in close proximity with each of the three passion predictions of 8:31; 9:31; and 10:33. Furthermore, Mark employs this expression in the group of formal OT quotations (Exod 23:20; Mal 3:1; Isa 40:3) at the opening of the gospel (1:2–3).

However, beyond these examples the use of the concept of "the way" in Mark is very limited. Heil's outline below attaches the term "the way" to the concepts of "kingdom, followers, suffering/death and resurrection," but Mark himself does not specifically employ the term with these concepts. Furthermore, Derrett's picture of Jesus walking the way of all Israel through the OT narratives corresponds much better with the Gospel of Matthew than Mark's writing, as Dale Allison illustrates in his book, *A New Moses: The Matthean Typology*. Finally, the particular OT allusions do not coincide with Mark's description of certain scenes. As Cook sarcastically concludes, "Derrett's attempt seems to be forced, as the following example illustrates: Mark 6:30–44 finds its model in Joshua 1 where Joshua has the people gather manna."[40] Mark concentrates upon the themes of Christology and discipleship much more comprehensively than the motif of "the way."

Heil's outline centering upon "the way"[41]:
I. Preparation for the way of the Lord (1:1–13)
II. Jesus demonstrates the way of the kingdom (1:14—3:6).
III. The followers of the way receive the mystery of the kingdom (3:7—5:43).
IV. The followers of the way do not grasp the mystery (6:1—8:26).
V. The way of Jesus leads to suffering, death, and resurrection (8:27—10:52).
VI. On his way Jesus teaches in and about the temple (11:1—13:37).
VII. Jesus accomplishes the way of suffering and death (14:1—15:47).
VIII. The resurrection of Jesus and the way of the Lord (16:1–8).

Derrett's outline in which the way of Jesus recalls the way that Israel traveled through the Old Testament[42]:
I. Preparation for the trek (1:1—2:17)
II. Exodus (2:18—3:12)
III. The crossing (3:20—5:20)

---
40. Cook, *Structure and Persuasive Power*, 19.
41. Heil, *Gospel of Mark as a Model for Action*, 18.
42. Derrett, *Making of Mark*, 1:xff.

IV. Facing a rebellion (5:21—6:29)

V. Invasion of the land (6:30—9:1)

VI. Triumph (9:2—10:52)

VII. Provocation (11:1—12:44)

VIII. Woe to Jerusalem (Mark 13)

IX. Martyrdom (14:1—15:47)

X. Justification (16:1–8)

Structural Pattern 11: Christological Outlines

Christology stands central to Mark's purpose in the gospel.[43] Yet whether Mark employs christological titles to create structural transitions is another question. Contrary to Peace's outline, one particular title does not dominate each section. For instance, in the passion narrative the titles teacher (14:14, 45), Son of Man (14:21, 62); shepherd (14:27), Christ (14:61; 15:32), prophet (14:65), Nazarene (14:67), and King of the Jews (15:2, 18, 26, 32) are all employed, with Son of God only appearing once at the end (15:39).

The second outline below captures better the flow of Mark's gospel. As evident from the voice from heaven at Jesus' baptism (1:11), Mark emphasizes two aspects of Jesus' person: his Davidic messiahship from Psalm 2, evidenced in his miracle ministry; and the suffering servant nature of his identity from Isaiah 42, which dominates the central discipleship catechism and the passion narrative. The only drawback of this outline is that a purely christological structure cannot emphasize the theme of discipleship, which robustly competes for prominence in Mark's gospel with Christology.

Peace's christological titles outline[44]:

I. Jesus as Teacher (1:16—4:34)

II. Jesus the Prophet (4:35—6:30)

III. Jesus the Messiah (6:31—8:30)

IV. Jesus the Son of Man (8:31—10:45)

V. Jesus the Son of David (10:46—13:37)

VI. Jesus the Son of God (14:1—15:39)

---

43. Cf. Telford, *Theology of Mark*, 30ff.
44. Peace, *Conversion in the NT: Paul and the Twelve.*

OUTLINES OF THE STRUCTURE OF MARK

Messianic Son of David and suffering Son of Man christological outline:

I. The beginning of the gospel introduces Jesus as both the triumphant Messiah and the suffering Son of God (1:1-13).

   A. The prologue: Jesus Christ, the Son of God (1:1), with Jesus as Christ proclaimed at the turning point (8:29) and Jesus as Son of God proclaimed at the cross (15:39).

   B. Mark begins with Jesus' baptism since the voice from heaven ("You are my Son in whom I am well pleased," an allusion to Ps 2:7 and Isa 42:1) proclaims Jesus as the suffering servant Son of David (1:9-13) and the inclusio (σχιζομένους 1:10; ἐσχίσθη 15:38) narrates the opening of heavenly revelation both in Jesus' glory and passion.

II. Galilean ministry: the identity of Jesus as Messiah through his kingdom words and miraculous deeds (1:14—8:26)

   A. The introduction to the various aspects of Jesus' ministry and his popularity (1:15-45)

   B. Jesus the great debater and his rejection by the Jewish leaders (2:1—3:6) and his family (3:7-34)

   C. Jesus the parable teller with the crowd's and his disciples' response (4:1-34)

   D. Jesus the miracle worker displays his lordship (4:35—8:26).

      1. Sea-calming trip (4:35—6:34)

         a. Lord over nature: the winds and waves obey him (4:35-41).

         b. Lord over demons: Jesus delivers the Gerasene demoniac (5:1-20).

         c. Lord over disease and death: the healing of the woman with the unclean flow of blood and the raising of Jairus' daughter (5:21-43)

         d. Response to lordship (6:1-34)

      2. Sea-walking trip (6:35—7:37)

         a. Lord over food: feeding of the 5,000 (6:35-44)

         b. Lord over nature: Jesus walks on water (6:45-56).

         c. Lord in controversies: controversy with the Pharisees about cleanliness (7:1-23)

         d. Lord over all peoples: healing of the Syrophoenician's daughter (7:24-30)

         e. Lord over the body: healing of the deaf-mute (7:31-37)

      3. Sea-conversation trip (8:1-21)

a. Lord over food: feeding of the 4,000 (8:1–10)

b. Lord in controversies: Pharisees demand a sign from heaven (8:11–13).

c. Lord of multiplication: trip over the sea; the disciples forget bread (8:14–21)

III. Galilean ministry: Jesus as the Suffering Servant in his passion predictions (8:27—10:52)

A. Jesus conveys to his disciples that he is the Messiah (8:27–30).

B. Cycle 1: Jesus as the suffering Son of Man and Peter's rejection of this option (confirmation in the transfiguration that Jesus is the Son of God) (8:30—9:29)

C. Cycle 2: Jesus as the suffering Son of Man and the disciples' argument about who is the greatest (9:30—10:31)

D. Cycle 3: Jesus as the suffering Son of Man and the request of James and John for seats of precedence (10:32–52)

IV. Jerusalem ministry: Jesus as the messianic Son of David

A. Jesus' prophetic actions whereby he becomes king and replaces the temple (11:1–25)

B. Jesus silences and replaces the Jewish leaders in the conflict dialogues (11:26—12:44).

C. The future suffering of the disciples, Jerusalem, and the cosmos leads to the triumph of Jesus' vindication and coming (13:1–37).

V. Jerusalem ministry: Jesus as suffering Son of God through his passion and resurrection (14:1—16:8)

A. The woman anoints Jesus' body for burial ahead of time, indicating that God's plan is for the Messiah to suffer and die (14:1–11).

B. Jesus predicts his sufferings at the Last Supper (14:12–31).

C. Jesus suffers in his arrest, betrayal, desertion by the disciples, and through the Jewish and Roman trials (14:32—15:20).

D. Jesus' crucifixion climaxes in the centurion's words, "Surely this man was the Son of God" (15:21–41).

E. Joseph of Arimathea accomplishes his kingdom action (15:43) by burying the Messiah (15:42–47).

F. Mark omits the resurrection appearances to call attention to the cross where the Messiah suffers but is also triumphant (16:1–8).

Structural Pattern 12: Discipleship Outline in Five Cycles[45]

A consistent pattern of discipleship clearly emerges from the Gospel of Mark. Each section begins with a positive description of the disciples but then the section concludes with a rejection of the ministry of Jesus which challenges the faith of the disciples. In addition, each cycle provides a deeper call to discipleship so that the role assigned to the disciples increases. The failure of the disciples becomes the final theme since, faced with the rejection of Jesus' message, their bold and decisive choices for Jesus turn to fear, misunderstanding, and unfaithfulness. The disciples are unable to accept a suffering Messiah and the concomitant claim of a discipleship of the cross.

The first cycle embarks with the disciples dramatically choosing to follow Jesus by leaving their professions (1:16–18) and families (1:19–20). Then Mark inserts five controversies over various important issues in Jewish religious life (2:1—3:5) where Jesus is criticized in each case. This section concludes with the disciples and Mark's readers witnessing the rejection of Jesus' message by the Jewish leaders (3:6). Two parties with opposite political and religious agendas (the Pharisees and Herodians) unite to plot Jesus' demise and death.

In the second cycle Jesus appoints the Twelve as the new Israel, endows them with his own authority, and trains them as apostles (3:13–19). The Twelve are called to be with Jesus (μετ' αὐτοῦ), a more intimate position than merely following after Jesus. However, the disciples are immediately confronted with the rejection by blood relation (3:20–21, 31–34) as well as serious accusations against Jesus by their own religious authorities (3:22–30). This section finally terminates with a rejection of Jesus' ministry by his own town's people (6:1–6a).

In the third cycle the disciples take the lead in the gospel mission (6:7–30) while Jesus supervises their ministry. Jesus again calls the Twelve (προσκαλεῖται 6:7; 3:13), confers upon them authority (ἐξουσίαν 6:7; 3:15), and sends them out as apostles (ἀποστέλλειν 6:7; ἀποστέλλῃ 3:14) to preach Jesus' message (ἐκήρυξαν 6:12; κηρύσσειν 3:14). In order to deepen their discipleship Jesus commands the disciples to provide food for the people (6:37) at the feeding of the five thousand, and they take leadership by distributing the bread to the crowds (6:41; 8:6). Jesus compels his disciples to endure the journey across the sea by themselves (6:45–46) while he oversees their discipleship from the mountain as he prays (6:48). Jesus rebukes the disciples' lack of faith when they cannot cast out the demons in his absence (9:19). Even though the disciples are warned that they could become outsiders to the cause (4:13), in the end they are overcome with blindness, misunderstanding, forgetfulness, and obduracy (8:17–21). Whereas the Jewish leaders are previously described

---

45. Schweizer ("Portrayal of the Life," 388) also produces a discipleship outline where he contrasts the blindness of the Pharisees (1:16—3:12), the blindness of Jesus' fellow-citizens (3:13—6:6), and the blindness of the disciples (6:7—8:26) with the unveiled revelation of 8:27—10:52 on the subject of discipleship. Wegener (*Cruciformed*, 90–92) divides the Jerusalem ministry into two scenes and so has six cycles of discipleship.

as hard-hearted (3:5 πωρώσει τῆς καρδίας αὐτῶν), now this infection has entered the disciples (πεπωρωμένην ἔχετε τὴν καρδίαν ὑμῶν 8:17; 6:52).

This initial call, training, and sending forth in mission of the disciples leads to a fourth section where Jesus' devotees are tested in their ability to persevere in a discipleship of the cross. In 8:34 Jesus issues a new call: "Whoever wants to be my disciple must deny themselves and take up their cross and follow me." The identical elements that comprised their successful response in 1:16–20 are now applied to a discipleship of the cross. Their initial call involved:

1. Their identification by name (1:16, 19; 2:14).
2. The mention of their profession (1:16 casting a net; 1:19 preparing their nets; 2:14 sitting at the tax collector's booth).
3. Jesus looking (εἶδεν) them over (1:16, 19; 2:14).
4. Jesus summoning them with various words (1:17 δεῦτε ὀπίσω μου, 20 ἐκάλεσεν; 2:14 λέγει αὐτῷ, Ἀκολούθει μοι).
5. The leaving behind (ἀφέντες) of something extraneous to their mission (1:18, 20; implied in the rising of Levi in 2:14).
6. A movement of following (1:18; 2:14) after Jesus (ὀπίσω 1:17, 20).

These elements are central as well to 8:34, which includes 1) the naming of a disciple (τις); 2) Jesus' summons (προσκαλεσάμενος similar to 3:13 and 6:7); 3) the leaving through denial (ἀπαρνησάσθω ἑαυτόν); 4) a new profession, i.e., the cross (ἀράτω τὸν σταυρὸν); and 5) the following after Jesus (ὀπίσω μου ἀκολουθεῖν), with the look of Jesus (#3 above) occurring the verse before in 8:33 (ἰδὼν). So the disciples are taught everything they need to know to follow a crucified Messiah (8:27—10:52), but in the end they betray (14:43–45), deny (14:66–72), and abandon Jesus (14:50–52). Whereas earlier the Jewish people were scandalized by Jesus (6:3 ἐσκανδαλίζοντο ἐν αὐτῷ), now the disciples imitate their behavior (14:27 πάντες σκανδαλισθήσεσθε). The insiders become outsiders.

In the fifth cycle of discipleship the women replace the disciples and like their counterparts commence their discipleship by leaving all behind (15:40–41). They follow Jesus all the way from Galilee and according to Mark become the only loyalists present at the cross, although they stand at a distance. Yet the final scene pictures them close-mouthed and fearful at the prospect of following a crucified Messiah (16:8). As Danova explains, "the story of the women re-presents significant elements of the characterization of the (male) disciples of Jesus and establishes narrative grounds for aligning the women with the disciples, from their earlier positive presentation to their final negative valuation."[46] Thus discipleship failure casts its shadow over the entire gospel.

---

46. Danova, "Characterization and Narrative Function," 375.

Outlines of the Structure of Mark

This thematic discipleship outline captures a major emphasis of Mark's gospel, yet its inability to include Christology in its pattern could cause the reader to focus on the disciples at the expense of Jesus. In addition, it disregards Mark's habit of framing material of similar genre like the sea crossings around the miracle section, the healing of the blind men encircling the discipleship catechism, the sacrificial contribution of female disciples bracketing the eschatological discourse, and the burial attempts serving as book ends for the passion narrative. Finally, the section on discipleship of the cross (8:22—15:39) is considerably longer than the other sections and contains material from various genres like discipleship teaching, prophetic actions, controversy dialogues, an eschatological discourse, and a passion narrative. On the other hand, this discipleship outline explains perfectly the insertion of the rejection at Nazareth (6:1-6) and the mission of the disciples (6:7-30) into the miracles section.

Thus Mark appears to have superimposed a discipleship outline over a collection of material that was organized by genre in the oral tradition. Therefore, Mark employs two literary methods to provide structure to his gospel. First he has framed the various collections of genre like controversy dialogues, parables, miracle stories, and eschatological teaching in order to offer a theological commentary on the content of this material. Then he has superimposed upon these literary units a discipleship structure which narrates the inability of the disciples to remain faithful to a cause to which they had originally dedicated their entire lives. The unfaithfulness of the disciples, Jesus' family, and the women (who are together the heroes of the early church in Acts 1:12-14) must be seen as a foil to both rebuke and encourage the readers of the gospel in their attempts at completing a discipleship of the cross.

I. Introduction: the beginning of the gospel (1:1–15)

    A. The preparation for the gospel by John the Baptizer (1:1–8)

    B. The preparation of Jesus through his baptism and testing in the wilderness (1:9–15)

II. The call of the disciples: ministry in front of the disciples (1:16—3:6)

    A. Begins with a call of the disciples to leave everything and follow Jesus (1:16-20)

    B. Paradigmatic ministry of Jesus in view of the disciples (1:21–45)

    C. Five controversies with the religious leaders (2:1—3:5)

    D. This section ends with the *rejection* of Jesus by the Jewish leaders (3:6–12).

III. The appointment of the Twelve: ministry with the disciples (3:13—6:6) (3:14 ἵνα ὦσιν μετ' αὐτοῦ)

    A. Begins with Jesus appointing the twelve disciples and giving them authority (3:7–35)

APPENDIX 4

   B. Narrates Jesus' parables (4:1–34) and miracles (4:35—5:43) with the disciples' responses

   C. Ends with the *rejection* of Jesus by his hometown people and family (6:1–6)

IV. The mission of the disciples: the disciples exercise their leadership with Jesus supervising (6:7—8:21).

   A. Begins with the mission journeys of the disciples (6:7–30)

   B. Jesus trains the disciples in their increased ministry roles through boat trips and journeys (6:31—8:10).

   C. Ends in failure when the disciples are *forgetful* (8:14), *hard-hearted* (8:17), and *do not understand* (8:21) (like the Pharisees who seek a sign, 8:11–12), prefiguring their *rejection* of his sufferings.

V. The cross and discipleship (8:22—15:39)

   A. Jesus' new call to his disciples to follow the way of the cross (8:22—10:52)

      1. The two-stage healing of the blind man (8:22–26) displays the need for the discipleship catechism that follows (8:31—10:45).

      2. The turning point: Peter's confession and Jesus' turning toward Jerusalem (8:27–30)

      3. Training in the discipleship of the cross (three cycles)

         a. First passion prediction, misunderstanding, teaching on discipleship (8:31—9:29)

         b. Second passion prediction, misunderstanding, teaching on discipleship (9:30—10:31)

         c. Third passion prediction, misunderstanding, teaching on discipleship (10:32–52)

      4. Bartimaeus, the example of enlightened discipleship, who both proclaims Jesus as Son of David and follows along the way (10:46–52)

   B. Jesus' struggle with Judaism in his Jerusalem ministry (11:1—12:44)

      1. The first three days of his ministry (11:1—12:12)

      2. Three difficult questions from the Jewish leaders, which Jesus' answers (12:13–34)

      3. Three accusations of Jesus against the Jewish leaders (12:35–44)

   C. Jesus' eschatological discourse (13:1–37)

   D. The passion narrative: Jesus goes to the cross without his disciples (14:1—15:39).

      1. Jesus foresees and predicts the sufferings of his passion (14:1–15:39).

2. *Ends in failure* when the disciples *betray* (14:43–45), *deny* (14:66–72), and *abandon* Jesus (14:50–52)

VI. The woman and discipleship (15:40—16:8)

A. The women begin their discipleship with sacrifice by following Jesus from Galilee and through their presence at the cross (15:40–47).

B. Mary Magdalene, Mary the mother of James, and Salome (15:40; 16:1) replace Peter, James, and John as the visible disciples.

C. *Ends in failure*, where in spite of Jesus' resurrection the women *flee in fear* and are *silent* in the proclamation of the gospel (16:1–8)

1. The identical word "flee" (ἔφυγον) is employed in the final picture of the male disciples in 14:50 (ἔφυγον πάντες).

2. The same description of the women as afraid (ἐφοβοῦντο γάρ) is used of the disciples (οἱ δὲ ἀκολουθοῦντες ἐφοβοῦντο) when Jesus goes before them into Jerusalem to his calling of crucifixion at 10:32.

3. The women are trembling and bewildered in 16:8 (τρόμος καὶ ἔκστασις) just as the male disciples are astonished (ἐθαμβοῦντο) at 10:32.

Conclusions

The multiplicity of outlines for the Gospel of Mark[47] has caused some to despair and skeptically doubt that any structural exemplar will prove convincing.[48] Kee for instance concludes that "Mark no more lends itself to analysis by means of a detailed outline developed by simple addition of components than does a major contrapuntal work of music."[49] Certainly the divergent outlines call attention to different connections in the text whether they are literary, stylistic, geographic, episodic, or thematic. However, we have argued in chapter 3 that Markan frames around material of similar genre provide a clarifying structure for the Gospel of Mark. These frameworks around a summary of Jesus' ministry, controversy dialogues, parables, miracle stories, discipleship teaching, eschatological/apocalyptic literature, and the passion narrative offer a theological perspective upon this material organized by genre from the oral tradition. The first outline above, structured by Markan frames, illustrates that some of Mark's material was already grouped together by genre and frequently organized

---

47. Because a fully developed lectionary only occurred after Mark's time, we have not mentioned outlines that base Mark's structure upon the Jewish lectionary. Philip Carrington (*Primitive Christian Calendar* and *According to Mark*) proposes that the appearance of a one-year ministry in the Gospel of Mark derived from a lectionary based upon the calendar year. Ruddick ("Behold I Send My Messenger," especially 416–17) ties each section of Mark to a successive reading of Genesis and Exodus. See also Goulder, "Mark and His Successors," 241–306.

48. See Cook, *Structure and Persuasive Power*, 12.

49. Kee, *Community of the New Age*, 64. Cf. Nineham, *St. Mark*, 29; Gundry, *Mark*, 1048–49.

through the employment of a fivefold chiasm for memory retention. The placement of frames around this material organized by genre constitutes the first stage in Mark's organization of the gospel material.

In the final discipleship outline above (12), we have postulated that Mark superimposes upon this material a second phase of structuring the material. This consists of five cycles of discipleship each beginning with success but terminating with tragic failure.[50] The disciples leave vocations and family to single-mindedly follow Jesus (1:16–20), but Jesus' path is filled with controversy and finally a death plot (3:6). The call to discipleship turns into an appointment of the Twelve (3:13–18), who witness Jesus' teaching and miracles but also his rejection by his own townspeople and family (6:1–6). The third cycle begins with the successful mission of the disciples (6:7–13, 30–31) but concludes with their own hard-heartedness and lack of understanding (8:17–21). Discipleship rejection has progressively closed in and finally infiltrated into the disciples' own commitment. Peter begins the fourth cycle with a triumphant confession of Jesus' messiahship (8:27–30), but the disciples misunderstand the implications of this confession and finally abandon, deny, and betray Jesus in his passion. In the final fifth cycle the women replace the disciples so that Mary Magdalene, Mary the mother of James and Joseph, and Salome (15:40; 16:1) become the inner circle instead of Peter, James, and John. Similarly, these newly introduced characters begin as vigorously committed disciples who have followed all the way from Galilee to be present at Jesus' crucifixion and burial. But in a repeat performance of the male disciples, they exit the narrative as discipleship failures. Overcome by fear, they fail to proclaim the gospel message (16:8). Their flight (ἔφυγον) parallels that of the male disciples in 14:50 (ἔφυγον πάντες).

These discipleship cycles have been variously interpreted, but I follow Fowler, who explains that they "serve the useful purpose of furnishing the reader with a vivid, memorable, and instructive antithesis to faithful discipleship.... In Mark's story they fail, but if Mark's portrayal of their failure achieves its objective, the reader will be more faithful than they and their failure will not have been utterly in vain."[51] In this progression toward a deepening discipleship, the followers of Jesus are first called to come after Jesus (1:17, 20 ὀπίσω αὐτοῦ), then to be with him (3:14 μετ' αὐτοῦ), then to go before him (6:45 προάγειν) as he supervises them, and finally to take up their cross and follow him in his passion (8:34 ἀράτω τὸν σταυρὸν αὐτοῦ καὶ ἀκολουθείτω μοι). They progress from followers to companions to fully authorized agents of Jesus' mission to participants in Jesus' suffering and resurrection.

Therefore, a structure that emphasizes Markan frameworks as a literary device as well as an outline based upon discipleship are not competing paradigms since both

---

50. See Lincoln ("Promise and Failure," 293–94) for confirmation of this view, except that he misses the beginning of the last cycle. Stein (*Mark*, 287) agrees with the first three cycles but contends that the ending of Mark in 16:8 is positive.

51. Fowler, *Loaves and Fishes*, 147.

offer significant insight into the purpose of Mark's gospel. Mark employs both the theme of discipleship and the literary device of framework to provide theological undergirding to his narrative sequence. The construction of his gospel is therefore a two-stage project of collecting the oral traditions by genre, framing them to offer a theological perspective, and overlaying this material with a discipleship structure. Mark labels the book as a gospel since it is primarily "good news about Jesus the Messiah, the Son of God" (1:1), but as Donahue affirms, "the story of the disciples occupies a strong second position" to the gospel's "obvious christological thrust."[52] A Christology that culminates in the cross has as its obvious corollary a discipleship of the cross. A disciple is not greater than his or her master but follows Jesus wherever he goes.

---

52. Donahue, *Theology and Setting of Discipleship*, 2. Henderson goes further and states that "in Mark's Gospel the themes of discipleship and Christology are inherently intertwined" ("Concerning the Loaves," 7).

Bibliography

Abegg, Martin G. "Exile and the Dead Sea Scrolls." In *Exile: Old Testament, Jewish, and Christian Perspectives*, edited by James M. Scott, 111–26. Leiden: Brill, 1997.
Achtemeier, Paul. J. "'And He Followed Him': Miracles and Discipleship in Mark 10:46–52." *Semeia* 11 (1978) 115–45.
———. "'He Taught Them Many Things': Reflections on Marcan Christology." *CBQ* 42 (1980) 465–81.
———. *Mark*. Proclamation Commentaries. Philadelphia: Fortress, 1975.
———. "Mark as Interpreter of the Jesus Traditions." *Int* 32 (1978) 339–52.
———. "*Omne verbum sonat*: The New Testament and the Oral Environment of Late Western Antiquity." *JBL* 109 (1990) 3–27.
———. "The Origin and Function of the Pre-Marcan Miracle Catenae." *JBL* 91 (1972) 198–221.
———. "Person and Deed. Jesus and the Storm-Tossed Sea." *Int* 16 (1962) 169–76.
———. "Toward the Isolation of a Pre-Markan Miracle Catenae." *JBL* 89 (1970) 265–91.
Achtemeier, Paul, Joel Green, and Marianne Meye Thompson. *Introducing the New Testament: Its Literature and Theology*. Grand Rapids: Eerdmans, 2001.
Aland, Kurt. "Bemerkungen zum Schluss des Markusevangliums." In *Neotestamentica et Semitica: Studies in Honour of Matthew Black*, edited by E. Earle Ellis and Max Wilcox, 157–80. Edinburgh: T. & T. Clark, 1969.
———. "Der wiedergefundene Markusschluß? Eine methodologiche Bemerkung zur textkritischen Arbeit." *ZTK* 67 (1970) 1–13.
Albertz, Martin. *Die synoptische Streitgespräche: ein Beitrag zur Formgeschichte des Urchristentums*. Berlin: Trowitzsch & Sohn, 1921.
Allison, Dale C. *Jesus of Nazareth: Millenarian Prophet*. Minneapolis: Fortress, 1998.
———. *The Jesus Tradition in Q*. Harrisburg, PA: Trinity, 1997.
Alon, G. "The Levitical Uncleanness of Gentiles." In *Jews, Judaism, and the Classical World*. Jerusalem: Magnes, 1977.
Ambrozic, Aloysius M. *The Hidden Kingdom. A Redactional-Critical Study of the References to the Kingdom of God in Mark's Gospel*. Washington, DC: Catholic Biblical Association of America, 1972.
———. "New Teaching with Power (Mk. 1:27)." In *Word and Spirit: Essays in Honor of David Michael Stanley*, edited by J. Plevnik Willowdale, 113–49. Ohio: Regis College, 1975.
Anderson, Charles P. "The Trial of Jesus as Jewish-Christian Polarization: Blasphemy and Polemic in Mark's Gospel." In *Anti-Judaism in Early Christianity: Vol. 1 Paul and the Gospels*, edited by P. Richardson & D. Granskou, 107–25. Waterloo: Canadian Corporation for Studies in Religion, 1986.

Bibliography

Anderson, Hugh. *The Gospel of Mark*. New Century Bible Commentary. London: Butler and Tanner, 1976.

Anderson, Janice Capel and Stephen D. Moore. *Mark and Method: New Approaches in Biblical Studies*. Minneapolis: Fortress, 1992.

Aune, David E. "The Problem of the Messianic Secret." *NovT* 11 (1969) 1–31.

Aus, Roger David. *Caught in the Act, Walking on the Sea, and The Release of Barabbas Revisited*. Atlanta: Scholars, 1998.

Avi-Yonah, Michael. *A History of Israel and the Holy Land*. New York: Continuum, 2001.

Bacchiocchi, Samuele. *Anti-Judaism and the Origin of Sunday*. Rome: Pontifical Gregorian University Press, 1975.

———. *From Sabbath to Sunday: a Historical Investigation of the Rise of Sunday Observance in Early Christianity*. Rome: Pontifical Gregorian University Press, 1977.

Bacon, Benjamin Wisner *The Beginnings of Gospel Story*. New Haven, CT: Yale University Press, 1909..

———. "The 'Five Books' of Moses against the Jews." *The Expositor* 15 (1918) 56–66.

———. *The Gospel of Mark: its composition and date*. New Haven: Yale University Press, 1925.

Bailey, James L. and Lyle D. Vander Broek. *Literary Forms in the New Testament*. London: SPCK, 1992.

Bailey, Kenneth E. *Jesus Through Middle Eastern Eyes: Cultural Studies in the Gospels*. Downers Grove, IL: IVP Academic, 2008.

Baltzer, Klaus. *Deutero-Isaiah: A Commentary on Isaiah 40–55*. Minneapolis: Fortress, 2001.

Banks, Robert. *Jesus and the Law in the Synoptic Tradition*. Cambridge: Cambridge University Press, 1975.

Barclay, John M. G. "Mirror-Reading a Polemical Letter: Galatians as a Test Case." *JSNT* 31 (1987) 73–93.

Barrett, Charles Kingsley. "The Gentile Mission as an Eschatological Phenomenon." In *Eschatology and the New Testament: Essays in Honor of George Raymond Beasley-Murray*, edited by W. Hulitt Gloer, 65–76. Peabody, MA: Hendrickson, 1988.

———. "The House of Prayer and the Den of Thieves." In *Jesus und Paulus*, edited by E.E. Ellis and E. Grasser, 13–20. Göttingen: Vandenhoeck and Ruprescht, 1975.

———. "The Parallels Between Acts and John." In *Exploring the Gospel of John: in Honor of D. Moody Smith*, edited by R. Alan Culpeper and C. Clifton Black. Louisville: Westminster John Knox, 1996.

Barth, Gerhard, Gunther Bornkamm, and Heinz Joachim Held. *Tradition and Interpretation in Matthew*. Philadelphia: Westminster, 1963.

Barton, Stephen C. *Discipleship and Family Ties in Mark and Matthew*. Cambridge: Cambridge University Press, 1994.

———. "Mark as Narrative: The Story of the Anointing Woman (Mk. 14:3–9)." *ExpT* 102 (1991) 230–34.

Bateman, Herbert W. IV. "Defining the Titles 'Christ' and 'Son of God' in Mark's Narrative Presentation of Jesus." *JETS* 50 (2007) 537–59.

Batto, B. F. "The Sleeping God: An Ancient Near Eastern Motif of Divine Sovereignty." *Bib* 68 (1987) 153–77.

Bauckham, Richard. "For Whom Were the Gospels Written?" In *The Gospels for All Christians*, edited by Richard Bauckham, 13–22. Grand Rapids: Eerdmans, 1988.

———. "James, Peter, and the Gentiles." In *The Missions of James, Peter, and Paul: Tensions in Early Christianity*, edited by Bruce Chilton and Craig Evans, 91–142. Leiden: Brill, 2005.

———. "Jesus' Demonstration in the Temple." In *Law and Religion*, edited by Barnabas Lindars, 72–89. Cambridge: James Clarke, 1988.

———. "Papias on Mark and Matthew." In *Jesus and the Eyewitnesses: The Gospels as Eyewitness Testimony*. Grand Rapids: Eerdmans, 2006.

Beare, Francis Wright. "The Sabbath Was Made for Man?" *JBL* 79 (1960) 130–36.

Beasley-Murray, George R. *Jesus and the Future*. London: Macmillan, 1954.

———. *Jesus and the Kingdom of God*. Grand Rapids: Eerdmans, 1986.

Beavis, Mary Ann. *Mark's Audience: The Literary and Social Setting of Mark 4:11–12*. JSNTSS 33. Sheffield: JSOT, 1989.

Beck, Norman A. "Reclaiming a Biblical Text: The Mark 8.14–21 Discussion about Bread in a Boat." *CBQ* 43 (1981) 49–56.

Becker, Jürgen. *Jesus of Nazareth*. New York: De Gruyter, 1998.

Belo, Fernando. *A Materialist Reading of the Gospel of Mark*. Translated by Matthew J. O'Connell. Maryknoll, NY: Orbis, 1981.

Berger, Klaus. *Formgeschichte des Neuen Testaments*. Heidelberg: Quelle and Meyer, 1984.

Best, Ernest. *Disciples and Discipleship: Studies in the Gospel According to Mark*. Edinburgh: T. & T. Clark, 1986.

———. "Discipleship in Mark: Mark 8:22—10:52." *SJTh* 23 (1970) 323–37.

———. "An Early Sayings Collection." *NovT* 18 (1976) 1–16.

———. *Following Jesus: Discipleship in the Gospel of Mark*. JSNTSS 4. Sheffield: JSOT, 1981.

———. "The Gospel of Mark: Who was the Reader?" *IBS* 11 (1989) 124–32.

———. "Mark III.20, 21, 31–35." *NTS* 22 (1975–76) 309–19.

———. *Mark: The Gospel as Story*. Edinburgh: T. & T. Clark, 1983.

———. "Mark's Narrative Technique." *JSNT* 37 (1989) 43–58.

———. "Mark's Preservation of the Tradition." In *The Interpretation of Mark*, edited by W.R. Telford, 153–68. Edinburgh: T. & T. Clark, 1995.

———. "Mark's Redaction of the Transfiguration." *St. Ev.* 7:41–53.

———. "The Miracles in Mark." *REx* 75 (1978) 539–54.

———. "The Purpose of Mark." *Proceedings of the Irish Biblical Association* 6 (1982) 19–35.

———. *The Temptation and the Passion: The Marcan Soteriology*. Cambridge: Cambridge University Press, 1965.

Betz, Hans Dieter. "The Early Christian Miracle Story: Some Observations on the Form Critical Problem." *Semeia* 11 (1978) 69–81.

Betz, Otto. "The Concept of the So-Called 'Divine Man' in Mark's Christology." In *Studies in New Testament and Early Christian Literature: Essays in Honor of Allen Wikgren*, edited by David Aune, 229–40. Leiden: Brill, 1972.

Bilezikian, Gilbert G. *The Liberated Gospel: A Comparison of the Gospel of Mark and Greek Tragedy*. Grand Rapids: Baker, 1977.

Bird, C. H. "Some γαρ clauses in St Mark's Gospel." *JThS* 4 (1953) 171–87.

Bird, Michael. *Jesus and the Origins of the Gentile Mission*. London: T. & T. Clark, 2006.

Birdsal, J. Neville. "The Withering of the Fig Tree [Mark xi. 12–14, 20–22]." *ExpT* 73 (1961–62) 191.

Bishop, Eric F. F. *Jesus of Palestine: The Local Background to the Gospel Documents*. London: Lutterworth, 1955.

Black, C. Clifton. *The Disciples according to Mark: Markan Redaction in Current Debate.* JSNTSS 27. Sheffield: JSOT, 1989.

———. "Was Mark a Roman Gospel?" *ExpT* 105 (1993) 36–40.

Black, David Alan, ed. *Perspectives on the Ending of Mark: 4 Views.* Nashville: Broadman and Holman, 2008.

Black, Matthew. *An Aramaic Approach to the Gospels and Acts.* Oxford: Clarendon, 1967.

Blackburn, Barry. *Theios Anē[set macron over e]r and the Markan Miracle Traditions. A Critique of the Theios Anē[set macron over e]r Concept as an Interpretative background of the Miracle Traditions used by Mark.* Tübingen: Mohr-Siebeck, 1991.

Blevens, James L. *The Messianic Secret in Markan Research 1901–1976.* Washington, DC: University Press of America, 1981.

Bligh, Philip H. "A Note on *Huios Theou* in Mark 15.39." *ExpT* 80 (1968–69) 51–53.

Blomberg, Craig L. "The Law in Luke-Acts." *JSNT* 22 (1984) 53–80.

———. "The Miracles as Parables." In *Gospel Perspectives 6: The Miracles of Jesus*, edited by David Wenham and Craig Blomberg, 327–59. Sheffield: JSOT Press, 1986.

———. "The Structure of 2 Corinthians 1–7." *CTR* 4 (1989) 4–5.

Blount, Brian K. and Charles, Gary W. *Preaching Mark in Two Voices.* Louisville: Westminster John Knox, 2002.

Bock, Darrell L. *Blasphemy and Exaltation in Judaism and the Final Examination of Jesus: A Philosophical-Historical Study of Key Jewish Themes Impacting Mark 14:61–64.* Grand Rapids: Baker, 2000.

———. "Key Texts on Blasphemy and Exaltation in the Jewish Examination of Jesus." In *SBL Seminar Papers 1997*, 115–60. SBLASP 34. Atlanta: Scholars, 1997.

Bockmuehl, Markus. *Jewish Law in Gentile Churches: Halakhah and the Beginning of Christian Public Ethics.* Edinburgh: T. & T. Clark, 2000.

Bolt, Peter G. *Jesus' Defeat of Death: Persuading Mark's Early Readers.* Cambridge: Cambridge University Press, 2003.

Boman, K. "Das textkritische Problem des sogenanntes Aposteldekrets." *NovT* 7 (1952) 26–36.

Bonner, Campbell. "Traces of Thaumaturgic Technique in the Miracles." *HTR* 20 (1927) 171–78.

Boobyer, George H. "The Eucharistic Interpretation of the Miracles of the Loaves in St. Mark's Gospel." *JThS* 3 (1952) 161–71.

———. "Galilee and Galileans in St. Mark's Gospel." *BJRL* 35 (1952–53) 334–48.

———. "The Miracles of the Loaves and the Gentiles in St Mark's Gospel." *SJTh* 6 (1953) 77–87.

———. "St. Mark and the Transfiguration." *JTS* 41 (1940) 119–40.

Boomershine, Thomas Eugene. "Mark 16:8 and the Apostolic Commission." *JBL* 100 (1981) 225–39.

———. "Mark the Storyteller: A Rhetorical-Critical Investigation of Mark's Passion and Resurrection Narrative." PhD diss., Union Theological Seminary, 1974.

———. "Peter's Denial as Polemic or Confession." *Semeia* 39 (1987) 47–68.

———. and Gilbert L. Bartholomew. "The Narrative Technique of Mark 16:8." *JBL* 100 (1981) 213–23.

Booth, Roger P. *Contrasts: Gospel Evidence and Christian Beliefs.* Bognor Regis: Paget, 1990.

———. *Jesus and the Laws of Purity. Tradition History and Legal History in Mark 7.* JSNTS 13. Sheffield: JSOT Press, 1986.

Booth, Wayne. *A Rhetoric of Irony*. Chicago: University of Chicago Press, 1974.

Borgen, Pieter. "Catalogues of Vices, the Apostolic Decree, and the Jerusalem Meeting." In *The Social World of Formative Christianity and Judaism*, edited by Jacob Neusner et al., 126–41. Philadelphia: Fortress, 1988.

Boring, M. Eugene. *Mark: A Commentary*. The New Testament Library. Louisville: Westminster John Knox, 2006.

———. "Mark 1:1–15 and the Beginning of the Gospel." *Semeia* 52 (1990) 43–82.

———. *Truly Human Truly Divine*. St. Louis: CBP Press, 1984.

Bornkamm, Günther. "Das Doppelgebot der Liebe." In *Neutestamentliche Studien für Rudolf Bultmann zu sienem 70: Geburtstag am 20: August 1954*, edited by Walther Eltester, 85–93. 2nd rev. ed. Berlin: Töpelmann, 1957.

———. *Jesus of Nazareth*. New York: Harper and Row, 1960.

Borrell, Agustí. *The Good News of Peter's Denial: A Narrative and Rhetorical Reading of Mark 14:54, 66–72*. Translated by Sean Conlon. Atlanta: Scholars for the University of South Florida, 1998.

Bosch, David. *Die Heidenmission in der Zukunftschau Jesu*. Zürich: Zwingli-Verlag, 1959.

Boucher, Madeleine. *The Mysterious Parable: A Literary Study*. Washington, DC: Catholic Biblical Association of America, 1977.

Bowman, John. *The Gospel of Mark: The New Christian Jewish Passover Haggadah*. Leiden: Brill, 1965.

Braun, Michael A. "James' Use of Amos at the Jerusalem Council: Steps Toward a Possible Solution of the Textual and Theological Problems." *JETS* 20 (1977) 119–20.

Breck, John. *The Shape of Biblical Language: Chiasmus in the Scriptures and Beyond*. Crestwood, NY: St. Vladimir's Seminary Press, 1994.

Breytenbach, Cilliers. "The Gospel of Mark as an Episodic Narrative: Reflections on the Composition of the Second Gospel." *Scriptura* 4 (1989) 1–26.

Broadhead, Edwin K. "Christology as Polemic and Apologetic: the Priestly Portrait of Jesus in the Gospel of Mark." *JSNT* 47 (1992) 21–34.

———. *Teaching with Authority: Miracles and Christology in the Gospel of Mark*. JSNTSS 74. Sheffield: JSOT Press, 1992.

———. "Mark 1,44: The Witness of the Leper." *ZNW* 83 (1992) 257–65.

———. "Mark 14, 1–9, a Gospel within a Gospel." *Paradigms* 1 (1985) 32–41.

———. "Which Mountain is 'This Mountain'? A Critical Note on Mark 11:22–25." *Paradigms* 2 (1986) 33–38.

Brooke, George J. "4Q500 1 and the Use of Scripture in the Parable of the Vineyard." *Dead Sea Discoveries* 2 (1995) 268–94.

Brooks, J. A. *Mark*. New American Commentary 23. Nashville: Broadman, 1991.

Brouwer, Wayne. *The Literary Development of John 13–17: A Chiastic Reading*. Atlanta: SBL, 2000.

Brower, Kent. "Elijah in the Markan Passion Narratives." *JSNT* 18 (1983) 85–101.

Brown, Raymond. *Antioch and Rome: New Testament Cradles of Catholic Christianity*. London: Geoffrey Chapman, 1983.

———. *The Death of the Messiah: From Gethsemane to the Grave. A Commentary on the Passion Narratives in the Four Gospels*. 2 vols. New York: Doubleday, 1994.

———. *The Gospel According to John*. The Anchor Bible. 2 vols. Garden City, NY: Doubeday, 1966, 1970.

———. "Jesus and Elijah." *Perspective* 12 (1971) 85–104.

Brown, Schuyler. "The Secret of the Kingdom of God (MARK 4:11)." *JBL* 92 (1973) 60–74.
Bruce, Frederick Fyvie. "The End of the Second Gospel." *EvQ* 17 (1945) 169–81.
Bryan, Steven M. *Jesus and Israel's Traditions of Judgement and Restoration*. Cambridge: Cambridge University Press, 2002.
Budesheim, Thomas L. "Jesus and the Disciples in Conflict with Judaism." *ZNW* 62 (1971) 190–209.
Bultmann, Rudolph. *Die Geschichte der synoptischen Tradition*. 2nd ed. Göttingen, 1931.
———. *The History of the Synoptic Tradition*. Oxford: Blackwell, 1963.
———. *Theology of the New Testament*. New York: Scribner's, 1951.
Burkill, T. Alec. "The Cryptology of Parables in St. Mark's Gospel." *NovT* 1 (1956) 246–56.
———. "Mark 3:7–12 and the Alleged Dualism in the Evangelist's Miracle Material." *JBL* 87 (1968) 409–17.
———. *Mysterious Revelation: An Examination of the Philosophy of St. Mark's Gospel*. Ithaca, NY: Cornell University Press, 1963.
———. *New Light on the Earliest Gospel: Seven Markan Studies*. Ithaca and London: Cornell University Press, 1972.
———. "The Notion of Miracle with Special Reference to St. Mark's Gospel." *ZNW* 50 (1959) 33–48.
———. "Strain on the Secret: an Examination of Mark 11:1—13:37." *ZNW* 51 (1960) 31–46.
———. "The Syrophoenician Woman: The Congruence of Mark 7, 24–31." *ZNW* 57 (1966) 23–37.
Burney, Charles Fox. *The Poetry of Our Lord*. Oxford: Clarendon, 1925.
Burridge, Richard. *What are the Gospels? A Comparison with Graeco-Roman Biography*. 2nd ed. Grand Rapids: Eerdmans, 2004.
Burton, Christopher. *Stumbling on God: Faith and Vision in Mark's Gospel*. Grand Rapids: Eerdmans, 1990.
Cadbury, Henry J. *The Making of Luke-Acts*. New York: Macmillan, 1927.
———. *The Style and Literary Method of Luke*. Cambridge, MA: Harvard University Press, 1920.
Cahill, Michael. *The First Commentary on Mark: An Annotated Translation*. Oxford: Oxford University Press, 1998.
Camery-Hoggatt, Jerry. *Irony in Mark's Gospel*. Cambridge: Cambridge University Press, 1992.
Campbell, William Sanger. "'Why did you abandon me?' Abandonment Christology in Mark's Gospel." In *The Trial and Death of Jesus: Essays on the Passion Narrative in Mark*, edited by Geert Van Oyen and Tom Shepherd, 99–118. Leuven: Peeters, 2006.
Carlston, Charles E. *The Parables of the Triple Tradition*. Philadelphia: Fortress, 1975.
———. "The Things that Defile (Mark vii.14) and the Law in Matthew and Mark." *NTS* (1968) 75–96.
Carrington, Philip. *According to Mark*. Cambridge: Cambridge University Press, 1960.
———. *The Primitive Christian Calendar: A Study in the Marking of the Marcan Gospel*. Cambridge: Cambridge University Press, 1952.
Carson, Donald A. "Jesus and the Sabbath in the Four Gospels." In *From Sabbath to Lord's Day: A Biblical, Historical, and Theological Investigation*, 57–98. Grand Rapids: Zondervan, 1982.
Carson, Donald A., Douglas J. Moo, and Leon Morris. *An Introduction to the New Testament*. Grand Rapids: Zondervan, 1992.

Casey, Maurice. *The Solution to the 'Son of Man' Problem*. London: T and T Clark, 2007.

Catchpole, David R. "The Fearful Silence of the Women at the Tomb." *JThSA* 18 (1977) 3–10.

———. "Paul, James, and the Apostolic Decree." *NTS* 23 (1977) 428–44.

Cave, H. C. "The Leper: Mark 1:40–45." *NTS* 25 (1978–79) 245–50.

Chapman, Dean W. *The Orphan Gospel: Mark's Perspective on Jesus*. Sheffield: JSOT Press, 1993.

Charles, R. H. *The Apocrypha and Pseudepigrapha of the Old Testament in English*. Oxford: Clarendon, 1913.

Childs, Brevard S. *The New Testament as Canon: An Introduction*. Philadelphia: Fortress, 1984.

Chilton, Bruce. "The Brother of Jesus and the Interpretation of Scripture." In *The Use of Sacred Books in the Ancient World*, edited by Leonard V. Rudgers, 29–48. Leuven: Peeters, 1998.

———. "A Generative Exegesis of Mark 7:1–12." In *Jesus in Context: Temple, Piety, and Restoration*, edited by Bruce Chilton and Craig A. Evans, 297–318. Leiden: Brill, 1997.

———. *The Temple of Jesus: His Sacrificial Program Within a Cultural History of Sacrifice*. University Park, PA: Pennsylvania State University Press, 1992.

——— and Jacob Neusner. *Judaism in the New Testament: Practices and Beliefs*. New York: Routledge, 1995.

Chronis, Harry L. "The Torn Veil: Cultus and Christology in Mark 15:37–39." *JBL* 101 (1982) 97–114.

Clark, David J. "Criteria for Identifying Chiasm." *LingBib* 35 (1975) 63–72.

Clark, Kenneth W. "The Gentile Bias in Matthew." *JBL* 66 (1947) 165–72.

Clements, Ronald Ernest. *God and Temple*. Oxford: Blackwell, 1965.

Coakley, J. F. "The Anointing at Bethany and the Priority of John." *JBL* 107 (1988) 241–56.

Coates, Mary. "Women, Silence and Fear (Mark 16:8)." In *Women in the Biblical Tradition*, edited by G. J. Brooke, 150–66. Lewiston, NY: Mellen, 1992.

Collins, Adela Yarbro. "The Charge of Blasphemy in Mark 14:64." In *The Trial and Death of Jesus: Essays on the Passion Narrative in Mark*, edited by Geert Van Oyen and Tom Shepherd, 149–70. Leuven: Peeters, 2006.

———. "From Noble Death to Crucified Messiah." *NTS* 40 (1994) 497–98.

———. *Mark: A Commentary*. Hermeneia—A Critical and Historical Commentary on the Bible. Minneapolis: Fortress, 2007.

———. "Rulers, Divine Men, and Walking on the Water [Mark 6:45–52]." In *Religious Propaganda and Missionary Competition in the New Testament World: Essays Honoring Dieter Georgi*, edited by Lukas Bormann, Kelly Del Tredicin, and Angela Strandhartinger, 207–27. Leiden: Brill, 1994.

Colwell, E. C. "A Definite Rule for the Use of the Article in the Greek New Testament." *JBL* 52 (1933) 12–21.

Combrink, H. J. Bernard. "The Structure of the Gospel of Matthew as Narrative." TynBul 34 (1983) 61–90.

Cook, John G. *The Structure and Persuasive Power of Mark: A Linguistic Approach*. Atlanta: Scholars, 1995.

Cook, M. J. *Mark's Treatment of the Jewish Leaders*. Leiden: Brill, 1978.

Cotes, M. "Women, Silence, and Fear (Mk. 16:8)." In *Women in the Biblical Tradition*, edited by G. J. Brooke, 150–66. Lewiston, NY: Mellen, 1992.

Cotter, Wendy J. *The Christ of the Miracle Stories: Portrait through Encounter*. Grand Rapids: Baker, 2010.

———. "For it was not the Season for Figs." *CBQ* 48 (1986) 62–66.

———. "Mark's Hero of the Twelfth-Year Miracles: The Healing of the Woman with the Hemorrhage and the Raising of Jairus's Daughter (Mark 5:21–43)." In *A Feminist Companion to Mark*, edited by Amy-Jill Levine, 54–78. Sheffield: Sheffield Academic, 2001.

Countryman, Louis William. "How Many Baskets Full? Mark 8:14–21 and the Value of Miracles in Mark." *CBQ* 47 (1985) 643–55.

Cox, Steven Lynn. *A History and Critique of Scholarship Concerning the Markan Endings*. Lewiston, NY: Mellen, 1993.

Cranfield, Charles E. B. *The Gospel according to St. Mark*. Cambridge: Cambridge University Press, 1959.

Crossan, John Dominac. "A Form for Absence: The Markan Creation of Gospel." *Semeia* 12 (1978) 41–55.

———. *The Historical Jesus: The Life of a Mediterranean Jewish Peasant*. San Francisco: HarperSanFrancisco, 1991.

———. "Mark and the Relatives of Jesus." *NovT* 15 (1973) 81–113.

Crossley, James G. *The Date of Mark's Gospel: Insight from the Law in Earliest Christianity*. London: T. & T. Clark International, 2004.

Croy, N. Clayton. *The Mutilation of Mark's Gospel*. Nashville: Abingdon, 2003.

Culpepper, R. Alan. *Anatomy of the Fourth Gospel: A Study in Literary Design*. Philadelphia: Fortress, 1983.

———. "Mark 10:50: Why Mention the Garment?" *JBL* 101 (1982) 131–32.

———. "The Passion and Resurrection in Mark." *REx* 75 (1978) 583–600.

Cunningham, Philip J. *Mark: The Good News Preached to the Romans*. New York: Paulist, 1995.

Dahl, Nils A. "The Purpose of Mark's Gospel." *Jesus in the Memory of the Early Church*, 52–65. Minneapolis: Augsburg, 1976.

———. "The Story of Abraham in Luke-Acts." In *Studies in Luke-Acts*, edited by Leander E. Keck and J. Louis Martyn. Nashville: Abingdon, 1966.

D'Angelo, Mary Rose. "Gender and Power in the Gospel of Mark: The Daughter of Jairus and the Woman with the Flow of Blood." In *Miracles in Jewish and Christian Antiquity*, edited by John C. Cavadini, 83–109. Notre Dame: University of Notre Dame Press, 1999.

Danker, Frederick. W. "The Demonic Secret in Mark: A Reexamination of the Cry of Dereliction (15:34)." *ZNW* 61 (1970) 48–69.

———. "Double-entendre in Mark XIII 9." *NovT* 10 (1968) 162–63.

———. "The Literary Unity of Mark 14,1–25." *JBL* 85 (1966) 467–72.

———. "Mark 8:3." *JBL* 82 (1963) 215–16.

Danove, Paul L. "The Characterization and Narrative Function of the Women at the Tomb (Mark 15,40–41, 47; 16,1–8)." *Bib* 77 (1996) 375–97.

———. *The End of Mark's Story: A Methodological Study*. Leiden: Brill, 1983.

Daube, David. "The Anointing at Bethany and Jesus' Burial." In *The New Testament and Rabbinic Judaism*, 312–24. London: Athlone, 1956.

Davies, Graham I. "The Presence of God in the Second Temple and Rabbinic Doctrine." In *Templum Amicitiae: Essays on the Second Temple Presented to Ernst Bammel*, edited by William Horbury, 32–36. Sheffield: JSOT, 1991.

Davies, William David. *Torah in the Messianic Age and / or The Age to Come*. Philadelphia: SBL, 1952.

Davies, William David and Dale C. Allison. *A Critical and Exegetical Commentary According to Saint Matthew*. 3 vols. Edinburgh: T. & T. Clark, 1988.

Davis, Philip. "Christology, Discipleship, and Self-Understanding in the Gospel of Mark." In *Self-Definition and Self-Discovery in Early Christianity*, edited by David J. Hawkin and Tom Robinson, 101–20. Lewiston, NY: Mellen, 1990.

———. "Mark's Christological Paradox." *JSNT* 35 (1989) 3–18.

Dean-Otting, Miriam. "Biblical Sources for Pronouncement Stories in the Gospels." *Semeia* 64 (1993) 92–115.

Deconick, April D. *The Original Gospel of Thomas in Translation*. London: T and T Clark International, 2006.

De Lacey, Douglas R. "The Sabbath / Sunday Question and the Law in the Pauline Corpus." In *From Sabbath to Lord's Day: A Biblical, Historical, and Theological Investigation*, 159–98. Grand Rapids: Zondervan, 1982.

Delorme, Jean. "John the Baptist's Head—The Word Perverted: A Reading of a Narrative (Mark 6:14–29)." *Semeia* 81 (1998) 115–30.

Deppe, Dean B. "Charting the Future or a Perspective on the Present? The Paraenetic Purpose of Mark 13." *CTJ* 41 (2006) 89–101.

———. *All Roads Lead to the Text: Eight Methods of Inquiry into the Bible*. Grand Rapids: Eerdmans, 2011.

De Jonge, Marinus, "Mark 14:25 among Jesus' Words about the Kingdom of God." In *Sayings of Jesus: Canonical and Non-Canonical: Essays in Honour of Tjitze Baarda*, edited by William L. Petersen, Johan S. Vos, and Henk J. De Jonge. Brill: Leiden, 1997.

Dibelius, Martin. *From Tradition to Gospel*. Translated by Bertram L. Woolf. Cambridge: James Clarke & Co., 1971.

Denis, Albert-Marie. "Jesus' Walking on the Waters: A Contribution to the History of the Pericope in the Gospel Tradition." *Louvain Studies* 1 (1967) 284–97.

Derrett, J. Duncan M. "Cursing Jesus (1 Cor XII.3): The Jews as Religious 'Persecutors,'" *NTS* 21 (1975) 544–554.

———. "Eating Up the Houses of Widows: Jesus' Comment on Lawyers." *NovT* 14 (1972) 1–9.

———. "Figtrees in the New Testament." *Heythrop Journal* 14 (1973) 249–65.

———. *The Making of Mark: The Scriptural Bases of the Earliest Gospel*. 2 vols. Shipston-on-Stour: Drinkwater, 1985.

———. "Mark's Technique: The Hemorrhaging Woman and Jairus' Daughter." *Bib* 63 (1982) 474–505.

Dewey, Joanna. "The Literary Structure of the Controversy Stories in Mark 2:1—3:6." *JBL* 92 (1973) 394–401. Reprinted in *The Interpretation of Mark*, edited by W.R. Telford, 141–51. Minneapolis: SPCK, 1995.

———. "Mark as Aural Narrative: Structures as Clues to Understanding." *SThR* 36 (1992) 45–56.

———. "Mark as Interwoven Tapestry: Forecasts and Echoes for a Listening Audience." *CBQ* 53 (1991) 221–36.

———. *Markan Public Debate: Literary Technique, Concentric Structure, and Theology in Mark 2:1—3:6*. Chico, CA: Scholars, 1980.

———. "Oral Methods of Structuring Narrative in Mark." *Int* 63 (1989) 32–44.

Dewey, Kim E. "Peter's Curse and Cursed Peter (Mark 14:53–54, 66–72)." In *The Passion in Mark*, edited by Werner Kelber, 96–114. Philadelphia: Fortress, 1976.

———. "Peter's Denial Reexamined: John's Knowledge of Mark's Gospel." In *SBL Seminar Papers*, 1:109–12. Missoula, MO: Scholars, 1979.
Dihle, Albrecht. "The Gospels and Greek Biography." In *The Gospel and the Gospels*, edited by edited by Peter Stuhlmacher, 361–86. Grand Rapids: Eerdmans, 1991.
Dobschütz, Ernst von. "Zur Erzählungskunst des Markus." *ZNW* 27 (1928) 193–98.
Dodd, Charles Harold. "The Appearances of the Risen Christ: An Essay in Form-Criticism of the Gospels." In *Studies in the Gospels: Essays in Memory of R.H. Lightfoot*, edited by D. E. Nineham, 23–24. Oxford: Blackwell, 1955.
———. "The Framework of the Gospel Narrative." *ExpT* 43 (1931–32) 396–400.
Donahue, John R. *Are You the Christ? The Trial Narrative in the Gospel of Mark*. Missoula: Scholars, 1973.
———. *Gospel as Parable: Metaphor, Narrative, and Theology in the Synoptic Gospels*. Philadelphia: Fortress, 1988.
———. "Introduction: From Passion Traditions to Passion Narrative." In *The Passion in Mark*, edited by Werner Kelber, 1–20. Philadelphia: Fortress, 1976.
———. "Jesus as the Parable of God in the Gospel of Mark." *Int* 32 (1978) 369–86.
———. "A Neglected Factor in the Theology of Mark." *JBL* 101 (1982) 563–94.
———. "The Quest for the Community of Mark's Gospel." In *The Four Gospels 1992: Festschrift F. Neirynck*, edited by F. Van Segbroeck et al., 817–38. Leuven: Leuven University Press, 1992.
———. "Temple, Trial, and Royal Christology (Mark 14:53–65)." In *The Passion in Mark*, edited by Werner Kelber, 61–79. Philadelphia: Fortress, 1976.
———. *The Theology and Setting of Discipleship in the Gospel of Mark*. Milwaukee: Marquette University Press, 1983.
——— and Daniel J. Harrington. *The Gospel of Mark*. Collegeville, MN: Liturgical, 2002.
Donfried, Karl P. "The Feeding Narratives and the Marcan Community." In *Kirche: Festschrift für Günther Bornkamm*, edited by D. Lührmann and G. Strecker, 95–103. Tübingen: Mohr, 1980.
Dormeyer, Detlev. *Die Passion Jesus als Verhaltensmodel*. Münster: Aschendorff, 1974.
Dowd, Sharyn Echols. *Reading Mark: A Literary and Theological Commentary on the Second Gospel*. Macon, GA: Smyth and Helwys, 2000.
———. *Prayer, Power, and the Problem of Suffering: Mark 11:22–25 in the Context of Markan Theology*. Atlanta: Scholars, 1988.
——— and Elizabeth Struthers Malbon. "The Significance of Jesus' Death in Mark: Narrative Context and Authorial Audience." In *The Trial and Death of Jesus: Essays on the Passion Narrative in Mark*, edited by Geert Van Oyen and Tom Shepherd, 1–32. Leuven: Peeters, 2006.
Dowda, Robert E. "The Cleansing of the Temple in the Synoptic Gospels." PhD diss., Duke University, 1972.
Droge, A. J. "Call Stories in Greek Biography and the Gospels." In *SBL Seminar Papers 1983*, 245–57. Chico, CA: Scholars, 1983.
Drury, John. "Mark." In *The Literary Guide to the Bible*, edited by Robert Alter and Frank Kermode, 402–17. Cambridge: Harvard University Press, 1987.
Dubis, Kevin M. "The Use of Amos 9:11–12 in Acts 15." ThM diss., Calvin Theological Seminary, 1989.
Dunn, James D.G. "Jesus and Ritual Purity: A Study of the Tradition-History of Mark 7:15." In *Jesus, Paul, and the Law: Studies in Mark and Galatians*, 37–60. London: SPCK, 1990.

———. *Jesus Remembered*. Vol. 1, *Christianity in the Making*. Grand Rapids: Eerdmans, 2003.

———. "Mark 2:1—3:6: A Bridge between Jesus and Paul on the Question of the Law." *NTS* 30 (1984) 395–415.

———. "Matthew's Awareness of Markan Redaction." In *The Four Gospels 1992: Festschrift F. Neirynck*, edited by F. Van Segbroeck et al., 1349–60. Leuven: Leuven University Press, 1992.

———. *The Partings of the Ways: Between Christianity and Judaism and their Significance for the Character of Christianity*. London: SCM, 1991.

———. *Romans 9–16*. Word Biblical Commentary. Dallas: Word, 2002.

Dwyer, Timothy. *The Motif of Wonder in the Gospel of Mark*. Sheffield: Sheffield Academic, 1996.

Dyer, Keith D. *The Prophecy on the Mount: Mark 13 and the Gathering of the New Community*. Berne: Peter Lang, 1998.

Edwards, James R. *The Gospel according to Mark*. Pillar New Testament Commentary. Grand Rapids: Eerdmans, 2002.

———. "Markan Sandwiches: The Significance of Interpretations in Markan Narratives." *NovT* 31 (1989) 193–216.

Ehrman, Bart D. "A Leper in the Hands of an Angry Jesus." In *New Testament Greek and Exegesis: Essays in Honor of Gerald F. Hawthorn*, 77–98. Grand Rapids: Eerdmans, 2003.

———. *The Orthodox Corruption of Scripture: The Effect of Early Christological Controversies on the Text of the New Testament*. Oxford: University Press, 1993.

———. "The Text of Mark in the Hands of the Orthodox." In *Biblical Hermeneutics in Historical Perspective*, edited by Mark Burrows and Paul Rorem, 19–31. Philadelphia: Fortress, 1991.

Egger, Wilhelm. *Frohbotschaft und Lehre: Die Sammelberichte des Wirkens Jesu im Markusevangelium*. Frankfurt: Knecht, 1976.

Elliot, James K. "The Anointing of Jesus." *ExpT* 85 (1973–74) 105–7.

———. "The Conclusion of the Pericope of the Healing of the Leper and Mark i 45." *JTS* 22 (1971) 153–57.

———. "The Healing of the Leper in the Synoptic Parallels." *ThZ* 34 (1978) 175–76.

———. "The Text and Language of the Endings to Mark's Gospel." *TZ* 27 (1971) 258–62

Ellis, Peter F. *The Genius of John*. Collegeville, MN: Liturgical, 1984.

———. "Patterns and Structures of Mark's Gospel." In *Biblical Studies in Contemporary Thought*, edited by Mirium Ward, 88–103. Somerville, MA: Greeno, Haddno, and Co., 1975.

Elwell, Walter and Robert Yarbrough. *Encountering the New Testament: A Historical and Theological Survey*. Grand Rapids: Baker, 1998.

Enslin, Mortin S. "The Artistry of Mark." *JBL* 66 (1947) 385–99.

Ernst, Josef. *Das Evangelium nach Markus*. Regensburg: Pustet, 1981.

Esler, Philip F. "Community and Gospel in Early Christianity: A Response to Richard Bauckham's *Gospels for All Christians*." *SJTh* 51 (1998) 235–48.

Evans, Craig A. "In What Sense 'Blasphemy'? Jesus before Caiaphas in Mark 14:61–64." In *Jesus and His Contemporaries: Comparative Studies*, 407–36. Leiden: Brill, 2001.

———. "Jesus' Action in the Temple: Cleansing or Portent of Destruction?" *CBQ* 51 (1989) 237–70.

———. "Jesus and the 'Cave of Robbers': Toward a Jewish Context for the Temple Action." *BBR* (1993) 93–110.

———. "Jesus and the Continuing Exile of Israel." In *Jesus and the Restoration of Israel: A Critical Assessment of N.T. Wright's Jesus and the Victory of God*, edited by Carey C. Newman. Downers Grove, IL: InterVarsity, 1999.

———. "Jesus and Zechariah's Messianic Hope." In *Authenticating the Activities of Jesus*. Leiden: Brill, 2002.

———. *Mark 8:27—16:20*. Word Biblical Commentary 34b. Nashville: Nelson, 2001.

———. "'Peter Warming Himself': The Problem of an Editorial 'Seam.'" *JBL* 101 (1982) 245–49.

———. "'Who Touched Me?' Jesus and the Ritually Impure." In *Jesus in Context: Temple, Piety, and Restoration*, edited by Bruce Chilton and Craig A. Evans, 353–76. Leiden: Brill, 1997.

Evans, C. F. "I Will Go Before You Into Galilee." *JTS* 5 (1954) 3–18.

———. *Resurrection and the New Testament*. London: SCM, 1970.

Farla, P. J. *Jezus' Oordeel over Israel: Een Form- en Redaktionsgeschichtliche Analyse van Mc. 10,46—12,40*. Kampen: Kok, 1978.

Farmer, William P. *The Last Twelve Verses of Mark*. London: Cambridge University Press, 1974.

Farrer, Austin. *A Study in St. Mark*. Westminster: Dacre Press, 1951.

Faw, Chalmer E. "The Outline of Mark." *JBR* 25 (1957) 19–23.

Fay, Greg. "Introduction to Incomprehension: The Literary Structure of Mark 4:1–34." *CBQ* 51 (1989) 65–81.

Feagin, Glyndle M. Jr. *Irony and the Kingdom in Mark: A Literary-Critical Study*. Lewiston, NY: Mellen, 1997.

Fenton, John C. "Paul and Mark." In *Studies in the Gospels: Essays in Memory of R. H. Lightfoot*, edited by D.E. Nineham, 89–112. Oxford: Blackwell, 1957.

———. *Saint Matthew*. Baltimore: Penguin Books, 1964.

Finegan, Jack. *Handbook of Biblical Chronology*. Rev. ed. Peabody, MA: Hendrickson, 1998.

Fiorenza, Elisabeth Schüssler. *In Memory of Her: A Feminist Theological Reconstruction of Christian Origins*. London: SCM, 1983.

Fisher, Kathleen M. and Urban C. von Wahlde. "The Miracles of Mark 4:35—5:43: Their Meaning and Function in the Gospel Framework." *BTB* 11 (1981) 13–16.

Fitzmyer, Joseph A. *The Gospel According to Luke*. 2 vols. Garden City, NY: Doubleday, 1981, 1985.

———. *The Gospel According to Luke I-IX*. Garden City, NY: Doubleday, 1979.

———. "The Jewish People and the Mosaic Law in Luke-Acts." *Luke the Theologian: Aspects of His Teaching*. Mahwah: Paulist, 1989.

Fitzpatrick, Michael. "The Structure of St. Mark's Gospel: With a Reconsideration of the Hypothesis of Pre-Markan Collections in Mk. 1–10." Diss., Leuven, 1975.

Fleddermann, Harry T. "The Flight of a Naked Young Man (Mark 14:51–52)." *CBQ* 41 (1979) 412–18.

———. "And He Wanted to Pass by Them (Mk. 6:48a)." *CBQ* 45 (1983) 389–95.

———. "A Warning against the Scribes (Mark 12:37b–40)." *CBQ* 44 (1982) 52–67.

Fleer, David and Bland, David. *Preaching Mark's Unsettling Messiah*. St. Louis: Chalice, 2006.

Flusser, David. "Do you Prefer New Wine." *Immanuel* 9 (1979) 26–31.

Fonrobert, Charlotte, "The Woman with a Blood-Flow (Mark 5:24–34) Revisited: Menstrual Laws and Jewish Culture in Christian Feminist Hermeneutics." In *Early Christian Interpretation of the Scriptures of Israel*, edited by Craig A. Evans and James A. Sanders, 121–40. Sheffield: Sheffield Academic, 1997.

Ford, J. Massyngberde. "Money Bags in the Temple (Mk. 11,16)." *Bib* 57 (1976) 249–53.

Fortna, Robert T. "Jesus and Peter at the High Priest's House: A Test Case for the Question of the Relation between Mark's and John's Gospels." *NTS* 24 (1978) 371–83.

Fowler, Robert M. *Let the Reader Understand: Reader-Response Criticism and the Gospel of Mark*. Harrisburg, PA: Trinity, 1996.

———. *Loaves and Fishes: The Function of the Feeding Stories in the Gospel of Mark*. SBLDS 54. Chico: Scholars, 1981.

———. "The Rhetoric or Direction and Indirection in the Gospel of Mark." *Semeia* 48 (1989) 115–34.

Fraade, Steven D. "Moses and the Commandments: Can Hermeneutics, History, and Rhetoric Be Disentangled?" In *The Idea of Biblical Interpretation: Essays in Honor of James Kugel*, edited by Hindy Najman and Judith H. Newman, 399–422. Leiden: Brill, 2004.

France, Richard Thomas. *The Gospel of Mark: A Commentary on the Greek Text*. Grand Rapids: Eerdmans, 2002.

Franklin, Eric. *Luke: Interpreter of Paul, Critic of Matthew*. Sheffield: Sheffield Academic, 1994.

Freedman, H. and M. Simon, eds. *Midrash Rabba Leviticus*. London: Soncino, 1939.

Freyne, Sean. "The Geography of Restoration: Galilee-Jerusalem Relations in Early Jewish and Christian Experience." In *Restoration: Old Testament, Jewish, and Christian Perspectives*, edited by James M. Scott, 405–33. Leiden: Brill, 2001.

———. "Locality and Doctrine: Mark and John Revisited." In *The Four Gospels 1992: Festschrift F. Neirynck*, edited by F. Van Segbroeck et al., 1889–1900. Leuven: Leuven University Press, 1992.

Friedrich, G. "Die beiden Erzählungen von der Speisung in Mark 6:31–44; 8:1–9." *ThZ* 20 (1964) 10–22.

Fuller, Reginald H. *The Formation of the Resurrection Narratives*. New York: MacMillan, 1971.

———. *Interpreting the Miracles*. London: SCM, 1963.

Fullmer, Paul M. *Resurrection in Mark's Literary-Historical Perspective*. London: T. & T. Clark, 2007.

Funk, Robert W. *The Acts of Jesus: the Search for the Authentic Deeds of Jesus*. San Francisco: Harper San Francisco, 1998.

———. "The Form of the New Testament Healing Miracle Story." *Semeia* 12 (1978) 57–96.

Furnish, Victor Paul. *The Love Command in the New Testament*. Nashville: Abingdon, 1972.

Gaechter, Paul. *Das Matthäus Evanglium*. Tyrolia-Verlag, 1963.

Gärtner, Bertil. *The Temple and the Community in Qumran and the New Testament*. Society for New Testament Studies Monograph Series 1. Cambridge, 1965.

Gaston, Lloyd. *No Stone on Another: Studies in the Significance of the Fall of Jerusalem in the Synoptic Gospels*. Leiden: Brill, 1970.

Gaventa, Beverly R. and Patrick D. Miller, eds. *The Ending of Mark and the Ends of God: Essays in Memory of Donald Harrisville Juel*. Louisville: Westminster John Knox, 2005.

Geddert, Timothy J. *Mark: Believers Church Bible Commentary*. Scottdale, PA: Herald, 2001.

———. *Watchwords: Mark 13 in Markan Eschatology*. JSNTSS 26. Sheffield: JSOT, 1989.

Gerhardsson, Birger. "Confession and Denial before Men: Observations on Matt. 26:57—27:2." *JSNT* 13 (1981) 46–66.

Geyer, Douglas W. *Fear, Anomaly, and Uncertainty in the Gospel of Mark*. Lanham, MD: Scarecrow, 2002.

Gibson, Jeffrey B. "The Function of the Charge of Blasphemy in Mark 14:64." In *The Trial and Death of Jesus: Essays on the Passion Narrative in Mark*, edited by Geert Van Oyen and Tom Shepherd, 171–88. Leuven: Peeters, 2006.

———. "The Rebuke of the Disciples in Mark 8:14–21." *JSNT* 27 (1986) 31–47.

Giesen, H. "Der verdotted Feigenbaum—Eine symbolische Aussage? Zu Mk. 11,12–14. 20f." *BZ* 20 (1976) 95–111.

Globe A. "The Caesarean Omission of the Phrase 'Son of God' in Mark 1:1." *HTR* 75 (1982) 209–18.

Glasswell, Mark Erril. "The Use of Miracles in the Markan Gospel." In *Miracles*, edited by C. F. D. Moule, 149–62. London: Mowbray, 1965.

Good, R. S. "Jesus, Protagonist of the Old in Lk. 5:33–39." *NovT* 25 (1983) 19–36.

Goodacre, Mark. *The Case Against Q: Studies in Markan Priority and the Synoptic Problem*. Harrisburg, PA: Trinity, 2002.

———. "Scripturalization in Mark's Crucifixion Narrative." In *The Trial and Death of Jesus: Essays on the Passion Narrative in Mark*, edited by Geert Van Oyen and Tom Shepherd, 33–48. Leuven: Peeters, 2006.

Gould, Ezra P. *The Gospel According to St. Mark*. ICC. New York: Scribner's, 1896.

Goulder, Michael D. "Mark and His Successors." In *The Evangelist's Calendar*, 241–306. London: SPCK, 1978.

———. "A Pauline in a Jacobite Church." In *The Four Gospels 1992: Festschrift F. Neirynck*, edited by F. Van Segbroeck et al., 859–76. Leuven: Leuven University Press, 1992.

Graham, Helen. "A Passion Prediction for Mark's Community: Mark 13:9–13." *BTB* 16 (1986) 18–22.

Grant, Robert M. "The Coming of the Kingdom." *JBL* 67 (1948) 297–303.

Grässer, Erich. "Jesus in Nazareth (Mark vi 1–6a): Notes on the Redaction and Theology of St. Mark." *NTS* 16 (1969) 1–23.

Grassi, Joseph A. "The Eucharist in the Gospel of Mark." *AER* 168 (1974) 595–608.

———. *Loaves and Fishes: The Gospel Feeding Narratives*. Collegeville, MN: Liturgical, 1991.

———. *The Hidden Heroes of the Gospels: Female Counterparts to Jesus*. Collegeville, MN: Liturgical, 1989.

Gray, Timothy C. *The Temple in the Gospel of Mark: A Study in its Narrative Role*. Tübingen: Mohr Siebeck, 2009.

Grayston, K. "The Study of Mark XIII." *BJRL* 56 (1973–74) 371–87.

Green, H. B. "The Structure of St. Matthew's Gospel." *StEv* IV (1968) 47–59.

Green, Joel B. *The Death of Jesus: Tradition and Interpretation in the Passion Narrative*. Tübingen: Mohr, 1988.

———. *The Gospel of Luke*. Grand Rapids: Eerdmans, 1997.

Green, M. P. "The Meaning of Cross Bearing." *BSac* 140 (1983) 117–33.

Greimas, A. J. *Sémantique structural*. Paris: Larousse, 1966.

Guelich, Robert A. "The Gospel Genre." In *The Gospel and the Gospels*, edited by Peter Stuhlmacher, 173–208. Grand Rapids: Eerdmans, 1991.

———. *Mark 1—8:26*. Word Biblical Commentary 34a. Dallas: Word Books, 1989.

Gundry, Robert H. *Mark: A Commentary on His Apology for the Cross*. Grand Rapids: Eerdmans, 1993.

Guy, Harold A. *The Origin of the Gospel of Mark*. New York: Harper and Brothers, 1955.

Haber, Susan. *"They Shall Purify Themselves": Essays on Purity in Early Judaism*. Atlanta: Society of Biblical Literature, 2008

Hägerland, Tobias. "John's Gospel: A Two-Level Drama?" JSNT 25 (2003) 309-22.

Hagner, Donald A. "Jesus and the Synoptic Sabbath Controversies." BBR 19 (2009) 215-48.

———. *Matthew*. Word Biblical Commentary 33. 2 vols. Dallas: Word, 1993, 95.

Hahn, Ferdinand. *Mission in the New Testament*. London: SCM, 1965.

Hamerton-Kelly, R. G. "Sacred Violence and the Messiah: The Markan Passion Narrative as a Redefinition of Messianology." In *The Messiah*, edited by James H. Charlesworth, 461-93. Minneapolis: Fortress, 1992.

Hamilton, Neill Q. "Resurrection Tradition and the Composition of Mark." JBL 84 (1965) 415-21.

———. "Temple Cleansing and Temple Bank." JBL 83 (1964) 365-72.

Hanhart, Karel. *The Open Tomb: A New Approach, Mark's Passover Haggadah*. Collegeville, MN: Liturgical, 1995.

———. "The Structure of John 1:35—4:54." In *Studies in John: Presented to Professor Dr. J. N. Sevenster on the Occasion of his Seventieth Birthday*. Leiden: Brill, 1970.

Hare, Douglas R. A. *The Son of Man Tradition*. Minneapolis: Fortress, 1990.

Harrington, Wilfrid. *Mark*. New Testament Message, A Biblical-Theological Commentary. Vol. 4. Wilmington, DE.: Michael Glazier, 1979.

Harris, W.V. *Ancient Literacy*. Cambridge: Harvard University Press, 1989.

Hartmann, G. "Mark 3,20f." BZ 11 (1913) 249-79.

Harvey, John D. "Mission in Jesus' Teaching." In *Mission in the New Testament: An Evangelical Approach*, edited by William J. Larkin Jr. and Joel F. Williams. Maryknoll, NY: Orbis, 1990.

Hawkin, David J. "The Incomprehension of the Disciples in the Marcan Redaction." JBL 91 (1972) 491-500.

———. "The Markan Horizon of Meaning." In *Self-Definition and Self-Discovery in Early Christianity*, edited by David J. Hawkin and Tom Robinson, 1-30. Lewiston, NY: Mellen, 1990.

———. "The Symbolism and Structure of the Marcan Redaction." EvQ 49 (1977) 98-110.

Hawkins, John C. *Horae Synopoticae: Contributions to the Study of the Synoptic Problem*. Oxford: Clarendon, 1909.

Head, Peter M. "A Text-Critical Study of Mark 1.1 'The Beginning of the Gospel of Jesus Christ.'" NTS 37 (1991) 621-29.

Healy, Mary. *The Gospel of Mark*. Grand Rapids: Baker Academic, 2008.

Hebert, A. G. "History in the Feeding of the Five Thousand." StEv 2: 65-72. Berlin: Akademie-Verlag, 1964.

Hedrick, Charles W. *When History and Faith Collide: Studying Jesus*. Peabody: Hendrickson, 1999.

———. "Miracles in Mark: A Study in Markan Theology and Its Implications for Modern Religious Thought." PRS 34, no. 3 (2007) 297-313.

———. "The Role of Summary Statements in the Composition of the Gospel of Mark: A Dialogue with Karl Schmidt and Norman Perrin." NovT 26 (1984) 289-311.

Bibliography

Heil, John Paul. *The Gospel of Mark as Model for Action: A Reader-Response Commentary.* Mahwah, NJ: Paulist, 1992.

———. *Jesus Walking on the Sea: Meaning and Gospel Functions of Matthew 14:22–33, Mark 6:45–52 and John 6:15b–21.* Rome: Biblical Institute Press, 1981.

———. *The Transfiguration of Jesus: Narrative Meaning and Function of Mark 9:2–8, Matt. 17:1–8 and Luke 9:28–36.* Rome: Editrice Pontificio Istituto Biblico, 2000.

Hemer, Colin J. *The Book of Acts in the Setting of Hellenistic History.* Tübingen: Mohr, 1989.

Henderson, Suzanne Watts. *Christology and Discipleship in the Gospel of Mark.* Cambridge: Cambridge University Press, 2006.

———. "'Concerning the Loaves': Comprehending Incomprehension in Mark 6.45–52." *JSNT* 83 (2001) 3–26.

Hendrickx, Herman. *The Miracle Stories of the Synoptic Gospels.* San Francisco: Harper and Row, 1987.

Hendriksen, William. *Mark.* Edinburgh: The Banner of Truth Trust, 1976.

Hengel, Martin. *Between Jesus and Paul: Studies in the Earliest History of Christianity.* Translated by John Bowden. London: SCM, 1983.

———. *The Charismatic Leader and his Followers.* Translated by James Greig. New York: Crossroad, 1981.

———. "Christological Titles in Early Christianity." In *Studies in Early Christianity*, 359–89. Edinburgh: T. & T. Clark, 1995.

———. *The Four Gospels and the One Gospel of Jesus Christ: An Investigation of the Collection and Origin of the Canonical Gospels.* Translated by John Bowden. Harrisburg: Trinity, 2000.

———. *Studies in the Gospel of Mark.* London: SCM, 1985.

Hester, J. David. "Dramatic Inconclusion: Irony and the Narrative Rhetoric of the Ending of Mark." *JSNT* 57 (1995) 61–86.

Herron, Robert W. Jr. *Mark's Account of Peter's Denial of Jesus: A History of Interpretation of Its Interpretation.* Lanham, MD: University Press of America, 1992.

Hicks, John Mark. "The Sabbath Controversy in Matthew: An Exegesis of Matthew 12:1–14." *ResQ* 27 (1984) 79–91.

Hiebert, D. Edmond. *Mark: A Portrait of the Servant.* Chicago: Moody Press, 1974.

Hiers, Richard H. "Purification of the Temple: Preparation for the Kingdom of God." *JBL* 90 (1971) 82–90.

———. "Not the Season for Figs." *JBL* 87 (1968) 394–400.

Hilgert, Earle. "The Son of Timaeus: Blindness, Sight, Ascent, Vision in Mark." In *Reimagining Christian Origins: A Colloquium Honoring Burton I. Mack*, edited by Elizabeth A. Castelli and Hal Taussig, 185–98. Valley Forge, PA: Trinity, 1996.

Hill, David. *The Gospel of Matthew.* The New Century Bible Commentary. London: Marshall, Morgan & Scott, 1972.

———. "On the Use and Meaning of Hosea vi.6 in Matthew's Gospel." *NTS* 24 (1977) 107–119.

Hobbs, Edward C. "The Gospel of Mark and the Exodus." PhD diss., University of Chicago, 1958.

Holding, James Patrick. "Did the Gospel End at 16:8—and Would That Be a Problem?" No pages. Online: http://www.tektonics.org/lp/markend.html.

Holladay, Carl. *Theios Aner in Hellenistic-Judaism: A Critique of the Use of This Category in New Testament Christology.* Missoula: Scholars, 1977.

Holmén, Tom. *Jesus and Jewish Covenant Thinking*. Leiden: Brill, 2001.

Holmes, Michael W. *The Apostolic Fathers: Greek Texts and English Translations*. Grand Rapids: Baker, 1999.

Holst, Robert. "The One Anointing of Jesus." *JBL* 95 (1976) 435–46.

Holtzmann, Heinrich J. *Die Synoptiker: Hand-Commentar zum Neuen Testament*. Tübingen: Mohr, 1901.

Hooker, Morna D. "Mark's Parables of the Kingdom (Mark 4:1–34)." In *The Challenge of Jesus' Parables*, edited by Richard N. Longenecker. Grand Rapids: Eerdmans, 2000.

———. *Endings: Invitations to Discipleship*. Peabody, MA: Hendrickson, 2003.

———. *The Gospel According to St. Mark*. Black's New Testament Commentaries. London: Black, 1991.

———. *The Message of Mark*. London: Epworth, 1983.

———. *The Son of Man in Mark*. London: SPCK, 1967.

Horn, Robert C. "The Use of the Greek New Testament." *The Lutheran Quarterly* 1 (1949) 301.

Hort, Fenton John Anthony. "A Note by the Late Dr. Hort on the Words κόφινος, σπυρίς, σαργάνη." *JTS* 10 (1909) 567–71.

Hoskyns, E. C. "Adversaria Exegetica." *Theology* 7 (1923) 147–55.

Hubbard, Benjamin J. "Commissioning Stories in Luke-Acts: A Study of Their Antecedents, Form, and Content." *Semeia* 8 (1977) 103–26.

Hull, John M. *Hellenistic Magic and the Synoptic Tradition*. London: SCM, 1974.

Hultgren, Arland J. "The Formation of the Sabbath Pericope in Mark 2:23–28." *JBL* 91 (1972) 38–43.

———. "Interpreting the Gospel of Luke." In Interpreting the Gospels, edited by J. L. Mays. Philadelphia: Fortress, 1981.

———. *Jesus and His Adversaries: The Form and Function of the Conflict Stories in the Synoptic Tradition*. Minneapolis: Augsburg, 1979.

Humphrey, Hugh M. *"He is Risen!" A New Reading of Mark's Gospel*. New York: Paulist, 1992.

Hurtado, Larry W. "The Gospel of Mark: Evolutionary or Revolutionary Document?" *JSNT* 40 (1990) 15–32.

———. *Mark: New International Biblical Commentary*. Peabody, MA: Hendrickson, 1983.

Incigneri, Brian J. *The Gospel to the Romans: The Setting and Rhetoric of Mark's Gospel*. Leiden: Brill, 2003.

Iverson, Kelly R. "A Further Word on Final Γάρ (Mark 16:8)." *CBQ* 68 (2006) 79–94.

Jackson, Howard M. "The Death of Jesus in Mark and the Miracle from the Cross." *NTS* 33 (1987) 16–37.

———. "Why the Youth Shed His Cloak and Fled Naked: The Meaning and Purpose of Mark 14:51–52." *JBL* 116 (1997) 273–89.

Jenkins, Luke H. "A Markan Doublet: Mark 6:31—7:37 and 8:1–26." In *Studies in History and Religion: Presented to H. Wheeler Robinson*, edited by Ernest Payne, 87–111. London: Lutterworth, 1942.

Jeremias, Joachim. "Die Salbungsgeschichte Mc 14,3–9." *ZNW* 35 (1936) 77–82.

———. *The Eucharistic Words of Jesus*. London: SCM, 1966.

———. *Jesus' Promise to the Nations*. Translated by S. H. Hooke. Naperville, IL: Alec R. Allenson, 1958.

———. *Infant Baptism in the First Four Centuries*. London: SCM, 1960.

———. "Mc 14,9." *ZNW* 44 (1952–53) 103–7.

———. *New Testament Theology: The Proclamation of Jesus*. London: SCM, 1971.
———. *The Parables of Jesus*. Rev. ed. London: SCM, 1963.
Jervell, Jacob. *Luke and the People of God: A New Look at Luke-Acts*. Minneapolis: Augsburg, 1972.
———. *The Theology of the Acts of the Apostles*. Cambridge: Cambridge University Press, 1996.
Jewett, Paul K. *The Lord's Day*. Grand Rapids: Eerdmans, 1971.
Johnson, Earl S. "Is Mark 15.39 the Key to Mark's Christology?" *JSNT* 31 (1987) 3–22.
Johnson, Lewis. "Who is the Beloved Disciple?" *ExpT* 77 (1965–66) 158.
Johnson, Luke Timothy. *The Writings of the New Testament: An Interpretation*. Rev. ed. Minneapolis: Fortress, 1999.
Johnson, Sherman E. *A Commentary on the Gospel According to St. Mark*. London: Adam & Charles Black, 1960.
———. "Mark viii. 22–26: The Blind Man from Bethsaida." *NTS* 25 (1979) 370–83.
Johnson, S. R. "The Identity and Significance of the *Neaniskos* in Mark." *Forum* 8 (1992) 123–39.
Josephus, F. and W. Whiston. *The Works of Josephus: Complete and Unabridged*. Peabody: Hendrickson, 1996.
Juel, Donald. *Mark*. Minneapolis: Augsburg, 1990.
———. *A Master of Surprise: Mark Interpreted*. Minneapolis: Fortress, 1994.
———. *Messiah and Temple: The Trial of Jesus in the Gospel of Mark*. SBLDS 31. Missoula: Scholars, 1977.
Kahl, Brigitte, "Jairus und die verlorenen Töchter Israels. Sozioliterarische Überlegungen zum Problem der Grenzüberschreitung in Mk 5,21–43." In *Von der Wurzel getragen: Christlich-feministische Exegese in Auseinandersetzung mit Antijudaismus*, edited by L. Schottroff and M.-T. Wacker, 61–78. Leiden: Brill, 1996.
Kahl, Werner. *New Testament Miracle Stories in their Religious-Historical Setting*. Göttingen: Vandenhoeck & Ruprecht, 1994.
Kähler, Martin. *The So-called Historical Jesus and the Historic Biblical Christ*. Philadelphia: Fortress, 1964. First published 1892.
Kallas, James. *The Significance of the Synoptic Miracles*. London: SPCK, 1961.
Kanjirakompil, Cherian. "New Wine Into Fresh Wineskins: An Exegetical Study on Mk. 2:21–22." *Biblehashyam* 23 (1997) 245–55.
Karnetzski, M. "Die Galiläische Redaktion im Marcusevangelium." *ZNW* 52 (1961) 238–72.
Kazen, Thomas. *Jesus and Purity Halakhah: Was Jesus Indifferent to Impurity?* Stockholm: Almqvist & Wiksell, 2002.
Kazmierski, Carl R. "Evangelist and Leper: A Socio-Cultural Study of Mark 1.40–45." *NTS* 38 (1992) 37–50.
———. *Jesus, the Son of God: a Study of the Markan Tradition and its Redaction by the Evangelist*. Wurzburg: Echter, 1979.
Keck, Leander E. "Mark 3:7–12 and Mark's Christology." *JBL* 84 (1965) 341–58.
———. "The Introduction to Mark's Gospel." *NTS* 12 (1965–66) 352–70.
Kee, Alistair. "The Old Coat and the New Wine: A Parable of Repentance." *NovT* 12 (1970) 13–22.
Kee, Howard Clark. "Aretalogy and Gospel." *JBL* 92 (1973) 402–22.
———. *Community of the New Age: Studies in Mark's Gospel*. Philadelphia: Westminster, 1977.

———. "Mark as Redactor and Theologian." *JBL* 90 (1971) 333–36.

Keerankeri, George. *The Love Command in Mark: An Exegetico-Theological Study of Mk. 12,28–34*. Roma: Pontificio Instituto Biblico, 2003.

Kelber, Werner. H. "From Passion Narrative to Gospel." In *The Passion of Mark*, edited by W. H. Kelber. Philadelphia: Fortress, 1976.

———. "The Hour of the Son of Man and the Temptation of the Disciples (Mark 14:32–42)." In *The Passion in Mark*, edited by Werner Kelber, 41–60. Philadelphia: Fortress, 1976.

———. *Kingdom and Parousia in the Gospel of Mark*. PhD diss., University of Chicago, 1970.

———. *The Kingdom in Mark. A New Place and a New Time*. Philadelphia: Fortress, 1974.

———. *Mark's Story of Jesus*. Philadelphia: Fortress, 1979.

———. *The Oral and Written Gospel*. Philadelphia: Fortress, 1983.

Kennard, J. S. "The Reconciliation *Tendenz* in Matthew." *Anglican Theological Review* 28 (1946) 159–63.

Kermode, Frank. *The Genesis of Secrecy: On the Interpretation of Narrative*. Cambridge: Harvard University Press, 1979.

Kernaghan, Ronald J. *Mark*. The IVP New Testament Commentary Series. Downers Grove, IL: InterVarsity, 2007

Kertelge, Karl. *Die Wunder Jesu im Markusevangelium: Eine redaktionsgechichtliche Untersuchung*. Munich: Kösel, 1970.

Kilpatrick, George Dunbar. "The Gentile Mission in Mark and Mark 13:9–11." In *Studies in the Gospels. Essays in Memory of R. H. Lightfoot*, edited by D. E. Nineham, 145–58. Oxford: Blackwell, 1955.

Kim, Tae Hun. "The Anarthrous υἱὸς θεοῦ in Mark 15,39 and the Roman Imperial Cult." *Bib.* 79 (1998) 221–41.

King, Zachary. "The Ethical Admonition of Watchfulness and the Timing of the *Parousia*." ThM Diss., Calvin Theological Seminary, 2005.

Kingsbury, Jack Dean. *The Christology of Mark's Gospel*. Philadelphia: Fortress, 1983.

———. *Conflict in Mark: Jesus, Authorities, Disciples*. Minneapolis: Fortress, 1989.

———. "The 'Divine Man' as the Key to Mark's Christology—the End of an Era?" *Int* 35 (1981) 243–57.

———. "Retelling the Old, Old Story: The Miracle of the Leper as an Approach to the Theology of Mark." *Currents in Theology and Mission* 4 (1977) 342–49.

Kirchhevel, Gordon D. "The 'Son of Man' Passages in Mark." *BBR* 9 (1999) 181–87.

Klauck, Hans-Josef. *Allegorie und Allegorese in synoptischen Gleichnistexten*. Münster: Aschendorff, 1978.

Klostermann, Erich. *Das Markusevangelium*. 2nd ed. Tübingen: Mohr, 1950. First published 1926.

Knowles, Michael. "Reading Matthew: The Gospel as Oral Performance." In *Reading the Gospels Today*, edited by Stanley E. Porter. Grand Rapids: Eerdmans, 2004.

Knox, B. M. W. "Silent Reading in Antiquity." *Greek, Roman, and Byzantine Studies* 9 (1968) 421–35.

Knox, Wilfred L. "The End of St. Mark's Gospel." *HTR* 35 (1942) 13–23.

———. *The Sources of the Synoptic Gospels*. Vol. 1 of *St. Mark*. Cambridge: Cambridge University Press, 1953.

Koch, Detrich-Alex. *Die Bedeutung der Wundererzählungen für Christologie des Markusevangeliums*. Berlin: de Gruyter, 1975.

———. "Inhaltliche Gliederung und geographischer Aufriss im Markusevanglium." *NTS* 29 (1983) 145–66.

Koester, Craig R. *Symbolism in the Fourth Gospel: Meaning, Mystery, Community*. Minneapolis: Fortress, 1995.

Krause, Deborah. "Narrative Prophecy in Mark 11.12–21: The Divine Authorization of Judgment." In *The Gospels and the Scriptures of Israel*, edited by Craig A. Evans and W. Richard Stegner, 235–48. Sheffield: Sheffield Academic, 1994.

———. "Simon Peter's Mother-in-Law—Disciple or Domestic Servant? Feminist Biblical Hermeneutics and the Interpretation of Mark 1.29–31." In *A Feminist Companion to Mark*, edited by Amy-Jill Levine, 37–53. Sheffield: Sheffield Academic, 2001.

Kuhn, Heinz-Wolfgang. *Ältere Sammlungen im Markusevangelium*. Göttingen: Vandenhoeck & Ruprecht, 1971.

Kümmel, Werner Georg. *Introduction to the New Testament*. Rev. ed. Translated by Howard Clark Kee. Nashville: Abingdon, 1975.

Ladd, George Elton. *Theology of the New Testament*. Rev. ed. Grand Rapids: Eerdmans, 1993.

Lake, Kirsopp. "ΕΜΒΡΙΜΗΣΑΜΕΝΟΣ and 'ΟΡΓΙΣΘΕΙΣ, Mark 1:40–43." *HTR* 16 (1926) 197–98.

Lambrecht, Jan. *Die Redaktion der Markus-Apokalypse: Literarische Analyse und Strukturuntersuchung*. Rome: Päpstliches Bibelinstitut, 1967.

———. "Jesus and the Law: An Investigation of Mk 7,1–23." *ETL* 53 (1977) 24–82.

———. "La structure de Mc. XIII." In *De Jésus aux Évangiles*, edited by I. de La Potterie, 141–64. Gembloux: Duculet, 1967.

———. *Marcus Interpretator: Stijl en Boodschap in Mc. 3,20—4,34*. Brugge-Utrecht: Desclee de Brouwer, 1969.

———. "Redaction and Theology in Mk. IV." In *L' Evangile selon Marc*, edited by M. Sabbe, 269–307. Leuven: Leuven University Press, 1988.

———. "The Relatives of Jesus in Mark." *NovT* 16 (1974) 241–58.

Lampe, Geoffrey W. H. "St. Peter's Denial." *BJRL* 55 (1972–73) 346–68.

Lange, Friedrich G. "Kompositionsanalyse des Markusevangeliums." *ZTK* 74 (1977) 1–24.

Lane, William L. *The Gospel According to Mark*. Grand Rapids: Eerdmans, 1974.

———. "*Theois Aner* Christology and the Gospel of Mark." In *New Dimensions in New Testament Study*, edited by R. Longenecker and M. C. Tenney, 144–61. Grand Rapids: Zondervan, 1974.

Lapham, Fred F. *An Introduction to the New Testament Apocrypha*. London: T. & T. Clark, 2003.

Larsen, Kevin W. "A Focused Christological Reading of Mark 8:22—9:13." *Trinity Journal* 26 (2005) 33–46.

———. "The Structure of Mark's Gospel: Current Proposals." *Currents in Biblical Research* 3 (2004) 140–60.

Latourelle, Rene. *The Miracles of Jesus and the Theology of Miracles*. Translated by M. O' Connell. New York: Paulist, 1988.

LaVerdiere, Eugene A. *The Beginning of the Gospel: Introducing the Gospel according to Mark*. Vol. 1. Collegeville, MN: Liturgical, 1999.

———. "Feed My Sheep: Eucharistic Tradition in Mark 6:34–44." In *Bread from Heaven*, edited by Paul Berneier, 45–58. Toronto: Paulist, 1977.

Lefevre, F. "De tempel polemiek in der redactie van Marcus. Tempelreiniging – Sanhedrinverhoor—Kruisscène." Diss., Leuven, 1975.

Legault, A. "An Application of the Form-Critique Method to the Anointings in Galilee (Lk 7,36–50) and Bethany (Mt 26,6–13; Mk 14,3–9; Jn 12,1–8)." *CBQ* 16 (1954) 131–45.

Lee-Pollard, Dorothy A. "Powerlessness as Power: A Key Emphasis in the Gospel of Mark." *SJTh* 40 (1987) 173–88.

Lemcio, Eugene E. "External Evidence for the Structure and Function of Mark iv 1–20, vii 14–23, and viii 14–21." *JTS* 29 (1978) 323–38.

———. "The Intention of the Evangelist, Mark." *NTS* 32 (1986) 187–206.

Levine, Amy-Jill. "Discharging Responsibility: Matthean Jesus, Biblical Law, and Hemorrhaging Woman." In *A Feminist Companion to the Gospel of Matthew*, 70–87. Sheffield: Sheffield Academic, 2001.

Lightfoot, J. B. *St. Paul's Epistle to the Galatians*. London: Macmillan, 1874.

Lightfoot, Robert Henry. *History and Interpretation of the Gospels*. London: Hodder and Stoughton, 1935.

———. *The Gospel Message of St. Mark*. Oxford: Oxford University Press, 1950.

———. *Locality and Doctrine in the Gospels*. London: Hodder and Stoughton, 1938.

Lincoln, Andrew T. "The Promise and the Failure: Mark 16.7, 8." *JBL* 108 (1989) 283–300.

Lindars, Barnabas. "'All Foods Clean': Thoughts on Jesus and the Law." In *Law and Religion: Essays on the Place of the Law in Israel and Early Christianity*, edited by B. Lindars, 61–71. Cambridge: Clarke, 1988.

———. *Jesus Son of Man: A Fresh Examination of the Son of Man Sayings in the Gospels in the Light of Recent Research*. London: SPCK, 1983.

———. *New Testament Apologetic: The Doctrinal Significance of the Old Testament Quotations*. London: SCM, 1961.

Lindemann, Andreas. "Die Osterbotschaft des Markus. Zur theologischen Interpretation von Mark 16.1–8." *NTS* 26 (1979–80) 298–317.

Linton, Olof. "The Demand for a Sign from Heaven (Mk. 8:11–12 and Parallels)." *StTh* 19 (1965) 112–29.

Loader, William. "Challenged at the Boundaries: A Conservative Jesus in Mark's Tradition." *JSNT* 63 (1996) 45–61.

———. *Jesus' Attitude towards the Law: A Study of the Gospels*. Grand Rapids: Eerdmans, 2002.

———. "Son of David, Blindness, Possession, and Duality." *CBQ* 44 (1982) 570–85.

Lohmeyer, Ernst. *Lord of the Temple: A Study of the Relation between Cult and Gospel*. Translated by Stewart Todd. Edinburgh: Oliver and Boyd, 1961.

———. *Das Evangelium des Markus*. Göttingen: Vanderhoeck & Ruprecht, 1953.

———. *Galiläa und Jerusalem*. Göttingen: Vandenhoeck and Reprecht, 1936.

Lohr, C. H. "Oral Techniques in the Gospel of Matthew." *CBQ* 23 (1961) 425.

Loisy, Alfred. *L'évangile selon Marc*. Paris: Nourry, 1912.

Louw, J. P. and E. A. Nida. *Greek-English Lexicon of the New Testament: Based on Semantic Domains*. New York: United Bible Societies, 1989.

———. *Greek-English Lexicon of the New Testament: Based on Semantic Domains*. 2nd ed. Electronic ed. New York: United Bible Societies, 1996.

Lüderitz, Gert. "Rhetorik, Poetik, Kompositionstechnik im Markusevangelium." In *Markus-Philologie*, edited by Hubert Cancik, 165–203. Tübingen: Mohr, 1984.

Lund, Nils Wilhelm. *Chiasmus in the New Testament*. Chapel Hill: University of North Carolina Press, 1942.

Luz, Ulrich. "The Secrecy Motif and the Marcan Christology." In *The Messianic Secret*, edited by C. M. Tuckett, 75–96. Philadelphia: Fortress, 1983.

Maartens, P. J. "Mark 2:18–22. An Exercise in Theoretically-Founded Exegesis." *Scriptura: Tydskrif vir Bybelkunde* 2 (1980) 1–54.

Mack, Burton L. "The Anointing of Jesus: Elaboration within a *Chreia*." In *Patterns of Persuasion in the Gospels*, edited by B. L. Mack and V. K. Robbins, 85–106. Sonoma: Polebridge, 1989.

———. *Mark and Christian Origins: A Myth of Innocence*. Philadelphia: Fortress, 1988.

Mackrell, Gerard. *The Healing Miracles in Mark's Gospel: The Passion and Compassion of Jesus*. Middlegreen, UK: St. Paul, 1987.

Madden, Patrick J. *Jesus Walking on the Sea: An Investigation of the Origin of the Narrative Account*. Berlin: De Gruyter, 1997.

Magness, J. Lee. *Sense and Absence: Structure and Suspension in the Ending of Mark's Gospel*. Chico, CA: Scholars, 1986.

Malbon, Elizabeth Struthers. "Disciples, Crowds, Whoever: Markan Characters and Readers." *NovT* 28 (1986) 104–30.

———. "Fallible Followers: Women and Men in the Gospel of Mark." *Semeia* 28 (1983) 29–48.

———. "Galilee and Jerusalem: History and Literature in Marcan Interpretation." In *The Interpretation of Mark*, edited by W. R. Telford, 253–68. Edinburgh: T. & T. Clark, 1995.

———. *Hearing Mark: A Listener's Guide*. Harrisburg, PA: Trinity, 2002.

———. "The Jesus of Mark and the Sea of Galilee." *JBL* 103 (1984) 363–77.

———. *Narrative Space and Mythic Meaning in Mark*. San Francisco: Harper and Row, 1986.

———. "OIKIA AYTOY: Mark 2:15 in Context." *NTS* 31 (1985) 282–92.

———. "The Poor Widow in Mark and Her Poor Rich Readers." *CBQ* 53 (1991) 589–604.

———. "Text and Contexts: Interpreting the Disciples in Mark." *Semeia* 62 (1993) 81–102.

Malina, Bruce J. "A Conflict Approach to Mark 7." *Forum* 4 (1988) 3–30.

Malina, Bruce and Richard Rohrbaugh. *A Social-Science Commentary on the Synoptic Gospels*. Minneapolis: Fortress, 1992.

Mally, Edward J. "The Gospel According to Mark." In *The Jerome Biblical Commentary*, 21–61. London: Geoffrey Chapman, 1968.

Maloney, Elliott C. *Semitic Interference in Marcan Context*. Chico, CA: Scholars, 1981.

Mann, Christopher Stephen. *Mark: A New Translation with Introduction and Commentary*. Garden City, NY: Doubleday, 1986.

Manson, Thomas Walter. "The Cleansing of the Temple." *BJRL* 33 (1950–1951) 271–82.

———. *Jesus and the Non-Jews*. London: Athlone, 1955.

———. "Mark viii 14–21." *JThS* 30 (1929) 45–47.

Marcus, Joel. "The Jewish War and the *Sitz im Leben* of Mark." *JBL* 111 (1992) 441–62.

———. *Mark 1–8: A New Translation with Introduction and Commentary*. The Anchor Bible. New York: Doubleday, 2000.

———. *Mark 8–16: A New Translation with Introduction and Commentary*. The Anchor Yale Bible. New Haven, CT: Yale University Press, 2009.

———. "Mark—Interpreter of Paul." *NTS* 46 (2000) 473–87.

———. "Mark 14:61: 'Are You the Messiah-Son of God?'" *NovT* 31 (1989) 125–41.

———. *The Mystery of the Kingdom of God*. Atlanta: Scholars, 1986.

———. *The Way of the Lord: Christological Exegesis of the Old Testament in the Gospel of Mark*. London: T. & T. Clark, 1992.

Marshall, Christopher D. *Faith as a Theme in Mark's Narrative.* SNTSMS 64. Cambridge: Cambridge University Press, 1989.

Marshall, I. Howard. *Commentary on Luke.* Grand Rapids: Eerdmans, 1978.

Martin, Ernest L. *Secrets of Golgotha: The Forgotten History of Christ's Crucifixion.* Alhambre, CA: ASK Publications, 1988.

Martin, Ralph P. "A Gospel in search of a Life-Setting." *ExpT* 80 (1968–69) 361–64.

———. *Mark: Evangelist and Theologian.* Grand Rapids: Zondervan, 1972.

Martyn, J. Louis. *History and Theology in the Fourth Gospel.* New York: Harper and Row, 1968.

Marxsen, Willi. *Mark the Evangelist: Studies on the Redaction History of the Gospel.* Translated by J. Boyce, D. Juel, and W. Poehlmann. Nashville: Abingdon, 1969.

Masuda, Sanae. "The Good News of the Miracle of the Bread: The Tradition and its Markan Redaction." *NTS* 28 (1982) 191–219.

Matera, Frank J. "'He Saved Others; He Cannot Save Himself': A Literary-Critical Perspective on the Markan Miracles." *Int* 47 (1993) 15–26.

———. "The Incomprehension of the Disciples and Peter's Confession (Mark 6,14—8,30)." *Biblica* 70 (1989) 153–72.

———. *The Kingship of Jesus: Composition and Theology in Mark 15.* Chico, CA: Scholars, 1982.

———. "The Prologue as the Interpretive Key to Mark's Gospel." In *The Interpretation of Mark*, edited by William R. Telford, 289–306. Edinburgh: T. & T. Clark, 1995.

———. *Passion Narratives and Gospel Theologies: Interpreting the Synoptics through their Passion Stories.* New York: Paulist, 1986.

———. *What are they saying about Mark?* New York: Paulist, 1987.

Matthew, Sam P. *Temple-Criticism in Mark's Gospel: The Economic Role of the Jerusalem Temple During the First Century.* Delhi: ISPCK, 1999.

Maurer, Christian. "σχίζω, σχίσμα." *TDNT* 7 (1971) 959–64.

May, David M. "Mark 3:20–35 from the Perspective of Shame / Honor." *BTB* 17 (1987) 83–87.

McCaffrey, U. P. "Psalm Quotations in the Passion Narratives of the Gospels." *Neotestamentica* 14 (1981) 73–89.

McGinley, Laurence J. "Form-Criticism of the Synoptic Healing Narratives." *TS* 3 (1947) 203–30.

McKinnis, R. "An analysis of Mark X 32–34." *NovT* 18 (1976) 81–100.

McWhirter, Jocelyn. "Messianic Exegesis in Mark's Passion Narrative." In *The Trial and Death of Jesus: Essays on the Passion Narrative in Mark*, edited by Geert Van Oyen and Tom Shepherd, 69–98. Leuven: Peeters, 2006.

Mead, A. H. "The βασιλικός in John 4:46–53." *JSNT* 23 (1985) 69–72.

Mead, R. T. "The Healing of the Paralytic—A Unit?" *JBL* 80 (1961) 348–54.

Meagher, John. *Clumsy Construction in Mark's Gospel: A Critique of Form- and Redaktionsgeschichte.* Lewiston, NY: Mellen, 1979.

Mearns, C. L. "Parables, Secrecy, and Eschatology in Mark's Gospel." *SJTh* 44 (1991) 423–42.

Meier, John P. "The Circle of the Twelve: Did It Exist during Jesus' Public Ministry?" *JBL* 116 (1997) 635–72.

———. *A Marginal Jew: Rethinking the Historical Jesus.* 3 vols. New York: Doubleday, 1991.

Meinertz, Max. *Jesus und die Heidenmission.* Münster: Aschendorff, 1925.

Menzies, Allan. Allan Menzies, *The Earliest Gospel.* New York: MacMillan, 1901

Merkel, Helmut. "The Opposition between Jesus and Judaism." In *Jesus and the Politics of His Day*, edited by E. Bammel and C. F. D. Moule, 129–44. Cambridge: Cambridge University Press, 1984.

———. "Peter's Curse." In *The Trial of Jesus. Cambridge Studies in Honour of C. F. D. Moule*, edited by E. Bammel, 66–71. London: SCM, 1970.

Metzger, Bruce M. *A Textual Commentary on the Greek New Testament*. 2nd ed. New York: United Bible Societies, 1994.

Meye, Robert P. *Jesus and the Twelve: Discipleship and Revelation in Mark's Gospel*. Grand Rapids: Eerdmans, 1968.

Meyer, Ben F. *The Aims of Jesus*. London: SCM, 1979.

———. *Christus Faber: The Master-Builder and the House of God*. Allison Park, PA: Pickwick, 1992.

Meyers, Carol L. and Eric M. Meyers. *Zechariah 9–14*. The Anchor Bible. New York: Doubleday, 1993.

Michaels, J. Ramsey. *Servant and Son: Jesus in Parable and Gospel*. Atlanta: John Knox, 1981.

Michel, Otto. "ναός." *TDNT* 4 (1967) 880–90.

Millard, Alan. *Reading and Writing in the Time of Jesus*. Sheffield: Sheffield Academic, 2000.

Miller, Dale. *The Gospel of Mark as Midrash on Earlier Jewish and New Testament Literature*. Lewiston, NY: Mellen, 1990.

Miller, Susan. *Women in Mark's Gospel*. London: T. & T. Clark, 2004.

Mitchell, Joan L. *Beyond Fear and Silence: A Feminist-Literary Approach to the Gospel of Mark*. New York: Continuum, 2001.

Moiser, Jeremy. "'She was Twelve Years Old' (Mk. 5:42): A Note on Jewish-Gentile Controversy in Mark's Gospel." *IBS* 3 (1981) 179–86.

Moloney, Francis. J. "The Vocation of the Disciples in the Gospel of Mark." *Salesianum* 43 (1981) 493–515.

Montefiore, Hugh and H. E. W. Turner. *Thomas and the Evangelists*. London: SCM, 1962.

Moo, Douglas J. *The Epistle to the Romans*. NICNT. Grand Rapids: Eerdmans, 1996.

———. *The Old Testament in the Gospel Passion Narratives*. Sheffield: Almond Press, 1983.

Moore, W. E. "'Outside and Inside': A Markan Motif." *ExpT* 98 (1986) 39–43.

Motyer, J. Alec. *Isaiah: An Introduction and Commentary*. Downers Grove, IL.: InterVarsity, 1999.

Motyer, Stephen. "The Rending of the Veil: A Markan Pentecost." *NTS* 33 (1987) 155–57.

Moule, Charles Francis Digby. *The Gospel according to Mark*. Cambridge: Cambridge University Press, 1965.

———. "St. Mark XVI.8 Once More." *NTS* 2 (1955–56) 58–59.

———. *The Phenomenon of the New Testament: Inquiry into the Implications of Certain Features of the New Testament*. London: SCM, 1967.

Mudiso Mbâ Mundla, J.-G. *Jesus und die Führer Israels: Studien zu den sog; Jerusalemer Streitgespräche*. Münster: Aschendorff, 1984.

Münderlein, Gerhard. "Die Verfluckung des Feigenbaumes (MK. XI:12–14)." *NTS* 10 (1963) 89–104.

Munro, Winsome. "Woman Disciples in Mark?" *CBQ* 44 (1982) 225–41.

Myers, Ched. *Binding the Strong Man: A Political Reading of Mark's Story of Jesus*. Maryknoll, NY: Orbis, 1988.

———. *Say to this Mountain: Mark's Story of Discipleship*. Maryknoll, NY: Orbis, 1996.

Neirynck, Frans. *Duality in Mark: Contributions to the Study of the Markan Redaction*. Leuven: Leuven University Press, 1972.

———. "Jesus and the Sabbath: Some Observations on Mark II,27." In *Jésus aux origines de la christologie*, edited by J. Dupont, 227–70. Leuven: Leuven University Press, 1975.

Neusner, Jacob. *The Idea of Purity in Ancient Judaism*. Leiden: Brill, 1973.

———. *The Mishnah: A New Translation*. New Haven, CT: Yale University Press, 1988.

———. "Money-Changers in the Temple: The Mishnah Explanation." *NTS* 35 (1989) 287–90.

Neyrey, Jerome H. "The Idea of Purity in Mark's Gospel." *Semeia* 35 (1986) 91–128.

———. "A Symbolic Approach to Mark 7." *Forum* 4 (1988) 63–91.

Nineham, Dennis E. *The Gospel of St. Mark*. London: Adam and Charles Black, 1963.

———. "The Order of Events in St. Mark's Gospel—an examination of Dr. Dodd's Hypothesis." *Studies in the Gospels: essays in memory of R. H. Lightfoot*, 223–339. Oxford: Blackwell, 1955.

O'Collins, Gerald. "The Fearful Silence of Three Women (Mark 16:8c)." *Gregorianum* 69 (1988) 489–503.

O'Neill, J. C. "The Charge of Blasphemy at Jesus' Trial Before the Sanhedrin." In *Jesus and the Politics of His Day*, edited by E. Bammel and C. F. D. Moule, 72–77. Cambridge: Cambridge University Press, 1984.

Orchard, Bernard. "Mark and the Fusion of Traditions." In *The Four Gospels 1992: Festschrift F. Neirynck*, edited by F. Van Segbroeck et al., 779–800. Leuven: Leuven University Press, 1992.

Orton, David E., ed. *The Composition of Mark's Gospel: Selected Studies from Novum Testamentum*. Leiden: Brill, 1999.

———. *The Understanding Scribe: Matthew and the Apocalyptic Ideal*. Sheffield: JSOT, 1989.

Oswald, John. *The Book of Isaiah: Chapters 40–66*. Grand Rapids: Eerdmans, 1998.

Ourisman, David J. *From Gospel to Sermon: Preaching Synoptic Texts*. St. Louis: Chalice: 2000.

Painter, John. *Mark's Gospel: Worlds in Conflict*. London: Routledge, 1997.

Parker, D. C. *Codex Bezae: An early Christian manuscript and its text*. Cambridge: Cambridge University Press, 1992.

Parrott, H. W. "Blind Bartimaeus Cries Out Again." *EvQ* 32 (1960) 25–29.

Parrott, Rod. "Conflict and Rhetoric in Mark 2:23–28." *Semeia* 64 (1993) 117–37.

Patten, Priscilla. "The Form and Function of Parable in Select Apocalyptic Literature and their Significance for Parables in the Gospel of Mark." *NTS* 29 (1983) 246–58.

Patterson, Stephen J. *The Gospel of Thomas and Jesus*. Sonoma, CA: Polebridge, 1993.

Payne, Philip Barton. "The Authenticity of the Parable of the Sower and its Interpretation." In *Gospel Perspectives*, vol. 1 of *Studies of History and Tradition in the Four Gospels*, edited by R. T. France and David Wenham, 163–207. Sheffield: JSOT, 1980.

Peabody, David Barrett. *Mark as Composer*. Macon, GA: Mercer University Press, 1987.

Peppard, Michael. *The Son of God in the Roman World: Divine Sonship in Its Social and Political Context*. New York: Oxford University Press, 2011.

Perrin, Norman. "The Christology of Mark: A Study in Methodology." In *The Interpretation of Mark*, edited by William Telford, 95–108. Philadelphia: Fortress, 1995.

———. "The Creative Use of the Son of Man Traditions by Mark." *USQR* 23 (1968) 357–65.

———. *The New Testament, an Introduction: Proclamation and Parenesis, Myth and History*. New York: Harcourt Brace Javanovich, 1974.

———. *Rediscovering the Teaching of Jesus*. New York: Harper and Row, 1967.

———. "Towards an Interpretation of the Gospel of Mark." In *Christology and a Modern Pilgrimage: A Discussion with Norman Perrin*, edited by Hans Dieter Betz, 1–78. Claremont: New Testament Colloquium, 1971.

———. *What is Redaction Criticism?* Philadelphia: Fortress, 1969.

Pesch, Rudolph. *Das Markusevangelium*. 2 vols. Freiburg: Herder, 1977.

———. "Ein Tag vollmächtige Wirkens Jesu in Kapharnaum (Mk 1,21–34, 35–39)." *BibLeb* 9 (1968) 114–95.

———. "The Markan Version of the Healing of the Gerasene Demoniac." *Ecumenical Review* 23 (1971) 349–76.

———. *Naherwartungen: Tradition und Redaktion in Mk. 13*. Düsseldorf: Patmos, 1968.

Petersen, Norman R. "The Composition of Mark 4:1—8:26." *HTR* 73 (1980) 185–217.

———. "When is the End not the End? Literary Reflections on the Ending of Mark's Narrative." *Int* 34 (1980) 151–66.

Peterson, Dwight N. *The Origins of Mark: The Markan Community in Current Debate*. Leiden: Brill, 2000.

Pettem, Michael. "Luke's Great Omission and His View of the Law." *NTS* 42 (1996) 35–54.

Phillips, Victoria. "The Failure of the Women who Followed Jesus in the Gospel of Mark." In *A Feminist Companion to Mark*, edited by Amy-Jill Levine, 222–34. Sheffield: Sheffield Academic, 2001.

Pobee, John. "The Cry of the Centurion—A Cry of Defeat." In *The Trial of Jesus: Cambridge Studies in Honour of C. F. D. Moule*, edited by Ernst Bammel, 91–102. London: SCM, 1970.

Polhill, John B. "Perspectives on the Miracle Stories." *REx* 74 (1977) 389–99.

Poitiers, Hilary of. "On Matthew 14:10." In *Sources chrétiennes*, 258:20–22.

Porter, Stanley. "Philippians as a Macro-Chiasm." *NTS* 44 (1998) 219–20.

Preuss, Julius. *Biblical and Talmudic Medicine*. Translated by Fred Rosner. New York: Sanhedrin Press, 1978.

Pryke, E. J. *Redactional Style in the Marcan Gospel*. SNTSMS 33. Cambridge University Press, 1978.

Quesnell, Quentin. *The Mind of Mark: Interpretation and Method through the Exegesis of Mark 6,52*. Rome: Pontifical Biblical Institute, 1969.

Radcliffe, Timothy. "'The Coming of the Son of Man,' Mark's Gospel, and the Subversion of the Apocalyptic Imagination." In *Language, Meaning, and God: Essays in Honor of Herbert McCabe*, edited by B. Davies, 167–89. London: Chapman, 1987.

Räisänen, Heikki. "Jesus and the Food Laws: Reflections on Mark 7:15." *JSNT* 16 (1982) 79–100.

———. *The Messianic Secret in Mark*. Translated by C. Tuckett. Edinburgh: T. & T. Clark, 1990.

———. *Paul and the Law*. Tübingen: Mohr, 1983.

Rau, G. "Das Markusevangelium: Komposition und Intention der ersten Darstellung christlicher Mission." In *Aufstieg und Niedergang der römischen Welt: II.25.3*, 2036–57. Berlin: de Gruyer, 1985.

Rawlinson, A. E. J. *The Gospel according to St. Mark*. Westminster Commentaries. London: Methuen, 1925.

Regev, Eyal. "Pure Individualism: The Idea of Non-Priestly Purity in Ancient Judaism." *Journal for the Study of Judaism* 31 (2000) 176–202.

BIBLIOGRAPHY

Reid, Daniel G. "Jesus: New Exodus, New Conquest." In *God is a Warrior: Studies in Old Testament Biblical Theology*, edited by Tremper Longman III and Daniel G. Reid, 91–118. Grand Rapids: Zondervan, 1995.

Reid, Robert Stephen. *Preaching Mark*. St. Louis: Chalice, 1999.

Reploh, Karl-Georg. *Markus—Lehrer der Gemeinde. Eine redaktionsgeschichtliche Studie zu den Jüngerperikopen des Markus-Evangeliums*. Stuttgart: Katholisches Bibelwerk, 1969.

Rhoads, David and Michie, Donald. *Mark as Story: An Introduction to the Narrative of a Gospel*. Philadelphia: Fortress, 1982.

Richardson, Alan. "The Feeding of the Five Thousand." *Int* 9 (1955) 144–49.

———. *The Miracle Stories of the Gospels*. London: SCM, 1941.

Riches, John Kenneth. *Jesus and the Transformation of Judaism*. New York: Seabury, 1980.

Riddle, Donald W. "The Martyr Motif in the Gospel of Mark." *JR* 4 (1924) 397–410.

Riesenfeld, Harald. *The Gospel Tradition*. Oxford: Blackwell, 1970.

———. "On the Composition of the Gospel of Mark." *The Gospel Tradition: Essays by Harald Riesenfeld*. Philadelphia: Fortress, 1970.

Riley, Harold. *The Making of Mark: An Exploration*. Macon, GA: Mercer University Press, 1989.

Roberts, Alexander, James Donaldson, A. Cleveland Coxe, Allan Menzies, Ernest Cushing Richardson, and Bernhard Pick, eds. *The Ante-Nicene Fathers*. Grand Rapids: Eerdmans, 1978.

Robin, A. De Q. "The Cursing of the Fig Tree in Mark xi. A Hypothesis." *NTS* 8 (1962) 276–81.

Robinson, Maurice A. and William G. Piermont. *The New Testament in the Original Greek according to the Majority Textform*. Atlanta: Original Word Publications, 1991.

Robbins, Vernon K. "Dynamis and Sē[set macron over e]meia in Mark." *BR* 18 (1973) 5–20.

———. *Jesus the Teacher*. Philadelphia: Fortress, 1984.

———. "The Healing of Blind Bartimaeus (10:46–52) in the Markan Theology." In *New Boundaries in Old Territory: Form and Social Rhetoric in Mark*, 37–57. New York: Lang, 1994.

———. "Last Meal: Preparation, Betrayal, and Absence (Mark 14:12–25)." In *The Passion in Mark*, edited by Werner Kelber, 21–40. Philadelphia: Fortress, 1976.

———. "Summons and Outline in Mark: The Three-Step Progression." *NovT* 23 (1981) 97–114.

———. "The Woman Who Touched Jesus' Garment: Socio-Rhetorical Analysis of the Synoptic Accounts." *NTS* 33 (1987) 502–15.

Robinson, James M. "The Problem of History in Mark, Reconsidered." *USRQ* 20 (1964) 131–47.

Romaniuk, K. "Le Problème des Paulinismes dans l'Èvangile de Marc." *NTS* 23 (1977) 266–74.

Rordorf, Willy. *Sunday: The History of the Day of Rest and Worship in the Earliest Centuries of the Christian Church*. Philadelphia: Westminster, 1968.

Roskam, Hendrika N. *The Purpose of Mark in Its Historical and Social Context*. Leiden: Brill, 2004.

Rossé, Gérard, *The Cry of Jesus on the Cross: A Biblical and Theological Study*. Translated by Stephen Arndt. New York: Paulist, 1987.

Roth, Cecil. "The Cleansing of the Temple and Zechariah xiv 21." *NovT* 4 (1960) 174–81.

Ruddick, Chester Townsend. "Behold I Send my Messenger." *JBL* 88 (1969) 381–417.

Rudolph, David J. "Jesus and the Food Laws: A Reassessment of Mark 7:19b." *EvQ* 74 (2002) 291–311.

Ruhland, Maria. *Die Markuspassion aus der Sicht der Verleugnung.* Eilsbrunn: Ko'amar, 1987.

Salyer, Gregory. "Rhetoric, Purity, and Play Aspects of Mark 7:1–23." *Semeia* 64 (1993) 139–69.

Samuel, Simon. *A Postcolonial Reading of Mark's Story of Jesus.* London: T. & T. Clark, 2007.

Sanders, E. P. *Jesus and Judaism.* Philadelphia: Fortress, 1985.

———. *Jewish Law from Jesus to the Mishnah: Five Studies.* London: SCM, 1990.

———. *Judaism: Practice and Belief 63 BCE–66 CE.* London: SCM, 1992.

———. and Margaret Davies. *Studying the Synoptic Gospels.* Philadelphia: Trinity, 1989.

Sanders, Jack T. *The Jews in Luke-Acts.* London: SCM, 1987.

Sandmel, Samuel. *Judaism and Christian Beginnings.* New York: Oxford University Press, 1978.

———. "Prolegomena to a Commentary on Mark." *JBR* 31 (1963) 294–300.

Sariola, H. *Markus und das Gesetz: Eine redaktionsgeschichliche Untersuchung.* Helsinki: Suomalainen Tiedeakatemia, 1990.

Sawyer, Harry. "The Marcan Framework." *SJTh* 14 (1961) 279–94.

Schenke, Ludger. *Glory and the Way of the Cross: The Gospel of Mark.* Chicago: Franciscan Herald, 1972.

———. *Studien zur Passiongeschichte des Markus.* Wüzburg: Echter, 1971.

———. *Die Wundererzählungen des Markusevangeliums.* Stuttgart: Verlag Katholisches Bibelwerk, 1974.

Schille, Gottfried. "Die Seesturmerzählung Marcus 4 35–41 als Beispiel Neutestamentliche Aktualisierung." *ZNW* 56 (1965) 30–40.

Schmid, Josef. *Das Evangelium nach Markus.* Regensburg: F. Pustet, 1958.

Schniewind, Julius. *Das Evangelium nach Markus.* Translated by Herman Strathmann. Das Neue Testament Deutsch. Göttingen: Vandenhoeck & Ruprecht, 1971.

Schnabel, Eckhard J. "Jesus and the Beginnings of the Mission to the Gentiles." In *Jesus of Nazareth: Lord and Christ*, edited by Joel Green and Max Turner, 37–58. Grand Rapids: Eerdmans, 1994.

Schneemelcher, Wilhelm, ed. *New Testament Apocrypha.* Louisville: Westminster / John Knox, 1992.

Scholtissek, K. *Die Vollmacht Jesu: traditions und redaktionsgeschichtliche Analyse zu einem Leitmotiv markinischer Christologie.* Münster: Aschendorff, 1992.

Schreiber, Johanus. "Die Christologie des Markusevangeliums." *ZTK* 58 (1961) 154–82.

Schroeder, H. H. *Eltern und Kinder in der Verkündigung Jesu.* Hamburg-Bergstedt: Reich, 1972.

Schweizer, Eduard. *The Good News According to Mark.* Translated by Donald Madvig. Atlanta: John Knox, 1970.

———. "The Portrayal of the Life of Faith in the Gospel of Mark." *Int* 32 (1978) 387–99.

———. "The Question of the Messianic Secret in Mark." In *The Messianic Secret*, edited by C. Tuckett. Philadephia: Fortress, 1983.

Scobie, Charles H. "Jesus or Paul? The Origin of the Universal Mission of the Christian Church." In *From Jesus to Paul: Studies in Honour of Francis Wright Beare*, edited by Peter Richardson and John C. Hurd, 47–60. Waterloo, ON: Wilfrid Laurier University Press, 1984.

———. *John the Baptist.* Philadelphia: Fortress, 1964.

Scott, James M. "Exile and the Self-understanding of Diaspora Jews." In *Exile: Old Testament, Jewish, and Christian Perspectives*, 173–218. Leiden: Brill, 1997.

———. *Restoration: Old Testament, Jewish, and Christian Perspectives*. Leiden: Brill, 2001.

Scott, M. Philip. "Chiastic Structure: A Key to the Interpretation of Mark's Gospel." *BTB* 15 (1985) 17–26.

Scroggs, Robin and Kent I. Groff. "Baptism in Mark: Dying and Rising with Christ." *JBL* 92 (1973) 531–48.

———, Kelber, Werner, and Kolenkow, Anitra. "Reflection on the Question: Was There a Pre-Markan Passion Narrative?" *SBLASP* 2 (1971) 504–85.

Seeley, David. "Jesus' Temple Act." *CBQ* 55 (1993) 263–83.

Seifrid, M. A. "Jesus and the Law in Acts." *JSNT* 30 (1987) 39–57.

Seitz, Oscar J.F. "Peter's 'Profanity': Mark 14,71 in the Light of Matthew 16,22." *StEv* 1: 516–19. Berlin: Akademie-Verlag, 1959.

Sellin, Gerhard. "Einige symbolische und esoterische Züge im Markus-Evangelium." In *Jesu Rede von Gott und ihre Nachgeschichte im frühen Christentum: Beiträge zur Verkündigung Jesus und zum Kerygma der Kirche: Festschrift für Willi Marxsen*, edited by D. A. Koch et al., 74–90. Gütersloh: Mohn, 1980.

Sellew, Philip. "Composition of Didactic Scenes in Mark's Gospel." *JBL* 108 (1989) 613–634.

———. "Oral and Written Sources in Mark 4:1–34." *NTS* 36 (1990) 234–67.

Selvidge, Marla J. "Mark 5:25–34 and Leviticus 15:19–20: A Reaction to Restrictive Purity Regulations." *JBL* 103 (1984) 619–23.

———. *Woman, Cult, and Miracle Recital: A Redactional-Critical Investigation on Mark 5.24–34*. Lewisburg, PA: Bucknell University Press, 1990.

Senior, Donald. "The Eucharist in Mark: Mission, Reconciliation, Hope." *BTB* 12 (1982) 67–72.

———. *The Passion of Jesus in the Gospel of Mark*. Wilmington: Michael Glazier, 1984.

Sergeant, John. *Lion Let Loose: The Structure and Meaning of St. Mark's Gospel*. Carlisle: Paternoster, 1988.

Shaw, A. "The Marcan Feeding Narratives." *Church Quarterly Review* 161 (1961) 268–78.

Shepherd, Thomas. "Intercalation in Mark and the Synoptic Problem." *SBL 1991 Seminar Papers*, 687–97. Chico, CA: Scholars, 1991.

———. *Markan Sandwich Stories. Narration, Definition, and Function*. Andrews University Seminary Doctoral Dissertaion Series 18. Berrien Springs: Andrews University Press, 1993.

———. "The Narrative Function of Markan Intercalation." *NTS* 41 (1995) 522–40.

Sherwin-White, A. N. *The Letters of Pliny: A Social and Historical Commentary*. Oxford: Clarendon, 1985.

Shiner, Whitney T. "The Ambiguous Pronouncement of the Centurion and the Shrouding of the Meaning in Mark." *JSNT* 78 (2000) 3–22.

———. *Follow Me! Disciples in Markan Rhetoric*. Atlanta: Scholars, 1995.

———. *Proclaiming the Gospel: First-Century Performance of Mark*. Harrisburg, PA: Trinity, 2003.

Shipley, Joseph T. *Dictionary of World Literature, Criticism, Forms, Technique*. New York: Philosophical Library, 1943.

Sim, David C. "The Gospel of Matthew and the Gentiles." *JSNT* 57 (1995) 19–48.

———. "The Gospels for All Christians? A Response to Richard Bauckham." *JSNT* 84 (2001) 3–27.

Slomp, J. "Are the Words 'Son of God' in Mark 1.1 Original?" *BTr* 28 (1977) 143–50.
Smith, Charles W.F. "No Time for Figs." *JBL* 79 (1960) 315–27.
Smith, Derwood. "Proselyte Baptism and the Baptism of John." *ResQ* 1 (1982) 24–37.
Smith, Dwight Moody. *Interpreting the Gospels for Preaching*. Philadelphia: Fortress, 1980.
Smith, Marion. "The Composition of Mark 11–16." *Heythrop Journal* 22 (1981) 363–77.
Smith, Morton. "Forms, Motives, and Omissions in Mark's Account of the Teaching of Jesus." In *M. S. Enslin, Festschrift, Understanding the Sacred Text*, edited by J. Reumann, 155–64. Valley Forge, PA: Judson, 1972.
Smith, Stephen H. "Bethsaida via Gennesaret: The Enigma of the Sea-Crossing in Mark 6,45–53." *Bib* 77 (1996) 349–74.
———. "The Literary Structure of Mark 11:1—12:40." *NovT* 31 (1989) 104–24. Reprinted in *The Composition of Mark's Gospel*, edited by David Orton, 171–91. Leiden: Brill, 1999.
———. "Mark 3,1–6: Form, Redaction, and Community Function." *Bib* 75 (1994) 153–74.
Snoy, Thierry. "Marc 6,48: 'et il voulait les dépasser.'" In *L'Evangile selon Marc*, edited by M. Sabbe, 339–60. Gembloux: Duculot, 1974.
Spitta, Friedrich. *Jesus und die Heidenmission*. Geissen: Alfred Töpelmann, 1909.
Stacy, R. W. "Fear in the Gospel of Mark." PhD Diss., Southern Baptist Seminary, 1979.
Standaert, Benoit. *L' Evangile selon Marc: Composition et genre littéraire*. Zevenkerken-Brugge: Stichting Studentenpers Nijmegen, 1978.
Stanton, Graham N. *A Gospel for a New People: Studies in Matthew*. Louisville: Westminster / John Knox, 1993.
Starobinski, Jean. "The Struggle with Legion: A Literary Analysis of Mark 5:1–20." *New Literary History* 4 (1973) 331–56.
Stauffer, Ethelbert. "Realistische Jesusworte." In *The New Testament Age: Essays in Honor of Bo Reiche*, edited by W. C. Weinrich, 503–10. Macon, GA: Mercer, 1984.
———. "Zum apokalyptischen Festmahl in Mc. 6:34ff." *ZNW* 46 (1955) 264–66.
Stegner, William Richard. "Jesus' Walking on the Water: Mark 6.45–52." In *The Gospels and the Scriptures of Israel*, edited by Craig A. Evans and W. Richard Stegner, 212–34. Sheffield: Sheffield Academic, 1994.
Stein, Robert H. "The Cleansing of the Temple in Mark (11:15–19): Reformation or Judgment?" In *Gospels and Tradition: Studies on Redaction Criticism of the Synoptic Gospels*, 21–33. Grand Rapids: Baker, 1991.
———. "The Ending of Mark." *BBR* 18 (2008) 79–98.
———. "Is Our Reading the Bible the Same as the Original Audience's Hearing It? A Case Study in the Gospel of Mark." *JETS* 46 (2003) 63–78.
———. "Is the Transfiguration (Mark 9:2–8) a Misplaced Resurrection-Account?" *JBL* 95 (1976) 79–96.
———. *Mark*. Baker Exegetical Commentary of the New Testament. Grand Rapids: Baker, 2008.
———. "The Proper Methodology for Ascertaining a Markan Redaction History." *NovT* 13 (1971) 181–98. Reprinted in *The Composition of Mark's Gospel*, edited by David Orton, 34–51. Leiden: Brill, 1999.
———. *The Synoptic Problem*. Grand Rapids: Baker, 1987.
Steinhauser, Michael G. "The Form of the Bartimaeus Narrative (Mark 10.46–52)." *NTS* 32 (1986) 583–95.
———. "Part of a Call Story?" *ExpT* 94 (1983) 204–6.
Stek, John. "Elijah." In *ISBE* 67.

Stemberger, Günther. "Galilee—Land of Salvation?" Appendix 4 in *The Gospel and the Land: Early Christianity and Jewish Territorial Doctrine*, by W.D. Davies, 409–38. Berkeley: University of California Press, 1974.

Stenger, Werner. "Die Grundlegung des Evangeliums von Jesus Christus: Zur kompositionellen Struktur der Markusevangeliums." *LingBib* 61 (1988) 7–56.

Stock, Augustine. *Call to Discipleship: A Literary Study of Mark's Gospel*. Wilmington, DE: Michael Glazier, 1982.

———. "Hinge Transitions in Mark's Gospel." *BTB* 15 (1985) 27–31.

———. *The Method and Message of Mark*. Wilmington, DE: Michael Glazier, 1989.

———. "The Structure of Mark." *The Bible Today* 23 (1985) 291–96.

———. *The Way in the Wilderness: Exodus, Wilderness, and Moses Themes in the Old Testament and New*. Collegeville, MN: Liturgical, 1969.

Stock, Klemens. "Gliederung und Zusammenhang in Mk. 11–12." *Bib* 59 (1978) 481–515.

Stonehouse, Ned. *The Witness of Matthew and Mark to Christ*. Philadelphia: Presbyterian Guardian, 1944.

Strathmann, H. "μάρτυς." In *TDNT* 4:502–4.

Streeter, Burnett Hillman. *The Four Gospels: A Study of Origins, Treating of the Manuscript Tradition, Sources, Authorship, and Dates*. New York: Macmillan, 1925.

Sugirtharajah, R. S. "The Widow's Mites Revalued." *ExpT* 103 (1991) 42–43.

Suggitt, J. N. "Bartimaeus and Christian Discipleship (Mark 10:46–52)." *Journal of Theology for South Africa* 74 (1991) 57–63.

Suhl, Alfred. *Die Funktion der alttestamentlichen Zitate und Anspielungen im Markusevangelium*. Gütersloh: Gerd Mohn, 1965.

Sunderwirth, Alfred Durand. "The Use of Miracle Stories in Mark's Gospel." PhD diss., Columbia University, 1975.

Svartvik, Jesper. *Mark and Mission: Mk. 7:1–23 in its Narrative and Historical Contexts*. Stockholm: Almqvist and Wiksell International, 2000.

Swartley, Willard M. "The Structural Function of the Term 'Way' (*Hodos*) in Mark's Gospel." In *The New Way of Jesus*, edited by W. Klassen, 73–86. Newton, KS: Faith and Life, 1980.

Swete, Henry Barclay. *The Gospel according to St. Mark*. London: Macmillan, 1920.

Synge, Francis Charles. "Intruded Middles." *ExpT* 92 (1981) 329–33.

———. "Mark 16:1–8." *JThSA* 11 (1975) 71–73.

Tannehill, Robert C. "The Disciples in Mark: The Function of a Narrative Role." *JR* 57 (1977) 386–405.

———. "The Gospel of Mark as Narrative Christology." *Semeia* 16 (1979) 57–95.

———. "Tension in Synoptic Sayings and Stories." *Int* 34 (1980) 138–50.

———. "Varieties of Synoptic Pronouncement Sayings." *Semeia* 20 (1981) 101–19.

Taylor, Joan E. "Golgotha: A Reconsideration of the Evidence for the Sites of Jesus' Crucifixion and Burial." *NTS* 44 (1998) 184–86.

———. *The Immerser: John the Baptist Within Second Temple Judaism*. Grand Rapids: Eerdmans, 1997.

Taylor, Vincent. *The Gospel According to St. Mark*. London: MacMillan, 1959.

———. "The Messianic Secret in Mark." *ExpT* 49 (1947–48) 146–51.

Telford, William R. *The Barren Temple and the Withered Tree: A Redaction-Critical Analysis of the Cursing of the Fig-tree Pericope in Mark's Gospel and its Relation to the Cleansing of the Temple Tradition*. Sheffield: JSOT, 1980.

———. "Introduction: The Interpretation of Mark. A History of Developments and Issues." In *The Interpretation of Mark*. 2nd ed. Edinburgh: T. & T. Clark, 1995.

———. *The Theology of the Gospel of Mark*. Cambridge: Cambridge University Press, 1999.

Theissen, Gerd. *The Gospels in Context: Social and Political History in the Synoptic Tradition*. Edinburgh: T. & T. Clark, 1992.

———. "Lokal- und Socialkolorit in der Geschichte von der syrophönikischen Frau (Mk 7 24–30)." *ZNW* 75 (1984) 202–25.

———. *The Miracle Stories of the Early Christian Tradition*. Translated by Francis McDonagh. Edinburgh: T. & T. Clark, 1983.

Thimmes, Pamela. *Studies in the Biblical Sea-Storm Type-Scene: Convention and Invention*. Lewiston, NY: Mellen, 1992.

Thompson, Mary R. *The Role of Disbelief in Mark: A New Approach to the Second Gospel*. New York: Paulist, 1989.

Thomson, Ian H. *Chiasmus in the Pauline Letters*. Sheffield: Sheffield Academic, 1995.

Thrall, Margaret E. "Elijah and Moses in Mark's Account of the Transfiguration." *NTS* 16 (1970) 305–17.

Thurston, Bonnie Bowman. "Faith and Fear in Mark's Gospel." *Bible Today* 23 (1985) 305–10.

———. *Preaching Mark*. Minneapolis: Fortress, 2002.

Tolbert, Mary Ann. "How the Gospel of Mark Builds Character." In *Gospel Interpretation*, edited by Jack Dean Kingsbury, 71–82. Harrisburg, PA: Trinity, 1997.

———. *Sowing the Gospel: Mark's World in Literary-Historical Perspective*. Minneapolis: Fortress, 1989.

Tomson, Peter J. *'If This Be From Heaven. . .': Jesus and the New Testament Authors in their Relationship to Judaism*. Sheffield: Sheffield Academic, 2001.

Torrey, C. C. *Our Translated Gospels*. New York: Harper and Brothers, 1936.

Trench, Richard C. *Notes on the Miracles of Our Lord*. London: Kegen, Paul, Trench, 1889.

———. *Synonyms of the New Testament*. London: Kegan, Pual, Trench, and Trübner, 1915.

Trocmé, Etienne. *The Formation of the Gospel According to Mark*. Translated by Pamela Gaughan. Philadelphia: Westminster, 1975.

Trompf, G. W. "The First Resurrection Appearance and the Ending of Mark's Gospel." *NTS* 18 (1971–72) 308–30.

Tuckett, Christopher. *The Messianic Secret*. Philadephia: Fortress, 1983.

Turner, C. H. "The Chronology of the New Testament." In Vol. 1 of *A Dictionary of the Bible*, edited by James Hastings, 403–25. New York: Scribner's, 1900.

———. *The Gospel according to St. Mark*. Edited by C. Gore, H. L. Goudge, and A. Guillaume. London: SPCK, 1928.

———. "Marcan Usage IV: Parenthetical Clauses in Mark." *JTS* 26 (1925) 145–56.

———. "A Textual Commentary on Mark I." *JTS* 28 (1927) 145–58.

Turner, Max B. "The Sabbath, Sunday, and the Law in Luke / Acts." In *From Sabbath to Lord's Day: A Biblical, Historical, and Theological Investigation*, 99–158. Grand Rapids: Zondervan, 1982.

Turner, Nigel. "The Style of St. Mark's Eucharistic Words." *JTS* 8 (1957) 108–11.

Twelftree, Graham H. *Jesus: The Miracle Worker: A Historical and Theological Study*. Downers Grove, IL: InterVarsity, 1999.

Tyson, Joseph B. "The Blindness of the Disciples in Mark." *JBL* 80 (1961) 261–68.

Ulansey, David. "The Heavenly Veil Torn: Mark's Cosmic Inclusio." *JBL* 110 (1991) 123–25.

Van der Hoerst, P. W. "Can a Book End with GAR? A Note on Mark XVI.8." *JTS* 23 (1972) 121–24.

Van der Loos, Hendrik. *The Miracles of Jesus.* Leiden: Brill, 1965.

Van Iersel, Bas M. F. "Concentric Structures in Mark 2,1—3,6 and 3,7—4,1: A Case Study." In *The Synoptic Gospels: Source Criticism and the New Literary Criticism*, edited by Camile Focant, 521-30. Leuven University Press, 1993.

———. "Failed Followers in Mark: Mark 13:12 as a Key for the Identification of the Intended Readers." *CBQ* 58 (1996) 244–63.

———. "The Gospel According to St. Mark—Written for a Persecuted Community?" *Nederlands Theologisch Tijdschrift* 34 (1980) 15–36.

———. "ΚΑΙ ΗΘΕΛΕΝ ΠΑΡΕΛΘΕΙΝ ΑΥΤΟΥΣ Another Look at Mk 6,48d." In *The Four Gospels 1992: Festschrift F. Neirynck*, edited by F. Van Segbroeck et al., 1065–76. Leuven: Leuven University Press, 1992.

———. *Mark: A Reader-Response Commentary.* Translated by W. H. Bisscheroux. JSNTSS 164. Sheffield: Sheffield Academic, 1998.

———. "The Reader of Mark as Operator of a System of Connotations." *Semeia* 48 (1989) 84–114.

———. *Reading Mark.* Translated by W. H. Bisscheroux. Collegeville, MN: Liturgical, 1988.

———. "De thuishaven van Marcus." *TTh* 32 (1992) 125–42.

———. "Die wunderbare Speisung und das Abendmahl in der synoptischen Tradition." *NovT* 7 (1964) 167–94.

Van Iersel, Bas M. F., and Linmans, A. J. M. "The Storm on the Lake, Mk iv 35–41 and Mt viii 18–27 in the Light of Form-Criticism, Redaktionsgeschichte, and Structural Analysis." In *Miscellanea Neotestamentica*, edited by T. Baarda, 2:18–48. Leiden: Brill, 1978.

Van Iersel, Bas M. F., and Nuchelmans, J. "De zoon van Timeüs en de zoon van David: Marcus 10,46–52 gelezen door een grieks-romeinse bril." *TTh* 35 (1995) 107–24.

Van Oyen, Geert. "Intercalation and Irony in the Gospel of Mark." In *The Four Gospels 1992: Festschrift Frans Neirynck*, 949–74. Leuven: Leuven University Press, 1992.

Via, Dan Otto Jr. *The Ethics of Mark's Gospel—in the Middle of Time.* Philadelphia: Fortress, 1985.

———. "Irony as Hope in Mark's Gospel: A Reply to Werner Kelber." *Semeia* 43 (1988) 21–28.

Vines, Michael E. *The Problem of Markan Genre: The Gospel of Mark and the Jewish Novel.* Atlanta: SBL, 2002.

Vorster, Willem S. "The Function of the Use of the Old Testament in Mark." *Neot* 14 (1981) 62–72.

———. "Literary Reflections on Mark 13:5-37: A Narrated Speech of Jesus." In *The Interpretation of Mark*, edited by W. R. Telford, 269-88. Edinburgh: T. & T. Clark, 1995.

Waetjen, Herman C. *A Reordering of Power: A Socio-Political Reading of Mark's Gospel.* Minneapolis: Fortress, 1989.

Wainwright, Elaine. "The Gospel of Matthew." In *Searching the Scriptures: A Feminist Commentary*, edited by Elisabeth Schüssler Fiorenza, 635–77. New York: Crossroad, 1994.

Waitz, H. "Das problem des sogenannten Aposteldekrets." *ZKG* 55 (1936) 277.

Wallace, Daniel B. *Greek Grammar Beyond the Basics.* Grand Rapids: Zondervan, 1996.

Wansbrough, Henry. "Mark III.21: Was Jesus Out of His Mind?" *NTS* (1971–72) 233–35.

Watts, Rikki E. *Isaiah's New Exodus in Mark.* Grand Rapids: Baker Academic, 2000.

Watty, William W. "Jesus and the Temple—Cleansing or Cursing?" *ExpT* 93 (1982) 235-39.
Watson, Francis. "The Social Function of Mark's Secrecy Motif." *JSNT* 24 (1985) 49-69.
———. "Toward a Literal Reading of the Gospels." In *The Gospels for All Christians: Rethinking the Gospel Audiences*, edited by Richard Bauckham. Grand Rapids: Eerdmans, 1998.
Webb, Robert L. *John the Baptizer and Prophet: A Socio-Historical Study*. Sheffield: JSOT, 1991.
Wedderburn, A. J. M. *Beyond Resurrection*. Peabody, MA: Hendrickson, 1999.
Weeden, Theodore J. "The Heresy that Necessitated Mark's Gospel." *ZNW* 59 (1968) 145-58.
———. *Mark: Traditions in Conflict*. Philadelphia: Fortress, 1971.
Wefald, Eric K. "The Separate Gentile Mission in Mark: A Narrative Explanation of Markan Geography, the Two Feeding Accounts and Exorcisms." *JSNT* 60 (1995) 3-26.
Wegener, Mark I. *Cruciformed: The Literary Impact of Mark's Story of Jesus and His Disciples*. Lanham, MD: University Press of America, 1995.
Weissenrieder, Annette. "The Plague of Uncleanness? The Ancient Illness construct 'Issue of blood' in Luke 8:43-48." In *The Social Setting of Jesus and the Gospels*, edited by Wolfgang Stegemann et al., 207-22. Minneapolis: Fortress, 2002.
Wendling, E. *Die Entstehung des Markusevangeliums*. Tübingen, 1908.
Wenham, David. "The Meaning of Mark III.21." *NTS* 21 (1974-75) 295-300.
———. *The Rediscovery of Jesus' Eschatological Discourse*. Sheffield: JSOT, 1984.
Werner, M. *Der Einfluss paulinischer Theologie im Markusevangelium: Eine Studie zur neutestamentlichen Theologie*. Giessen: Töpelmann, 1923.
Westerholm, Stephen. *Jesus and Scribal Authority*. Doctrinal Thesis at Lund University: Gleerup, 1978.
Westermann, Claus. *Isaiah 40-66: A Commentary*. Philadelphia: Westminster, 1969.
Wikgren, A. "ΑΡΧΗ ΤΟΥ ΕΥΑΓΓΕΛΙΟΥ." *JBL* 61 (1942) 16-19.
Wilde, J. A. "A Social Description of the Community Reflected in the Gospel of Mark." PhD diss., Drew University, 1978.
Wilder, Amos N. *Early Christian Rhetoric: The Language of the Gospels*. New York: Harper and Row, 1964.
Wilhelm, Dawn Ottoni. *Preaching the Gospel of Mark: Proclaiming the Power of God*. Louisville: Westminster John Knox, 2008.
Wilcox, Max. "The Denial-Sequence in Mark XIV." *NTS* 17 (1970-71) 426-36.
Wilkinson, John. "The Case of the Epileptic Boy." *ExpT* 79 (1967-68) 38-42.
Williams, James G. *Gospel Against Parable: Mark's Language of Mystery*. Sheffield: JSOT, 1985.
Williams, Joel F. "Does Mark's Gospel Have an Outline?" *JETS* 49 (2006) 505-26.
———. "Literary Approaches to the End of Mark's Gospel." *JETS* 42 (1999) 21-35.
———. *Other Followers of Jesus: Minor Characters as Major Figures in Mark's Gospel*. Sheffield: Sheffield Academic, 1994.
Wilson, Stephen G. *The Gentiles and the Gentile Mission in Luke-Acts*. Cambridge: Cambridge University Press, 1973.
———. *Luke and the Law*. Cambridge: Cambridge University Press, 1983.
Wire, Antoinette Clark. "The Structure of the Gospel Miracle Stories and Their Tellers." *Semeia* 11 (1978) 83-113.
Wisse, Frederick. "Historical Method and the Johannine Community." *ARC* 20 (1992) 35-42.
Witherington, Ben III. *The Gospel of Mark: A Socio-Rhetorical Commentary*. Grand Rapids: Eerdmans, 2001.

Bibliography

———. "John the Baptist." In *Dictionary of Jesus and the Gospels*, edited by Joel B. Green, Scot McKnight, and I. Howard Marshall, 384–85. Downers Grove, IL: InterVarsity, 1992.

Wojciechowski, M. "The Touching of the Leper (Mark 1,40–45) as a Historical and Symbolic Act of Jesus." *BZ* 33 (1989) 114–19.

Wolff, C. "Zur Bedeutung Johannes des Täufers im Markusevangeliums." *TLZ* 102 (1977) 857–65.

Wright, Addison G. "The Widow's Mites: Praise or Lament?—A Matter of Context." *CBQ* 44 (1982) 256–65.

Wright, George Al Jr. "Markan Intercalations: A Study in the Plot of the Gospel." PhD diss., Southern Baptist Theological Seminary, 1985.

Wright, N. Thomas. *Jesus and the Victory of God*. Minneapolis: Fortress, 1996.

———. *The New Testament and the People of God*. Minneapolis: Fortress, 1992.

———. *Scripture and the Authority of God: How to Read the Bible Today*. New York: HarperOne, 2011.

Young, Brad H. *Jesus the Jewish Theologian*. Peabody, MA: Hendrickson, 1995.

Zahn, Theodor. *Introduction to the New Testament*. Grand Rapids: Kregel, 1953.

Zodhiates, S., ed. *The Complete Word Study Dictionary: New Testament*. Electronic ed. Chattanooga, TN: AMG, 2000.

Ziener, P. G. "Die Brotwunder im Markusevangelium." *BZ* 4 (1960) 282–85.

Ziesler, John A. "The Transformation Story and the Markan Soteriology." *ET* 81 (1970) 263–68.

www.ingramcontent.com/pod-product-compliance
Lightning Source LLC
Chambersburg PA
CBHW080529300426
44111CB00017B/2654